"An excellent volume covering a huge amount of material. The editors introduce the wide range of topics and variety of perspectives considered and, in every case, encouraged me to want to read further into the book on all the aspects highlighted."

—**Sara Horrell,** *London School of Economics and Political Science, UK*

20th Century Britain

20th Century Britain provides an authoritative and accessible survey of contemporary research on economic activity, society, political development and culture. Written by leading academics, it examines recent advances in scholarship and gives a grounding in established approaches and topics.

The first part comprises thematic essays covering the whole of the twentieth century, including chapters on the economy, economic management, big business, parliamentary politics, leisure, work, health, international economic relations and empire. It uncovers key areas of equality and diversity in chapters on women, living standards, social mobility, ethnicity and multiculturalism, and gender and sexuality. The most recent subfields of historical studies are also explored, including disability history and environmental economic history. The second part focuses on seismic events and topics covering shorter timeframes, including the World Wars, interwar Depression, Britain and European integration, sexual behaviours, civil society, the 1960s cultural revolution and resisting racism.

This collection provides an essential guide to current academic thinking on the most important elements of twentieth-century British history and is a useful tool for all students and scholars interested in modern Britain.

Nicole Robertson is Associate Professor in Modern British History at Sheffield Hallam University. She has published widely on women and the clerical sector, the co-operative movement, consumerism, and the Labour Party. Her current research project explores gender, activism and identity among white-collar workers.

John Singleton is Emeritus Professor of Economic and Business History at Sheffield Hallam University. He has published widely on British business history, economic policy in New Zealand, the development of central banking and the history of disasters and industrial safety.

Avram Taylor is Senior Lecturer in History at Northumbria University. His research reflects his interest in the relationship between class, gender and ethnicity. His thesis was published as *Working Class Credit and Community since 1918* (2002). He has subsequently published a number of articles on Jews in Britain.

20th Century Britain
Economic, Cultural and Social Change

Third Edition

Edited by Nicole Robertson, John Singleton and Avram Taylor

Routledge
Taylor & Francis Group

LONDON AND NEW YORK

Cover image: Woodhorn Museum © Museums Northumberland

Third edition published 2023
by Routledge
4 Park Square, Milton Park, Abingdon, Oxon, OX14 4RN

and by Routledge
605 Third Avenue, New York, NY 10158

Routledge is an imprint of the Taylor & Francis Group, an informa business

© 2023 selection and editorial matter, Economic History Society, Nicole
Robertson, John Singleton and Avram Taylor; individual chapters, the
contributors

The right of Economic History Society, Nicole Robertson, John Singleton and
Avram

First edition published by Pearson Education Limited 1994
Second edition published by Routledge 2007

British Library Cataloguing in Publication Data
A catalogue record for this book is available from the British Library

Library of Congress Cataloging-in-Publication Data
Names: Robertson, Nicole, editor. | Singleton, John, 1960- editor. |
    Taylor, Avram, 1962- editor.
Title: 20th century Britain : economic, cultural and social change /
    edited by Nicole Robertson, John Singleton and Avram Taylor.
Other titles: Twentieth-century Britain
Description: Third edition. | Abingdon, Oxon : New York, NY :
    Routledge, 2023. | Includes bibliographical references and index.
Identifiers: LCCN 2022036701 (print) | LCCN 2022036702 (ebook)
Subjects: LCSH: Great Britain—History—20th century.
Classification: LCC DA566 .T844 2023 (print) | LCC DA566 (ebook) |
    DDC 941.082—dc23/eng/20220802
LC record available at https://lccn.loc.gov/2022036701
LC ebook record available at https://lccn.loc.gov/2022036702

ISBN: 978-0-367-42657-6 (hbk)
ISBN: 978-0-367-42656-9 (pbk)
ISBN: 978-1-003-03711-8 (ebk)

DOI: 10.4324/9781003037118

Typeset in Sabon
by Apex CoVantage, LLC

Contents

Images

Figures

Tables

Contributors

Victoria Bates is Associate Professor in Modern Medical History at the University of Bristol. Her research expertise ranges from Victorian forensic medicine to the history of NHS hospitals and current-day sensory studies. Her current UKRI Future Leaders Fellowship, 'Sensing Spaces of Healthcare' brings together history, medical humanities, sensory studies and design for the first time.

Stephen Brooke is Professor of History at York University, Toronto. He is the author of *Sexual Politics* (Oxford, 2011) and articles dealing with photography, gender, sexuality and politics in twentieth-century Britain.

Hannah Charnock is Lecturer in British History at the University of Bristol. Her research explores social relationships, gender and sexuality in twentieth-century Britain. She has published articles on the history of marriage in the interwar period and on teenage sexuality in post war England.

Martin Chick is Professor of Economic History at the University of Edinburgh. He has written three books to date on a ragbag of topics which include economic planning, electricity and energy policy and the development of the British economy since 1951. He is currently trying to write another book, this time on the economic use of the sea.

Marcus Collins is Reader in Contemporary History at Loughborough University. He is author of *Modern Love* (2003) and *The Beatles and Sixties Britain* (2020), co-author of *Why Study History?* (2020) and editor of *The Permissive Society and Its Enemies* (2007). His current projects include *The Beatles' World* and *Broadcasting and Homosexuality from Wolfenden to AIDS*.

Kate Fisher is Professor of Social and Cultural History at the University of Exeter. Her books include, *Birth Control, Sex, and Marriage in Britain, c1918–1960*; *Sex before the Sexual Revolution* (with Prof. Simon Szreter) and *Sex, Knowledge and Receptions of the Past* (with Prof. Rebecca Langlands). She is currently directing *Rethinking Sexology* (with Prof. Jana Funke), http://rethinkingsexology.exeter. ac.uk/. She co-directs *Sex & History*, which uses historical material to improve sexuality education, http://blogs.exeter.ac.uk/sexandhistory/.

Sarah Hackett is Professor in Modern European History at Bath Spa University. She is a specialist in Europe's immigration history and researches migration and integration policies and Muslim minorities. She is author of *Foreigners, Minorities and Integration: The Muslim Immigrant Experience in Britain and Germany* (MUP,

2013) and *Britain's Rural Muslims: Rethinking Integration* (MUP, 2020) and co-editor of the *Journal of Migration History*.

Vicky Long is Senior Lecturer in 20th Century British History at Newcastle University. She is the author of *The Rise and Fall of the Healthy Factory: The Politics of Industrial Health in Britain, 1914–60* (Palgrave, 2011) and *Destigmatising Mental Illness? Professional Politics and Public Education in Britain, 1870–1970* (Manchester, 2014). She is currently researching the history of prenatal screening in late twentieth-century Britain.

Helen McCarthy is Reader in Modern and Contemporary British History at the University of Cambridge. She is author of three books: *The British People and the League of Nations: Democracy, Citizenship and Internationalism* (Manchester University Press, 2011); *Women of the World: The Rise of the Female Diplomat* (Bloomsbury, 2014); and *Double Lives: A History of Working Motherhood* (Bloomsbury, 2020), which was shortlisted for the Wolfson History Prize.

Andrew Miles is Professor of Sociology at the University of Manchester, where he works on issues of culture, stratification and social mobility. He has written the only systematic study of historical social mobility in Britain to date (Miles 1999). More recently, he was a member of the high-profile *Great British Class Survey* project and a co-author of the best-selling Pelican book *Social Class in the 21st Century* (Savage *et al.* 2015). In 2018, he edited a special issue of new work on social mobility for *The British Journal of Sociology*.

Anandi Ramamurthy is Professor in Media and Culture at Sheffield Hallam University. She is the author of *Imperial Persuaders: Images of Africa and Asian in British Advertising* (2003) and *Black Star: Britain's Asian Youth Movements* (2013) and founder of www.tandana.org, a digital archive of public documents produced by the AYMs.

Linsey Robb is Senior Lecturer in Modern British History at Northumbria University. She is a social and cultural historian specializing in the study of gender in the Second World War. Key publications include *Men at Work* (Palgrave, 2015) and *Men in Reserve* (2017). She is currently researching British conscientious objection during the Second World War.

Nicole Robertson is Associate Professor in Modern British History at Sheffield Hallam University. She has published widely on women and the clerical sector, the co-operative movement, consumerism and the Labour Party. Her current research project explores gender, activism and identity among white-collar workers.

Neil Rollings is Professor of Economic and Business History at the University of Glasgow. He writes mainly on historical aspects of business-government relations and of business and European integration.

Catherine R. Schenk is Professor of Economic and Social History at the University of Oxford. She has held academic posts in New Zealand, London and Glasgow and was visiting researcher at the IMF and the Bank for International Settlements. She has written many articles and books on international economic relations.

Peter Scott is Professor of International Business History at the University of Reading's Henley Business School. His research mainly focuses on twentieth-century Britain and the United States, including income and wealth inequality, living standards, household consumption, consumer durables, the housing sector, working hours, regional development and path dependence.

John Singleton is Emeritus Professor of Economic and Business History at Sheffield Hallam University. He has published widely on British business history, economic policy in New Zealand, the development of central banking and the history of disasters and industrial safety.

Avram Taylor is Senior Lecturer in History at Northumbria University. His research reflects his interest in the relationship between class, gender and ethnicity. His thesis was published as *Working Class Credit and Community since 1918* (Palgrave, 2002.) He has subsequently published a number of articles on Jews in Britain.

Pat Thane is a visiting professor in history at Birkbeck College London. Her publications include *The Foundations of the Welfare State* (Longman, 2nd ed. 1996); *Old Age in English History. Past Experiences, Present Issues* (OUP, 2000); *Unequal Britain. Equalities in Britain since 1945*, ed. (Bloomsbury 2010); *Women and Citizenship in Britain and Ireland in the Twentieth Century*, co-ed with Esther Breitenbach (Bloomsbury, 2010); *Sinners? Scroungers? Saints? Unmarried Motherhood in Twentieth Century England*, with Tanya Evans (OUP 2012); and *Divided Kingdom. A History of Britain 1900 to the Present* (CUP 2018).

Jim Tomlinson is Professor of Economic and Social History at the University of Glasgow. He has published widely on the historical political economy of modern Britain, most recently *Managing the Economy, Managing the People. Narratives of British Economic Life from Brexit to Beveridge* (Oxford University Press, 2017) and *Dundee and the Empire: Juteopolis 1850–1939* (Edinburgh University Press, 2014).

Richard Toye is Professor of Modern History at the University of Exeter. He has published numerous books on British political history, including (with David Thackeray) *Age of Promises: Electoral Pledges in Twentieth Century Britain* (Oxford University Press, 2021).

James T. Walker is Professor and Director of Research at the Henley Business School at the University of Reading. Currently, his research is exploring the causes and consequences of changing levels of inequality over the last 100 years and the unintended consequences of research evaluation on the generation of knowledge.

Paul Ward is Professor of Public History and Community Heritage at Edge Hill University. He taught at Edge Hill University and the University of Huddersfield until 2021. He has written *Red Flag and Union Jack: Englishness, Patriotism and the British Left, 1881–1924* (1998) and *Britishness since 1870* (2004). He is co-writing a book called *Making History Together: A Practical Guide to Doing Collaborative Research*.

Stephanie Ward is Senior Lecturer in Modern Welsh History at Cardiff University. She is an historian of the working class in interwar Britain and is primarily interested in histories of masculinity, political identities, social policy and protest movements.

John F. Wilson is Professor of Business History, Newcastle Business School, Northumbria University. He has published extensively in the fields of business and management history. He is especially interested in issues related to management strategy and organizational structure, as well as corporate governance and business networking. Current projects include an analysis of how business history can make a bigger impact on business performance and policy.

Chris Wrigley is Emeritus Professor of Modern British History at the University of Nottingham. He has published *David Lloyd George and the British Labour Movement* (1976), *Lloyd George and the Challenge of Labour* (1990), *British Trade Unions since 1933* (2002), *AJP Taylor* (2006), *A History of British Industrial Relations 1875–1979*, 3 volumes (1982–96) and *The First World War and the International Economy* (2000).

Foreword

The Economic History Society, established in 1926 to support research, teaching and publications in economic and social history, broadly defined, is especially pleased to sponsor this third edition of *Twentieth-Century Britain: Economic, Cultural and Social History*. The editors and contributors are to be congratulated for overcoming the challenges of the pandemic, not least the closure of archives, and for producing a comprehensive range of chapters examining the economic, social, cultural and political history of twentieth-century Britain from the perspective of the first two decades of the twenty-first century. This edition is an admirable successor to the first edition, published in 1994 (edited by Paul Johnson), and the second edition, published in 2007 (edited by Julie-Marie Strange and Francesca Carnevali), reflecting new contemporary concerns and developments in scholarship, as well as established approaches and topics. Directed at undergraduates, it offers sufficient flexibility to provide the basis for a year-long course about twentieth-century Britain or chapters to drop into.

In their introduction, the editors highlight interrelationships among the economic, cultural, social and political and set out overarching themes: economic prosperity and decline, equality and inequality and social mobility. Departing from the structures of previous editions, the editors do not use the First or Second World Wars to divide the twentieth century but provide in the first section an overview of important issues between 1900 and the early twenty-first century in order to draw the attention of students to the main elements of change and continuity across a wide range of topics, including the British political system; the economy since 1900: living standards, economic inequality and welfare provision; linkages between the UK and the world economy; the formulation of economic policy; work, the labour market and trade unions; leisure, consumption and consumerism; environmental history; business and management; empire and decolonization; ethnicity, identity and multiculturalism; women and inequalities; disability and the experience of disabled people; social mobility; and gender and sexuality.

Topics over a shorter time frame are the focus of chapters in the second section, including comparison of the First and Second World Wars; the interwar depression; civil society, citizenship and voluntary action from 1918 to the 1960s; sexual attitudes and behaviours; cultural revolution in the 1960s; Britain and Europe since 1945; and the experience of young South Asians.

Of particular note are two features of all chapters, which enable students to delve more deeply. An 'In Focus' box addresses a specific issue in more detail, and 'Debates and Interpretations' offers a discussion of an aspect of the chapter's topic that has provoked controversy among historians and suggestions for further reading. In addition, there is a glossary of terms, and in the economic history chapters, there are explanations of why and how some features of the economy are measured, providing an introduction to key concepts for historians and non-economists.

Finally, special thanks go to Eve Setch, for initiating the third edition, and to her team at Taylor & Francis; to the editors – Nicole Robertson, John Singleton and Avram Taylor – as well as to Barry Doyle, the original editor, forced to bow out due to additional work responsibilities – for taking on the project and for their efficiency, skill, clear focus and good humour throughout, and to the distinguished team of contributors for sharing their expertise and enthusiasm for understanding and interpreting the past for the present – a challenging mission of enduring importance.

Marguerite Dupree
Chair, Publications Committee
Economic History Society

Acknowledgements

We are grateful to the following for permission to reproduce copyright material:
  Woodhorn Museum, BBC, the National Archives, Leeds Postcards, Peter Trimming, Library of Congress Prints and Photographs and Tandana.org.
  Every effort has been made to contact copyright holders. Please advise the publisher of any errors or omissions, and these will be corrected in subsequent editions.

Editors' acknowledgements

Firstly, we are extremely grateful to the contributors for all the hard work and commitment that has gone into the volume and the Economic History Society for sponsoring the project. Thank you to the readers and the Economic History Society Publications committee for their very constructive advice and suggestions. We are grateful to Museums Northumberland for their kind permission to use the cover image of Woodhorn Museum, Northumberland. We would also like to thank Eve Setch, Zoe Thomson and staff at Taylor and Francis for their invaluable assistance. We had the pleasure of working with Barry Doyle, whose expertise and vision were essential in this book's earlier stages. Finally, special thanks to Marguerite Dupree for her generous encouragement and support throughout this project.

1 Introduction

Twentieth-century Britain

Nicole Robertson, John Singleton and Avram Taylor

One way to start thinking about the past is to consider our own place within society and how that has been shaped by history. A good way to approach the period that this book covers is to think about how this volume is itself a product of some of the significant social changes that have shaped the course of the twentieth century. The historical context for this book is both the expansion of the discipline of history, which saw it move way beyond its traditional concerns with high politics, and also the expansion of education in general, and higher education in particular in twentieth-century Britain.[1] The main readership for this book will be undergraduate students, who may be studying in a variety of different types of institution, which is, in itself, a manifestation of a significant social and cultural shift in British society since 1900. This is the third edition of this particular volume. Texts like the current one are in demand because of the expansion of higher education since the 1960s. There were approximately 250,000 students in higher education in 1962, and by the academic year 2012/13, this had risen to 2.3 million (Mahoney and Lim 2015, p. 75). This meant that, after 1945, a lot of young people from working-class backgrounds became the first members of their family to attend university.

This was a profound social change that not only greatly increased social mobility, an issue we will be returning to later, but also made many who had benefited from it critical of the society they lived in and its history. The then Labour leader, Neil Kinnock, spoke for many of his generation in a famous speech in 1987, when he asked: 'Why am I the first Kinnock for a thousand generations to be able to get to University?' (Chaytor 2004). There was also an expansion in the number of universities to cope with this influx of students, and new universities were created in 1992 as a result of the Further and Higher Education Act (1992), in which institutions originally called polytechnics became universities. In addition, many further education colleges are now able to award degrees as part of the general expansion of the number and type of institutions that can confer higher education awards (Mahoney and Lim 2015, pp. 74–75). While we should all welcome the expansion of higher education that has taken place since 1945, it is also necessary to go beyond the increase in the total number of students cited previously and consider the extent to which a university education really is open to everyone, regardless of background, as we will see in the following.

As this discussion of higher education suggests, at first sight it seems obvious that the history of the twentieth century was one of continual progress in every aspect of British life. As we will see, the standard of living increased, and the rights of women and minorities have been increasingly recognized through legislative measures that

DOI: 10.4324/9781003037118-1

would seem to make discrimination 'impossible' in today's society. However, not only do we need to look beyond superficial assessments of the century, but recent events also suggest that British society may not be as 'equal' as it appears to be, and that it has still not come to terms with the legacy of its past and the history of slavery and Empire in particular. As Paul Ward points out in his chapter on Empire in this book, the legacy of the imperial past is literally built into British towns and cities. In 2020 the statue of the slave trader Edward Colston was removed from its plinth and thrown into Bristol docks as part of a Black Lives Matter protest in that city. Colston's statue had caused considerable controversy for some time, but after the killing of George Floyd by police officers in the United States in 2020 there was a wave of protests that quickly spread to the United Kingdom in which protestors raised questions about racism in this country. The issue of young Black men being disproportionately targeted by the police as a result of the stop and search policy, for example, had long caused tensions between the Black community and the police. The co-founder of Black Lives Matter UK, Natalie Jeffers, pointed out that there were fewer guns in the United Kingdom, but institutional racism meant that 'there is a war going on against black people' (McVeigh 2016).

Statues of the businessman and imperialist Cecil Rhodes have also been the subject of an intense protest campaign called Rhodes Must Fall that began in South Africa and was then taken up in Britain and directed against a statue of Rhodes at Oxford University. This sparked a media controversy, as some commentators felt that the protestors were attempting to rewrite the history of the British Empire (Chaudhuri 2016). This illustrates not only how views of the British Empire have been reshaped as we move further away from the process of decolonization but also how the imperial legacy is still contested, as the loss of Empire is at the heart of discussions of 'British decline'.

Economic prosperity or decline?

In 1900 people in the United Kingdom were poor by the standards of developed countries nowadays. Income per person in the United Kingdom in about 1900 was roughly the same as it is now in Guatemala, Jamaica or the Philippines.[2] People in other European countries were even poorer than those in Britain. Yet, as historical drama series remind us, the United Kingdom also had quite a few rich people in 1900 and was the centre of an empire over which the sun never set. So, as people often say, it 'was a different world', and we should beware of examining the past through the lens of the 2020s.

Since 1900 the United Kingdom has enjoyed remarkable improvements in living standards, quality of life, longevity, health and education. The chapters in this book that deal most directly with the economy, its management and its impact can be located within the subdisciplines of economic history, business history and environmental history.

Economic history seeks to explain this growing material prosperity, which may not be obvious over brief periods but which is startling over longer ones. It does so by drawing on the tools of economics, a discipline quite different from those underpinning social and cultural history.[3]

Economics investigates the behaviour of consumers, workers, businesses and government officials, not in isolation, but as they engage with each other in markets.

A market could be a group of cheese stalls, an online job search site or the London Stock Exchange – it is not necessary for people to meet in person for a market to exist. Markets bring together buyers and sellers of goods and services to determine prices and the quantities sold and consumed. Markets send signals that prompt firms and individuals to adjust their behaviour. There are markets for new ideas (intellectual property) and for new and improved goods and services (better machinery, the internet, vaccines) that embody those ideas. Through the emergence of knowledge, its application in the form of new technology and, more prosaically, the accumulation of productive assets (like aircraft or supermarkets), the economy grows and living standards rise. As people become better off, they can be taxed to fund government services like healthcare and education. This – all of it – is what has happened since 1900, not only in the United Kingdom but also in other successful countries, including the United States, France, Germany, Japan, Australia and New Zealand.

Economists and economic historians try to measure the changes outlined earlier, partly to make international comparisons and partly to understand the processes involved. Consequently, economic historians use (and sometimes construct) statistics, and some develop mathematical models to show how the economy fits together.

But, if you read much British economic history, you will soon discover a strong current of pessimism, perhaps even an obsession with failure and decline. Why? In the 1850s, the UK was the top dog in the world economy, with the largest and most modern industries, such as cotton textiles, coal mining, iron and steel making and engineering. By the late nineteenth century, however, the United States and Germany had in some areas overtaken British industry. This process continued, with other countries catching up and sometimes leapfrogging British industrial output and efficiency. Much of the handwringing is over *relative* decline, the fact that instead of being the world leader in industry and technology, and the owner of the biggest empire, the UK became an also-ran, albeit a wealthy one, with no empire to speak of except the Falklands, Gibraltar and a chunk of the Antarctic. 'Declinists' sometimes look with nostalgia to the days when industries such as cotton and coal ruled supreme in some districts. But the gradual replacement of manual industrial occupations by jobs in the service industries was a global phenomenon and not a sign of British failure. Nevertheless, the transition was painful for the regions and workers affected, recreating the North-South divide. Despite the UK's loss of status since the Second World War, the population as a whole continued to enjoy rising living standards.

Long-term perspectives must be qualified with mention of shorter fluctuations. The economy did contract at times, including during the depression of the early 1930s and the financial crisis of 2008–09. Those episodes saw the imposition of policies of austerity which exacerbated inequality.

Of the disciplines most closely related to economic history, business history is the most prominent. Whereas economic history is taught, if at all, in university economics or history departments, business historians often reside in business or management schools. Business history draws on concepts and theories from the management and organizational disciplines. Business historians endeavour to understand the behaviour and assess the performance of firms and groups of firms. This often involves examining how they were organized and led, how they formulated and implemented strategies and how they interacted with other firms and the government. Over the twentieth century, the way in which businesses were managed evolved. As firms grew, they became more difficult to manage, and a more systematic approach emerged (Wilson

1995). Although there is sometimes a tendency to regard UK business as less efficient than its overseas counterparts, many UK-based firms have developed into successful multinationals: for example, Astra Zeneca, GSK, BP and Unilever.

Economic historians have until recently given little attention to the environmental impact of economic activity. Britain is densely populated, and much land has been built over, not to say trashed. Damage to the environment and health arising from economic activity is hard to measure and value, which may explain the slowness of economic historians to address the topic. If you could go back in time to a British city in 1900, you would be shocked at how dirty everything was. The modern world may not seem as dirty, but it also contains serious environmental hazards that threaten our wellbeing and the sustainability of our civilization.

(In)equality

The Equality Act (2010) strengthened discrimination legislation passed in the closing decades of the twentieth century. The law protected certain characteristics: age, disability, gender reassignment, marriage and civil partnership, pregnancy and maternity, race, religion or belief, sex and sexual orientation. This legislation would have been unimaginable in 1900. The twentieth century saw intense campaigning and significant progress for equal rights associated with disability, gender, LGBTQ+ and race. But inequalities remain, and there is a vibrant scholarship exploring this.

Disability studies and disability history draw on an interdisciplinary field, with war, social policy and activists' work being a particular focus of interest. The First World War heightened awareness of physical impairments and mental wellbeing as troops returned with life-changing injuries and significant trauma. During the interwar years, some support became available. For example, the Blind Persons Act (1920) required local authorities to make arrangements for the visually impaired, work on prosthetics advanced and sheltered employment opportunities were available, including the British Legion poppy factory (London) and Painted Fabrics (Sheffield) (Cohen 2001). The NHS's launch in 1948 revolutionized healthcare, providing nationalized medical care that was no longer exclusive to those who could afford it and assisting those who previously were forced to rely on charity. Disabled people were not passive in campaigning against discrimination, establishing disability charities and support groups. From the 1960s and 1970s, disabled people took direct action against inequality and discrimination, increasingly driven by a social rather than a medical model of disability.

Campaigning against inequality and exclusion was also central to women's rights in the twentieth century. In 1900 women could not vote in general elections, were barred from certain professions and educational opportunities and had no right to equal pay. The early 1900s saw widespread campaigns for electoral equality with men. Organizations including the National Union of Women's Suffrage Societies, Women's Social and Political Union and the Co-operative Women's Guild used various tactics. But they faced opposition, such as the National League for Opposing Women's Suffrage. The Representation of the People Act (1918) awarded certain women the right to vote (also abolishing almost all property qualifications to men); full suffrage on the same basis as men was granted in 1928. Inequality could vary across countries. For example, in England and Wales, before the 1923 Matrimonial Causes Act, a husband could end the marriage after proving adultery. A woman needed proof of adultery plus additional faults. However, in Scotland, men and women divorced on equal terms

(Thane 2018, pp. 25, 100). The twentieth century saw further campaigns for equality, including employment, education and training. Significant progress was made with the Equal Pay Act 1970 (Clementina Black moved the first TUC equal pay resolution in 1888) and the Employment Protection Act 1975 (which introduced Britain's first maternity leave legislation and made sacking women for becoming pregnant illegal).

Whilst it was illegal to pay men and women different amounts for doing the same job, the first gender pay gap report in 2018 revealed gender pay gaps over 40 per cent were not uncommon, and 78 per cent of organizations had pay gaps in favour of men (Gender Pay Gap Reporting 2019). Expensive childcare, employer resistance to flexible working and the effect of maternity leave on a woman's career are some of the challenges. The Royal Historical Society noted,

> there are still major barriers to gender equality in the historical profession, both formal and informal . . . in many key ways gender continues fundamentally to shape historians' experience of work at universities, in ways that make women's careers harder than those of men.
>
> (2018, p. 7)

During the twentieth century, documenting women's history became a vibrant area of enquiry. Following first-wave feminism, work on women and industry, trade unions and the vote was published. Writing women's history and feminist history was particularly buoyant during the 1970s and 1980s. Interest remains strong, for example, with studies on second-wave feminism and diversity within the women's movement (Setch 2002; Thomlinson 2015). Expanding since the mid-1970s, gender history 'is based on the fundamental idea that what it means to be defined as man or woman has a history', and it traces the impact of gender on difference, events and institutions over time (Rose 2010, p. 2). Using gender as a tool of historical analysis is not without controversies; whether gender history is 'hiding' women from history once again is debated (Bailey and Arnold 2005). Gender history has produced a range of dynamic work; for example, on race, empire, war and fatherhood (Matera 2015; Strange 2015).

Sex also has a history. Since the 1970s, a new, critical history of sexuality developed, engaging with a broad range of topics, including fertility, sex work, marriage (same-sex and other-sex), singleness, cohabitation, sexual health and campaigns for and against LGBTQ+ rights (Weeks 2016, pp. 3–4). As Weeks highlights, 'Sexuality research in general and LGBTQ history in particular are no longer marginal activities: they have become a major aspect of the historical endeavour' (2016, p. 124).

He notes that many of those early writers were research students, independent scholars and activists in the women's or gay movements (2016, p. 2). In twentieth-century Britain, sexual preferences and identities were denied equality in law. The Criminal Law Amendment Act (1885) made *any* male homosexual act illegal, including those conducted in private. Not until 1967 did the Sexual Offences Act partially decriminalize same-sex acts between men undertaken in private. This applied in England and Wales. It took until 1980 for the law to change in Scotland and 1982 for Northern Ireland. More than two men having sex together remained illegal, and in 1998 the Bolton Seven, a group of gay and bisexual men, was convicted of gross indecency. Section 28 of the Local Government Act (1988) forbade local authorities to 'promote homosexuality', remaining enforceable until 2000 in Scotland and 2003 in England and Wales. Denied equality, campaigns for legal and social change for the LGBTQ+ community were crucial. This included work by North Western Homosexual Law Reform Committee (established 1964, becoming the Campaign for Homosexual Equality in 1971), Gay Liberation Front (established 1970), the gay and lesbian Trade Union Congress (established 1977), the Black Lesbian and Gay Centre (opened in 1982 to provide advice and counselling) and the Terrence Higgins Trust (established in 1982 as the first charity in the UK set up in response to HIV and AIDS).

Social mobility: opportunity for everyone?

As this discussion of discrimination and inequality illustrates, the view of the twentieth century as simply one of progress always has to be qualified as we consider the persistence of prejudice and inequalities across British society. As legal barriers to education and employment have been removed during the course of the century, it is easy to imagine that we live in an age of social mobility in which there are opportunities for everyone regardless of their background, and we should now consider how class and ethnicity have shaped people's experience during the course of the century.

There have been some significant historical studies of social mobility in Britain, the most recent of which is by Selina Todd, who argues that social mobility was greatest

Image 1.1 Female University of London graduates, wearing traditional caps and gowns, arriving at the Albert Hall for the presentation of degrees on 'Presentation Day', 1937

Source: © SZ Photo/Scherl/Bridgeman Images.

in periods when people enjoyed the benefits of a strong economy and a comprehensive welfare system:

> No single generation enjoyed all of these benefits but those who came closest were the breakthrough generation (born between 1920 and 1934) and the golden generation (born between 1935 and 1955.) The golden generation enjoyed far more upward mobility than any before or since.
>
> (2021, p. 6)

However, as Todd herself has pointed out, despite the expansion of education for working-class children after the Second World War and the new employment opportunities this created for them, 'Most of the fortunate few only travelled a short distance up the social ladder' (2014, p. 233).

These arguments are explored in depth in a special issue of the journal *Cultural and Social History*, and the introduction to this provides an excellent overview of the literature. The key themes identified in this review of the literature are that social mobility was the result of economic and social change rather than government policies, that men and women had different experiences of social mobility and that social mobility cannot be reduced to 'a linear movement up or down a social hierarchy' (de Bellaigue, Mills and Worth 2019, p. 4). The piece also identifies the importance of the racial discrimination faced by ethnic minorities in British society, and we should now move on to discuss this.

As Sarah Hackett points out in her chapter on ethnic minorities in this book, 'Migrants' experiences in Britain have been diverse and have varied according to either ethnic group or location, or both. They have been characterized by discrimination, hostility and constraint, but also integration, success and self-determination' (Chapter 12). This is an important point, as it is not only necessary to understand the vastly differing experiences of ethnic minorities, but it is also the case that experiences within a single minority can vary greatly. For example, as Panikos Panayi points out, 'Indians or Chinese people may have higher rates of unemployment than the "White British", yet a larger percentage of their populations work as professionals' (2010, p. 106).

The East European Jews who arrived in Britain at the end of the nineteenth century are usually identified as the archetypal immigrant 'success story' in terms of their integration and social mobility (Panayi 2010, p. 107). This is because they initially worked in occupations that would limit their contact with non-Jews, and, even though they were often employed by their co-religionists, they were still very poorly paid, and many worked in 'sweatshop' conditions. During the interwar years there was a degree of social mobility among the children of Jewish immigrants, but a lot of the second generation continued to work in 'immigrant trades', and very few went to university. There was a transformation of the social structure of the Jewish community in Britain after the Second World War, but this was very gradual. However, by the 1960s more Jewish children were attending university, Jewish families had moved out of the old immigrant areas, and increasing numbers of Jews had joined the professions. There was also a decline in religious observance amongst the mainstream Jewish population after the Second World War (Taylor 2019, pp. 472–473; Endelman 2002, pp. 239–241). This example raises many issues, such as the role of residential segregation and the 'immigrant economy' in creating the conditions for social mobility and also what happens to the identity of an ethnic community when they achieve this level of 'successful integration'.

This discussion of Jewish social mobility, which suggests that the barriers to a university education were removed during the course of the century, returns us to the issue that we considered at the start of the introduction: access to higher education. A 2017 study of this issue found that, although people from all social backgrounds benefited from the expansion of higher education, poorer children were still less likely to attend university than children who came from rich families. Thus, although by the early twenty-first century it was more likely that children from lower social class backgrounds would go to university than it was in 1900, there were still significant differences in 'university participation' between this group and the children of graduate parents. As the authors of the report point out, this difference was particularly marked amongst those children who received free school meals: 'teenagers from families not receiving free meals were two and a half times more likely to go to university than their peers in low-income families who qualified for this benefit' (Crawford *et al.* 2017, p. 4).

However, university attendance, although important, is not the only indicator of social mobility. We also need to consider how graduates fare in the labour market and the extent to which ethnic minorities still face discrimination when seeking employment. David Olusoga points out that, despite the successful social integration of Black Britons, significant disadvantages remain, as Black graduates in Britain are paid less than their white contemporaries, and young people from ethnic minorities have experienced an increase in unemployment, while there has been a decrease in unemployment amongst their white peers (2016, p. 525). The history of social mobility in Britain clearly demonstrates some of the ways in which Britain has been transformed since 1900 and the increased opportunities which many people have benefited from, particularly after the Second World War. However, as we saw when we considered women's position in the labour market and gender discrimination, despite the considerable progress that has been made in overcoming prejudice in society, an individual's class and ethnicity still have a significant impact on their life chances even after a century of protest and legislation to create a more 'equal' Britain.

Twentieth-Century Britain: economic, cultural and social change

Twentieth-Century Britain is divided into two parts, A and B. Part A consists of 16 chapters that provide an overview of important issues in British history between 1900 and the early twenty-first century. The editors chose not to break twentieth-century British history in two at the Second World War. As we get further away from 1945, the division between pre– and post–Second World War is becoming increasingly arbitrary and in some cases may obscure changes or continuities while overemphasizing the importance of some topics. The broader perspective will allow for greater flexibility in teaching. There is also a practical reason for this decision: it avoided the need to double the number of chapters. Of necessity, each chapter must take a broad-brush approach because it deals with at least one hundred years.

The purpose of the chapters in Part A is to draw the attention of students to the main elements of change, whether sharp or gradual, across a range of topics. However, these chapters also highlight areas of continuity in British experience. Each chapter also contains two features that stand out from the main text, first an 'In Focus' box which addresses in more detail a particular issue and second a 'Debates and Interpretations' section which discusses an aspect of the chapter's theme that has provoked controversy amongst historians. The 'Debates and Interpretations' also provide an introduction to the relevant historiography.

Part A begins with a summary of UK political history and institutions, which is designed to give students a framework for considering the role of government, political parties and their supporters in shaping, or at least influencing, many of the developments described subsequently. The next group of chapters address broadly economic issues: the development of the British economy since 1900; living standards, economic inequality and welfare provision; the evolution of the trade and financial linkages between the UK and the world economy; and the formulation and implementation of economic policy. Some chapters span several different approaches to British history. The chapter on work, the labour market and trade unions combines social and economic history, whilst that on leisure, consumption and consumerism is even more eclectic addressing matters of interest to cultural historians. Next comes environmental history, a branch of history in its own right but which once more is of increasing importance to economic, cultural and social historians. The chapter on business and management, like that on the environment, tackles a distinct branch of history, albeit one closely related to economic history. The chapter on empire and decolonization explores the imperial context, its impact on British culture and the demise of empire. The next set of chapters deal with broadly social and cultural issues, although these are also ones that have a significant impact on the economy: ethnicity, identity and multiculturalism; women and inequalities; disability and disabled people; social mobility; gender and sexuality; and healthcare, health and wellbeing. These focus on key areas of (in)equality, diversity and wellbeing in twentieth-century Britain.

The chapters in Part B deal with a selection of topics over a shorter time frame. Although it would have been possible to offer separate chapters on the First and Second World Wars, there is merit in comparing those two seismic events. The interwar depression is the most important episode in the peacetime history of Britain in the first half of the twentieth century. The importance of civil society and voluntary action from 1918 to the rise of radical social movements 50 years later provides an understanding of citizenship that sits alongside traditionally defined political systems. There is a large historical scholarship on sexual attitudes and behaviours, and this chapter in Part B adopts a 'queer' approach to understanding the practice and experience of heterosexual identity and desire from the aftermath of the First World War to the beginning of the women's liberation movement. The UK's tricky relationship with the EU is also a matter of the greatest importance deserving a separate chapter. The next chapter spotlights the cultural revolution of the 1960s – arguably a pivotal moment in British history. The selection closes by exploring the formation of independent grassroots organizations amongst Asian youth during the 1970s and 1980s. It offers an important understanding of how this generation defended their communities and addresses key aspects of British identity and culture.

Both the first and second editions of *Twentieth-Century Britain* (1994 edited by Paul Johnson; 2007 edited by Francesca Carnevali and Julie-Marie Strange) provided excellent coverage of shifts in British history. The accessibility of these two volumes made them important teaching tools. It is in this same vein that we have commissioned and recommissioned essays that provide coverage of recent developments in scholarship whilst also giving a grounding in established approaches and topics studied by students of history and related disciplines. Both these early editions, alongside

Matthew Hilton's chapter on a revised *Twentieth-Century Britain* textbook (2017), have influenced this revised collection.

Some aspects of British history are left out of the current volume. Except for relations with the EU, there is little or nothing on foreign policy; military history, history of science and religious history are also neglected, and it would be easy to think of other omissions. The book is already quite large, and there is bound to be a trade-off between coverage and manageability. We hope, however, to provide first- and second-year undergraduates with an essential guide to the current state of academic thinking on most important elements of twentieth-century British history, with a view to encouraging them to dig deeper by following up the references.

Notes

1 To clarify, Great Britain comprises England, Scotland and Wales. The United Kingdom of Great Britain and Northern Ireland includes England, Scotland, Wales and Northern Ireland. As in everyday usage, contributors often use Britain and the UK interchangeably. For important comparative and historical reasons, at times this book on twentieth-century Britain includes reference to all four countries.
2 If you'd like to compare estimates of income per person (or real GDP per capita in technical language) in different countries over time, visit the Maddison Project Database, but remember that such *estimates* are subject to a wide variety of errors (Bolt *et al.* 2018).
3 For a more advanced textbook on British economic history, see Floud *et al.* (2014). For a fact-filled, narrative approach, see Pollard (1992).

References

Bailey, J., and Arnold, J., 2005. *Is the rise of gender history 'hiding' women from history once again?* Available from: https://archives.history.ac.uk/history-in-focus/Gender/articles.html.
Bolt, J., Inklaar, R., de Jong, H., and van Zanden, J.L., 2018. *Rebasing 'Maddison': New income comparisons and the shape of long-run economic development.* Available from: www.rug.nl/ggdc/historicaldevelopment/maddison/releases/maddison-project-database-2018.
Chaudhuri, A., 2016. The real meaning of Rhodes must fall. *The Guardian*, 16 March. Available from: https://www.theguardian.com/uk-news/2016/mar/16/the-real-meaning-of-rhodes-must-fall.
Chaytor, D., 2004. Socialism actually. *The Guardian*, 23 January. Available from: https://www.theguardian.com/education/2004/jan/23/highereducation.uk.
Cohen, D., 2001. *The war come home: Disabled veterans in Britain and Germany 1914–1939.* Berkeley: University of California Press.
Crawford, C., Dearden, L., Micklewright, J., and Vignoles, A., 2017. *Family background & university success: Differences in higher education access and outcomes in England.* Oxford: Oxford University Press.
de Bellaigue, C., Mills, H., and Worth, E., 2019. 'Rags to Riches?' New histories of social mobility in modern Britain – introduction. *Cultural and Social History*, 16 (2), 1–11.
Endelman, T.M., 2002. *The Jews of Britain, 1656 to 2000.* Berkeley and Los Angeles: University of California Press.
Floud, R., Humphries, J., and Johnson, P., eds., 2014. *The Cambridge economic history of modern Britain, Vol. 2, Growth and decline, 1870 to the present.* 2nd ed. Cambridge: Cambridge University Press.
Gender Pay Gap Reporting, 2019. Available from: www.equalpayportal.co.uk/gender-pay-gap-reporting.
Hilton, M., 2017. Twentieth-century British history: Perspectives, trajectories and some thoughts on a revised textbook. *In*: P. Di Martino, A. Popp and P. Scott, eds. *People, markets,*

goods: *Economies and societies in history: Essays in honour of Francesca Carnevali*. Woodbridge: Boydell & Brewer, 155–175.

Mahoney, C., and Lim, H., 2015. Democratizing higher education in the United Kingdom: A case study. *In*: P. Blessinger and J.P. Anchan, eds. *Democratizing higher education: International comparative perspective*. New York and London: Routledge, 74–91.

Matera, M., 2015. *Black London: The imperial metropolis and decolonisation in the twentieth century*. Oakland: University of California Press.

McVeigh, T., 2016. Why activists brought the Black Lives Matter movement to the UK. *The Guardian*, 6 August. Available from: https://www.theguardian.com/uk-news/2016/aug/06/black-lives-matter-uk-found-vital-social-justice.

Olusoga, D., 2016. *Black and British: A forgotten history*. London: Pan Books.

Panayi, P., 2010. *An immigration history of Britain: Multicultural racism since 1800*. Harlow: Pearson.

Pollard, S., 1992. *The development of the British economy, 1914–1990*. 4th ed. London: Edward Arnold.

Rose, S.O., 2010. *What is gender history?* Cambridge: Polity Press.

Setch, E., 2002. The face of metropolitan feminism: The London Women's Liberation Workshop, 1969–1979. *Twentieth Century British History*, 13 (2), 171–190.

Strange, J.-M., 2015. *Fatherhood and the British working class, 1865–1914*. Cambridge: Cambridge University Press.

Taylor, A., 2019. 'We have never employed Jewish people.' Young Jewish women's experiences of education and employment in Glasgow from the 1920s to the 1950s. *Cultural and Social History*, 16 (4), 467–489.

Thane, P., 2018. *Divided kingdom: A history of Britain, 1900 to the present*. Cambridge: Cambridge University Press.

The Royal Historical Society, 2018. *Promoting gender equality in UK history*. Available from: https://royalhistsoc.org/genderreport2018/.

Thomlinson, N., 2015. *Race, ethnicity and the women's movement in Britain, 1968–1993*. London: Palgrave Macmillan.

Todd, S., 2014. *The people: The rise and fall of the working class 1910–2010*. London: John Murray.

Todd, S., 2021. *Snakes and ladders: The Great British social mobility myth*. London: Chatto & Windus.

Weeks, J., 2016. *What is sexual history?* Cambridge: Polity Press.

Wilson, J.F., 1995. *British business history, 1720–1994*. Manchester: Manchester University Press.

Part A
Britain since 1900

2 The British political system

Richard Toye

Introduction

The 'British political system' and the 'British constitution' are closely interrelated, but they are not quite the same thing. The constitution is a set of rules and understandings about how the country is governed, which in the UK (unlike in some countries) is not codified in a single document. The political system incorporates the constitution but also includes electoral culture and questions such as which parties tend to dominate. Thus in the first part of the twentieth century the Liberal versus Conservative 'two-party system' was replaced by the Labour versus Conservative 'two party system'. Yet in itself this did not involve any constitutional alteration (although it may have been the cause and consequence of it). Rather than attempt to describe the entire political system over a period of over 100 years, this chapter will show how three distinct eras were defined by different kinds of formal and informal change.

The United Kingdom's political system has often been regarded rather complacently. Its most fervent admirers have frequently linked its apparent stability with the supposed equanimity and moderation of the British national character. It is certainly true that, during the interwar years, neither fascism nor communism secured the levels of success that they obtained elsewhere. For the most part, the country did not see the extremely rapid changes in government that characterised the Third and Fourth Republics in France or post-war Italy. The loss of Britain's empire after 1945 occurred without major domestic upheaval.

Yet, as will be seen in the following pages, the political system underwent a fundamental crisis in the Edwardian period. After the First World War, the Irish Revolutionary War/War of Independence resulted in Westminster losing its authority over the bulk of the island of Ireland. The unfinished business of that conflict surged up again in the late 1960s, leading to nearly three decades of violence during the Northern Irish 'Troubles'. The UK also experienced large-scale industrial unrest during the 1970s and 1980s. The growth of nationalist feeling in Scotland and Wales led to new systems of devolved government in the 1990s. Nationalism was fuelled by the sense that English politicians were remote, dictatorial, and neglectful of Scottish and Welsh economic and social problems (Duclos 2017). Perceived threats to the Welsh language were also a factor. The demand for Scottish independence was defeated in a 2014 referendum by the fairly narrow margin of 55% to 45%. A further referendum, on the question of Britain's withdrawal from the European Union (EU) succeeded by 52% to 48%. This triggered years of political chaos, a crisis which was only partially resolved by the sweeping victory of the Conservative Party at the 2019 general election. Brexit finally

DOI: 10.4324/9781003037118-3

took place on 31 January 2020, but instability continued, exacerbated by the Corona-virus pandemic, the global energy crisis, and Russia's war with Ukraine.

An obvious point of comparison is the constitution of the United States. That enforces a strict separation of powers between the president (the executive branch), the congress (the legislative branch), and the judiciary. In the UK, although the judici-ary is also independent from government, the executive is drawn from the legislature, that is to say government ministers are members of Parliament (either of the House of Commons or of the House of Lords). This means that ministers are responsible to Par-liament, which can call them to account by asking for information or to justify their actions. For example, the phenomenon of Prime Minister's Question Time – which developed into its modern form from the 1960s – has no parallel in the United States, where the president only addresses Congress on formal, set-piece occasions. It should also be noted that in the UK, the monarch is the head of state, whereas in the United States, the president is the head of state. Furthermore, the UK has a permanent, politi-cally neutral civil service (albeit now supplemented by special advisers appointed from outside who give political advice to ministers). In the United States, by contrast, some high-level appointments are filled by political appointees.

Undoubtedly, the British political system has had significant strengths, not least that of adaptability. However, at various times it has seemed close to the breaking point. The genuine and substantive continuities across the period since 1900 should not dis-tract from the equally important changes that occurred. The fact that the system for a long time proved fairly resilient in the face of challenges should not lead us to the conclusion that it will inevitably always do so in the future.

1900–1945

These decades saw a reduction in the powers of the House of Lords and radical exten-sions of the franchise (including to women) as well a culture of powerful local govern-ment. Coalition governments and shifting party labels were quite common, but the post-1931 settlement and the experience of the Second World War created the condi-tions for the emergence of a more rigid two-party system.

Were a politician from the Edwardian era to be transported to the House of Com-mons in the year 2023, some things would appear recognisable. These would include the rowdiness of many MPs' behaviour, the Speaker's cries of 'Order! Order!', and the basic structure and codes of debate. By contrast the TV cameras (introduced in 1985 in the House of Lords and four years later in the House of Commons) would clearly be unfamiliar. The presence of a large number of women members might be less of a shock, given that debates about female suffrage raged in the years before 1914. Out-side Parliament, the time-traveller might be surprised and perturbed at the virtual disappearance of the mass meeting, a phenomenon that played a key role in electoral culture up to the 1970s (Lawrence 2009).

Other changes in the system, although profound, might not be as immediately obvi-ous. The first moves towards the introduction of the welfare state were introduced by Britain's last exclusively Liberal government before the First World War. But state power was in many ways still quite limited. At the same time, it was less centralised than it would later become. Levels of local government spending rivalled those of central government. There was a strong municipal civic culture which was both sig-nificant as a phenomenon in its own right and for the fact that experience of serving on local councils provided a respected route to higher electoral office. Neville Chamberlain, for example, was Lord Mayor of Birmingham prior to being elected as an MP at the age of 49. He went on to become prime minister, although by subsequent standards he was a very late starter.

The Edwardian period also saw the elected House of Commons assert its dominance over the unelected House of Lords. After Lord Salisbury retired from Downing Street in 1902, it came gradually to be accepted that a peer could not be prime minister. (When Lord Home was selected in 1963 he disclaimed his peerage and was elected, as Alec Douglas-Home, to the Commons at a by-election.) More dramatically, the Liberal government clashed with the Lords when the latter used its power of veto against David Lloyd George's radical, tax-raising 'People's Budget' of 1909.

After two inconclusive general elections, fought on the theme of 'the Peers versus the People', the Liberals succeeded in abolishing the Lords' veto. The Parliament Act (1911) gave the Lords instead a two-year delaying power over most legislation. The monarchy declined as a factor in politics throughout the century, although various monarchs did, on a few rare occasions, make significant interventions at moments of crisis.

The coming of the First World War created conditions which split the Liberal Party and allowed Lloyd George to emerge, in 1916, as the prime minister of a coalition government in alliance with Conservatives and the nascent Labour Party. The election that took place after the Armistice in 1918 was the first fought on the basis of universal manhood suffrage. Women over 30 who met a property qualification were also allowed to vote; the franchise was equalised in 1928. This, however, was not the end of franchise reform (Gottlieb and Toye 2013). University representation (which

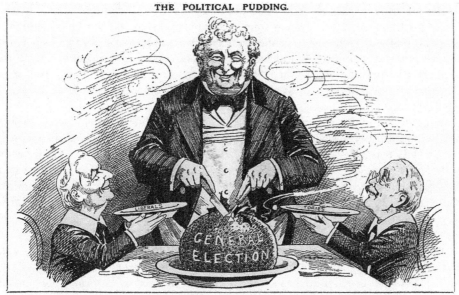

THE POLITICAL PUDDING.

MASTERS ASQUITH AND BALFOUR: "Give ME the biggest piece, Uncle John!"

Image 2.1 1910 General Election – British political cartoon – Asquith and Balfour asking John Bull for a bigger slice of the General Election votes

Source: © Colin Waters/Alamy Stock Photo.

allowed plural voting for graduates) was not abolished until 1948, and 18–21-year-olds were only given the vote in 1969. Debates about whether 16- and 17-year-olds should be allowed to vote continue to this day.

1918 saw the election of seventy-three MPs from the radical Irish nationalist party Sinn Féin (including the first female Member of Parliament, Constance Markievicz). As they refused to take their seats, and as the Irish Free State became an independent country in 1922, they did not become a factor in Westminster politics; the general effect was to cement Conservative dominance.

Under the Government of Ireland Act (1920) a Northern Irish parliament was established at Stormont covering the remaining six counties. Throughout its life it was heavily dominated by the Conservative Party's Unionist allies. The Labour Party and the Liberals did not contest Stormont elections themselves, but they had sister parties that did. In general, British politicians preferred to keep the province at arm's length. If they found Northern Ireland's religious sectarianism distasteful, then they also tended to relegate its associated politics to the status of 'somebody else's problem'.

In mainland Britain, the 1920s was a period of genuine three-party politics. Although the Liberals were much weakened, they could not be wholly ruled out of contention. The Labour Party held power for the first time in 1924 for just over nine months, and again in 1929–31, but did not obtain a parliamentary majority. Historians of all stripes have rightly argued that Labour was committed to parliamentary methods. What has been forgotten is that there was considerable debate within the party about how Parliament should be used.

Not only was Labour's commitment to Parliament challenged by its critics, who alleged extremism and disregard of the conventions of the Commons, but Labour itself accused its opponents of riding roughshod over parliamentary liberties. Thus, the decision of some left-wing MPs to use parliamentary disruption tactics in their quest to present themselves as spokesmen of the unemployed was depicted by them as a proper use of the Commons to challenge capitalism and by Conservatives as proof of Labour's innate extremism and unfitness to govern. But unlike its would-be rival, the Communist Party of Great Britain (CPGB), Labour increasingly distanced itself from older forms of local street protest in order to present itself as a respectable 'national' party rather than as a class-based one (Petrie 2013).

Labour's (admittedly limited) electoral successes in the 1920s could be seen as a partial vindication of that strategy, but the general election that followed the financial crisis of 1931 was a devastating setback. The party was reduced to around fifty MPs, but the result was even worse for the Liberals, who, following a temporary reunion in 1923, had split into three separate factions (Thorpe 1991). The effect was to confirm Labour as the main opposition party, and thus almost inevitably as an alternative party of government, even if there seemed little prospect of it holding power in the near future.

A new two-party system was now solidifying. Up until 1945, parliamentary candidates were often flexible in their choices of party labels, reflecting local conditions and their personal proclivities; central party control was relatively weak. Independent candidates and minor parties had some success. During its lifetime the Communist Party of Great Britain secured four MPs, although none after 1950. (The British Union of Fascists did not normally contest Westminster elections, though it did fight three by-elections in 1940, securing no more than a few hundred votes each time.) Coalitions and other forms of alliance were quite common, and governments often changed between elections, due to changes in the balance of forces in the Commons rather than as an immediate consequence of them (Edgerton 2018, pp. 35–36). In 1931, for example, the Labour Government fell to be replaced by a Conservative-dominated coalition that branded itself the 'National Government'. An election followed, but by the government's own choice.

Labour, which (from 1918) was explicitly pledged to bringing about the common ownership of the means of production, was in important ways a different kind of party from its rivals. (In the 1990s, the removal of this commitment from the party's constitution was a totem of Tony Blair's commitment to ideological modernisation.) The party drove change within the political system as a whole – for example, through offering voters increasingly specific policy programmes rather simply articulating general principles. It acted as an innovator in terms of how politics was conducted, in spite of its comparative lack of electoral success. Labour also achieved specific policy victories, even sometimes when out of power. For example, the MP Ellen Wilkinson successfully sponsored 1938 legislation to regulate Hire Purchase, a form of credit widely used in working-class communities (Taylor 2002, p. 31).

In Focus: party leadership elections

Although choosing party leaders via an election process is now a regular feature of political life, the way in which this came about was haphazard. In the nineteenth century, parties were far less centralised, and at the same time their leaders in Parliament were not expected to be accountable to ordinary Liberals or Conservatives. It was the birth of the Labour Party which, in the longer run, shaped more general expectations of how leaders should be chosen. With its electoral breakthrough in 1906, Keir Hardie was narrowly elected as the first Chairman of the Parliamentary Labour Party (PLP). Another close battle took place in 1922, after Labour emerged as the official Opposition for the first time. Ramsay MacDonald saw off J.R. Clynes and was thus in position to become Labour's first prime minister after the general election of 1923. Until 1981, the PLP retained the right to elect the leader each year during periods when the party was out of power. In fact, there were only eight such contests.

At this time, would-be Tory leaders did not compete openly for the post but rather 'emerged' as the result of informal soundings. The avoidance of undignified public contests was an advantage of this method, but in 1963 the choice of the Lord Home to succeed Harold Macmillan threatened to bring the 'magic circle' process into disrepute. A system of elections (by MPs) was instituted in 1965, and Edward Heath was the first victor. But it was these same rules that allowed Margaret Thatcher to bring him down ten years later, and she in turn fell victim to them in 1990. Five years after that, John Major called the bluff of his critics by calling and winning a leadership election himself; but he soon suffered a landslide general election loss nonetheless.

The first party to involve its membership in a leadership election was the Liberals, when David Steel was chosen in 1976. Labour followed suit with the creation of an electoral college system which gave MPs 30% of the vote,

Constituency Labour Parties 30%, and affiliated unions 40%. This arrangement was replaced by the (rather misleadingly titled) One Member One Vote system in 1993. Although intended to break the power of left-wing unions, its long-term impact has been to empower radical constituency activists – as seen in the clash between MPs and party members when Owen Smith unsuccessfully challenged Jeremy Corbyn in 2016.

Similarly, the Conservative Party's 1998 reforms led, the first time they were tested, to the election of a leader, Iain Duncan-Smith, who was to the taste of party activists rather than to the majority of MPs. He didn't last long. In 2019, under the same system, Boris Johnson was chosen by party members after Conservative MPs had whittled down the choice to two candidates. Liz Truss was elected in the same way in 2022. Critics alleged that this was undemocratic because it left the final choice of prime minister to a small, unrepresentative, and self-selected clique. The question of how to choose party leaders in a way that combines efficiency with democracy and legitimacy has not yet been fully resolved.

1945–74

This period was the apex of the Labour versus Conservative two-party system, which has often been taken as the norm but which was threatened by the rise of nationalist parties from the 1960s. It also saw the elevation in status of the party manifesto as part of a more general shift from 'discursive' to 'programmatic' politics.

By contrast with 1914–18, the Second World War was not notably disruptive of the political system. But, by involving Labour in Churchill's coalition government, it did create the conditions in which the party, in 1945, secured a parliamentary majority for the first time. The party's manifesto was significant for two reasons. First, as implemented, it brought about a dramatic expansion of the welfare state and the extension of state control over a large swathe of industry via nationalisation. This meant that politicians and civil servants were faced with greater responsibilities. Second, it drove the Conservatives further in the direction of programmatic, future-oriented politics. Increasingly, all parties felt obliged to offer the electorate detailed, specific, and 'costed' policy promises rather than running mainly on the basis of political principles and past performance (Thackeray and Toye 2020a, 2020b).

The Conservatives now accepted that if a policy had been included in another party's winning manifesto, they would not use their in-built majority in the Lords to block it. The House of Lords remained somewhat controversial – the Attlee government reduced its power of delay to one year via the Parliament Act (1949) using the previous (1911) Parliament Act in order to do so. On the whole, though, the constitution was not a major flash-point of political debate. The introduction of life peerages in 1958 helped secure the long-term future of the Lords; Labour wanted more fundamental reform but did not implement it when returned to government.

In terms of the political process, there was a fair level of accord about what 'the rules of the game were', even if politicians frequently accused each other of breaching their spirit. Whether or not there was a broader 'post-war consensus' – defined as an unusual degree of substantive political agreement between the parties – has been the subject of a long-running debate. Addison (1975) made the case for consensus; challenges have been made by many, including Pimlott (1989). What is certain is that, when they returned to office in 1951, the Conservatives denationalised (privatised) only the iron and steel and road haulage industries. Nor did they take any radical steps to dismantle the welfare state.

In 1961, the Macmillan government established the National Economic Development-ment Council (NEDC). The purpose of this 'corporatist' body was to involve business and union representatives in efforts to tackle Britain's relative economic decline. It marked the acceptance by both main parties that unions deserved to be consulted on the government's major economic decisions. This accord would not survive the 1970s.

In 1969 large-scale violence broke out in Northern Ireland. The army was sent in in an attempt to restore order. The British state responded to the ensuing terrorist campaign by the Provisional Irish Republican Army (IRA) in ways which cast doubt upon its even-handedness between the Catholic and Protestant communities and upon its commitment to the rule of law. The introduction of internment without trial for IRA suspects led to protests; on 'Bloody Sunday' in 1972, British soldiers shot unarmed demonstrators dead. The original official enquiry was a whitewash; a later one led to an official apology in 2010.

Weeks after Bloody Sunday, the British government imposed direct rule from Westminster. The Stormont parliament was suspended and then abolished. A new Northern Ireland Assembly was created in 1973, and an executive was created with the aim of sharing power between the two communities. In 1974 the new arrangements collapsed in the face of a general strike called by Unionists.

The story of Northern Ireland complicates any effort to present the thirty years after 1945 as ones of political harmony. Moreover, although there were important consensus-seeking elements of the (Westminster-based) post-war settlement, the system as a whole remained, in the procedural sense, majoritarian rather than consensual. In many countries elections do not always lead to a clear transfer of power. Post-election coalition negotiations often determine how power is allocated. But Britain's First Past the Post (FPTP) electoral system usually delivered a clear majority to one party. There was no formal coalition in the UK between 1945 and 2010. At the same time, MPs were increasingly expected to act as representatives of their parties rather than as individuals exercising their own independent judgement.

This did not, however, preclude serious splits developing within parties, and these became more obvious as deteriorating economic conditions placed the political system under increasing pressure. The two-party system had reached its high-water mark in 1951, when between them Labour and the Conservatives monopolised 97.8% of the vote. By February 1974 this figure had fallen to 76.8% (although at later elections it increased again). The difference is explained in part by a revival of the Liberals and by breakthroughs for the Scottish National Party and the Welsh nationalist party Plaid Cymru. Simultaneously, the period's large-scale industrial unrest raised questions about whether the UK's governing institutions were fit for purpose.

1975–2020

Britain's membership of the European Economic Community (EEC) had important implications for the political system. The 1975 referendum that confirmed Britain's membership set a precedent that would have far-reaching repercussions forty years later (Saunders 2018) – in combination with other constitutional developments such as the 2011 Fixed Term Parliaments Act (FTPA).

In the 1960s, the United Kingdom had made two failed applications to join the Community. It finally succeeded and became a member in 1973 – at the same time, significantly, as the Republic of Ireland. However, the issue divided both Labour and the Conservatives. Labour returned to power in 1974 on the basis of pledge to renegotiate the British terms of entry and to put them to a confirmatory public vote. As a result, there took place the first UK-wide referendum, although the 1973 Northern Ireland 'border poll' formed a precedent of a kind.

The 'Yes' side won the EEC referendum heavily. Indisputably, EEC membership had major repercussions for UK sovereignty. Contrary to later allegations, this was not disguised from the public at the time. However, the EEC did evolve in ways that could not have been fully anticipated at the point Britain joined (and it was superseded by the EU in 1993). Britain's system of government became closely integrated with it, even if public enthusiasm declined significantly after the high point of the referendum.

From 1979, the UK participated in direct elections to the European Parliament. Turnout in these five-yearly contests was low: in the first one, less than a third of eligible voters took part, whereas in the general election the previous month, over three quarters did so. Moreover, the activities of Britain's MEPs attracted little interest or media attention. The elections did, however, offer the electorate the chance to deliver a protest vote against the governing party. From 1999, the use of a proportional voting system offered the United Kingdom Independence Party (UKIP) and (in 2019) the Brexit Party the chance to obtain more seats than they would likely have won under FPTP. A proposed switch to the Alternative Vote system for Westminster elections was heavily defeated in a national referendum in 2011.

Party conferences had long been a significant part of the political system. It would be easy to dismiss these televised annual rituals merely as theatre. To an extent this was true of Conservative conferences, which were largely rallies designed to boost the party's electoral standing. The Labour conference, on the other hand, was the party's supreme policy-making body, at least in theory (Minkin 1980); it was certainly a site for the exposure of ideological divisions. However, its claims to democratic legitimacy were questionable, because the block votes exercised by affiliated trades unions heavily outweighed those of the Constituency Labour Parties (CLPs) which represented individual party members. Conferences provided many memorable moments. In 1984, the IRA succeeded in blowing up the Grand Hotel in Brighton, in which Prime Minister Margaret Thatcher was staying. She was uninjured and gave her conference speech the next day.

At the time, the UK was in the middle of a year-long strike by the National Union of Mineworkers (NUM), which eventually failed in its bid to halt large-scale pit closures. Thatcher's successful efforts to restrict the power of the unions was at one with her broader project of 'rolling back the frontiers of the state'. Privatisation of state-owned industries was accompanied by important reforms of the civil service. A (modified) welfare state remained in place, but in some respects central government was now doing less. Concurrently, though, it was exerting more control over local government (which had been the subject of large-scale shake-up in 1974). But an attempt to reform the problematic system of local government finance ('the Rates') with a new community charge (or 'poll tax') proved an important factor in Thatcher's political downfall.

The 1980s saw a partial revival of three-party politics. The Social Democratic Party (SDP) was formed in 1981 as a result of split within Labour's ranks; the new party formed an Alliance with the Liberals. Early hopes of an electoral breakthrough were disappointed, and the bulk of the SDP merged with the Liberals in 1988. The Liberal Democrats (as they were eventually renamed) built on the old Liberal Party's style of localised 'pavement politics'. Over time they built up their parliamentary strength to the point where, in 2010, they were able to enter a coalition with the Conservatives – but five years later they lost almost all their seats.

The Alliance parties had a strong interest in constitutional reform which Labour and the Conservatives did not match. (However, the creation in 1979 of Departmental Select Committees, which had cross-party support, offered a significant extension of Parliament's power of scrutiny.) By the late 1980s, there was a new mood in favour of change, influenced in part by the belief that the Thatcher government had often behaved in an overbearing and secretive manner. The pressure group Charter 88 drew up a list of demands, including fixed-term parliaments, which corresponded in many respects with reforms that later came to pass.

The election of a Labour government led to important innovations. These included the Human Rights Act (1998) and the Freedom of Information Act (2000). The hereditary element of the House of Lords was reduced but not eliminated. New devolved governments for Scotland and Wales were paralleled by the new Northern Ireland Assembly established under the terms of the 1998 Good Friday Agreement (a major step in the peace process). At the time of writing, however, Stormont is once again in limbo, on account of the latest crisis in the power-sharing arrangements. Here is evidence that the Northern Ireland part of the UK's political system remains profoundly dysfunctional.

Yet the Northern Irish log-jam cannot be dismissed simply as the product of localised pathologies. The 2016 UK-wide referendum on membership of the EU led to years of political paralysis after voters chose to leave by 52% to 48%. It might be tempting to blame politicians as a class for their failure to resolve speedily the stalemate surrounding the attempt to secure a withdrawal agreement. The real cause of the problem, though, was an unresolved tension in the system. The 1975 referendum had established an understanding that this type of plebiscite was a legitimate way of establishing the popular will. This did not matter so long as this popular will did not conflict with the people's will as expressed through their choice of representatives in Parliament. But over Brexit it did. The Parliament elected in 2017, which could not resolve definitely to leave, had been chosen by the same electorate that had delivered the referendum result. The Conservative election victory of December 2019 created the conditions for the UK to formally implement Brexit, though key aspects of the UK's future trading relationship with the EU remained unresolved.

The Brexit debates also showed the impact of Northern Ireland directly on Westminster politics, in spite of the neglectful attitude of the political classes over many decades. The question of how uninhibited trade across the Irish border and the obligations of the Good Friday Agreement could be satisfactorily reconciled with Brexit did not receive nearly enough attention during the referendum campaign. When, in 2017, Theresa May called a snap election and lost her majority, she became reliant on the votes of the Democratic Unionist Party (DUP). The continued refusal of Sinn Féin MPs to take up their seats had an effect on the balance of power in the Commons as well. The British political system as a whole had disregarded Northern Ireland to its considerable peril.

It is also worth noting that Brexit threw the UK Supreme Court into the spotlight. The court was established in 2009, taking over the judicial functions previously exercised by the House of Lords. Two cases in particular received attention. One (the 'Miller Case', decided in 2017) determined that the government could not trigger Article 50 of the Lisbon Treaty, and thereby give notice of intent to withdraw from the EU, without an Act of Parliament. The second, in 2019, overturned the decision of Prime Minister Boris Johnson to prorogue (suspend) Parliament for five weeks, an action it was widely suspected that he had taken in order to force through Brexit.

Although the judges attracted considerable media hostility on account of these judgements, they were not, as alleged, becoming involved in politics. Rather, they had asserted the primacy of Parliament over the executive. One of the most striking features of the Brexit era is the revival of the Commons as a major site and focus of national debate. It even projected John Bercow (the speaker from 2009 to 2019) into global media stardom.

Debates and Interpretations: prime ministerial power

For many years, the debate about prime ministerial power was dominated by two alternative models. In 1963, the Labour MP Richard Crossman suggested that 'the post-war epoch has seen the final transformation of Cabinet Government into Prime Ministerial Government' (pp. 51–52) He claimed that the prime minister's control of patronage and of the cabinet agenda, already amounting to 'near-Presidential powers', had been progressively increased by the centralisation of the party machine and of government bureaucracy. Yet at the time that he wrote this, Crossman had not yet seen the government machine from the inside; his subsequent experience as a Cabinet minister under Harold Wilson revealed that the situation was more complex than he had suggested.

An alternative point of view to Crossman's was advanced by the political scientist G.W. Jones. Jones (1969, p. 190) wrote that the prime minister 'is not the all powerful individual which many have recently claimed him to be. . . . A Prime Minister who can carry his colleagues with him can be in a very powerful position, but he is only as strong as they let him be'. This was the so-called 'chairmanship' model. In the 1990s, a new approach emerged, known as the 'core executive' model. This emphasised that senior actors in government do not possess and deploy a fixed stock of power. Rather, they are part of mutually interdependent networks; their power depends on context, circumstance, and the use that they make of their varying resources (Rhodes and Dunleavy 1995; Smith 1999).

Yet although the core executive approach reflected a sophisticated approach to the problem, its advocates did not expand the scope of the debate beyond the machinery of government and the functions of the core executive. More attention needs to be paid to the public role of the prime minister and in particular to the rhetorical functions of the office. Any occupant of 10 Downing Street needs not only to operate the levers of bureaucracy and party but also to present themselves, through various forms of rhetoric, as a party and above all national leader (Toye 2011).

Advancing the debate further will require more attention to the international dimension of the problem. When prime ministers are described as 'presidential', the comparison is often to the US presidency, which tends to be considered very powerful. But the latter assumption may not be fully accurate, and one can also point to countries where the power of the president is very limited. There is also the question of how the prime minister's power may wax and wane along with shifts in the UK's influence on the global stage. It remains to be seen whether current developments will result in significant changes in the power of No. 10, both in relation to Britain's European neighbours and relative to the recent self-assertion by Parliament during the discussions over Brexit.

Conclusion

When one is very well acquainted with a political system, it is possible to take some of its most important features for granted. In the UK's case, one of these features is the reliance of political parties on large armies of volunteer workers who carry out tasks such as canvassing and leafleting out of conviction rather than hope of reward. It would be a brave analyst, though, who asserted that British politics is not corrupt. In fact, the Labour Party has consistently asserted that the Conservatives are in the pay of big business, while the Tories have argued that Labour are in the pockets of their 'union paymasters'. Lloyd George was brought down in part by revelations about the sale of honours of 1922, but since then Liberals have generally not had enough money to make their influence worth complaining about. Still, it is notable, for example, that the 'cash for questions' affair of the 1990s, and the parliamentary expenses exposé of 2009, involved sums that, considered in global perspective, were comparatively trivial. This does not excuse politicians' misbehaviour, but it is significant that some of those who defrauded the taxpayer went to prison, and many others were publicly shamed. Nevertheless, the abuse of public procurement procedures during the Coronavirus pandemic raised questions about corruption on a much larger scale.

Other familiar aspects of the system are discomfiting. The election of four Black and Asian MPs in 1987 was something of a landmark, but, in spite of growing diversity in Parliament and at Cabinet level, at the time of writing there are no MPs from ethnic minorities representing seats in Scotland, Wales, or Northern Ireland. It was not until 1997 that the number of female MPs in the House of Commons at one time breached the ceiling of 100 (out of 659 at that time). Since then women MPs have become a particular target of abuse and harassment. Equality still seems some way off.

This chapter has tried to address another habitual blind spot: Northern Ireland. Historians have tended to treat this as a special problem, quite separate from the politics of the mainland. This is understandable, as that is what many politicians have done, too. Integrating the province's history with that of the UK is challenging. But there is no excuse for neglecting it. On the one hand, it is now clear that the causes and consequences of Brexit, a seismic event, cannot be understood in its absence. On the other hand, removing Northern Ireland from the equation permits the creation of a narrative of British stability that is quite misleading.

Finally, the much-vaunted flexibility of the British system has proved a double-edged sword. For example, the Fixed-Term Parliaments Act had a persuasive rationale – to remove the prime minister's power to exploit the timing of elections for partisan advantage. Yet it had unintended consequences. It was now possible for MPs to vote down a government's major proposals without them having to face a general election, which would previously have been the likely consequence of such an action. In this scenario, which recurred repeatedly in 2018 to 2019, ministers were left in office but not in power. Had the FTPA not been in place, it is certain that the parliamentary wrangling over Brexit would have played out differently. The Act was repealed in

2022. The broader lesson is that the United Kingdom's political system is vulnerable to hidden flaws which may only reveal themselves in moments of crisis.

Further reading

There are many excellent histories that cover the politics of the bulk of the period in relation to economic and social developments. Particularly recommended is Peter Clarke's *Hope and Glory: Britain 1900–2000* (Penguin 2004). Jon Lawrence's *Electing Our Masters: The Hustings in British Politics from Hogarth to Blair* (Oxford University Press, 2009) offers a stimulating and wide-ranging account of electoral culture. Not all politics takes place in Parliament or at election times. In *The British People and the League of Nations: Democracy, Citizenship and Internationalism, c.1918–45* (Manchester University Press, 2011), Helen McCarthy explores popular engagement with foreign policy issues. In *Thinking Black: Britain, 1964–1985* (University of California Press, 2018) Rob Waters illuminates Black radical politics. Julie Gottlieb examines the intersection between gender and extremism in *Feminine Fascism: Women in Britain's Fascist Movement, 1923–45* (I.B. Tauris, 2000).

Yet while there is a wealth of publications covering particular parties and individuals and key themes and events, it is less easy to find work that deals with the evolution of the whole political system since 1900. *The Oxford Handbook of Modern British Political History, 1800–2000*, edited by Brown, Pentland and Crowcroft (Oxford University Press, 2018) is a good starting point. There is still much to be learnt from older works such as Lewis Minkin's *The Labour Party Conference* (Manchester University Press, 1980). There is perhaps no better way to learn about the system than reading the diaries or memoirs of politicians who interest you: although there is no guarantee that these people understood the system themselves!

Timeline

Prime ministers since 1895. The party label is that of the prime minister in question rather than that of his/her government; it does not necessarily imply that s/he was the leader of her/his party. For example, Winston Churchill, a Conservative, took office in May 1940 as the head of a cross-party national coalition, but he did not become leader of the Conservative Party until later in the year when Neville Chamberlain retired from politics.

1895 Robert Gascoyne-Cecil, 3rd Marquess of Salisbury (Conservative)
1902 Arthur Balfour (Conservative)
1905 Sir Henry Campbell-Bannerman (Liberal)
1908 Herbert Henry Asquith (Liberal)
1916 David Lloyd George (Liberal)
1922 Andrew Bonar Law (Conservative)
1923 Stanley Baldwin (Conservative)
1924 Ramsay MacDonald (Labour)
1924 Stanley Baldwin (Conservative)
1929 Ramsay MacDonald (Labour; National Labour from 1931)
1935 Stanley Baldwin (Conservative)
1937 Neville Chamberlain (Conservative)
1940 Winston Churchill (Conservative)

1945 Clement Attlee (Labour)
1951 Winston Churchill (Conservative)
1955 Anthony Eden (Conservative)
1957 Harold Macmillan (Conservative)
1963 Alec Douglas-Home (Conservative)
1964 Harold Wilson (Labour)
1970 Edward Heath (Conservative)
1974 Harold Wilson (Labour)
1976 James Callaghan (Labour)
1979 Margaret Thatcher (Conservative)
1990 John Major (Conservative)
1997 Tony Blair (Labour)
2007 Gordon Brown (Labour)
2010 David Cameron (Conservative)
2016 Theresa May (Conservative)
2019 Boris Johnson (Conservative)
2022 Liz Truss (Conservative)
2022 Rishi Sunak (Conservative)

References

Addison, P., 1975. *The road to 1945*. London: Jonathan Cape.

Brown, D., Pentland, G., and Crowcroft, R., eds., 2018. *The Oxford handbook of modern British political history, 1800–2000*. Oxford: Oxford University Press.

Clarke, P., 2004. *Hope and glory: Britain 1900–2000*. London: Penguin.

Crossman, R., 1963. Introduction. *In:* W. Bagehot, ed. *The English constiution*. London: Fontana.

Duclos, N., 2017. The 1970s: A "Paradoxical Decade" for the Scottish National Party. *Revue Française de Civilisation Britannique*, XXII, 1–18.

Edgerton, D., 2018. *The rise and fall of the British nation: A twentieth century history*. London: Allen Lane.

Gottlieb, J., 2000. *Feminine fascism: Women in Britain's fascist movement, 1923–45*. London: I.B. Tauris.

Gottlieb, J.V., and Toye, R., eds., 2013. *The aftermath of suffrage: Women, gender, and politics in Britain, 1918–1945*. Houndmills and Basingstoke: Palgrave Macmillan.

Jones, G., 1969. The prime minister's power. *In:* A. King, ed. *The British prime minister: A reader*. London: Macmillan.

Lawrence, J., 2009. *Electing our masters: The hustings in British politics from Hogarth to Blair*. Oxford: Oxford University Press.

McCarthy, H., 2011. *The British people and the league of nations: Democracy, citizenship and internationalism, c. 1918–45*. Manchester: Manchester University Press.

Minkin, L., 1980. *The Labour party conference: A study in the politics of intra-party democracy*. Manchester: Manchester University Press.

Petrie, M.R., 2013. Public politics and traditions of popular protest: Demonstrations of the unemployed in Dundee and Edinburgh, c.1921–1939. *Contemporary British History*, 27 (4), 490–513.

Pimlott, B., 1989. Is the 'postwar consensus' a myth? *Contemporary Record*, 2 (6), 12–14.

Rhodes, R.A.W., and Dunleavy, R.R., ed., 1995. *Prime minister, cabinet and core executive*. Basingstoke: Palgrave Macmillan.

Saunders, R., 2018. *Yes to Europe! The 1975 referendum and seventies Britain*. Cambridge: Cambridge University Press.

Smith, M.J., 1999. *The core executive in Britain*. Basingstoke: Palgrave.

Taylor, A., 2002. *Working class credit and community since 1918*. Basingstoke: Palgrave Macmillan.

Thackeray, D., and Toye, R., eds., 2020a. *Electoral pledges in Britain since 1918: The politics of promises*. Basingstoke: Palgrave Macmillan.

Thackeray, D., and Toye, R., 2020b. An age of promises: British election manifestos and addresses 1900–97. *Twentieth Century British History*, 31 (1), 1–26.

Thorpe, A., 1991. *The British general election of 1931*. Oxford: Clarendon Press.

Toye, R., 2011. The rhetorical premiership: A new perspective on prime ministerial power since 1945. *Parliamentary History*, 30 (2), 175–192.

3   The British economy

John Singleton

Introduction

Economic activity – the production, distribution, and consumption of goods and services – is crucial to the life of any community. Without a satisfactory level of production, and an effective mechanism for distributing goods and services, a community will not be able to provide adequately for its members, and it may even struggle to defend itself against external threats. The United Kingdom was the world's most dynamic economy during the Industrial Revolution of the late eighteenth and early nineteenth centuries, and it remained one of the globe's largest and most prosperous economies in the early twenty-first century. In the century after 1900, the British economy continued to evolve and to grow in both size and sophistication. The overwhelming majority of people in early twenty-first century Britain lived longer, and were better housed and educated, than their Victorian ancestors. Modern Britons also consumed a far greater quantity and variety of goods and services than their forebears.

Nevertheless, debate over the long-run performance of the UK economy has often stressed the themes of failure and decline. Britain's inability to maintain the advantage over other western economies in technology and industry that was celebrated at the Great Exhibition in 1851 has troubled economic historians, economists, and politicians. Other countries caught up with (and some overtook) the UK economy. When improved economic statistics became available after the Second World War, it became possible to make more reliable international comparisons. The speed of economic growth in the UK was compared unfavourably with that in other western European countries and Japan. Economic decline, however, was *relative*, not *absolute*. With few interruptions, British workers continued to become more productive, and British consumers more prosperous; it was simply that their counterparts in certain other countries were doing even better. It is conceivable that future generations will regard the fixation of twentieth-century commentators on relatively small differences in economic performance as misguided. They may regard issues that were largely overlooked in the twentieth century – one candidate being the impact of the economy on the environment – as of far greater significance.

The first section discusses how economic activity is measured at the national level. The second outlines the UK's economic performance since 1900. In the third section we examine structural change, that is, shifts in the relative importance of the three main sectors of the economy: farming, industry, and services. This section also considers regional developments. The fourth section introduces the methods used by economic historians to investigate the sources of economic growth. In the fifth section we discuss fluctuations in economic activity and their effects on unemployment and the

DOI: 10.4324/9781003037118-4

price level. Lack of space means that several important issues, including living standards and inequality, international trade and finance, the business sector, and economic
policy, are left for other chapters to address.

How to measure the economy

The standard approach to measuring economic activity at the national (or macroeconomic) level was invented in the mid-twentieth century. During the Second World
War, the British and American governments developed aggregate measures of output,
income, and expenditure to help with war planning. After the war, international committees of economists and statisticians devised a set of conventions for use by other
countries in the construction of national income accounts.

The most widely used measure of national income is gross domestic product (GDP).
GDP is the sum of the 'value added' of each industry, as well as farming, services
(e.g. tourism and banking), and government production (e.g. the NHS), over a given
time span such as twelve months. Value added is the money value of an industry's
sales minus the cost of non-human inputs. For example, the value added of the car
industry is the value of cars sold minus the cost of steel, glass, power, and other non-
human inputs used in car production. It would be misleading to include steel twice in
the contributions to output of the steel *and* car industries. Another way of putting it
is that GDP measures the economy's output of *final* goods and services, whether sold
domestically or exported.

GDP may be calculated, as previously, by aggregating the value added of each industry. Aggregating the incomes (wages, rent, profits) generated by production should
lead to the same answer, as also should aggregating spending on goods and services
produced in the UK. In practice, there are always some 'measurement errors'.[1]

So far, so good. But there are problems. Working out the value added of parts of the
service sector is difficult. Restaurants are easy because people pay for their meals. But
what is the value added of the NHS or South Yorkshire Police, entities that do not sell
services to customers? Statisticians are compelled to fudge an answer in such cases.
Moreover, services produced within the household, such as washing up or looking after
children, are by convention excluded from standard national income statistics. Standard
GDP figures also take no account of damage to the environment caused by economic
activity. If we could start again, we might design a better set of national income accounting conventions, and some economists have indeed constructed alternative measures
that address, for example, the household and environmental questions (Coyle 2014).

In this chapter, we adopt the standard approach to national income accounting
because the bulk of existing research follows its conventions. Nevertheless, we should
bear in mind that, rather than an objective measure of economic activity, GDP is simply the most popular out of a range of constructed measures.

The record: economic growth and productivity

An increase in GDP over time is known as economic growth. Because the price
level also changes over time – rising in most, but not all, years in a process known
as inflation – we would overestimate economic growth if we used unadjusted or
'nominal' GDP figures. The solution is to 'deflate' nominal GDP figures to remove
the effect of inflation: this operation leaves us with 'real' GDP figures for each year

Figure 3.1 Real GDP, United Kingdom, 1900–2016 (£billion, 2013 prices)
Note: United Kingdom consists of England, Scotland, Northern Ireland, and Wales.
Source: Thomas and Dimsdale (2017), spreadsheet A1, column D.

that show the changing *volume* of final output. Whenever we mention GDP either in the text or in charts and tables, we mean *real GDP*.

Figure 3.1 shows the changing volume of final goods and services produced within the UK between 1900 and 2016. Clearly, the economy grew most of the time, but there were a few downturns. The output of final goods and services in 2016 was more than ten times as much as in 1900.

Some of the increase in GDP may be explained by a rise in population. Other things being equal, population growth increases the size of the labour force. As Figure 3.2 illustrates, the UK population expanded from 38 million in 1900 to 66 million in 2016. Population reached 55 million by 1970 and hovered around that level for a while before rising again in the late 1980s. Although increasing life expectancy boosted population, the growing preference of women for fewer children worked in the opposite direction. Until the mid-1980s, annual emigration, typically to Australia, Canada, or the United States, exceeded immigration into the United Kingdom. Thereafter the UK became a country of net immigration. Annual net inflows rose from 0.1 per cent of the population in 1985 to 0.5 per cent in 2015.

The impact of population growth on the amount of paid work performed in the economy was not straightforward. Young people began to stay in education for longer, whilst old people lived longer in retirement. Most people worked shorter hours as the century wore on. Adjusting for holidays and sickness, the average working week fell from 57 hours in 1900 to 32 in 2016 (Thomas and Dimsdale 2017, spreadsheet A54, column AV), a phenomenon explained by a reduction in standard hours, increased holiday entitlement, and more part-time working. More working-age women, including those with children, found paid work in addition to their unpaid jobs at home. Women's employment is looked at in greater detail in other chapters.

By dividing each year's GDP by the population, we obtain another measure of economic activity known as GDP per capita. GDP per capita means GDP per person, and the number of persons includes babies and children and retirees, as well as men and women of working age. The course of the United Kingdom's GDP per capita between 1900 and 2016 is shown in Figure 3.3. As a result of population growth, GDP per capita did not rise as fast as GDP; nevertheless, GDP per capita in 2016 was six times as high as in 1900. This does not mean that people were exactly six times

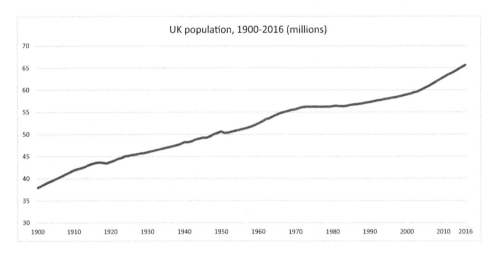

Figure 3.2 UK population, 1900–2016 (millions)

Note: United Kingdom consists of England, Scotland, Northern Ireland, and Wales.
Source: Thomas and Dimsdale (2017), Spreadsheet A1, column Y.

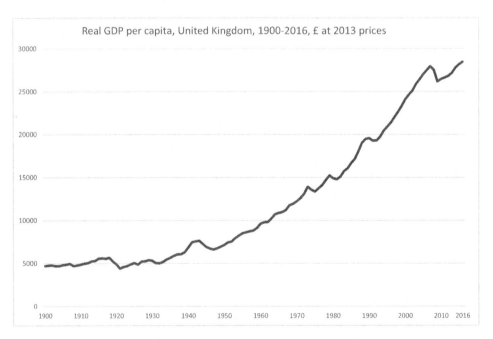

Figure 3.3 Real GDP per capita, United Kingdom, 1900–2016, £ at 2013 prices

Note: United Kingdom consists of England, Scotland, Northern Ireland, and Wales.
Source: Thomas and Dimsdale (2017), spreadsheet A21, column X.

Table 3.1 Growth rates of real GDP and real GDP per capita in the UK (% per year)

	Maddison GDP	Crafts GDP	Maddison GDP per capita	Crafts GDP per capita
1870–1913	1.90	1.90	1.01	1.01
1913–1950	1.19		0.92	
1929–1937		1.99		1.55
1950–1973	2.93		2.44	
1950–1979		2.63		2.23
1973–1998	2.00		1.79	
1979–2007		2.54		2.22

Sources: Maddison (2006, pp. 186, 187); Crafts (2018, pp. 9–10).

better off in 2016 than in 1900. GDP is not a precise measure of welfare: later chapters will examine wages, living standards, and the distribution of income. Moreover, GDP includes investment goods, such as new factories, offices, and machinery, that are not consumed by households but promise more consumption in the future. Some consumer goods and services are exported to other countries and therefore unavailable to British consumers; at the same time, imports from abroad offer households a wider choice.

GDP and GDP per capita statistics are interrogated mercilessly by economists and economic historians. They calculate the annual percentage growth rates in GDP and GDP per capita and then debate the trends and fluctuations in national economic performance. Even when they draw upon the same source of data, the way in which they divide up time can influence the stories they tell. We can see this in Table 3.1, which shows estimates of economic growth published by two leading economic historians, Angus Maddison (2006) and Nick Crafts (2018). Although both use data generated by Maddison, they select different groups of years for comparison. Maddison observes a marked deterioration in UK growth rates (both GDP and GDP per capita) between 1870–1913 and 1913–1950, a period blighted by the world wars. Crafts, however, excludes from his study the abnormal years of the world wars and post-war recoveries. Having done so, he finds that economic growth was higher between 1929 and 1937 – a period marked by depression and recovery – than between 1870 and 1913. The decay in economic performance identified by Maddison now disappears, or at least becomes more questionable. Maddison and Crafts agree that there was an improvement in growth rates between 1950 and the 1970s. However, whereas Maddison finds a marked deterioration between 1973 and 1998, Crafts, whose study extends into the early 2000s, does not observe any deceleration in the growth of GDP per capita. Crafts's approach lends a more benign interpretation to the effects of the economic reforms initiated by the Thatcher government in the 1980s. Who is right? We cannot be sure: the message to take away is that the interpretation of economic statistics involves judgement as well as technique.

Productivity is a measure of the efficiency with which inputs (such as labour) are transformed into outputs. Labour productivity is defined as output per worker over a certain period, such as an hour or a year, and depends on the quantity of capital and the technology available as well as individual effort. (In the next section we discuss an alternative measure called total factor productivity or TFP.) A pizza delivery person with more capital equipment – a bigger delivery bag – can deliver more pizzas per hour. Adopting a more advanced technology – a car rather than a skateboard – should

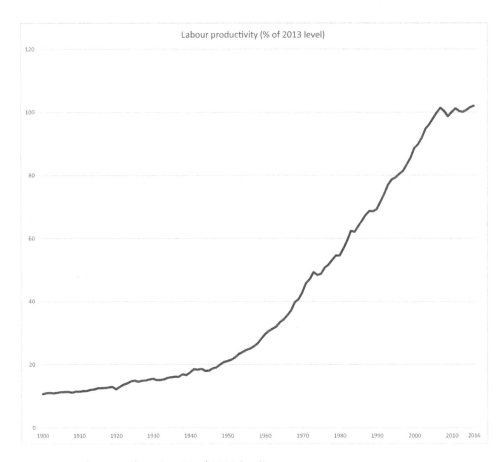

Figure 3.4 Labour productivity (% of 2013 level)

Note: Labour productivity is defined here as real GDP per hour worked.

Source: Thomas and Dimsdale (2017), spreadsheet A1, column AG.

also increase labour productivity.[2] Figure 3.4 depicts the course of labour productivity in the UK economy since 1900. The average worker in 2016 produced 9.5 times as much per hour as a worker in 1900. It is also worth noting that a worker in 2016 produced twice as much per hour as their grandparents did in the mid-1970s. Despite the rising trend, there were several periods of stagnation in labour productivity – in the early 1900s, the early 1930s, the mid-1970s, and, most worryingly for current policymakers, after the financial crisis of the early 2000s.

Seen from the perspective of 1900 or even the 1950s, early twenty-first-century Britain possessed a thriving economy with rising levels of output and output per capita and an increasingly productive labour force.

Structural change, deindustrialization, and the regions

All modern economies experience structural change. The relative importance of the three sectors of the economy – agriculture, industry (including mining), and services (comprising all other activities) – evolves over time. Agriculture accounted for the largest share of the labour force in the United Kingdom until the early nineteenth century, when it was overtaken by industry. Agriculture continued to dwindle in relative importance as an employer throughout the nineteenth and twentieth centuries. Industry and services were dominant by 1901, as Table 3.2 shows.

Mid-twentieth-century Britain was a highly industrialized society. Starting in the 1960s, however, industry lost ground relative to the service sector. Other developed nations experienced a similar transition to a service economy, but that shift began early in the UK and was uncomfortably sharp, prompting fears of terminal deindustrialization. In fact, the grim forecasts of the 1970s and 1980s proved exaggerated. Aggregate industrial output continued to grow, albeit with some dips, but improvements in productivity meant that fewer workers were required. Nevertheless, several branches of industry that had risen to prominence during the Industrial Revolution had effectively disappeared by the early twenty-first century. The cotton industry, based in Lancashire and Greater Manchester, disintegrated in the 1960s under competitive pressure from factories in Asia that could make cotton goods more cheaply (Singleton 1991). The last British coal mine closed in 2015 (Thomas *et al.* 2019).[3] Adjustment was difficult for areas in which such industries had been important. Whilst new jobs were created, they were often a poor fit for older workers shed by manufacturing and mining. By contrast, banking and finance, activities in which Britain excelled internationally, were expanding strongly. Occupations associated with health and education services also witnessed rapid growth. Unfortunately, a substantial proportion of new jobs, including care giving and working on the checkouts, were poorly paid and insecure (Tomlinson 2016, p. 90). Naturally, the story differed from occupation to occupation. After seeming moribund in the 1970s, the car industry had recovered under foreign ownership by 2000. By contrast, domestic service, a massive employer in the early twentieth century, subsequently entered a steep decline. In principle, it is

Table 3.2 Sectoral workforce shares in the UK 1901–2016 (%)

	Agriculture	*Industry*	*Services*
1901	12.96	43.90	43.15
1911	11.77	44.09	44.14
1921	8.47	38.53	52.99
1931	6.94	36.71	56.35
1938	5.40	38.24	56.36
1951	4.45	42.20	53.35
1961	3.57	43.00	53.43
1971	2.21	38.92	58.87
1981	1.87	31.78	66.35
1991	1.75	24.71	73.54
2001	1.20	20.32	78.48
2011	1.32	15.81	82.87
2016	1.12	15.29	83.59

Notes: All figures include employees, employers, and the self-employed.

Agriculture: Agriculture, forestry, and fishing.

Industry: Mining and quarrying, manufacturing, construction, gas, electricity, and water.

Services: All other activities.

Source: Thomas and Dimsdale (2017), spreadsheet A53.

Table 3.3 Regional shares in the United Kingdom's GDP, 1901–2011 (%)

	1901	1911	1921	1931	1951	1961	1971	1981	1991	2001	2011
South East	33.4	33.4	34.0	38.3	33.4	35.1	35.4	35.4	35.9	39.1	41.5
(London)	21.2	20.9	21.0	22.8	20.1	19.9	19.3	15.4	15.0	17.6	20.2
(Rest of South East)	12.2	12.5	13.0	15.4	13.3	15.2	16.0	19.9	20.9	21.5	21.3
East Anglia	2.3	2.3	2.2	2.1	2.3	2.5	2.8	3.2	3.6	3.8	3.9
South West	6.2	6.0	5.8	5.8	5.9	6.0	6.5	7.3	7.8	7.8	7.7
West Midlands	6.8	7.2	6.6	7.9	9.2	9.5	9.5	8.4	8.5	8.0	7.3
East Midlands	5.7	5.9	5.3	5.3	6.1	6.2	5.9	6.6	6.8	6.5	6.2
North West	14.7	14.7	14.9	11.9	13.3	11.9	11.7	10.8	10.0	9.4	8.8
North	5.7	5.7	5.7	4.3	5.6	5.6	5.2	5.2	4.8	4.0	3.8
Yorkshire and Humberside	8.0	8.2	8.2	7.9	8.5	8.0	8.1	8.0	7.5	7.3	6.8
Wales	4.3	4.8	4.7	4.6	4.4	4.6	4.3	4.2	4.3	3.8	3.6
Scotland	10.7	10.0	10.3	10.0	9.1	8.8	8.7	8.9	8.6	8.0	8.1
N. Ireland	2.1	1.8	2.2	1.9	2.0	2.0	2.1	2.0	2.2	2.3	2.2

Source: Geary and Stark (2019, p. 336)

desirable that an economy should adapt to changing circumstances and patterns of demand. International competitiveness will always be falling in some activities and rising in others. As incomes rose, moreover, British households spent relatively more on services like restaurant meals and holidays (but not servants) and less on basic goods such as towels and pies. They also expected the state to provide a higher quality of health care and education.

Structural change also has a vital regional dimension. The relative contribution of each region to national GDP has evolved since the start of the twentieth century, albeit quite slowly (see Table 3.3). Between 1901 and 2001, the share of regions in southern and central England increased, whilst the share of regions in northern England, Scotland, and Wales all dropped. Once more, we are concerned here with relative rather than aggregate change: the output of all regions grew, though at varying rates.

Before the Industrial Revolution, London and South-East England were dominant in every respect. By 1900, strong and self-confident regional economies had emerged around cities such as Birmingham, Manchester, Liverpool, Sheffield, Leeds, Bradford, Newcastle, and Glasgow based on their prowess in industry and trade. The twentieth and early twenty-first centuries saw the reassertion of South Eastern dominance, as industries on the periphery struggled to fend off foreign competition. The North–South divide made its debut in the interwar era. Even the West Midlands, which did well until the early 1970s, lost ground in the 1970s and 1980s, partly because of the crisis in the car industry. Although the relative expansion of the South East owed much to the buoyancy of services, this region also contained some successful modern industries, including light engineering and food processing. Whilst the share in national GDP of London – that is, Greater London – fell between 1901 and 2001, London's tentacles were spreading. There was more space for new development in the rest of the South East, a region we might call 'Greater Greater London'. Rapid expansion of the university sector in the late twentieth century brought some respite to otherwise declining northern towns and cities like Sheffield, Preston, and Huddersfield.

Image 3.1 Mersey Tunnel Opening, Liverpool, July 1934, by King George IV and Queen Mary
Source: © Trinity Mirror/Mirrorpix/Alamy Stock Photo.

Scotland, Wales, and Northern Ireland were significant industrial regions in 1900. Clydeside, the district around Glasgow, was a global centre of shipbuilding and engineering. Scotland also had large coal, steel, and textile industries. South Wales was principally a coal mining area, with some iron and steel production. Belfast was home to the UK linen industry and an important shipbuilding centre responsible for the *Titanic*. By the 1920s, the 'staple' industries of Victorian Britain were in trouble. Amongst the problems faced by Scottish, Welsh, and Northern Irish industry were low demand in the UK, rising tariffs abroad, and vigorous foreign competition. The Second World War and post-war boom brought some temporary respite. Investment by English, American, and Japanese firms in electrical engineering and other industries helped between the 1960s and 1980s, but such ventures often lacked resilience. Similar problems were experienced by peripheral English regions. Edinburgh and Cardiff enjoyed revivals in the late twentieth and early twenty-first centuries, largely because of devolution and the associated job creation and investment.

Explaining economic growth

So far, we have focused largely on *describing* trends in the economy. In this section we try to *explain* economic growth using concepts and theories developed by economists. History students without some training in economics need not worry: the more technical bits will go into an appendix.

Economists have always been fascinated by economic growth and its sources, but it was not until the emergence of national income accounting in the 1940s and 1950s that it became possible to discuss growth with any precision. 'Neoclassical' growth models – simplified algebraic depictions of the economy – then began to appear in the academic journals. When economic information was fed into such models, they could estimate how much of any increase in real GDP could be credited to the use of (i) more inputs of labour, (ii) more inputs of capital (that is buildings, machinery, roads, and so forth), and (iii) more inputs of land (including natural resources). There was always a 'residual' contribution to growth that could not be attributed to additional labour, capital, or land. The residual (also known as total factor productivity) was assumed to incorporate *anything else* that might contribute to growth, especially improvements in technology and management. Early studies with such models suggested that TFP and capital accumulation were the leading contributors to growth in developed economies; additions to the workforce and land were less important. The neoclassical growth model could also estimate the contribution to the growth of GDP *per capita* (or GDP per worker or GDP per hour worked) of changes in capital per worker and changes in TFP. See the appendix for the algebra.

After the 1950s and 1960s, growth accounting techniques became more refined. The crude assumption that units of labour (or workers) were identical was dropped. Members of the labour force differ enormously in education and training, or 'human capital' in economic jargon. Years spent in education offers a rough proxy for labour force quality. A more highly educated workforce should be more productive and innovative. Other research showed that major new technologies, including electric power in the early twentieth century, and computers after the Second World War, were slow to have an impact on economic growth. Not until they were perfected and came down in price were they used widely enough to make much difference.

Nick Crafts estimates that between 1899 and 1913 the principal sources of growth in GDP per hour worked in the UK were an increase in capital per worker and more education; by contrast, TFP was falling. Between 1924 and 1937, rising TFP and longer education were the main drivers of growth in GDP per hour worked (Crafts 2018, pp. 45, 67). Throughout the period between 1950 and 2007, rising TFP and more capital per worker, with more education a distant third, were the main contributors to growth in GDP per hour worked (Crafts 2018, pp. 87, 109–110). In short, new technology and investment have propelled growth since the Second World War.

Growth models identify the *proximate* causes of growth: more labour, more capital, improved technology, and more education. To grasp the *underlying* sources of economic growth we must consider processes that sometimes resist quantification. Unfortunately, there is only enough space to mention a couple of those factors. Secure property rights – the enforcement of laws to protect private property from confiscation by the state or criminals – are vital to the promotion of enterprise. As well as houses and land, property encompasses businesses; financial assets such as shares and bonds; and intellectual property, including the ideas behind new products and techniques. Property rights were already strong in the UK before the Industrial Revolution. In their absence, investing in a business or developing a new technology would have been far riskier, deterring many entrepreneurs. Other institutional arrangements may also influence economic growth, whether positively or negatively. Economic growth could be hampered by dysfunctional business and labour institutions. Collusive agreements between firms to raise profits through price-fixing rather than by increasing productivity, and the antipathy to change of some trade unions, may have constrained growth between the 1930s and 1970s. Although the contribution of good and bad economic policy may also have been substantial, this topic is left for a later chapter. Clearly, the debate over the underlying causes of growth is unlikely to reach a consensus. Economists' understanding of the economy continues to evolve along with the available range of econometric techniques.

Appendix: simple neoclassical growth model

[a] The most basic neoclassical growth accounting equation is as follows (Crafts 2018, p. 23):

$$\Delta Y/Y = \alpha \Delta K/K + \beta \Delta L/L + \gamma \Delta N/N + \Delta A/A$$

where $\Delta Y/Y$ is the rate of change in GDP; $\Delta K/K$ is the rate of change in the quantity of capital; $\Delta L/L$ is the rate of change in the quantity of labour; $\Delta N/N$ is the rate of change in the amount of land, and $\Delta A/A$ is the rate of change in the residual.

K, L, and N are weighted according to their shares in GDP by the income method: α is the share of profits, β is the share of wages, and γ is the share of rent.

Note that the symbols used may differ from author to author.

[b] The previous equation may be rearranged to focus on the determinants of the rate of growth in labour productivity or GDP per worker:

$$\Delta \ln(Y/L) = \alpha \Delta \ln(K/L) + \gamma \Delta \ln(N/L) + \Delta \ln A$$

where ln stands for natural logarithm.

Students with an interest in economic growth and some background in economics might like to explore Crafts (2018), Helpman (2004), and Maddison (1991).

Economic cycles, inflation, and unemployment

Growth does not occur at a constant pace. Economic activity is cyclical: growth may be vigorous for several years but then slacken for a while. Sometimes that slackening may lead to a recession in which GDP contracts before recovering. The length of each cycle varies, but around seven years from peak to peak is typical. GDP follows a wavelike path with an upward trend. Occasionally, a recession may be particularly sharp or prolonged. Excluding the world wars, the most serious economic crises in the United Kingdom were at the start of the 1920s, in the global depression of the early 1930s, during the oil crisis of the mid 1970s, in the early 1980s, and during the Anglo-American financial crisis of 2007–2009. Turning points in economic cycles may be triggered by various events, such as a shift in government policy, an economic crisis overseas, or a reversal in business or consumer confidence.

The annual rate of increase in the price level – inflation for short – usually accelerates during the upswing of the cycle, then decelerates when growth slackens. Very occasionally the price level may fall. Inflation is bad because it erodes living standards, industrial competitiveness, and savings and provokes conflict in the labour market over compensatory wage increases. Unemployment tends to follow an inverse pattern to inflation, dropping during the upswing but rising in the downswing when workers are laid off. Figure 3.5 shows the course of inflation and unemployment in the UK since 1900. Inflation peaked during the First and Second World Wars when there were serious shortages of consumer goods and between the mid-1970s and early 1980s when economic conditions were volatile. Unemployment was low during wartime and between 1945 and the early 1970s but high in the interwar era and to a lesser extent during the 1980s and early 1990s. The unemployment rate shown in Figure 3.5 is for all occupations; in the depression of the early 1930s, the unemployment rate among industrial workers was far higher.

Figure 3.5's misery index, a crude measure of economic stress (and not of whether people were feeling subjectively miserable), is calculated by adding the inflation and unemployment rates. High levels of economic stress in wartime may not be surprising. More intriguingly, the detrimental effect of high unemployment in the 1920s and 1930s was tempered somewhat by falling living costs. The 1970s witnessed a startling increase in economic stress, driven mainly by surging inflation combined with rising unemployment. In the middle of this decade there was a serious recession, caused in part by a dramatic rise in the price of imported oil, as Middle Eastern and other suppliers took advantage of the bargaining power placed in their hands by the growing dependence of western countries on oil since 1945.[4] The UK did not return to the low 1960s level of economic stress until the early 2000s. Between the mid-1950s and the mid-1960s, the British were not troubled by either unemployment or inflation, lending credence to the boast of Harold Macmillan, prime minister between 1957 and 1963, that they had never had it so good.

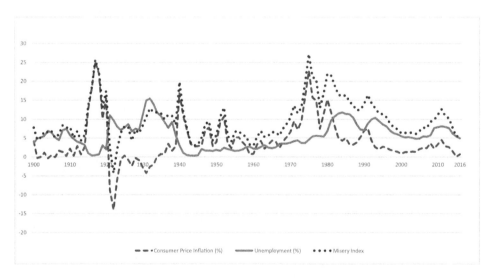

Figure 3.5 Inflation, unemployment, and 'misery' in the UK, 1900–2016

Note: Misery is measured as the inflation rate plus the unemployment rate.

Source: Thomas and Dimsdale (2017), spreadsheet A1, columns AB, AP.

In Focus: Britain in the Global Financial Crisis

Visiting the London School of Economics in November 2008, Queen Elizabeth II described the Global Financial Crisis (GFC), which destabilized the British banking system, prompting a large fall in share prices, and pushing the economy into recession, as 'awful' and asked why economists had not seen it coming. It was estimated that the GFC reduced the value of Her Majesty's own £100 million investment portfolio by 25 per cent. The GFC was the worst and most prolonged economic crisis – disaster is a more appropriate term – since the early 1930s. GDP in the United Kingdom did not return to the 2007 level until 2013. Several banks, beginning with Northern Rock and followed by the much larger Royal Bank of Scotland (RBS) and Halifax Bank of Scotland (HBOS), needed rescuing from impending collapse by the authorities. Indeed, the years 2007 to 2009 saw the most serious banking crisis in British history. Prior to 2007, the UK had experienced over a decade of relatively smooth economic growth, combined with low inflation and low unemployment, so, to return to the concerns raised by the Queen, what had gone wrong?

Banks in the United States, the United Kingdom, Ireland, and some other countries became more aggressive in their lending in the early 2000s. Much of this lending poured into the housing market, and it was funded not by rising consumer deposits but by borrowing, often very short term, from other banks and financial institutions with spare cash. In retrospect, this was not what an old-fashioned banker would call 'prudent' behaviour. An unexpected downturn in the US housing market placed American banks and financial institutions in serious difficulties. Many US housing loans could not be repaid, and the resale value of dwellings was falling. Some British banks, including RBS, were affected directly through their US subsidiaries. RBS also made the serious mistake in the early stages of the GFC of launching an expensive takeover of the Dutch bank ABN Amro. As the American crisis deepened, the global interbank lending market contracted sharply, and British banks, including Northern Rock and RBS, found it difficult to borrow to replace funds due for repayment. Without help from the Bank of England and the government, they would have shut down. What was the alternative to keeping the banks running at the taxpayers' expense? (It should be stressed that bank shareholders were not rescued.) Panic would have spread throughout the UK after the closure of an important bank. Customers would have lost access to their accounts, businesses would have been unable to borrow, and the payments system that processed transactions between customers of different banks would have jammed (Singleton 2016, pp. 159–176).

Although the GFC could have been far worse, it certainly ended the illusion that under New Labour the British economy had entered a golden age of stability. The tardiness of the recovery from the GFC was also disappointing. Economists were puzzled by the stagnation of productivity in the decade after the crisis.

Debates and Interpretations: Britain's economic performance in the international mirror

Is the glass half full or half empty? Economists, economic historians, and politicians have generally said half empty when comparing the economic performance of the UK and its main rivals from the late nineteenth century through to the present. Instead of focusing on the impressive growth in Britain's real GDP per capita since 1900, as shown in Figure 3.3, they lament that some other countries enjoyed even faster economic growth. Table 3.4 shows that in 1870 the United States, Germany, and France all had lower levels of GDP per capita than the UK. By 1913, however, the United States had overtaken the UK and thereafter extended its lead. Germany and France were closing the gap, and by 1979 they too had overtaken the UK. By the eve of the GFC, Britain had regained at least some lost ground.

For much of the twentieth century, British economic growth was comparatively lacklustre; hence the popularity of various brands of 'declinism'. The superior performance of the United States is easiest to explain. American business gained from ready access to land and other natural resources. Population was growing rapidly. With a vast internal market, US firms could operate on a larger scale than their European counterparts, adopting capital-intensive methods and achieving substantial cost reductions which to some extent were shared with consumers and workers. Accounting for the higher rates of economic growth enjoyed by Germany and France is harder because they had more in common with the UK in terms of size and endowments of land and natural resources. Germany and France suffered far more economic damage than Britain did in the Second World War, yet both managed to bounce back strongly after 1950. One possibility is that the disruption experienced by Germany and France enabled those countries to start afresh in 1945, creating new and more efficient types of business and labour organizations, whereas the UK was stuck with sleepy old family firms, collusive agreements that disadvantaged consumers, and awkward trade unions. Olson (1982) argued that the British economy was sclerotic, a medical term describing the slow clogging of the arteries in some patients.

Comparative economic statistics were produced in greater detail from the 1950s onwards, supplying economists with plenty of raw material for analysing economic

Table 3.4 Real GDP per capita as % of UK level, 1870–2013

	United States	*West Germany*	*France*
1870	76.6	57.6	58.8
1913	107.8	74.1	70.8
1929	125.3	73.6	85.6
1950	137.7	61.7	74.7
1979	142.7	115.9	111.1
2007	124.3	101.9	87.4
2013	132.2	107.8	89.8

Note: West Germany requires a little explanation. Figures for 1870, 1913, and 1929 are for the whole of Germany. The figures for 1950 to 2013 are for the more economically developed West Germany only; the poorer East Germany, under communist rule until 1990, is excluded even after reunification.

Source: Crafts (2015, p. R17).

growth. Somewhat paradoxically, the golden years of the mid-1950s to the early 1970s were marked by renewed fascination with British decline. The UK economy was growing strongly, but competitors in western Europe (not to mention Japan) were advancing even more rapidly. Economic growth in Western Europe and Japan was boosted by a transfer of labour from agriculture into more productive activities. The United Kingdom underwent that transition in the nineteenth century. Futile attempts to maintain Britain's world power status after 1945 were burdensome. Industrial resources, including talented researchers, were wasted on the design and production of weapons. Between 1973 and 1979, the UK economy and British manufacturing industry performed exceptional badly, helping Germany and France to establish significant leads in GDP per capita. Whereas in 1972 labour productivity in West German manufacturing was 21 per cent above the British level, by 1977 the gap had widened to 49 per cent (Broadberry 1997, p. 50). Industrial declinism threatened to give way to despair. Perhaps the obsession with industrial performance was overdone, however, for it was in fact the UK's tardiness to raise efficiency in services, especially in transport, communications, and distribution (which includes shops), that contributed most to the UK's weak economic performance relative to the United States and Germany over the twentieth century (Broadberry 2006).

The 1980s are still the most controversial decade in twentieth-century British history. Many of today's senior academic economists were young in the 1980s, and for them the clashes of the Thatcher era stick in the memory. Following a recession at the beginning of the 1980s, the British economy began to experience strong growth that continued, with a brief interruption in the early 1990s, until the onset of the Global Financial Crisis of 2007–2009. Perhaps the reforms of the Thatcher years helped to overcome some of the sclerotic features of British institutions. The UK's entry into the European Economic Community in 1973 may also have helped by exposing inefficient firms and industries to competition that either destroyed them or compelled them to adopt more efficient technologies and methods of working (Crafts 2019).

Conclusion

By the early 2000s the United Kingdom was a fairly typical Western European country in terms of income levels. It was still one of the ten largest economies in the world measured by GDP but no longer a superpower. From the perspective of the early 1900s, such *relative* decline would have seemed disastrous. Speaking at the London Guildhall in 1904, the imperial statesman Joseph Chamberlain MP drew attention to the growing industrial might of the United States and Germany (Our Special Correspondent 1904). He warned that Britain would be relegated to the status of a second-rank power unless it overcame that challenge. Subsequent debates over British economic performance betrayed a similar anxiety, albeit stripped of Chamberlain's obsession with empire. Chamberlain, however, was also a social reformer who sought to improve the economic condition of the masses. Stark inequalities persist, but the United Kingdom today is far wealthier than it was in 1904. Although no longer as dependent on manufacturing, the UK continues to prosper by producing the services (and still many of the goods) demanded in a modern society. Chamberlain's geopolitical concerns are not relevant to the twenty-first century.

Further reading

The most authoritative, though quite demanding, text on twentieth-century British economic history is Floud *et al.* (2014). Earlier versions of this text are also useful. For an older, more narrative approach, see Pollard (1992). For the work of Nick Crafts – cited more than any other author in this chapter – see his *Forging Ahead, Falling Behind and Fighting Back* (2018), which covers the period from the Industrial Revolution to the very recent past. Students interested in European comparisons may consult the volume edited by Broadberry and O'Rourke (2010). Britain's manufacturing sector and its performance are examined in detail in Broadberry (1997). There is a companion volume on services (Broadberry 2006). Those who just want the numbers should go to the database compiled by Thomas and Dimsdale and posted on the Bank of England website.

Notes

1 The key components of the expenditure method are shown in the following national income equation:

$$Y = C + I + G + (X - M)$$

where Y is GDP, C is consumer spending, I is investment spending, G is government spending, X is export receipts, and M is import spending. The terms on the right-hand side of the equation are the components of aggregate expenditure.

2 Hence technology is important not just within sophisticated manufacturing industries but also in the provision of everyday services.

3 At the time of writing, however, there were plans to build a new coal mine on the Cumbrian coast.

4 The occasion for the flexing of oil producer muscle was Arab resentment at western support for Israel during the 1973 Yom Kippur War. The UK did not become a large oil producer until several years after this crisis (Pollard 1992, pp. 240–241).

References

Broadberry, S.N., 1997. *The productivity race: British manufacturing in international perspective, 1850–1990*. Cambridge: Cambridge University Press.

Broadberry, S.N., 2006. *Market services and the productivity race 1850–2000. British performance in international perspective*. Cambridge: Cambridge University Press.

Broadberry, S.N., and O'Rourke, K.H., 2010. *The Cambridge economic history of modern Europe*. Vol. 2. Cambridge: Cambridge University Press.

Coyle, D., 2014. *GDP: A brief but affectionate history*. Princeton: Princeton University Press.

Crafts, N., 2015. UK economic growth since 2010: Is it as bad as it seems? *National Institute Economic Review*, 231, R17–R29.

Crafts, N., 2018. *Forging ahead, falling behind and fighting back: British economic growth from the industrial revolution to the financial crisis*. Cambridge: Cambridge University Press.

Crafts, N., 2019. Persistent productivity failure in the UK; Is the EU really to blame? *National Institute Economic Review*, 247, R10–R18.

Floud, R., Humphries, J., and Johnson, P., eds., 2014. *The Cambridge economic history of modern Britain, Vol. 2, Growth and decline, 1870 to the present*. 2nd ed. Cambridge: Cambridge University Press.

Geary, F., and Stark, T., 2019. 150 years of regional GDP: United Kingdom and Ireland. *In:* J.R. Rosés and N. Wolf, eds. *The economic development of Europe's regions: A quantitative history since 1900*. London: Routledge, 330–362.

Helpman, E., 2004. *The mystery of economic growth*. Cambridge, MA: Belknap.

Maddison, A., 1991. *Dynamic forces in capitalist development*. Oxford: Oxford University Press.

Maddison, A., 2006. *The world economy. Vol. II, Historical statistics*. Paris: OECD.

Olson, M., 1982. *The rise and decline of nations: Economic growth, stagnation and social rigidities*. New Haven: Yale University Press.

Our Special Correspondent, 1904. Mr. Chamberlain in the city. *The Times*, 20 January, p. 10.

Pollard, S., 1992. *The development of the British economy, 1914–1990*. 4th ed. London: Edward Arnold.

Singleton, J., 1991. *Lancashire on the scrapheap: The cotton industry, 1945–1970*. Oxford: Oxford University Press.

Singleton, J., 2016. *Economic and natural disasters since 1900*. Cheltenham: Edward Elgar.

Thomas, N., Hook, L., and Tighe, C., 2019. How Britain ended its coal addiction. *Financial Times*, 1 October. Available from: https://www.ft.com/content/a05d1dd4-dddd-11e9-9743-db5a370481bc.

Thomas, R., and Dimsdale, N., 2017. *A millennium of UK data*. Available from: www.bankofengland.co.uk/statistics/research-datasets [Accessed 20 May 2020].

Tomlinson, J., 2016. De-industrialization not decline: A new meta-narrative for post-war British history. *Twentieth Century British History*, 27 (1), 76–99.

4 Inequality, living standards, and welfare provision

Peter Scott and James T. Walker

Introduction

We are all born into inequality: in potential height, strength, intellect, and all the other elements that reflect the diversity of our species. However, much inequality is socially constructed and, therefore, of salience to social scientists and policy-makers. Inequality can arise from discrimination: by ethnicity, class, gender, religion, and other characteristics. Institutional discrimination can also occur indirectly owing to differences in parental income, which have strong impacts on children's life chances, encompassing such important factors as educational attainment, access to higher-paying careers, and even life expectancy.

In 1900 the chances of the child of a manual worker rising to the professional classes were virtually zero, owing the very limited education he/she could access, together with a formidable class system. Seventy years later, despite the playing field remaining deeply uneven, the life chances of working-class children had been transformed, with a reduction in income inequality and the development of a welfare state that provided financial support to those in need, plus a range of services, from housing to education. However, the process of equalising life-chances has since stalled and reversed.[1]

Apart from the obvious welfare and social justice arguments, high inequality and low social mobility are likely to negatively impact economic efficiency, as a society that is 'closed' to meritocratic entry into higher-earning occupations is likely to exclude many of its potentially most talented individuals. Thus it is plausible that the tax and welfare state reforms of the 1980s, which were defended in terms of their positive impacts on efficiency and competitiveness (by boosting incentives), may actually have had the opposite long-term effect.

We first examine changes in the distribution of income and wealth over the twentieth century, and beyond, together with their drivers. We then review changes in living standards and related issues such as social mobility, equality of opportunity, and poverty. This is followed by a discussion of the rise and fall of the welfare state. Finally, we examine whether changes in inequality and living standards are driven primarily by long-run technological change or the ebb and flow of globalisation.

Trends in income and wealth inequality

Income inequality statistics are generally based on income tax data and cover 'tax units' – a man and wife, or a single adult (or a child with income in his/her own right), plus dependents. Pre-1939 data are generally restricted to higher earners, as

DOI: 10.4324/9781003037118-5

these were the only ones who then paid income tax. However, such 'top incomes' are important, because income redistributions in western countries have typically been dominated by changes in the shares of this group, especially the top 1 percent (Piketty and Saez 2006, pp. 201–202). Table 4.1 shows the income shares of the top 0.01–10.0 of the population, together with the bottom 90 percent.

The UK's (then including Ireland's) 1911 income distribution was extremely unequal. The top 1 percent of the population enjoyed some 30 percent of total personal income, while the top 0.01 percent had 4.6 percent of personal income (460 times more than the average person). The First World War witnessed a substantial reduction in income inequality, while the inter-war years saw some further reduction in inequality within the top income range but little change for the top 5 or 10 percent. The Second World War witnessed a significant further redistribution, with the share of the bottom 90 percent rising from around 64 percent in 1937 to 68 percent in 1949. However, UK income inequality in 1949 was still greater than that for France and the United States, as it had been in 1911 and 1937 (Scott and Walker 2020; Piketty 2003, p. 1037; Piketty and Saez 2003, pp. 8–9). The trend towards greater equality continued until the 1970s but was reversed from around 1980, with the income share of the bottom 90 percent falling below its 1919 level by the end of the century and experiencing a further slight decline by 2014.

These figures cover pre-tax incomes. Changes in after-tax income from 1911–2000 are examined in Table 4.2. In 1911 a top income tax rate of 5.8 percent (plus a maximum 2.5 percent 'super-tax' for the rich) left after-tax income shares little different from pre-tax shares. However, by 1937, partly owing to rearmament, much higher income taxes substantially reduced the shares of the top 0.1–5 percent but had only a small impact on the top 10 percent. The bottom 90 percent received a growing share of post-tax income until the 1970s, while the tax and benefits system became much more redistributive, largely due to the development of the post-war welfare state.

Table 4.1 The distribution of pre-tax personal income in the UK, 1911–2014

Top income shares (%)	0.01	0.1	1.0	5	10	Bottom 90%
1911	4.60	13.81	30.15	44.97	n.a.	n.a.
1919	3.32	8.98	19.48	31.44	37.21	62.79
1937	2.17	6.73	16.90	31.73	36.18	63.82
1949	1.06	3.00	11.42	23.38	32.33	67.67
1954	0.67	2.72	9.67	21.22	30.63	69.37
1959	0.60	2.30	8.60	20.26	29.96	70.04
1965	0.62	2.28	8.55	20.10	29.88	70.12
1970	0.42	1.64	7.05	18.65	28.82	71.18
1975	0.31	1.40	6.10	17.40	27.82	72.18
1981	n.a.	1.53	6.67	19.45	31.03	68.97
1985	n.a.	1.86	7.55	21.04	32.94	67.06
1990	n.a.	n.a.	9.80	24.43	36.90	63.10
1995	n.a.	3.24	10.75	25.80	38.51	61.49
2000	n.a.	4.64	12.67	27.04	38.43	61.57
2014	n.a.	5.48	13.88	28.53	39.99	60.01

Sources: 1911–1949, Scott and Walker (2020); 1954–2000, Atkinson (2007): 93–95; 2014 World Inequality Database (2019). Note that the data range for the 1911 estimate is close to the 5% share at 4.9% and estimated by extrapolation.

Table 4.2 The distribution of after-tax personal income, 1911–2000

Top income shares (%)	0.1	1	5	10	Bottom 90%
1911	12.15	27.93	42.24	n.a.	n.a.
1937	3.65	12.57	26.1	35.64	64.36
1949	1.23	6.76	18.75	28.75	71.25
1959	0.95	5.51	16.21	25.91	74.09
1970	0.73	4.83	15.33	25.27	74.73
1985	1.18	5.79	18.25	29.94	70.06
2000	3.50	10.03	23.09	34.31	65.69

Source: 1911, Scott and Walker (2020); 1937–2000, Atkinson (2007, pp. 104–105).

Note that the 5% interval for 1911 was within the data income range and is calculated directly.

However, redistribution was reversed from the 1980s, with the bottom 90 percent's income share falling back to just over its 1937 level by 2000. Meanwhile the top 0.1 percent – the biggest losers in terms of post-tax income shares over 1911–1970 (from 12.34 to 0.73 percent) – saw their losses reversed, recovering to almost their 1937 shares.

Table 4.3 examines changes in the distribution of personal wealth (based on 'net worth': the value of assets owned by individuals, net of their debts) over the twentieth century. These include both financial assets (stocks and bonds etc.), plus 'real' assets, such as property or an unincorporated family business. The table is based on

Table 4.3 The distribution of personal wealth in the UK: 1895–2009

Year	Bottom 90%	Top 10%	Top 5%	Top 1%	Top 0.5%	Top 0.1%
1900	7.3	92.7	89.1	70.7	59.0	36.4
1910	8.1	91.9	87.8	68.8	57.8	37.3
1920	12.0	88.0	81.4	57.3	45.6	27.8
1925	11.8	88.2	82.0	60.3	50.5	33.8
1930	13.9	86.1	79.2	56.9	47.0	29.5
1935	14.1	85.9	78.2	54.0	43.6	25.8
1938	15.0	85.0	77.5	54.1	43.8	27.0
1946	16.5	83.5	72.7	46.1	36.1	19.3
1950	20.1	79.9	69.0	43.0	33.3	20.1
1955	24.7	75.3	62.2	37.9	28.9	15.8
1960	29.5	70.5	59.1	35.0	26.6	13.6
1965	31.8	68.2	55.2	30.9	23.0	10.6
1970	35.5	64.5	50.1	27.4	20.2	9.9
1975	41.3	58.7	44.0	22.1	16.1	7.1
1980	47.9	52.1	38.3	18.8	13.8	6.6
1985	51.3	48.7	35.2	15.8	10.9	4.6
1990	54.0	46.0	33.8	16.3	12.0	5.9
1995	53.1	46.9	34.6	16.2	11.6	5.4
2000	49.4	50.6	38.1	18.5	13.4	5.9
2009	46.0	54.0	40.3	20.6	15.6	8.2

Source: Alvaredo et al. (2018), online Appendix Table G1.

recent research by Alvaredo *et al.* (2018), who use data from the estates of deceased persons, with adjustments to allow for the fact that mortality is weighted towards older age groups. The table indicates that wealth has been substantially more concentrated than income. This partly reflects a general pattern across nations for wealth concentration to be stronger than income concentration. However, Britain had an unusually high concentration of wealth compared to other western nations, reflecting its extreme concentration of land in the hands of the aristocracy and gentry (Lindert 1991, pp. 220–224). In 1900 the bottom 90 percent held only 7.3 percent of personal wealth, and even in 1938 they held only 15 percent. The trend towards greater wealth equality accelerated after the Second World War but slowed in the 1980s and reversed from the 1990s – following the economic liberalisation policies of the Thatcher and Major Conservative governments.

Why is the post-1979 upward trend for wealth inequality much weaker than that for income inequality? One important factor is the extension of owner-occupation, which has distributed a major source of wealth more widely (Alvaredo *et al.* 2018, pp. 36–37). House price inflation has magnified this trend, given that many people who purchased their house several decades ago own homes that they could not now afford to buy on mortgage. Another potentially important factor concerns the declining importance of capital incomes (incomes flowing from wealth) compared to the early twentieth century. Prior to 1939 top incomes were typically dominated by 'capital incomes' (dividends, interest, rents, etc.) in Britain and other western nations. However capital incomes have played a relatively minor role in the post-1980 surge in top income shares compared to salaries and business/entrepreneurial incomes (Atkinson *et al.* 2011, pp. 6–8).

In Focus: the Gini coefficient as a summary measure of inequality

Although data on top income or wealth shares are useful, we also need some overall summary measure of inequality. The most widely used summary statistic is the Gini coefficient (developed by the Italian statistician and sociologist Corrado Gini). Gini provides an absolute, 0–1, index of inequality, with zero indicating perfect equality and 1 representing complete inequality (one person having all the income or wealth). Values greater than 1 are also theoretically possible – if people have negative income (i.e. their debt payments outweigh their income).

The Gini coefficient can be most easily interpreted geometrically, using the Lorenz curve, shown in Figure 4.1. The diagram plots cumulative shares of population against cumulative shares of income. If income were perfectly equal, it would follow the 45 degree 'line of equality'. The Lorenz curve shows the extent to which income/wealth distribution departs from equity. Therefore:

$$\text{Gini coefficient} = \frac{(\text{Area A})}{(\text{Area A} + \text{Area B})}$$

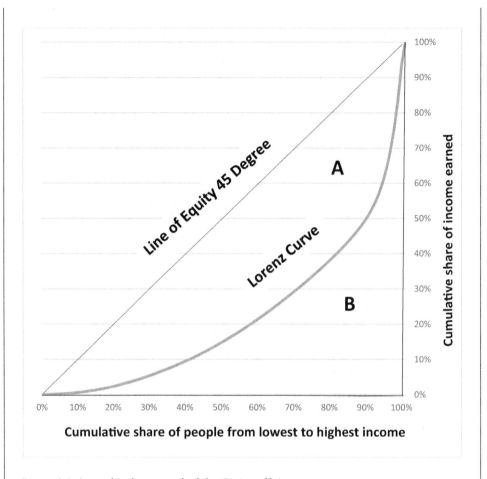

Figure 4.1 A graphical portrayal of the Gini coefficient

The appendix provides a mathematical definition of the Gini coefficient. Long-term comparisons of Britain's Gini coefficient have been hampered by incompatibilities in the ways it has been calculated for different periods. Atkinson and Jenkins (2020) provide a linked series from 1937 to 2012. This shows the expected U-shaped curve, with Gini falling to a low of 0.37 in 1978 and then rising to around 0.50 in the 2000s (above even its 1937 value). Figure 4.2 shows a comparison of the Gini coefficient and the income share of the top 5 percent (for convenience, the Gini is graphed as a percentage rather than a fraction of 1, to make it directly comparable with the 5 percent income share). Changes in the top 5 percent's income share appear to dominate the changes in Gini, reflecting the fact that this group were major gainers from the neo-liberal job market, tax, and benefit reforms initiated in the 1980s.

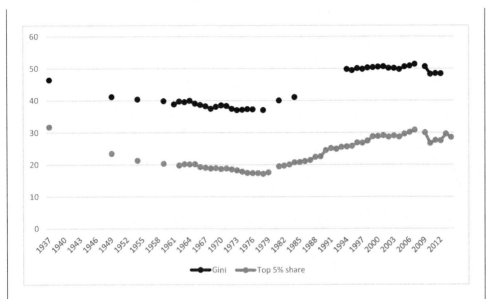

Figure 4.2 A linked series for the UK Gini coefficient for income, together with the income share of the top 5 percent

Notes: Atkinson and Jenkins' preferred series, for gross (pre-tax) incomes. For convenience, the Gini is shown as a percentage rather than a fraction of 1.

Source: Atkinson and Jenkins (2020, p. 263).

Living standards, equality of opportunity, and poverty

Figure 4.3 shows the growth in average UK real pre-tax earnings from 1900–2018. Virtually flat real earnings during 1900–1913 (with a decline from 1908–1913) were followed by more rapid growth in the inter-war era, sustained growth from the 1950s to 2007, and finally the longest peacetime earnings fall following the onset of the 2008 'credit crunch'. Overall, the twentieth century has seen a huge leap in living standards, with the average worker in 2018 earning around 3.7 times the real income of his/her ancestor in 1900, while the early twenty-first century shows no clear trend. However, for households, income growth would have been faster during the second half of the twentieth century, due to a dramatic rise in the number of married women in the formal labour market.

Twentieth-century Britain also witnessed a major compression in the initially huge income differentials between different classes of worker, illustrated (for adult males) in Figure 4.4. In 1911–14 higher professionals (e.g. doctors, lawyers, accountants) received 3.49 times the average male earnings, while lower professionals (e.g. nurses, teachers, laboratory technicians) received 1.65 times and managerial workers 2.13 times. Conversely semi-skilled and unskilled workers received 73 and 67 percent of the average, respectively, while clerks (among the least well paid of all 'white-collar workers') and skilled manual workers typically received just over the average. By 1978 the gap between the highest and lowest groups had markedly narrowed. Higher professionals still led the field, but with only 1.73 times average earnings.

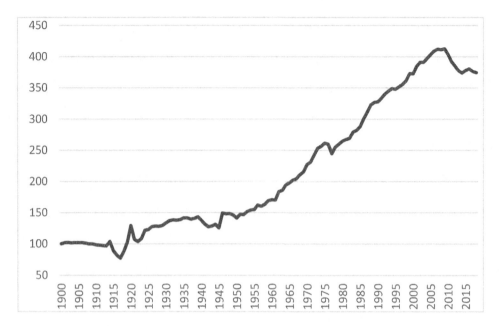

Figure 4.3 Average real pre-tax earnings in the UK (in 2010 £s), 1900–2018

Notes: Deflated by the retail price index.

Source: Clark 2019.

Managers and lower professionals had also moved much closer to the mean, while clerks' relative incomes had fallen to around those of semi-skilled workers. Yet the relative position of manual workers had not greatly improved, and despite some decline in their proportion of all male workers (from 78 percent in 1911 to 62 percent in 1971; Routh 1980, pp. 6–7), they still constituted the bulk of male, and total, employment.

Meanwhile the large pay differentials between men and women had declined, mainly during 1939–47 (owing to very tight labour markets) and the 1970s (owing to anti-sex discrimination legislation) (Joshi *et al.* 1985, p. S158). This legislation also ended the widespread practice of employers' 'marriage bars', prohibiting women from working after marriage. Marriage bars were often justified on moral grounds (the need for the wife to be at home to look after children), though they provided major cost savings for employers by segmenting their labour force. By providing a relatively uncontroversial means of dismissing older female workers and replacing them with cheaper juvenile girls, they reduced costs for un/semi-skilled work (that was often assigned to female workers). Meanwhile more skilled work – requiring years, rather than weeks or months, to fully master – was reserved for male workers, who were regarded as part of their permanent labour force (Scott 2007, pp. 194–196).

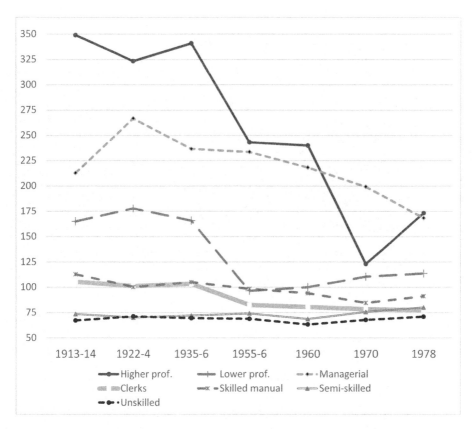

Figure 4.4 Earnings of adult male British higher professionals; lower professionals; managerial
workers; clerks; and skilled, semi-skilled, and unskilled manual workers, relative to
mean adult male earnings, 1913–14 to 1978

Notes: Mean income is the mean for seven occupational groups, including foremen (who are not shown
in the graph) based on current weights for numbers of employees, for the nearest population census year.
Source: Routh 1980, pp. 120–121.

The range of occupations open to women had also expanded greatly, again assisted
by legislation, such as the Sex Disqualification (Removal) Act 1919, which prohibited discriminatory practices that had excluded women from many professions. However – in common with legislation to outlaw job discrimination by race – real change
proved very slow, and even today women and many racial minorities are substantially
under-represented and under-paid in corporate board rooms and some professional
and high-status occupations.

Discrimination by class has also proved intransigent (in some respects more so
than gender). Prior to the 1940s only a very small proportion of working-class
children entered secondary education (which was necessary for most clerical jobs
and improved the chances of entering skilled manual occupations). In 1932 it was

Image 4.1 Social immobility, as depicted on *The Frost Report*, 7 April 1966
Source: Courtesy of the BBC.

estimated that, for children of equal ability, seven fee-paying children entered secondary education for every child that won a free place (McKibbin 1998, p. 260). The post-war decline of manual occupations and the rapid expansion of the service sector created an impression of a more open society (by creating more white-collar jobs). However, studies in the 1970s noted that relative mobility rates by social class had not greatly increased (Heath and Payne 2000, pp. 255–257). This partly reflects persistent inequalities in education. Edgerton and Halsey (1993) noted that while there had been a substantial reduction in gender inequality with regard to higher education, there had been no diminution in social class inequality, with parental occupation remaining a strong predictor of a child's odds of getting into tertiary education and, particularly, elite universities (that expanded much more slowly than the overall university sector).

An influential report for the Social Mobility Commission (Friedman *et al.* 2017) found that the odds of children from professional backgrounds ending up in professional jobs were 2.5 times higher than those from less-advantaged groups (much higher than the odds differences for males and females of all classes; see Office for National Statistics 2018). An extreme example is medicine: 73 percent of doctors are the children of professionals and managers, and less than 6 percent have working-class backgrounds (Friedman *et al.* 2017, p. 1). Thus, while opportunities for social mobility had increased universally – with the expansion of professional/managerial occupations – for the children of working-class parents the odds of pursuing such high-status careers remain very much against them.[2]

Meanwhile poverty remains a major economic and social problem, despite a 275 percent increase in real pre-tax incomes from 1900–2018. Britain's unusually high pre-1914 income inequality meant that its high GDP per capita was not reflected in working-class living standards. British life expectancy was only 53 in 1913, lower than the Netherlands, Denmark, and Sweden – despite higher British per capita incomes; with many people being so malnourished that they were stunted in height (Scott 2007, pp. 1 & 33).

Prior to the 1940s poverty was a constant risk for most families, should the main bread-winner become ill, incapacitated, or unemployed (accentuated by the fact that women's wages were only around half those of men, and wages for juveniles were markedly lower). Meanwhile even many families with the father working full-time were in poverty – on account of low wages. The inter-war years witnessed rising living standards for those in work and significantly higher state unemployment assistance, but mass unemployment greatly increased the risk of long-term poverty, especially for people working in the staple industries or living in the industrial heartlands of northern England, Scotland, and Wales.

The post-war full employment welfare state reduced, but did not eradicate, poverty. Absolute poverty (based on a minimum income deemed sufficient for all *essentials*) fell to comparatively very low levels, but relative poverty – defined as household incomes less than half of the median (middle of the range) – remained around 5–10 percent even in the 1960s and 1970s. Figure 4.5 shows relative poverty rates from 1961 to the 2017–18 financial year, before and after housing costs. During the 1960s and 1970s Britain had low relative poverty, which was broadly similar before and after housing costs. However, during the 1980s relative poverty soared to around 14–15 percent after housing costs, boosted by housing cost inflation (especially in London and the South East). If the relative poverty rate is set at half the *mean* (average) income, rather than half the *median* income, there is a sharper rise in after housing cost poverty, from around 10 percent in the 1960s and 1970s to around 25 percent in the 1990s.

From the 1990s relative poverty rates (as shown in Figure 4.5) before housing costs have declined somewhat, but relative poverty after housing costs has stayed around its peak levels. Significantly, the sharp fall in headline unemployment since 1990 appears to have had little impact on relative poverty, especially after housing costs – suggesting that there may be major elements of under-employment or under-reported employment not captured in official statistics.

Figure 4.5 Relative poverty rates before and after housing costs, 1961–2017/18

Notes: Based on 50 percent of the contemporary medium income. Data from 1961 to 2001–02 are for Great Britain, and subsequent data are for the UK.

Source: Institute of Fiscal Studies 2019.

Tempering inequality: the welfare state and its critics

In 1900 the state's role in social welfare was largely limited to regulation, primary education, and the Poor Law. Meanwhile the proportion of families who could realistically guard against destitution in the event of the main breadwinner becoming unable to work – through savings or insurance – was very small, certainly less than 5 percent. Most working and lower-middle class families relied on a patchwork of self-help; mutual-aid; and religious, charitable, or philanthropic institutions, such as friendly societies, trade unions, building societies, retail co-operatives, and 'industrial' (burial) insurance companies. However, these were inadequate even in periods of prosperity, let alone during a protracted trade depression (Finlayson 1994, pp. 107–200).

The 1906 and 1910 Liberal governments introduced some tentative welfare measures, including a modest pension for people over 70, via the 1908 Old Age Pensions Act. This was followed by the 1911 National Insurance Act, which provided sickness and unemployment benefits for certain classes of workers. The 1911 Act introduced the principle of a state-supported insurance system, funded by the contributions of workers, which still underpins a major strand of the British welfare state. Germany had already introduced a similar system, which strongly influenced British policy (Hill 1990, pp. 18–19).

The next phase of innovation occurred towards the end of the First World War. Policy-makers became concerned about potential popular unrest if demobbed soldiers returned to civilian life to find they had no jobs or homes. Fears were expressed that this might even lead to revolution (as happened in Russia and parts of Eastern Europe). An 'out-of work donation' for the unemployed, which became known as 'the dole', was introduced, followed by the 1920 Unemployment Insurance Act, which extended the 1911 social security legislation to all manual workers and non-manual workers on less than £250 per annum.

Meanwhile, partly to create work, the government introduced the 1919 Housing and Town Planning Act, subsidising local councils to build 'homes for heroes' (Scott 2013, pp. 37–38). These were generally located on greenfield areas beyond existing urban boundaries (capitalising on transport improvements accelerated by the war). Their design marked a major improvement in size, utilities, and garden space compared to pre-1914 working-class housing and established the blueprint for the interwar suburban semi-detached house. Although the original post-Armistice 'homes for heroes' council housing programme was beset with delays and, later, drastic expenditure cuts, these recommendations formed the basis of a series of major house building programmes over the next 20 years, resulting in the construction of 1,320,000 municipal homes (Scott 2013, pp. 7 & 82).

Unemployment benefits were also subject to retrenchment as costs escalated following the emergence of mass unemployment during the 1921–22 recession. A further increase in unemployment during the 1929–32 world depression prompted the introduction of the hated 'means test' by the new "National government" in November 1931. This subjected households to examination by investigators to ensure that they had no other means of subsistence (for example, household items that might be sold) and that any payments were kept to the lowest possible level compatible with avoiding starvation.

The Second World War transformed the relationship between the state and its people, with public expenditure on social services (equivalent to only 2.3 percent of GDP in 1900 and 4.9 percent in 1920) jumping to over 10 percent by 1948 (Johnson 2004, p. 216). War mobilisation rapidly transformed Britain into a 'command economy' with tight control over the allocation of resources – including the vast majority of people, who were subject to some form of conscription, even for civilians. This environment influenced war-time social services and post-war reconstruction planning – based on the Beveridge (1942) report: *Social Insurance and Allied Services*. Beveridge proposed a comprehensive policy of income maintenance to address what he described as 'five giants . . . Want, Disease, Ignorance, Squalor and Idleness', via a mainly insurance-based system following the precedent of the 1911 Act. This would be supplemented by non-contributory means-tested 'social assistance' benefits for circumstances not covered by the insurance-based benefits. The system would provide protection against loss of income during sickness and unemployment, together with pensions and a range of other benefits.

Despite Treasury opposition, the 1945 Labour landslide election victory ensured that there would be no return to the policies of the 1930s. The 1946 National Insurance Act, 1946 National Insurance (Industrial Injuries) Act, and 1948 National Assistance Act launched a comprehensive social insurance and welfare system (Hill 1990, p. 31). Together with the foundation of the National Health Service (assumed in Beveridge's report) in 1948 and the 1944 Education Act, providing universal education up to age 15, the key features of the post-war welfare state were in place. Its success was facilitated by buoyant economic growth and full employment up to the 1970s, together with rapid medical advances. Further waves of council housing also assisted low-income families.

The welfare state was subject to substantial cuts from the 1980s, discussed in the next section. The most recent round of welfare reforms, introduced in the wake of the credit crunch, has again raised the spectre of destitution for those unable to work. The 2012 Welfare Reform Act replaced unemployment-related and income benefits by 'Universal Credit.' While this had some positive features (such as rationalising the benefits system), it required claimants to wait at least five weeks before receiving their first income payment. As many claimants had little or no savings, waiting five or six weeks for money often led to eviction from their homes and/or amassing huge debts to 'pay-day lenders' charging extortionate interest rates. Despite regulation of pay-day loans from 2015, following a Competition and Markets Authority investigation, Universal Credit continues to plunge substantial numbers of families into the type of deep absolute poverty not seen in Britain since the 1930s – including several cases where vulnerable people refused benefits have died of starvation (Butler 2020).

Has Britain over-spent on social welfare?

The election of Margaret Thatcher's government in 1979 witnessed a sharp break with previous Conservative administrations, with a commitment to 'rolling back the welfare state' as part of a wider initiative to cut public expenditure. In some respects it was successful, particularly in council housing, which was sold off at heavily discounted prices, mainly to sitting tenants (thereby eliminating most of the social housing sector). However, despite cuts in social security provision, the overall cost of the welfare state continued to rise, owing to the temporary return of mass unemployment during the 1980s and the longer-term trend towards higher life expectancy – increasing medical and pension costs. Government thus reinforced its attack on the welfare state. In addition to opposition in principle to the state playing a major role in people's lives, through taxation and benefits, the system was branded expensive and inefficient. To what extent are these arguments justified?

One proximate measure is spending comparisons with other nations. Advocates of reform claimed that a large welfare state represented a key ingredient in a specific 'British malaise' (Slater 2012) that gave Britain a competitive disadvantage. Table 4.4 compares long-term changes in three important elements of public social welfare spending – education, health, and pensions – in the UK, France, Germany, Sweden, and the United States. All five nations show long-term trends of rising welfare expenditures, as expected, given that services such as pensions and health are 'superior goods,' demand for which grows more than proportionately with economic growth. Moreover, productivity growth for health and other social services (both public and private sector) is generally slower than in manufacturing (De Vries 2008, p. 238). In 1960 UK welfare spending was roughly on a par with the other four countries (except for pensions, where it was the lowest spender, relative to GDP). However, in 1980, when the welfare state was allegedly 'bloated,' UK public health spending accounted for a lower proportion of GDP than the other countries (with the exception of the United States); Britain's pensions expenditure was the lowest in the table; and its education spending was broadly in line with the other nations. A similar pattern is evident for 2013.

These figures do not include some important elements of welfare spending, particularly unemployment benefits, which vary considerably over the economic cycle and are thus best measured over several years. Figure 4.6 examines total public social expenditure for the UK and eight OECD countries. Britain was towards the bottom of

Table 4.4 Public expenditure on education, health, and pensions for Britain and four other western nations from the early twentieth century to 2013 (% of GDP)

Education	1913	1930s	1960	1980	1993–4	2013
UK	1.1	4.0	4.3	5.6	5.4	5.2
France	1.5	1.3	2.4	5.0	5.8	4.7
Germany	2.7	n.a.	2.9	4.7	4.8	3.7
Sweden	n.a.	n.a.	5.1	9.0	8.4	5.2
USA	1.5	3.1	4.0	5.3	5.5	4.2

Health	c. 1910	1930s	1960	1980	1993–4	2013
UK	0.3	0.6	3.3	5.2	5.8	7.8
France	0.3	0.3	2.5	6.1	7.6	8.7
Germany	0.5	0.7	3.2	6.5	7.0	9.2
Sweden	0.3	0.9	3.4	8.8	6.4	9.2
USA	0.3	0.3	1.3	4.1	6.3	7.9

Pensions	1920	1930s	1960	1980	1993–4	2013
UK	2.2	1.0	4.0	5.9	7.3	6.1
France	1.6	n.a.	6.0	10.5	12.3	13.8
Germany	2.1	n.a.	9.7	12.8	12.4	10.1
Sweden	0.5	n.a.	4.4	9.9	12.8	7.7
USA	0.7	n.a.	4.1	7.0	7.5	7.0

Sources: Education, USA, 1913, 1930s, 2005 and 2017, US spending from 1900 dataset (2019); education, 2013, OECD (2019a); health, 2013, OECD (2019d); pensions, 2013, OECD (2019b). All other data Tanzi and Schuknecht (2000, pp. 43–41).

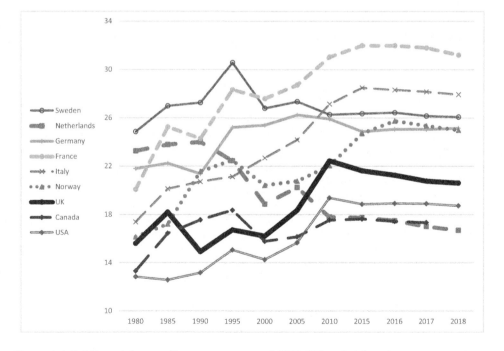

Figure 4.6 Public social expenditure as a percent of GDP, UK and eight other western nations
Source: OECD 2019c.

the league table of social welfare spending in 1980 and, despite some increase during the Blair and Brown Labour governments, has remained in the lower half.

Expenditure is only one side of the value for money equation, though the fact that Britain had a relatively low ratio of public welfare expenditure to GDP suggests that any 'crowding out' of private investment could not have disadvantaged it relative to other more successful economies, which typically had higher social spending. Assessing value for money is problematic, given that there are no clear 'prices' for goods that are free at the point of delivery. However, a review of the literature by Johnson (2004, pp. 224–228) found that many studies on the efficiency of public sector provision are inconclusive or obviously biased – owing to nonsensical assumptions such as non-market activities being inherently non-productive and market services inherently productive (which would mean that private education or health spending would benefit the economy, by definition, while public education and health spending would not). Johnson concluded that the argument that public welfare provision inevitably harms economic performance remains unproven, though badly designed and/or administered welfare systems can have adverse economic impacts. Much of the literature also ignores the 'agency' risks of private welfare provision – for example, insurers refusing to pay out on private health insurance policies or the mis-selling of private pensions (which became a scandal during the 1980s).

Debates and Interpretations: why did income inequality fall from 1900 to the 1970s, and why has it risen since 1980?

Most large industrial nations followed Britain's pattern of falling income inequality from 1914 to the late 1970s, followed by either a reversal or a flattening of this trend since 1980. There are two main explanations: the first identifies technology and sectoral change as the major drivers, and the second focuses on economic shocks, the reactions of policy-makers, and non-market mechanisms such as labour institutions.

The leading American growth and development economist Simon Kuznets (1955) proposed a model based on the relative value of skills during industrialisation in the old sector (agriculture) versus the new one (industry). As a primarily agrarian society is transformed into an industrial society, workers will switch from low-wage agricultural work to higher-wage industrial employment, leading to rising income inequalities between the two sectors. The initial scarcity of skills required for the new sector (including technical and managerial skills) would further raise inequalities. However, over time the new sector, and its associated skills, come to dominate the economy, thereby reducing inequality. This 'Kuznets wave' model predicts an inverted u-shaped pattern of inequality during the development process.

It has been suggested that deindustrialisation and the information and communications technology (ICT) revolution have triggered a second Kuznets wave, again driven primarily by the greater potential income generation available in the new (ICT and services) sector relative to manufacturing. This 'augmented' Kuznets wave model – shown in Figure 4.7 – has proved attractive to policy-makers, as it portrays the post-1980 rise in inequality as an inevitable phenomenon rather than a reversible consequence of public policy. Moreover, the model predicts that the problem of inequality is ultimately self-correcting once the new sector becomes dominant.

However, Kuznets's model has been widely criticised as not being supported by the empirical evidence. As three of the leading scholars of global inequality, Tony

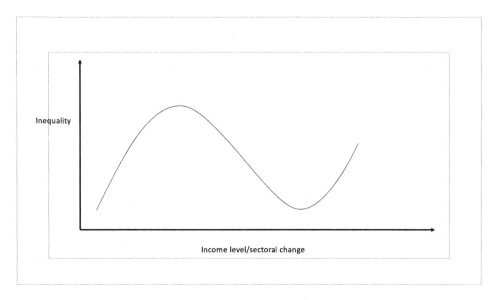

Figure 4.7 The augmented Kuznets curve, showing the first wave and the start of the second

Atkinson, Thomas Piketty, and Emmanuel Saez (2011, p. 57), note, 'it has little pur-chase in explaining top income shares,' as it essentially focuses on labour incomes rather than capital (investment) incomes which, historically, have dominated the incomes of the rich. Moreover, they note that much of the recent change in income distribution has taken place within the top 10 percent, where workers have very simi-lar skills (university education). The model also ignores inherited wealth, which can make income inequality persistent. Finally, not all countries have experienced sub-stantially rising inequality after the 1970s. France, Germany, Switzerland, the Neth-erlands, Japan, and Singapore enjoyed relatively stable inequality, in contrast to the English-speaking countries (United States, Canada, Ireland, UK, Australia, and New Zealand), which were in the vanguard of the move to globalisation and deregulation (Atkinson *et al.* 2011, pp. 41–49).

It is also worth noting that Kuznets's wave model was more a 'conjecture' than a theory. Indeed, Kuznets (1955, p. 26) noted that it was based on, 'perhaps 5 per cent empirical information and 95 per cent speculation, some of it possibly tainted by wishful thinking.' Moreover, Piketty (2003, p. 1036) argues that this theory was not supported by Kuznets's own data, while Kuznets's discussion of the importance of shocks has been overly neglected by economists.

An alternative argument explains the inequality reduction from c. 1914–c. 1979 as being driven by a series of economic shocks and policy responses, together with non-market mechanisms such as labour institutions. The principal shocks were the two world wars, together with the 1920–21 and 1929–32 depressions (Atkinson 2007, pp. 167–168; Atkinson *et al.* 2011, p. 5). This explanation fits well with evidence for Britain, where the top 1 percent of incomes in 1911 were mainly 'rentiers' (peo-ple who live primarily on property and investment income), but rentier-dominated incomes encompassed only the top 0.4 percent in 1937 and the top 0.026 percent in 1949 (Scott and Walker 2020). War-time inflation reduced the real value of fixed-interest securities, land values declined substantially, and rising taxation impacted even 'pre-tax' personal incomes (for example, through corporation tax). Meanwhile some of the economic gains for lower income groups during the two world wars and their aftermaths – such as the welfare state – proved persistent (Atkinson *et al.* 2011, pp. 65–67; Scott and Walker 2020).

In contrast the post-1979 globalisation – driven by trade and capital control liberalisation, shortly followed by changes in the incidence of taxes and benefits that redistributed resources from low to higher income groups – has witnessed shocks, policy responses, and institutional changes that have acted to increase, rather than reduce, inequality. This largely reflects a change in the balance of power between the economic elite and the state. Globalisation and economic liberalisation have made it far easier for the rich to offshore their assets, or themselves, in search of lower taxes or other policies favourable to protecting their wealth. Rising international labour mobility has also increased the bargaining power of top executives when pressing for higher salaries (in relation to profits), based on the need to bench-mark salaries against a 'global market for talent' that has persistently driven up top executive incomes. Meanwhile, for the vast bulk of workers, being 'competitive' has typically involved accepting lower wage growth and less attractive conditions to meet competition from lower-wage countries that enthusiastically embraced globalisation, such as China and India.

The rapidity of the switch from falling to rising income and wealth inequality since 1980 is more plausibly explained by the radical liberalisation agenda triggered by the elections of Margaret Thatcher in Britain and Ronald Reagan in the United States than by technological change (which tends to be a more gradual, cumulative process). This would also explain why countries that have resisted the liberalisation agenda (for example, France and Germany) have witnessed stagnant, rather than rising, inequality – an outcome difficult to reconcile with Kuznets wave models. However, it is nevertheless plausible that technological change has played some role in this process, alongside globalisation.

Conclusions

The evidence reviewed previously regarding the inequality of wealth and income, and the incidence of relative poverty, all point to a long-term U-shaped pattern, with inequality falling from c. 1914–c. 1979 and rising thereafter. The welfare impacts of these trends have been amplified by the development of a comprehensive welfare state in the middle decades of the twentieth century, followed by attempts to 'roll it back' from the 1980s. In some respects post-1980 globalisation appears to have reintroduced some of the key characteristics of pre-1914 globalisation to Britain and other western nations – high inequality, a small state, and greater economic instability (including the return of frequent financial crises). This, in turn, appears to have increased political instability (again paralleling the downfall of the previous globalisation), including Brexit, Trumpism in the United States, and social unrest related to austerity, such as France's 'gilet jaunes' movement or the riots in Chile (both triggered by higher state-imposed transport costs). It is conceivable that such instability may eventually lead to a collapse of the current globalisation – paralleling world events during 1914 to the 1950s.

APPENDIX: THE MATHEMATICAL FORMULA FOR THE GINI COEFFICIENT

The Gini coefficient can be calculated as equivalent to the Lorenz curve at half the relative mean absolute difference (Sen 1977). The mean absolute difference is the average absolute difference of pairs of items of the population, while the relative mean absolute difference is the mean absolute difference divided by the average ($\bar{x}$). If x_i is the income of person i, j is the income of person j, and there are n persons, then the Gini coefficient G is given by:

$$G = \frac{\sum_{i=1}^{n}\sum_{j=1}^{n} |x_i - x_j|}{2\sum_{i=1}^{n}\sum_{i=1}^{n} x_j} = \frac{\sum_{i=1}^{n}\sum_{j=1}^{n} |x_i - x_j|}{2n^2 x}$$

Further reading

Useful studies of income and wealth inequality include Lindert (1991); Atkinson (2007); Alvaredo *et al.* (2018); Atkinson and Jenkins (2020); Scott and Walker (2020); and, internationally, Atkinson *et al.* (2011). Good sources for British living standards, inequality of opportunity, social mobility, and poverty include Routh (1980), Joshi *et al.* (1985), Edgerton and Halsey (1993), McKibbin (1998), Heath and Payne (2000), Friedman *et al.* (2017), and Clark (2019) (for statistical data). Studies on the welfare state include Hill (1990), Johnson (2004), and Slater (2012). For the debate on long-term causes of inequality changes over time, see Kuznets (1955), Atkinson *et al.* (2011), Piketty (2003), Atkinson (2007), and Scott and Walker (2020).

Notes

1 See Chapter 15 of this volume for a detailed analysis of social mobility and life chances.
2 For more on social mobility, see Chapter 15.

References

Alvaredo, F., Atkinson, A.B., and Morelli, S., 2018. Top wealth shares in the UK over more than a century. *Journal of Public Economics*, 162, 26–47.
Atkinson, A.B., 2007. The distribution of top incomes in the United Kingdom, 1908–2000. *In:* A.B. Atkinson and T. Piketty, eds. *Top incomes over the twentieth century*. Oxford: Oxford University Press.
Atkinson, A.B., and Jenkins, S.P., 2020. A different perspective on the evolution of UK income inequality. *Review of Income and Wealth*, 66 (2), 253–266.
Atkinson, A.B., Piketty, T., and Saez, E., 2011. Top incomes in the long run of history. *Journal of Economic Literature*, 49 (1), 3–71.
Beveridge, W., 1942. *Social insurance and allied services*. London: HMSO.
Butler, P., 2020. Disabled man starved to death after DWP stopped his benefits. *Guardian. com*, 28 January. Available from: www.theguardian.com/society/2020/jan/28/disabled-man-starved-to-death-after-dwp-stopped-his-benefits.
Clark, G., 2019. What were the British earnings and prices then? (new series). *Measuring Worth*. Available from: www.measuringworth.com/ukearncpi/ [Accessed 25 October 2019].

De Vries, J., 2008. *The industrious revolution: Consumer behavior and the household economy, 1650 to the present*. Cambridge: Cambridge University Press.

Edgerton, M., and Halsey, A.H., 1993. Trends by social class and gender in access to higher education in Britain. *Oxford Review of Education*, 19 (2), 183–194.

Finlayson, G., 1994. *Citizen, state, and social welfare in Britain 1830–1990*. Oxford: Clarendon.

Friedman, S., Laurison, D., and Macmillan, L., 2017. *Social mobility, the class pay gap and inter-generational worklessness: New insights from the Labour Force Survey* (Report). Available from: www.lse.ac.uk/business-and-consultancy/consulting/consulting-reports/social-mobility-the-class-pay-gap-and-intergenerational-worklessness.

Heath, A., and Payne, C., 2000. Social mobility. *In*: A.H. Halsey and J. Web, eds., *Twentieth century British social trends*. Basingstoke: Macmillan, 254–278.

Hill, M., 1990. *Social security in Britain*. Aldershot: Edward Elgar.

Institute of Fiscal Studies, 2019. *Living standards, inequality and poverty spreadsheet* [dataset]. Available from: www.ifs.org.uk/tools_and_resources/incomes_in_uk [Accessed 28 October 2019].

Johnson, P., 2004. The welfare state and living standards. *In*: R. Floud and P. Johnson, eds, *The Cambridge economic history of modern Britain, volume III: Structural change and growth, 1939–2000*. Cambridge: Cambridge University Press, 213–237.

Joshi, H.E., Layard, R., and Owen, S.J., 1985. Why are more women working in Britain. *Journal of Labor Economics*, 3 (1), S147–S176.

Kuznets, S., 1955. Economic growth and income inequality. *American Economic Review*, 45 (1), 1–28.

Lindert, P.H., 1991. Towards a comparative history of income and wealth inequality. *In*: Y.S. Brenner, H. Kaelble and M. Thomas, eds. *Income distribution in historical perspective*. Cambridge: Cambridge University Press, 212–231.

McKibbin, R., 1998. *Classses and masses. England 1918–1951*. Oxford: Oxford University Press.

OECD, 2019a. *OECD family database*. Available from: www.oecd.org/els/family/database.htm [Accessed 10 September 2019].

OECD, 2019b. *OECD Library.org*. Available from: www.oecd-ilibrary.org/docserver/pension_glance-2017-30 en.pdf?expires=1569401792&id=id&accname=guest&checksum=0622814 F492EB8B7AE3B7B85E334308E [Accessed 25 September 2019].

OECD, 2019c. *SOCX database*. Available from: www.oecd.org/social/expenditure.htm [Accessed 26 October 2019].

OECD, 2019d. *OECD. Stat, database*. Available from: https://stats.oecd.org/Index.aspx?DataSetCode=SHA [Accessed 26 October 2019].

Office for National Statistics, 2018. *Dataset EMP04: Employment by occupation*. Available from: www.ons.gov.uk/employmentandlabourmarket/peopleinwork/employmentandemployeetypes/datasets/employmentbyoccupationemp04.

Piketty, T., 2003. Income inequality in France, 1901–1998. *Journal of Political Economy*, 111 (5), 1004–1042.

Piketty, T., and Saez, E., 2003. Income inequality in the United States, 1913–1998. *Quarterly Journal of Economics*, 118 (1), 1–39.

Piketty, T., and Saez, E., 2006. The evolution of top incomes: A historical and international perspective. *American Economic Review*, 96 (2), 200–205.

Routh, G., 1980. *Occupation and pay in Great Britain 1906–79*. London: Macmillan.

Scott, P., 2007. *Triumph of the south. A regional economic history of early twentieth century Britain*. Aldershot: Ashgate.

Scott, P., 2013. *The making of the modern British home. The suburban semi and family life between the wars*. Oxford: Oxford University Press.

Scott, P., and Walker, J., 2020. The comfortable, the rich, and the super-rich. What really happened to top British incomes during the first half of the twentieth century? *Journal of Economic History*, 80 (1), 38–68.

Sen, A., 1977. *On economic inequality*. 2nd ed. Oxford: Oxford University Press.

Slater, T., 2012. The myth of 'broken Britain': Welfare reform and the production of ignorance. *Antipode*, 46 (4), 948–969.

Tanzi, V., and Schuknecht, L., 2000. *Public spending in the 20th century*. Cambridge: Cambridge University Press.

U.S. spending history from 1900 dataset, 2019. Available from: www.usgovernmentspending. com/education_spending [Accessed 10 September 2019].

World Inequality Database. Available from: https://wid.world/ [Accessed 1 November 2019].

5 Britain's changing position in the international economy

Catherine R. Schenk

Introduction

This chapter traces the changing role of Britain in the international economy by focusing on four important international economic relations: international trade, international investment, international migration and international monetary relations. A major theme of this chapter is how Britain's trade and investment flows changed during the century as Britain receded as the dominant manufacturer in the decades running up to the First World War and then struggled through the interwar period before emerging into the new environment of the post-war era to face the challenges of the new globalisation.

International trade

Figure 5.1 shows that Britain accounted for about 40–45% of the world's manufactured exports from 1850–1870, but from 1872 this dominant position was steadily eroded as Germany and the United States industrialised, so that by 1913 Britain's share had fallen to 28%. This pattern closely followed the decline in Britain's share of world manufacturing output. While other countries adopted more protectionist policies after 1880, British governments resolutely held to free trade right through to the outbreak of the First World War.

Figure 5.2 picks up the continuing decline of Britain's share of international trade after the disruption of the wars and interwar great depression. Here the data show the steady decline in Britain's share of trade in all goods (not just manufactures) during the Long Boom of 1950–73. These were years of rapid growth in world trade as quotas and then tariffs were reduced under successive rounds of the General Agreement on Tariffs and Trade and due to the development of the common market in continental Europe. From the time of the oil crisis in 1973, however, Britain's long-term declining share ceased and was even reversed at the beginning of the 1980s due to exports of North Sea Oil. With the entry of new export competitors in the Far East such as China, the decline in Britain's share of merchandise exports resumed. The retreat was particularly evident after the Great Financial Crisis of 2007.

Figure 5.3 shows the value of international trade compared to the size of the British economy. This shows that the persistent deficit in the balance of trade after 1945 was by no means a new phenomenon. Indeed, the deficit on the goods account was larger in the first half of the century than after, ranging from 6–10% of GDP in the years 1900–1918 compared to 0–2% of GDP after 1950. During the early decades

DOI: 10.4324/9781003037118-6

Figure 5.1 UK share of world exports of manufactures, 1850–1913
Source: B.R. Mitchell (1988).

Figure 5.2 UK share of world merchandise exports, 1948–2018
Source: B.R. Mitchell (1988).

Image 5.1 An image of a tractor made in Ford's Dagenham factory being loaded for shipment
to the United States in August 1953

Source: © Keystone/Zuma/Bridgeman Images.

of the century, the trade deficit was offset by earnings from overseas investments as
well as export of services. An interesting feature of Figure 5.3 is that exports in relation to GDP are almost the same at the beginning and at the end of the century. In
between, however, there was considerable variation. During the heyday of the first

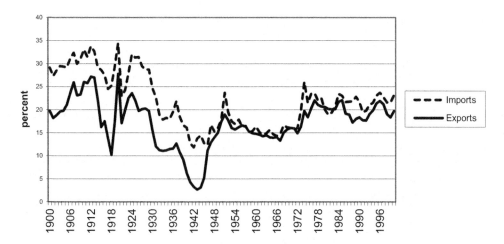

Figure 5.3 Goods trade as a percent of GDP, 1900–2000

Source: B.R. Mitchell (1988), ONS for post-1945.

era of globalisation in the run-up to the First World War, trade grew much faster than GDP. This was interrupted by the war and then by the great depression when the value of world trade collapsed. In the 1930s the nominal value of British exports fell from a peak of £1.55 billion in the restocking boom of 1920 to a trough of £416 million in 1932. During the Long Boom after the Second World War, both imports and exports were fairly consistently about 15% of GDP as both output and trade increased steadily, but at a slower rate than world trade. Trade increased relative to GDP from 1973–2000 to about 20% due to oil exports and Britain's accession to the EEC in 1973 and because of the general rise in world trade during the second and more profound era of globalisation.

Throughout the twentieth century, while Britain's share of world goods trade fell, it remained an important part of the British economy. Britain's place in the global trading system receded both as other countries expanded their trade and as Britain's own economy shifted from manufacturing to services. The prominence of the City of London and its financial and associated activities, however, meant that Britain remained a more important part of global services trade than was the case for trade in goods. From 1980–2013, British services exports were 6–9% of the world total compared to 2–5% of world goods trade. This was partly due to the legacy of Britain's role in international investment, discussed in the next section.

International investment

The amount of foreign investment in the second half of the nineteenth century is subject to some dispute – what is not disputed is that the 60 years up to 1913 saw an unprecedented and dramatic increase in flows of capital overseas. British investments abroad were about £1 billion in 1875 and rose to £4 billion by 1913, accounting for about 43% of the global total foreign investment. The reasons for the increase in overseas investment included increased financial sophistication and specialisation of institutions that made it easier to invest abroad, especially through London. Technological innovations such as communications and transport also improved the awareness of opportunities for investment. In this way the increase in international trade and migration generated increases in foreign investment and vice versa. Immigrant populations in places like Canada, the United States and Australia sought investment in construction and infrastructure, particularly railroads, to bring their abundant raw materials to the coasts and thence to the European markets. Indeed, about 40% of British overseas investment was in railways in this period.

In 1870 about one third of British investments were in the British empire and dominions, but by 1914 this share had risen to almost half, mainly due to investment in Australia and Canada after 1880. Two world wars and the great depression interrupted investment flows in the same way that they disrupted trade. Both wars resulted in the accumulation of debt, although the outcomes were very different. During the First World War the British government lent vital cash to support its allied partners, particularly France, Italy and Russia. In turn, Britain had to borrow from the United States to help finance its own war effort. The result was that at the time of the Armistice, Britain owed almost US$4 billion to the United States and was owed US$7 billion by other allied powers (Hardach 1973). Unfortunately, Britain's debtors had few resources with which to repay their debt, and this left Britain exposed in its own obligations to the United States. The result was a damaging cycle of international debt throughout the interwar period in which the allies depended on extracting reparations from the defeated German state in order to repay their allied creditors. When the reparations were not forthcoming, the cycle broke, and an international financial crisis ensued in 1931. Throughout the interwar depression, international investment was severely curtailed.

Although international opinion was firmly in favour of freer trade after 1945, there was consensus that short-term capital flows should remain controlled to protect national economies from the vagaries of speculators and to support independent national economic policies. As a result, while trade restrictions fell dramatically in the 1950s and 1960s, investment flows were only gradually liberalised. Long-term and foreign direct investment were freed first during the 1950s, but the final controls on short-term capital flows were not relaxed in Britain until 1979.

There were significant changes in the long-term investment position of the British economy after 1945. The 1960s marked the beginning of the 'American Challenge' (Servan-Schreiber 1967) as US companies increased their presence abroad to exploit their managerial, scale, and technological advantages. Multinational corporations, such as IBM and Ford, set up factories, research facilities, sales outlets and warehouses as well as other forms of investment that entailed a form of control or ownership. This type of investment, where the investor owns part of the target enterprise, is known as foreign direct investment (or FDI). In the 1950s the value of US FDI in Britain grew from $542 million to $1.6 billion, and 230 subsidiaries of foreign companies were opened in Britain, of which 187 were American. US companies favoured Britain for the common language and familiar culture compared with other European countries. The inflow of US firms was particularly striking in the banking industry, where the culture of the City of London was rudely shaken out of its traditional values by the more competitive practices of American bankers. By 1971 almost 10% of US outward FDI was in banking and insurance.

This form of investment had an impact on the structure of production. In 1963 foreign companies accounted for about 10% of net output of British manufacturing (Steuer *et al.* 1973). The stock of inward FDI in Britain amounted to about 6.5% of GDP in 1960, rising to 27% by the end of 1999 (Pain 2001). British companies also invested abroad and were responsible for about 13% of the world's FDI flows in the 1960s, but this was well behind the United States with 65% of world FDI. Britain also had a much higher share of both inward and outward FDI than other European countries and accounted for about 40% of all outward FDI from Western Europe in the 1960s.

Figure 5.4 shows the trends in flows of FDI relative to domestic investment for the UK compared to Western Europe as a whole (including the UK). Values above zero record gross inflows and below zero are outflows. It is clear that inflows of foreign investment are more important for Britain than for other European economies. The huge surge in the final years of the 1990s reflected a few very large trans-border mergers and acquisitions, particularly among telecommunications companies. Once this flurry of activity was over, outward FDI fell back to 14% of domestic investment. Britain also remained an important target for foreign companies. By 2000 the inward stock of FDI amounted to 30% of GDP compared with 12% in 1980. The traditional role of Britain as an active part of global investment patterns had reduced, but foreign investors still played an important role in the British economy.

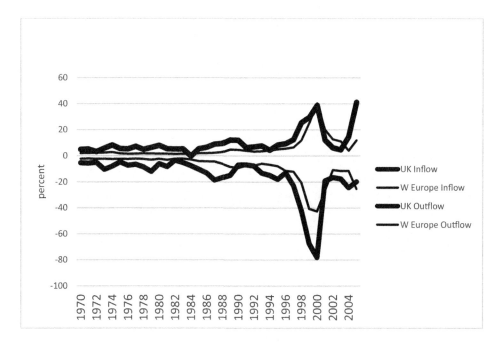

Figure 5.4 Flows of foreign direct investment as a percentage of domestic capital formation, 1970–2005

Source: unctadstat.unctad.org.

International migration

We have seen that Britain was a major contributor to the globalisation of the inter-national economy through trade and investment in the late nineteenth century. In the period from 1880–1914, while the share of the world's total migrants coming from Britain fell to 28%, the number increased sharply to 8.9 million people as trans-port became less risky and costly, information on opportunities for migrants spread and infrastructure improved. Most emigrants were destined for the United States and dominions where they settled and farmed or engaged in industrial activity in these fast-growing countries, where labour was relatively scarce and incomes were higher compared to Britain.

Figure 5.5 shows that the number of emigrants from Britain to countries beyond Europe never repeated the scale of the years before 1914. Falling incomes and unem-ployment around the world reduced opportunities and resources for emigration in the 1930s and was also accompanied by stricter controls on migration in many countries to protect domestic jobs. After 1945 thousands of migrants came from colonies and new commonwealth countries for whom entry to the UK was not restricted, including India, Pakistan and the Caribbean. They helped overcome the shortage of skills and labour in manufacturing and services in the immediate post-war period. In addition to the data presented in Figure 5.5, Britain was also the destination for hundreds of thousands of refugees and other people displaced by the war in Europe, including from Poland, Hungary and Ukraine. Despite the contribution to the UK's cultural and economic life, political tensions over unrestricted migration led to stronger controls on immigration from the Commonwealth and elsewhere in the 1960s and 1970s.

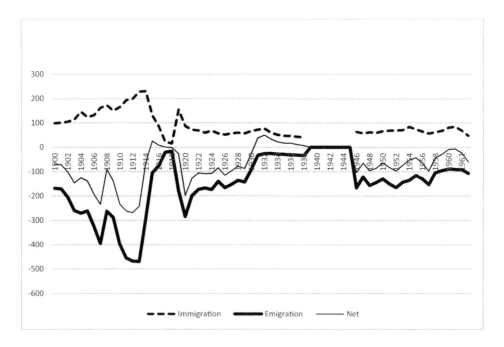

Figure 5.5 International migration into and out of the UK, 1900–1963 (thousands of people)

Source: B.R. Mitchell (1988). Excludes migration to and from European countries.

Figure 5.6 shows the transition from net emigration to net immigration from the 1980s, particularly due to migrants from Europe, with the creation of the single market. The share of total immigrants coming from Europe increased from 10.5% in 1971 before Britain joined the European community to a peak of 31% in 1996. Immigration from Europe was fairly evenly matched by emigration to Europe until 2004 when more countries joined the EU.[1] Emigration out of Britain also rose in the 2000s, but not as fast as the number of people coming to the country. Hostility to net immigration began to mount from 2005 and intensified after the global financial crisis of 2008 threatened jobs and services. Net immigration peaked in 2015, the year before the British referendum on exiting the European Union. But these broad trends become more complex when looked at closely. First, a significant proportion of recorded immigrants were British citizens returning home after living abroad. In the 1980s and 1990s the number of UK citizens immigrating to the UK was fairly stable at about 80–100,000 per year, although they were a declining proportion of total immigrants (falling from 40% in 1990 to 21% in 2000 and 13% by 2015). Second, an important reason citizens of other countries came to the UK was to study at colleges and universities. In the early 1990s about 50,000 people arrived in the UK on student visas each year, and this number rose steadily, reaching about 230,000 in 2010 (close to 40% of total immigrants) (Office for National Statistics 2016). Finally, while immigration may generate cultural and political tensions as well as benefits, there is some consensus that the overall impact on productivity, skills and the government's budget is positive, although there may be higher costs for low-skilled and low-paid workers already in Britain (Portes 2018). Thus, the direction and motivation for international migration have changed during the twentieth century in response to shifting political, cultural and economic opportunities.

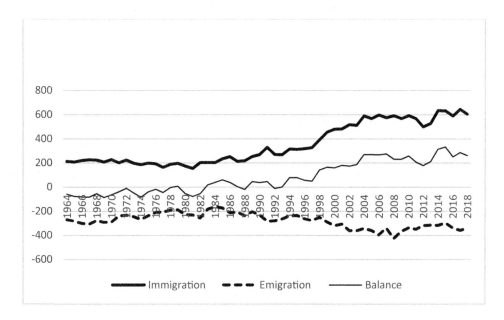

Figure 5.6 Long-term international migration, 1964–2018 (thousands)

Source: Office for National Statistics. Includes migration within the EU.

Britain and the international monetary system

Underlying all international transactions is the means of payment. It is only the ability to convert national currencies that allows international trade to take place on a multilateral basis. If currencies are not convertible, then trade can only take place through barter or by balancing all bilateral trade between two countries. When currencies are convertible, a surplus earned from exports to one country can be used to pay for imports from another country, and this allows traders to buy in the cheapest market and sell where they can get the best price, thus improving the scale and efficiency of international trade. The rules that govern convertibility are known as the international monetary system, which has taken various forms throughout the twentieth century. By 1880 most countries participating in the international economy had currencies convertible to gold at a fixed exchange rate. The international gold standard operated as the international monetary system, offering a fixed exchange rate and convertible currencies to ease the accelerating international trade and capital flows of the late nineteenth century.

While gold was the nominal anchor of the system, in practice sterling played a vital role in its success. Shipping gold internationally to settle outstanding balances was costly and risky, and the supply of gold was relatively fixed by the need to discover and mine it. Because of Britain's importance in trade, and the concentration of finance, merchanting, shipping and insurance in the City of London, most trade was contracted and paid for in sterling rather than gold. This meant that countries did not have to compete for scarce gold supplies. Instead many governments fixed the exchange rates of their national currencies to sterling, which was in turn firmly pegged to gold. The period from 1880–1914, the classic gold standard, was a period of rapid growth in international trade and payments, partly due to the high levels of confidence and reduction in transactions costs delivered by this fixed exchange rate system with Britain at its centre. It was achievable in the late nineteenth century because the dominance of Britain and the City of London generated confidence in the gold value of sterling.

After the disruption of the First World War, it was generally assumed that a return to a fixed exchange rate system should be the goal of all countries to resume international economic relations on the same scale as before the war. In practice, however, this proved difficult to achieve. Once again, Britain took a leadership role, although the British economy had suffered during the war, reducing even further its competitiveness, particularly compared to the United States. The British government's decision to return to a revised gold standard in 1925 at the same exchange rate as had been used before the war is generally considered one of the great policy mistakes of the twentieth century. It has a particular historical significance because it showed the perils of a fixed exchange rate that was inappropriate, particularly the difficulties that ensue from an overvalued exchange rate. This experience should have taught policy-makers of the future the importance of getting the rate right in any fixed exchange rate system.

The decision to return to the pre-war exchange rate was taken partly for political reasons; the public expected it, the rate had a symbolic resonance of Britain's leadership in the international economy and a lower rate would disappoint overseas holders of sterling by devaluing their assets. At the time, moreover, expectations had led the market price to near the pre-war rate in any case, so it seemed realistic. The extent of overvaluation is open to some dispute, but is generally agreed to have been about 10%

too high – thus requiring a 10% reduction in domestic costs and prices to maintain exports and balance of payments equilibrium. The consequent need to pursue deflationary policies during the growing international economic crisis after 1925 increased the impact of the depression on British producers and workers.

After struggling through the second half of the 1920s, the government finally had to abandon the fixed exchange rate under the pressure of the financial crisis of 1931, and the depreciation of the pound marked the beginning of Britain's recovery from the depression. Nevertheless, the uncertainty and crisis of the international monetary system in the 1930s led the public and governments still to hanker after a workable system of fixed exchange rates. During the Second World War the British and American governments agreed to start planning for the post-war era, and the coordination of the international monetary system was at the forefront of their minds.

The goal for the post-war period was agreed between the British and Americans in a series of formal agreements that stemmed from aid offered by the United States to Britain before the United States officially declared war. Under the so-called Lend Lease arrangements of 1942, the United States offered munitions and supplies to Britain in return for an undertaking from the British government that they would agree to help reconstruct the international economy after the war along the lines of freer multilateral trade and payments. A requirement for multilateral trade, as we have seen, is convertible currencies. It was also agreed that a fixed exchange rate should be the framework for the international monetary system to enhance confidence and coordination. Anglo-American wartime planning culminated in the Bretton Woods meeting in New Hampshire in July 1944, when 730 delegates representing 44 members of the United and Associated Nations met to finalise a blueprint for the international monetary system.

The Bretton Woods system, as it became known, comprised two main institutions: the International Monetary Fund (IMF) and the International Bank for Reconstruction and Development (later the World Bank). The IMF was supposed to provide the short-term credit needed to give countries the confidence to free up their trade and payments at fixed exchange rates. In the event, however, currencies were generally not made convertible until the end of 1958. Already from 1960 the fixed exchange rate system came under strain due to persistent surpluses by West Germany and deficits in the UK. The UK struggled through several crises to maintain the parity of sterling until November 1967, when it was devalued by 14%. This marked the beginning of the end of the pegged rate system as speculators put pressure on other currencies until, in August 1971, the United States unilaterally devalued the US$ against gold. A brief interim system was reconstructed in December 1971 called the Smithsonian Agreement, but by June 1972 sterling was forced to float. The dollar, the yen and European currencies then floated free of the Bretton Woods system from the spring of 1973.

Since this time, a global fixed exchange rate system has not been a goal of policymakers. Instead, countries manage their exchange rates independently, although Britain and other members of the G8 co-operated at times through the 1980s and 1990s to stabilise rates among the most important currencies in the world. While a global rate system was out of the question, European countries sought to stabilise exchange rates among themselves. Their economies were so open to each others' trade that the transactions costs of fluctuations were very high. Even more importantly, the institutions of the EEC (especially the Common Agricultural Policy) did not function efficiently when exchange rates among members changed frequently. From 1969, therefore, continental Europe progressed toward elimination of exchange rate fluctuations in a process that culminated in the introduction of the single currency in 1999. Although Britain was a member of the EEC from 1973, it did not share the enthusiasm for exchange rate stability and the convergence of economic policy that this requires. Britain reluctantly joined the Exchange Rate Mechanism (ERM) in 1990, pegging within +/-6% to a grid of European currencies with the Deutsche Mark (DM) at its core. In 1992, however, the pound was spectacularly forced out of the ERM by speculators who recognised that the rate was unsustainable. This expensive experience (both financially and politically) further discouraged British governments from engaging in Europe's plans for economic and monetary union, and Britain did not adopt the Euro in 1999. Twenty years later, not being part of the Euro made it easier to leave the EU altogether in 2020 (O'Rourke 2019).

In Focus: sterling as an international currency since 1945

As noted, during the Second World War, the US government was determined not to allow a repeat of the interwar debt problem and made special arrangements to 'lend-lease' vital supplies to Britain and the allies rather than forcing them to accumulate debt. However, Britain did accumulate large debts to its colonies in South Asia, members of the Commonwealth and others such as Egypt and Argentina. By 1945, the territories that would become the states of India, Pakistan and Ceylon held £1.3 billion of short-term British government debt denominated in sterling. These assets became known as sterling balances and represented claims on the British economy or foreign exchange reserves. The total overseas sterling debt remained remarkably stable between £2.5–£3.0 billion or about three times Britain's foreign exchange reserves from 1950–1970. However, the total figure disguises shifts in the geographical distribution of these sterling balances during the 1950s and 1960s. The extraordinary war debts to South Asia were quickly reduced, mainly through British exports to these territories and development spending. By the mid-1950s they were replaced by assets held in African colonies as a result of the primary materials boom associated with the Korean War. By the 1960s territories in the Middle East and Far East were accumulating sterling assets. This was due to the denomination of some oil trade in sterling, which boosted the sterling denominated foreign exchange reserves of Middle Eastern countries like Kuwait and Libya and also due to the industrialisation and growth of Singapore, Hong Kong and Malaysia in the Far East, which increased their reserves. After the oil crisis of 1973, OPEC countries came to hold about 40% of outstanding overseas short-term sterling debt, although this share fell to 20% by 1990. Another dramatic change was in the type of holders of overseas sterling assets. Until 1976, about 60% of them were held by central banks or other official monetary institutions, but this share fell steadily to 20% by 1980. This reflected the decline of sterling as a reserve asset and the dramatic increase in private banking and money market holdings of sterling overseas (from £10 billion in 1980 to £80 billion in 1990) due to the increase in the overall value of international trade and payments.

In summary, Britain was the leader of the pre-1914 and interwar gold standards. This influence shifted more toward the United States after 1945 with the design of the Bretton Woods system. By the time that Britain re-oriented its economic relations to Europe, governments there had already embarked on a path to economic and monetary integration that left Britain out of the leadership role since these goals of policy convergence did not match Britain's view of its role in the international economy and its domestic economic and political interests. Since the 1970s sterling has become primarily a domestic currency, while the City of London does most of its international financial business in foreign currencies like the dollar or the Euro and is a major centre for Chinese RMB. Nevertheless, the value of the pound still matters because declines make imports more expensive for British consumers and business, while a rise in the value of the pound adversely affects the competitiveness of British exports. For this reason, sterling's international position is still hotly debated.

Debates and Interpretations: Britain's role in the international economy

A central question about Britain's role in the international economy throughout the long twentieth century has been whether international economic relations and Britain's policy of openness had a positive or negative impact on the performance of the British economy. These debates are reflected in the continuing disagreement today about Britain's role in the world and the costs and benefits of international economic relations with Europe and other trading partners.

The fact that British prominence as an international investor at the end of the nineteenth century coincided with relatively low domestic investment rates compared with Germany and the United States has raised the question of whether foreign investment diverted scarce resources abroad to the detriment of the domestic economy. This was the argument put forward by Sidney Pollard in the 1980s (1989). He calculated that the annual outflow of capital amounted to an average of 5% of national income from 1874–1913 and approached 9% of national income in 1911–13. He blamed biases in the capital market in the City of London that channelled domestic savings toward overseas portfolio investment rather than domestic industrial investment. On the other hand, the relatively slow growth at home could be a cause as well as an effect of high rates of overseas investment, since returns on overseas assets were higher. In this way investors were reacting rationally to get the highest returns on their money.

Britain's trade policy has also been controversial. This debate pits advocates of free markets against those who believe the government should more actively support and protect domestic producers against their foreign competitors. Thus, some historians have argued that the adherence to free trade until 1931 allowed competitors to penetrate the British market, while foreign countries were protecting their producers with tariffs and so putting British industry at a disadvantage. In 1990 Kitson and Solomou

rejected the prevailing advocacy of free markets to argue that the switch to protectionism in 1931 was important for the recovery of Britain from the depression. Capie
(1983, 1991), however, showed that the effective protection was not focused on those
sectors that led the recovery, which suggests that the tariffs were not instrumental in
the process. Moreover, the impact of trade barriers on the total volume of trade in the
depression has been questioned, for example, by Irwin (1998), who showed that falling incomes rather than trade barriers were responsible for most of the collapse in US
trade. This finding was confirmed for the UK in the interwar period by de Bromhead
et al. (2019). Nevertheless, there were strong political pressures that explain the introduction of tariffs to protect domestic industry during the economic downturn (Rooth
1992).

The impact of the system of Imperial Preference, whereby members of the British
Empire and Commonwealth offered lower or preferential tariffs to each other from
1932, is also controversial. It seemed effective, since UK imports from the Empire
increased from 30% in 1929 to 42% by 1938. Despite the US insistence at the time
that Imperial Preference was an important drag on world trade and discriminated
against US products, historians have found that preference itself had less impact on
trade within the Empire than previously supposed (Wolf and Ritschl 2011). Partly
this is because these countries already traded more with each other before the formal
preferential agreements (Eichengreen and Irwin 1995). Using more detailed evidence
of the tariffs on particular products rather than an average overall tariff, however,
de Bromhead *et al.* (2019) find that Imperial Preference did have an effect in shifting
Britain's trade to these territories. The impact of tariffs is difficult to measure because
of their complexity and the assumptions that must be made about what would have
happened without them.

After 1945, there was considerably more protection through tariffs and quotas and
through preferential access to imperial markets. Some, such as Pollard (1982), argued
that this lulled British industry into complacency and left it unable to compete with the
more dynamic European producers. However, Schenk (1994) argued that this analysis
overestimated the 'softness' of commonwealth markets, where British producers were
increasingly encountering stiff competition from American and European producers.
On the other hand, Milward and Brennan (1996) calculated that controls on imports
in the 1950s were more effective than contemporaries believed, and that this misap-
prehension led to an exaggerated view of Britain's industrial competitiveness, which
in turn contributed to the government's decision to remain outside the EEC until the
1960s. The impact of trade policy is still very much a subject of debate.

Another long-standing subject of debate is the relationship between economics and
empire. Hobson (1902) and Lenin (1917) famously equated late nineteenth-century
imperialism with economic exploitation and explained the expansion of the British
empire in terms of the export of capital, the control of raw materials and the creation
of captive markets for British industrial production. In the 1990s Cain and Hopkins
(1993) revived economic motivations in their concept of 'gentlemanly capitalism'.
They argued that the important economic driver for imperialism was not manufacturing industry but the service sector. Thus, bankers and merchants in the City of London
established economic relations with territories that did not necessarily overlap with
the formal constitutional British empire. Nevertheless, due to their social and political
influence in Britain, the interests of these 'gentlemen' were supported through imperial
political and strategic relationships. This thesis was challenged by various case studies

of business interests in particular territories where the link between business elites and political elites was not compelling (Dumett 1999; Akita 2002).

The relationship between economics and empire was also explored for the period of decolonisation in the 1950s. Krozewski (2001) argued that the financial links of empire supported British economic recovery in these years and help to explain a reluctant approach to decolonisation. Hinds (2001) put more emphasis on the costs of colonial development policy in determining the pace of decolonisation. Both historians are critical of Britain's failure to meet the development priorities of its colonies during the 1940s and 1950s. Thus, Britain's international relations need also to be viewed from the perspective of its political as well as economic links.

Conclusions

Although British leadership of the global economy disappeared after the nineteenth century with respect to trade, investment and currency, the UK remained part of the core group of countries that promoted international economic cooperation. The Group of 7 industrialised economies (UK, United States, France, Germany, Italy, Japan, Canada) began to meet in the mid-1970s to share their views on the international economic system and to promote cooperation. Russia joined from 1998 to 2014, and the group was renamed the G8. In recognition that these countries had a declining share of global GDP, particularly since the return of China to global trade, the Group of 20 (G20) was formed in 1999, and Britain continued to play a role in global governance through this institution. The importance of the financial institutions in the City of London for international financial stability means that Britain has always had a prominent influence in the development of international financial regulation, for example, at the Bank for International Settlements, where global standards are set, and the Financial Stability Board (chaired by the Bank of England Governor Mark Carney from 2011–2018). While Britain's influence in global trade and output has declined, it retains an important role in international finance.

When the Global Financial Crisis struck in 2008 the G20 quickly came together to implement reforms to improve financial stability. In April 2009, UK Prime Minister Gordon Brown hosted a follow-up conference in London where countries committed to more immediate and practical action, including trebling the resources available to the IMF. They also agreed to expand government budgets collectively by $5 trillion as part of 'the largest fiscal and monetary stimulus and the most comprehensive support programme for the financial sector in modern times'. This was a landmark in international cooperation led by Britain and demonstrated the country's continued global influence. It was widely credited at the time with avoiding even greater economic fallout from the crisis. While the fiscal commitment was relatively short lived, the monetary expansion persisted for almost a decade after the crisis, contributing to an unprecedentedly long period of low interest rates globally. The COVID crisis in the spring of 2020 prompted renewed monetary easing and international economic cooperation.

As the prospects for a full recovery from the effects of the Global Financial Crisis seemed more and more distant, a vigorous and often passionate public debate emerged over Britain's future role in the international economy, culminating in the 2016 referendum result to take Britain out of the EU. A majority of the voting public believed that the UK's future should be pursued more independently from EU institutions, particularly with respect to migration and legal frameworks. But it proved more challenging than anticipated to extricate the UK from almost 50 years of historical links. Subsequent negotiations between the UK and the EU finally concluded with a new trade agreement at the end of 2020. The economic and social crisis caused by the global COVID-19 pandemic will no doubt intensify the importance of Britain's international economic relations, and the decisions taken from 2020 onward will no doubt be the foundation of many historical debates of the future.

Further reading

There are several excellent introductions to the development of the international economy which put Britain's history into context, including Graff *et al.* (2013), Eichengreen (2019) and Schenk (2021). Alford (1996) gives greater detail on the changes in Britain's international economic relations up to the 1980s, while Crafts (2002) provides a succinct overview of Britain's economy from a comparative perspective.

Note

1 Cyprus, Czech Republic, Estonia, Hungary, Latvia, Lithuania, Malta, Poland, Slovakia and Slovenia joined the EU in May 2004. Bulgaria and Romania joined in 2007.

References

Akita, S., ed., 2002. *Gentlemanly capitalism, imperialism and global history.* Basingstoke: Macmillan.

Alford, B., 1996. *Britain in the world economy since 1880.* London: Longman.

Cain, P., and Hopkins, A.G., 1993. *British imperialism: Crisis and deconstruction 1914–1990.* London: Longman.

Capie, F., 1983. *Depression and protectionism: Britain between the wars.* London: Allen and Unwin.

Capie, F., 1991. Effective protection and economic recovery in Britain 1932–1937. *Economic History Review,* 44 (2), 339–342.

Crafts, N.F.R., 2002. *Britain's relative economic performance 1870–1999.* London: IEA.

de Bromhead, A., Fernihough, A., Lampe, M., and O'Rourke, K.H., 2019. When Britain turned inward: The impact of interwar British protection. *American Economic Review,* 109 (2), 325–352.

Dumett, R.E., ed., 1999. *Gentlemanly capitalism and British imperialism: The new debate on empire.* London: Longman.

Eichengreen, B., 2019. *Globalizing capital: A history of the international monetary system.* 3rd ed. Princeton: Princeton University Press.

Eichengreen, B., and Irwin, D.A., 1995. Trade blocs, currency blocs and the reorientation of world trade in the 1930s. *Journal of International Economics,* 38, 1–24.

Graff, M., Kenwood, A.G., and Lougheed, A.L., 2013. *Growth of the international economy, 1820–2015.* London: Routledge.

Hardach, G., 1973. *The First World War 1914–1918.* London: Penguin.

Hinds, A., 2001. *Britain's sterling colonial policy and decolonization 1939–1958.* Westport: Greenwood Press.

Hobson, J.A., 1902. *Imperialism: A study.* London: George Allen & Unwin.

Irwin, D., 1998. The Smoot-Hawley tariff: A quantitative assessment. *Review of Economics and Statistics,* 80 (2), 326–334.

Kitson, M., and Solomou, S., 1990. *Protectionism and economic revival: The British interwar economy*. Cambridge: Cambridge University Press.

Krozewski, G., 2001. *Money and the end of empire: British international economic policy and the colonies, 1947–58*. Basingstoke: Palgrave.

Lenin, V.I., 1917. *Imperialism: The last stage of capitalism*. London: Communist Party of Great Britain.

Milward, A.S., and Brennan, G., 1996. *Britain's place in the world: A historical enquiry into import controls 1945–60*. London: Routledge.

Mitchell, B.R., 1988. *British historical statistics*. Cambridge: Cambridge University Press.

Office for National Statistics, 2016. Population briefing 'international student migration: What do the statistics tell us?', January 2016. Available from: https://www.gov.uk/government/statistics/student-migration-what-do-the-statistics-tell-us.

O'Rourke, K.H., 2019. *A short history of Brexit: From Brentry to Backstop*. London: Pelican Books.

Pain, N., 2001. The growth and impact of inward investment in the UK: Introduction and overview. *In:* N. Pain, ed. *Inward investment, technological change and growth*. London: NIESR.

Pollard, S., 1982. *The wasting of the British economy: British economic policy 1945 to the present*. London: Croom Helm.

Pollard, S., 1989. *Britain's prime and Britain's decline: The British economy 1870–1914*. London: Edward Arnold.

Portes, J., 2018. New evidence on the economics of immigration to the UK. 04 October. *Vox CEPR Policy Portal*. Available from: https://voxeu.org/article/new-evidence-economics-immigration-uk.

Rooth, T., 1992. *British protectionism and the international economy: overseas commercial policy in the 1930s*. Cambridge: Cambridge University Press.

Schenk, C.R., 1994. *Britain and the sterling area*. London: Routledge.

Schenk, C.R., 2021. *International economic relations since 1945* 2nd edn. London: Routledge.

Servan-Schreiber, J., 1967. *Le Defi Americain*. Paris: Denoel.

Steuer, M.D., Abell, P., Gennard, J., Perlman, M., Rees, R., Scott, B., and Wallis, K., 1973. *The impact of foreign direct investment on the UK*. London: HMSO.

Wolf, N., and Ritschl, A., 2011. Endogeneity of currency areas and trade blocs: Evidence from a natural experiment. *Kyklos*, 64 (2), 291–312.

6 Managing the economy, managing the people

Jim Tomlinson

Introduction

This chapter charts the rise of the managed economy from the 1930s to the 2010s. This rise is linked to the parallel attempts by governments to shape popular under-standing of the economy-to 'manage the people'. After summarising the development of national economic management, the chapter analyses the parallel evolution of gov-ernment attempts to mobilise economic opinion under wartime and post-war plan-ning, down to developments in the purportedly 'anti-statist' climate from the 1980s onwards. The final section discusses the interpretative challenges of this approach to Britain's economic history, including how far economic management and representa-tion of the economy were shaped by structural change, especially deindustrialisation.

Chronology of national economic management

1) 1931 to 1951

In 1931 Britain left the gold standard and imposed tariffs, and in doing so broke decisively with the pre-1914 'liberal' international regime which minimised the role of the state in the economy, a regime that had been largely if insecurely reconstructed in the 1920s. The decisions of 1931 were driven by crisis; between 1931 and 1940 they created a space for moves towards economic management, albeit tentative and contested. But thereafter this all changed, as the Coalition faced the requirements of total war, necessitating an unprecedented scale of government intervention to stabilise the economy and maximise resources for the war effort.

In the First World War planning of the economy had grown incrementally as the war unexpectedly developed as one of intense attrition. In the Second World War the government was much better prepared and quickly implemented plans for rationing and allocating all major resources. Plans aimed to minimise non-essential imports and investment, conscript and allocate labour to war industries, ration consumer goods to provide 'fair shares' and sustain popular morale.

Sustaining morale was vital. In the First World War popular support for the war had been threatened by price rises and shortages but also by a belief that profiteering showed how the burdens of the war were shared unequally. In the Second World War there was a determination to prevent any recurrence of discontent. Prices were controlled and rationing was widespread. But from the point of view of economic management, the key innovation was the use of the budget to control the level of aggregate demand in the

DOI: 10.4324/9781003037118-7

economy. In the 1920s and 1930s economists such as Keynes had advocated the use of the budget to expand demand to reduce unemployment. Such efforts had been rebuffed. But in wartime, when the need was to *constrain* demand to prevent inflation and maintain resources for the war effort, such budgeting became central to economic management. So 'the first Keynesian budget' of 1941 was not just about controlling wartime taxing and spending but doing so in order to manage the overall economy.

If the war saw a major enhancement of the powers of government, it also saw the government taking on new political responsibilities. Driven in part by the radicalisation of wartime public opinion, the Coalition began a process of expansion of state provision with free secondary education under the 1944 Education Act and family allowances in 1945. The Labour government led by Clement Attlee, elected in 1945, greatly extended such initiatives, with comprehensive social security (largely as proposed in the Beveridge Committee Report of 1942) and the creation of the NHS in 1948. Alongside these welfare developments the government accepted the duty to pursue 'high and stable' levels of employment following the pledges of the 1944 White Paper on *Employment Policy*. This duty was to underpin economic management down to the 1970s (Middleton 2014).

The Attlee government sought to influence the economy by a changing mix of direct controls and macroeconomic management through use of taxation and public spending. It significantly expanded the scope of government by its welfare state measures and through public ownership, including coal, railways, gas and electricity. However, this public ownership programme embraced neither most of the manufacturing sector nor finance (the Bank of England was nationalised in 1946, to little practical effect). In addition, the extent of government responsibility for these new 'public' industries was ambiguous, given that the public corporations which ran the industries had considerable autonomy. Rather than being the 'commanding heights' of the economy under government control, as many socialists had hoped, they turned out to be concentrated mainly in declining sectors. This meant that down to the 1980s, when many of them were privatised, the performance of these industries was a major cause of controversy, but without governments having full control of their actions.

The welfare reforms of the 1940s created an 'austerity welfare state.' Social security payments were miserly, and the post-war decline in poverty was mainly due to full employment. The NHS provided much-needed access to free medical care, but it did so in mainly rundown buildings. Rundown infrastructure was also the norm in schools, where provision struggled to keep pace with rising pupil numbers. Large numbers of houses were built, not least because of the enormous scale of destruction in the stock during the war, but even here the expansion lagged behind growth in demand. This 'physical austerity' followed the priority given by the government to industrial and commercial building when bricks, wood, construction steel and building labour were in short supply (Cairncross 1986).

Total spending on welfare expanded across the war period, but less than might be expected, given the notion of this period as the key moment in the creation of a welfare state. This was partly because of the factors noted in the previous paragraph but also because the high level of employment greatly reduced demands on social security. Conversely, military spending fell more slowly than would be expected after the end of the war, partly because of the onset of the Cold War and partly because of Britain's continuing ambition to be a world power. Throughout the 1950s and 1960s Britain spent historically high levels of money in peacetime on the military, more than any country in Western Europe (except briefly France in the early 1960s, when that country was defending *its* empire) (Edgerton 2018)

A key issue in managing the British economy in the 1960s was the balance of payments (on the international environment, see Schenk in this volume). Contemporaries saw this balance as in continuous crisis in the 50s and 60s, but we need to be careful to note exactly what the balance of payments 'problem' was.

In the war Britain had thrown caution to the winds in reducing exports to divert resources into the war effort. Imports were paid for by selling foreign assets, borrowing from India and Egypt (the 'sterling balances') and by receipt of lend-lease from the United States. After 1945 a major effort was put into restoring exports, with some success, helped by devaluation of the pound in 1949. Improvement was derailed by the Korean War (1950–52), which hugely increased import prices, but in the 1950s the payments position was greatly helped by a fall in import relative to export prices. For the 1950s and most of the 1960s the current account of the balance of payments was healthily in surplus, helped by subsidies for domestic agriculture reducing the demand for food imports. But the overall situation was weakened by the high military spending and commitment to allow large-scale outward foreign investment. Such expenditures, plus the fact that the pound remained a major international reserve currency, were the cause of the periodic payment 'crises', not some fundamental problem of competitiveness.

2) *1951 to 1979*

Balance of payments crises were part of the policy cycle of the 1950s and 1960s, called 'stop-go'. In these cycles governments used Keynesian-style fiscal and monetary policy to expand the economy when the level of unemployment was seen as approaching unacceptable levels, a stance which was then reversed when the payments situation deteriorated or inflation threatened. These frequent policy reversals were highly controversial, attracting much political criticism, though with the benefit of hindsight we might think this was 'much ado about nothing'. We can now see that throughout the 1950s and 1960s Britain enjoyed a 'golden age' of low inflation, low unemployment and high growth rates.

British growth rates were high by her own historic standards, aiding the creation of considerable affluence amongst the working class, even while there continued to be significant pockets of poverty. However, contemporaries were increasingly exercised by the fact that Britain's near neighbours in Western Europe were experiencing substantially faster growth rates. Much of this gap can be explained by Britain's position as the pioneer industrial country, which underpinned much higher living standards than most of the rest of Europe. After 1945, countries like West Germany, France and Italy caught up with Britain, especially by transferring large numbers of low-productivity agricultural workers into high-productivity industrial jobs.

The performance of the British economy started to deteriorate in the late 1960s and was massively affected by the crisis of 1973/4, when the Organisation of Petroleum Exporting Countries (OPEC) quadrupled the price of oil. For a major oil importer like Britain, this was a multiple problem. Higher oil prices fed through into much higher inflation. The need to channel more resources into paying for the oil exerted a deflationary impetus. Before OPEC the Conservative government under Edward

Heath (1970–74) initiated a major expansionary 'go' phase in policy in response to unemployment going above a million for the first time since the 1940s. This stimulated an inflationary surge, exacerbated by rising oil prices. The Labour government elected in 1974 faced a combination of major inflationary pressure alongside the first significant recession since the war. The government sought to contain inflation by a 'Social Contract' with the trade unions, aimed to bargain wage restraint against delivering on policies favoured by the unions. But this project was undermined both by increasing inflation (which peaked at 25 per cent in 1975) and the government's shift to focussing macroeconomic policy on reducing the public sector deficit and reducing inflation, announced in a landmark budget statement in 1975. But the impact of this policy shift took time to work through; only when trade union leaders looked into the abyss of accelerating inflation did they seek to make the Social Contract effective (Artis and Cobham 1991).

The crisis of the mid-1970s was much less one of recession and unemployment (certainly compared with the three recessions of the 1980s, 1990s and 2000s) but rather of inflation and public borrowing. The latter had ballooned because of the increased spending begun under Heath, coupled with the impact of the recession. Labour sought to reduce this deficit whilst simultaneously conciliating the trade

Image 6.1 Inflation. We Can Beat It Together. Newspaper advertisement by the government's Counter-Inflation publicity unit

Source: Image taken by the author. Courtesy of the National Archives.

unions and its traditional working-class supporters. As noted, they began to cut back spending from 1975, but it was only after the traumatic political battle surrounding Britain's loan from the IMF in 1976 that it became apparent that a new direction had been consolidated. From 1976 to 1978 the public deficit and inflation fell, the pound strengthened (helped by the beginnings of North Sea Oil) and the economy grew. But the government sought to cut inflation further by continuing the Social Contract with a 5 per cent wage limit in 1978/9 (inflation was running at around 10 per cent). Such a limit could only readily be enforced in the public sector, and there it implied a continuing significant fall in real wages, especially amongst low-paid workers in local authorities and the NHS. The result was a 'Winter of Discontent' that pitched these workers against the government and undermined the key claim of Labour to be able to work with the trade unions. In the election of 1979 the Conservatives, led by Margaret Thatcher, came to power, promising a radical new departure in economic policy (Jackson and Saunders 2012).

3) 1979 to 2019

This departure involved tight control of the money supply to reduce inflation, backed by big public spending cuts aimed at both 'rolling back the state' and reducing public borrowing. The initial impact of the policy shift was an unprecedented appreciation of the pound, which rendered much of the tradeable sector of the economy uncompetitive and led to a collapse of manufacturing employment, 1.7 million jobs being lost between 1979 and 1983. The resulting rise in unemployment led to panic in government circles in 1980–82, when joblessness rose to over three million, and was expected to seriously undermine support for the government. In the event, in the election of 1983, it proved possible for the government to retain power (indeed, increase its majority) despite this level of unemployment. A focus on inflation at the expense of unemployment now seemed to bear fewer political costs than had been assumed ever since the 1940s (Britton 1991, Chapter 4).

After 1983 the Conservative government had much more leeway to pursue their policies, focusing their attention on reducing the role of the state via privatisation of publicly owned assets, sales of council houses and deregulation of the City of London. The labour market was an especial focus of attention, with policies aimed at eroding worker's rights and a very substantial tightening in the legal framework governing the actions of trade unions. Some parts of public spending were sharply cut, such as expenditure on housing and unemployment pay, though the trend of total public spending was broadly flat (with sharp cyclical fluctuations), as military spending increased and also spending on the NHS and pensions.

Looking at the long-run statistics of the British economy, the most obvious change in this period was an unprecedentedly sharp rise in income inequality (Figure 6.1; see also discussion of income inequality in Chapter 4). This pattern was driven by the beginnings of greater dispersion of wages in the labour market, originating well before 1979 but reinforced by a range of policy measures after that year, including benefit cuts, weakening trade unions and greater capital mobility, which shifted bargaining power away from workers.

The core claim of the Conservatives was that their policies would enhance economic efficiency. A traditional key measure of this, labour productivity in the manufacturing sector, recovered sharply from the very poor performance of the 1970s, though only

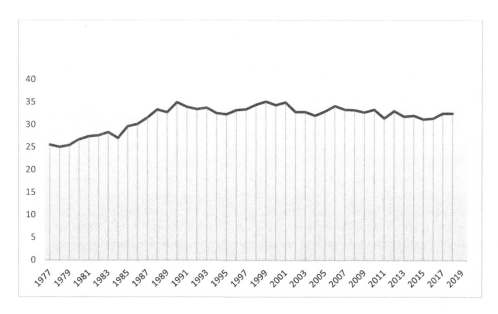

Figure 6.1 Gini coefficient of disposable income, UK, 1977–2019

Source: ONS database.

back to the rate of increase of the 1950s and 1960s, and in the 1980s deindustrialisa-tion, the shrinking of the share of the economy's output and employment in industry, meant the role of manufacturing in the whole economy's performance was signifi-cantly less than previously (Figure 6.2).

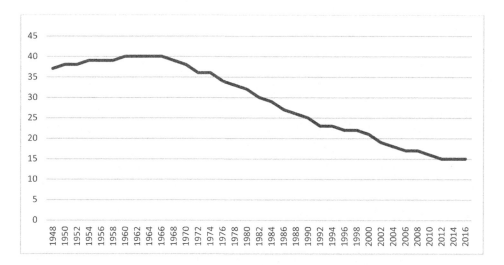

Figure 6.2 Industrial employment as percentage of total employment, UK, 1948–2016 (does not include mining)

Source: www.ons.gov.uk/economy/nationalaccounts/uksectoraccounts/compendium/economicreview/april2019/ longtermtrendsinukemployment1861to2018.

The government's commitment to inflation reduction proved hard to implement. After falling rapidly in the early 1980s, the rate rose again later in that decade. Policies to address this caused major divisions in the government, especially as it overlapped with issues concerning Britain's relationship with the EEC. At the beginning of the 1990s attempts to anchor inflation by tying the pound to the Deutschmark (which required Britain to match Germany's low inflation rate by a similar tight monetary policy) led to a crisis and a sharp recession. In response, the government of John Major (1992–1997) pursued a markedly reflationary fiscal policy, very different from that in the early 1980s under Thatcher (Thompson 2014).

The New Labour government elected in 1997 was determined to assert its difference from previous Labour governments, leading to major innovations in policy (Balls 1998). The Bank of England was made independent, with a mandate to focus on controlling inflation. Fiscal policy was to be constrained by rules limiting both the acceptable budget deficit and the total of the national debt to gross domestic product (GDP). These innovations were presented as steps necessary for the government to sustain credibility with financial markets in an increasingly globalised world. Much of the deregulation introduced under the preceding Conservative governments was retained, though an important shift was made by the introduction of a national minimum wage.

The government after 1997 inherited an upswing in the economy originating in the early 1990s, which continued until 2007, with only minor slowdowns. This was part of a much wider international experience, the years of the 'Great Complacency'. In this favourable context Labour was able to pursue policies involving (eventually) huge increases in public spending on health and education, along with greatly expanding cash payments to the working poor, whose numbers were increasing significantly.

The Global Financial Crisis (GFC) of 2007/8, followed by the most serious recession since the 1930s, derailed this trajectory, as the automatic stabilisers and bank bailouts drove up the deficit, leading to the politics of austerity discussed in 'In Focus'.

After 2010 economic recovery was slow. Inflation was very low, and employment expanded fast, the latter in part the result of increasing hours worked and increased labour market participation as households sought to increase their living standards in the face of sustained stagnation in real wages. The Brexit vote in 2016 further slowed the economy, at the same time stimulating a search for policies to respond to the economic discontent which was widely perceived to have pushed many older working-class people to support departing from the EU and at the margins to have driven the Leave majority. The complex politics of Brexit thus led to a shift away from austerity policies across the political spectrum. The legacy from the GFC of extremely low interest rates provided a convenient framework for downplaying the significance of public borrowing, as all parties in the 2019 general election sought to reverse the spending policies of the previous decade.

In Focus: austerity 1945–51, 2010–2019

In both of these periods governments pursued 'austerity', seeking to reduce public spending in order to cut public borrowing and public debts after a period when borrowing and debts had shot up. The first followed the Second World War, the second the GFC.

But there were big differences in both the economics and politics of the episodes.

In the 1940s austerity meant holding back the growth of private consumption so that resources could be transferred from the war effort to civilian uses, especially exports and investment. In economic terms this policy was very successful; between 1946 and 1952 consumer spending rose by 5.9 per cent but fixed investment by 57.9 per cent and exports by 77 per cent (see Table 6.1). Politically the consequences were problematic for the Labour government. The holding back of consumption, and the rationing and controls which accompanied this restriction, allowed the Conservatives to mount an effective campaign to 'set the people free', which seems to have been especially effective amongst women, who bore the daily brunt of dealing with shortages of goods for everyday consumption. Labour's majority was minimal in the general election of 1950, and the government lost office in 1951. This result emphasises the limits to the effectiveness of government propaganda.

Table 6.1 Change in allocation of resources in the UK 1946–52

	Change in value, £m. in 1948 prices	Percentage change
Consumers' expenditure	486	5.9
Public spending (current)*	−322	−12.4
Gross domestic fixed capital formation	613	57.9
Increase in stocks	63	n/a
Exports of goods and services	1,145	77.3
Total final expenditure	1,985	14.9
Imports of goods and services	417	14.5
Gross domestic product	1,568	15.0
Net property income from abroad	25	24.5
Gross national product	1,593	15.3

*Almost all this fall was in 1946 and 1947.

Source: Cairncross (1986, p. 24).

The austerity of the 1940s was driven by two imperatives: to correct the balance of payments and to invest to expand the economy. Contemporary propaganda about the balance of payments focused on the private sector and the current account, the key slogan of 'export or die' obscuring the extent to which foreign exchange was flowing into overseas military spending and foreign investment. But within this framing of the issue, policy was highly successful, with the payments position corrected, until the onset of the Korean War brought further problems. But, while international conditions were undoubtedly favourable, the political commitment to correcting the payments position, despite the consequential starving of the powerful demands of the home market, is striking.

Unlike austerity after 2010, that of the 1940s was accompanied by expanding welfare provision. The 1940s were the years of the inauguration of the NHS, expansion of education and a major increase in social security provision. However, three points about this much-emphasised expansion of the welfare state are worth highlighting. First, because of buoyant demand for labour, expenditure on social security rose much more slowly than had been budgeted for in war-time planning. Second, this expansion was of entitlement to very low standards of support. The newly expanded national insurance system, offering flat-rate benefits for flat-rate contributions, had to have contribution levels affordable by the low paid and hence offered benefits which mean we can rightly talk of an 'austerity welfare state'. Third, while entitlement to welfare greatly expanded in the 1940s, physical provision in the form of schools and hospitals was heavily constrained by the priority given to industrial investment. Despite the hopes entertained at the founding of the NHS, only one new district general hospital was opened before the 1960s. Military spending was cut, though quite slowly because of Britain's ambitions to be a world power.

The GFC led to big deficits mainly through 'automatic stabilisers' (where tax revenues fall and public spending increases as output declines) but also increases in spending, especially on bank rescues. Austerity after the GFC is associated with the Coalition government elected in 2010, but cutbacks were also advocated by Labour in the run-up to the election, arguing that it had been right to use 'Keynesian' methods to fight the impact of the Crisis, but once the economy showed signs of recovery, the government needed to reduce the deficit (Labour suggested slightly more tax increases and slightly fewer expenditure cuts than proposed by the Coalition). The cuts imposed after 2010 were very uneven in impact. In order to shift the political blame, cuts were concentrated on local government, with benefits for those of working age also hard hit. In contrast, pensioners' incomes were protected. The cuts did not reduce the deficit as fast as hoped because they themselves delayed the recovery. In the run-up to the 2019 election, austerity policies were abandoned in a 'bidding war' to increase spending. This helped the Conservatives win the election.

Austerity after 2010 was presented as required by the previous period of 'over-spending' and the need to eliminate deficits and debts. During the whole course of the Labour government from 1997 the public sector debt was below the level inherited in that year (40 per cent), until the GFC had its effects in 2008/9. The government ran a tight fiscal policy in its early years, loosened the stance in the early 2000s and tightened again after 2005/6, until the GFC intervened. So the scale of deficits and debts in 2010 was largely the result of the GFC but was successfully presented by the Conservatives and their Liberal Democrat allies as the result of Labour's extravagance. Homely analogies about countries like households needing to balance their budgets effectively caricatured what had occurred and who was to blame.

In his first budget after the 2010 election the new chancellor of the exchequer, George Osborne, echoed key themes from the 1940s: 'Our policy is to raise from the ruins of an economy built on debt, a new, balanced, economy where we save, invest and export' (House of Commons 22 June 2010, col 167). But no such re-balancing took place, and there was no switching of resources into investment and exports as had occurred in the later 1940s.

Austerity aimed at 'rebalancing' the economy in favour of exports and invest-ment and away from consumption is easier in circumstances of excess demand, such as in the 1940s, where government has leverage to direct resources in the desired direction. In a situation of excess supply, as after 2010, taking resources out of public consumption and from the incomes of the poor does nothing directly to encourage the growth of exports or investment. There was little sign of rebalancing after 2010. Despite the fall in the exchange rate (around 25 per cent from its pre-crash level to 2019), there was no 'export-led' recovery, and investment stagnated (see Figure 6.3).

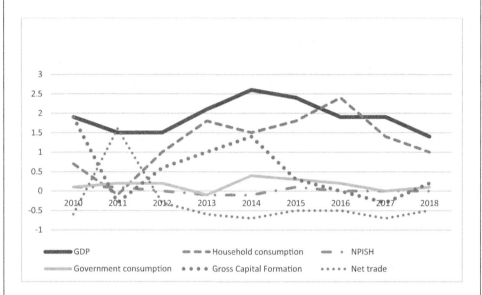

Figure 6.3 Re-balancing? Contributions to annual real growth of UK GDP, 2010–2018

Source: ONS database (NPISH = non-profit institutions serving households).

Managing the people

The 'economy' is not a natural object, available simply to be observed and described, but a socially constructed one. Our understanding of it is, in the words of Adam Tooze (1998, p. 214), 'the product of a dramatic process of imaginative abstraction and representational labour'. The account of economic management given so far in this chapter relies on a whole series of very well-established conventions about how we think about the economy. The concepts used, such as 'growth', 'unemployment' and 'the balance of payments', have gained great power in thinking about the economy, but none of them has an indisputable meaning.

This broad point matters especially for our approach to twentieth-century Britain because in that period understanding of something called 'the economy' became much more prominent in public debate, and popular understanding of the economy was widely perceived to be a key factor in political behaviour. The slogan 'it's the economy, stupid' summed up the view that electoral success for governments rested on their capacity to persuade the electorate that the economy was performing well. To achieve a successful outcome required not only the use of whatever instruments governments possessed to shape the economy but the use of their powers to shape how the public perceived the economy and how they behaved in consequence. Hence they sought to 'manage the people' as well as managing the economy.

Of all the understandings that have underpinned political representations of 'the economy' none has been as sustained as the concept of 'growth'. It was in the 1950s that growth became the central concern of economic policy, building on the formalisation and quantification of concepts like gross domestic product. As Singleton explains in Chapter 3, this concept is deeply flawed as a measure of economic welfare. But the political benefits of the figure meant it became, and has remained, deeply entrenched in public discourse. As a single number GDP is attractive in representing the economy in simple terms, and it fits happily into homely analogies about the economy as a 'pie', which can be cut up in different ways but also, by growth, turned into a bigger 'pie'. Such a narrative was immensely attractive in the 1950s, because it suggested the possibility of a politics that didn't fight over shares of a fixed 'pie' but promised that more of *everything* was possible. Contests for resources between 'guns and butter', between investment and consumption, between higher public spending and lower taxes could all be happily resolved by growth. In addition, in the context of the Cold War, the idea of growth was crucial to the West's claims to be able to provide greater economic welfare than Communism. So it was towards the end of that decade that the prime minister, Harold Macmillan, was able to proclaim that the British public had 'never had it so good' because of growth in previous years.

The propagation of growth to the public as the key measure of economic success was undoubtedly successful. It reshaped public and political debate, so that in the 1960s governments vied with each other to promise faster expansion. But if growth was the measure by which governments wanted to persuade the public to judge them, it could also be a measure of failure if growth was deemed too slow. In the early 1960s the perception that Britain was indeed growing 'too slowly' became widespread, and the promise of growth rebounded on governments as their critics blamed them for an 'under-performing' economy. The word that became central to this perception was 'decline', often vaguely understood, but at its most focused stressing the slow growth of the British economy in comparison with other Western European countries. ('Decline' was also commonly used in relation to Britain's loss of empire, much of which also occurred in this period.) By transferring huge amounts of labour from the rural to the urban economy, these countries were able to achieve growth rates that Britain, which had transferred most of that labour in the nineteenth century, could not hope to match. This structural difference accounts for most of the disparity in growth rates, and as these countries caught up with Britain, their rates of growth also slowed.

But such structural, largely inescapable patterns were not politically attractive explanations; rather, these focused on the alleged culpability of some combination of mistaken policies/trade unions/management/banks and often wider, if less well-specified, factors like an 'anti-entrepreneurial culture'. These declinist notions became popular across the political spectrum, from Marxists to free-marketeers, though the chosen *culprits* for 'decline' differed.

Notions of British 'decline' originated outside party political circles but were taken up by political parties to criticise their opponent's performance. Most effectively, notions of decline were deployed very aggressively by the Conservatives under Thatcher after she became party leader in 1975. In this narrative, Britain's evident problems with inflation, public deficits and trade union discontent in the 1970s were not about the difficulty of managing the British economy following the dislocations caused by OPEC but about a fundamental malaise in British society which could only be corrected by a sharp turn in policy in a market fundamentalist direction. The widespread labour unrest of the 1978/9 period preceding the May 1979 election gave credence to this narrative, feeding into the Conservative success in that election. (But see Table 6.2, which suggests that amongst the West European big four economies, it was West Germany's exceptionally good performance in the 1970s that stands out, not Britain's as particularly poor.)

The focus on growth as the over-arching economic policy objective since the 1950s has been accompanied by recurrent emphasis on raising productivity. In the 1940s the Labour government under Attlee devoted enormous resources seeking to persuade workers that higher productivity would deliver 'a better life sooner', though the 'better life' was framed as a relief from short-run shortages and rationing rather than the vista of continuous expansion in consumption offered by prospective perpetual growth.

In the 1950s the Conservatives re-framed the productivity issue as all about growth, to be achieved by enhancing incentives to work and invest, though with a persistent undertow of propaganda about 'restrictive practices', especially as pursued by trade unions. Conversely, when Labour came back to power in 1964, productivity propaganda focussed on raising investment and finding ways to improve co-operation at work, with trade unions represented as key partners rather than potential antagonists in the pursuit of higher efficiency.

The pursuit of higher productivity from the 1940s to the 1960s led all governments to give substantial attention to one particular group – industrial workers. This focus followed on from two assumptions: that the key to productivity change lay in the

Table 6.2 Comparative economic performance in the Western European 'big four', 1974–79

	France	Italy	West Germany	UK
Output growth (%p.a.)	3.1	2.3	2.7	2.0
Unemployment (national definitions)	4.5	6.6	3.6	4.5
Inflation (GDP deflator)	10.4	16.9	4.3	16.3
Balance of payments current account (% GDP)	-0.6	-0.2	1.0	-1.3

Source: Based on Artis and Cobham (1991, p. 267).

industrial sector and that the beliefs and behaviour of industrial workers were the key to changing productivity. The propaganda effort aimed at this group faded away from the 1970s, partly because other policy goals briefly loomed large (especially inflation in the 1970s), but more profoundly because the industrial sector was a declining proportion of the economy, and the industrial working class was shrinking, so the focus on this group made less sense.

Despite the sector's declining overall significance, the measurement of productivity in *manufacturing* was central to many political arguments about economic performance, partly because the fluctuations in this sector were so marked. Table 6.3 shows the data for Britain and West Germany, the commonest comparator. These show clearly that claims about a fundamental change in the 1980s draw on comparison with the very poor levels of the mid-1970s, but in a longer perspective, the growth of that decade looks like a return to the post-war 'norm' (see also discussion in Singleton in this volume).

This process of employment deindustrialisation began in the 1950s and is discussed in the 'Debates and Interpretations' section later. In the short term at least one of its major impacts was on the level of unemployment. From the 1940s to the 1980s the conventional wisdom across the political spectrum was that mass unemployment was to be avoided like the plague, because its recurrence would be not only economically and socially wasteful but fatal to the electoral chances of the governing party. As outlined, this assumption was strongly present at the beginning of the 1980s but seriously undermined by the 1983 election when the ruling party was returned to power despite the (official) numbers of unemployed exceeding three million.

This political outcome did not mean issues around employment disappeared from economic argument, but they were re-framed. The new departure in macroeconomic policy of the 1980s was formalised by the chancellor, Nigel Lawson, shifting the key aim of government from controlling the level of employment to controlling inflation (by monetary policy). In this account, government would stabilise the economy, but the impact of that stability on output and employment would largely depend upon the behaviour of trade unions in determining wages. If workers and their unions pushed too hard, *they* would be the cause of unemployment. In this way government policy distanced itself from responsibility for unemployment. The aim of government propaganda was *not* to suggest that unemployment didn't matter but that its causes lay elsewhere than in the policies of government. In this framing, reducing unemployment benefit was presented as encouraging popular 'realism' about the nature of the labour market, by cutting obstacles to wages falling to appropriate levels (Rieger 2018). While 'managing the people' has by no means always worked as intended by governments, this strategy of continuing to emphasise the importance of unemployment, while

Table 6.3 Manufacturing labour productivity in the UK and West Germany 1951–1989 (% increase per annum per person engaged)

	UK	West Germany
1951–64	4.50	5.32
1964–73	4.18	4.52
1973–79	0.68	3.47
1979–89	4.14	1.92

Source: Based on Broadberry and Crafts (2003, p. 723).

disclaiming government's capacity to directly influence its level, could be counted a governmental success.

Despite employment expansion, 'hidden' unemployment in Britain has been high since the 1970s (Beatty *et al.* 2007). But since the 1980s it has not been the central concern of macroeconomic policy. A focus on microeconomic policy (liberalising the labour market) in the context of deindustrialisation has led to the multiplication of low-paid jobs. So, ironically, 'market liberalisation' has been accompanied by a great expansion of labour market subsidies and a decisive increase in state control of prices in that market in the form of a national minimum wage.

No account of national economic management in post-war Britain would be complete without some discussion of the fact that 'the nation' no longer means what it did in 1945. In particular, the devolution of economic powers to Scotland, beginning with the devolution settlement of 1999 but subsequently expanded, has challenged the idea of a UK-wide 'national economy'.

Historically the Scottish economy was both highly integrated with the rest of the UK and highly globalised. Deindustrialisation has reduced the scale of those links. Scotland, like the rest of the UK, has seen a long-term increase in employment in the public sector (including in 'para-state' sectors, funded from taxation but sub-contracted to private companies). So there has been a process of 'de-globalisation' as the economic welfare of Scots has come to rely less on events outwith the country and more on levels of public spending and taxation in the country. Fiscal devolution has been slow and limited but has been set on a trajectory that emphasises that some levers of economic policy no longer operate across the UK in the old way. Of course, a radical divergence of policy in Scotland from the UK would require much greater devolution of fiscal powers and some form of monetary separation from the rest of the UK.

Debates and Interpretations: deindustrialisation

Deindustrialisation began in the 1950s when several of the old staple industries (coal, textiles, railways) shed large numbers of workers but was accentuated from the 1960s when manufacturing employment peaked. As already noted, the loss of industrial jobs in the early 1980s was enormous, but the process continued thereafter, so that by 2016 only 16 per cent of all workers were in that sector (manufacturing plus construction). It should be emphasised that this process affected the whole country, though with particularly serious effects in much of the North (Baker and Billinge 2011, ch. 1). In absolute terms the biggest losses were in London (where from 1981 to 1991 alone manufacturing jobs fell from almost 700,000 to 359,000), large numbers were lost in cities like Edinburgh and small towns spread across the UK were hit especially hard (Graham and Spence 1995; Tomlinson 2020). Deindustrialisation measured by employment has gone along with flat or slowly rising industrial *output*, as trend labour productivity in the sector has increased at around 4 per cent a year (Broadberry and Leunig 2013, table 5b).

The decline of industrial employment led to a much more polarised labour market, with growing numbers of well-paid, skilled jobs in the service sector for those with good educational qualifications but many lousy jobs with low wages, insecure contracts and poor prospects (Goos and Manning 2007). The governmental response to this polarisation has been to continue to claim that 'work is the route out of poverty' whilst only making such a claim credible by two major policy innovations. First, a huge expansion of in-work benefits (wage subsidies), begun on a very small scale in the 1970s, expanded significantly in the 1990s and 2000s, cut back somewhat under post-2010 austerity but continuing in 2019 as a major component of public spending (Tomlinson 2016). Second, a national minimum wage, introduced by Labour in 1998 in the face of great hostility from the Conservatives (on the grounds that it would cause unemployment), but subsequently embraced with enthusiasm by the post-GFC Conservative-led government, with a national living wage announced in 2015 (Budget 2015).

Deindustrialisation has diminished the size and political significance of the industrial working class, with peak of that class's influence coming in the 1970s (Hobsbawm in Jacques and Mulhern 1981). One sign of this is how industrial workers have ceased to be the key audience for governmental attempts at shaping economic understanding. The propaganda poster above (Image 6.1) from the 1970s is clearly aimed at a working-class audience. However, the perceived concerns of the (much-reduced) working class in the so-called 'old industrial areas' of Britain came back into focus in the 2019 General Election, as they were widely seen as the key swing voters in the politics of Brexit (Thompson 2017).

Conclusion

The British economy in 2021 looks radically different from that in 1931. It is more prosperous, much less industrial and much more oriented to Europe. It is also much more globalised, and this weakens attempts to differentiate the *national* from the *international* economy. The crash of 2008/9 and then the economic impact of COVID-19 have shown how fragile economic prosperity has become. Nevertheless, British (and Scottish) governments continue to attempt to manage their economies in pursuit of providing economic wellbeing and security to their electorates. But a world of much greater insecurity and fragility makes it much harder to persuade that electorate that 'success' is being achieved.

Further reading

For work using the same approach as this chapter, see Tomlinson (2017). A variety of views on the economic history of this period can be found in Floud *et al.* (2014). On the important narrative of 'decline' see Crafts (1995), Tomlinson (2009) and Edgerton (1991). On austerity, see Blyth (2013).

References

Artis, M., and Cobham, D., eds., 1991. *Labour's economic policies, 1974–79*. Manchester: Manchester University Press.

Baker, A., and Billinge, M., 2011. *Geographies of England: The North South divide, material and imagined*. Cambridge: Cambridge University Press.

Balls, E., 1998. Open macroeconomics in an open economy. *Scottish Journal of Political Economy*, 45, 113–132.

Beatty, C., Fothergill, S., Gore, T., and Powell, R., 2007. *The real level of unemployment, 2007*. Sheffield: Sheffield Hallam University.

Blyth, M., 2013. *Austerity. The history of a dangerous idea*. Oxford: Oxford University Press.

Britton, A.J.C., 1991. *Macroeconomic policy in Britain 1974–87*. Cambridge: Cambridge University Press.

Broadberry, S., and Crafts, N., 2003. A re-statement of the Broadberry–Crafts view. *Economic History Review*, 56, 718–735.

Broadberry, S., and Leunig, T., 2013. *The impact of government policy on UK manufacturing since 1945*. London: Government Office for Science.

Budget, 2015. Available from: www.gov.uk/government/news/summer-budget-2015-key-announcements.

Cairncross, A., 1986. *Years of recovery, British economic policy, 1945–51*. London: Methuen.

Crafts, N., 1995. The golden age of economic growth in Western Europe, 1950–1973. *Economic History Review*, 48, 429–447.

Edgerton, D., 1991. *England and the aeroplane*. Basingstoke: Palgrave Macmillan.

Edgerton, D., 2018. *The rise and fall of the British Nation*. London: Allen Lane.

Floud, R., Humphries, J., and Johnson, P., eds., 2014. *The Cambridge economic history of modern Britain, vol. 2, growth and decline, 1870 to the present*. 2nd ed. Cambridge: Cambridge University Press.

Goos, M., and Manning, A., 2007. Lousy and lovely jobs: The rising polarization of work in Britain. *Review of Economics and Statistics*, 89, 118–133.

Graham, D., and Spence, N., 1995. Contemporary deindustrialisation and tertiarisation in the London economy. *Urban Studies*, 32, 885–911.

Jackson, B., and Saunders, R., eds., 2012. *Making Thatcher's Britain*. Cambridge: Cambridge University Press.

Jacques, E., and Mulhern, F., eds., 1981. *The forward march of labour halted?* London: New Left Books.

Middleton, R., 2014. Economic policy and management. *In*: R.C. Floud *et al.*, eds. *The Cambridge economic history of Modern Britain*. Cambridge: Cambridge University Press

Rieger, B., 2018. Making Britain work again: Unemployment and the remaking of British social policy in the eighties. *English Historical Review*, 133, 634–666.

Thompson, H., 2014. The Thatcherite economic legacy. *In*: S. Farrall and C. Hay, eds., *The legacy of Thatcherism*. Oxford: Oxford University Press.

Thompson, H., 2017. Inevitability and contingency: The political economy of Brexit. *British Journal of Politics and International Relations*, 19, 434–449.

Tomlinson, J., 2009. Thrice denied: 'Declinism' as a recurrent theme in British history in the long twentieth century'. *Twentieth Century British History*, 20, 227–251.

Tomlinson, J., 2016. De-industrialization not decline. A new meta-narrative for post-war British history. *Twentieth Century British History*, 27, 76–99.

Tomlinson, J., 2017. *Managing the economy, managing the people*. Oxford: Oxford University Press.

Tomlinson, J., 2020. Deindustrialisation: Strengths and weaknesses of a key concept for understanding post-war British history. *Urban History*, 47, 199–219.

Tooze, A., 1998. Imagining national economies: National and international economic statistics, 1900–1950. *In*: G. Cubitt, ed. *Imagining nations*. Manchester: Manchester University Press.

7 Work, the labour market and trade unions

Chris Wrigley

Introduction

The structure of the British economy changed greatly between 1901 and the start of 2020 (before the coronavirus pandemic), with accompanying great changes to working lives. In the labour market there was a decline in demand for unskilled labour and a growth in white-collar work. Women workers continued to be paid substantially less than men for similar jobs, whether manual or white-collar. Trade unions changed from being predominantly male to predominantly female. This chapter examines the impact of these changes on working lives and industrial relations over the 120 years.

Working lives and the labour market

In 1901, Britain was the world's third largest manufacturer, with a huge industrial and coalmining labour force. However, according to Professor Stephen Broadberry, as early as 1911 employment in services in the UK accounted for as much employment as in industry. Britain, which had had the first industrial revolution, was among the first countries to deindustrialise. By the early twenty-first century, far more people were employed by the service sector than in manufacturing.

Changes in the school leaving age greatly affected entry into the labour market. From 1899, children were not allowed to go into full-time employment until the age of 12, but many worked out of school hours, and up to a sixth of children were absent from school each day. It has been estimated that 21 per cent of boys and 12 per cent of girls aged 10–14 were working at the start of the twentieth century (Horrell 2007, p. 124). The school leaving age was raised to 14 (1921), 15 (1944), 16 (1972), 17 (2013) and 18 (2015).

At the other end of working lives, by the 1960s state and private pension provision saw some 70 per cent of men leave the labour market at or before the age of 65 either through poor health or if they had good pensions. 6.1 million state pensions and 1.8 million occupational pensions were paid in 1963. By 1979, when the population over 65 had risen by 30.2 per cent since 1963, the provision of state pensions had risen by 45.9 per cent (to 8.9 million) and occupational pensions by 105.6 per cent (to 3.7 million). This was in marked contrast to 1901, when two-thirds of men were working aged 65–69. Men who began work in the mid-1870s worked on average 50 years

DOI: 10.4324/9781003037118-8

Table 7.1 Employment by sector, UK (%)

	1911	1930	1950	1990
Agriculture	22.2	7.6	5.1	2.0
Mineral extraction	4.0	5.4	5.7	0.6
Manufacturing	33.5	31.7	34.9	20.1
Construction	4.7	5.4	6.3	6.7
Utilities	0.2	1.2	1.6	1.1
Transport and communications	5.4	8.3	7.0	5.5
Distribution	7.5	14.3	12.2	19.5
Finance and services	19.5	20.9	19.5	37.5
Government	4.2	5.2	8.8	7.0
Total	100	100	100	100

Source: Broadberry (2006, p. 42).

between the ages of 15 and 69, whereas those who began work in the late 1980s are likely to work on average 41 years (Johnson and Zaida 2007, pp. 102 and 114).

The employment pattern of paid work for women during the twentieth century was notably different from that of men. At the start of the century, larger families shortened the length of time women were in the labour market, especially those in low-paid jobs who could not afford childcare, compared to a century later. Women who began work in the mid-1870s worked for pay on average 16 years between the ages of 15 and 69. Women in white-collar work, such as in the civil service, teaching, banking and secretarial work in industry, were usually subject to the marriage bar until 1944 in teaching (though there were regions where the bar was not applied), 1946 in the home civil service, 1973 in the Foreign Office and various times in private industry. This discrimination was despite the Sex Disqualification (Removal) Act, 1919, which banned discrimination in employment by sex or marriage, an act which appears to have been treated as permissive by employers. Women worked in unpaid labour most, or all, of their lives, often beginning young minding younger siblings. With the rise in the state pension age in stages from 60 to 65 by 2018 under the Pensions Act, 2011, fewer women have retired between 60 and 65. More women with dependent children have worked in the early twenty-first century, the proportion rising from two-thirds to three-quarters, 2000–2019. However, in 2019, 30 per cent of working mothers said that they had reduced their hours of work to help with childcare, most of whom attributed the need to do so to long working hours or unpredictable and difficult working schedules (Office for National Statistics 2019).

In the early 1970s roughly half of the employed population were in occupational pension schemes. These schemes had more members as the over-65 population grew (from 2 million in 1900 to 6.3 million in 1963 and close to 12 million in 2019) and as savings grew with the rise in the standard of living, especially after the Second World War. Occupational pensions were paid to about 100,000 people in 1900, 1.8 million in 1963, 3.7 million in 1979 and 10.4 million in 2016 (Hannah 1986, pp. 125–126).

Image 7.1 Low pay/sex difference, 1984, LP247

Source: © Leeds Postcards.

Table 7.2 Occupational and private pension scheme membership, UK (in millions) 1983–2016

Year	1983	1987	1991	1995	2000	2004	2008	2012	2016
Active	11.1	10.9	10.7	10.3	9.1	9.8	9.0	7.8	13.5
Pensioners	5.0	6.0	7.0	8.5	8.2	9.0	8.8	9.5	10.4
Entitlements	2.8	3.5	4.5	7.0	6.7	9.3	9.9	10.2	15.4
Total	18.9	20.4	22.2	25.8	25.0	28.1	27.7	27.5	39.3

Note: Active are those currently contributing to the schemes; preserved pension entitlements (deferred members) are those who paid in before moving to another job or have been moved into another scheme by their employer.

Source: Hannah (1986); Office for National Statistics, Occupational Pension Scheme Survey, UK, 2018.

In the pre–First World War years, several of the manufacturing industries of the Industrial Revolution and mid-Victorian Britain, such as cotton and engineering, each employed over a million people, as did coal mining. Textiles experienced a final boom in the period before the First World War. In 1913, 1,509,000 people (639,000 men and 870,000 women) were employed in textiles. The number of coalminers peaked at 1,127,900 in 1913.

Before 1914 agriculture was still a major employer. In 1901, 1,539,000 men were employed, with 1,436,000 there in 1911. The census figures for women working in agriculture – 67,000 in 1901 and 60,000 in 1911 – under-represent the work done by women. Women made important contributions to the household income through paid work, but this was often seasonal and intermittent and not always recorded in the census (Verdon 2017, pp. 57–59, 65 and 113). After the Second World War, the National Union of Agricultural Workers was more mindful of its women members and in 1976 successfully represented three women in a case of sex discrimination in agricultural pay, a result which had favourable repercussions for other female farm labour (Wynn 1993, p. 277).

During the First World War, the demands of war skewed industrial output heavily towards metals, engineering and chemicals. Although the numbers of people employed in civil employment fell by 12 per cent between 1914 and 1918, the numbers working in the metal trades rose by 32.6 per cent from 2,094,400 to 2,777,000, with women going from 8.2 to 22.8 per cent of the labour force. Employment also rose markedly in the various branches of engineering and chemicals. In contrast, between July 1914 and July 1918 employment fell 49.4 per cent in building; 27.6 per cent in cotton; 14.0 per cent in food, drink and tobacco; and 13.7 per cent in paper and printing (Buxton and McKay 1977, pp. 76–81). Women's employment in the First World War highlighted discrepancies between women's and men's pay for the same or similar jobs. After the war, women's employment reverted to pre-war patterns other than in shops, banking and other clerical work.

The wartime and post-war booms (1915–20) were followed by a severe recession (1921–2). Unemployment remained high until 1940, with the average rate in 1923–38 being 10.9 per cent compared with 6.2 per cent in 1892–1913 (Hatton 2003, p. 371). The hardest-hit sectors were the old industries of the Industrial Revolution, which were predominantly located in the north of England, South Wales, the Clyde Valley in Scotland and Belfast and the Lagan Valley in Northern Ireland. In the case of cotton, employment in Britain fell by 36.7 per cent as exports fell. These areas still had resid-ual patterns of unemployment in the early twenty-first century (Table 7.3).

There was much migration from the North East and Wales, with impressive growth of employment in newer industries in London and the Home Counties, the South East, the South West and the Midlands. Taking the sizes of new industries in 1935 and giving them indices of 100, electrical goods had grown from 55 in 1924 to 67 in 1930, while the indices for electricity supply were 45 and 71, cars and cycles were 42 and 61, aircraft 23 and 65 and silk and rayon 29 and 47 (Pollard 1992, pp. 40–62). Indeed, for those in work, the interwar years were a period of rising incomes and increased discretionary spending (see the chapter by Peter Scott in this volume).

Table 7.3 (a): GB: Insured unemployment rates by country and English region, 1923–1938

Year	Scotland	Wales	London	South East	South West	Midlands	North East	North West
1923	14.3	6.4	10.1	9.2	10.6	10.7	12.2	14.5
1929	12.1	19.3	5.6	5.6	8.1	9.3	13.7	13.3
1932	27.7	36.5	13.5	14.3	17.1	20.1	28.5	25.8
1938	16.4	24.8	8.0	8.0	8.2	10.3	13.6	17.9

Source: Department of Employment (1971, pp. 306–310 and 424–426).

Table 7.3 (b): GB: Unemployment rates by country and English region, 2004–2019

Year	Scotland	Wales	London	South East	South West	East Mid	West Mid	East	Yorks + Humb
2004/5	5.3	4.8	7.2	3.7	3.5	4.3	5.1	3.8	4.4
2008/9	5.9	7.6	8.3	5.0	5.3	6.8	8.5	5.8	7.5
2012/3	7.8	8.2	9.1	6.2	5.7	7.9	9.2	6.5	7.1
2016/7	4.5	4.7	5.5	3.5	3.7	4.4	5.1	3.9	5.0
2019	4.1	4.2	4.7	3.1	3.1	4.6	4.7	3.2	4.5

Year	North East	North West
2004/5	5.8	4.7
2008/9	8.7	7.5
2012/3	9.9	8.1
2016/7	6.5	4.7
2019	5.7	4.0

Sources: Andrew Powell, House of Commons Briefing, 7950, Labour Market Statistics (October 2019). Office of National Statistics, Labour Force Surveys, 2004–20.

Until the 1960s, there were more than double the number of manual workers to white-collar workers. In 1911, there were 13,585,000 manual and 3,433,999 white-collar workers. In 1961 the number of manual workers had only risen to 14,020,000, while the number of white-collar workers had risen to 8,479,000. There was an ongoing wage gap between skilled and unskilled workers. The different proficiencies of skilled, semi-skilled and unskilled were apparent in the munitions industries during the First World War.

Equal pay for women became a major issue in the post–Second World War boom when labour was again at a premium. It was highlighted by the successful strike at Ford's Dagenham factory in 1968 by women sewing-machinists demanding pay equal to that received by men for their skills. The Dagenham strike contributed to the introduction of the Equal Pay Act, 1970, which came into full effect at the end of 1975. There was an immediate impact, with a rise in UK women's industrial basic weekly wages going from 53.7 to 64.3 per cent and for basic hourly wages from 63.7 to 73.5 per cent of men's pay between 1970 and 1976. The main features of the Equal Pay Act, 1970, were incorporated into the Equality Act, 2010. From April 2017, employers with over 250 staff were required to report the gap, if any, between men and women's wages. The findings published in 2019 showed that 80 per cent of these big firms still paid men more than women, with men also holding more senior posts and receiving higher bonuses.

The gender pay gap is the difference between average hourly earnings (excluding overtime) of men and women as a proportion of average hourly earnings (excluding overtime) of men's wages. There were substantial gender pay gaps throughout the twentieth and early twenty-first centuries. Table 7.4 reports the gradual narrowing of the gender pay gap since 1997.

There have also been substantial disparities in pay among ethnic workers. In 2018, the biggest variants were among Chinese people, who earned on average 30.9 per cent more than the median pay of white British people, and Bangladeshi people, who earned on average 20.2 per cent less than the median pay of white British people. However, both Chinese and Bangladeshi people made up small parts of the British workforce aged 16–64, the Chinese being 0.7 per cent and the Bangladeshi 0.5 per cent. There were more self-employed among Chinese people (22.5 per cent) than Pakistani/Bangladeshi (19 per cent), Indian (14 per cent) or Black (7 per cent) in 1996–7 (Office for National Statistics 2019 and *Social Trends*, 1998, p. 79).

Table 7.4 Gender wage gap for median gross hourly earnings (excluding overtime), UK, 1997–2019 (percentages)

Year	All workers	Full-time workers
1997	27.5	17.4
1999	26.9	16.4
2001	26.3	16.4
2003	25.1	14.6
2005	22.6	13.0
2007	21.9	12.5
2009	22.0	12.2
2011	20.2	10.5
2013	19.8	10.0
2017	18.4	9.1
2019	17.3	8.9

Sources: Office for National Statistics, Gender Pay Gap 2018 and 2019.

Trade unions 1900–45

British trade unions were the biggest and oldest in the world in 1900. British unions grew from 1,908,000 members in 1900 to a pre–Second World War high of 8,253,000 in 1920. The 1920 membership total was not surpassed until 1946. British trade unionism reached its greatest size in 1979, with 13,212,000 members. By 2018, membership had shrunk to 6,098,000.

While trade union membership numbers are one indicator of trade union strength, union density is another which suggests likely bargaining strength. Density is the proportion of those in a union out of those legally able to join a union. Hence a union with 500 members out of a specialist trade of 1000 workers is in a stronger position than a trade union of 5000 members in a trade with 500,000 employed.

In 1901, the density of British trade unions was 13.0 per cent, with densities of 17.2 per cent for males and 2.9 per cent for females. The important feature of this density was that it was not evenly spread. In 1901, the sectors most organised by the unions were coal mining (density of 68.7 per cent), postal and telecommunications (42.7), ports and inland water transport (38.2), printing (31.6), cotton (28.8), metals and engineering (26.4) and construction (25.4). These strong unions were able to secure better pay and conditions of work through collective bargaining with the employers. In 1889, only in cotton weaving was there a national agreement that had been negotiated between unions and employers. By 1910, there were seven further areas where national agreements had been signed by the unions and employers. Collective bargaining was a sign of the strength of British trade unionism as well as of the relatively liberal conditions in Britain.

The unions were committed to voluntary solutions in industrial relations, and most leaders sought to make gains through union strength in collective bargaining, not legislation. However, a series of legal decisions culminating in the Taff Vale Judgement, 1901, undercut rights to take strike action that the unions believed had been established in legislation in 1871–75 and was followed by the railway union involved paying £42,000 (equivalent to £5.3 million in 2020) in damages and legal costs. The trade unions secured the reversal of the Taff Vale Judgement and additional immunities from legal action for damages with the Trade Disputes Act, 1906. For most of the period 1906 to 1980, British industrial relations were organised by voluntary agreements rather than by legal regulations. Other than on issues of law and order, British governments usually avoided intervening in industrial disputes.

The needs of war ensured that the wartime governments intervened in the labour market. The government needed the cooperation of the trade unions, especially in engineering, shipbuilding, coal mining and chemicals. The great majority of trade unionists supported the war effort despite the soaring cost of living. Unlike the Second World War, in which there were cost of living subsidies and rationing from early on, in July 1914 to July 1917 the cost of living rose by 80 per cent, while wage rates rose by 35–40 per cent. In contrast, in 1944, the cost of living had risen by 30 per cent and wage rates by 43 per cent over September 1939 (Hancock and Gowing 1949, p. 142). In the First World War, by working the longer hours available, working people could absorb the inflated cost of living. Once the war was over, restraint ended and wages caught up with the cost of living by July 1919.

The government controlled much of the economy through the Munitions of War Act, 1915; the Defence of the Realm Act; the Military Service Acts; and the Corn Production Act, 1917. Under the wartime legislation industrial disputes in controlled industries were to be settled by arbitration by the Committee on Production. However, the government sought agreements before going to arbitration. Labour's strength in the economy encouraged the setting up of joint committees ranging from industry-wide bodies, such as the Cotton Control Board, set up in June 1917, to those in individual factories. Collective bargaining was often a result of increased trade union membership, especially in industries and geographic areas where trade unionism had been weak before the war. Good examples of big increases in trade union membership between the 1911 and the 1921 census were in gas (from 20.2 to 56.4 per cent density), electricity (20.2 to 56.4 per cent), bricks and building materials (14.7 to 47.0 per cent), chemicals (9.6 to 23.6 per cent) and pottery (14.7 to 50.1 per cent) (Bain and Price 1980, pp. 49, 56, 57, 64 and 65). In turn, benefits stemming from collective bargaining further boosted trade union membership.

Trade union membership grew markedly in areas it had hitherto been weak. This was especially so among women workers. In 1914, there were 436,000 women in trade unions, many of whom were in textiles, clothing and health services. In 1918 the number of female trade unionists had risen to 1,182, 000 (the density rising from 8.6 to 22.8 per cent) across many types of employment. The number of white-collar union members rose from 534,500 in 1914 to 815,600 in 1918, a rise in density of about 14.4 to 24.5 per cent. White-collar unionism reached 1,129,200 in 1920 and fell back to 992,700 (a density of 24.2 per cent) in 1921.

The First World War and its aftermath saw changes that were to be critical to British trade unionism over the next century. Although female trade unionism halved in terms of density between 1920, its pre-1941 peak, and 1933, its interwar lowest point, it remained substantially above its 1914 level. In 1939, there were 928,000 (a density of 16.0 per cent) female trade unionists. A notable feature of white-collar trade unionism was that it never fell back to the 1918 level, let alone the much lower 1914 level, averaging 940,000 members from 1922 to 1929. By 1939, white-collar trade unions had 1,458,300 members. However, the rapid growths in female and white-collar trade unionism (categories that overlap) came after the Second World War.

British trade union membership fell quickly from 8,253,000 in 1920 to 4,350,000 in 1933, a fall in union density from 48.2 to 23.9 per cent. Trade union membership recovered slowly in the 1930s, the pace quickening from 1936 with economic recovery and rearmament. There was considerable growth in hitherto weakly unionised areas such as food and drink (the density rising from 14.9 to 23.7 per cent) and in clothing (from 12.3 to 23.6 per cent) between 1933 and 1939. Other unions reached new levels of membership, such as road transport (the density rising from 47.3 to 68.4 per cent). There was also substantial recovery in some major unions affected by the 1926 general strike, when the TUC called out several unions in a solidarity strike with the coal miners. The coal miners improved their union density from 52.4 to 81.1 per cent, railway-workers from 56.9 to 67.2 per cent and those in printing and publishing from 43.0 to 51.4 per cent between 1933 and 1939 (Wrigley 2002, p. 8).

In the Second World War, the number of men in the armed forces reached its peak at 4,653,000 in June 1945, while the Women's Auxiliary Service reached its highest number of 467,500 in December 1943. As in the First World War, the government needed the co-operation of the trade unions. British trade union membership rose from 6,519,000 (a density of 33.4 per cent) in 1940 to 7,684,000 (a density of 38.6 per cent) in 1945.

Trade union strength was rarely exercised during the Second World War. Coal mining accounted for nearly 60 per cent of days lost through industrial disputes, with engineering and shipbuilding a long way behind. Churchill paid tribute to the trade unions in 1941, writing, 'I . . . cannot forget the support and encouragement which trade unions, themselves in the forefront of the battle, gave in the darkest days in 1940 and are giving with all their heart today' (Wrigley 2001, p. 64). The government took powers to be able to regulate labour. A Schedule of Reserved Occupations was drawn up before the war, unlike waiting until 1917 in the First World War; competitive bidding by employers for scarce labour was stopped by the Control of Employment Act, 1939; and the Minister of National Service had wide powers which were used frequently under the Emergency Powers (Defence) Act 1940. By December 1944 Essential Work Orders covered 67,400 workplaces and 8,569,000 people, of whom 28 per cent were women (Parker 1957, p. 499).

The government encouraged the spread of collective bargaining, especially industry-wide agreements. In engineering, by late 1943 up to 60 per cent of engineering firms that employed 60 or more workers as well as the Royal Ordnance factories had joint committees of trade union and employer representatives to boost production (Inman 1957, pp. 380–381). There were also district production committees in the coal industry.

In Focus: strikes

The level of strike activity generally went up during upturns in the economy when labour was in a stronger bargaining position. This was so in 1908–14 and during the two World Wars. Although strikes and lockouts were illegal for much of the two World Wars, the numbers of days lost through strikes and the numbers of those involved in strikes were substantial. In 1915–18, 37.8 per cent of those people directly or indirectly involved in strikes worked in mining and quarrying and 29.2 per cent in metals, engineering and shipbuilding. In 1940–44, most strikers were also in coal mining (58.5 per cent) and metals, engineering and shipbuilding (28.2 per cent). After the post-war boom of 1919–20, the trade unions were on the defensive, with defeats in engineering in 1922, coal mining in 1926 and in wool in 1930. In the 1930s there was a low level of strikes. Coal strikes accounted for nearly half of all strikes, and these usually affected only one colliery, with close to half of these occurring in Scotland (Church and Outram 1998).

In 1952, the statistician K.J.G.C. Knowles analysed strike-proneness in 1911 to 1945 by dividing the percentage of the industrial population of a region by the percentage of strikers. With the UK as 1.0 (having 100 per cent of both strikers and industrial population), the countries and regions with above-average levels for strike proneness were South Wales (4.8), the West Riding of Yorkshire (2.4), Lancashire and Cheshire (2.0) and Scotland (1.1). The presence of strike-prone industries contributed to the areas with high levels of strikes; thus, South Wales would have been at 1.3 were it not for coal mining. Coal mining (6.7) was the most strike-prone industry in these years, with textiles (4.3) second (Knowles 1952). Further studies for later periods have also emphasised the geography of strikes. David Gilbert has pointed to the development of new industries 'away from the older heartlands of union organization, militancy, and established industrial communities, has led to relatively low levels of strike activity'. He also found that 'the history of strikes also exhibits some degree of . . . "regional resilience"' (Gilbert 1996, p. 151).

The first national strike for 20 years came in 1953, a one-day engineering strike. There were strike waves in 1955–58, 1968–74 and 1977–80 associated with wage issues. There were political strikes against proposed trade union laws and the legislation, most notably against the Heath government's Industrial Relations Act, 1971. There were high numbers of days lost through strikes in the UK in 1970–74, peaking at 23,900,000 in 1972. There was a further wave of strikes in 1977–80, linked to wage demands thwarted by the Labour government's incomes policies, peaking at 29,474,000 in 1979 (the 'Winter of Discontent').

In 1984, because of the mining dispute, there was again a huge number of days lost in disputes, 27,135,000. At the height of the 1984–5 coal dispute, some 242,000 miners were on strike, primarily over pit closures. Closure of pits proceeded quickly after the end of the strike. The Conservative government privatised the mines in 1994. In 1983 there were 174 working deep mines, by 2000, 33 deep mines remained. In July 2018, the last working deep mine, Kellingley, closed.

Trade unions after 1945

The post-war years from 1945 to 1979 were a golden age for the British trade unions. Trade union membership rose from 7,684,000, of whom 20.6 per cent were women, to 13,212,00, of whom 46.2 per cent were women. Unemployment was low, running between 1.5 and 2.6 per cent from 1949 to 1971 (Mitchell 1988, p. 126). Employers were keen to hold their labour force. Part of the explanation for rapid trade union growth in the post-war years also lies with the economic pressure of retail price inflation, notably in the late 1960s and the 1970s (Bain and Elsheikh 1976, pp. 26–70). Yet while the pressure of inflation is a major part of the reason trade unionism grew rapidly in 1968–79 and earlier in 1915–20, in other periods such as 1950–52 and 1959–62 there was retail price inflation but relatively little trade union growth.

Another explanation offered for trade union strength in Britain and similar economies is favourable political conditions. In a study of 18 countries between 1950 and 1990, Bruce Western concluded that trade unions were strongest where working-class parties who favoured trade unions were in office, where centralised collective bargaining took place and where trade union management of welfare schemes enabled them to hold on to the support of those in weak negotiating positions (Western 1997, p. 3). In Britain, Labour in office in 1945–51, 1964–70 and 1974–9 helped trade union development, including through continuing the tripartite (government, employers and trade unions) discussions of 1961–64.

The trade union growth of 1945–79 took place despite changes in industrial structure which adversely affected some the strongest unionised sectors. Coal, cotton and human-made fibres were bastions of trade unionism in 1948, with densities of membership of 86.4, 78.3 and 88.7, respectively. By 1979, they had fallen by nearly 30 per cent as a proportion of British trade unionists, but their densities had risen to 92.7, 87.6 and 96.8 per cent, respectively. The higher union densities reflected the appeal of unions to working people whose jobs were under threat. Another group of employees highly unionised but declining in relative importance was manual workers, whose numbers fell by 14.7 per cent but whose union density rose by 5.9 per cent between 1951 and 1979.

The British trade union movement shrank from 1980 to 2018. One outstanding feature of this was that the fall in female trade unionists was slower than male. Since 2002 there have been fewer men than women in trade unions. In 1901, women were 6.5 per cent of trade unionists. In 2018, women were 55.4 per cent of British trade unionists. Although women did not secure half of senior trade union posts, Frances O'Grady was general secretary of the TUC, 2013–22.

The long fall in trade union membership returned British trade union membership by 2018 to near its pre–Second World War level in numbers, 6,098,000, but lower in density (1938: 5,969,000 and density of 30.8 per cent). Trade unionism remained strong in the public sector, both for male and female employees. Public sector trade union density was 52.5 per cent, whereas private sector trade union membership had shrunk to 13.2 per cent, with males at 14.4 per cent to females 11.8 per cent. As before the First World War, trade union membership was concentrated in several sectors. In 2020, these were professional occupations (where female trade union density was 53.1 per cent to male 26.4); associated professional and technical, caring leisure and other services; process, plant and machine operatives; and skilled trades. In terms of services, the most unionised were education and health and social work, followed by transport and storage, electricity and gas, and water supply and sewage. Trade union membership was strongest among older workers, 26.5 per cent of those 35–49 and 29.3 per cent of those 50 and over, while weakest among young workers, 8.4 per cent of 16–24 and 18.9 per cent of 25–34. Trade union membership was still highest in the former industrial areas of the North, North-East and North-West and lowest in London and the South-East.

Table 7.5 GB trade union membership (000s) and density, 1901–2018

Year	Total	Density	Male	Density	Female	Density
1901	1908	13.0	1356	17.2	124	2.9
1911	3129	19.0	2799	24.5	331	6.6
1921	6512	37.9	5526	46.3	986	18.8
1931	4569	24.3	3820	29.5	749	12.4
1941	7048	36.0	5664	42.4	1384	22.2
1951	9266	44.7	7515	55.2	1751	24.7
1961	9518	43.2	7587	52.7	1931	25.2
1971	10518	47.0	7923	56.4	2595	31.2
1981	11628	50.5	7934	57.9	3694	39.7
1991	8602	37.5		42.0		32.0
2001	6800	29.0	3479	29.9	3319	28.6
2011	6219	25.8	2969	23.4	3250	28.6
2018	6098	23.0	2739	20.7	3359	26.2

Sources: Bain and Price (1980, pp. 39–40). Waddington (1992). Office of National Statistics, *Labour Market Trends*, July 2002.

Debates and Interpretations: trade unions, industrial relations and equality

There have been political and academic debates over the merits of the British voluntary approach to industrial relations which, apart from the two world wars, was dominant until 1980. This view, promoted by such academics as Hugh Clegg and Otto Kahn-Freund, praised collective bargaining and the relative lack of state intervention in Britain (Flanders and Clegg 1954, pp. 43–44; Wrigley 2007). It was a view echoed by the report of the Royal Commission on Trade Unions and Employers' Associations, 1968. The voluntary approach was increasingly challenged by those who believed industrial relations should be regulated by law, a view expressed by the Society of Conservative Lawyers in its influential pamphlet, *A Giant's Strength* (1958). After Wilson's Labour government unsuccessfully proposed legal changes in a white paper, *In Place of Strife* (1969), and Edward Heath's Industrial Relations Act 1971 failed, the Thatcher and Major Conservative governments (1979–1997) restricted trade unions in stages by legislation between 1980 and 1993.

The trade union legislation was made against claims that high strike levels were 'the British disease'. Such views have been refuted by international comparisons. The Donovan Report (1968) put Britain neither in a group of the worst affected countries by strikes, which included Australia, Canada, the United States, Ireland and Italy, nor in a group notable for relatively few strikes, which included France and Japan, but in an intermediate group. From 1969 to 1989 British strike levels varied, but throughout Britain's position stayed broadly the same even during the Thatcher years (1979–90). British strike levels went up and down broadly in line with strike levels in other countries. Changes in the international economy are a substantial part of the explanation (Wrigley 2002, pp. 49–53).

Studies of post-1945 strikes have often drawn attention to strike-prone plants or mines, or even parts of them (Prais 1978; Durcan *et al.* 1983). A detailed Department of the Employment–sponsored study of the turbulent industrial unrest of 1971–73 found that 'only five per cent of plants had stoppages and of those over two-thirds had only one stoppage'. Within this 5 per cent, 5 per cent accounted for two-thirds of days lost through strikes. The authors concluded, 'It is abundantly clear that Britain does not have a widespread strike problem but rather a problem of stoppages concentrated in a small minority of manufacturing plants and in certain non-manufacturing sectors' (Smith *et al.* 1978, pp. 63 and 86–87).

Another controversy has been over free-market views of trade unions affecting economic competitiveness through the trade union wage premium, which is the difference in pay and other benefits between union and non-union labour. The gap between union and non-union pay has shrunk. In 1995 the gap in the public sector was 30 per cent and in the private sector 15 per cent, but by 2018 these gaps had reduced to 11.6 per cent and 2.6 per cent, respectively. This has been affected to a certain extent by about a quarter of pay being settled for union and non-union labour alike by collective bargaining (Department for Business, Energy and Industrial Strategy, *Trade Union Statistics 2018*, 2019). The smaller union wage premium has made the union impact on investment, productivity and profitability smaller, though there is little evidence that in the past unions have affected investment and some suggestions that highly unionised plants have encouraged employers 'to increase capital intensity and introduce more efficient work methods' (Aldcroft and Oliver 2000).

Despite the fall in membership, trade unions have retained their appeal for many people, not least low-paid workers, including ethnic-minority and disabled workers.

David Metcalf, a leading authority on British industrial relations, has commented on unions' 'sword of justice' role: 'Unions narrow the distribution of pay, promote equal opportunity and family friendly policies, and lower the rate of industrial injuries' (2003, p. 180). The TUC has run annual Black Workers Conferences since 1998, and, at the 2001 TUC, affiliated unions undertook 'to promote equality for all and to eliminate all forms of harassment, prejudice and unfair discrimination, both within its own structures and through all its activities, including its own employment practices'. The TUC held Disability Forums and in 2000 drew up a Disability Action Plan for all its affiliated unions. The TUC also held annual Lesbian and Gay Conferences from 1998 and sought anti-discrimination legislation comparable to that covering sex and race (Wrigley 2002, pp. 30–31). The trade unions have also attempted, with some success, to lessen job losses and to avoid people being reduced to needing benefits or even foodbanks while in work as part of 'flexible' self-employed labour without most employment rights, such as proper sick pay and paid holidays. As women have been especially subject to such insecurity, many have turned to trade unions for support.

Conclusion

The UK labour market continued to change substantially in the first two decades of the twenty-first century, even before the impact of the coronavirus and Brexit. For instance, online shopping adversely impacted British high street shops, and more people relied on electronic rather than printed news. Employment for life continued to become rarer.

While British trade unionism fell by over half (53.8 per cent) in size between 1979 and 2018, it remained bigger than French trade unionism had been at its biggest in 1946 (5,424,000) (Visser 1989, p. 680). However, British trade unionism fell faster than German, which reached its post-war peak in 1981 and then fell by 29.7 per cent by 2018. British trade unionism was still important in the public sector of the economy.

Further reading

For work and the labour market, see the essays in: Crafts, N., Gazeley, I., and Newell, A., eds., *Work and Pay in Twentieth Century Britain* (Oxford: Oxford University Press, 2007) as well as in Gregg, P., and Wadsworth, J., *The Labour Market in Winter: The State of Working Britain* (Oxford: Oxford University Press, 2011). For shrewd overviews of work, see also McIvor, A.J., *A History of Work in Britain 1880–1950* and *Working Lives: Work in Britain since 1945* (Basingstoke: Palgrave Macmillan, 2001 and 2013). For the economic background, see Pollard, S., *The Development of the British Economy, 1914–1990* (London: Arnold, 1992) and Booth, A., *The British Economy in the Twentieth Century* (London: Macmillan, 2001). For occupational pension schemes, see Hannah, L., *Inventing Retirement: The Development of Occupational Pensions in Britain* (Cambridge: Cambridge University Press, 1996). For the importance of the service sector, see Broadberry, S., *Market Services and the Productivity Race 1850–2000* (Cambridge: Cambridge University Press, 2006) Broadberry, S., *The productivity race: British Manufacturing in International Perspective 1850–1990* (Cambridge: Cambridge University Press, 1997). For trade union development, see Clegg, H., and Fox, A., *The History of British Trade Unionism since 1889*, Volume 2: 1911–1933 and Volume 3: 1934–1951 (Oxford: Clarendon Press, 1985 and 1994) and, more briefly, Wrigley, C., *British Trade Unions since 1933* (Cambridge: Cambridge University Press, 2002). For strikes in the coal industry, see Church, R., and Outram, Q., *Strikes and Solidarity, Coalfield Conflict in Britain, 1889–1966* (Cambridge: Cambridge University Press, 1998).

References

Aldcroft, D., and Oliver, M., 2000. *Trade unions and the economy*. Aldershot: Ashgate.

Bain, G.S., and Elsheikh, F., 1976. *Union growth and the trade cycle: An econometric analysis*. Oxford: Blackwell.

Bain, G.S., and Price, R., 1980. *Profiles of union growth: A comparative statistical portrait of eight countries*. Oxford: Blackwell.

Broadberry, S., 1997. *The productivity race: British manufacturing in international perspective 1850–1990*. Cambridge: Cambridge University Press.

Broadberry, S., 2006. *Market services and the productivity race 1850–2000*. Cambridge: Cambridge University Press.

Buxton, N.K., and McKay, D.I., 1977. *British employment statistics*. Oxford: Blackwell.

Church, R., and Outram, Q., 1998. *Strikes and solidarity, coalfield conflict in Britain, 1889–1966*. Cambridge: Cambridge University Press.

Crafts, N., Gazeley, I., and Newell, A., eds., 2007. *Work and pay in twentieth century Britain*. Oxford: Oxford University Press.

Department for Business, Energy and Industrial Strategy, 2019. *Trade union statistics 2018*, https://www.gov.uk/government/statistics/trade-union-statistics-2018.

Department of the Employment, 1971. *British labour statistics: Historical abstract 1886–1968*. London: HMSO.

Durcan, J., McCarthy, W., and Redman, G., 1983. *Strikes in post-war Britain*. London: Allen and Unwin.

Flanders, A., and Clegg, H., eds., 1954. *The system of industrial relations in Britain*. Oxford: Blackwell.

Gilbert, D., 1996. Strikes in post-war Britain. *In*: C. Wrigley, ed. *A history of British industrial relations, 1939–1979*. Cheltenham: Edward Elgar, 128–161.

Gregg, P., and Wadsworth, J., 2011. *The labour market in winter*. Oxford: Oxford University Press.

Hancock, L., and Gowing, M., 1949. *British war economy*. London: HMSO.

Hannah, L., 1986. *Inventing retirement: The development of occupational pensions in Britain*. Cambridge: Cambridge University Press.

Hatton, T., 2003. Unemployment and the labour market, 1870–1939. *In*: R.C. Floud and P.A. Johnson, eds. *The Cambridge economic history of modern Britain*. Cambridge: Cambridge University Press, 344–373.

Horrell, S., 2007. The household and the labour market. *In*: N. Crafts, I. Gazeley and A. Newell, eds. *Work and pay in twentieth century Britain*. Oxford: Oxford University Press, 117–141.

Inman, P., 1957. *Labour in the munitions industries*. London: HMSO.

Inns of Court Conservative and Unionist Society, October 1958. *A giant's strength*. Inns of Court Conservative and Unionist Society (pamphlet series).

Johnson, P., and Zaida, A., 2007. Work over the life course. *In*: N. Crafts, I. Gazeley and A. Newell, eds. *Work and pay in twentieth century Britain*. Oxford: Oxford University Press, 98–116.

Knowles, K.G.J.C., 1952. *Strikes: A study in conflict*. Oxford: Blackwell.

Metcalf, D., 2003. Trade unions. *In*: R. Dickens, P. Gregg and J. Wadsworth, eds. *The labour market under new labour*. Basingstoke: Palgrave Macmillan, 170–187.

Mitchell, B.R., 1988. *British historical statistics*. Cambridge: Cambridge University Press.

Office for National Statistics, 1998. *Social Trends*. London: HMSO.

Office for National Statistics, 2019. *Families and the labour market, UK: 2019*, Release date: 24 October 2019. Available from: https://www.ons.gov.uk/employmentandlabourmarket/peopleinwork/employmentandemployeetypes/articles/familiesandthelabourmarketengland/2019.

Parker, H.M.D., 1957. *Manpower: A study in war-time policy and administration*. London: HMSO.

Phillips, J., 2019. *Scottish coal miners in the twentieth century*. Edinburgh: Edinburgh University Press.

Pollard, S., 1992. *The development of the British economy, 1914–1990*. London: Arnold.

Prais, S., 1978. The strike-proneness of large plants. *Journal of the Royal Statistical Society*, 141, 368–384.

Smith, C., Clifton, R., Makcham, P., Creigh, S., and Burns, R., 1978. *Strikes in Britain*. London: HMSO.

Verdon, N., 2017. *Working the land: A history of the farmworkers in England from 1850 to the present day*. London: Palgrave Macmillan.

Visser, J., 1989. *European trade unionism in figures*. Deventer, Netherlands: Kluwer Law and Taxation Publishers.

Waddington, J., 1992. Trade union membership in Britain 1980–1987. *British Journal of Industrial Relations*, 30 (2), 287–324.

Western, B., 1997. *Between class and market. Post-war unionization in capitalist democracies*. Princeton: Princeton University Press.

Wrigley, C., 2001. Churchill and the trade unions. *Transactions of the Royal Historical Society*, 11, 273–293.

Wrigley, C., 2002. *British trade unions since 1933*. Cambridge: Cambridge University Press.

Wrigley, C., 2007. Industrial relations. *In*: N. Crafts, I. Gazeley and A. Newell, eds. *Work and pay in twentieth century Britain*. Oxford: Oxford University Press, 203–224.

Wynn, B., 1993. *Skilled at all trades: The history of the farmworkers' union, 1947–1984*. London: TGWU/Frontline.

8 Leisure, consumption and consumerism

Peter Scott

Introduction

Prior to 1914 the vast majority of Britain's population lived in various states of severe poverty; occupying small, rented homes, which were spartanly furnished (with the possible exception of the front parlour). The twentieth century, and particularly the period from around 1950–1980, witnessed what previous generations would have considered a miraculous rise in living standards and mass affluence in Britain and most western countries. Two key elements in the improving lifestyles of especially working and lower-middle class families were increased access to leisure and to discretionary spending (spending after taking care of 'essentials' such as food, fuel, accommodation, and commuting). This chapter examines the key drivers of these trends and their impacts on individuals and households. We also discuss whether the twenty-first century has witnessed a halt, or even reversal, of the march towards a mass affluence, mass leisure society.

Leisure has two meanings – 'positive' leisure, that is, partaking of leisure activities, and 'free time' – not committed to paid work, housework, education and training, commuting, or sleep. Both were in very short supply at the start of the twentieth century. In 1900 a typical male industrial worker had a working week of around 54 hours, plus overtime (often compulsory and sometimes unpaid). Moreover, his working life started early, at around age 12, and would continue until he was no longer fit to undertake full-time paid work. Then, given the absence of state old age pensions or wages high enough to fund retirement savings, he would most likely have to turn to the workhouse – where he would be separated from his wife and compelled to do whatever work he could manage until he was completely invalided.

Working-class girls also commenced paid work at around age 12, often in domestic service – which involved a substantially longer working week than industrial employment, together with severe constraints on their personal liberty. And while the majority of working-class women did not work in the formal labour market after marriage, running the household involved long hours of often heavy labour, such as carrying large amounts of water into the house, heating it, and then manually washing the family's clothes or, in Scotland, carrying and manually washing the clothes in the public wash house or 'steamie'. Meanwhile both working and lower-middle class people had very limited access to commercial leisure, given their low discretionary income and the fact that most leisure venues (with the obvious exception of churches) were closed on Sundays – the one day that was free from paid work.

DOI: 10.4324/9781003037118-9

By the 1970s mass access to leisure, in terms of both free time and the money to make use of it, was regarded as a 'necessity' for all classes. People typically began work aged 16–21; the welfare state and private pensions had replaced the workhouse; almost every home had several entertainment durables, while labour-saving durables took most of the effort, and much of the time, out of housework. Meanwhile 'consumerism' – a belief that all classes should have access to a prosperous life, evidenced by ownership of a house, car, and a range of household durables – had become one of the dominant ideas of the age – promoted during the cold war as proof that capitalism could offer a better life than communism. This chapter explores how rising incomes, technological innovation, and other factors transformed Britain into a 'consumer society' and threatened to turn it into a 'leisure society,' together with the post-1980 trend towards people being faced with an endlessly multiplying range of leisure activities while having diminishing time, and often income, to enjoy them.

Inter-war Britain – the dawn of mass consumerism?

Although the First World War was an unprecedented humanitarian catastrophe, it also acted as a catalyst for socio-economic changes that created Britain's embryonic mass leisure sector and brought about major increases in incomes, and discretionary spending, for those lucky enough to remain in work during the mass unemployment era of the 1920s and 1930s. One of the key pre-1914 barriers to any major improvement in working-class living standards was the high cost of good-quality housing, largely owing to low working-class personal mobility. As most industrial buildings were located in urban areas and manual workers typically walked to work, housing land costs were forced up by the pressure of demand from people who had little choice but to live nearby. This incentivised developers to economise on land by building densely packed streets of cramped, low-quality terraces or back-to-back housing or, in Scotland, tenements, typically four or five storeys high.

The War witnessed substantial redistributions of income, both from the upper and middle classes to the working class and from skilled to less-skilled manual workers. There was also a general acceleration in income growth over 1913–1920 compared to the Edwardian era (Boyer 2004, p. 284). Families could thus potentially devote more income to accommodation, while the balance of housing and land costs tilted in favour of lower-density houses, owing to a relative fall in land prices. It was estimated in December 1919 that the additional cost per plot when developing at twelve houses per acre rather than twenty-one had fallen from 19 per cent in 1914 to less than 4 per cent (Swenarton 1981, p. 143). Meanwhile the War had accelerated technological innovation in transport, including motor trucks (often sold off as war surplus and converted into buses), together with cheaper and more efficient bicycles and motorbikes (Lloyd-Jones and Lewis 2000, pp. 105–107).

Increased personal mobility, enabling workers to commute longer distances, was further assisted by the introduction of 'daylight saving' from 1916, which reduced the number of days bicycle journeys would have to be taken in darkness. Then in the immediate aftermath of the War, trade unions (in Britain and most industrial nations) successfully pressed for a 48-hour week for industrial workers – compared to the 1900 norm of around 54. Collectively, these changes made much longer commutes viable. According to research by Pooley and Turnbull (1999), the average journey to work increased from 3.9 km for men and 3.2 km for women in 1900–09 to 6.8 and 6.1 km, respectively, in 1920–29. For the first time, large numbers of manual workers could move beyond the edges of their towns, where land for houses was both more plentiful and cheaper.

Government, wishing to avoid potential civil unrest by demobbed soldiers returning to find themselves unemployed, planned a 'homes for heroes' municipal house-building programme. They followed the advice of leading planners such as Raymond Unwin, who advocated housing provision in the form of self-contained cottages, generally with at least three bedrooms, a bathroom or fixed bath, modern utilities, a scullery kitchen, and, wherever possible, a parlour. They were to be built at low densities (twelve or fewer houses per acre, compared to the thirty or more per acre in new Edwardian working-class neighbourhoods) to allow for generous gardens (Ravetz 2001, p. 62). Although the original post-Armistice 'homes for heroes' council housing programme was beset with delays and, later, drastic expenditure cuts, these recommendations formed the basis of a series of major inter-war council house building programmes, creating 1,320,000 British municipal homes (more than 90 per cent on suburban estates) (Scott 2013, pp. 7 & 82).

This model of housing was also used by private housing developers, as the suburban semi was economical to build and proved popular with purchasers. However, speculative developers were careful to externally style their homes to immediately distinguish them from council houses – creating the 'Tudorbethan' inter-war semi that remains, for many, the ideal home (see Image 8.1). Affordability was also greatly extended from the late 1920s, with the introduction of 25-year building society mortgages for new houses, with a minimum deposit of only 5 per cent of the purchase price. It has been estimated that during the inter-war era, around 25 per cent of the urban working class migrated to suburban estates (13 per cent to suburban council estates, 9 per cent to owner-occupied estates, and perhaps 3 per cent to private rentals), together with a substantially larger proportion of non-manual workers (Scott 2013, p. 10).

Working-class family migration to suburban estates was found to be associated with substantial changes in social norms, the home and family increasingly being viewed as 'an intense domestic unit enclosed from the wider world' (Hughes and Hunt 1992, p. 92). This new, aspirational respectability emphasised high standards of personal and domestic hygiene, 'privatised' family- and home-centred lifestyles, and an increased commitment of resources to the welfare and material advancement of the next generation (Hughes and Hunt 1992, p. 92; Szreter 1996, p. 528; Gittins 1982, pp. 175–176). As De Vries (2008, p. 189) noted, together with improved diets, these preferences formed a 'complex of consumption goals' which required clear household strategies to deliver them. Such trends were strongest in new suburban estates, which were initially communities of 'strangers,' drawn from different parts of town, with no yardstick for judging respectability or status (Scott 2013, Chapter 6).

Rising inter-war incomes (for those in work) both facilitated this transition and increased households' discretionary spending – much of which was devoted to leisure activities (broadly defined) and durables. Household durables' share of British consumer expenditure rose from 3.85 per cent in 1913 to 7.28 per cent in 1936 (Feinstein 1972, pp. T65–7). However, even in 1939, diffusion rates for labour-saving appliances were low both in absolute terms and in comparison with the United States. Some 30 per cent of British homes wired for electricity had vacuums, compared to 48 per cent in the United States (both boosted by high-pressure door-to-door selling). However, comparisons were less favourable for electric washing machines (59.6 per cent

Image 8.1 The inter-war speculative semi (left panel) and its more austere municipal counter-
         part (right panel)
Source: Scrapbook of house plans (c. 1939), held privately by the author.

diffusion to wired homes in the United States but only 3.6 per cent for the UK) or electric refrigerators (56.0 per cent United States, 2.3 per cent UK). Similarly, while the
number of cars on Britain's roads doubled during the decade to 1938, they were still
confined to only 15.4 per cent of households, compared to around 44 per cent in the
United States by the mid-1930s (Political and Economic Planning 1945, pp. 211–212;
Scott 2017, pp. 261–262).

High purchase costs severely limited diffusion, even if spread over several years via
'hire purchase' credit (an instalment payment system where goods were technically
hired until the final payment was made and could therefore be repossessed without a
court order). For example, a high-powered Hoover vacuum cost around £21 in the
1930s, the equivalent of £1,469 in 2019 prices. This was not clearly better value for
money than employing a char lady a few hours each week (especially given that she
could be sacked if household finances were strained, while hire purchase payments
could not be terminated without losing the vacuum and all the instalments paid) (Scott
2017, pp. 239–245). Car ownership was also prohibitively expensive for most families, reflecting high running costs (£1.50–£2 *per week*, or £105–£140 in 2019 prices),
partly due to Britain's exceptionally high road and petrol taxes (Scott 2017, Chapter 11). Conversely, entertainment durables, such as the radio, had much more rapid
diffusion, as an hour of entertainment was perceived to be more important than an
hour saved from housework. Similarly, leisure spending was higher than spending on
durables, averaging 8.3 per cent of household consumption for working-class families
(Scott *et al.* 2015) and 15 per cent of disposable income for all households (Bakker
2008, p. 102) by the late 1930s.

In Focus: working-class commercial leisure during the 1930s

A long-term trend towards rising working-class leisure expenditure was evident from the late nineteenth century, though this accelerated during the inter-war years and, particularly, the 1930s (Bakker 2008, pp. 11–152; Holt 1989, pp. 144–148). Employment in entertainment and sport, which had risen from 101,700 in 1920 to 129,600 in 1929, mushroomed to 247,900 by 1938 (Jones 1986, pp. 42–47.) Research using Britain's first official national working-class family expenditure survey returns (covering four survey weeks – spaced at quarterly intervals over the year beginning October 1937) quantifies non-rural working-class leisure expenditure in the late 1930s. Table 8.1 examines commercial leisure in the context of overall working-class expenditure. Leisure-related activities represented some 18 per cent of 'disposable income,' (defined as total expenditure minus food, accommodation, and journey to work costs). The table also shows the proportion of non-rural working-class households that recorded some expenditure on each activity in any one of the four survey weeks.

Table 8.1 Working-class household expenditure on leisure and other activities (%) and participation rates, 1937/38 (UK)

	Percentage distribution of household expenditure			Participation
	All items	*Leisure items*	*Disposable expenditure*	*(% in four weeks)*
Total expenditure	100.0			
Food	40.0			
Accommodation	12.3			
Transport to work	1.6			
Disposable expenditure	46.1			
Low-commitment leisure				
Cinema	1.1	12.8	2.3	71
Newspapers	1.2	14.5	2.6	98
Books	0.2	2.8	0.5	64
High-commitment leisure				
Theatre etc.	0.2	3.0	0.5	32
Sport	0.3	3.2	0.6	39
Holidays	0.9	10.9	2.0	22
Education	0.3	3.7	0.7	11
Addictive leisure				
Smoking	3.1	37.5	6.7	86
Drink	1.0	11.7	2.1	53
Total leisure	8.3	100.0	18.0	n.a.

Source: Scott *et al.* (2015).

Notes: Participation rates show participation by any family member over any of the four weeks. 'Holiday' participation includes savings for holidays.

Inter-war leisure can be usefully classified into low-commitment activities (reading, cinema-going), high-commitment activities (theatre, sport, holidays, piano lessons), and addictive activities (smoking, drinking). Low-commitment activities were typically low cost (relative to the time spent) and could be accessed with little or no forward planning. This contributed to very high participation. For example, expenditure on reading matter (books, newspapers, magazines, and comics) represented 3.1 per cent of average disposable expenditure, significantly higher than for cinema (which is generally regarded as the leading form of working-class commercial leisure at this time). Working-class 'time budgets' for Liverpool in 1931 show reading to have the highest participation rate of any commercial leisure activity, with some 83 per cent of men and 84 per cent of women doing some leisure reading each week (Middleton 1931, pp. 146, 179–180). Almost everyone subscribed to a newspaper and/or magazine, while book sales witnessed a major boom, from 7.2 million books sold in 1928 to 26.8 million in 1939 (Rowntree 1941, pp. 371–376; Beaven 2005, p. 181). Most were accessed through libraries, yet – given that many towns had very few branch public libraries – people often found it both more convenient and cheaper (factoring in travel costs) to use local commercial 'two penny libraries' or purchase one of the large selection of six-penny books at Woolworths.

Cinema is shown to be the third most popular leisure activity after reading and tobacco. Around half of working-class households spent some money on cinema-going each week, purchasing several hours of entertainment (including a main feature, 'B' feature, and newsreel) for around 6d (or 3d in the cheapest venues). Sedgwick (2000, p. 46), estimated that the average Briton aged 15 or over spent the equivalent of one-and-a-half to two working weeks watching films each year, yet cinema accounted for little more than 1 per cent of total consumer expenditure. Cinema was also one of the few commercial leisure activities with high female participation rates (Davies 1992, p. 77; Langhamer 2000, p. 166), though the survey found that this largely represented married women having higher participation than their husbands. The gender imbalance for juveniles – who were among the most intensive cinema-goers – was found to be much weaker (Scott *et al.* 2015, pp. 664–665).

Activities such as dancing, spectator sports, and theatres/music halls typically involved a significantly greater minimum commitment than majority leisure pursuits such as reading and cinema, in terms of longer journeys to venues, higher admission costs, and the investment of time and energy required to gain full appreciation. As a result weekly participation rates were only a fraction of those for cinema, yet for large numbers of working-class people, a visit to a dance hall or football match could be the highlight of their week, assuming an importance out of all proportion to the time spent. Holidays also represented a high-commitment activity, as they typically required systematic savings over several months, though the loss of income during holiday weeks was eventually addressed by the 1938 Holidays with Pay Act (Walton 2000, p. 59). Around 20 per cent of working-class households, and a third of all households, went on holiday (typically at the seaside) each year (Scott *et al.* 2015, pp 666–667; Brunner 1945, p. 3; Walton 2000, pp. 58–60).

Addictive substances had low minimum costs of participation but high typical expenditures for participants. The inter-war era marked the highpoint of smoking, which was ubiquitous among the adult male population, while women's proportionate consumption rose from 1.0 per cent in 1922 to 9.4 per cent in 1938 (Alford 1973, pp. 340, 362; Pugh 2009, pp. 221–223). Conversely, alcohol consumption had declined substantially since the late Victorian era. Davies (1992, pp. 28–30 & 56) identifies drink, gambling, and sport as cornerstones of traditional, male-oriented, working-class culture. However, in common with smoking, female drinking increased during the inter-war years, while many younger people often preferred newer forms of leisure, such as dancing and cinema (Pugh 2009, pp. 224–228).

There were, of course, other popular activities that fell outside the commercial leisure sector, such as amateur sport, hiking, and gardening (which became a national pastime during the 1930s, encompassing all classes, owing largely to the proliferation of new suburban homes and the expansion of allotments following the Allotments Act of 1925). Finally, the importance of the radio (not itemised in the working-class expenditure survey) should not be underestimated. By the late 1930s virtually all households had a 'wireless' (licensed or unlicensed), which provided entertainment at extremely low cost per hour and could be enjoyed even when doing the housework. Until the mid-1950s radio represented the only form of broadcast entertainment in most homes and was generally considered a household 'essential'.

Consumption and leisure during the post-war 'long boom'

In common with other western countries, Britain witnessed unprecedented long-term growth in living standards during 1945–1980 (though less so than many West European nations). Other important trends in household consumption during this era included a shift from production within the household to market purchases (for example, from home-cooked to ready meals), greater reliance on labour-saving consumption technologies, reduced income pooling by household members, and rising proportionate spending on services (De Vries 2008, p. 238). Growing affluence was underpinned by the expansion of the welfare state, low fertility rates (though higher than in the 1930s), full employment, and rapid economic growth. Real earnings growth averaged 2.16 per cent per annum over 1946–80 (slowing from 2.25 per cent over 1946–67 to 2.02 per cent over 1967–80) (Williamson 2020).

Real incomes for typical households grew faster, owing to rising women's labour force participation and a reduction in income inequality (boosted by tight labour markets and the welfare state). Married women's labour force participation (typically part-time) increased by 35 percentage points over 1931–71, compared to only 6 percentage points for single, widowed, and divorced women (who already had very high participation rates). During the 1950s and 1960s the ratio of aggregate hours worked by women to those of men remained roughly stable, despite an increase in female activity rates from 36.3 to 51.5 per cent, with more women, working but for lower average hours. However, from the 1970s both women's participation rates and aggregate hours jointly rose (Joshi *et al.* 1985, p. S154).

Higher and more secure incomes encouraged longer household planning horizons. Ferdinand Zweig's *The Worker in an Affluent Society* (1961) argued that workers were adjusting to a climate of greater economic security by developing a more future-oriented outlook, based around rising material expectations; more home and family-oriented lifestyles; improved standards of domestic comfort in better houses with modern consumer durables; and higher aspirations for the next generation. Zweig's thesis was challenged during the 1960s by sociologists including John Goldthorpe, David Lockwood, Frank Bechhofer, and Jennifer Platt, culminating in Goldthorpe *et al.*'s *The Affluent Worker in the Class Struggle* (1969), yet remains influential.

Investing resources in the well-being and human capital of children became a rising priority in household financial planning. Children can be viewed as a 'positional good' (a good which ranks a household's social status) (Offer 2006, pp. 248–264). Children (or rather their parents) compete for the best educational and career entry opportunities, which bids up the cost of raising each child – giving families an incentive to have fewer children so that each could be better resourced. Thus, despite the extension of state secondary and tertiary education, family income remained a major determinant of educational success; even in the 1980s only around 22 per cent of university entrants were from manual workers' households, though these made up almost 60 per cent of the population (Pearson 1991, pp. 83–94).

These trends were strongest among the middle classes and in new suburban communities and government-sponsored 'new towns'. Housing was a high government priority in the early post-war period, to compensate for the cessation of building during six years of war and the effective destruction of 475,000 houses by bombing. Building 300,000 new homes per year was a key Conservative pledge in the 1951 election, which may have been responsible for their return to power (with a very slim initial majority). Yet this promise proved short lived.

The Treasury, seeking to support the value of sterling (see Chapter 5) and pave the way for the resumption of the City of London's role as a major financial centre, introduced 'stop-go' aggregate demand management policies (see Chapter 6) to control inflationary pressures on the exchange rate. To reduce investment demand, the government quietly abandoned its 300,000 homes promise in 1955 and began covertly restricting house-building – a policy which was followed, to varying degrees, for most years until the early 1980s. Municipal house-building was restricted by cutting back local authority housing budgets, while private house-building was restricted principally by covertly pressuring the Building Societies Association (the building societies' cartel) to reduce the interest rate offered to savers (which thereby starved them of funds for mortgage lending) (Scott and Walker 2019).

The Conservatives also suspended Labour's New Towns programme and blocked house-building beyond urban boundaries – by creating 'green belts' around towns and cities and by refusing urban boundary extensions. In addition to a desire to reduce house-building, Conservative governments of the 1950s and early 1960s also had party-political motives – seeking to block the migration of urban working-class families into rural areas which were 'Conservative seats, and usually marginal' (see Scott 2020, p. 553). As a result of these pressures, annual house-building from the mid-1950s to the late 1970s was substantially lower than for the inter-war years,

Table 8.2 Gross fixed capital formation in housing as a percentage of GNP/GDP for the UK and nine West European countries, 1954–59

Country	Belgium	France	Italy	Netherlands	W. Germany	Denmark	Finland	Norway	Sweden	UK
Average:										
1955–59	4.3	4.7	5.9	4.6	5.2	2.8	5.7	4.5	5.2	2.8
1960–64	4.9	5.1	6.7	4.1	5.6	3.6	5.8	4.2	5.4	3.2
1965–69	5.7	6.7	6.5	5.3	5.6	4.6	5.5	4.6	5.7	3.5
1970–74	5.2	7.0	6.3	5.9	6.1	5.6	7.0	5.2	5.4	3.6
1975–79	6.8	7.0	5.6	5.6	5.9	6.0	7.0	5.3	4.4	3.5
Coefficient of variation										
1955–62	0.11	0.05	0.08	0.12	0.07	0.14	0.12	0.08	0.02	0.08
1963–70	0.12	0.09	0.09	0.12	0.04	0.13	0.08	0.11	0.07	0.09
1971–79	0.19	0.06	0.09	0.08	0.06	0.16	0.06	0.02	0.14	0.11

Sources: Scott and Walker (2019, p. 731).

Notes: Data are expressed as a proportion of GNP until 1969 for averages and until 1970 for the coefficient of variation, then as a proportion of GDP thereafter, owing to changes in how the figures were reported.

while Britain's gross fixed capital formation in housing was substantially lower than that for other West European nations (Scott and Walker 2019), as shown in Table 8.2.

Much of the money spent on public-sector housing was diverted by government into high tower-block projects, which often had to be demolished within a few decades after their completion owing to serious structural and/or social problems. The Ministry of Housing and Local Government was aware from an early stage that high tower blocks were both more expensive to build than conventional housing (including land costs) and were problematic in various respects – for example, being unsuitable for children. However, the priority of successive Conservative governments to avoid large-scale population outflows from Labour-voting towns into Conservative-voting rural areas overrode cost and safety considerations. Ironically, many Labour urban councils supported tower block development, partly because they were not keen to lose Labour-voting constituents through out-migration (Scott 2020).

Stop-go policy also severely restricted the demand for consumer durables by raising purchase tax (the predecessor of VAT) on durables, the tax sometimes being equivalent to two thirds of the wholesale price. Government also periodically tightened hire purchase regulations to reduce durables' sales – raising minimum down-payments and reducing the maximum time over which loans could be repaid. Given that consumer durables often cost the equivalent of several weeks' wages, this effectively priced cars, refrigerators, washing machines, and other high-value durables beyond the reach of many families. For example, in 1957 less than 10 per cent of British homes had refrigerators, compared to 12 per cent in France; 14 per cent in West Germany; 25 per cent in Denmark; 26 per cent in New Zealand; and 50 per cent or more in Sweden, Australia, Canada, and the United States (Scott and Walker 2017). However, there was one exception – television – which experienced rapid diffusion, from less than 1 per cent of households in 1948 to 36.4 per cent in 1955 and 90.4 per cent in 1965. Despite being expensive, with poor picture quality and limited hours of programming, by the late 1950s the collective experience of sitting around the television in the evening to watch a mix of news, drama, and light enter-tainment was regarded as an essential by most households (Moran 2013). Many TVs were rented, rather than purchased, an arrangement that avoided paying a large hire purchase deposit and also ensured that if the TV broke down (as they were prone to do prior to the 1970s), the rental firm's repair man would soon be round to fix it, at no extra charge.

Debates and Interpretations: the emergence of the 'teenager' in post-war Britain?

To what extent was a distinct 'teenage' culture evident before 1939? Historians have traced 'teenage' lifestyles back to the inter-war years and even the Edwardian era (Davies 1992, pp. 82; 171; Fowler 2008, Chapter 1). However, others have argued that while the inter-war era witnessed growing purchasing power for young people – evidenced by higher participation in commercial leisure (and therefore 'visibility') – the emergence of a distinct 'youth culture' was a post-1945 phenomenon (Todd 2006). One important factor was that teenagers typically had much more money than even their 1930s predecessors. Full employment, raising the school leaving age to 15 in 1948, and the removal of 18–20-year-old males from the labour force for two years compulsory National Service made juvenile workers relatively scarce, raising their wages relative to adults (inter-war juvenile males and females received only around a third and a quarter of adult male wages, respectively). Moreover, young single women on 'adult' wage rates, who constituted most of the full-time female labour force in the 1950s, saw their relative wages rise from 47 per cent of adult male wages in the late 1930s to around 60 per cent after 1945 (where they remained until the early 1970s) (Joshi *et al.* 1985, p. S158).

The proportion of earnings young people retained for their own expenditure also rose substantially. Juveniles had traditionally either given their wages to their mother and received spending money back, or paid board (Davies 1992, pp. 84–85; Lang-hamer 2000, p. 102). After 1945 full employment and rising wages put less pressure on working children to financially support the family. Furthermore, juveniles were now earning enough to threaten to set up home by themselves if they were not satisfied with their retained earnings. Financial self-sufficiency is reflected in a continual fall in the average age of first marriage, from 26.1 for men and 23.5 for women in 1945 to an all-time low of 23.1 for men and 21.4 for women in 1969 (Office for National Statistics 2011, Table 5).

Discretionary spending power boosted the visibility of teenagers and young adults from the 1950s, including distinctive 'tribes,' reflected in music, dress, and codes of behaviour, such as teddy boys, mods, rockers, skinheads, and punks – though the majority of young people lived outside, or on the fringes of, such subcultures (Todd 2006, p. 719). Youth spending power was soon capitalised on by the commercial lei-sure sector, with the proliferation of milk bars, cafés, and record and clothes shops, together with the reorientation of existing leisure venues, such as dance halls, to appeal to this market. 1950s youth culture was strongly influenced by American fashion, including rock and roll (mainly accessed via juke boxes and record shops, as the BBC frowned on American popular music). However, rather than being just passive 'con-sumers,' youth culture increasingly created styles 'from the ground up,' an important

Image 8.2 Young lads gather around the fountain in Stevenage Town Centre, Hertfordshire.13th
October 1959

factor behind Britain's emergence from the 1960s as a youth and popular culture hub
ranking second only to the United States.

Discretionary spending and leisure in an age of slower growth, crises, and austerity: 1980–2019

By the 1970s Britain (in common with other industrial nations) appeared to be on a
path towards what futurologists termed the 'leisure society,' where all classes would
have access to affluent lifestyles and work would constitute only a relatively small part
of people's lives. Obviously, things haven't worked out that way.

Consumer durables became ubiquitous without demanding a rising share of income,
owing to considerable long-term falls in their real (inflation-adjusted) prices, which
made them almost universally available. This partly reflected a switch in their production to lower-wage countries specialising in these sectors, especially in East and
South-East Asia. Meanwhile entertainment durables underwent spectacular product
innovation, owing to the ICT revolution – which both created new products (such as
video game consoles and computers) and improved the functionality of existing ones
(such as televisions and telephones).

In contrast, housing (officially classed as a service but sharing the key characteristics of consumer durables) became ever more expensive, while council housing – the main alternative to owner occupation, was largely transferred to the private sector. The Housing Act 1980 allowed all council tenants of more than three years' residence to purchase their homes on discounts of up to 50 per cent of assessed value, depending on the length of tenancy. Given the weak legal rights of private tenants, the huge difficulties in obtaining social housing, and the growing importance of housing as a source of household wealth, home ownership became a key priority for many families, driving up prices.

In 1970 the average house cost the equivalent of 3.1 years average adult earnings, which was little changed in 1982 (3.2 years). Then a series of house price booms raised the ratio of house prices to earnings to 3.6 by 1993, 5.1 by 2002, 6.5 by 2009, and an unprecedented 7.8 years' earnings in 2018 (Scott 2013, pp. 243–245; Office for National Statistics 2019a. Data for 2002–2018 are for England and Wales only). This also reflected decades of inadequate house building, together with an acceleration in the growth of households – driven by high net immigration and a trend towards smaller households.

This in turn has important generational impacts, as shown in Figure 8.1, which charts owner-occupation rates by age cohort from 1961–2017. Prior to the early 1980s there was a relatively narrow gap in owner-occupation rates by age. However, this subsequently widened until, from the early 1990s, the 25–34 and 35–44 cohorts had declining owner-occupation rates both absolutely and relative to older groups. By 2017 owner-occupation rates for the 25–34 cohort had fallen to a lower level than for 1961, while the 35–44 cohort had fallen to its lowest level since 1975. This raises the spectre of future generations typically only getting on the housing ladder by inheriting their parents' homes. Housing has thus been transformed from a major opportunity for 'saving' (broadly defined) in the 1960s–1980s to an increasingly problematic cost item for a large proportion of especially younger households.

Meanwhile growing numbers of families, especially in the bottom half of the income distribution, have found it increasingly difficult to fund the lifestyles they aspire to. While the period from 1911 to the late 1970s saw a marked reduction in income inequality, this trend sharply reversed from 1980 (see the chapter on inequality). This reflects both deteriorating income growth for un/semi-skilled workers and changes in the tax and benefits system, initiated by the Thatcher governments, which shifted more of the burden of taxation onto lower-income families while reducing the services they received (Atkinson 2000, p. 370).

Lower-income families reacted by increasing their reliance on female earnings, while a similar, though weaker, trend towards the 'feminisation' of household income generation was evident for all families, with men's employment contribution to total household income falling from 68 to 46 per cent over 1968 to 2008–09 and women's rising from 15 to 26 per cent (Brewster and Wren-Lewis 2011, pp. 16 & 27). Households also became increasingly reliant on credit (particularly credit cards and mortgages) to bridge the gap between their incomes and desired lifestyles. As Figure 8.2 shows, by 1987 total household debt was already equivalent to 80 per cent of household income. Indebtedness grew to 92 per cent in 1990 but then fell to 86 per cent in 1993 following the recession and housing market crash. However, it subsequently expanded to 93 per cent by 2000 and jumped to 147 per cent in 2007.

Figure 8.1 Owner-occupation rates by age cohort, 1961–2017, UK
Source: Resolution Foundation (2019).

The credit crunch saw a second dip, to a low of 130 per cent in 2015, though debt rose again with the onset of recovery. Growing indebtedness for home owners also reflects a belief that personal debts could be balanced against above-inflation rises in house values.

Another important long-term trend in household expenditure is the rising importance of services, which now dominate total household expenditure (Office for National Statistics 2019b). Services increasingly strain family budgets, owing to their rising shares of family expenditure and above-inflation price rises. For example, an Office for National Statistics (ONS) analysis of price rises for 52 product/service categories from 2005–2016 found that five of the six items with the highest price rises were services: education (159% price rise), gas (125%), insurance connected with transport (118 per cent), health and other insurance (102 per cent) and electricity (98%). The only good with a price hike in the same range was tobacco (reflecting rising taxation). Meanwhile the consumer prices index (including occupiers' housing costs: CIPH) had increased by only 27.2 per cent over this period (ONS 2017). Many services have characteristics such as complexity and non-transparency (e.g. insurance and financial and professional services), imperfect markets (e.g. utilities, train fares, and financial and professional services), or inelastic supply (e.g. housing, private schools, elite universities) that enable inflation-busting price rises.

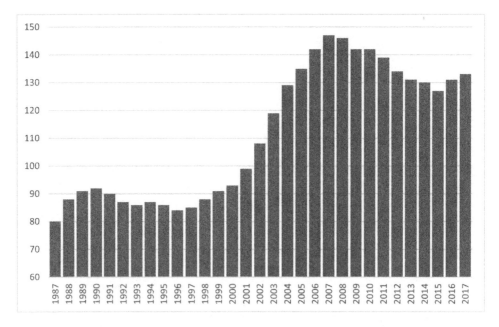

Figure 8.2 Household debt as a percentage of total household income, UK, 1987–2017
Source: Office for National Statistics (2018).

Some also have strong 'positional' characteristics – implying that as societies become wealthier, competition for them will intensify, pushing up prices. Thus, in contrast to goods, where standardisation, long production runs, and product and process innovation create 'mass markets' characterised by falling long-run prices, the outlook for 'Fordist' solutions to the high costs of services is much less positive.

Conclusions

It is still too early to tell whether the twentieth-century 'affluent society' represented part of a longer-term upward trend in consumption or a one-off transition from a high-hours, low-wage economy to a higher-wage, lower-hours society, or even a golden age of affluence that will be reversed over the twenty-first century. The twentieth century certainly had distinctive characteristics, including the impacts of the two world wars and the cold war, which incentivised policy-makers to distribute the gains from economic growth more widely in order to ensure mass participation and support. Moreover, the 1914–1980 era marked a move away from globalisation, which made it more difficult for the richest individuals (who lost out in terms of their income shares) to 'offshore' their wealth or themselves.

Conversely, from the 1980s, the abolition of capital export controls, a partial dismantling of the welfare state, moves towards more regressive taxation, and deregulation of financial and other markets have boosted globalisation but apportioned most of the gains to the very top of the income distribution. This era has also witnessed the return of financial crises, the costs of which fall disproportionately on lower-income groups. For example, the 2008 'credit crunch' heralded the first protracted peacetime fall in real incomes for British households since the nineteenth century. There has also been a retreat from the relatively leisured lives of late twentieth-century workers, with the partial deregulation of working hours and planned increases in the statutory retirement age to 66 in October 2020, 67 between 2026 and 2028, and 68 between 2037 and 2039. While we know a great deal about the history of leisure and consumption, predicting even its broad trajectory over the next several decades is now a much more problematic task than that which faced the optimistic futurologists of the 1960s and 1970s.

Further reading

Good general studies of the evolution of British leisure include Jones (1986), Offer (2006), Scott *et al.* (2015), and, internationally, Bakker (2008). There is also a rich literature on working-class leisure (e.g. Beaven 2005; Davies 1992; Jones 1986), juvenile leisure (Fowler 2008; Todd 2006), and female leisure (Langhamer 2000). Accessible introductions to particular leisure activities include: Holt (1989), sport; Sedgwick (2000), films; Moran (2013), television; and Walton (2000), holidays. For an introduction to the literature on consumer durables, including housing, see Scott (2017).

References

Alford, B.W.E., 1973. *W. D. & H. O. Wills and the development of the U.K. tobacco industry 1786–1965*. London: Methuen.

Atkinson, A.B., 2000. The distribution of income and wealth in Britain over the twentieth century. *In*: A.H. Halsey and J. Webb, eds. *British social trends*. London: Macmillan, 38–381.

Bakker, G., 2008. *Entertainment industrialised: The emergence of the international film industry, 1890–1940*. Cambridge: Cambridge University Press.

Beaven, B., 2005. *Leisure, citizenship, and working-class men in Britain 1850–1945*. Manchester: Manchester University Press.

Boyer, G.R., 2004. Living standards 1860–1939. *In*: R. Floud and P. Johnson, eds. *The Cambridge economic history of modern Britain, volume 2. economic maturity, 1860–1939*. Cambridge: Cambridge University Press, 280–313.

Brewster, M., and Wren-Lewis, L., 2011. "Why did Britain's households get richer? Decomposing UK household income growth between 1968 and 2008–09", IFS Briefing Note 125, Institute for Fiscal Studies.

Brunner, E., 1945. *Holiday making and the holiday trades*. Oxford: Oxford University Press.

Davies, A., 1992. *Leisure, gender, and poverty: Working-class culture in Salford and Manchester, 1900–1939*. Buckingham: Open University Press.

De Vries, J., 2008. *The industrious revolution: Consumer behavior and the household economy, 1650 to the present*. Cambridge: Cambridge University Press.

Feinstein, C.H., 1972. *National expenditure and output in the United Kingdom 1855–1965*. Cambridge: Cambridge University Press.

Fowler, D., 2008. *Youth culture in modern Britain, c. 1920 – c.1970*. Houndmills: Palgrave Macmillan.

Gittins, D., 1982. *Fair sex: Family size and structure, 1900–39*. London: Hutchinson.

Goldthorpe, J.H., Lockwood, D., Bechhofer, F., and Platt, J., eds., 1969. *The affluent worker in the class structure*. Cambridge: Cambridge University Press.

Holt, R., 1989. *Sport and the British: A modern history*. Oxford: Oxford University Press.

Hughes, A., and Hunt, K., 1992. A culture transformed? Women's lives in Wythenshawe in the 1930s. *In*: A. Davies and S. Fielding, eds. *Workers' worlds: Cultures and communities in Manchester and Salford, 1880–1939*. Manchester: Manchester University Press, 74–101.

Jones, S.G., 1986. *Workers at play: A social and economic history of leisure 1918–1939*. London: Routledge.

Joshi, H.E., Layard, R., and Owen, S.J., 1985. Why are more women working in Britain. *Journal of Labor Economics*, 3 (1), S147–S176.

Langhamer, C., 2000. *Women's leisure in England 1920–60*. Manchester: Manchester University Press.

Lloyd-Jones, R., and Lewis, M.J., 2000. *Raleigh and the British bicycle industry. An economic and business history, 1870–1960*. Aldershot: Ashgate.

Middleton, T.M., 1931. *An enquiry into the use of leisure amongst the working classes of Liverpool*. Unpublished. M.A. thesis. University of Liverpool.

Moran, J., 2013. *Armchair nation. An intimate history of Britain in front of the TV*. London: Profile.

Offer, A., 2006. *The challenge of affluence: Self-control and well-being in the United States and Britain since 1950*. Oxford: Oxford University Press.

Office for National Statistics (ONS). 2011. *Marriages in England and Wales (provisional), 2009*. Available from: www.ons.gov.uk/ons/publications/re-reference-tables.html?edition=tcm: 77-210946.

Office for National Statistics (ONS). 2017. *The changing price of everyday goods and services*. Available from: https://www.ons.gov.uk/economy/inflationandpriceindices/articles/thechanging priceofeverydaygoodsandservices/2017-07-11.

Office for National Statistics (ONS). 2018. *Quarterly sector accounts, UK: October to December 2017*. Available from: www.ons.gov.uk/economy/nationalaccounts/uksectoraccounts/bulletins/quarterlysectoraccounts/octobertodecember2017.

Office for National Statistics (ONS). 2019a. *House price to residence-based earnings ratio*. Available from: www.ons.gov.uk/peoplepopulationandcommunity/housing/datasets/ratioofhouse pricetoresidencebasedearningslowerquartileandmedian.

Office for National Statistics (ONS). 2019b. *Consumer trends, UK: October to December 2018*, 29 March. Available from: www.ons.gov.uk/economy/nationalaccounts/satelliteaccounts/bulletins/consumertrends/octobertodecember2018.

Pearson, M., 1991. Maintenance support during education. *In*: S. Smith, ed. *Economic policy and the division of income within the family*. London: IFS, 71–96.

Political and Economic Planning, 1945. *The market for household appliances*. London: PEP.

Pooley C.G., and Turnbull, J., 1999. The journey to work: A century of change. *Area*, 31 (3), 281–292.

Pugh, M., 2009. *We danced all night. A social history of Britain between the wars*. London: Vintage.

Ravetz, A., 2001. *Council housing and culture. The history of a social experiment*. London: Routledge.

Resolution Foundation, 2019. *Home ownership in the UK*. Available from: www.resolution-foundation.org/data/housing/.

Rowntree, S., 1941. *Poverty and progress: A second social survey of York*. London: Longmans.

Scott, P., 2013. *The making of the modern British home. The suburban semi and family life between the wars*. Oxford: Oxford University Press.

Scott, P., 2017. *The market makers: creating mass markets for consumer durables in inter-war Britain*. Oxford: Oxford University Press.

Scott, P., 2020. Friends in high-places: Government-industry relations in public sector house-building during Britain's tower block era. *Business History*, 62 (4), 545–565.

Scott, P., and Walker, J.T., 2017. The impact of 'stop-go' demand management policy on Britain's consumer durables industries, 1952–65. *Economic History Review*, 70 (4), 1321–1345.

Scott, P., and Walker, J.T., 2019. 'Stop-go' policy and the restriction of post-war British house-building. *Economic History Review*, 72 (2), 716–737.

Scott, P., Walker, J.T., and Miskell, P., 2015. British working-class household composition, labour supply, and commercial leisure participation during the 1930s. *Economic History Review*, 68 (2), 657–682.

Sedgwick, J., 2000. *Popular film-going in 1930s Britain: A choice of pleasures*. Exeter: University of Exeter Press.

Swenarton, M., 1981. *Homes fit for heroes: The politics and architecture of early state housing in Britain*. Gateshead: Heinemann.

Szreter, S., 1996. *Fertility, class and gender in Britain, 1860–1940*. Cambridge: Cambridge University Press.

Todd, S., 2006. Flappers and factory lads: Youth and youth culture in inter-war Britain. *History Compass*, 4 (4), 715–730.

Walton, J.K., 2000. *The British seaside: Holidays and resorts in the twentieth century*. Manchester: Manchester University Press.

Williamson, S.H., 2020. Annualized growth rate of various historical economic series. *Measuring Worth*. Available from: www.measuringworth.com/calculators/growth/.

Zweig, F., 1961. *The worker in an affluent society*. London: Heinemann.

9   The environment and environmental policy

Martin Chick

Introduction

One way of viewing modern environmental history is through the optic of time and space. In temporal terms, concerns lengthened from such immediate preoccupations as the smells rising from the polluted canal or the air-borne grit falling on the washing hung out to dry to the current consideration of the impact of climate change on as-yet-unborn generations. As the temporal and spatial concerns respectively lengthened and widened, so too did UK environmental policy come to enjoy a higher political profile while also interacting increasingly with international and global environmental policies. In the process, considerations of international co-operation and of seeking to discourage free-riding arose, free-riding being the decision by countries not to contribute to investments from which they benefited in the belief that other countries would invest anyway. In some cases, such as the depletion of ozone in the atmosphere with springtime peaks around the poles, free-riding countries were carried by the United States, which financed programmes to reduce CFC emissions in their countries. In the case of climate change, free-riding behaviour proved more difficult to overcome. Yet for all that UK environmental policy became increasingly enmeshed with global environmental issues, so too could local issues still carry force at a national level. Some of these tensions were evident in sea fishing, and this is considered in a separate section.(See 'In Focus' section on fisheries) In all considerations of environmental policy, the issue of time was central, albeit of differing lengths in fishing, ozone depletion and climate change. One means of mediating between the obligations of the present to the future is by means of the discount rate (See 'Debates and Interpretations' on discounting).

Different spaces: from local to international

Just as the temporal perspectives in environmental policy discussions changed over time, so too in spatial terms was there a changing interaction between local action and increasing national and international environmental legislation and regulation. Local groups campaigned and acted to improve the quality of their local environment, whether it was in the rivers Tyne or Thames or to protect areas such as Epping Forest near London or Thirlmere in the English Lake District (Skelton 2017; Warde *et al*. 2016, p. 3). As the spatial dimension widened and the temporal perspective lengthened, so too did the objects of concern become less visible. The 40,000 tonnes of Kuwaiti crude oil which was washed on to Cornish beaches from the Liberian-registered oil

DOI: 10.4324/9781003037118-10

Image 9.1 Policeman on point duty seen here using flares to guide the traffic during a heavy smog in London. 8 December 1952

Source: © Trinity Mirror/Mirrorpix/Alamy Stock Photo.

tanker the *Torrey Canyon* as it lay stranded between the Isles of Scilly and Land's End on 18 March 1967, and the coal slag heap which slid down onto the village school in Aberfan on 21 October 1966, killing 144 people, 116 of them children, were two all too visible events. Yet paradoxically, visible, tangible, physical evidence of environmental problems was not what the environmental movement thrived on. Slag heaps, smog and oil spills could all potentially be stopped or at least reduced. It was when environmental problems were less visible, because they were at a distance in space and/or in time, that they seemed to acquire a heightened grip. It was when fauna and flora could no longer be seen that their absence caused worry. One instance of this was the international reaction to the publication of Rachel Carson's (1962) book *Silent Spring*, which attributed the reduced biodiversity, the missing fauna and flora, to the careless use of pesticides.

Acid rain

At a local level, the smog which enveloped London between 5 and 8 December 1952 was visible and tangible. You could taste it, feel it in your hair. The seeping of this smog into Sadler's Wells on 6 December 1952 so reduced visibility that the performance of *La Traviata* was stopped, as many of the audience could no longer see the stage. At least 4,000 people in the Greater London area were thought to have died as smog, this physical and linguistic mix of smoke and fog, weighed on a population for whom bronchitis was a common condition (Gloag 1981, p. 723). One response to smog was to build taller chimneys so as to push pollution higher into the atmosphere. One unintended effect was to push sulphur across the North Sea, to export the previously local problem. While most of the sulphur emitted reached the ground within 100 km of the point of emission, some, whether from high-level or low-level sources, travelled long distances (in some cases 1,000 km or more). As sulphur dioxide along with nitrogen oxides and chlorides precipitated over the mountains of southern Scandinavia, it fell as an acid-rain mix of sulphuric acid, nitric acid and hydrochloric acid. The UK was a net exporter of airborne sulphur and the largest single contributor to the acid rain falling on southern Norway. In time, the effects of acid rain became apparent as trees died, lakes became acidified and fish were killed. In 1969, the Scandinavians successfully pushed for the UN General Assembly to convene an international conference to discuss acid rain, and this call in turn provided an important backdrop to the first United Nations Conference on the Human Environment in Stockholm in 1972 (Chick 2020, pp. 263–266).

The 1972 UN Conference on the Human Environment reflected and signalled the important and growing role for the United Nations in investigating and seeking to resolve global environmental problems. Steadily, environmental problems were addressed at a national, a supranational (as in the European Economic Community) and a global level. The holding of the first UN Conference on the Human Environment in 1972 was also in step with the tenor of the times. Reflecting an increased interest in environmental issues, the UK government established the Royal Commission on Environmental Pollution in 1970 as well as the world's first Department of the Environment (Grove-White 2001, p. 45). Some of the prevailing concerns were with a loss of habitat and species, as reflected in the activities of the Nature Conservancy Council, Wildlife Conservation and the Royal Society for the Protection of Birds. Embedded in the language of conservation and preservation was an implicit concern for the future (Alexander 2015; Moore 1987, 2001).

Stocks and flows: natural resources, population and the Commons

Within broad concerns with the environment, there were also issues of specific concern. One was with the industrialisation of agriculture. In the forty years following the Second World War, about 95% of lowland meadow was lost, 80% of chalk downland, 60% of lowland bogs, 50% of lowland marsh and 40% of lowland heath. The length of hedgerows declined from 495,000 miles in 1947 to 386,000 miles in 1985 as fields were enlarged and agriculture became more specialised. Arable cropping and cereals were increasingly concentrated in the eastern counties, the west specialising in grazing livestock. Pig and poultry production became more concentrated in specialist production units (Dwyer and Hodge 2001, pp. 117–118). Forestry too became industrialised as serried monoculture was pursued in an effort to improve forestry's economic returns. Forests such as that at Kielder in Northumberland which had been planted by the newly established Forestry Commission in 1919 as a response to the strategic shortages of wood revealed during the First World War were, by the 1960s, expected by the Treasury to demonstrate an ability to earn something like a commercial rate of return. Where fast-growing Sitka spruce trees could be planted on marginal low-value land, as in Scotland, then meeting such targets was easier, although still not easy, than on high-value land such as that in Thetford, Norfolk (Foot 2002; Gill 2016, p. 236). This tougher government approach to the complex economics of forestry came at the same time as the growing amenity value of natural areas was recognised, as in the establishment of national parks from the 1950s. In 1980, some of the objections to the industrialisation of the countryside were raised in *The Theft of the Countryside* by Marion Shoard (1980) of the Council for the Protection of Rural England (CPRE), and slowly the Forestry Commission moved from mono-block coniferous culture to planting a more mixed form of woodland.

Roughly coinciding with this heightened interest in environmental issues was a revival of Malthusian anxieties concerning population growth outstripping available resources. In 1968, Paul Ehrlich's book *The Population Bomb* excited much attention, and in 1972 he became president of the Conservation Society (ConSoc), whose membership peaked at 8,700 in November 1973 (Ehrlich 1968). It subsequently lost ground to new groups like Friends of the Earth (founded in late 1970) whose members (termed 'supporters') grew from 1,000 by the end of 1971 to 5,000 in 1976 and 16,000 by 1979 (Herring 2001). Malthusian concerns were also evident in the Club of Rome *Report* of 1972 (Meadows *et al.* 1972). Two other popular books, Edward Mishan's 1967 *The Costs of Economic Growth* and E. F. Schumacher's *Small Is Beautiful* in 1973, were written respectively by a reader in economics at the London School of Economics and a former economic adviser (1950–1970) at the National Coal Board (Mishan 1967; Schumacher 1973). Yet while it was striking that economists were to the fore in writing popular books on environmental issues, this did not mean that there was agreement amongst the ranks of economists as to the extent and nature of any environmental problem. The Oxford economist Wilfred Beckerman was initially happy to review Mishan's book favourably and to urge the importance of environmental issues so strongly on his friend Anthony Crosland that he, Beckerman, found himself appointed to the Royal Commission on Environmental Pollution which Crosland established in 1970. It was only then that, as Beckerman recalled,

> within a few weeks of taking up my appointment and studying the evidence, I discovered, somewhat to my embarrassment, that the impression I had gained from the media, and from much environmentalist literature about pollution trends or the exhaustion of finite resources, was quite false.

(1995, p. 6)

Later, amidst concern about global warming, Beckerman (1995) was to express his politically incorrect scepticism in a book entitled with a taunting nod towards Schumacher, *Small Is Stupid: Blowing the Whistle on the Greens*.

As well as the increased national and international interest in environmental issues, from the late 1960s there was also a developing approach as to how stocks of natural resources should be managed. Where, as with fish and air, resources were renewable, some of the approach centred on a stock-flow model of management. This approach involved not only restricting access to the stock but also seeking to establish a sustainable flow of use of the stock. In economics, discussion of limiting access to a stock of natural resources usually cites an article, 'The Tragedy of the Commons', in 1968 by Garrett Hardin, a professor of biology in the United States who studied the effects of population pressure on the use and availability of natural resources. Hardin's article had a Malthusian underpinning, although his concern was with a particular type of pressure on the Commons, namely with population density in relation to local environmental resources, rather than with population size in aggregate. Nonetheless some of its strictures on breeding were striking, as in the section headed 'Freedom to Breed Is Intolerable', where Hardin stated that 'to couple the concept of freedom to breed with the belief that everyone born has an equal right to the commons is to lock the world into a tragic course of action' (Hardin 1968, p. 1246). Although often cited, in particular areas such as fishing, few of Hardin's arguments were new. Many of these issues affecting fisheries were set out more clearly by Scott and Gordon some fifteen years before Hardin's article (Scott 1955; Gordon 1954; Levhari and Mirman 1980; Turvey 1964). (See 'In Focus' on fisheries.)

In Focus: fisheries

In fishing, technological progress in navigation, in communication and in fishing itself increased the efficiency of fishing and in so doing raised the issue of conservation (Nadelson 1992, p. 477; Loftas 1981, p. 237). Recognising that technological externalities (gear, sonar) were changing the economics of fishing, it was argued that entry to the fishery should be restricted where marginal social cost exceeded marginal private cost (Butlin 1975, pp. 97–8; Cheung 1970). This interest in establishing and asserting property rights over fisheries roughly coincided with leading national governments' wish to claim ownership of the economic resources of the sea (fish, whales) and of the continental shelf (oil) off and contiguous to their coastlines. After the Second World War, the international basis for restricting access to fish was negotiated under the auspices of the United Nations in a drawn-out series of international Law of the Sea Conferences (LOSC). Both before and during these negotiations, individual and groups of countries made their own claims. In 1952, Chile, Ecuador and Peru adopted the Maritime Zone Declaration or Santiago Declaration, and in a series of 'Cod Wars' against the UK, mainly in the 1970s, Iceland also claimed a 200-nm Exclusive Economic Zone (EEZ). Many of these unilateral declarations did in fact become formally encoded in the Law of the Sea Convention. Since an estimated 90% of fisheries yield was taken within 200 nm of coastlines, most fisheries came under national jurisdiction (Costa 1987).

In Britain, the approach to the Law of the Sea Conferences was increasingly complicated by the growing importance of off-shore oil. Initially, the concern was with the differing interests of the inshore and distant-water fishing fleets. Inshore, pelagic fish like herring and mackerel were caught near the surface of the sea. Demersal fish like cod, haddock and plaice were trawled from the bottom of the sea. Demersal fish formed about 75% of the British catch by volume and about 90% by value. Half of the UK demersal catch was caught in third-country waters, with as much as 70% of the total cod catch being so. The UK distant-water fleet fished to depths of 1,200 feet off Newfoundland, Labrador,

Greenland, Iceland, the Norway Coast, Bear Island and grounds in the Barents Sea. Almost without exception these grounds would fall within the UN-projected 200 mile EEZs of other states (Chick 2020, p. 275).

In early UN LOSC negotiations, UK negotiators favoured narrow EEZs so as to protect the interests of the distant-water fishing fleets. However, with the discovery of North Sea oil and gas reserves, UK negotiators switched to arguing for wider EEZs. Although legally different, since drilling rights to oil and gas arose from Continental Shelf legislation, negotiators became concerned that disparities between the areas covered in EEZ and Continental Shelf agreements and laws would make it difficult to oversee and develop oil drilling and exploration activities in the North Sea. Essentially, the Treasury viewed the economic prospects of oil much more highly than those of fishing and did all it could to protect and encourage its oil interests. In Scotland most of the fisheries were inshore, and increasingly, as the interest in oil began to overtake that in gas, the offshore oil and gas industry also moved into the Scottish section of the North Sea. For the UK, matters came to a head in 1973 in the Third LOSC, at which the approaches to setting the limits of the EEZs and Continental Shelves were grouped together. In discussing its approach to the EEZs, UK negotiators in 1973 were also discussing their continental shelf oil interests. UK thinking on the extent of its sea-bed interests was enlivened from 1970 by an increased prospect of finding oil in the shelf surrounding Rockall, an uninhabited granite rock, 230 miles to the west of North Uist (TNA 1970). In 1973, in discussions ahead of the LOSC, the Treasury made it clear 'that the hydrocarbon resources on the UK continental shelf represent our major economic interest in all this' and that where conflicts of interest arose between fishing and oil, then 'there can surely be no doubt that we should be prepared to sacrifice our distant-water fishing rights' (TNA 1973). Ultimately the UK government agreed that from 1 December 1976 British vessels would not fish within the 200-mile limit, a decision which fell hard on the fishing towns of Grimsby, Hull and Fleetwood. The number of distant-water vessels declined from 535 in 1969 to 126 at the end of March 1976, while the number of larger inshore vessels increased from 1,400 in 1965 to 2,140 in 1975 (TNA 1976). With accession to the EEC in 1973 and the phased introduction of the Common Fisheries Policy, distant-water fleets were further hit as EEC fishing rights were calculated on a historic basis, reflecting the previous fishing activity within EEC waters. The effect on fishing communities of UN and EEC negotiations pointed to the interplay between global and local interests in sea fishing. National and local action remained important, even as environmental resources became subject to international legislation and regulation. For all of the global and international agreements in fisheries, the effective operation and monitoring of catch quotas relied on the co-operation of local producer organisations and boat owners. Similarly, even as economic considerations led to the ending of the last commercial whaling operation in Britain with Salvesen's closure at Leith, Edinburgh, it was local pressure on MPs as well as campaigns by Greenpeace and Friends of the Earth which forced a reduction in the use of whale products and a ban on their import from 1973.

Mechanisms and incentives: the Clean Air Act of 1956

As stock-flow approaches were adopted to the management of natural resources, so too was there a move away from an administrative to a market-based approach to the allocation of access to the resources. This was true of natural resources as different as fish and air. The initial belated response to the smogs had been legislative, notably in the Clean Air Act 1956, which arose slowly out of the work of the Beaver Com-mittee on Air Pollution which was (eventually) appointed in July 1953 (Ashby and Anderson 1977). The 1956 Clean Air Act gave local authorities powers to control dark smoke emissions and to declare areas 'smokeless'. By far the greatest progress was made in Greater London, where by 1970 nearly three-quarters of its acreage and premises were covered with control orders. In contrast, the local authorities in the Northern Region and the Midlands had accomplished only about one-third or less of their targets (Scarrow 1972). Of sixty-six authorities which had attained progress of 50 per cent or more, sixty were contiguous to another in the group, and of the forty-seven authorities which had reached less than 10 per cent of their goal, forty-one were contiguous. Reducing your emissions benefited your free-riding neighbour, who might then continue to pollute your shared atmosphere. The smaller the author-ity, then the more likely this was to be so. Smoke emissions reduced even when local authorities did little. In York, the local authorities did not start to implement smoke control zoning until 1970, but York experienced its greatest decline in concentrations between 1960 and 1970 (Brimblecombe and Bowler 1992). Within smokeless areas, householders had often already converted to smokeless appliances by the time their area was scheduled to become smokeless and therefore did not apply for a conversion grant. The increasing use of gas and electricity for domestic heating allied to changes in household occupation as more women entered the labour market and increased efficiency of fuel burn and dispersion from industrial and commercial sources all con-tributed to the fall in smoke emissions. Smogs continued to occur, but less often and with less serious consequences. Between 3 and 7 December 1962, smog in London was associated with an estimated 340 deaths (Newbery 1990, p. 310). While the sul-phur dioxide concentrations in December 1962 were similar to those of 1952, there was now less smoke. As smoke reduced, so visibility improved. It became possible to see right across London most of the winter as the average hours of winter sunshine in London doubled during the 1960s, and average winter visibility improved from being one mile in 1958 to averaging four by the early 1970s. In general, pollution improved sufficiently in London for magpies to return to nesting in Hyde Park for the first time in living ornithological memory.

Higher spaces: CFCs and GHGs

As the spatial and temporal dimensions of air pollution changed, as in concern with the widening of the ozone hole over the poles, and with climate change, then so too did approaches to addressing such problems also change. Given the difficulties of addressing climate change, the ability to address the ozone hole problem was instruc-tive. The problem centred on the release of chlorofluorocarbons (CFCs), which by the early 1970s were widely used in aerosol sprays, refrigerators, air conditioning units and plastic foam. Ostensibly, the restriction of CFCs required a global agree-ment for all to stop using CFCs and to switch to alternatives. Theoretically, efforts to reach international agreement and to take effective action would be bedevilled by the problem of free riding. In practice, however, because the United States was so directly affected by the depletion of the ozone layer, it was prepared to carry free riders. This motivation was greatly bolstered by two Environmental Protection Agency reports in 1987 which estimated that a 50% cut in CFC emissions from 1986 levels could save the United States $64 trillion by 2075 in reduced costs associated with skin cancers. In the long run the costs from cutting CFC use were estimated at anywhere between $20 and $40 billion during the 1989–2075 period, given the projected CFC use growth rates (Sandler 2004, p. 214). So, unlike acid rain, which was rival (what landed in one place did not land elsewhere), the depletion of the ozone layer was a global good (or bad) whose consequences significantly affected the developed economies, notably the United States. The willingness of the United States to finance moves towards the use of available substitutes and to carry free riders was crucial to the success of the Montreal Protocol on Substances That Deplete the Ozone Layer of 1987 (hereafter Montreal Protocol). Cost-benefit calculations by Scott Barrett indicated that for the United States, the benefit which it would receive by implementing the Montreal Protocol, assuming that other countries did nothing, exceeded the cost by 65 to 1. Such calculations rested in part on estimates of the opportunity cost of saving a statistical life, that is, what would it cost to reduce the number of deaths each year by some other means such as improving road safety. While not enjoying such a high benefit:cost ratio as the United States, many developed countries were also willing to finance the implementation of the Montreal Protocol. Belgium, Canada, Norway, Sweden and the UK all banned the use of CFCs in aerosols at the same time as the United States. In the first renegotiation of the Montreal Protocol, held in London in 1990, the industrialised country parties agreed to pay for the 'incremental costs' of implementation by developing countries. This meant that developing countries could not be made worse off by acceding to the agreement; they could only gain (Barrett 2007, pp. 76–81).

In sharp contrast, in the case of greenhouses gases (GHGs), the United States was the largest producer of carbon dioxide, and the worst effects of climate change would not be visited on it but on the less-developed economies. In 1996 of the world's total emissions of carbon dioxide, the United States accounted for 22.2%, China 14.1%, Russian Federation 6.6%, Japan 4.9%, India 4.2%, Germany 3.6% and the UK 2.3% (Sandler 2004, p. 222). In contrast to the effects of CFCs, the main effects of a rise in global warming were likely to fall on the tropical and sub-tropical low-income regions of the world. These poorer countries were the least able to mitigate climate change. The incentives to carry free riders were seriously reduced and made notions of basing the 1992 Kyoto Protocol on climate change on the 1987 Montreal Protocol inappropriate. In the case of GHGs, the incentives to inaction were significant. The marginal cost of abatement rose as the marginal benefit fell, essentially as the easiest and cheapest means of making reductions were tried first and completed. Investment to reduce emissions had opportunity costs not least in terms of investment in adapting to, rather than resisting, climate change.

Time and incentives: taxing carbon

The discussions of how to respond to climate change also raised issues of what mechanisms should be used, as well as how much should be done in the present to help a distant future. (See 'Debates and Interpretations' on discounting.) In addressing the externality of GHGs, the economists' preference was for the use of a carbon tax which would reflect the rising social marginal cost of emissions as it added to the existing stock of CO_2. As the social cost of emissions rose as they added to the stock of CO_2, then so too could the tax be increased. The trend of a rising carbon tax would also be reasonably predictable and would provide clear signals to those investing in new capital equipment that they should favour a plant which was as emissions efficient as possible. In practice, it proved difficult to introduce such a tax. Internationally, developing economies raised objections to being penalised for adding to a long-lasting (over 100 years) stock of CO_2 which was largely not of their making. A political preference for equity over efficiency favoured the allocation of permits for pollution both spatially across the global economy as well as temporally in not penalising those who were saddled with older plants bought in the past (the grandfathering principle). At a more pecuniary level, there was also more money for the private sector in developing and operating carbon trading than in allowing the public collection of a carbon tax. Yet while a tax sets a price and allows quantity to adjust, permits set a quantity for which price adjustments are made through trading (Sorrell and Sijm 2003). A predetermined quantity before trading occurred is rigid and potentially out of kilter with subsequent economic development. In the EU Emissions Trading System (ETS), in which the UK participated, the limits were determined before the 2008 financial crash, such that there was a surplus of emissions rights which was unlikely to be removed before mid-2020. Subsequent rounds of decisions on the size of permitted emissions and the arrangements for trading will be subject to lobbying by interested groups, and the outcomes are unpredictable. This provides less guidance for those making fixed capital investment decisions than does a carbon tax. While some forms of carbon taxation, such as the UK Climate Change Levy (2001–) have been introduced, and particular states and countries have had more success than others, the global nature of the CO_2 problem means that the resistance to carbon taxation on a cross-international level is of concern. At a local level, where price increases are targeted on particular groups, then resistance can be fierce. The protests of road haulage drivers in the UK in 2000 and France in 2018 are examples of this. More likely to succeed is a carbon tax levied at borders on non-carbon taxed imports with the proceeds earmarked for clear public purposes. One such idea is for countries to form a Carbon Club in which members accept that the social cost of carbon is at least $36 (2018, $ per ton of CO_2) and that members would invest as if the target carbon price were $50 per ton CO_2. At present carbon taxes are around $3, so 10% of the estimated social cost of carbon at a time when the annual growth of CO_2 emissions is around 1.8% p.a. (1970–2017). Those who did not join the club would be subject to a tariff of 3% (Nordhaus 2015). The function of the club approach is to address the issue of free riding, which is itself a function of the spatial widening of problems of pollution.

Debates and Interpretations: discounting

Discounting is an approach to thinking about the value of benefits in the future in terms of their current cost. It is a central concept in environmental economics. A simple way to think of discounting is as the reverse of an interest rate. So £1 saved today at 5% p.a. is worth £1.05 in one year's time. Ignoring the finer points of the maths, roughly speaking, that £1.05 in one year's time can be viewed as having a 'present value' today of £1. Thinking about the present value of future benefits is important in deciding whether to proceed with investment projects and in considering how much the present generation should invest for the benefit of often richer and technologically wiser future generations. To the fore of the early twentieth-century thinkers on discounting was Frank Ramsey, a friend of J.M. Keynes. Ramsey's article 'A Mathematical Theory of Saving' was published in *The Economic Journal* in 1928, of which J.M. Keynes was editor (Ramsey 1928). Ramsey considered the temporal issue of what proportion of its income a society should save for the purposes of investment. The thinking of Ramsey and other interwar economists like Pigou remains important. In July 2005 the UK government appointed a team led by the economist Nicholas Stern to examine the economics of climate change, or more formally to assess 'the economics of moving to a low-carbon global economy, focussing on the medium to long-term perspective, and drawing implications for the timescales for action, and the choice of policies and institutions' (Stern 2007, p. ix). Seven of the 37 bibliographical references in Chapter 2 of the Stern review on 'Economics, Ethics and Climate Change' were published between 1921 and 1931. Yet while the early work of Ramsey had concerned the effects of discounting across one and, perhaps, a succeeding overlapping generation, the use of discount rates in climate change discussions involved the discounting of benefits to a very distant generation. Indeed, given the length of time between investment in the present to mitigate some effects of climate change and the distant beneficiaries of such change, the common approach to discounting was awkward. The choice of the discount rate to be used to compare the costs of future action now with benefits in a very distant future proved highly contentious (Broome 1992). In part because of the effect of this length of time on the discounting of distant benefits back to a present value, the Stern report favoured a low social discount rate. This view of Stern was at odds with those of his fellow economists like William Nordhaus, who viewed a real discount rate of 5% as socially efficient (Nordhaus 2006, 2008, 2013; Wagner and Weitzman 2015). Estimating the net present value of the future damages generated by one more tonne of CO_2 emitted at $8, Nordhaus suggested that much of the expenditure on carbon sequestration, wind generation, solar power or biofuel technologies was not socially desirable and that funds would be better spent on R&D as part of a slowly rising ramped response as technology costs fell and demand rose. Stern's use of a smaller real discount rate of 1.4% produced a present value calculation of around $85 per tonne of CO_2 (Gollier 2013, p. 6). Matters are further complicated in climate change discussions by the discount rate being prescriptive rather than descriptive (reflecting current opportunity costs of capital) and also distributive across space, most of the investment made in the present tending to be by developed economies at least as much, if not more, for the benefit of future distant less developed countries (Schelling 1999).

Conclusion

This chapter has pointed to the changing spatial and temporal characteristics of environmental issues and policy, as well as recognising the paradoxes which exist within that perspective. As the spatial dimensions of such issues as air pollution and the use of the seas widened, so too could local initiatives remain important. As the temporal perspectives on what the present should do for the benefit of the future developed, so too did the present reveal a reluctance to pay the true cost of its resource use. For all of the discussion of GHGs and climate change, the resistance to paying a carbon tax has been ingenious and striking. Legal and administrative approaches to the conservation of resources, as in the negotiation of property rights in the sea, have been important, as too has been the use of economic mechanisms in distributing the fishing quotas. In shaping future environmental policy, the mix of administrative and market mechanisms chosen for implementing policies will be at least as important as the stated policy aims.

Further reading

For an insight into key issues in environmental economics, see Stern (2007). On discounting, Price (1993) is clear and perceptive, and on Frank Ramsey, see Misak (2020). International environmental treaty negotiations are discussed by Barrett (2003); fisheries by Clark (2006); and the countryside, woodlands and forests by Smout (2002), Rackham (2006), Mabey (2007) and Williamson *et al.* (2017). In addition to his *Flora Britannica* (Mabey 1996), Mabey (2006) also wrote movingly of the curative effects of nature in easing depression. For an interesting discussion of military spaces and nature, see Dudley (2012), and for enlightening and highly readable discussions of various aspects of environmental history, read Smout (2009).

References

Alexander, I., 2015. *The English love affair with nature*. Oxford and Shrewsbury: Youcaxton Publications.

Ashby, E., and Anderson, M., 1977. Studies in the politics of environmental protection: The historical roots of the British Clean Air Act, 1956. II. The ripening of public opinion, 1898–1952. *Interdisciplinary Science Review*, 2, 190–206.

Barrett, S., 2003. *Environment & statecraft: The strategy of environmental treaty-making*. Oxford: Oxford University Press.

Barrett, S., 2007. *Why cooperate? The incentive to supply public goods*. Oxford: Oxford University Press.

Beckerman, W., 1995. *Small is stupid: Blowing the whistle on the greens*. London: Duckworth.

Brimblecombe, P., and Bowler, C., 1992. The history of air pollution in York, England. *Journal of Air Waste Management Association*, 42, 1562–1566.

Broome, J., 1992. *Counting the cost of global warming*. Cambridge: White Horse.

Butlin, J., 1975. Optimal depletion of a replenish-able resource: An evaluation of recent contributions to fisheries economics. *In:* D. Pearce, ed. *The economics of natural resource depletion*. New York: Wiley, 85–114.

Carson, R., 1962. *Silent spring*. Boston: Houghton Mifflin.

Cheung, S.N.S., 1970. The structure of a contract and the theory of a non-exclusive resource. *Journal of Land Economics*, 13 (1), 49–70.

Chick, M., 2020. *Changing times: Economics, policies, and resource allocation in Britain since 1951*. Oxford: Oxford University Press.

Clark, C.W., 2006. *The worldwide crisis in fisheries: Economic models and human behaviour*. Cambridge: Cambridge University Press.

Costa, E.F., 1987. Peru and the law of the sea convention. *Marine Policy*, January, 45–57.

Dudley, M., 2012. *An environmental history of the U.K. defence estate, 1945 to the present*. London: Continuum.

Dwyer, J., and Hodge, I., 2001. The challenge of change: Demands and expectations for farmed land. *In:* T.C. Smout, ed. *Nature, landscape and people since the Second World War*. East Lothian: Tuckwell Press, 117–134.

Ehrlich, P., 1968. *The population bomb*. New York: Ballantine.

Foot, D., 2002. The twentieth century: Forestry takes off. *In:* T.C. Smout, ed. *People and woods in Scotland: A history.* Edinburgh: Edinburgh University Press, 158–194.

Gill, G., 2016. Kielder forest. *In:* P. Warde, P. Coates and D. Moon, eds. *Local places, global processes.* Oxford: Oxbow Books, 233–238.

Gloag, D., 1981. Air pollutants: The 'classical' pollutants. *British Medical Journal,* 282, 723–725.

Gollier, C., 2013. *Pricing the planet's future: The economics of discounting in an uncertain world.* Princeton: Princeton University Press.

Gordon, S.H., 1954. The economic theory of a common-property resource: The fishery. *Journal of Political Economy,* 62 (2), 124–142.

Grove-White, R., 2001. The rise of the environmental movement, 1970–1990. *In:* T.C. Smout, ed., *Nature, landscape and people since the Second World War.* East Lothian: Tuckwell, 44–51.

Hardin, G., 1968. The tragedy of the commons. *Science,* 162 (3859), 1243–1248.

Herring, H., 2001. The conservation society: Harbinger of the 1970s environment movement in the UK. *Environment and History,* 7, 381–401.

Levhari, D., and Mirman, L.J., 1980. The great fish war: An example using a dynamic Cournot-Nash solution. *Bell Journal of Economics,* 11 (1), 322–334.

Loftas, T., 1981. FAO's EEZ Programme: Assisting a new era in fisheries. *Marine Policy,* July, 229–239.

Mabey, R., 1996. *Flora Britannica.* London: Sinclair-Stevenson.

Mabey, R., 2006. *Nature cure.* London: Pimlico.

Mabey, R., 2007. *Beechcombings: The narratives of trees.* London: Chatto & Windus.

Meadows, D.H., Meadows, D.L., Randers, J., and Behrens, W.W., III, 1972. *The limits to growth: A report for the club of Rome's project on the predicament of mankind.* London: A Potomac Associates Book, Earth Island Limited.

Misak, C., 2020. *Frank Ramsey: A sheer excess of powers.* Oxford: Oxford University Press.

Mishan, E.J., 1967. *The costs of economic growth.* London: Staples Press.

Moore, N.W., 1987. *The bird of time: The science and politics of nature conservation.* Cambridge: Cambridge University Press.

Moore, N.W., 2001. Toxic chemicals and wildlife: Raising awareness and reducing damage. *In:* T.C. Smout, ed. *Nature, landscape and people since the Second World War.* East Lothian: Tuckwell, 25–31.

Nadelson, R., 1992. The exclusive economic zone: State claims and the LOS convention. *Marine Policy,* November, 463–487.

Newbery, D.M., 1990. Acid rain. *Economic Policy,* 5 (11), 297–346.

Nordhaus, W.D., 2006. The Stern review on the economics of climate change, National Bureau of Economic Research, Working Paper, no. 12741, November.

Nordhaus, W.D., 2008. *A question of balance: Weighing the options on global warming policies.* New Haven: Yale University Press.

Nordhaus, W.D., 2013. *The climate casino: Risk, uncertainty and economics for a warming world.* New Haven: Yale University Press.

Nordhaus, W.D., 2015. Climate clubs: Overcoming free-riding in international climate policy. *American Economic Review,* 105 (4), 1339–1370.

Price, C., 1993. *Time, discounting and value.* Oxford: Blackwell.

Rackham, O., 2006. *Woodlands.* London: Collins.

Ramsey, F., 1928. A mathematical theory of saving. *Economic Journal,* 38 (4), 543–559.

Sandler, T., 2004. *Global collective action.* Cambridge: Cambridge University Press.

Scarrow, H.A., 1972. The impact of British domestic air pollution. *British Journal of Political Science,* 2 (3), 261–282.

Schelling, T.G., 1999. Intergenerational discounting. *In:* P.R. Portney and J.P. Weyant, eds. *Discounting and intergenerational equity.* Washington, DC: Resources for the Future, 99–109.

Schumacher, E.F., 1973. *Small is beautiful: A study of economics as if people mattered*. London: Blond & Briggs.

Scott, A., 1955. The fishery: The objectives of sole ownership. *Journal of Political Economy*, 63 (2), 116–124.

Shoard, M., 1980. *The theft of the countryside*. London: Temple Smith.

Skelton, L.J., 2017. *Tyne after Tyne: An environmental history of a river's battle for protection, 1529–2015*. Winwick: White Horse.

Smout, T.C., 2002. *People and woods in Scotland: A history*. Edinburgh: Edinburgh University Press.

Smout, T.C., 2009. *Exploring environmental history: Selected essays*. Edinburgh: Edinburgh University Press.

Sorrell, S., and Sijm, J., 2003. Carbon trading in the policy mix. *Oxford Review of Economic Policy*, 19 (3), 420–437.

Stern, N., 2007. *The economics of climate change: The Stern review*. Cambridge: Cambridge University Press.

The National Archives, Kew (henceforth TNA), 1970. CAB 148/107, Defence and Overseas Policy Committee (70) 6, The Peaceful Use of the Sea-Bed Beyond the Limits of National Jurisdiction, 'Future British Policy in United Nations Seabed Committee', 15 December.

TNA, 1973. T224/3092, Note, Law of the Sea, DOP(73)20, 6 March.

TNA, 1976. CAB 164/1353, Policy for the fishing industry, June.

Turvey, R., 1964. Optimisation and sub-optimisation in fisheries regulation. *American Economic Review*, 54 (2), Part 1, 64–76.

Wagner, G., and Weitzman, M., 2015. *Climate shock: The economic consequences of a hotter planet*. Princeton: Princeton University Press.

Warde, P., Coates, P., and Moon, D., 2016. Local places, global processes: In search of the environment. *In*: P. Warde, P. Coates and D. Moon, eds. *Local places, global processes*. Oxford: Oxbow Books, 1–15.

Williamson, T., Barnes, G., and Pillatt, T., 2017. *Trees in England: Management and disease since 1600*. Hatfield: University of Hertfordshire Press.

10 Big business and management in Britain

John F. Wilson

Introduction

Charting the evolution of big business and management in Britain over the course of the twentieth century provides some fascinating insights into both the nature of these activities and the way in which they interact with many other aspects of a highly complex socio-economic environment. First, it is important to highlight several continuous features of the business scene, such as the role of the City of London, alongside the growth in multinational transactions. At the same time, there were many fundamental discontinuities, for example, the scale and scope of business operations, attitudes to the practice of and training for management, state-business relations and the impact of foreign firms and investors on business practices. The key drivers that influenced change in British business and management were a combination of external elements (market-cum-technological and institutional-cultural factors) and the internal dynamics associated with business policy and practice. While an extensive evaluation of these drivers would occupy too much space (Wilson and Thomson 2006a, 2006b), it is vital to bear in mind how external and internal factors combined to precipitate change in both the scale and nature of business operations over a century that featured a wide range of different challenges and opportunities.

Starting with a brief insight into the nature of business and management in the late nineteenth century, a key feature of this chapter will be the vital importance of merger activity, precipitating the creation of multi-billion-pound business empires. It is consequently important to explain why acquisition became such a vital dimension of corporate strategy. Similarly, nationalisation of key sectors in the 1940s, and later privatisation from the 1980s, would further facilitate the increased scale of business, while the policies of certain governments in the 1930s and 1960s encouraged oligopolistic concentration in both staple and new industries. Crucially, these influences would stimulate a demand for more sophisticated management structures, which in turn helped to persuade universities to develop management education, imitating especially the American practice of establishing university business schools as a major source of managerial talent. Indeed, as the century progressed international influences on the strategy and structure of British business became ever more prevalent, a decisive trend that was accentuated even further from the 1980s as both multinational activity intensified and the equity quoted on the London Stock Exchange passed into the hands of overseas investors. The latter in particular was also associated with the rise of what has come to be known as 'financialisation', which, alongside its attendant corporate scandals and deep concerns about executive behaviour, has come to dominate

DOI: 10.4324/9781003037118-11

British business strategy (Froud *et al.* 2006). It is consequently unclear whether the way in which business and management had evolved was greeted with enthusiasm, providing a challenging conclusion to this chapter.

Business and management up to the 1940s

Until recently, one of the most dominant depictions of British business in the period up to the 1940s was the preponderance of what Chandler (1990) refers to as 'Personal Capitalism', or rather a system based on family control and ownership, with limited managerial hierarchies that recruited relatively few professional managers. Chandler (1990) also contrasted what he felt were Britain's relatively small-scale, specialist firms with the integrated, large-scale 'Managerial Capitalism' of the United States. Others (Payne 1984; Wilson 1995) were also convinced that family firms dominated British business, possibly until the 1970s, providing abundant evidence to support the paradigm. Over the last thirty years, however, extensive research has revised aspects of this view, highlighting that in 1914 not only were British firms as large as their American and European counterparts (Wardley 1991), but also the divorce between control and ownership was greater than in any other economy, including the United States (Foreman-Peck and Hannah 2012). While these revelations have done much to alter our view of pre-1914 British business, it is essential to remember that most of the large-scale firms that had emerged by that time were dominated by the holding company structure, which can be regarded as an intermediate stage between the family firm and a managerial form. Although Quail (2002) has coined the term 'Proprietorial Capitalism' to describe this system, it is important to remember that the holding company was still dominated by a board of directors populated by the principal shareholders, who brooked little interference from managers in the way that the business operated.

Another dimension of Chandler's (1990) critique was his claim that British competitiveness was undermined by the failure to make interdependent investments in production, marketing and management. This highlights how the 'Chandlerian Model' was driven by the internalisation of scale and scope economies made possible by the Second Industrial Revolution, adopting the large multidivisional form (M-form) of organisation as an effective vehicle to manage increasingly diversified and integrated operations. As Wilson and Popp (2003) demonstrated, however, well into the twentieth century, most British industries operated in deeply embedded districts that offered considerable advantages to those willing to externalise their business activities, whether in terms of either production and labour management or marketing and sales. This limited the development of management as the main internal mechanism for operationalising transactions, demonstrating how in the long term British business was consequently disadvantaged by the extensive externalisation of functions (Wilson and Thomson 2006a).

Another key factor in this scenario is the socio-cultural environment in which business and management operated. While there are many dimensions to this debate (Wilson 1995), it is clear that manufacturing industry has never attained the prestigious social and political positions achieved by finance and commerce, significantly undermining the former's ability to recruit the best talent into its managerial hierarchies. This in part reflected a geographical dimension, with industry focused above a line from the Severn to the Wash and finance and commerce below it, with London as the hub of Empire and of power. Moreover, from the early days of industry, a considerable

Table 10.1 Merger activity in UK manufacturing industry, 1880–1950

	No. of firms disappearing	Values (at current prices) £m	Values (at 1961 prices) £m	Merger value as % of TIE[a]
1880–9	207	10	136	–
1890–9	769	42	401	–
1900–9	659	55	483	–
1910–9	750	161–173[b]	998–1060[b]	–
1920–9	1884	360–411[b]	1654–1886[b]	32
1930–9	1414	184–218[b]	759–907	21[c]
1940–9	778	–	–	–

Source: Hannah (1983, p. 178).

Key:

[a] TIE – total investment expenditure.

[b] There was a major break in the series at these dates, leading Hannah to offer a range of estimates.

[c] For 1930–1938 only.

section of public opinion regarded manufacturing as exploitative, in contrast to the dignity and traditions of the professions, ancient universities and landed interests. As we shall see later, the education system was also less than supportive of vocational training, with universities taking over eighty years before they imitated the American system of management education that emerged in the 1880s (Wilson 1995).

Having noted these prominent features of the British scene up to the 1940s, it is equally important to evaluate some of the key developments in an era dominated by world wars and global economic depression. Crucially, merger activity had been rife in several industries (cotton textiles, brewing, heavy engineering and mining) since the 1880s, as Table 10.1 illustrates, while in the interwar era this activity intensified and corporate giants such as ICI, Unilever and Cadbury-Fry were formed. No less than 22 of the Top 100 firms in 1970 were created at that time (Hannah 1983), resulting in the development of an oligopolistic trading structure across most British industries. This prominent characteristic was also reinforced from the 1930s by the creation of strong trade associations that cartelised market structures through price and market controls, exploiting the shelter afforded by the introduction of protectionism in 1931 and the limited international competition of the 1940s. The impact of these developments can be seen in Figure 10.1, because while the concentration of manufacturing output in the Top 100 firms had been increasing since the turn of the century, there was a hiatus during the 1930s and 1940s. Even though by the late 1960s anti-monopoly legislation had broken up the previously dominant trade associations, oligopolistic market structures had become a permanent feature of the British business scene, largely as a result of further waves of merger and acquisition activity.

Although in many ways these British trends mirrored those in the United States, Japan and Germany, one must bear in mind Hannah's (1980) warning that distinctive national characteristics played key roles in fashioning organisational outcomes. In particular, it is clear that managerial hierarchies had failed to evolve from the

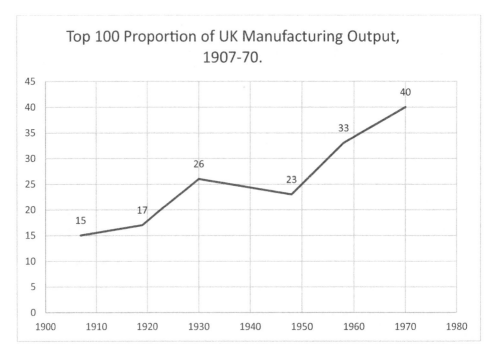

Figure 10.1 Top 100 proportion of UK manufacturing output, 1907–70

Source: Hannah (1983).

'Proprietorial' system mentioned earlier into a more 'Managerial' form, most British companies preferring a holding company pattern of organisation that limited the opportunities to exploit both scale and scope economies (Wilson and Thomson 2006a). This again highlights the earlier point that while British business had since the late nineteenth century been experiencing an extensive divorce between control and ownership, corporate governance remained extremely weak, with shareholders rarely challenging the actions of executive directors (Tilba 2017). At the same time, the attitude towards the recruitment and development of managers had barely changed by the 1950s, Woodward (1965) arguing that there was a prejudicial attitudes towards professional qualifications. Chartered accountants proved an exception to this rule (Matthews *et al.* 1998), primarily because of the need to conform to increasingly complex accounting regulations rather than providing a degree of professionalism on company boards.

Business transformation in the late twentieth century

Starting in the 1960s, and accelerating rapidly after the economically traumatic 1970s and 1980s, business and management in Britain experienced a transformation. The principal drivers of change were the market-cum-technological environment alongside legal and financial reforms that obliged senior management to follow especially

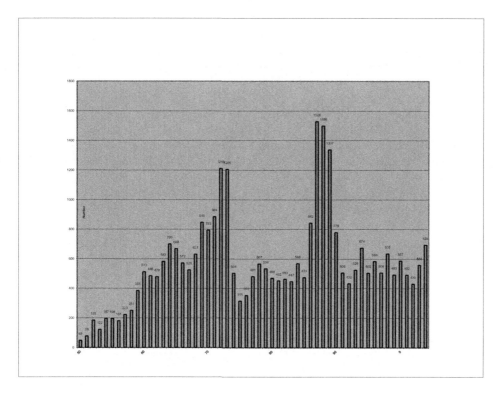

Figure 10.2 Number of companies acquired in UK mergers, 1950–2004

Source: Wilson and Thomson (2006a).

American approaches to management and organisation. One of the most obvious manifestations of this transformation was the internationalisation of British business, because while up to the 1950s many firms had developed overseas ventures, by the 1990s these operations had become highly integrated multinational operations with extensive cross-border supply chains (Dicken 1986). Moreover, foreign investors were eagerly buying the equity of British companies floated on the London Stock Exchange, precipitating later debates about whether big firms could be classified as 'British' and how control of investment strategies was moving overseas.

Although we have already emphasised the role of merger and acquisition activity in significantly altering the British business landscape prior to 1940, it is apparent from Figure 10.2 that, especially in the 1960s and 1970s, an even greater number of firms disappeared as a direct result of predatory behaviour. A key driver behind these waves was the overwhelming desire for market control, a point illustrated in Figure 10.1, with concentration levels in manufacturing continuing to rise after the 1940s hiatus. A distinctly new feature of the post-1950 era, however, was the emergence of the take-over bid, a technique that had hardly been recognised in previous decades but which in the late twentieth century became a major feature of business strategy. The essential context for this development was a recognition by aggressive entrepreneurs such as Charles Clore and Hugh Fraser in the early 1950s that they could bid directly to large numbers of passive shareholders rather than negotiate with boards of directors, wresting control of assets by offering better returns on investments. This highlighted the increased importance of the City of London and the financial institutions and intermediaries that populated the 'square mile' (Michie 1999). Indeed, over this period the City moved from being a provider of financial services to a principal driver of business strategy, with executives fearful of a takeover bid from rivals unless they maintained a healthy dividend income and improvements in share prices. These pressures inevitably resulted in the development of a short-termist mentality amongst British executives, accentuated by a desire for scale as an effective defence against predators. Crucially, by the 1960s an institutionalised market for corporate control had taken a decisive grip of business activity on both sides of the Atlantic (Chandler 1992), resulting in the emergence of 'financialisation' as the key driver of corporate strategy.

Having highlighted this decisive switch in emphasis across British merger activity from the 1950s, it is also important to remember the other forces that strongly encouraged the growth in scale. In this context, we exclude those industries (coalmining, railways and canals, gas and electricity supply and steel) that were nationalised after the Second World War by a Labour government intent on maintaining full employment. In any case, these monopolistic entities failed to demonstrate any of the advantages of concentration, because they were not only managed in a highly bureaucratic way, but restrictive governmental interference and a legacy of under-investment significantly hampered performance (Millward 2017). More importantly, the market-cum-technological environment and institutional-cultural factors contributed decisively to the urge to concentrate business activity. Other chapters in this volume will explain and analyse the improvements in living standards after the wartime and post-war restrictions had faded by the early 1950s, creating a vibrant domestic market that was characterised by full employment and rising incomes (Pollard 1992).

At the same time, successive governments moved decisively to stimulate competition by severely restricting the influence of trade associations and their price-fixing activities (Walshe 1991). Ironically, however, by eliminating restrictive practices, firms responded by seeking more mergers in order to effect greater market control (Newbould 1970). It was also increasingly evident that as a signatory to the General Agreement on Tariffs and Trade (GATT) in 1948, British business could no longer be protected against foreign competition. Of course, it was not until the late 1950s and 1960s that British industry started to feel the full effects of foreign competition in the domestic market, Germany and Japan especially having been obliged to focus on recovery after 1945. Nevertheless, in key growth sectors (automobiles, domestic appliances and electronics), it was increasingly apparent that foreign products were better designed and more efficient, British firms having failed to invest in modern production technology when competition was limited (Broadberry 1997).

As a direct result of these factors, and especially the fear that British industry was falling behind in key sectors, in the late 1960s another Labour government experimented with a state-led vehicle for concentration, the Industrial Reorganisation Corporation (IRC). Earlier in the decade, prompted by overcapacity in the industry and the need to combine resources in order to fund increasingly expensive development projects (Gardner 1981), a Conservative government had persuaded twenty aircraft companies to merge into three groups. The IRC, on the other hand, was created specifically with the intention of concentrating business activity in bigger firms across key high-technology sectors in order to compete with much larger American corporations

Image 10.1 Aerial view of the City of London: the Gherkin

Source: © APS(UK)/Alamy Stock photo.

that were coming to dominate international markets. In total, the IRC was involved in ninety projects, the most outstanding of which were mergers resulting in the creation of British Leyland (automobiles), GEC (electrical and electronic engineering), ICL (computers) and Swann-Hunter (shipbuilding) (Hague 1983).

While many contemporaries supported the IRC's drive for scale, one might argue that given the intense merger wave of the late 1960s (see Figure 10.2), when over 2,200 companies disappeared through acquisitions, government intervention was unnecessary. Similarly, even though GEC proved highly durable, many of the new ventures were short lived, while British Leyland (see 'Debates and Interpretations') required another Labour government to provide extensive subsidies and fresh management when the conglomerate went bust (Cowling 1980). On the other hand, the IRC simply reflected the universal drive to scale across British business, with the City playing an increasingly influential role as a catalyst. Moreover, it was City institutions and intermediaries that benefitted most from mergers, while executives in predator companies would appear to have secured both enhanced prestige and significant increases in remuneration (Cowling 1980). This highlights another key conclusion from the research into merger activity, because, as Walshe (1991) concluded, rarely did merger activity result in greater industrial efficiency. One might add to this damning conclusion by reemphasising that short-termism had come to dominate investment strategies by the 1970s, with City interests exerting enormous influence over executives whose only focus would appear to have been maximising shareholder value.

Who were the shareholders? As Figure 10.3 reveals, from the early 1960s decisive changes occurred in the nature of shareholding, with the proportion owned by individuals falling precipitously and institutional shareholders coming to dominate activity. This reflected a significant change in investment behaviour, because individuals

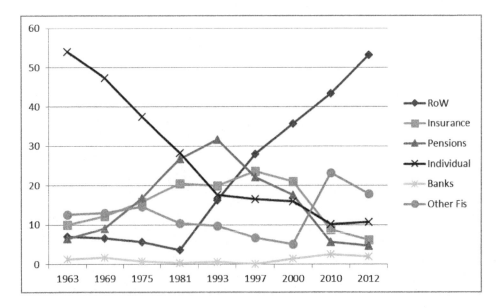

Figure 10.3 Beneficial ownership of UK equities, 1963–2010

Source: Buchnea et al. (2019).

increasingly preferred to invest their savings through pension funds, insurance companies and investment trusts, in the belief that these professionals could generate better returns. Although overseas investors ('RoW' [rest of the world] in Figure 10.3) would by the turn of the century become the largest single group, institutional investors have since the 1960s been major players on the London Stock Exchange. At the same time, one must always remember that they rarely interfered directly with the fashioning of corporate strategy, preferring instead to influence executives through the buying and selling of shares (Tilba and Wilson 2017).

Having highlighted the disengaged relationship between shareholders and companies, Scott (1987) noted that a new corporate class had evolved, characterised by intense intercorporate links across both financial and non-financial enterprises. This conclusion has recently been substantiated by the detailed research of Wilson *et al.* (2017), which highlighted how by the 1970s financial institutions were extensively connected to the Top 250 firms through interlinking directorships. Indeed, by the time of the 'Big Bang' in 1986, when City practices were radically transformed as a result of both computerisation and the liberalisation of traditional restrictive practices (Thomas 1986), big business and financial institutions had become intimately interconnected. It is also worth adding that while trade associations had been significantly undermined by anti-monopoly legislation, there was still a considerable amount of intra-industry connectivity, providing extensive opportunities for information sharing and collaboration. Although a long series of corporate governance reforms stretching from 1992 to 2019 helped to break up this kind of business interaction (Tilba 2017), and British corporate networks dissipated somewhat from the 1990s (Buchnea *et al.* 2019), it is fair to conclude that financialisation dominated British business (Froud *et al.* 2006).

Management, managers and corporate culture

With big business in Britain coming to be dominated by the market for corporate control, and scale continually being regarded as both a defence against take-overs and a base for achieving greater economies of scale, it is equally important to examine the way in which management and corporate structures responded to various organisational challenges. One of these was associated with scale and scope, with Prais (1976) calculating that while in 1958 the 100 largest manufacturing companies had an average of 27 plants, by 1972 this number had risen to 72. Channon (1973) has also noted that, whereas only 25 of the top 100 companies could be considered diversified in 1950, this had increased to 60 per cent by 1970. A decisive feature of these processes was the emergence of conglomerates, or firms that operated across different, unrelated industries, with Hanson Trust and Trafalgar House being the most prominent. Often associated with asset stripping and highly speculative investments, conglomerates enjoyed a period of dominance up to the 1990s when they encapsulated the market for corporate control and short-termism.

Perhaps the most significant organisational challenge facing British firms at that time was how effectively to manage their overseas activities. Across the twentieth century, the UK has consistently contributed more than any other economy except the United States to global foreign direct investment (FDI). Jones (1986) has revealed that overseas subsidiaries rarely performed well financially, and most were located in Empire markets that lacked sophistication and depth (Jones 1985; Dunning 1983). From the 1960s, however, Western Europe became the main focus of attention (Rollings

2007), given the rapid development of those economies that initiated the Common Market (now the European Union). In the late twentieth century, British business also increased its reliance on overseas investment, because by 1990 the stock of FDI accounted for 25.1 per cent of UK GDP, compared to just 7.9 per cent in the United States and 6.8 per cent in Japan (Stopford and Turner 1985).

Another feature of globalisation was the establishment of subsidiaries in Britain by foreign companies, especially in the high-growth sectors of electronics, automobiles, domestic appliances and petro-chemicals (Bostock and Jones 1994). Again, this was not unique to the post-1950 era, because industries such as electrical engineering and automobiles had featured especially American subsidiaries since the 1890s, often reaching dominant positions as a result of their larger investments in new technologies. This characteristic was also a key feature of the late twentieth century, as substantial Japanese investments in automobile and electronics production effectively ensured that these industries survived in Britain (Trevor 1987). Apart from benefitting directly from these investments in what have continued to be high-growth sectors of the world economy, British business was able to imitate the management and organisational techniques that had made these foreign multinationals so successful. Moreover, and especially given the prominent role played by the City of London in funding international trade, shipping and insurance, this provided significant support to Britain's consistently weak balance of payments.

In this context, one must return to Chandler's (1990) view that British managerial hierarchies had been slow to evolve up to the 1940s, given the extensive preference for a holding company form that limited the degree of cohesion required in large-scale firms. In the United States, on the other hand, the multidivisional form (M-form) had evolved, largely in the highly diversified sectors such as chemicals and engineering. The key point about the M-form was its ability to effect the kind of integration which was essential when managing a diversified and vertically integrated range of operations. Although there has been some debate amongst American business historians about the nature and effectiveness of the M-form as it functioned in the United States (Freeland 2001), it is interesting to note that by 1950 only 12 of the Top 100 British firms had adopted this structure (Channon 1973). By 1993, however, 90 of the Top 100 were classified as M-forms (Whittington and Mayer 2002), indicating clearly how executives had responded to the organisational pressures imposed by their strategies. A key influence on these executives had been American consultancy firms such as McKinsey & Co, and, although Channon (1973) was critical of the extent to which British M-forms matched their American counterparts, at the very least there had been significant organisational progress. Indeed, Quail (2000, p. 14) has concluded that by 1990 a significant shift had taken place in terms of organisational refinement and management recruitment, reflecting the increased dominance of executive power at a time when the legal status of trade unions had been significantly diminished.

Another decisive dimension to this narrative was the internalisation of labour management. Although in the context of a full employment economy up to the 1970s, management struggled to impose its will on a strong trade union movement, increasingly over the post-war decades control of the shopfloor swung in favour of the former (Gospel 2005). The decisive moves came in the early 1980s, when a Conservative government enacted legislation that significantly undermined trade union effectiveness, providing management with an opportunity to develop more elaborate control systems. In addition, management accountancy became a much more intrinsic feature of business operations, reflecting the desire by management to introduce financial planning and control techniques after decades of neglect in this respect.

As a direct result of these developments, there was an enormous increase in demand for managers, as firms built larger and more sophisticated organisations that were run from top to bottom by those who owned either none or very little of the equity. Crucially, merit was increasingly recognised as the essential criterion for recruitment, rather than social background (Thomson *et al*. 2001). As Perkin (1990) indicates, this reflected a more general development associated with the rise of a 'professional society', indicating how changes in the socio-cultural environment were positively benefiting business. This resulted in management as a career becoming much more socially acceptable, with professional associations expanding their membership (Wilson and Thomson 2006a) and universities establishing business and management programmes that rapidly grew in scale and scope (see the 'In Focus' section). Although only 30 per cent of managers possessed degrees in 2000, the vast majority had undergone some training for their role, often through the increased number of management traineeships that had emerged for graduates.

An important caveat in this respect, however, is the acute gender imbalance in British management, because while the proportion of women managers had increased from 1.8 per cent in 1974 to 31.1 per cent by 2004 (CMI 2004), only 13.2 per cent of company directors were women by the end of that period. Indeed, women in business generally remains an area in need of considerable research (Doe 2017), as well as analysis of why management has been perceived as an essentially masculine activity. Although university business schools are leading the way in achieving an improved gender balance in management, because women account for almost one-half of all graduates and positive recruitment strategies are being enacted (Wilson and Thomson 2006a), women are still grossly underrepresented at executive and board levels of management. Among the largest publicly listed companies in the European Union in 2019, only 17.6 per cent of executives and 6.9 per cent of CEOs were women, indicating that this was not solely a British phenomenon (EIGE 2019).

In Focus: the rise of management education

A key feature of the British management scene by the 1990s was the rapid expansion of management education at university level. Although it was 1965 before two business schools had been formed, by London and Manchester universities, over eighty years after American universities had started to invest in this application of social science disciplines (Wilson 1995), by the 1990s there were more undergraduate students studying business than any other subject. Moreover, this ascendancy has continued up to 2020, indicating the extent to which students (especially after the introduction of tuition fees in 1997) gravitated towards what in the past had been regarded as a vocational education. One might even argue that the rapid and sustained expansion of business studies has been fundamental to the expansion of British universities since the 1990s, because not only have a growing number of British students enrolled in these programmes, but international students have also been willing to pay even higher fees, especially on business school master's programmes. Crucially, as far as British business and management are concerned, this created a much-expanded pool of talent.

Debates and Interpretations: British Leyland

Formed in 1968 by combining British Motor Holdings Ltd (BMH) with the Leyland Motor Co, British Leyland (BL) was a direct result of IRC intervention (Davis 1970, pp. 94–109). Prime Minister Harold Wilson chose Sir Donald Stokes as managing director, because he was regarded as one of the dynamic new breed of managers capable of building businesses which would be capable of competing with large American multinationals such as Ford and General Motors. By 1975, however, having accounted for 40 per cent of new car registrations at the time of its merger, BL's share (31 per cent) had fallen below the import sector's (33 per cent) for the first time. Even though an M-form structure was introduced in 1969, the group still remained largely unconsolidated seven years after the merger, and few of the advantages of merger were ever achieved (Channon 1973, p. 106). Indeed, severe financial difficulties featured prominently (Cowling 1980, pp. 186–190), resulting in another Labour government nationalising the company in 1975. This is a damning indictment of the largest merger of this period, as it was obliged to fall under the management of the new Labour government's agent for industrial intervention, the National Enterprise Board (NEB), and by 1977 a new chief executive, Sir Michael Edwardes. Even though this South African introduced fundamental changes to the organisation (Edwardes 1983, pp. 36–59), there was loud criticism of BL's 'market-led failure', because the new models introduced in 1981 (Metro) and 1983 (Maestro) were initially produced in insufficient numbers either to cover total charges or boost market share (Church 1994). Edwardes was also replaced by the Canadian Graham Day in 1982, because the Conservative government lost faith in Edwardes' ability to engineer a financial recovery at BL. Day experienced a similar challenge, finally acquiescing to the overwhelming power of foreign (and especially Japanese) competition by selling the car division to British Aerospace in 1988 for just £150 million. By that time what had been renamed The Rover Group held just 13 per cent of the British car market, while Japanese multinationals such as Nissan, Honda and Toyota established substantial subsidiaries in Britain during the 1980s, dominating the industry for the next thirty years. While a single case study cannot be regarded as symbolic of all British business, BL demonstrates how strategies and structures went wrong so badly at a time when foreign competitors were more successful in the high-growth sectors of world trade.

Conclusion

It is clear that by 2000 British business and management had evolved significantly when compared to 1900. These changes had happened because business was responding energetically to the market-cum-technological and institutional-cultural drivers that had featured so prominently over the century (Wilson and Thomson 2006a). In particular, the status of business and management had altered dramatically, elevating itself as a direct result of both socio-cultural changes and increased interaction with the state. The role played by the City of London has been an especially powerful force in these respects, giving rise to a business world dominated by financialisation. Although Higgins and Toms (2013) have demonstrated that even by the 1990s family firms were more profitable than those in which there had been an extensive divorce between control and ownership, the latter were by then extremely powerful agents of economic and political power because of their scale and connections (Buchnea *et al.* 2019).

Having noted these decisive changes in the status and influence of business and management, fundamental questions have been asked about the nature of capitalistic enterprise, especially after the 2007–08 global financial crisis precipitated a major debate about financialisation. With banks and other major financial institutions either collapsing entirely or requiring substantial state bail-outs, it was clear to many that change was required. The global financial crisis had also been preceded by a plethora of cases in which corporate executives had abused the lack of engagement by either regulators or shareholders, precipitating corporate collapses measured in hundreds of millions of dollars. Space limitations prevent a detailed analysis of these cases (van Driel 2019), but the very mention of Guinness, Ferranti, Polly Peck, Mirror Group Newspapers, the dot.com crash of 2001, Enron, Royal Bank of Scotland and Halifax Bank of Scotland resonate with the chorus of demands to curb excesses perpetrated by uncontrolled executives. As Kay (2019, p. 1136) has emphasised, one of the direct consequences of the Anglo-American preoccupation with shareholder value had been the emergence of the 'cult of the heroic CEO', directly personalising financial success with an individual whose power went largely uncontested. This acute lack of accountability also proved a challenge to the evolving corporate governance codes enacted from 1992, because while a series of these featured over the period 1992–2019, few regard them as effective in curbing executive excess. Clearly, while in the United States a strong legislative framework was put in place after the Enron scandal, in the form of the Sarbanes Oxley Act of 2003, the British codes failed to prevent further corporate crises precipitated by executive malfeasance (Tilba 2017; Toms 2017).

The challenge to financialisation has recently become a major debate on both sides of the Atlantic, involving academics, practitioners and policy-makers. This debate has focused primarily on the nature of the Anglo-Saxon corporation and specifically the relationship between owners and managers, highlighting the acute dangers associated with the disengaged relationship that is characteristic of financialisation. In this context, business ethics has become a major focus of attention, alongside a drive to encourage executives to adopt much more responsible strategies that not only sustain the business for which they are responsible but also limit waste and reduce carbon footprints. While it is clear that only slowly are British companies responding to these pressures, increasingly influential voices are beginning to be heard in boardrooms. The British Academy has recently funded a major research project headed by Colin Mayer to examine 'the future of the corporation', challenging the ethical basis of strategies aimed solely at increasing shareholder value and obliging companies to align more effectively business and public interests. Whether this will restore trust in corporate executives, and especially the financial institutions that underpin the whole financialisation edifice, is debatable, but at least the debate is continuing and traditional practices are being challenged.

Further reading

Apart from the long-term studies by Wilson (1995) and Wilson and Thomson (2006a), the most useful sources are by Hannah (1983) and Buchnea *et al.* (2019). On the subject of financialisation, Froud *et al.* (2006) provide extensive detail, while Michie (1999) covers the history of the London Stock Exchange.

References

Bostock, F., and Jones, G., 1994. Foreign multinationals in British manufacturing, 1850–1962. *Business History*, 36 (1).

Broadberry, S., 1997. *Productivity race: British manufacturing in international perspective, 1850–1990*. Cambridge: Cambridge University Press.

Buchnea, E., Tilba, A., and Wilson, J.F., 2019. British corporate networks, 1976–2010: Extending the study of finance–industry relationships. *Business History*, 61 (4).

Chandler, A.D., 1990. *Scale and scope: The dynamics of industrial capitalism*. Cambridge: Harvard University Press.

Chandler, A.D., 1992. Managerial enterprise and competitive capabilities. *In:* C. Harvey and G. Jones, eds. *Organisational capability and competitive advantage*, Special Issue of *Business History*, 34. London: Frank Cass.

Channon, D., 1973. *Strategy and structure of British enterprise*. Cambridge: Harvard University Press.

Chartered Management Institute (CMI), 2004. *Business continuity survey*. London: HMSO.

Church, R., 1994. *Rise and decline of the British motor industry*. London: Macmillan.

Cowling, K., 1980. *Mergers and economic performance*. Cambridge: Cambridge University Press.

Davis, W., 1970. *Merger mania*. London: Constable.

Dicken, P., 1986. *Global shift*. London: Sage.

Doe, H., 2017. Gender and business: Women in business or businesswomen? An assessment of the history of entrepreneurial women. *In:* J.F. Wilson, *et al.*, eds. *Routledge companion to business history*. Abingdon: Routledge, 347–357.

Dunning, J., 1983. Changes in the level and structure of international production: The last 100 years. *In:* M. Casson, ed. *Growth of international business*. London: George Allen & Unwin, 25–34.

Edwardes, M., 1983. *Back from the brink: An apocalyptic experience*. London: Pan.

European Institute for Gender Equality, 2019. Largest listed companies: CEOs, executives and non-executives. *Gender Statistics Database*. Available from: https://eige.europa.eu.

Foreman-Peck, J., and Hannah, L., 2012. Some consequences of the early twentieth-century divorce of ownership from control. *Business History*, 55 (4).

Freeland, R.F., 2001. *The struggle for control of the modern corporation. Organizational change at General Motors, 1920s to the 1970s*. Cambridge: Cambridge University Press.

Froud, J., Johal, S., Leaver, A., and Williams, K., 2006. *Financialisation and strategy. Narrative and numbers*. Abingdon: Routledge.

Gardner, C., 1981. *British Aircraft Corporation: A history*. London: Batsford.

Gospel, H., 2005. *Markets, firms and the management of labour*. Cambridge: Cambridge University Press.

Hague, D., 1983. *IRC: An experiment in industrial intervention*. London: George Allen & Unwin.

Hannah, L., 1980. Visible and invisible hands in Great Britain. *In:* A.D. Chandler and H. Daems, eds., *Managerial hierarchies: Comparative perspectives on the rise of the modern Industrial enterprise*. Cambridge: Harvard University Press, 1–24.

Hannah, L., 1983. *Rise of the corporate economy*. London: Methuen.

Higgins, D.M., and Toms, S., 2013. Explaining corporate success: The structure and performance of British firms, 1950–84. *Business History*, special issue on 'Mapping European Corporations', 56 (2).

Jones, G., 1986. Origins, management and performance. *In:* G. Jones, ed. *British multinationals: Origins, management and performance*. London: Gower, 1–12.

Kay, J., 2019. The concept of the corporation. Special Issue: Leslie Hannah Festschrift, *Business History*, 61 (7).

Matthews, D., Anderson, M., and Edwards, J., 1998. *Priesthood of industry: The rise of the professional accountant in British management*. Oxford: Oxford University Press.

Michie, R., 1999. *The London stock exchange. A history*. Oxford: Oxford University Press.

Millward, R., 2017. Business institutions and the state. *In:* J.F. Wilson, *et al.*, eds. *Routledge companion to business history*. Abingdon: Routledge, 274–299.

Newbould, G.D., 1970. *Management and merger activity*. London: Guthstead.

Payne, P., 1984. Family business in Britain: An historical and analytical survey. *In:* A. Okochi and S. Yasuoka, eds. *Family business in the era of industrial growth*. Tokyo: Tokyo University Press, 1–26.

Perkin, W., 1990. *Rise of professional society: England since 1880*. Abingdon: Routledge.

Pollard, S., 1992. *Development of the British economy, 1914–1990*. London: Edward Arnold.

Prais, S.J., 1976. *Evolution of giant firms: A study of the growth of concentration in manufacturing industry in Britain*. Cambridge: Cambridge University Press.

Quail, J., 2000. The proprietorial theory of the firm and its consequences. *Journal of Industrial History*, 3 (1).

Quail, J., 2002. Visible hands and invisible hands: Understanding the managerial revolution in the UK. *Journal of Industrial History*, 5 (2).

Rollings, N., 2007. *British business in the formative years of European integration, 1945–1973*. Cambridge: Cambridge University Press.

Scott, J., 1987. *Directors of industry. The British corporate network, 1904–76*. London: Polity Press.

Stopford, J.M., and Turner, L., 1985. *Britain and the multinationals*. London: John Wiley & Sons.

Thomas, W.A., 1986. *Finance of British industry, 1918–1976*. London: Methuen.

Thomson, A., Mabey, C., Storey, J., Gray, C., and Iles, P., 2001. *Changing patterns of management development*. Oxford: Oxford University Press.

Tilba, A., 2017. Evolution of UK corporate ownership and control: Codification, governance, transition and context. *In:* J.F. Wilson, *et al.*, eds. *Routledge companion to business history*. Abingdon: Routledge, 300–315.

Tilba, A., and Wilson, J.F., 2017. Vocabularies of motive and temporal perspectives: Examples of pension fund engagement and disengagement. *British Journal of Management*, 28 (3), 502–518.

Toms, S., 2017. Fraud and financial scandals. In J.F. Wilson, *et al.*, eds. *Routledge companion to business history*. Abingdon: Routledge.

Trevor, M., 1987. Japanese Companies in the UK. *In:* M. Trevor, ed. *Internationalisation of Japanese business: European and Japanese perspectives*. Boulder: Westview Press, 24–42.

van Driel, H., 2019. Financial fraud, scandals, and regulations: A conceptual framework and literature review. *Business History*, 61 (8).

Walshe, J.G., 1991. Industrial organisation and competition policy. *In:* N.F.R. Crafts and N.W.C. Woodward, eds. *British economy since 1945*. Oxford: Oxford University Press.

Wardley, P., 1991. The anatomy of big business: Aspects of corporate development in the twentieth century. *Business History*, 33 (2).

Whittington, R., and Mayer, M., 2002. *European corporation. Strategy, structure and social science*. Oxford: Oxford University Press.

Wilson, J.F., 1995. *British business history, 1720–1994*. Manchester: Manchester University Press.

Wilson, J.F., Buchnea, E., and Tilba, A., 2017. The British corporate network, 1904–1976: Revisiting the finance – industry relationship. *Business History*, 60 (6).

Wilson, J.F., and Popp, A., eds., 2003. *Clusters and networks in English industrial districts*. London: Ashgate.

Wilson, J.F., and Thomson, A., 2006a. *Making of modern management. British management in historical perspective*. Oxford: Oxford University Press.

Wilson, J.F., and Thomson, A., 2006b. Management in historical perspective: Stages and paradigms. *Competition and Change*, 10 (4).

Woodward, J., 1965. *Industrial organization theory and practice*. Oxford: Oxford University Press.

11 Empire and decolonisation

Paul Ward

Introduction

In 1900, Britain was an imperial nation. Evidence of Britain's global dominion could be seen across the world and also in the United Kingdom – on billboards and commercial advertising and packaging, in urban streetscapes, in shops, newspapers, literature and classrooms. By 1970, while Britain had won two world wars, it had lost its empire and, in withdrawing military bases from 'East of Suez', had curtailed its imperial pretensions. This chapter blurs the boundary between Empire and metropole to explore how such imperial changes were played out 'at home' and how, from the 1940s onwards, the realities of decolonisation in Asia, Africa and the West Indies affected the identities of British people. In 1945, about 700 million people lived in the British Empire outside the UK. After the return of Hong Kong to China in 1997, there were just 2 million in areas controlled by the UK. Inevitably, the extent to which empire and its loss impacted the British people is contested, often quite bitterly, with some commentators suggesting that empire's effects were ubiquitous, while others consider that Britons were largely indifferent to its rise and fall. At the same time, some celebrate Britain's past imperial role, while others are critical. This chapter provides a brief overview of the imperial context and its impact on British culture between 1900 and 1939, around the unspoken assumptions about Britain's global role. It then explores the post-war years up to 1970, when celebration of victory in the Second World War was tempered by the demise of empire.

Imperial interactions 1900–1945

In 1900 many people believed that Empire was the keystone of British power. In 1901, for example, the British viceroy (governor) of India, Lord Curzon, wrote that, 'As long as we rule India, we are the greatest power in the world. If we lose it, we shall straight away drop to a third-rate power'. Such a statement, which is widely quoted, reveals an attitude to power and also to British identity. It locates being British in relation to other nations in the world and sees no middle ground. Britain was either top dog, based on its ability to maintain Empire, or ramshackle and powerless. Such anxiety about Britain's future was pervasive at the opening of the century and appears frequently in debates about Britain's global position later in the century. It was based on a fear of decolonisation. At the beginning of the twentieth century, Britain's elites considered the empire a 'weary titan', overstretched across the globe, facing threats from all comers. Governments, therefore, sought foreign relations that defended the

DOI: 10.4324/9781003037118-12

Empire from danger in different parts of the world by appeasing them – an Entente Cordiale with France in 1904 reduced chances of conflict in Africa, and an Anglo-Russian entente in 1907 lessened risks to India. Nationalism in Ireland and India were resisted in case concession might precede a flood of similar demands elsewhere. In April 1919 British soldiers opened fire on a nationalist demonstration in the Jallianwala Bagh in Amritsar, India, killing at least 379 and wounding a thousand more. In the following year, the 'Black and Tans', temporary recruits to the police, were sent into Ireland to fight the Irish Republican Army, gaining a reputation for their brutality towards civilians.

Yet alongside the anxious politics of imperial defence and decline, British society, at least until the end of the Second World War, was suffused with imperial themes. The imperial historian John Mackenzie (1984) has argued that empire was everywhere in Britain. There is substantial evidence to support this proposition. At the head of British society, the monarchy had been made imperial in the 1870s when Queen Victoria was proclaimed Empress of India, and the coronation of Elizabeth II in 1953, which was 'in many ways the first post-imperial crowning', saw the new monarch remain queen of Canada, Australia, New Zealand and South Africa, 'not [as] a unitary monarch but [as] symbol of association' (Cannadine 2001, pp. 158–159). Royal events were attended by dignitaries from across the Empire, bringing them to London as imperial capital. Also in attendance at such events were the British armed forces, whose main role (other than between 1914–18 and 1939–45) was imperial defence and offence. As late as 1914, the War Office published a manual called *Small Wars*, which were defined as 'expeditions against savages and semi-civilised races by disciplined soldiers' (MacKenzie 1992, pp. 6–7). The armed forces were portrayed as defending a benevolent empire in popular culture as well as public ritual. One example was at the annual Hendon Air Pageants, staged by the Royal Air Force, which included air races, 'crazy flying' and mock battles between fighters and bombers. *The Aeroplane* magazine in 1922 described planes which 'machine-gunned funny fellows in flowing robes' so that the set burned 'like the shop of an over-insured Jew' (Omissi 1992, pp. 203–204). Empire and racism went hand in hand, emphasising something special about what was considered the British imperial stock.

Politicians lived their lives within an imperial culture. They reveal how Empire and imperialism infected all parts of the British home nations. Two examples from Scotland show imperialist sentiment in unexpected places and provide support the argument that, 'So intense was Scottish engagement with empire that it had an impact on almost every nook and cranny of Scottish life over these two centuries: economy, identity, politics, intellectual activity, popular culture, consumerism, religion, demographic trends and much else' (Devine 2006, p. 168). Tom Johnston, left-wing Labour MP for a variety of Scottish seats between the wars, helped to form the Commonwealth Labour Group in 1922, which he hoped could build on the ties of kinship within the Empire for socialist ends. He saw the 'Commonwealth of Nations . . . coming together as free and equal partners in a Commonwealth representative of all peoples at present living under the British flag' (Ward 2005, p. 48). Priscilla Buchan, Baroness Tweedsmuir of Belhelvie, Conservative MP for Aberdeen South from 1946 to 1966, told the House of Commons in 1950 that, 'Surely we cannot think of Britain as just Britain. Britain is part of the Commonwealth, and one of our major points of policy should be to allow a greater number of emigrants to spread our ideas and spread our British stock throughout the world'. Her family home in Aberdeen was full of hunting trophies, and her husband called these the 'reminders of the extent of our wanderings, mostly on duties concerned with Britain's old responsibilities of Empire' (Ward 2005, p. 66). Johnston and Tweedsmuir and many other Britons thought in terms of British kin or stock across the world sharing physical characteristics and affinities.

The everyday lives of most Britons were affected by Empire in other ways. Young people found themselves part of the imperial project at school. They learnt about colonial exploration and wars, missionary work and the infinite variety of people and produce in the Empire. One school geography text from 1910 argued that: 'The greatest overseas Empire that ever existed under one flag is a heritage to be proud of. . . . Civilisation has followed the Union Jack wherever it has been unfurled' (Maddrell 1996, pp. 380–381). Juvenile imperial literature often provided prizes for good academic performance and behaviour. Children were a captive audience for a variety of imperial pressure groups such as the Imperial Institute and were voluntary participants in youth organisations such as the Boy Scouts and Girl Guides that had imperial origins. Between 1904 and 1958, children participated in Empire Day on 24 May each year, a patriotic festival to celebrate imperialism, which was:

> presented as the righteous celebration of what was generally held to be a set of social facts – the primacy and destiny of the Anglo-Saxon race, the virtuous progression of the British empire, and the common bond of an 'imagined community' inhabiting a vast and far flung empire.
>
> (English 2006, p. 249)

There is conflicting evidence about how children responded to Empire Day, but most probably viewed it positively, since they were allowed out of school early after the ritual had finished.

Complex responses were also likely in relation to imperialism associated with leisure. People went to the music hall, theatre, concerts and cinema for a variety of reasons – enjoyment, courtship, sociability and so on – but in each arena they encountered imperial messages. MacKenzie emphasises that imperial films were made well into the post-1945 end of empire period, such as *King Solomon's Mines* (1950), *King of the Khyber Rifles* (1954) and *Storm over the Nile* (1955). Similarly, radio provided a 'modern' outlet for imperial themes. George V made the first Christmas Day broadcast to the Empire in 1932, preceded by an hour-long programme with imperial greetings called 'All the World Over' (Constantine 1986, p. 181).

In 1935, a BBC series called *The Empire at Work* about imperial occupations aimed to 'show the Empire, not as an achievement in the past, but as a day-to-day reality' (Nicholas 2003, p. 206). This narrative was reinforced through considerable efforts to show the importance of Empire to the British economy. The volume of British imports from Australia and Canada more than doubled in the 1930s, whereas they fell from non-imperial sources. Two-thirds of Britain's wheat came from Australia and Canada. The Empire Marketing Board (EMB) was established in 1926 to promote imperial trade in Britain, and it did so very effectively with extensive advertising.

Image 11.1 Empire Marketing Board poster 1927–1933, Making the Empire Christmas Pudding. Propaganda brought the economics of Empire into British homes. Housewives were encouraged to use Empire products, for example, in their Christmas pudding, for which recipes were supplied by the EMB

Source: Credit Line: Artist F C Harrison. The National Archives, CO 956/62.

It spent £1.96 million on marketing and research and £1.22 million on publicity between 1926 and 1933 (Constantine 1986, p. 199). These were not enormous sums but showed state commitment to imperial propaganda. The EMB produced 10 million leaflets and pamphlets and had 1,800 billboards in 450 towns and cities, displaying colourful posters with a tale of imperial progress and metropolitan benefits, instructing that 'The Empire is at home as well as overseas' and 'Buy Empire Goods from Home and Overseas'. Such official publicity supported the banal imperialism of other advertising on product packaging and cigarette and tea cards. The EMB's life was curtailed in 1933 when the Conservative-dominated national government introduced Imperial Preference – favourable trading terms for the Commonwealth and Empire, which made the board unnecessary. Pressure groups continued to champion imperial economics, such as the British Empire Union, founded in 1915, which was supported by companies such as Castrol, Tate and Lyle and Ty-phoo Tea. It was still in existence at the end of the 1950s, campaigning forlornly against decolonisation (MacKenzie 1984, pp. 156–157).

Historians debate the degree to which imperial messages were accepted by the British public (see 'Debates and Interpretations'), but all accept their abundance. It was impossible for Britons not to know that they presided over a global empire, whatever they thought about it or how little they knew of its extent. A small number were virulently opposed to Empire, and more still wanted the way it was run reformed. Priyamvada Gopal (2019) has shown how radical groups of anti-imperialists in Britain were influenced by resistance within the Empire in what she calls 'reverse tutelage': instead of British ideas of liberty and democracy having an impact on colonial nationalists, she argues that imperial visitors to Britain, such as Gandhi, C.L.R. James and George Padmore, influenced many British radicals. The transnational League Against Imperialism, for example, was founded in 1927 with Fenner Brockway as chair, encouraging anti-imperialism in the labour movement.

From the British perspective, the Second World War has largely been portrayed as a war fought at home, with bombing of British cities developing a Blitz spirit, participation by millions of men and women on the home front and the foundation of the welfare state by the Labour government elected in 1945 – a people's peace following the People's War. However, Wendy Webster has argued that:

> A racial community of Britons was one prominent theme of empire propaganda, highlighting the role of white Australians, Canadians, New Zealanders, and South Africans as 'sons of empire'. This showed the efforts of the common people in empire, united with the common people of Britain in a fight for justice and freedom.
>
> (Webster 2005, p. 22)

Britain emerged victorious from the war, thanks to its Soviet and American allies, with its Empire restored despite historic defeats in Singapore in the east Asia and Gazala in north Africa. Even Labour's victory in 1945 can be linked to imperial concerns. In 1940, after defeat at Dunkirk, left-wing propagandists attacked the Conservative government as 'guilty men' 'who took over a great empire, supreme in arms and secure in liberty . . . [and] conducted it to the edge of national annihilation' (Cato 1940, p. 19).

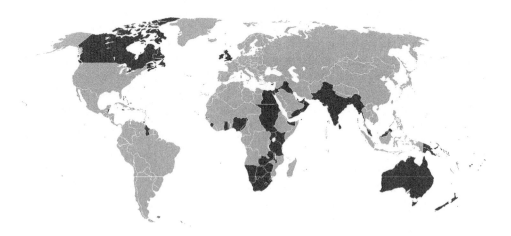

Image 11.2 Map of the Empire at its peak in 1921

Source: By Vadac. Own work. Public domain, https://commons.wikimedia.org/w/index.php?curid=1436172.

Imperial illusion 1945–1956

After the Second World War, the Labour government sought to rebuild Britain in a socialist mould, nationalising significant parts of the economy, founding the National Health Service and developing a comprehensive welfare state. Simultaneously, India achieved independence as a result of nationalist campaigns such as the Quit India movement. Britain also withdrew from Palestine. This might have been seen as the end of Britain's imperial intentions but instead resulted in an imperial illusion. Post-war governments, Labour and Conservative, were convinced that Britain could restore empire to maintain its global role. For two decades after the war, many Britons persuaded themselves that Britain was unchanged, indeed was stronger as a result of victory in war and restoration of the Empire on which the sun never set.

There were plans to restore imperial power though schemes in Africa, labelled as colonial development but driven mostly by the need for resources. As Charlotte Lydia Riley argues,

> For . . . the Attlee Government [in the 1940s], colonial development policies were an 'ethical' way of doing imperialism; for . . . Wilson's governments [in the 1960s], development was a way of maintaining colonial ties in a postcolonial world and forging a new identity for Britain in a world without empires.
>
> (2017, p. 59)

Similarly, Walter Elliot, a senior Scottish Conservative, saw himself contributing to development rather than end of empire when in 1954 he headed a delegation to the newly formed Central African Federation assembly. He took a replica of the mace of the House of Commons as a reminder of British influence. The federation was a compromise aimed at accommodating white settler nationalism in Southern Rhodesia with the desires of the British government to maintain control without provoking Black nationalism. As Empire elsewhere disintegrated, the economic importance of sub-Saharan Africa, in the Gold Coast, Nigeria and central Africa were all increasingly recognised, and intricate negotiations with conflicting interests taxed British diplomatic minds.

When such overtures failed, as Jordana Bailkin (2012, p. 4) argues, 'The imperial mission was revitalized with interventions in British Guiana, counterinsurgency campaigns in Cyprus, Malaya, and Kenya, and a dedication to Commonwealth relations'. Britain fought a series of brutal wars to quell colonial nationalism. The campaigns were described euphemistically as 'Emergencies'. In Malaya between 1948 and 1960, British forces killed about 12,000 and 'resettled' 400,000 people. Its rubber and tin made it economically more valuable than New Zealand, especially since they were sold for dollars which helped pay Britain's astronomical debt to the United States (Schwarz 2005, p. 488). Another 'Emergency' flared in Kenya (1952–60). Some Kikuyu people, known as Mau Mau, began a nationalist guerrilla campaign against British rule, including attacks on fellow Kikuyu who had collaborated with the British. Much of the British media saw Black Africans as 'demonic and viral' (Gopal 2019, p. 396), which allowed British forces free rein to inflict brutality on those suspected of being part of the rising. Hundreds of thousands of Kenyans were interned, interrogated and tortured, and tens of thousands were killed, some in appalling circumstances, such as Hola, the latter a prison camp where eighty-eight people were brutally clubbed for refusing to work. Eleven were killed. David Anderson (2005), Caroline Elkins and Huw Bennett found that there was systematic destruction of records to prevent history judging the British for such acts. In 2013 the British government reached a settlement with many Kenyan victims of brutality. Between 1955 and 1959, British troops sought to suppress nationalism in Cyprus (the British government paid compensation to victims of its torture in 2019), and between 1963 and 1967 the British Army dealt similarly with Arab nationalism in Aden.

While some counter-insurgency operations were successful in the short term, empire crumbled. Decolonisation was unplanned, an outcome of weakness and inability to act independently in a world dominated by the United States, whose conflict with the Communist bloc in the Cold War increasingly impacted British policy. In the Middle East, a coup in Egypt threatened Britain's weakening grip in the region, and in 1956 the nationalisation of the Suez Canal, Britain's lifeline to the east, led prime minister Anthony Eden to collude with France and Israel to launch a military operation designed to secure the canal. Britain was humiliated into immediate withdrawal by American pressure on sterling. Recognition of Britain's inability to act independently accelerated decolonisation after Suez. In Africa, Harold Macmillan, the Conservative prime minister, claimed he felt 'the winds of change', seeking to sound prophetic and altruistic about the collapse of British power. British conceit meant that they had to give the appearance of far-sightedness rather than failure. Emily Lowrance-Floyd (2012, p. 4) has suggested that 'as decolonization itself progressed, British imperial identity maintained a deliberate continuity through a political discourse that invoked traditions of the empire of liberty and a vision of the British civilizing mission culminating in eventual colonial self-government'. This mentality enabled the British to convince themselves that they handled things better than other decolonising powers such as France and Portugal (Buettner 2016).

The role of the monarch was important in this narrative. The accession of a young queen in 1952 created 'a new Elizabethan age' of transition from Empire to Commonwealth, from domination to association. The Coronation in 1953 was global and spectacular, and the Queen revelled in her role as head of the Commonwealth. In coronation year, mountaineers reached the summit of Mount Everest, the world's highest mountain. The *Daily Express* noted that, 'Everest was conquered by a New Zealander. What could be more joyfully appropriate than such a reminder that the spirit of old Britain has spread through the whole of the young Commonwealth?' (Webster 2005, p. 27).

Imperial ideas remained widely visible in British society. Webster (1998) has shown how films combined themes of Englishness, gender and Empire, with women often blamed for crumbling imperial boundaries. *Where No Vultures Fly* (1951) was about modernisation in Africa; *The Planter's Wife* (1952) was set in Malaya; and *Simba* (1955) was set in Kenya, starring Virginia McKenna and Dirk Bogarde. In the early 1960s, David Lean's *Lawrence of Arabia* (1962) and Cy Endfield's *Zulu* (1964) focused more on men building empire than women dismantling it. British culture on the eve of the swinging 1960s persistently refused to be post-imperial (Howe 2005, p. 234).

Debates and Interpretations: imperialism and decolonisation

Bernard Porter is probably the most quoted historian on the impact of imperialism and decolonisation on British society. He argues that Britain was much less imperially minded than most historians suggest. Much propaganda, he thinks, was due to imperial evangelists in pressure groups and mainly right-wing political parties, and there was, therefore 'no widespread imperial "mentality"' (Porter 2006, p. 320). This would explain, if accurate, the lack of obvious opposition to the decline of the Empire. Porter stands firmly against those who argue imperialism was ubiquitous in British society and that the effects of the end of Empire have been under-researched. In the mid-1980s, following Britain's 'imperial' war in the South Atlantic, many historians began to study the impact of Empire on the metropolis and a 'new imperial history' developed, which sought to collapse the boundaries between home and empire (see Burton 1998). MacKenzie led the way in 1984 with *Propaganda and Empire: The Manipulation of British Public Opinion, 1880–1960*, which resulted in a highly successful series called 'Studies in Imperialism' published by Manchester University Press. The series now has more than 120 volumes. Not all its volumes argue that the impact of imperialism was pervasive, and they shed much light on the complexities of its effects in the United Kingdom. Stuart Ward (2001b) pointed out how little historians had researched decolonisation. A number of scholars have addressed this gap. Elizabeth Buettner (2016) has argued that that end of empire had deep impact but in different ways in different national contexts. A range of recent work on specific groups in civil and political society is discussed in the main text of this chapter. Finding so many examples of imperial legacies in the late twentieth century leads some to argue that Britain is not yet post-colonial – such as historian Bill Schwarz in *The White Man's World: Memories of Empire* (2013).

Student historians seeking a moderate line might find the conclusion to Andrew Thompson's book *The Empire Strikes Back? The Impact of Imperialism on Britain from the Mid-Nineteenth Century* appealing. Thompson argues that 'The "big theory" behind [his] book is that there is no "big theory": no uniform imperial impact, no joined-up or monolithic ideology of imperialism, no single source of enthusiasm or propaganda for the empire, no cohesive imperial movement' (2005, p. 241). Rather than see this as middle ground, it could be taken as a call to research the many complexities of the impact of imperialism and decolonisation on British society – including at the micro level feasible for undergraduate dissertations.

After Suez 1956–1970

The rise in living standards caused by a global economic boom created much optimism about being British in the 1950s and 1960s, often expressed through youth, sport and popular culture and especially music. But differences from the economic performance of other nations and a continuing sense that the Empire had been integral to British greatness encouraged parallel pessimistic and sometimes apocalyptic voices. By the end of the 1960s, Britain's formal global rule was much diminished, even while it remained one of the world's leading economies. Britain's imperial role was almost at its end as the trickle of colonies becoming independent in the 1950s became a flood in the 1960s, including Uganda, Jamaica, Kenya, Zambia, Barbados and Guyana between 1962 and 1968. Commentators declared British society stagnant as a result of its outdated Establishment, which was mercilessly satirised in an expanding media. The satire boom of the 1960s included people like Peter Cook, whose forebears had played a role in empire from Kuala Lumpur to Nigeria. It was assumed that Cook would have a career in the Foreign Office after studying languages at Cambridge, but instead he mocked authority figures who had once ruled an empire (Ward 2001a, p. 96).

Some rejected the imperial past, such as Enoch Powell, who had cried when India was granted independence in 1947 but subsequently called for a new Conservatism based on a post-imperial racialised British identity. Powell denied the possibility of Englishness for migrants: 'The West Indian or Asian does not, by being born in England, become an Englishman. In law he becomes a United Kingdom citizen by birth; in fact he is a West Indian or an Asian still' (Schofield 2013). Post-war population fluidity brought migrants to Britain, but their association with British decline encouraged a particularly British racism. Webster (1998, p. xv) argues that,

> The construction of black and Asian people as primitive acquired new meanings when the colonial encounter was reversed through migration to the metropolis, and was no longer represented in terms of colonizers bringing civilization to the primitive, but of 'immigrants' bringing physical and moral decline to the civilised.

For example, one commentator, Elspeth Huxley, considered in the 1960s that

> Caribbean domestic habits and customs collide with our own. Most West Indians . . . like loud music, noise in general . . . keeping late hours at weekends, dancing and jiving. . . . Most English prefer to keep themselves to themselves.
> (Webster 1998, p. 67)

The Empire had come home, for as David Dabydeen commented, the half million West Indians in Britain in the late twentieth century meant 'England today is the largest West Indian island after Jamaica and Trinidad' (in Burton 1998, p. 9). This had a profound impact on Britain: Paul Gilroy (2004, p. xi) has identified one outcome as 'conviviality' or 'the processes of cohabitation and interaction that have made multiculture an ordinary feature of social life in Britain's urban areas and in postcolonial cities elsewhere'. This powerfully countered but did not overcome post-imperial racism.

It seemed also that end of empire brought disruption to the unity of the United Kingdom. David Marquand (1995, pp. 277–278), for example, has seen end of empire as the crucial factor forcing questioning of the Union. He has argued that

> The British state was, by definition, a global state . . . imperialist Britain was Britain. . . . Empire was not an optional extra for the British . . . it was their reason for being British as opposed to English or Scots or Welsh.

Nationalism rose in Scotland and Wales in the 1960s, and Northern Ireland saw civil war, with the British state adopting much that it had learned in policing colonial wars.

The end of Empire seemed entirely destructive and culturally problematic. Yet it happened in parallel to other developments and could be accommodated without considerable political upheaval. It was hoped by many that the Commonwealth of Nations would maintain the gravitas of British power in a changing world, but apart from the Queen, few other Britons celebrated its subsequent role. Historians have recently explored the response of different groups of people and institutions adjusting to change in the period of decolonisation. Anna Bocking-Welch (2019, p. 4) has suggested that many in British civic society, residing in the village hall, the local church and the small-town assembly room, 'chose to read [decolonisation] through a pre-existing narrative of global benevolence in which they, as British citizens and participants in associational life, could play an active part'. Similarly, Sarah Stockwell (2020) has identified an on-going sense of imperial mission in the Royal Mint, the Oxbridge universities and Sandhurst Military Academy through their advice to new Commonwealth states. Jodi Burkett (2013) has shown how radical 'people and groups who were fundamentally opposed to empire' reconstructed Britain as post-imperial but through a belief in British moral superiority necessitating maintaining a global role. Anna Claeys (2018, p. 824) has argued that in education, change was portrayed as positive: 'English schools embellished the idea of a powerful Commonwealth to depict the continuation of Britain's global might during dramatic imperial decline'.

While end of empire may not have resulted in radical political change, it was noticed in a variety of cultural forms. In 1969, the Kinks, one of the most influential bands of the decade, released an album telling the nostalgic story of a working-class man's life in a period of substantial change, and called it *Arthur (Or the Decline and Fall of the British Empire)*. Philip Larkin, university librarian and poet, wrote of the Labour government's decision to withdraw military bases from 'East of Suez': 'Next year we are going to bring the soldiers home/For lack of money, and it is all right' (Thompson 2005, p. 111). Talbot Rothwell, who had served in the Palestine police in the 1930s, penned many of the *Carry On* comedy films, including *Carry On Up the Khyber* (1968), filmed in Snowdonia (Chapman and Cull 2009, Chapter 8). The BBC and ITV consistently screened factual and fictional imperial programmes. Much of the media culturally demonised Asian refugees from decolonised countries in East Africa expelled or encouraged to leave by 'Africanising' governments. The League of Empire Loyalists, tiny but nasty, was particularly vocal in its hostility, joining with other racists to become the National Front in 1967, which infected football hooliganism in the 1970s.

By 1970, though, Britain was no longer an imperial nation. Britons knew little about the empire and its history but knew that it had once been important. Some congratulated themselves on its passing, with many convincing themselves that ending empire was a British gift to former colonies. Harold Macmillan, who had scuttled from Empire in 1960, affirmed British benevolence in giving up:

> It is a vulgar but false jibe that the British people by a series of gestures unique in history abandoned their Empire in a fit of frivolity or impatience. They had not lost the will or even the power to rule. . . . It was rather their duty to spread to other nations those advantages which through the long course of the centuries they had won for themselves.
>
> (Quoted in Lowrance-Floyd 2012, p. 1)

In Focus: sketches of empire in British towns and cities

While millions of Britons travelled to the empire overseas, the majority did not, yet they experienced empire architecture and streetscapes in the towns and cities in which they lived. These traces of empire remain in the present, providing persistent reminders of Britain's imperial past. As the British Empire was dismantled, people could walk through their cities with scenes of Britain's rule over large parts of the world in their sightline. This was perhaps most obvious in London, the imperial capital, where state and civic architecture in the nineteenth and early twentieth centuries celebrated the world role of conquest, dominion and colonial development. In 1912, for instance, a statue of 'Clive of India' designed by John Tweed was unveiled in Whitehall.

Other cities celebrated their commercial and administrative roles in Empire. Liverpool built a town hall in the eighteenth century that stands to the present, with motifs of camels, crocodiles, elephants and African faces. The Mersey docks in Liverpool brought in the raw materials from West Africa, the West Indies and North America and then after processing in the northwest shipped them out again. The docks acted as a reminder of imperial wealth into the decades of post-industrial decline in the late twentieth century. Civic developers in smaller towns and cities also brought the empire home, and it

Image 11.3 Source: Statue of Robert Clive, London © Peter Trimming – geograph.org. uk/p/1764992 cc-by-sa/2.0

is not always apparent why and with what motives, but it suggests a way of seeing Britain as a global nation in an everyday way. In the 1920s and 1930s, as Burtons the Tailors expanded its retail empire, some of its stores included stylised elephants' heads, such as at Weston-Super-Mare and Halifax in West Yorkshire.

Image 11.4 Elephants in Halifax

Source: Paul Ward cc-by-sa/2.0.

Sometimes visitors to towns provided imperial context. For example, Mohandas Gandhi visited Lancashire in September 1931, when he met cotton workers in Bolton and Darwen. He was greeted by enthusiastic crowds despite the Indian boycott of British cotton goods, which he had come to explain (Thompson 2005, pp. 77–78). Gandhi's point that 'the poorest man in Lancashire' was 'a king compared to our wealthiest [workers] in India' was accepted. Also in Lancashire, Learie Constantine, born in Trinidad in 1901, became a professional cricketer after 1929, playing for Nelson. He invited C.L.R. James, Trinidadian journalist and socialist, to stay with him, who wrote, 'I could forgive England all the vulgarity and all the depressing disappointment of London for the magnificent spirit of these north country working people' (Høgsbjerg 2014, p. 46). In Manchester, the Fifth Pan-African Congress was held in Chorlton Town Hall in October 1945. Kwame Nkrumah, Hastings Banda, Jomo Kenyatta, George Padmore, W.E.B. Du Bois and Amy Ashwood Garvey attended. People therefore contributed to the imperial and post-colonial contexts of British towns and cities. The rise in immigration from Britain's former empire in the decades after the Second World War provided further intimations of bygone global rule. Reggae and sound systems in London, Bristol, Birmingham, Leeds – and Huddersfield – with bass-heavy sounds and critiques of imperialism and oppression brought Jamaica and the West Indies into urban spaces, impacting the pop charts. Similarly, Bollywood, popular films from India, were played in the West Midlands, West London and West Yorkshire. 'The Empire Strikes Back', the Centre for Contemporary Cultural Studies at the University of Birmingham, declared (1982).

Conclusion

The twentieth century was both imperial and post-imperial for Britain. Despite witnessing imperial retreat after 1945, many Britons remained proud of the empire, and its legacy continued to play a part in subsequent political and cultural developments. The unilateral declaration of independence by white British-origin settlers in Rhodesia in 1964 was not resolved until 1980. Rhodesia returned to British rule briefly in December 1979 to be granted independence as Zimbabwe the following year. A couple of years later, in 1982, Britain fought and won an imperial war in the South Atlantic to recapture the Falkland Islands after invasion by Argentina. In her speech celebrating victory, Margaret Thatcher, the prime minister, argued that triumph showed that Britain was still 'the nation that had built an Empire and ruled a quarter of the world' (1982). Thirty years later still, the vote to leave the European Union in 2016 has been seen by some as renewing imperial vigour, restoring Britain to its global role after a European detour. To other voices, it seems like the last gasp of imperial nostalgia.

Further reading

MacKenzie (1984) remains essential reading for the ubiquity of imperial feeling in British society, and Porter is equally crucial for the counter argument. Thompson (2005) should be next on the list. For a comparative European approach, Buettner

Table 11.1 Timeline of decolonisation 1900–1970. Dates of independence do not necessarily signify the loss of British control or influence

1919	Afghanistan
1922	Egypt, Ireland
1931	Statute of Westminster enabled dominion independence: Australia, Canada, New Zealand, South Africa
1932	Iraq
1946	Transjordan
1947	India, Pakistan
1948	Burma, Ceylon, Palestine
1951	Libya, Muscat and Oman
1956	Sudan
1957	Gold Coast and Togoland, Malaya, North Borneo, Singapore, Sarawak
1960	British Somaliland Protectorate, Cyprus, Nigeria
1961	Cameroon, Kuwait, Sierra Leone, Tanganyika
1962	Basutoland, Jamaica, Trinidad and Tobago, Uganda
1963	Kenya
1964	Malta, Malawi, Nyasaland, Northern Rhodesia
1965	Gambia, Maldives
1966	British Guiana, Bechuanaland, Basutoland, Barbados
1967	Decision to withdraw military forces from 'East of Suez'. Aden Colony and Protectorate
1968	Mauritius, Nauru, Swaziland
1970	Tonga, Fiji

(2016) is a sophisticated analysis of the reconfiguration of nations by returnees and migrants. Thomas (2014) contrasts the British and French experiences. Gopal (2019) is indispensable for opposition to empire.

Despite the supposed move away from grand narrative history, there are some bold interpretations of the rise and fall of the British Empire. In a highly influential thesis, Cain and Hopkins (1993) argue that imperialism was essential to Britain's 'gentlemanly capitalism'. This created a powerful social and financial elite based in the southeast of England and the City of London. Once it no longer made financial sense to them to retain it, empire could be allowed to slip away after 1945. Complementing Cain and Hopkins, Darwin (2009) argues that Empire was a project held together by the white dominions, India and the City, and dissembled as two pillars fell away. There are also several historians who are defenders of empire and its legacy who claim to be neglected in academic discussion but appear frequently in the national media.

There are some excellent resources available online, though not to be used uncritically. Colonial Film (colonialfilm.org.uk) and Pathé News are fruitful for searches on imperial topics. The National Army Museum website at www.nam.ac.uk/subjects/empire is interesting, and the Empire Marketing Board posters are available on a number of websites, such as Manchester Art Gallery. The Cabinet Papers at the National Archives are rich in discussion of post-imperial themes at www.nationalarchives.gov.uk/cabinetpapers/themes/empire-commonwealth.htm.

References

Anderson, D., 2005. *Histories of the hanged: The dirty war in Kenya and the end of empire.* London: Norton & Co.

Bailkin, J., 2012. *The afterlife of empire*. Berkeley: University of California Press.

Bocking-Welch, A., 2019. *British civic society at the end of empire: Decolonisation, globalisation and international responsibility*. Manchester: Manchester University Press.

Buettner, E., 2016. *Europe after empire: Decolonization, society, and culture*. Cambridge: Cambridge University Press.

Burkett, J., 2013. *Constructing post-imperial Britain: Britishness, 'race' and the radical left in the 1960s*. London: Palgrave Macmillan.

Burton, A., 1998. *At the heart of the Empire: Indians and the colonial encounter in late-Victorian Britain*. Berkeley: University of California Press.

Cain, P.J., and Hopkins A.G., 1993. *British imperialism: Crisis and Deconstruction*. London: Longman.

Cannadine, D., 2001. *Ornamentalism*. Oxford: Oxford University Press.

Cato, 1940. *Guilty Men*. London: Victor Gollancz.

Centre for Contemporary Cultural Studies, 1982. *The empire strikes back: Race and racism in 70s Britain*. London: Hutchinson.

Chapman, J., and Cull, N.J., 2009. *Projecting empire: Imperialism and popular cinema*. London: I.B. Tauris.

Claeys, A., 2018. Britannia's children grow up: English education at empire's end. *History of Education*, 47 (6), 823–839.

Constantine, S., 1986. 'Bringing the Empire alive': The empire marketing board and imperial propaganda, 1926–33. *In:* J.M. MacKenzie, ed. *Imperialism and popular culture*. Manchester: Manchester University Press.

Darwin, J., 2009. *The empire project: The rise and fall of the British world-system, 1830–1970*. Cambridge: Cambridge University Press.

Devine, T., 2006. The break-up of Britain? Scotland and the end of Empire. *Transactions of the Royal Historical Society*, 16, 163–180.

English, J., 2006. Empire day in Britain, 1904–1958. *Historical Journal*, 49 (1), 247–276.

Gilroy, P., 2004. *After empire: Melancholia or convivial culture?* London: Routledge.

Gopal, P., 2019. *Insurgent empire: Anticolonial resistance and British dissent*. London: Verso.

Høgsbjerg, C., 2014. *C.L.R. James in Imperial Britain*. Durham: Duke University Press.

Howe, S., 2005. When if ever did Empire end? Recent studies of imperialism and decolonization. *Journal of Contemporary History*, 40 (3), 585–599.

Lowrance-Floyd, E., 2012. *Losing an empire, losing a role? The Commonwealth Vision, British identity and African decolonization, 1959–1963*. PhD Thesis. University of Kansas.

MacKenzie, J., 1984. *Propaganda and empire: The manipulation of British public opinion, 1880–1960*. Manchester: Manchester University Press.

MacKenzie, J., ed., 1992. *Popular imperialism and the military 1850–1950*. Manchester: Manchester University Press.

Maddrell, A.M.C., 1996. Empire, emigration and school geography: Changing discourses of imperial citizenship, 1880–1925. *Journal of Historical Geography*, 22 (4), 373–387.

Marquand, D., 1995. How united is the modern United Kingdom? *In:* A. Grant and K. Stringer, eds. *Uniting the Kingdom: The making of British history*. London: Taylor and Francis.

Nicholas, S., 2003. 'Brushing up your Empire': Dominion and colonial propaganda on BBC's Home Services, 1939–45. *In:* C. Bridge and K. Fedorowich, eds. *The British World: Diaspora, culture and identity*. London: Taylor and Francis.

Omissi, D., 1992. The Hendon Air Pageant, 1920–37. *In:* J.M. MacKenzie, ed. *Popular imperialism and the military 1850–1950*. Manchester: Manchester University Press, 198–220.

Porter, B., 2006. *The absent-minded imperialists: Empire, society, and culture in Britain*. Revised ed. Oxford: Oxford University Press.

Riley, C.L., 2017. 'The winds of change are blowing economically': The Labour Party and British overseas development, 1940s–1960s. *In:* A.W. Smith and C. Jeppesen, eds. *Britain, France and the decolonization of Africa: Future imperfect?* London: UCL Press.

Schofield, C., 2013. *Enoch Powell and the making of postcolonial Britain.* Cambridge: Cambridge University Press.

Schwarz, B., 2005. The end of empire. *In:* P. Addison and H. Jones, eds. *A companion to contemporary Britain 1939–2000.* Oxford: Blackwell, 489–504.

Schwarz, B., 2013. *The white man's world: Memories of empire.* Oxford: Oxford University Press.

Stockwell, S., 2020. *The British end of the British empire.* Cambridge: Cambridge University Press.

Thatcher, M., 1982. *Speech to Conservative rally at Cheltenham.* Available from: www.margaretthatcher.org/document/104989 [Accessed 5 August 2020].

Thomas, M., 2014. *Fight or flight: Britain, France, and their roads from empire.* Oxford: Oxford University Press.

Thompson, A., 2005. *The Empire strikes back? The impact of imperialism on Britain from the mid-nineteenth century.* Harlow: Pearson.

Ward, P., 2005. *Unionism in the United Kingdom, 1918–1970.* Basingstoke: Palgrave Macmillan.

Ward, S., 2001a. 'No nation could be broker': The satire boom and the demise of Britain's world role. *In:* S. Ward, ed. *British culture and the end of empire.* Manchester: Manchester University Press.

Ward, S., ed., 2001b. *British culture and the end of empire.* Manchester: Manchester University Press.

Webster, W., 1998. *Imagining home: Gender, 'race' and national identity, 1945–64.* London: UCL Press.

Webster, W., 2005. *Englishness and empire, 1939–1965.* Oxford: Oxford University Press.

12 Ethnicity, identity and multiculturalism

Sarah Hackett

Introduction

> Blood alone does not define our national identity. How can we separate out the Celtic, the Roman, the Saxon, the Norman, the Huguenot, the Jewish, the Asian and the Caribbean and all the other nations that have come and settled here? Why should we want to? It is precisely this rich mix that has made all of us what we are today.
>
> (Blair 2000)

Setting out his vision of Britishness, Prime Minister Tony Blair's words reflected a New Labour Britain that, on the surface at least, celebrated its ethnic and religious minorities. These were the days of 'Cool Britannia', a 'new' Britain rooted in notions of cosmopolitanism, diversity and multiculturalism. How had Britain arrived at this point by the turn of the twenty-first century? Which groups have made up Britain's migrant communities, and what have their experiences been? Which issues and themes have characterised political and public discourses surrounding immigration? These are some of the questions this chapter addresses by examining ethnicity, identity and multiculturalism in Britain since 1900. It argues that this history cannot be fully understood without reference to empire and an awareness of existing local, regional and national variations.

Migration to twentieth-century Britain

Whilst the post-1945 years receive the most attention, pre-1945 Britain also experienced continuous immigration. Although often eclipsed by more visible migrant communities, it was the Irish who, linked to Britain through empire, made up its largest foreign-born population across the 1900s (Delaney 2007, p. 2). Building upon centuries of migration, a significant number of Irish, many of whom were Catholic, continued to find Britain an attractive destination, largely due to the economic opportunities it offered. Between 1931 and 1937, the number of Irish migrating to Britain underwent a fivefold increase, and, during the Second World War, more than 250,000 Irish men and women arrived to Britain to carry out war work and volunteer for the armed forces (MacRaild 2011, p. 30; Webster 2018, p. 6). Ireland remained a crucial source for economic migrants during the post-war reconstruction period, and more than one million Irish migrated to Britain across the second half of the twentieth century (Delaney 2007, p. 2).

DOI: 10.4324/9781003037118-13

On a much smaller scale, an estimated 120,000–150,000 Eastern European Jews escaping anti-Semitism and economic hardship settled in Britain between 1881 and 1914, transforming its existing Jewish population of around 60,000 (Field 2019, p. 67). Other exile populations who sought refuge in Britain during the first half of the twentieth century included Belgian refugees during the First World War, Basque children during the Spanish Civil War and Jews fleeing Nazi Germany. Britain's other minorities before 1945 included the French, Germans, Italians, Chinese and South Asians. A group that has frequently been overlooked are the Muslim lascars from countries like Somalia and Yemen who, due to Britain's empire and the opening of the Suez Canal, worked on British merchant ships and began settling in port cities and towns by the late nineteenth century.

It was, however, during the post-1945 years that immigration accelerated and became more international in scope and to which the roots of Britain's present-day multicultural society can be largely traced. As a result of economic growth and labour shortages during the late 1940s and early 1950s, the British government made efforts to attract white European immigrants. 115,000 Poles arrived under the Polish Resettlement Scheme, and around 90,000 labour migrants, many of whom were from Eastern European countries including Estonia, Latvia and Lithuania and were recruited from refugee camps in Germany, moved to Britain as a result of the European Volunteer Workers scheme (Anwar 1986, p. 7). Furthermore, the post-war years and subsequent decades witnessed the settlement of additional Europeans, including German and Italian prisoners of war, Cypriot and Maltese economic migrants and Hungarian and Yugoslavian refugees following the 1956 uprising and the Cold War, respectively.

Despite a preference for white Europeans, it was the 'coloured' colonial workers who, connected to Britain through empire, began to settle in ever-greater numbers. The first major influx consisted of West Indians, primarily those from Jamaica, Barbados and Trinidad, who began arriving to the 'mother country' during the late 1940s and 1950s. Some had served Britain during the Second World War, whilst others were attracted to its economic opportunities. The second group were the South Asians from India, Pakistan and subsequently Bangladesh, who began migrating to Britain from the 1950s due to the partition of India, the displacement caused by the construction of the Mangla Dam in the Mirpur district of Azad Kashmir, the socio-economic prospects available and subsequently family reunification. Furthermore, chain migration played an important role in the settlement of both West Indians and South Asians, whereby immigrants in Britain were joined by relatives and friends. By the early 1970s when West Indian migration to Britain was coming to an end, the population stood at around 550,000 (Peach 1991). By the same time, Britain's South Asian population had reached 516,000, a figure that by the early 2000s had risen to over two million (Peach 2006, p. 134).

Other immigrant and refugee groups are also noteworthy. During the 1960s and 1970s, an estimated 155,000 East African Asians, the majority of whom were from Uganda, but also Kenya and Malawi, settled in Britain (Bloch 2002, p. 35). These British passport-holders, with their roots in the Indian sub-continent, were political refugees fleeing post-independence Africanisation policies. Smaller refugee movements included Chilean refugees following the 1973 coup, those from south-east Asia throughout the late 1970s and 1980s following the Vietnam War and Kurdish refugees of the late 1980s and early 1990s fleeing persecution in Turkey. During the late twentieth century, and as a result of the European Union's free movement of workers principle, Britain received migrants from France, Germany, Ireland, Italy, Poland, Romania and Spain. Other frequently overlooked ethnic minority groups include Moroccans, Somalis and Turks, and there also exists a heterogeneous group of 'hidden' undocumented immigrants. Overall, whilst it often proved difficult to capture the size of Britain's individual migrant populations, the 1991 Census, the first to include a question on ethnicity, made great strides in doing so and in offering insights into their experiences in a range of areas, including education, employment and housing.

Patterns of settlement and variations in experiences

Local, regional and national variations in patterns of ethnic minority settlement mean it proves impossible to refer to one homogenous history of immigration in Britain since 1900. England has traditionally experienced much greater levels of immigration than Scotland and Wales, and it has been particular cities that have become centres of ethnic and cultural diversity. Many of the Irish who had settled by the turn of the twentieth century were concentrated in London, Glasgow, Liverpool and Manchester. Similarly, around half of the Eastern European Jews who arrived during the late 1800s and early 1900s settled in London and in the East End especially, whilst other communities emerged in Birmingham, Glasgow, Leeds, Liverpool and Manchester. Simultaneously, Arab Muslim lascars put down roots in port cities and towns, including Cardiff and South Shields, and London was the hub of Britain's German and Italian communities. The majority of Belgian refugees who arrived during the First World War settled in England and much smaller numbers in Scotland and Wales.

This uneven distribution extended into the post-1945 period. Many Polish migrants of the immediate post-war years settled in London, Manchester and Bradford, whilst the Irish continued to be drawn to London but also Birmingham, Coventry and Leicester. West Indians became concentrated in the capital but also in cities like Birmingham and Bristol, and sizeable South Asian communities emerged in Birmingham, Bradford, Leeds, Leicester, London and Manchester. Furthermore, many Ugandan Asians settled in Leicester, and London became the ethnic, cultural and religious nucleus for numerous groups, including Moroccans and Turks. Indeed, it is the English city in particular that has long been at the centre of Britain's twentieth-century immigration history. In contrast, Scotland overwhelmingly remained a country of emigration until the 1980s, though it did receive Chinese, Indian and Pakistani immigrants from the 1950s, albeit in much smaller numbers than in England, many of whom settled in Glasgow and Edinburgh. More recently, EU post-Accession migrant communities from Poland in particular have emerged in cities but also in more rural areas, including Aberdeenshire and the Highlands. In Wales, ethnic minorities from Bangladeshi, Indian, Pakistani and Chinese backgrounds have frequently been concentrated in Cardiff, Newport and Swansea, whilst areas like Flintshire and Blaenau Gwent have remained overwhelmingly white.

Migrants' experiences in Britain have been diverse and have varied according to either ethnic group or location or both. They have been characterised by discrimination, hostility and constraint but also integration, success and self-determination. Regarding employment, Eastern European Jews at the turn of the twentieth century often worked in low-skilled jobs in London's garment and tailoring industries, as well as in shoe, boot and furniture manufacturing and market trading. During the first half of the 1900s, Irish males worked in unskilled labour, agriculture and the building trade and women in domestic services, the clothing trade and clerical work. During the First World War, Indian and Yemeni seafarers worked on ships out of Cardiff and Tyneside, whilst others found employment in Manchester's chemical and munitions factories. A number of Eastern Europeans who settled in Bradford after the Second World War were employed in textile mills, and the Irish who migrated during the post-1945 period became concentrated in agriculture, coal mining and construction, with some women working as nurses and midwives. Turks and Moroccans who arrived during the 1960s frequently worked in the textile industry and in hotels and catering in London, respectively, and this decade also witnessed a growth of Chinese restaurants and takeaways across Britain.

Regarding Commonwealth immigration, during the late 1940s and 1950s, West Indians were actively recruited by transport companies and the NHS, where a number of women worked as nurses. Some could only secure unskilled and semi-skilled jobs, with many carrying out manual labour, and this group suffered high levels of unemployment, something frequently attributed to racial prejudice. Many South Asians who began settling in Britain during the 1950s carried out work that was predominantly unskilled, poorly paid and unattractive to the average British worker. In England, many found employment in manufacturing and steel and textile mills in the North West and West Midlands, as well as in the catering and service industries. In Scotland, South Asians were employed in jute mills and in industry and transport. Some were professionals who worked as doctors in practices across Britain, from London to the Welsh Valleys. At least partially due to Britain's industrial decline, unemployment and labour market discrimination, South Asians increasingly moved into self-employment, the service sector in particular. This led to the rise of South Asian–run restaurants and takeaways, corner shops and taxi services across Britain. Ugandan Asians also became successful entrepreneurs, with some running shops and manufacturing businesses. Amongst the younger generations, Bangladeshi, Pakistani and West Indian migrants especially have experienced higher rates of unemployment and fewer chances for upward occupational mobility.

Migrants' housing experiences have been characterised by segregation, disadvantage, the formation of ethnically and culturally diverse neighbourhoods and some dispersal. Impoverished Jewish neighbourhoods during the early 1900s, especially that in Stepney in London, were overcrowded, noisy and renowned for slum housing and unsanitary conditions but benefited from a network of social services and charitable and welfare organisations provided by the Jewish community. Muslim lascars in early twentieth-century Tiger Bay in Cardiff and Holborn in South Shields often lived in Arab-owned boarding houses that provided *halal* food and prayer spaces and helped them secure work. Italians in London's Holborn endured overcrowding and unsanitary conditions during the early 1900s and, in Cardiff and Liverpool, the Chinese were residentially concentrated near the docks. The Irish experienced some dispersal during the early 1900s, and this continued during the post-war years, with some moving out of areas like London's Hammersmith and Paddington and Birmingham's Handsworth and Sparkhill. Moroccans in London during the 1960s became concentrated in North Kensington and, initially unable to access council housing, often lived in bed-sits and properties in multiple occupation, yet many chose to stay in the area to remain part of the community.

During the 1950s and 1960s, West Indians were drawn to inner-city areas like Hackney in London and St Pauls in Bristol due to chain migration and proximity to the workplace but have since experienced dispersal into the suburbs. Similarly, as a result of property prices, housing market discrimination and a preference to live amongst their own ethnic and religious communities, many Bangladeshi and Pakistani Muslims became clustered in terraced housing in central wards in cities like Bradford, London and Manchester during the 1960s. The London borough of Tower Hamlets, home to almost one-quarter of the British Bangladeshi community by the 1990s, was perhaps the most pronounced example of residential segregation (Peach 1998, p. 1663). Although Bangladeshis and Pakistanis also experienced residential segregation in Scotland, such as that amongst Pakistanis in the East Pollokshields area of Glasgow, this was less pronounced than in many English cities. Compared to other groups, Indians often secured housing in more modern industrial areas in the East Midlands and Outer London. Differences between groups also emerged regarding housing tenure, with Indians and Pakistanis traditionally preferring owner-occupation and Bangladeshis and West Indians depending more on social housing. Furthermore, during their initial years of settlement, multi-occupation was not uncommon amongst any of the groups, and Bangladeshis and West Indians especially endured overcrowding.

Negative and racist attitudes have long characterised migrants' daily lives in Britain beyond employment and housing. By the early 1900s, Jewish immigrants had become the main victims of anti-immigrant anxiety and hostility and were replaced by Germans during the First World War. Across the post-1945 period, it was the 'coloured' Commonwealth immigrants who undoubtedly endured the most racism and discrimination in Britain. In education, at least partially the legacy of an empire mindset, West Indian and South Asian children were frequently placed in schools and classrooms designed for educationally 'subnormal' children, and their schooling was often defined by racial prejudice and underachievement. During the 1960s, racism became explicit in British politics through individuals like Peter Griffiths and Enoch Powell, and the far-right National Front enjoyed electoral success during the 1970s especially. The 1958 Notting Hill and Nottingham race riots; the 1981 urban riots in Brixton, Handsworth and Toxteth; and the 1993 murder of Stephen Lawrence in south-east London are but some of the most notorious consequences of inner-city deprivation and racist attitudes, tensions and violence. Ethnic minorities have also been victims of racism at the hands of the police, as was exposed in the 1981 Scarman Report and the 1999 Macpherson Inquiry, which were commissioned following the Brixton riots and Stephen Lawrence's murder, respectively. Furthermore, the 2001 and 2011 riots are evidence that racism and disadvantage remained a fact of life in Britain into the twenty-first century.

Yet Caribbean and South Asian communities have also become progressively integrated into British society and achieved recognition, representation and success. There is evidence of increased educational attainment at schools and universities, and many proved successful in establishing and running their own businesses. They have engaged with British politics and have secured political representation through ethnic minority MPs and local councillors. They have set up ethnic and religious community organisations that provide them with voices and work with local authorities on issues of integration and race relations. There is a history of inter-ethnic relationships and marriages amongst West Indians, and English became the main language of communication for many South Asians growing up in Britain. These groups developed new, and often hybrid, identities, including 'Black British', 'Scottish Asian' and 'Welsh Muslim', as well as those at the regional and local level. Furthermore, the discrimination and xenophobia West Indians and South Asians have endured, as well as their distinct ethnic, cultural and religious identities, have increasingly been recognised in government legislation.

Immigration control and race relations legislation

At the turn of the twentieth century, immigrants settled in Britain with relative ease. However, the British state subsequently implemented a series of immigration and nationality laws that were increasingly strict and exclusionary in nature. These were influenced by notions of empire and the Commonwealth, negative public opinion regarding immigration and the concepts of 'race' and 'ethnicity' being applied to immigration and integration legislation. British immigration control began with the Aliens Act of 1905, which was a response to anxiety and public pressure regarding Eastern European Jews, those who had settled in London's East End in particular. These Jewish communities were seen to have displaced the local population; as being unsanitary, physically weak and 'too different' to fit into British society; and as posing unwanted competition for jobs and threatening Britain's physical health and imperial standing. The Act limited authorised points of arrival to a number of ports and introduced controls whereby immigrants deemed undesirable could be refused entry. Whilst its actual impact has been questioned, it nevertheless constituted what Vaughan Bevan termed a 'watershed for aliens' entry' (1986, p. 70) and laid the foundation for future legislation. Subsequent controls included the 1914 Aliens Restriction Act and the 1919 Aliens Restriction (Amendment) Act. Both were the result of wartime anxiety over national security issues and a rise in anti-foreigner sentiment regarding Germans in Britain in particular, required foreigners to register with the police and made it so that aliens could be denied entry and deported. The subsequent 1925 Coloured Alien Seamen Order was Britain's first attempt to restrict 'coloured' workers and mandated that undocumented 'coloured' seamen had to register as aliens, a policy that Laura Tabili has described as being 'the first instance of state-sanctioned race discrimination inside Britain to come to widespread notice' (1994, p. 56).

The second half of the twentieth century saw ever-stricter immigration controls introduced, which were largely a response to the legacy of empire and the settlement of Black and Asian Commonwealth immigrants. Whilst the British Nationality Act of 1948, the first to define British citizenship, was never intended to enable mass immigration (Hansen 2000, p. 35), it gave an estimated 800 million Commonwealth citizens the right to reside in Britain. Though the majority of immigrants during the late 1940s and 1950s came from the Irish Republic and white Commonwealth and neighbouring European countries, it was non-white colonial immigrants who caused anxiety. It was feared they would prove hard to integrate, and they were perceived as posing a threat to British society and as belonging to the empire rather than to Britain itself. Indeed, the measures introduced by the British government to deter Black immigration already during the immediate post-war period have caused some to challenge the notion that the period between 1948 and 1962 was an 'age of innocence' after which restrictions were eventually brought in (Solomos 2003, pp. 52–53). Nevertheless, the 1962 Commonwealth Immigrants Act, which subjected Commonwealth passport holders to immigration controls and required that they obtain a work voucher in order to gain entry to Britain, is frequently described as a turning point in British immigration politics (Hansen 2000, p. 123). It was strengthened by the 1968 Commonwealth Immigrants Act, which mandated that only those with at least one parent or grandparent born in Britain could enter without restriction, thus purposefully excluding non-white immigrants in particular. Concerns about 'coloured' immigration from the Commonwealth continued to drive policy in subsequent years as was seen with the 1971 and 1981 Immigration Acts, which replaced the 1948 British Nationality Act and rendered Commonwealth citizens subject to the same controls as other immigrants. Stricter immigration controls and deterrents with regard to asylum seekers, family and irregular migrants and non-white arrivals from beyond Europe were introduced towards the end of the twentieth century.

Non-white immigrants from the former empire were also the main targets of race relations policies. The Race Relations Acts of 1965, 1968 and 1976, which banned racial discrimination in areas like employment, housing and public spaces, stemmed from the belief that the growing presence of Black Commonwealth immigrants could lead to social conflict and that they needed help achieving integration. Yet this race relation legislation was not applied evenly at the local level. From the 1980s, local authorities in areas with sizeable ethnic minority populations especially, such as Brent and Hackney in London, Birmingham and Bradford, had begun to draw up policies that addressed equal opportunities and racial equality. Yet it was arguably not until the 1999 Macpherson Report and the Race Relations (Amendment) Act 2000, which extended the 1976 Act and required public institutions to promote racial equality, that some local authorities in non-metropolitan areas with smaller ethnic minority communities considered such policies in earnest.

Image 12.1 The children of the Templeton family seen here arriving in the United Kingdom from Jamaica to join their parents who had emigrated to Britain earlier. 25 November 1954

Source: © Trinity Mirror/Mirrorpix/Alamy Stock Photo.

Multiculturalism

Historians remind us that ethnic and cultural diversity has a long history in Britain. Writing during the 1980s, and no doubt spurred on by the race riots and racism of the time, activists like Peter Fryer (1984) and Rozina Visram (1986) produced groundbreaking histories of Black and Asian communities that showcased the vast contributions they had made to Britain and thus the inherent multicultural nature of British history and society. Yet it was not until the 1980s that the concept of multiculturalism, associated with post-empire 'coloured' immigration in particular, became commonplace in debates on integration. In a shift from the policy of assimilation of the 1950s and 1960s whereby ethnic minorities were largely expected to abandon their cultures and assimilate into that of the British majority, multiculturalism consisted of recognising ethnic groups' diverse origins, cultures and traditions and their distinct experiences and needs. At least partially encouraged by the establishment of the Commission for Racial Equality in 1976 and the 1981 Scarman Report, a series of multiculturalist policies were implemented during the 1980s and 1990s, often at the local level in urban areas with sizeable migrant populations. For example, changes in council housing distribution and social services delivery were made in attempts to prevent racial discrimination, and schools were encouraged to teach ethnic minority languages, as well as about the multicultural and multi-racial make-up of Britain.

Multiculturalism became an intrinsic part of Tony Blair's vision for a 'new Britain' following New Labour's 1997 victory. As well as the 1999 Macpherson Report and the Race Relations (Amendment) Act 2000, this was reflected in other initiatives, which recognised and supported religious diversity, such as state-funded faith schools and the establishment of the Muslim Council for Britain. Furthermore, the report produced by the Commission on the Future of Multi-Ethnic Britain in 2000 outlined an optimistic vision of 'a relaxed and self-confident multicultural Britain with which all its citizens can identify' and of a Britain made up of 'a community of communities' (pp. x, 105). Yet it was precisely this perception regarding diverse and separate ethnic and cultural communities that caused some to challenge the concept of multiculturalism by the beginning of the twenty-first century. The 2001 riots in Bradford, Burnley and Oldham, for example, led to allegations of ethnic minorities, and Muslim communities in particular, living so-called 'parallel lives'. A few years later, Gilles Kepel went as far as to argue that the 7/7 bombers 'were the children of Britain's own multicultural society' (2005). Thus, there was a growing belief that multiculturalism had encouraged separateness between communities and that a more cohesive British society was needed.

Nevertheless, grassroots multiculturalism has long been an integral part of British daily life. Lenny Henry, the son of Jamaican immigrants, first appeared on television screens during the mid-1970s; the soap *Eastenders* has featured South Asian characters since the mid-1980s; and presenters and newscasters like George Alagiah, Trevor McDonald, Krishnan Guru-Murthy and Naga Munchetty have become household names. The comedy series, *Goodness Gracious Me*, which featured a British Asian cast, enjoyed widespread success during the late 1990s, and a number of films, including *Pressure* (1975) and *Bhaji on the Beach* (1993), addressed life in multicultural Britain and attracted a general audience. Popular Black musicians born in Britain during the first half of the twentieth century include Ray Ellington and Shirley Bassey. Across the post-war period, Britain's multicultural society was reflected in a range of music genres, including bhangra, drum 'n' bass and jungle. British reggae bands like Aswad and Steel Pulse developed a distinctive approach to the genre, and Two Tone bands like The Selecter and The Specials combined ska, reggae, punk and New Wave sounds to create a uniquely British sound. By the 1990s, a mainstream audience was enjoying the Asian Underground scene through artists and bands like Apache Indian and Cornershop.

In sport, Gaelic Athletic Association clubs were active in Britain across the 1900s and promoted Gaelic football and hurling amongst Irish communities. More recently, following Viv Anderson and John Barnes, ethnic minority footballers have achieved great success despite ongoing racism, and athletes like Jessica Ennis and Mo Farah have been hailed as examples of successful British multiculturalism. Britain's migrant communities have also influenced other aspects of British life, whether through novelists like Salman Rushdie and Zadie Smith; politicians like Paul Boateng and Sayeeda Warsi; or neighbourhoods that are pebble-dashed with mosques, synagogues, temples, Chinese and Indian restaurants and takeaways and Asian clothing and *halal* meat stores. At the city level, London's multiculturalism was successfully marketed as a reason it should host the 2012 Olympic Games, and Leicester has been proclaimed a model of multiculturalism. Furthermore, the ever-growing multicultural diversity of Scottish and Welsh cities like Edinburgh, Glasgow, Cardiff and Swansea is increasingly apparent.

In Focus: the multicultural history of British food

Multicultural food became a central aspect of life in twentieth-century Britain. Panikos Panayi has traced the multicultural history of British food to the Victorian period and outlined how immigration has transformed eating habits and food culture (2008). Italian vendors of the late nineteenth century played a key role in establishing the practice of selling ice cream in Glasgow, Leeds and Manchester, for example, whilst Chinese restaurants and Eastern European Jewish peddlers sold chop suey and bagels in Liverpool and London's East End during the early 1900s, respectively. Across the first half of the twentieth century, London became home to an ever-greater number of German food shops and restaurants that sold German meats, pastries and beers; French restaurants that served gourmet meals to the British upper classes; and Greek, Indian and Spanish eateries that catered to both diasporic communities and Londoners.

After 1945, the influence of immigration on British food intensified and was increasingly seen beyond London and other cities. It has been the curry in particular that has embodied British multiculturalism. Whilst a small number of Indian restaurants had existed in Britain previously, it was as a result of post–Second World War immigration from the Sylhet region of Bangladesh in particular that 'going for an Indian' became an unequivocal part of everyday British life. For many, establishing and running 'Indian' curry houses presented attractive entrepreneurial opportunities. Not only have these establishments traditionally catered to an overwhelmingly white British clientele, but they have also served dishes created by the South Asian diaspora in Britain with Western tastes in mind. Tandoori dishes emerged in London during the 1960s, whilst the balti was invented in Birmingham during the 1970s and 1980s. The most-cited example of a hybrid British-Indian dish is undoubtedly chicken tikka masala, which the late Foreign Secretary Robin Cook proclaimed was 'a true British national dish' (2001). This was due to its popularity but also because it was an Indian recipe to which sauce had been added to satisfy British tastes. Although most visible in curry capitals like Birmingham's Balti Triangle and Leicester's Golden Mile, by the end of the twentieth century, 'Indian' restaurants and takeaways had spread to towns and even villages across Britain.

Immigration has also influenced British food and eating culture in other ways. Restaurants and takeaways opened by migrants from Cyprus, Italy, Turkey, Thailand, and Hong Kong and mainland China introduced moussaka, pasta dishes, kebabs, pad thai and chow mein to ever-greater numbers of British consumers. Some also crossed cultural divides and tried to satisfy more traditional British tastes by selling products like burgers, fish and chips and chips with curry sauce. Chefs and television personalities like Ken Hom, Madhur Jaffrey and Jamie Oliver played an important part in introducing Britain to American, Chinese, French, Indian and Italian cuisines. Furthermore, pub menus began to feature 'foreign' dishes like chicken curry and lasagne, and supermarkets stocked Chinese and Indian ready-meals, Italian cooking sauces and South Asian spices.

The rise of Muslim identity and Islamophobia

Ethnic identities were traditionally the key markers of difference in Britain's debates on race relations. To a large extent, this changed following the 1989 Rushdie Affair, frequently identified as the watershed moment that facilitated the rise of a Muslim identity. It is said to have united what were British Muslim communities fragmented along ethnic and sectarian lines, giving them a collective voice and sense of politicisation. Enraged by what they saw as blasphemous content in Salman Rushdie's novel *The Satanic Verses* (1988), some British South Asian Muslims participated in protests, campaigns and the infamous Bradford book burning. Perhaps most importantly, the affair signalled the beginning of Muslim self-determination as a distinct minority group and raised questions regarding what it meant to be a British Muslim. It also caused something of a backlash against Muslims who were perceived as unable to conform to Western values regarding freedom of expression.

Muslim communities became increasingly vocal about their status and experiences, as well as the place and recognition of Islam. During the 1980s and 1990s, there was a growing perception amongst British Muslims that Muslim schools were essential if their children were to learn about Islam and if their communities were to develop and maintain an Islamic way of life. Other religious needs and demands addressed the provision of *halal* food and dress codes in schools; taking time off work for religious holidays; and the establishment of mosques, prayer rooms and Muslim burial grounds. Furthermore, wanting to have their concerns and religious identities recognised, Britain's Muslims began to organise. Some mosques liaised with institutions like hospitals and the police regarding Muslims' needs, the Muslim Educational Trust played a key role in promoting Islamic religious education in state schools and the formation of organisations like the UK Action Committee on Islamic Affairs and the Muslim Council of Britain undertook efforts to secure national representation for British Muslims. Indeed, Muslims in Britain gradually had their religious identities recognised: they secured the right to state-funded faith schools and were represented by Muslim councillors and MPs, and the 2001 Census included a question on religious affiliation for the first time.

However, this growing prevalence and recognition of Muslim identity also led to an awareness that British Muslims suffered structural and social disadvantages, especially regarding employment, housing, education and health. Compared to other minority groups, they were often more likely to be confined to semi-skilled and unskilled work and be unemployed; endure residential deprivation, overcrowding and segregation; experience lower educational attainment and teacher expectations; and suffer from higher rates of ill-health. Furthermore, one major obstacle to Muslim integration in Britain has been Islamophobia. Although coined during the late 1980s, the term 'Islamophobia' was developed in the Runnymede Trust's 1997 landmark report, which was written in response to a growing anti-Muslim sentiment in Britain, and argued that this 'unfounded hostility towards Islam' 'is a new reality which needs naming' (p. 4). Indeed, by the 1990s, the Muslim had become 'the other' in British society, a development that had no doubt been spurred by the Rushdie Affair and the first Gulf War. More recently, the targeting of Muslims has been influenced by Islamic radicalism and rising levels of populism.

Debates and Interpretations: the prevalence of Islamophobia and anti-Muslim prejudice

Whilst Islamophobia and anti-Muslim prejudice in Britain are often understood to have developed during the late twentieth century in earnest, some interpretations remind us of their deeper historical roots. The Runnymede Trust's 1997 report raised the possibility of 'a continuous line from the Crusades of medieval times through the Ottoman Empire and European colonialism to the Islamophobia of the 1990s' (p. 5). Regarding colonialism specifically, at the centre of the British Empire's expansion into the Islamic world lay the notion that Muslims were 'backward', 'inferior' and 'uncivilised'. Inherently linked to this is Orientalism, a concept that Edward Said outlined in his highly influential book (1978) and used to describe the way in which 'the West' has long applied a series of stereotypes to the Middle East and its people, and by extension Islam, perceiving them to be different, static and threatening. As scholars like Kate Zebiri contend, they have to some extent laid the foundations for anti-Muslim discourse in contemporary postcolonial Britain (2008).

Some argue that Islamophobia constitutes a distinct, and possibly new, form of cultural racism (Modood 2019), whilst others maintain it is not a type of racism at all, as Islam is not a race but a religion (Miles and Brown 2003). Yet others challenge the use of the term altogether, pointing out that it incorrectly implies that British Muslims are culturally and racially homogenous and that contemporary alarmism has developed regarding Muslims as individuals rather than Islam as a religion (Halliday 1999). Regardless of the terminology, anti-Muslim sentiment has become the most prevalent type of religious prejudice in Britain and has been increasingly recognised and debated, not least in the Runnymede Trust's 2017 twentieth-anniversary report. It outlined the broad reach that Islamophobic attacks, sentiments and narratives have on Muslims' lives. The effects can be behavioural, emotional, financial, physical and psychological and are reflected in political campaigns and discourses, counter-terrorism strategies, the media, debates about gender and integration and religious recognition and accommodation. Furthermore, as Clive Field's research has shown, Islamophobic attitudes have increased since 2001 due to 9/11, 7/7 and the war on terror, and Muslims are linked to slow integration, limited patriotism and anti-Western values (2007, 2012). Islamophobic stereotypes include the notions that young Muslim men constitute the 'fundamentalist other' (Hopkins 2007), and veiled Muslim women are threatening, self-segregated and unwilling to integrate into British society (Chakraborti and Zempi 2012). There is also a growing awareness that there exists considerable variation within Britain, with Scotland perceived to be less Islamophobic than England (Bonino 2017), and anti-Muslim prejudice in more rural areas developing and being experienced differently to that in cities (Hackett 2020).

Conclusion

Overall, despite racism and hostility, migration to Britain continued, and indeed accelerated, during the late twentieth century and into the twenty-first. This was due to the economic opportunities Britain offered but also family reunification and a rise in international students and asylum applications. Yet Britain's multicultural history and inherent and ever-increasing ethnic and cultural diversity have by no means negated intolerance and discrimination but rather continued to develop alongside them. Thus, whilst Britain's migrant populations have long enjoyed economic and social integration and success, racism has evolved and Muslims have emerged as the principal victims of prejudicial attitudes and discourse.

Further reading

Important migration histories of Britain include Colin Holmes (1988) and Panikos Panayi (2010). Relatively few general works exist on Scotland and Wales specifically, yet there are two valuable edited collections in particular: T.M. Devine and Angela McCarthy (2018) and Charlotte Williams *et al.* (2015). For an accessible insight into the history of refugees in Britain at the national and local level, see Tony Kushner and Katharine Knox (1999). Excellent studies on Caribbean and South Asian migrants include those of Pnina Werbner (1990) and Margaret Byron (1994). For material on policy and legislation, see Kathleen Paul (1997) and Randall Hansen (2000). The most important historical work on Muslims in modern Britain is that of Humayun Ansari (2004). For British multiculturalism and Islamophobia, see Tariq Modood (2013) and Chris Allen (2016), respectively. For an excellent discussion on the history and development of South Asian restaurants in relation to multiculturalism, see Elizabeth Buettner (2008).

References

Allen, C., 2016. *Islamophobia*. London: Routledge.
Ansari, H., 2004. *'The infidel within': Muslims in Britain since 1800*. London: Hurst.
Anwar, M., 1986. *Race and politics: Ethnic minorities and the British political system*. London: Tavistock.

Bevan, V., 1986. *The development of British immigration law*. London: Croom Helm.

Blair, T., 2000. Britain speech. *The Guardian*, 28 March. Available from: www.theguardian.com/uk/2000/mar/28/britishidentity.tonyblair [Accessed 19 February 2021].

Bloch, A., 2002. *The Migration and Settlement of Refugees in Britain*. Basingstoke: Palgrave Macmillan.

Bonino, S., 2017. *Muslims in Scotland: The making of community in a post-9/11 world*. Edinburgh: Edinburgh University Press.

Buettner, E., 2008. "Going for an Indian": South Asian restaurants and the limits of multiculturalism in Britain. *The Journal of Modern History*, 80 (4), 865–901.

Byron, M., 1994. *Post-war Caribbean migration to Britain: The unfinished cycle*. Aldershot: Avebury.

Chakraborti, N., and Zempi, I., 2012. The veil under attack: Gendered dimensions of Islamophobic victimization. *International Review of Victimology*, 18 (3), 269–284.

Commission on the Future of Multi-Ethnic Britain, 2000. *The future of multi-ethnic Britain: The Parekh report*. London: Profile Books.

Cook, R., 2001. Robin Cook's chicken tikka masala speech. *The Guardian*, 19 April. Available from: www.theguardian.com/world/2001/apr/19/race.britishidentity [Accessed 8 September 2020].

Delaney, E., 2007. *The Irish in post-war Britain*. Oxford: Oxford University Press.

Devine, T., and McCarthy, A., eds., 2018. *New Scots: Scotland's immigrant communities since 1945*. Edinburgh: Edinburgh University Press.

Field, C., 2007. Islamophobia in contemporary Britain: The evidence of the opinion polls, 1988–2006. *Islam and Christian-Muslim Relations*, 18 (4), 447–477.

Field, C., 2012. Revisiting Islamophobia in contemporary Britain, 2007–10. *In:* M. Helbling, ed. *Islamophobia in the West: Measuring and explaining individual attitudes*. Abingdon: Routledge, 147–161.

Field, C., 2019. *Periodizing secularization: Religious allegiance and attendance in Britain, 1880–1945*. Oxford: Oxford University Press.

Fryer, P., 1984. *Staying power: The history of black people in Britain*. London: Pluto Press.

Hackett, S., 2020. *Britain's rural Muslims: Rethinking integration*. Manchester: Manchester University Press.

Halliday, F., 1999. 'Islamophobia' reconsidered. *Ethnic and Racial Studies*, 22 (5), 892–902.

Hansen, R., 2000. *Citizenship and immigration in post-war Britain*. Oxford: Oxford University Press.

Holmes, C., 1988. *John Bull's island: Immigration and British society, 1871–1971*. Basingstoke: Macmillan.

Hopkins, P., 2007. Global events, national politics, local lives: Young Muslim men in Scotland. *Environment and Planning A*, 39 (5), 1119–1133.

Kepel, G., 2005. Europe's answer to Londonistan [online]. *Open Democracy*. Available from: www.opendemocracy.net/en/londonistan_2775jsp/ [Accessed 8 September 2020].

Kushner, T., and Knox, K., 1999. *Refugees in an age of genocide: Global, national and local perspectives during the twentieth century*. London: Frank Cass.

MacRaild, D., 2011. *The Irish diaspora in Britain, 1750–1939*. Basingstoke: Palgrave Macmillan.

Miles, R., and Brown, M., 2003. *Racism*. London: Routledge.

Modood, T., 2013. *Multiculturalism: A civic idea*. Cambridge: Polity.

Modood, T., 2019. *Essays on secularism and multiculturalism*. London: ECPR Press.

Panayi, P., 2008. *Spicing up Britain: The multicultural history of British food*. London: Reaktion.

Panayi, P., 2010. *An immigration history of Britain: Multicultural racism since 1800*. Harlow: Longman.

Paul, K., 1997. *Whitewashing Britain: Race and citizenship in the postwar era*. Ithaca: Cornell University Press.

Peach, C., 1991. The Caribbean in Europe: Contrasting patterns of migration and settlement in Britain, France and the Netherlands. *Research Paper in Ethnic Relations*, 15.

Peach, C., 1998. South Asian and Caribbean ethnic minority housing choice in Britain. *Urban Studies*, 35 (10), 1657–1680.

Peach, C., 2006. South Asian migration and settlement in Great Britain, 1951–2001. *Contemporary South Asia*, 15 (2), 133–146.

Runnymede Trust, 1997. *Islamophobia: A challenge for us all*. London: Runnymede Trust.

Runnymede Trust, 2017. *Islamophobia: Still a challenge for us all*. London: Runnymede Trust.

Rushdie, S., 1988. *The satanic verses*. London: Penguin.

Said, E., 1978. *Orientalism*. London: Routledge & Kegan Paul.

Solomos, J., 2003. *Race and racism in Britain*. Basingstoke: Palgrave Macmillan.

Tabili, L., 1994. The construction of racial difference in twentieth-century Britain: The Special Restriction (Coloured Alien Seamen) Order, 1925. *Journal of British Studies*, 33 (1), 54–98.

Visram, R., 1986. *Ayahs, lascars and princes: Indians in Britain, 1700–1947*. London: Pluto Press.

Webster, W., 2018. *Mixing it: Diversity in World War Two Britain*. Oxford: Oxford University Press.

Werbner, P., 1990. *The migration process: Capital, gifts and offerings among British Pakistanis*. Oxford: Berg.

Williams, C., Evans, N., and O'Leary, P., eds., 2015. *A tolerant nation? Revisiting ethnic diversity in a devolved Wales*. Cardiff: University of Wales Press.

Zebiri, K., 2008. The redeployment of Orientalist themes in contemporary Islamophobia. *Studies in Contemporary Islam*, 10, 4–44.

13 Women and inequalities

Pat Thane

Introduction

That volumes such as this include chapters on 'women' but a comparable chapter surveying the history of 'men' is unimaginable says much about persistent gender inequality. One justification is that women throughout the twentieth century needed to protest against inequality, as men did not. This chapter focuses upon these inequalities and protests and their outcomes.

Votes for women

From the mid-nineteenth century the growing numbers of educated, independent middle-class women demanded equal rights, including to vote, to education, employment and in marriage. From 1869 property-holding women (exclusively better-off widows and unmarried women) could vote in local elections. Parliament accepted this because local authorities dealt mainly with social issues, including public health and poor relief, believed to suit women's capabilities as matters of state did not. After further struggles, they gained election to school boards and poor law guardians, then to county and borough councils in 1907. In 1900 there were about one million female electors and 1,589 elected women, by 1914, there were 2,488 (Hollis 1987).

Increasingly women lost patience, convinced that only the national vote would gain the equalities they desired. Northern textile workers, shop workers and members of the working-class Women's Co-operative Guild campaigned alongside middle- and upper-class women (Liddington and Norris 1978). The National Union of Women's Suffrage Societies (NUWSS) was formed in 1897 by Millicent Garrett Fawcett (Howarth 2004). As a tactical first step it demanded the vote on the same terms as men, which would have limited it, like local voting, to better-off, propertied women.

The Women's Social and Political Union (WSPU) was founded in 1903 by Emmeline Pankhurst, an ILP stalwart from Manchester, her daughters and friends, also supporting the limited franchise as an initial aim. It was committed to public campaigning, impatient with NUWSS's quiet lobbying, interrupting Ministers' speeches shouting 'Votes for Women', then driven to demonstrations, window-smashing and damaging property but not people. In 1911 unknown numbers of campaigners boycotted the census, claiming 'If we do not count, we will not be counted' (Liddington 2014). Horror at WSPU's 'unwomanly' behaviour drove the *Daily Mail* to label them 'suffragettes' – intended, wholly unsuccessfully, as disparaging (Adams 2014, p. 204). More seriously it provoked arrests and imprisonment, hunger strikes in prison and

DOI: 10.4324/9781003037118-14

resistance when forced feeding followed. Quiet lobbying and noisy demonstrations both sustained 'the Cause' until it was temporarily silenced by the 'Great' war.

Debates and Interpretations: women and wars

Studies of the impact of the World Wars on Britain, like most historiography at the time, paid little attention to women until in 1974 Arthur Marwick published *War and Social Change*. He argued that both wars gave women 'new economic and social freedoms, including in work' and a lasting 'change in consciousness', acquiring greater independence and assertiveness. As women's history began to flourish through the 1980s, Marwick was challenged from various perspectives. Susan Kingsley Kent (1988, 1990) argued that, on the contrary, the 'Great War' was followed by an 'anti-feminist backlash' and a revival of traditional gender roles, which were internalized by feminists, who became increasingly conservative and made little effective use of the vote. This was supported by Harold L. Smith (1986, 1990) who extended the argument to the Second World War, which he believed was followed by a 'marked revival of domesticity' and 'a strengthening of traditional sex roles rather than the emergence of new roles'. Martin Pugh (1990, 1992/2000) agreed, perceiving 'domesticity' as culturally dominant in the 1930s and again in the 1950s, which he described as 'the nadir of British feminism'.

More moderate critiques from Gail Braybon (1981, Braybon and Summerfield 1987) and Penny Summerfield (1984, 1986), mainly concerning women and work, contested Marwick's view that the wars transformed women's employment opportunities. They stressed the great diversity of women's experiences and that there were changes in women's work following both wars but argued that most women remained confined to low-status, low-paid employment. As women's history developed in the 1990s further research confirmed this diversity of work experience, by class, age and region, documenting limited improvements, especially for younger middle-class women following both wars, and the continuing, probably increased, strength, activism and effectiveness of feminist campaigning after the First World War (Law 1997; Thane 2001) and during and after the Second World War. Research now focused more on the actions and reactions of women, less on the rhetoric of anti-feminists. A picture emerged of both wars somewhat, though not massively, accelerating, rather than retarding, pre-war aspirations to equality, part of a long process of gradual change and compromise against persistent opposition and prejudice. Thereafter the debate around these issues became less intense as this more complex, well evidenced interpretation was widely shared, as expressed, for example, in Helen McCarthy's study of working motherhood since 1840 (2020). Current interpretations are summarized in the following.

Women's work opportunities certainly changed. In 1917 women were recruited to the armed services for the first time. Resistance from senior officers was overcome by the shortage of men. The Women's Army Auxiliary Corps and the Women's Royal Naval Reserve were formed for non-combatant tasks, to release men for the front, followed by the Women's Royal Air Force when the Royal Air Force was formed in April 1918. They continued into the next war, still serving behind the lines, forbidden to bear arms (Sherit 2020). In both wars, a Woman's Land Army replaced conscripted rural workers to maintain food production. In 1941 unmarried women aged 18–50 were conscripted for the services or essential work. By 1943, c. 7,250,000 were in civilian work, the services or civil defence, 46% of women aged 14–56.

Image 13.1 Women as British Army Auxiliaries – stretcher bearers
Source: © Library of Congress Prints and Photographs Division.

Domestic service was the largest employer of women before both wars. Many were dismissed early in the First World War; then the war economy opened new opportunities and others eagerly abandoned service for better pay, conditions and independence (Whiteside 1988, p. 92), as they did in the second war, when the decline of domestic service became permanent. It revived between the wars due to lack of alternatives for many working-class women, but they were less likely to 'live-in', acquiring more independence. In 1914, 5,966,000 women were employed, 7,311,000 in 1918. Almost one million worked in the metal and chemical industries compared with 200,000 before the war, 25% in munitions. Munitions work brought higher pay, but long hours in dangerous conditions caused sickness and stress. About 300 'munitionettes' died, and others were physically and/or mentally impaired by chemical poisoning or explosions (Thom 1998). Women drove trams, buses and ambulances. Where they took men's industrial jobs, unions and employers agreed to 'dilute' the work, redesigning skilled work into semi- and un-skilled tasks, enabling women to be paid less and assuaging male fears that women would permanently replace them. Women launched strikes for equal pay, with few successes but some gains in pay.

Illustrating the variety of women's work experience, medical training opened up to women when male doctors went to war. In London in 1914 women could study medicine at only one all-female medical school. Elsewhere medical schools admitted a few women. Gradually they admitted more, who performed well. After the war, places were severely cut: small quotas for female students survived until the Sex Dis-crimination Act, 1975 (Dyhouse 2006, pp. 137–155). In contrast, there was lasting expansion of employment for women as clerks, secretaries and telephonists, speeding up a pre-war trend as the scale of government and business grew during and after the war but still confining women to lower-level work. On average, women's pay in these occupations rose from half to two-thirds that of men, though none offered equal pay or equal opportunities for appointment or promotion (Glew 2016, pp. 100–121).

More women were mobilized in the Second World War. Female civil servants increased, 1939–45, from 14–54%; industrial workers from 28–39%; in commerce, banking, insurance and finance 31–63%, again mainly at lower levels. Again came strikes for equal pay, with some successes, including in engineering, where one in three workers were female by 1943. Women's weekly wages in manual work averaged 47% of men's in 1938 and 52% in 1945 (Summerfield 1986, pp. 187–188, 2012, p. 200). From 1941 mothers were encouraged into work by reduced working hours and unprecedented provision of day-nurseries. 8,770,000 women remained full-time 'housewives', exempted from conscription by voluntary service or as carers, including for evacuated children.

Suffrage campaigns revived from 1916 when conscription persuaded the govern-ment to extend the vote to the 40% of mainly working-class disfranchised men com-pelled to risk their lives for the country. For some, the war was a further reason to reject votes for women, because they did not fight; others argued that women deserved the vote for their essential wartime work. NUWSS resumed lobbying; WSPU did not. The Representation of the People Act, 1918, granted votes to all men at 21, or younger if they served in the war, and women at 30, if they or their husbands met the property qualification which the Act abolished for men. The voting age was unequal because politicians could not face the majority female electorate which would result from equality. Also they sought to limit the influence of a working-class electorate likely to support socialism and the growing Labour Party by enfranchising only older, better-off women expected to vote conservatively. Women became 43% of voters. About two million women aged over 30 were disfranchised. Suffragists accepted an unavoidable compromise and, far from giving up, fought on.

Following continuing inter-war campaigning, in the next war women again demanded equality and improved social provision. The Woman Power Committee of women MPs was formed and challenged inequalities, including unmarried male civilians receiving 7s pw more compensation for war-related injuries than unmarried women. Payments were equalized in 1943. Women were then infuriated by Churchill's cancellation of an equal pay clause inserted in the Education Bill, 1944, by female MPs and passed by the Commons. They formed the Equal Pay Campaign Committee (EPCC), uniting women's groups, still active after the war (Beaumont 2013, pp. 146–153). Women's political presence grew permanently in, and between, both wars, as we will see, as their work opportunities also, gradually and unevenly, expanded.

Women voters

Shortly after women partially gained the vote, they were allowed to stand for parlia-ment at age 21, before they could vote, as men had done when they were disfran-chised by the property qualification (Takanayagi 2012, pp. 16–37). Seventeen women stood in 1918. The one elected, Irish Nationalist Countess Constance Markiewicz, imprisoned in Holloway for her part in the Easter Rising, like all Sinn Feiners, refused to take her seat in parliament. The first woman MP, in 1919, was Conservative Nancy Astor, who replaced her husband when he inherited a seat in the Lords. She found parliament lonely and often hostile. When she spoke, 'I used to be shouted at for 5 or 10 minutes at a time' (Takanayagi 2012, p. 137). The largest number of women elected before 1945 was 15 in 1931. Women were willing to stand, but prejudice long prevented their selection for winnable seats.

They had more success in local government, where they were already established (Hollis 1987; Breitenbach 2010, pp. 65–67). As councillors they gained improvements to housing, health, welfare and other services (Beaumont 2013). Nationally, women used their votes, speaking at public meetings and showering politicians with letters. They engaged in extra-parliamentary campaigning almost certainly in larger numbers than before the war, on a wider range of issues. In 1918 NUWSS was re-named the National Union of Societies for Equal Citizenship (NUSEC), dedicated to helping women use the vote, informing them on political issues and campaigning with other organizations for equality. Women's organizations grew, including trade unions and professional, confessional and single-issue groups.

An early success was the Sex Disqualification (Removal) Act, 1919, which, in principle, abolished disqualification by sex or marriage in the professions or any public role. Again, it did not achieve all campaigners wanted but was all parliament would accept (Takanayagi 2012). In practice women 'white blouse' workers still experienced prejudice, restricted entry, limited promotion prospects and lower pay than men for the same work. Despite the law, the 'marriage bar', prohibiting employment of married women and requiring them to resign on marriage, spread throughout the public and much of the private sector despite campaigns by women trade unionists and others against this and other inequalities at work throughout the interwar years (Law 1997, pp. 82–84; Glew 2016). But the Act enabled women to become accountants, architects, lawyers and magistrates and sit on juries. The first women were called to the bar, though they faced discrimination (Bourne 2016). There were 1,600 female magistrates in England and Wales by 1927, out of a total of 25,000 (Logan 2008). No longer did women always face trial alone in courts wholly composed of men.

After the war the labour market again became gender divided, as ex-servicemen reclaimed their work. Many women returned reluctantly to domestic service: by 1931 there were 1,600,017 servants, the largest single occupation, male or female. It was difficult for working-class women to find alternative work, especially when unemployment rose from 1920. Young, unmarried, middle-class women were luckier, gaining (limited) opportunities in the civil service, local government, teaching, nursing, secretarial and clerical work (Glew 2016), and new freedoms – living independently, enjoying leisure activities and more relaxed dress. Employed females aged 15 to 24 increased from 47% to 63% 1911–21, mainly due to the middle-class influx. In 1921, 13% of women worked in textiles; 12% were clerks and typists; and 9% shop assistants, another expanding occupation (Todd, pp. 20–23). Most working-class women worked from age 14, some from 12 or 13. Women under 18 were the lowest paid, regarded as cheap, disposable labour, though their incomes were vital to their families as unemployment grew, or if their mother was widowed or separated with younger children. The standard argument for unequal pay, that men supported families, overlooked such realities.

Some campaigners called themselves 'feminists'; others, equally committed to gender equality, resisted an unpopular term. Among other demands for equality, both groups demanded better work conditions inside the home, insisting that housework should be valued as 'work', since supporting working men and raising children was as vital to society and the economy as paid work, requiring well-designed housing and access to communal services, including for laundry and child-care. This was not because they believed domesticity was woman's proper role. They thought women should be free to choose to work in or out of the home but recognized that the 'marriage bar' gave many women no choice and that the essential work they did was too often disparaged.

They also demanded protection of women and children from sexual and physical abuse, within and outside the family, through tighter laws and appointment of police-women to support victims. Women police could be appointed from 1920, though by 1939 there were just 174 among 65,000 police in England and Wales (Jackson 2006). Campaigning women achieved significant legal changes. In 1922 the age of (heterosexual) consent was raised from 13 to 16. The maximum maintenance for women and their children under separation orders was increased, helping them escape intolerable marriages, and the charge of murder was eliminated for women who killed their infants when they were proven to be suffering from what would now be called post-natal depression (Grey 2011). In 1923 an Act initially drafted by NUSEC created gender equality in divorce, enabling wives in England and Wales to gain divorce for adultery alone, as men had long done (Cretney 2003, pp. 196–318; Thane and Evans 2012, pp. 34–35; Frost 2008). In 1937 the grounds for divorce were extended further, but it remained expensive, difficult to obtain and stigmatizing for women. In 1925 mothers acquired equal rights with fathers to custody of their children over age 10, though, again, the costs were often prohibitive and the courts inclined to support fathers over mothers. The Bastardy Act, 1923, legitimated children following their parents' marriage, improved procedures whereby unmarried mothers claimed maintenance from the fathers of their children and doubled to £1 the maximum weekly maintenance (Thane and Evans 2012, pp. 29–53). In 1925 pensions were introduced for civilian widows and orphans. Most of these reforms resulted from Bills drafted by women's organizations and guided through parliament by sympathetic male MPs, since there were so few women. Most were modified in parliament and did not deliver everything women wanted, but they were significant moves towards gender equality (Thane 2001).

The fight for the equal franchise continued, with demonstrations, meetings and deputations to ministers, hinting increasingly at militancy (Law 1997, pp. 181–201). After much foot-dragging, in 1928 Conservative premier Stanley Baldwin announced a bill which passed easily through parliament. Women could vote on the same terms as men; the electorate became 53% female. This reinforced determination to remove remaining gender inequalities. Campaigns continued through the next war, as described previously.

Women in the Welfare State

Women's activism contributed to the creation of the post-1945 Welfare State. The National Health Service was a particular blessing to working-class women, who previously suffered major problems from lack of access to skilled health care, especially in childbirth (Spring M. Rice 1939/1981). Maternal and infant mortality continued to fall. Living standards gained from full (male) employment, for the first time in peacetime.

Most younger women gave up work to start families, encouraged by the government to maintain the rising birth-rate and the future workforce. Mothers experienced strong social pressure against working, and child-care became scarce again. But there was no overall return to domesticity for women. The marriage bar died permanently in most occupations during the war. Amid a growing labour shortage, the government encouraged older women to work, though a strict gender division of labour revived (Thane 1991, pp. 191–195). Women's work opportunities slowly improved, especially due to the expansion of social, health and education services, always deemed to lie within their sphere. The previous social prohibition against middle-class married women's employment declined, while more working-class women stayed home, at least while their children were small, as family incomes improved. A new pattern emerged: increasingly women of all classes worked until the birth of their first child, taking a break for child-rearing, returning later, often part-time. This was easier to combine with domestic responsibilities and suited employers, who were not required to give part-timers sickness or other benefits until 1999. Employed women increased by 300,000 each year 1947–50, 11.5% worked part-time in 1951, mostly 'returners' aged over 40 (Beechey and Perkins 1987, p. 16).

The Royal Commission on Equal Pay (a product of women's wartime campaigns) reported in 1946 that, on average, women earned 47% less than men in the largely gender-divided private sector. In the public sector men and women commonly did identical work for pay differences averaging 50% at lower levels, 10% at higher, where there were few women: women held only 7% of higher civil service posts (Glew 2016, pp. 150–159). In most professions, including university teaching, architecture, medicine and in parliament, equal pay formally existed but few women were appointed and even fewer promoted to high levels. In 1946 of 44,341 doctors, 7,198 were female; 325 of 9,375 architects; about 164 among 17,100 solicitors (*Report*, Royal Commission on Equal Pay 1946, p. 43). Women kept fighting until in 1955 the Conservative government, coveting women's votes, granted equal pay in the public sector but not equal opportunities (Glew 2016, pp. 159–171). Campaigns continued.

The 1960s and 1970s

Still by 1960 women had limited work and educational opportunities. In 1954–6 only 708 graduated in science and engineering and had few prospects of work in industry or scientific research. In 1961, of 249,000 employees in science and technology, only 18,300 were female, despite shortages of suitably trained workers. Employers in these fields expressed reluctance to employ women or promote them because they doubted their abilities and expected difficulties if women managed men. In 1960 just 4% of 18–21-year-olds attended university, only 25% female, 15% at Oxford and Cambridge, overwhelmingly studying arts subjects. A much higher proportion of females attended two-year teacher training colleges, a traditionally female occupation.

Gradual change followed. About 38% of married women were employed in 1960, c. 45% in 1970, 60% in 1980. More women were ambitious for careers, encouraged by improving education opportunities, while others were driven by inflation, especially of housing costs, and, increasingly, by single motherhood. Child-care remained scarce and expensive. Housework was eased by modern technology: two-thirds of households owned a washing machine by 1972. But domestic standards rose, and the time women, employed or not, spent on housework hardly changed between the 1930s and 1970s. Most men still contributed very little (Zweiniger-Bargielowska 2001, pp. 158–160).

Several long-held ambitions were fulfilled in the later 1960s. In 1967 Britain became the first country in Western Europe to legalize abortion, though on grounds more limited than supporters hoped. It did not apply in Northern Ireland until 2019. The birth control pill emerged, more effective than other methods, arousing hopes and fears of sexual liberation for women, but not until 1967 was birth control available on the NHS and only if local authorities chose, until it became universally free in 1974. The post-war 'baby-boom' ended in the late 1960s, and births declined.

In 1969 easier divorce was allowed in England and Wales on grounds of separation for at least two years. This was adopted in Scotland in 1975 and reluctantly in Northern Ireland in 1978, where it remained difficult to obtain. Divorces rose rapidly, most following petitions by wives (Halsey and Webb 1999, p. 62). Marriages declined permanently, unmarried cohabitation grew and there were more unconventional households, including gay couples and more single mothers due to divorce, separation or choice (Cook 2004).

Then came the Equal Pay Act, 1970, initiated by Barbara Castle, minister for employment. Labour appointed more women to the Cabinet than ever before: two. Castle was influenced by strikes for equal pay and equal work conditions by increasingly unionized women (Castle 1993, pp. 408–409). The Act required pay for the same or similar work to be assessed by job evaluation schemes, to be completed by

Image 13.2 Women's rights. Equal pay for women. Rally Trafalgar Square, London 1968
Source: © Homer Sykes/Alamy Stock Photo.

1975. It overlooked unequal access to promotion or appointment to higher-paid work. A gradual narrowing of gender pay differentials followed but not their elimination, as it was widely evaded (Halsey and Webb 1999, p. 354). Women remained concentrated in low-status, low-paid work.

In 1975 Labour introduced the Sex Discrimination Act, outlawing discrimination in employment, education, advertising and the provision of housing, goods or services, again with imperfect effects, but the Equal Opportunities Commission was established to investigate complaints and support women claiming discrimination. It helped them take successful cases concerning unequal pay and conditions to the European Court of Human Rights. The law forced medical schools to remove the quotas restricting women's entry: by the early 1990s women were over 50% of students. The proportion of female lawyers rose from 4% in 1971 to 27% in 1990 (Women and Equality Unit 2001).

In Focus: The Women's Liberation Movement

The UK branch of the Women's Liberation Movement (WLM) emerged in 1969 from a conference of the radical History Workshop, among women infuriated by the marginalization of women and women's history by socialist men demanding social equality (Rowbotham 1999). It began as a movement of white, middle-class intellectuals and largely remained so. Through the 1970s it made feminism public and flamboyant again, achieving government action on issues long neglected.

Despite previous feminist campaigns against domestic violence, police and the courts still insisted that 'domestic disputes' were private, beyond their powers to intervene. Women protested and founded refuges for 'battered wives' across Britain, revealing shocking numbers (Cretney 2003, pp. 753–755). At last in 1976 domestic violence became a legal offence. Again the law was imperfect, and still in the 21st century one in four women experienced domestic violence at some point in their lives, and two women a week were killed by partners (Amnesty International 2015). Still police did not always take complaints seriously, and campaigns and refuges continued, the latter severely reduced by 'austerity' spending cuts from 2010.

Rape was another suppressed issue exposed by WLM. Victims often failed to complain, fearing reprisals from the perpetrator, feeling shame or that they would be disbelieved and denigrated: police and the courts too often blamed victims, for drunkenness or wearing 'provocative' clothing (Jackson 2006, pp. 185–193). Feminists established rape crisis centres providing counselling, refuge and support, and in 1976 legislation guaranteed anonymity for victims (Bingham 2009, pp. 155–156). But still in the 21st century 167 women were reported to suffer rape every day; only one in five approached the police, for the same reasons as before.

WLM fought less successfully for men to share domestic work, for abortion on demand, improved nursery provision and improved pay and work conditions for low-paid women. It aspired to be inclusive, but few working-class women felt included or supported it (Stevenson 2020). Black and Asian women also felt unwelcome and formed their own organizations. The Organisation of Women of Asian and African Descent (OWAAD), formed 1978, and Southall Black Sisters (1979), with Brixton Black Women, Liverpool Black Sisters, Baheno Women's Organization in Leicester and others campaigned against restrictive immigration laws, virginity tests on women immigrants, domestic and sexual violence and discrimination, including in employment, which they experienced due to both race and gender. OWAAD organized the first national Black women's conference in 1979; 250 women attended (Thomlinson 2016).

There was tension, too, over whether to co-operate with men. WLM made valuable gains, but the divisions and then the implacable hostility of the governments of the 1980s brought it to an end.

The 1980s and 90s

Some hailed the election of Britain's first woman premier, Margaret Thatcher, in 1979 as a further signal of equality. But she was explicitly not a feminist and did not promote gender equality. She was concerned about what she saw as the decline of the 'traditional family', but, despite government rhetoric about 'preserving' the family, families had never changed so much. Births outside marriage rose from 11.5% of all UK births in 1980 to 33.6% in 1995, 78% registered by both parents, often living together. By 1992 one in five families with 2.1m children were headed by single parents, overwhelmingly mothers. They often found it hard to work in the absence of affordable childcare. Thatcher refused to fund childcare to avoid 'discouraging women from staying at home', as she had not (Thatcher 1993, pp. 630–631). Unemployment, poverty and income inequality rose to levels unseen since the 1930s, while benefits were cut. More women than men experienced poverty due to single motherhood; unemployment; or low-status, low-paid, often part-time work in the growing service sector, selling fast food or staffing call centres.

Thatcher's successor, John Major, resisted calls for stronger legislation on equal pay and sex discrimination, fearing to restrict the free market. Single mothers faced attacks by ministers, including blaming them for the rise in violent crime. Britain had the worst provision for working parents in the EU and trailed in most areas of gender equality. One hint of progress was that women were admitted to combat roles in all the armed services (though not in the front line until 2016) due to a shortage of male recruits and later than several other countries. The women's and men's services were amalgamated (Sherit 2020). Meanwhile, girls outperformed boys in education and more stayed on longer as their opportunities for work and higher education grew.

The most visible feminist activism was the women's peace camp outside the US airbase at Greenham Common (Berkshire) from 1981–91, protesting against nuclear missiles. As WLM declined feminists engaged more in formal politics as potentially more effective than public campaigns for challenging hostile governments. In 1993 the Labour Party introduced All-Women Shortlists in candidate selections for a significant number of seats. In the 1997 election, which brought Labour back to power, an unprecedented 120 women were elected, 102 Labour, 13 Conservatives. Thereafter women MPs slowly increased: in 2019, 220 women were elected, just 34% of MPs but more than ever before.

New Labour and beyond

Tony Blair appointed an unprecedented five women to his Cabinet (of 23). When Scotland and Wales gained devolution in 1998, women lobbied successfully for voting by proportional representation which, internationally, returned more elected women. Following the first devolved elections in 1999, in Wales 41.7% of elected representatives were female, in Scotland 37.2%, compared with 18% at Westminster. The second election, in 2002, returned 51.7% of female representatives in Wales, the first elected assembly in the world to achieve gender equality, remarkably when Wales had previously elected only four women to Westminster (Breitenbach and MacKay 2010, pp. 157–159; Chaney 2010, pp. 189–208).

Nationally, employment grew and poverty fell. Low incomes rose, assisted by improved benefits, while top incomes rose also and inequality grew, though more slowly than before. More single mothers found work, assisted by free child care while training or seeking work, though poverty remained highest in single-mother households. Britain's first minimum wage was introduced along with other EU-inspired improvements to employee rights, especially benefitting women: equal rights for part-timers, including to holiday and sickness pay; paid maternity leave extended from 14 to 26 weeks; women gained the right to return to their previous job, or a suitable equivalent, after maternity leave and could not be dismissed for any reason connected with pregnancy and maternity (though it remained all too common); parents could request flexible working hours to match their childcare responsibilities, though employers could refuse; discrimination at work on any grounds was prohibited, though it remained harder for women from minority ethnic backgrounds to gain good jobs.

By 2000 most mothers of children under five were employed, often part-time; grandparents provided much childcare. From 2001 the birth rate unexpectedly started to rise before levelling out in 2017–19. It was partly due to births to immigrant women but more to higher fertility among native-born women in their 30s and 40s, who delayed childbirth until they were established in a career and/or found a stable partner (Office for National Statistics 2011). Still about one-third of babies were born to unmarried parents. In 2001 marriages in UK fell to an all-time low (Office for National Statistics 2010, p. 20).

Conclusion

Women fought hard through the century for gender equality, but by the 21st century much inequality remained. Girls in all ethnic and socio-economic groups now out-performed boys at all levels of education, but few women studied sciences and engineering. Women, married and unmarried, with and without children, trailed men in employment opportunities and pay. In 2007/8 just 11% of directors of the top FTSE 100 companies were female (Equality and Human Rights Commission 2008, pp. 5–7). Women were 9.6% senior judges, 19.5% of local authority chief executives and 34% of secondary school heads (Equality and Human Rights Commission 2008). The average gender pay gap was 27.5% in 1997, 16.4% in 2010 and 13.1 % in 2019.

Progress slowed in the financial crisis of 2007–9, slowing further under the 'austerity' policies of governments from 2010.

Further reading

References throughout the chapter suggest further reading on specific topics. For more detail and deeper understanding of key topics and themes:

June Purvis and Sandra Stanley Holton eds. (2000), *Votes for Women*, provides an overview of the British suffrage movement to 1928. On women's activism between the wars, J. Gottlieb and R. Toye eds. (2013), *The Aftermath of Suffrage*. Krista Cowman (2010), *Women in British Politics c.1689–1979*, is a useful overview. Also, Jane Rendell ed. (1987), *Equal or different. Women's politics 1800–1914*. Kate Murphy (2016), *Behind the Wireless. A History of Early Women at the BBC*, is interesting on a new field of employment for women between the wars. Pat Thane (2018), *Divided Kingdom. A History of Britain, 1900 to the Present*, attempts to set gender inequalities through the period in the wider national context. On family size and related issues, E. Garrett, A. Reid, K. Schürer and S. Szreter (2001), *Changing family size in England and Wales. Place, Class and Demography, 1891–1911*. Kathleen Kiernan, Hilary Land and Jane Lewis (1998), *Lone motherhood in Twentieth Century Britain*. Simon Szreter and Kate Fisher (2010), *Sex before the Sexual Revolution: Intimate Life in England, 1918–1963*. A valuable survey of the experience of World War 1: J. M. Winter (1985), *The Great War and the British People*.

References

Adams, J., 2014. *Women and the vote. A world history.* Oxford: Oxford University Press.

Amnesty International, 2015. Available from: www.amnesty.org.uk/violence-against-women#. VMTOG1 [Accessed 25 January 2015].

Beaumont, C., 2013. *Housewives and citizens. Domesticity and the women's movement in England, 1928–1964.* Manchester: Manchester University Press.

Beechey, V., and Perkins, T., 1987. *A matter of hours.* Minneapolis: University of Minnesota Press.

Bingham, A., 2009. *Family newspapers. Sex, private life and the British Popular Press, 1918–1978.* Oxford: Oxford University Press.

Bourne, J., 2016. *Helena Normanton and the opening of the bar to women.* London: Waterside Press.

Braybon, G., 1981. *Women workers in the First World War.* London: Routledge.

Braybon, G., and Summerfield, P., 1987. *Out of the cage. Women's experiences in two world wars.* London: Pandora.

Breitenbach, E., 2010. Scottish women's organizations and the exercise of citizenship, c1900–c.1970. *In:* E. Breitenbach and P. Thane, eds. *Women and citizenship in Britain and Ireland in the twentieth century.* London: Bloomsbury, 63–78.

Breitenbach, E., and MacKay, F., 2010, Feminist politics in Scotland from the 1970s–2000s: Engaging with the changing state. *In:* E. Breitenbach and P. Thane, eds. *Women and citizenship.* London: Continuum, 153–170.

Castle, B., 1993. *Fighting all the way.* London: Pan.

Chaney, P., 2010. Devolution, citizenship and women's political representation in Wales. *In:* E. Breitenbach and P. Thane, eds. *Women and citizenship.* London: Continuum, 189–208.

Cook, H., 2004. *The long sexual revolution.* Oxford: Oxford University Press.

Cowman, K., 2010. *Women in British politics c.1689–1979.* Basingstoke: Palgrave Macmillan.

Cretney, S., 2003. *Family law in the twentieth century. A history*. Oxford: Oxford University Press.

Dyhouse, C., 2006. *Students: A gendered history*. London: Routledge.

Equality and Human Rights Commission, 2008. *Sex and power: Who runs Britain, 2008?* London: Equality and Human Rights Commission.

Frost, G.S., 2008. *Living in Sin. Cohabiting as husband and wife in nineteenth century England*. Manchester: Manchester University Press.

Garrett, E., Reid, A., Schürer, K., and Szreter S., 2001. *Changing family size in England and Wales. Place, class and demography, 1891–1911*. Cambridge: Cambridge University Press.

Glew, H., 2016. *Gender, rhetoric and regulation. Women's work in the civil service and the London County Council, 1900–55*. Manchester: Manchester University Press.

Gottlieb, J., and Toye, R., eds., 2013. *The aftermath of suffrage*. Basingstoke: Palgrave Macmillan.

Grey, D., 2011. Women's policy networks and the infanticide act, 1922. *Twentieth Century British History*, 21 (4), 441–463.

Halsey, A.H., and Webb, J., 1999. *Twentieth century British social trends*. Basingstoke: Macmillan.

Hollis, P., 1987. *Ladies elect. Women in English Local Government 1865–1914*. Oxford: Oxford University Press.

Howarth, J., 2004. Fawcett, Dame Millicent Garrett. In: *Oxford Dictionary of National Biography*. Oxford: Oxford University Press.

Jackson, L., 2006. *Women police. Gender, Welfare and surveillance in the twentieth century*. Manchester: Manchester University Press.

Kiernan, K., Land, H., and Lewis, J., 1998. *Lone motherhood in twentieth century Britain*. Oxford: Oxford University Press.

Kingsley Kent, S., 1988. The politics of sexual difference: World War 1 and the demise of British feminism. *Journal of British Studies*, 27 (3), 232–253.

Kingsley Kent, S., 1990. Gender reconstruction after the First World War. In: H.L. Smith, ed. *British feminism in the twentieth century*. Aldershot: Edward Elgar, 66–83.

Law, C., 1997. *Suffrage and power. The women's movement, 1918–1928*. London: I.B. Tauris.

Liddington, J., 2014. *Vanishing for the vote. Suffrage, citizenship and the battle for the census*. Manchester: Manchester University Press.

Liddington, J., and Norris, J., 1978. *One hand tied behind us. The rise of the women's suffrage movement*. London: Virago.

Logan, A., 2008. *Feminism and criminal justice. A historical perspective*. London: Palgrave Macmillan.

Marwick, A., 1974. *War and social change in the twentieth century*. London: Macmillan.

McCarthy, H., 2020. *Double lives. A history of working motherhood*. London: Bloomsbury.

Murphy, K., 2016. *Behind the wireless. A history of early women at the BBC*. London: Palgrave Macmillan.

Office for National Statistics, 2010. *Social Trends*, 40.

Office for National Statistics, 2011. Fertility. UK Fertility remains high. Available from: www.ons.gov.uk/index.html [Accessed 24 June 2020].

Pugh, M., 1990. Domesticity and the decline of feminism, 1930–1952. In: H.L. Smith, ed. *British feminism in the twentieth century*. Aldershot: Edward Elgar, 144–166.

Pugh, M., 1992/2000. *Women and the women's movement in Britain* (1st edition 1992, 2nd edition 2000). London: Macmillan Press.

Purvis, J., and Stanley Holton, S., eds, 2000. *Votes for women*. London: Routledge.

Rendell, J., ed., 1987. *Equal or different. Women's politics 1800–1914*. Oxford: Blackwell.

Rice, M.S., 1939. *Working class wives. Their health and conditions*. Harmondsworth: Penguin; 2nd ed. London: Virago, 1981.

Rowbotham, S., 1999. *Threads through time. Writings on history and autobiography.* London: Penguin.

Royal Commission on Equal Pay, 1946. *Report.* London: HMSO.

Sherit, K., 2020. *Women on the front line. British servicewomen's path to combat.* Stroud: Amberley.

Smith, H.L., 1986. The effect of the war on the status of women. *In*: H.L. Smith, ed. *War and social change.* Manchester: Manchester University Press, 208–229.

Smith, H.L., 1990. British Feminism in the 1920s. *In*: H.L. Smith, ed. *British feminism in the twentieth century.* Aldershot: Edward Elgar, 47–65.

Stevenson, G., 2020. *The women's liberation movement and the politics of class in Britain.* London: Bloomsbury.

Summerfield, P., 1984. *Women workers in the Second World War: Production and patriarchy in conflict.* London: Croom Helm.

Summerfield, P., 1986. The "levelling of class". *In*: H.L. Smith, ed. *War and social change.* Manchester: Manchester University Press, 179–207.

Szreter, S., and Fisher, K., 2010. *Sex before the sexual revolution: Intimate life in England, 1918–1963.* Cambridge: Cambridge University Press.

Takanayagi, M., 2012. *Parliament and women, c 1900–1945.* PhD thesis. King's College London.

Thane, P., 1991. Towards equal opportunities? Women in Britain since 1945. *In*: T. Gourvishand and A. O'Day, eds. *Britain since 1945.* London: Macmillan, 183–208.

Thane, P., 2001. What difference did the vote make? *In*: Amanda Vickery, ed. *Women, privilege and power. British politics 1750 to the present.* Stanford: Stanford University Press, 253–288.

Thane, P., 2010. Women and political participation. *In*: E. Breitenbach and P. Thane, eds. *Women and citizenship in Britain and Ireland.* London: Continuum, 11–28.

Thane, P., 2018. *Divided kingdom. A history of Britain 1900 to the present.* Cambridge: Cambridge University Press.

Thane, P., and Evans, T., 2012. *Sinners? Scroungers? Saints? Unmarried motherhood in twentieth century England.* Oxford: Oxford University Press.

Thatcher, M., 1993. *The downing St Years.* London: Harper Collins.

Thom, D., 1998. *Nice girls and rude girls. Women workers in world war 1.* London: I.B. Tauris.

Thomlinson, N., 2016. *Race, ethnicity and the women's movement in England, 1968–93.* London: Palgrave.

Todd, S., 2005. *Young women, work and family in England, 1918–1950.* Oxford: Oxford University Press.

Whiteside, N., 1988. The British population at war. *In*: J. Turner, ed. *Britain and the First World War.* London: Unwin, Hyman, 85–98.

Winter, J.M., 1985. *The great war and the British people.* London: Macmillan.

Women and Equality Unit, 2001. *Key indicators of women's position in Britain.* London: UK Government, Department of Trade and Industry.

Zweiniger-Bargielowska, I., 2001. Housewifery. *In*: I. Zweiniger-Bargielowska, ed. *Women in twentieth century Britain.* Harlow: Longman, 149–164.

14 Disability and disabled people

Vicky Long

Introduction

In 2001, the American historian Douglas Baynton claimed, 'disability is everywhere, once you begin looking for it, but conspicuously absent in the histories that we write' (2001, p. 52). Disability history has since moved from the margins to become a significant subfield of historical studies in the twenty-first century, revealing the impact of industrialization and the rise of institutional care on perceptions of disability and the experiences of disabled people.

This chapter examines twentieth-century Britain through the prism of disability, outlining how services for and experiences of people with physical disabilities, learning disabilities (permanent intellectual impairment, arising before adulthood, sometimes termed intellectual disabilities), and long-term mental health conditions changed throughout the century as integration policies displaced historical practices of segregation. It will analyse how both world wars and the development of the postwar Welfare State shaped government policies and provisions for disabled people. Finally, it considers how the emergence of the disability rights movement changed attitudes towards disability, emphasizing the barriers that prevented people from participating equally in society.

Definitions and demographics

Changing definitions and inconsistent data sources undermine efforts to quantify the prevalence of disability within Britain over the last century. The current UK legal definition of disability, derived from the 2010 Equality Act, designates disability as a physical or mental impairment that has a 'substantial' and 'long-term' negative effect on your ability to do normal daily activities. In 2017/18, 21 percent of people in the UK reported a disability, with the percentage rising through age groups: from 8 percent of children to 44 percent of state pension age adults (Department for Work and Pensions 2019, p. 7). By contrast, figures given in the 1901 census for England and Wales, derived from householder's responses to the occupier's schedule, suggest that 0.59 percent of the population were disabled (Census of England and Wales 1901 1903, pp. 282–283).

In part, broader demographic developments account for this dramatic increase in the percentage of the population identified as disabled. Life expectancy rose from 48.5 for men and 52.4 for women in 1900, to 76 for men and 80.6 for women in 2001 (ONS 2015). Consequently, the proportion of the population of state pension age has

DOI: 10.4324/9781003037118-15

increased significantly, and people within this cohort report the highest share of disabilities today. However, a cursory glance at the headings of the 1901 census figures – blind, deaf, deaf and dumb, lunatic, imbecile and feeble-minded – reminds us that early twentieth-century definitions of what constituted disability differ radically from our current-day definitions. These historical definitions linger on as pejorative terms, indicating how society has stigmatized disability.

People who experience long-term mental health conditions are legally defined as disabled today and historically were subjected to similar patterns of segregative care. My analysis includes their experiences while acknowledging that some prefer to self-define as survivors of the psychiatric system, resisting the disability label, which they feel medicalizes their distress as impairment (Plumb 1994).

Over the century a greater range of impairments were brought under the umbrella of disability; different measures of classifying and enumerating disability underpinned the doubling of the number of British people deemed disabled between 1971 – just over 3 million, or 7.8 percent of the population – to over 6 million by 1988 (Abberley 2007). The emergence of the social model of disability, outlined in the following section, also influenced how we define and measure disability. The social model asserts that people are disabled not by their impairments but by social and environmental constraints that inhibit their ability to participate fully in everyday life. If people's environments generate disability, we cannot calculate disability simply by enumerating the number of people with impairments.

Debates and Interpretations: the medical versus the social model of disability

Disability was long understood as a physical or intellectual impairment, which restricted an individual's movements, senses or capacity. Whether the impairment underpinning the disability was inborn or developed following accident or illness, disability was understood as a medical matter: doctors could identify the cause of the disability and could offer disabled people some interventions to ameliorate their impairments and enhance their capacity.

Disability activists began to formulate the social model of disability in the 1970s as a potent campaign tool against the social oppression of disabled people. In an influential 1976 circular, the Union of the Physically Impaired Against Segregation (UPIAS) argued that disability was preventable: it arose not because of impairment but because society discriminated against people with impairments. Vic Finkelstein, a UPIAS co-founder, was a prominent activist in South Africa's 1960s anti-apartheid movement, travelling to England in 1968 after release from imprisonment for his activism. A meeting with fellow disability activists, Paul and Judy Hunt, prompted Finkelstein to reflect on the similarities between apartheid and the systematic segregation of disabled people in UK institutions. He concluded that disability was not an attribute, but a social relationship between a person with an impairment and their social environment. Take, for example, a wheelchair user unable to access a building designed with stairs leading to its entrance: the medical model would attribute this to the wheelchair user's impairment; the social model would argue that the architect's choice to design stairs, as opposed to a ramp or lift, disabled the wheelchair user from accessing the building.

Finklestein, alongside the disability rights activists and researchers Colin Barnes and Mike Oliver, developed and disseminated the social model (Oliver 2013). It was an influential concept in disability studies and shaped the emerging disability history field. Disability historians, such as Catherine Kudlick, contended that medical history pathologized disability, conflated disability with illness, and privileged medicine's role in disabled peoples' histories (2008). She argued that medical historians, while alert to misogyny and racism in medical practice, overlooked the structural oppression of disabled people.

Yet Tom Shakespeare and Nicholas Watson, who both initially helped disseminate the social model of disability, now contend that it is a reductive approach that ignores disabled people's divergent experiences. They caution that the social model trivializes people's embodied experiences of living with impairment, which can entail pain, and may lead to the rejection of interventions that could reduce discomfort and maximize functioning. Nor is it straightforward to create an environment that is universally accessible, as removing obstacles for one individual may generate new obstacles for another. Tactile blister paving, for example, which offers guidance for visually impaired people approaching pedestrian crossings, affects gait and balance, constituting a trip hazard to people with balance impairments (Thies *et al.* 2011). Disability, contend Shakespeare and Watson, is 'a complex dialectic of biological, psychological, cultural and socio-political factors' (2001); it cannot be defined purely as impairment, but neither should it be attributed solely to societal barriers. Acknowledging the inherently fragile, embodied nature of human existence, which means that everyone experiences impairment at some stage in their lives, may now be a more productive approach to further disability rights.

Provision for disabled people in Britain c. 1900

In the early years of the century, services for disabled people primarily took the form of institutional provisions, many originating in the nineteenth century. These institutions usually catered to an age group or those with a designated disability and usually separated inhabitants by sex.

Voluntary specialist schools for disabled children, many operating on a charitable basis, originated in the late eighteenth century and segregated disabled children from their peers. The Royal Schools, for example, catered to deaf or blind children, primarily on a residential basis. They were charitable bodies with paying clientele but were sponsored by boards of guardians to offer places to working-class children. These schools aimed to transform students into productive citizens, capable of securing paid work, and taught religious instruction and vocational education, along gendered lines. The Heritage Craft Schools and Hospital, established by Grace Kimmins in 1903 at Chailey in Sussex, provided its residents with medical care, education, recreation, and physical training. Proclaiming Chailey the 'public school of crippledom', Kimmins displayed her pupils in theatrical performances to raise school funds (Koven 1994, p. 1175).

State intervention followed the 1870 Education Act, which mandated the education of all children in England and Wales between the ages of 5 and 12. The 1893 Elementary Education (Blind and Deaf) Act and 1899 Elementary Education (Defective and Epileptic Children) Act required local authorities to provide schools for blind and deaf children and empowered them to do the same for intellectually impaired children.

A 1918 Education Act mandated local authority provision of schools for children deemed physically and mentally defective. Collectively, these provisions led to a network of state-funded schools for disabled children.

Adults with physical impairments relied heavily on workhouses for support in the early twentieth century. A campaign after 1850 to reduce outdoor poor relief caused the percentage of adults deemed non-able bodied who were workhouse residents to jump from 11 to 28 percent between 1849 and 1899 (Borsay 2005, p. 25). Disabled and elderly residents were in principle afforded some privileges in terms of living conditions, diet, and work, yet such large-scale institutions remained bleak and regimented. Workhouses, renamed poor law institutions in 1913, came under the Ministry of Health's control in 1918. In 1929, the Local Government Act abolished poor law unions and boards of guardians, replacing these with public assistance committees and re-designating poor relief as public assistance. In practice, the former workhouses continued to operate similarly under the new label of public assistance institutions before 1948 and residential homes thereafter. While new homes were built over time, 35,000 elderly people were still resident in former public assistance institutions in 1960 (Borsay 2005, pp. 36–38).

The 1845 County Asylums Act and 1857 Lunacy (Scotland) Act obliged local authorities to establish asylums for pauper lunatics and established legal processes for certifying and committing people to asylums, usually involuntarily. By 1900, an asylum network operated across Britain, providing segregated institutional care for people deemed mentally ill. Some operated on a fee-paying basis for patients from wealthy families, but most housed paupers. Of the 106,611 individuals identified in January 1900 as lunatics by the Commissioners in Lunacy, a public body tasked with inspecting asylum conditions in England and Wales, 79,953 were held in county, borough or metropolitan district asylums, all intended for pauper patients, with a further 11,511 accommodated within workhouses (Commissioners in Lunacy 1900, p. 2). Local authorities purposefully constructed pauper asylums in rural settings where land was cheaper: psychiatrists argued that rural environments benefitted mental health, but this isolated patients from their families. Asylums functioned to some extent as self-sustaining communities staffed by their inhabitants, with farms to produce food and workshops to produce clothing and goods for the asylum.

The care and management of people with learning disabilities developed initially along similar lines: some were institutionalized in what were termed idiot asylums or in specialist schools for children. However, eugenics was more influential in shaping policies and services for people with learning disabilities. The Eugenics Education Society, founded in 1907, promulgated the belief that society should proactively manage the human race by encouraging healthy people to have children while preventing or discouraging those deemed unhealthy from doing so. It reflected growing concerns that the health of the race was deteriorating, both mentally and physically, a process termed degeneration. Eugenicists viewed learning disabilities, then termed mental deficiency, as heritable conditions marking the endpoint of degeneration: the genetic culmination of tuberculosis, alcoholism, sexual immorality, poverty, and insanity. The emerging field of criminology further stigmatized learning disability by asserting that mental deficiency was a causal factor in criminal behaviour. Such considerations influenced the 1913 Mental Deficiency Act, which established legal powers to compulsorily and permanently segregate people with learning disabilities, tasking local authorities with the duty of identifying, certifying, and, in some instances, detaining those deemed 'mentally defective'.

Eugenic Education Society lobbying in the interwar years highlighted once more care and management policies for people with learning disabilities. Unlike some Western countries, Britain did not enact proposals to compulsorily sterilize people diagnosed as mentally defective. However, local authorities did establish an increasing number of so-called mental deficiency colonies. Advocates of these large-scale institutions conjured images of a homely, village-like atmosphere that protected vulnerable residents from the outside world (Thomson 1998b). However, the term 'colony' was also associated more negatively with imperialism and racial segregation and was applied to punitive institutional solutions for crime and unemployment. Part of the colony solution's appeal was its affordability, with local authorities urged to spend less per capita on barracks-like accommodation for mentally defective patients than on mental hospitals or working-class housing.

Britain's industries, a major sector of employment in the early twentieth century, were typically hazardous, weakly regulated working environments, exposing workers to disabling accidents, industrial toxins, and lethal industrial diseases. Employers and the government did little to curb these risks in the nineteenth century, bar legal measures that restricted women and children's employment in some sectors but left male workers exposed. The 1897 Workmen's Compensation Act established employers' liability for employees injured at work. If incapacity lasted more than two weeks, injured workers could claim up to 50 percent of previous weekly earnings for full incapacity and a smaller sum for partial incapacity. A 1906 Act extended these provisions to compensate workers incapacitated through six industrial diseases connected to working processes, with further industrial diseases added later. While this provided some financial protection for employees incapacitated through work, it only covered a prescribed list of occupations and did little to prevent accidents and diseases from occurring (Bartrip 1987).

War and disability

The two world wars were turning points in social attitudes towards disabled people. Both conflicts propelled the development of statutory and voluntary services for disabled people. However, we should not overstate the extent of these provisions, for not all groups of disabled people benefitted. Typically, charities and the government designed services and legislation to meet the needs of war veterans and those disabled through industrial accidents. Sometimes these provisions extended to encompass other disabled people, but often as an afterthought.

The plight of men disabled through wartime combat inspired the establishment of rehabilitation provisions and measures to support and protect the employment of disabled people. By February 1915, around 360 disabled men returned to England and Wales on a weekly basis (Kowalsky 2007, p. 568). In 1922, war veteran George Howson persuaded the British Legion to contract the Disabled Society, which he had co-founded in 1920, to manufacture poppies. By 1924, Howson's factory employed 185 people, with an average disability of between 60 to 70 percent (Waller 2004). The King's National Roll Scheme, established in 1919, was a voluntary initiative, managed by the government, which urged companies to employ disabled ex-servicemen. The number of men employed through this scheme increased from 89,000 in

1920 to an average of 316,000 men a year between 1921 and 1938 (Kowalsky 2007, p. 573). The National Roll pioneered an integrationist approach, finding disabled workers employment in general firms, as opposed to segregating disabled people into sheltered workshops. Nevertheless, firms could meet the scheme's requirements by employing those with minor impairments, disadvantaging ex-servicemen with more severe impairments. During the Second World War, the scheme expanded to encompass disabled civilians and continued to operate until superseded by the 1944 Disabled Persons' Employment Act. Economic independence was a constitutive component of masculinity in early twentieth-century Britain. Yet all core elements of masculinity – appearance, economic independence, sporting prowess, white Britishness, and heterosexuality – were necessary to preserve men's identity, and postwar society's inability or reluctance to accomplish this raised questions about disabled veterans' roles in society (Bourke 2016).

Many men experienced lasting psychological damage following their wartime service, labelled shell shock during wartime. By 1939, 120,000 English First World War veterans had either received a final war award or ongoing pensions for psychiatric disability (Bogacz 1989, p. 251). Men invalided out of the army suffering from shell shock were treated in hospitals which had formerly served as asylums. Disquiet about these men's poor treatment fuelled a temporary surge of public interest in the nation's mental health services, but this concern rapidly dissipated in the postwar era, leaving little lasting imprint on civilian mental health services.

Wartime challenges also fostered the development of rehabilitation. The development of orthopaedics reduced the extent of long-term impairment arising from injury, but basic antiseptic techniques and the challenging environment of the battlefield meant that many injuries led to amputation. 41,050 ex-servicemen received prosthetic limbs, manufactured by Queen Mary's Hospital at Roehampton. Princess Louise Scottish Hospital for Limbless Sailors and Soldiers, known as Esrkine Hospital, opened in 1916 near Glasgow, serving a similar purpose in Scotland. Founded in 1916, the Ministry of Pensions awarded pensions to disabled ex-servicemen on a fractional basis, calculated by the type of amputation, impairment, or disfigurement experienced. It distributed pensions to 400,000 men in 1918 (Anderson 2011, p. 45). It also established workshops to train disabled veterans in occupations, transferring this responsibility to the Ministry of Labour after the War. St Dunstan's, established in 1914, provided specialist training and care for ex-servicemen who were blinded or sight impaired because of the War. It aimed to enable its residents to support themselves, and provided training and assistance in finding employment.

The demand for labour during the two world wars did create new employment opportunities for disabled civilians. Anderson (2006) describes the case of Ms B, a deaf woman, who found employment assembling shells. Deaf people were the preferred employees for this work, because it exposed workers to noise levels that damaged hearing. It was also a hazardous occupation, and Ms B experienced further disability when a detonator exploded, damaging her hands. Other forms of employment were still more exploitative. Noting approvingly that he was aware of 170 former mental deficiency school pupils who had enlisted to fight, Dr George Shuttleworth, a leading expert in mental deficiency, argued these recruits made good soldiers, as 'they had a good deal of drill, and were prompt in carrying out commands' (Thomson 1998b, p. 153).

Indeed, wartime developments largely privileged disabled ex-servicemen, not disabled civilians. The War Office requisitioned a number of asylums across the UK to provide accommodation for anticipated higher-status military casualties, redistributing existing residents to other asylums. Over the course of the First World War, asylum death rates in England and Wales doubled from 10 to 20 percent (Crammer 1992), largely a consequence of overcrowding; infectious disease, aided by lower nutritional standards; and a reduced asylum workforce, which hindered suicide prevention. After the war, veterans with pre-war histories of learning disability or mental illness were often denied the state pensions otherwise provided to those whose service had left them with enduring psychological trauma. The only legislative intervention to help disabled people secure employment after the First World War was the 1920 Blind Persons Act, which compelled local authorities to provide sheltered employment for blind people who were otherwise unable to secure employment. This Act was passed following a protest march by blind and partially sighted people to London, organized by the National League of the Blind, a trade union for blind workers.

A more systematic approach to rehabilitation was taken during the Second World War. Hospitals developed an integrated approach to help disabled ex-servicemen, offering occupation, exercise, and vocational rehabilitation. Their goal was to maximize efficiency by rapidly restoring injured soldiers to military service or the civilian workforce. Seeking primarily to develop services for disabled veterans, the Ministry of Labour and National Service established an inter-departmental committee in 1941 to make recommendations for the rehabilitation, training, and employment of 'disabled persons of all categories'. This committee's 1943 report paved the way for a new post-war system of rehabilitation and employment for disabled people.

Disabled people and the Welfare State

In the postwar era, segregated provisions slowly and unevenly gave way to integration policies, ushered in under the auspices of the Welfare State, with change evident in education, health provisions, work, benefits, and housing. We use the term 'Welfare State' to collectively describe a series of measures passed in the 1940s through which the government assumed responsibility for the welfare of its citizens, establishing core universal housing, education, and health services. The Welfare State's emergence has often been attributed to a sense of solidarity, seeking to establish services on the principle of universality and people's rights to access support and benefits. Yet while the acts that constituted the Welfare State provided some incremental gains for disabled people and implemented specific provisions for people disabled through industrial work and wartime service, they continued to mark disabled people out as second-class citizens. This was by design: while Beveridge acknowledged the deficiencies in provision for the physically disabled, he saw this as a matter for non-statutory bodies (Hampton 2016, p. 56).

The 1944 Disabled Persons (Employment) Act established a system to restore people to the workforce, operated by the Ministry of Labour. It obliged employers with 20 or more staff to hire 3 percent of their workforce from registered disabled people; introduced disablement resettlement officers to place people into employment; and provided segregated, sheltered work opportunities through the newly established body Remploy. The Act established industrial rehabilitation units to restore disabled people's working capacity and retrain them. Nominally, these provisions were open to all disabled people, but ministry officials curbed the number of people with learning disabilities and mental illness entering rehabilitation units and sheltered workshops, believing them to be more difficult to rehabilitate. In response, medical superintendents established sheltered workshops, termed industrial therapy units, within psychiatric hospitals in the 1950s and 1960s.

For workers disabled through a workplace accident or occupational illness, the 1946 National Insurance Act replaced the adversarial workmen's compensation system with industrial disablement benefit. This enabled disabled workers to claim sickness benefit indefinitely and introduced universal retirement pensions. While this measure removed some obstacles disabled workers had hitherto faced securing compensation, it offered little incentive to reduce the incidence of work-related disability. Alongside the government's decision to exclude occupational health services from the remit of the National Health Service, this was a missed opportunity to curb the incidence of occupational illness and disability, which disproportionately affected people working in heavy industries.

The new National Health Service, launched in 1948, incorporated hospitals for people with mental illness and learning disabilities. In practice, however, many of these institutions continued to operate independently from other hospitals. Admittance procedures also differed markedly: while the 1930 Mental Treatment Act enabled people to voluntarily seek hospital treatment, many patients were still admitted involuntarily. Psychiatrists introduced new therapeutic approaches in the early to mid-twentieth century, including electro-convulsive therapy, insulin coma therapy, psychosurgery, and psychotropic or antipsychotic drugs. However, inpatient numbers continued to rise, leading to overcrowding by the 1950s. Moreover, lack of funding meant that many hospitals remained bleak and seemingly little altered since their construction in the previous century. Describing one typical mental hospital, Jones and Sidebotham (1962, pp. 55–56) explained how:

> At one moment, one is in the setting of a good modern hospital, with pastel painted walls and chintz curtains as pleasant adjuncts to modern and efficient treatment. At the next, one is plunged back in the 'asylum' atmosphere of locked doors, long stone corridors, and large bare wards containing a hundred or more patients, many of them actively demented.

Although there were widespread issues with the quality of the hospital stock inherited by the NHS, resourcing for hospitals serving patients with mental illness and learning disability was markedly lower. While over £10 a week was spent maintaining patients in a general hospital, rising to £12–15 a week for maternity or sanatorium patients, less than half that sum – £5 a week – was apportioned to maintain a mental hospital patient (Bickford 1954). In practice, this meant that psychiatric hospital patients spent less time with medical staff and received less treatment than their counterparts in general hospitals. Similar parsimony affected the institutional care of people with learning disabilities, who by the mid-1970s were fed on a weekly sum of £3.59, as opposed to the £8.18 allotted to feed general hospital patients (Clare 1976).

One indirect consequence of the Welfare State's establishment was a greater willingness to create a more accessible environment for disabled people to navigate. In Britain, the architect Selwyn Goldsmith, partially paralyzed after contracting polio in 1956, was the driving force behind these changes. He concluded that many disabled people were, to some extent, dependent and that access provisions should be signposted to enable disabled people to identify and use them. This ethos furthered the development of signs and symbols designating disability. In 1963, Goldsmith wrote the first issue of *Designing for the Disabled*, commissioned and published by the Royal Institute of British Architects. This manual sought to provide comprehensive guidance on architectural planning for disabled access to buildings. Goldsmith also designed the dropped kerb, an innovation that facilitated travel across urban environments for wheelchair users. Developments in wheelchair design delivered greater mobility for many disabled people (Guffey 2018). The lightweight, robust, folding Everest and Jennings wheelchair, first developed in America in 1937, was easier to self-propel and handled different terrains more effectively than earlier models. In the 1970s and 1980s, innovations in special and adaptive seating, which tailored the seating to the user's body, generated wheelchairs that were more suitable for severely disabled people (Watson and Woods 2005).

Disability rights

By the 1960s and 1970s, disabled people began to establish their own campaign organizations and take charge of existing charities that had been set up on their behalf. These campaigners asserted that disabled people should shape policies and provisions that affected them, promoting a rights-based agenda covering integration, independent living, and an end to discrimination and institutionalization. The social model of disability increasingly underpinned these campaigns, alongside a rejection of the earlier medicalized approach that had attributed the challenges facing disabled people purely to bodily impairment.

Image 14.1 Wheelchair users from DAN (Disabled Action Network) handcuff themselves to a London bus on Westminster Bridge, London, in February 1995 as part of a series of protests about lack of disabled persons access to public transport, in the lead-up to the Disability Discrimination Act being debated in Parliament

Source: Credit Line: G.P. Essex/Alamay Stock Photo.

An early target for activists was the welfare state's failure to cater to all classes of disabled people. Campaigns for state compensation for children with limb and organ deformities, born to mothers prescribed thalidomide between 1958 and 1961, highlighted the absence of non-contributory state incomes for disabled civilians, aside from those who had acquired impairments through military service or industrial injury (Hampton 2016, pp. 163–168). In 1965, Megan du Boisson and Berit Thornberry attacked institutional care, which separated disabled people from their families, and called for the establishment of a disablement income group (DIG) to campaign for the rights of all disabled people – regardless of the cause of disablement – to access state pensions that would enable them to live independently. Led by disabled people, DIG membership numbered 6,000 by May 1969, spread across 46 local branches (Hampton 2016, 93). Its rallies attracted media coverage, raising awareness of the challenges facing disabled people. The 1970 Chronically Sick and Disabled Persons Act sought to address the prior neglect of disabled people's needs by the Welfare State, which created a division between the National Health Service and social care provided by local authorities. It compelled local authorities to provide community support services, such as practical assistance within the home, home adaptations, and access to recreational activities, and to ascertain how many disabled people required such services. In practice, however, variation in its implementation and a desire to restrict expenditure limited its scope.

Other disability rights activists believed that DIG's focus on income in isolation overlooked the pervasive discrimination experienced by disabled people. This approach was championed by UPIAS, co-founded in 1972 by the disability activist Paul Hunt, who had lived much of his life in institutions. Hunt had edited the 1966 book, *Stigma: The Experience of Disability*, a series of personal accounts authored by disabled people. In the booklet, 'Fundamental Principles of Disability' (1975), UPIAS asserted:

> it is society which disables physically impaired people. Disability is something imposed on top of our impairments, by the way we are unnecessarily isolated and excluded from full participation in society. Disabled people are therefore an oppressed group in society.

In 1981, nine disability organizations, led by disabled people, founded the British Council of Organisations of Disabled People, an umbrella organization designed to coordinate action on housing, education, and independent living. The Hampshire Centre for Independent Living, established by disabled people in 1984, sought to empower disabled people to leave institutional settings by securing financial support and social care to live independent lives in the community.

Similar changes affected mental health activism in this era. During the 1960s, the government formally adopted a policy of psychiatric deinstitutionalization, aiming to relocate people suffering from mental illness and learning disabilities into the community and close down long-stay hospitals. This policy sought to displace segregation with integration, but the government's failure to establish alternative community-based services meant that many people discharged from hospitals received inadequate support. It also discouraged any further investment in hospitals earmarked for closure, lowering staff morale and generating staffing shortages. These problems were particularly acute in hospitals and wards catering for people with learning disabilities and older patients with enduring mental health conditions. A series of hospital scandals in the 1960s which revealed extensive staff neglect and abuse of vulnerable patients and residents (Hilton 2017), and the high-profile anti-psychiatry movement of the 1970s, further incentivized the process of deinstitutionalization.

In the 1970s, mental patients' unions developed across the UK. Inspired by trade unionism and rights-based campaigning, these organizations asserted patients' rights to collectively campaign regarding their treatment. This led to the development of the service user or survivor movement, which fought vociferously for the rights of people who receive psychiatric treatment to shape the organization of psychiatric services.

Such developments impacted existing charities. The National Association of Mental Health, a philanthropic body led by healthcare professionals, adopted the 'MIND' campaign in 1971, deploying the language of patients' rights, critiquing societal apathetic indifference to the plight of people with mental health problems, and attacking the government's failure to develop substantive community care provisions. Alongside the Campaign for the Mentally Handicapped, a pressure group founded by *Guardian* journalist Anne Shearer and Anita Hunt of the Spastics Society (now Scope), the Association, which in 1972 adopted the name Mind, began calling for the closure of institutions for people with learning disabilities. It argued that learning disability was not a sickness that responded to medical treatment and pushed for learning disability's removal from legislation governing mental health, a step enacted in the 1983 Mental Health Act.

In Focus: prenatal screening and diagnosis

The history of prenatal screening and diagnosis in the UK reveals the impact of the disability rights movement, as well as the challenges it has faced. Today, the neutral language of choice shapes NHS prenatal screening programmes, emphasizing parents' rights to choose whether to accept screening for prenatally detected anomalies, and whether to continue their pregnancy when prenatally diagnosed conditions are detected. The NHS terms the likelihood of carrying a fetus affected by a particular condition as a chance, not a risk. However, when researchers first developed these technologies in the 1970s, they sought to prevent conditions that caused impairment and premature death through abortion (Löwy 2017). Researchers and the government justified these measures on the grounds of both cost (saving money that would otherwise be expended on care and education for disabled people) and the prevention of suffering.

Many disability rights activists have campaigned against prenatal screening and diagnosis, arguing that it discriminates against disabled people and devalues disabled lives. Some argue that it constitutes a renewed form of eugenics; a deliberate effort to improve the health of the human race by preventing the birth of disabled people (Duster 2003). Certainly, prenatal screening and diagnostic technologies were initially developed in a society that devalued disabled people's lives, and the profound structural discrimination experienced by disabled people was embedded within these practices. Notably, prenatal screening developed alongside ethical debates about providing or withholding life-saving surgical interventions to infants born with spina bifida, where the spinal cord does not fully develop, and Down's syndrome – the presence of an extra copy of chromosome 21 – which causes intellectual impairment and, for some individuals, cardiac defects and other physiological anomalies. In the 1960s, the surgeon John Lorber helped pioneer a new protocol of rapid surgical intervention for spina bifida babies, which dramatically reduced mortality rates. A decade later, he publicly renounced this approach, arguing that many survivors experienced a poor quality of life and asserting that surgical interventions should be restricted to only the most clinically promising cases (Lorber 1975). Meanwhile, the case of Dr Leonard Arthur, who in 1981 was found not guilty of murder after prescribing morphine to a newborn baby with Down's syndrome with the intent to end its life, revealed the discriminatory attitudes held by some doctors towards disabled people in this era (Wright 2011, pp. 165–166).

In practice, while we can identify a historical connection between prenatal screening and earlier eugenic ideas, we cannot determine if prenatal screening is eugenic in intent, because it is ambiguous whether its intended goal is to save money by improving the health of the population or to provide expectant mothers with more choice. However, it is arguably a reflection of the disability rights movement's success that we ask this question in the first place. By the 1980s, eugenics was a discredited science, and disability activists increasingly used the word pejoratively when describing prenatal screening and diagnosis in an attempt to link these practices with the Nazis. While prenatal screening and diagnosis provokes an ongoing animated debate about ethics and rights, the disability rights movement has influenced the scope of prenatal screening, underpinning the language of choice, as opposed to risk, which is evident today.

Conclusion

The 1995 Disability Discrimination Act in some ways reflects the achievements of the disability rights movement. It criminalized discrimination against disabled people in connection with employment; the provision of goods, facilities, and services; or the disposal or management of premises and obliged providers to make reasonable adjustments to enable disabled people to access their services. Yet we should exert caution before assuming that disabled people's rights were assured by the end of the century. As Mike Oliver observed (2016), the Disability Discrimination Act retained a medicalized definition of disability, and its emphasis on reasonable adjustment made it difficult to enforce. It was, moreover, enacted in an era of neoliberal welfare reform: in the same year, incapacity benefit replaced invalidity benefit, introducing tougher eligibility criteria to reduce the number of claimants.

Further reading

Disability history emerged from disability studies: see uploaded materials from activists and researchers in the Leeds Disability Archive (https://disability-studies.leeds.ac.uk/library/). Borsay (2005) remains the most comprehensive overview of disability in Britain. Other texts offer more detail on the relationship between disability and war (Anderson 2006), industrialization (Bohata *et al.* 2020), the Welfare State (Hampton

2016), and barrier-free architecture and signage (Guffey 2018). On learning disability, Thomson (1998a) analyses social policy, while Atkinson *et al.* (1997) reveal first-hand experiences of learning disabled people.

References

Abberley, P., 2007. Counting us out: A discussion of the OPCS disability surveys. *Disability and Society*, 7 (2), 139–155.

Anderson, J., 2006. British women, disability and the Second World War. *Contemporary British History*, 20 (1), 37–53.

Anderson, J., 2011. *War, disability and rehabilitation in Britain. 'Soul of a nation'*. Manchester: Manchester University Press.

Atkinson, D., Jackson, M., and Walmsley, J., 1997. *Forgotten lives: Exploring the history of learning disability*. Kidderminster: Bild Publications.

Bartrip, P.W.J., 1987. *Workmen's compensation in twentieth-century Britain: Law, history and social policy*. Aldershot: Gower.

Baynton, D.C., 2001. Disability and the justification of inequality in American history. *In*: P.K. Longmore and L. Umansky, eds. *The new disability history: American perspectives*. New York: New York University Press, 33–57.

Bickford, J.A.R., 1954. Treatment of the chronic mental patient. *The Lancet*, 263 (6818), 924–927.

Bogacz, T., 1989. War neurosis and cultural change in England, 1914–22: The work of the War Office Committee of Enquiry into 'Shell-Shock'. *Journal of Contemporary History*, 24 (2), 227–256.

Bohata, K., Jones, A., Mantin, M., and Thompson, S., 2020. *Disability in industrial Britain: A cultural and literary history of impairment in the coal industry, 1880–1948*. Manchester: Manchester University Press.

Borsay, A., 2005. *Disability and social policy in Britain since 1750: A history of exclusion*. Basingstoke: Palgrave Macmillan.

Bourke, J., 2016. Love and limblessness: Male heterosexuality, disability and the Great War. *Journal of War and Culture Studies*, 9 (1), 3–19.

Census of England and Wales 1901, 1903. *Summary tables. Areas, houses and population; also population classified by ages, condition as to marriage, occupations, birthplaces, and infirmities*. London: The Stationery Office.

Clare, A., 1976. *Psychiatry in dissent: Controversial issues in thought and practice*. London: Tavistock Publications.

Commissioners in Lunacy, 1900. *Fifty-fourth report of the Commissioners in Lunacy to the Lord Chancellor*. London: The Stationery Office.

Crammer, J.L., 1992. Extraordinary deaths of asylum inpatients during the 1914–1918 war. *Medical History*, 36 (4), 430–441.

Department for Work and Pensions, 2019. *Family resources survey 2017/2018*. London: The Stationery Office.

Duster, T., 2003. *Backdoor to eugenics*. London: Routledge.

Guffey, E., 2018. *Designing disability. Symbols, space and society*. London: Bloomsbury Academic.

Hampton, J., 2016. *Disability and the welfare state in Britain. Changes in perception and policy, 1948–79*. Bristol: Policy Press.

Hilton, C., 2017. *Improving psychiatric care for older people. Barbara Robb's campaign 1965–1975*. Basingstoke: Palgrave Macmillan.

Hunt, P., ed., 1966. *Stigma. The experience of disability*. London: Geoffrey Chapman.

Jones, K., and Sidebotham, R., 1962. *Mental hospitals at work*. London: Routledge & Keagan Paul.

Koven, S., 1994. Remembering and dismemberment: Crippled children, wounded soldiers, and the Great War in Great Britain. *The American Historical Review*, 99 (4), 1167–1202.

Kowalsky, M., 2007. 'This honourable obligation': The King's National Roll scheme for disabled ex-servicemen 1915–1944. *European Review of History*, 14 (4), 567–584.

Kudlick, C., 2008. *Disability history and history of medicine: Rival siblings or conjoined twins? (keynote address, Social History of Medicine Conference, Glasgow, Scotland, September 2008)*. Available from: www.academia.edu/1634239/_Disability_History_and_History_of_Medicine_Rival_Siblings_or_Conjoined_Twins_ [Accessed 16 February 2021.

Lorber, J., 1975. Ethical problems in the management of myelomeningocele and hydrocephalus. *Journal of the Royal College of Physicians of London*, 10 (1), 47–60.

Löwy, I., 2017. *Imperfect pregnancies. A history of birth defects and prenatal diagnosis*. Baltimore: John Hopkins University Press.

Office for National Statistics, 2015. *How has life expectancy changed over time?* Available from: www.ons.gov.uk/peoplepopulationandcommunity/birthsdeathsandmarriages/lifeexpectancies/articles/howhaslifeexpectancychangedovertime/2015-09-09 [Accessed 15 October 2019].

Oliver, M., 2013. The social model of disability: Thirty years on. *Disability and Society*, 28 (7), 1024–1026.

Oliver, M., 2016. Rewriting history: The case of the Disability Discrimination Act 1995. *Disability and Society*, 31 (7), 966–968.

Plumb, A., 1994. . . . Distress or disability? A discussion document. Reprinted. *In*: J. Anderson, B. Sapey and H. Spandler, eds. *Distress or disability? Proceedings of a symposium held at Lancaster University, 15–16 November 2011*. Centre for Disability Research, Lancaster University, 2–12. Available from: https://core.ac.uk/download/pdf/1441356.pdf [Accessed 25 November 2020].

Shakespeare, T., and Watson, N., 2001. The social model of disability: An outdated ideology? *Research in Social Science and Disability*, 2, 9–28.

Thies, S.B., Kenney, L.P.J., Howard, D., Nestera, C., Ormerod, M., Newton, R., Baker, R., Faruk, M., and MacLennan, H., 2011. Biomechanics for inclusive urban design: Effects of tactile paving on older adults' gait when crossing the street. *Journal of Biomechanics*, 44 (8), 1599–1604.

Thomson, M., 1998a. *The problem of mental deficiency. Eugenics, democracy, and social policy in Britain c. 1870–1959*. Oxford: Clarendon Press.

Thomson, M., 1998b. Status, manpower and mental fitness: Mental deficiency in the First World War. *In*: R. Cooter, M. Harrison and S. Sturdy, eds. *War, medicine and modernity*. Thrupp: Sutton Publishing, 149–166.

UPIAS and Disability Alliance, 1975. *Fundamental principles of disability: Being a summary of the discussion that was held on 22 November 1975*. Available from: https://disability-studies.leeds.ac.uk/wp-content/uploads/sites/40/library/UPIAS-fundamental-principles.pdf [Accessed 13 July 2020].

Waller, P., 2004. Howson, George (1886–1936). 23 September. Available from: https://doi-org.libproxy.ncl.ac.uk/10.1093/ref:odnb/37577.

Watson, N., and Woods, B., 2005. The origins and early developments of special/adaptive wheelchair seating. *Social History of Medicine*, 18 (3), 459–474.

Wright, D., 2011. *Downs: The history of a disability*. Oxford: Oxford University Press.

15 Social mobility

Andrew Miles

Introduction

In recent years social mobility has become a hot topic in the UK, drawing unprecedented attention from policymakers and featuring as a staple of media discourse. This level of concern stems from repeated claims that Britain is in the grip of a social mobility 'crisis', which has seen previously rising rates of mobility stagnate and even go into reverse. In 2010, a dedicated Parliamentary Commission on social mobility was established in response to cross-party consensus that 'more mobility' was needed. Since then the idea that mobility is in decline has become firmly embedded in the popular imagination.[1]

Behind the scenes, however, there is rather less consensus about the current state of mobility in Britain. It is the recent findings of economists that politicians have fastened upon in reaching their conclusion that there is a mobility crisis. Yet the main sociological tradition of social mobility research, which has dominated the field for the past 50 years, resolutely disputes this, arguing that the underlying rate of mobility has remained largely the same since the beginning of the twentieth century (Buscha and Sturgis 2017). Meanwhile, historians have recently joined with sociologists working outside of the mainstream tradition in mobility studies to argue that current debates revolve around too narrow a research agenda, limiting our view of what matters about mobility and how it operates (Lawler and Payne 2018, Miles 2018; de Bellaigue *et al.* 2019).

Such disciplinary disagreements speak to the complexity of social mobility as a concept and area of study that is highly sensitive to the differing interests, methodological standpoints and data sources that have been brought to bear on it. This, in turn, makes it impossible to tell a single, conclusive story about the nature of social mobility in Britain since 1900. However, in this chapter I will attempt to unravel the differences of approach and interpretation surrounding the topic, tracing how understandings of social mobility have developed since the early twentieth century and explaining what is at stake in contemporary conceptions of Britain's mobility crisis.

What is social mobility and why does it matter?

Social mobility is, essentially, movement in social space. However, there are various ways of understanding how social space is organised, what movement within or across it consists of, and how to represent, measure and interpret the transitions that take place (Sorokin 1927). The notion of mobility implies that social space is

DOI: 10.4324/9781003037118-16

structured in a relational or hierarchical way – in other words, that movement takes place between social positions that are differentiated by types and levels of resource, giving people more or less control over their own lives and, potentially, the lives of others. Movement in social space often coincides with movement in physical or geographical space, although social and spatial mobility have rarely been considered together.

In the UK, the predominant way of thinking about social mobility has been in terms of *social class*, usually based on people's job or occupational position, though more recently discussions of income mobility have come to the fore. Most often, the term 'social mobility' is used to refer to the *intergenerational* comparison between a person's social *origin*, or family background, and their *destination*, or the social position that they themselves occupy. This forms the basis of the standard approach to measuring changes in mobility using the two-way mobility table. Some studies have extended the intergenerational approach to include a *multi-* or *transgenerational* perspective. As well as comparisons between generations, researchers also refer, often by way of contrast, to social mobility as movement over the life course, which is known as *work-life, career* or *intragenerational* mobility. Other approaches to studying mobility have looked beyond the labour market to include people's changing status in terms of their educational qualifications or their social networks through marriage.

Social mobility matters because it affects how society is shaped, or structured, over time and also how that structure is justified culturally, politically and morally. By modulating the extent to which people share common experiences and resources in life, the rate, pace and direction of mobility conditions how likely it is that social groups will form, how people think about themselves in terms of identity and belonging and how they relate to others. Stemming from this, the nature and rate of social mobility have long been thought to influence the stability of society, with theorists arguing that both low and high rates of mobility are potential causes of tension and discord (Heath 1981).

What, then, constitutes the 'right' amount of mobility depends on expectations rooted in societal norms and political conventions. Central to expectations of mobility in Britain since the Second World War has been the concept of 'meritocracy'. A meritocratic society is one where people 'get ahead', or enter desirable, influential and well-paid jobs, on the basis of hard work, talent and 'equality of opportunity' rather than tradition, corruption or favour. In Western liberal nations with capitalist economies, meritocracy is proposed as a reasonable justification for the unequal rewards that accrue to different positions in the division of labour. These are seen to be acceptable if the outcome of social mobility is fair; that is, based on open access and achievement rather than ascription or hereditary privilege. It is further argued that the meritocratic process is beneficial to all, not just those who are mobile, because it puts 'the right people in the right place', thereby making the economy more competitive and the administration of society more efficient. However, it is precisely this set of expectations and justifications that has been called into question by the present day 'crisis' of social mobility.

The birth of social mobility

The picture we have of mobility at the beginning of the twentieth century is that it was heavily restricted but also, in certain respects, increasing. Research by historians backs up the contemporary account of working-class writer Robert Roberts who noted that while there were still distinct economic and cultural barriers between the skilled artisans and labourers in the Salford slum in which he grew up, 'the real social divide' in the period before the First World War was 'between those who, in earning their daily bread, dirtied hand and face, and those who do not' (Roberts 1973, pp. 13, 19).

Evidence taken from the occupations of marriage partners in church registers across England at the time shows that fewer than 10 per cent of those born to families engaged in manual work were upwardly mobile into the world of non-manual employment (Miles 1999). Almost all of these 'inter-class' travellers made it no further than the emerging lower middle class of 'white-collar' employment, populated by post-office sorters, elementary school teachers, travelling salesmen and the like or into small manufacturing and retail businesses. Their numbers were slowly increasing, but more change was in train within working-class communities, where the effects of the changing shape of the economy and urbanisation towards the end of the nineteenth century had started to eat away at the status distinctions between skilled and the unskilled workers noted by Roberts. By 1914, 40 per cent of workers' children experienced either 'short-range' upward or downward 'intra-class' mobility, compared to 20 per cent in the middle of the nineteenth century.

This trend was boosted by inflation and the demand for labour during the First World War. It continued in the interwar period as the decline of the staple industries, dilution, mass unemployment during the Great Depression and the bureaucratisation of work reduced the independence and power of skilled working men. At this point the gap to the middle classes looks to have increased. Here a parallel process of restructuring was underway, centred on the rise of salaried professional and managerial employment and a private house building boom in the South that far outstripped the rise of council house building in the North. Meanwhile, at the top of society, declining landed aristocratic fortunes were shored up by intermarriage with rising wealth elites in business and finance to create a more eclectic, plutocratic elite (Miles 2003).

The period after 1918 is covered by the first dedicated, national-level study of social mobility, based on a representative sample survey of more than 9,000 adults, which was carried out by David Glass and a team of researchers at the London School of Economics (LSE) in 1949 (Glass 1954). It was from this point on that the study of social mobility became synonymous with the emerging discipline of sociology. However, the groundwork for the field had been laid earlier by an assortment of civil servants, demographers, social biologists and statisticians, who sought to investigate the social structure of the population in the wake of claims by eugenicists that a growing 'underclass' risked undermining the quality of the British 'race'. Glass was a product of the more progressive elements in this wave of early twentieth-century social investigation, from whom he inherited a concern with social justice and the way that restrictions on access to the professions amounted to a waste of talent (Renwick 2018).

A key aim of the 1949 study was therefore to probe the distinctiveness of the civil service elite in the context of the wider educational and social reforms ushered in by the Second World War (Payne 2017). Accordingly, Glass placed most stress on his finding that sons with fathers in the highest of the seven status groups he identified were vastly overrepresented at this level by comparison with those whose fathers were in the lowest. Overall, Glass argued that there had been no significant trend in the overall pattern of intergenerational mobility in the interwar period, though here it should be noted that his data suggest that upward mobility continued to rise up until the 1930s depression, while his analysis also obscured key distinctions within the working class. It also excluded the experience of women and thus the dramatic rise in female clerical employment in the inter-war period, which nevertheless looks to have played an important role in helping to maintain the barriers to upward mobility for working-class men (Miles and Savage 2004).

The Nuffield 'paradigm' and the paradox of mobility

The LSE study remained influential in the way that sociologists thought about Britain's social structure in the 1950s and 60s. However, it is the work of John Goldthorpe that has dominated the field of social mobility and stratification in the UK for much of the last fifty years. Goldthorpe and his colleagues at Nuffield College, Oxford, carried out a second national mobility survey in 1972. In many respects this work was a consolidation of Glass's approach. Goldthorpe also came to study mobility through an interest in the goal of a fairer society, which he approached by quantifying the rate of male intergenerational mobility based on a comparison of the occupations of sample survey respondents with those of their fathers (Goldthorpe *et al.* 1987). Yet his approach to operationalising mobility in terms of movement within an occupational class structure, and the analytical distinction he made between 'absolute' and 'relative' mobility, was to redefine the field, making a profound impact on the development of UK sociology as a modern 'scientific' discipline in the process (Savage 2010).

Goldthorpe first tackled the issue of classifying occupation in a more objective way than the partly subjective, status-based, social grading approach adopted by Glass. His 'class structural' approach drew on Max Weber's theory of stratification to distinguish seven main groups of occupations according to their 'employment relations'; whether their incumbents were employers, self-employed or employees; and, in the latter case, how much security and autonomy their contracts of employment allowed. This approach now forms the basis of the modern-day National Statistics Socio-Economic Classification Scheme (NS-SEC), which is the official class scheme used by government agencies in the UK.

Goldthorpe was notable for being a member of a new generation of upwardly mobile academics from unconventional backgrounds. He had previously undertaken a landmark study of the impact of 'affluence' on the outlook of the postwar working class with David Lockwood. Turning to the subject of social mobility, his initial interest was in movement across the 'collar-line' between working-class and middle-class positions and how this affected the degree of 'class formation' in society (Savage 2000). This could be gauged by considering the 'absolute', or raw, percentages of people moving between class groups, either from the perspective of their origin class, termed 'outflow' mobility, or their destination class, known as 'inflow' mobility.

Altogether, the Oxford Mobility Study showed that the rate of mobility in Britain in the middle of the twentieth century was considerable. More than 70 per cent of people were found to be in a different social class to the one they were born into.

A comparison of survey respondents born in different decades also showed that the rate of upward mobility from the working and intermediate classes into the 'service' class – professional and managerial groups with the highest levels of expertise, delegated authority and salaried remuneration in a capitalist economy – had increased from 30 per cent of those reaching the age of 35 in the 1940s and 50s to 40 per cent in the 1960s and 70s.

As to the effect of these trends on the potential for class formation, Goldthorpe observed that the service class was in fact very diverse in terms of it class origins. Two-thirds of its membership were, in fact, class outsiders. By contrast, as more people left their working-class origins behind, that class became more self-recruiting and, continuing the trend from the first half of the twentieth century, internally homogenous. However, when the implications of these structural or 'demographic' patterns of class formation were explored in a follow-up study of survey respondents in 1974, there was little to suggest that members of the working class felt cut off from the rest of society or antagonistic towards other class groups or that the upwardly mobile felt out of place in their new class surroundings.

With absolute mobility rates seeming to offer little of substantive sociological interest, Goldthorpe turned his attention to what was driving the changes that could be observed in the cells of the mobility tables that provided the platform for his analysis. Here, by focusing on relative mobility rates, he revealed a crucial paradox. Although absolute rates indicated that mobility levels were high and upward mobility was increasing, this did not mean that British society had become more fluid, or 'open', in the sense that the competition for top jobs had become fairer. Modelling the 'odds' of people from different class backgrounds ending up in one class position rather than another, Goldthorpe revealed the persistence of marked inequalities in mobility chances between men born into families towards the top and the bottom of the class structure.

What had accounted for the rising rates of upward mobility was the expansion of the professional and managerial jobs brought about by the changing shape of the economy in the middle decades of the twentieth century. Between the 1930s and the 1980s the size of the professional and managerial sector in the UK doubled, from 15 per cent to 29 per cent (Routh 1987). This resulted in an 'upgrading' of the class structure, creating more 'room at the top'. Rather than the upwardly mobile sons of working-class fathers displacing the sons of the service class in the completion for professional and managerial positions, people from all class backgrounds had benefited equally from the expansion of these sectors. Ultimately, despite appearances to the contrary, rising rates of absolute upward mobility had not made Britain a more meritocratic society.

Goldthorpe's approach to relative mobility effectively controlled for the impact of the changing division of labour on the observable pattern of mobility. Exposing the underlying 'mobility regime', it facilitated a true comparison of how open societies are over time and between places. Subsequently, Goldthorpe went on to show that there had been no significant variation in relative mobility rates across nine European countries since the early twentieth century (Erikson and Goldthorpe 1992). On this basis he argued that modern industrial societies had probably always been characterised by unequal mobility regimes that were essentially constant and, at most, subject to 'trendless fluctuation'.

In Focus: measuring mobility

Concern about the consequences of the rate and pattern of social mobility in society has placed an emphasis on issues of quantification and measurement in terms of the way that the subject has been approached. In the UK, social scientists have traditionally measured mobility by comparing the occupations of survey respondents (until recently just males) with those of their parents (until recently just their father's) at two points in time by means of an origin-destination contingency table.

This is shown in Table 15.1, which is based on the 1972 Oxford Mobility Study (Goldthorpe *et al.* 1987). Here the seven occupational classes on which the main analyses from this survey were based have been collapsed into three in order to simplify the illustration. The vertical axis shows the occupational class of respondents' fathers when the respondents were 14 and the horizontal axis respondents' own occupational class at age 35 or older. The cells in the body of the table show the percentages of people with specific origin-destination combinations.

Table 15.1 Intergenerational social mobility of men in England and Wales aged 20–64 in 1972 (calculated from Goldthorpe *et al.* 1987, Tables 2.1 and 2.2)

Father's class (when son was 14)	Son's class (1972)			
	Service class	Intermediate class	Working class	Number in each class
Service class	59.4 / 32.0	25.3 / 12.2	15.2 / 5.0	1227
Intermediate class	29.9 / 34.6	35.8 / 37.3	34.3 / 24.2	2645
Working class	16.2 / 33.3	27.3 / 50.6	56.6 / 70.9	4703
Number in each class	2280	2540	3755	

■ Immobility   ▨ Downward mobility   ▨ Upward mobility

Note: Service-class occupations include large employers and those in professional and managerial roles, such as lawyers, teachers and chief executives; the intermediate class combines routine non-manual workers, such as bank clerks, with lower-grade technicians, like electricians, work-place supervisors and the self-employed; the working class includes skilled manual workers, like carpenters (if not self-employed), and those in routine manual jobs, like bus drivers.

The diagonal cells represent 'immobility', or those who were found in the same class as their father. Below the diagonal are those who were upwardly mobile and above it those who were downwardly mobile. Reading this table from left to right, by row, and focusing on the percentage in the top left of each cell gives us a measure of the 'outflow' from particular class origins to particular class destinations. Here it is evident that there is a degree of concentration at the two poles of the class structure, where around almost 60 per cent of those born into the service class and into the working class follow their fathers into similar types of jobs. However this also means that a substantial minority of people was either upwardly or downwardly mobile, with one step up or down into the intermediate class more likely than longer-range mobility.

Reading the table from top to bottom, by column, and focusing on the percentages in the bottom right of each cell shows us the effects of these patterns in terms of the 'inflow' to particular class destinations from particular class origins. The reason these percentages are not the same as the corresponding cell percentage for outflow mobility is, first, because the three classes are quite different in size and, second, because of the substantial relative expansion of the service class that took place between the two generations. Thus the men who followed their fathers into the service class, which was the majority experience (59.4 per cent) among this group, found themselves in the minority (32.4 per cent) of all service class employees in their own generation.

The fact that two-thirds of both the service class and the working class in 1972 were made up of class 'outsiders' by birth certainly gives the appearance of a quite fluid or 'open' society, which, in such 'absolute' terms, it was. Yet if we consider these patterns in terms of the relative mobility chances of those with different class origins, a rather different picture, of inequality and restriction, emerges. The fact that 59 per cent of those born into the service class achieved a service class position themselves, compared to just 16 per cent of those born into the working class, means that they started out with an advantage of almost four to one ($59.4/16.2 = 3.67$) in the competition for professional and managerial jobs. At the same time, they held a similarly sized advantage ($15.2/56.6 = 0.27$) over those growing up in the working class when it came to avoiding manual employment. Taken together, then, the relative odds of those born into the service class and the working class ending up in the service class rather than the working class ($3.67/0.27$) were more than 13:1 in favour of those who grew up in the more advantaged households. It follows that for the mobility chances of these two groups to be equal in this particular competition, relative to each other, which some consider the true test of social 'openness', rates of upward and downward mobility between the working class and the service class would have had to have been around double what they actually were.

The major strength of the mobility table is that it standardises the calibration and analysis of social mobility, enabling comparison over time and allowing it to be subjected to powerful statistical analysis. This includes the calculation and modelling of relative mobility, which indicates what accounts for changes in the surface pattern of inter-generational mobility transitions. However, by constructing mobility as a cross-sectional snapshot between individual members of different generations at two particular points in time, this approach tends to obscure what is actually a complex socio-temporal process (Savage 1997).

The standard mobility table also hides from view many of the social mechanisms that underpin and drive the patterns of movement it captures. These include, for example, the role of family relationships and strategies in producing the mobile individual (Shahrokni 2018). At the same time, it takes no account of people's subjective understandings of mobility, which is problematic when theorising about the impact of mobility and immobility on processes of class formation and questions of social identity. Here, for example, it has been argued that the identity of middle-class groups is more bound up with their own work-life trajectories and the prospective rewards associated with these rather than considerations of family background and intergenerational comparison (Savage 2000).

The challenge of the economists

For some time, the only challenge to the findings of the Nuffield paradigm came from historians studying class mobility in the nineteenth and early twentieth centuries, whose findings suggested that both absolute and relative mobility rates were rising at least up until the First World War, casting doubt on how far the 'constant flux' reaches back in time (Miles 1999, Lambert *et al.* 2007, Maas and van Leeuwen 2016). However, this changed quite dramatically following the publication of research in the early 2000s by a group of economists at the LSE working on income, as opposed to occupational class, mobility (Blanden *et al.* 2004; Elliot Major and Machin 2018).

Comparing data from the 1958 and 1970 birth cohort studies, the LSE researchers found that the earnings of men and women in the 1970 cohort at age 33–34 were more strongly associated with those of their parents than was the case among the earlier cohort. This meant that children from richer families who left school in the 1980s had, by the early 2000s, significantly increased their earnings advantage over poorer children as compared to the situation twelve years earlier. On this basis, the economists concluded that the rate of income mobility in Britain was both declining and one of the lowest among the world's economically developed nations. Extending the reach of their inquiry to include data from the British Household Panel Survey from the 1990s, the economists went on to argue that it was children from more affluent families that appeared to have benefitted most from the big expansion of higher education over this period, which in turn helped account for rising income inequalities.

This research quickly gained traction with policymakers. Suddenly, having been a relatively quiet preserve of academic research and debate for half a century, mobility became a political football. First the New Labour government of 1997, and then the subsequent Coalition and Conservative governments, blamed their opponents for failing to tackle its decline. Also in line with the economists' arguments, policy prescriptions, focusing on improving educational opportunities to produce 'more mobility', followed. These included 'Sure Start' and the Educational Maintenance Allowance on one side of the political divide and reform of the National Curriculum and the revival of grammar schools on the other. Meanwhile, the purchase of the 'decline thesis' was cemented in the popular imagination by the way it was consumed and repeated by media commentators.

Sociologists, including Goldthorpe, responded to this research with new studies of occupational class mobility. These also took advantage of the British cohort studies, as well as longitudinal census data, to extend their temporal focus (Buscha and Sturgis 2017), with the inclusion of women's occupational trajectories in these data finally giving a more rounded picture of mobility. In most respects these studies confirmed the core findings of the Nuffield paradigm. The absolute rate of occupational class mobility in Britain remains high and shows no sign of declining: consistently, between 1984 and 2011, three out of four people in Britain have ended up in a different class to the one they grew up in. Alongside this, relative mobility rates – referring to the inequalities in mobility chances between people originating in different class groups – have remained largely constant. If anything, these studies suggest a small *increase* in social fluidity, particularly among women, in the 1980s and 90s.

Moreover, it has also been shown that improving educational opportunities – assumed by the politicians to be the main solution to the problem of equalising mobility chances – was unlikely to succeed in isolation. Education can be thought of as a form of mobility in its own right, and in this sense the past seventy years have revolutionised educational attainment. In the first half of the twentieth century around 90 per cent of working-class children left school by the age of 13 (Floud 1954). This changed radically after the Second World War as a result of the 1944 Education Act, which made secondary education free, universal and compulsory until the age 15, rising to 16 in 1972. More recently, the expansion of higher education has seen a similarly profound shift, with the proportion of 18–21 year-olds going to university skyrocketing from just one in twenty-five in 1960 to effectively one in two today. Yet education was also intended by reformers to promote social mobility by making social selection, particularly for top jobs, more meritocratic, and this promise has not been met (Mandler 2020).

Evaluation of the postwar 'tripartite' education system soon showed that, rather than breaking the link between class background and relative educational attainment, it had maintained it (Halsey *et al.* 1980). Recent research confirms that this pattern continued through the era of comprehensivisation in secondary education and in spite of university expansion. As with the growth of professional and managerial employment, it is those born into economic and social advantage who have made the most of the new opportunities (Bukodi and Goldthorpe 2018). More damningly still for the prospects of meritocracy, it is also the case that indirect routes into top jobs – bypassing the need for A-levels and more recently degrees on entry – remain as important as ever, and in this respect, the relative class advantage of those from NS-SEC Classes 1 and 2 has actually increased by 40 per cent since the 1970s.

Mobility and the crisis of inequality

In terms of consistency, the weight of the evidence in the academic dispute about mobility in the UK seems to be against any sustained decline in relative social mobility.[2] On the other hand, we are not comparing like with like when it comes to occupational class and income mobility, leaving open the possibility that the contrasting findings of the sociologists and economists are a reflection of the different dynamics at play in the pattern of intergenerational association between different dimensions of socio-economic advantage (Buscha and Sturgis 2017).

One effect of the intervention of the economists is that it has helped to open up debate about the significance of perspectives on mobility, like income as opposed to occupation, that tended to become sidelined by the Nuffield paradigm's increasing focus on measuring macro-level trends in relative intergenerational mobility. These also include the important role of absolute mobility in shaping the subjective meanings it carries for people, the importance of intra-generational mobility and the mechanisms behind mobility, all of which are obscured by the two-way comparison of occupational origins and destinations of individuals in the standard mobility table.

Arguably, the disagreement about trends in relative mobility has become something of a distraction from more pressing issues. After all, both the economists' and the sociologists' data describe a situation where relative mobility chances, whether they are changing slightly or not, remain profoundly unequal. The more important and interesting issue questions would therefore seem to be why, since the 1940s, people born into in the NS-SEC Class 1 have been around *twenty times* more likely to end up in Class 1 rather than Class 7 when compared to those born into Class 7 (Bukodi and Goldthorpe 2018), and why, given the extent and consistency of this disparity, is it only in the past 15 years that mobility has come to the fore as a social problem?

There are, in fact, good historical and sociological reasons, bound up with the pattern and process of mobility itself, for the *perception* of stalling or declining mobility taking root in both political debate and in wider society. A key factor here has been the more general rise in economic and social inequalities since the 1980s (Elliot Major and Machin 2018) and the way in which this has coincided with a profound demographic shift brought about by the end of what is now understood to have been, in absolute if not relative terms, a 'golden age' of mobility beginning in the 1940s.

As we know from Goldthorpe's original study, the expansion of the upper reaches of the class structure during the period of economic growth after 1945 sponsored an increase in upward mobility that was widely shared across the population. At the same time, classes lower down the social structure contracted, making downward mobility less likely. Between the 1980s and the early years of this century, however, this pattern went into reverse. The likelihood of becoming upwardly mobile fell, while downward mobility became more common. Simultaneously, the post-war expansion of professional and managerial jobs that had encouraged more upward mobility from the working class, as well as allowing more sons from middle-class families to maintain their status, changed the composition of the class structure. More people have been starting out from middle-class homes, but with the expansion of professional and managerial positions now stalling, their risk of falling in social space has begun to rise.

So, even while the sociologists' findings suggest no significant change in social fluidity, it is clear that their data also show that there is cause for *increasing* alarm about mobility. Today, younger people's mobility prospects are rather more obviously *less* favourable than those of their parents and include the spectre of more downward mobility. Meanwhile, the upgrading of the class structure also means those who do make the transition from a contracting working-class environment into an expanded middle class are less likely to find themselves among people from the same background who have experienced a similar upwardly mobile trajectory.

Here we should note that, unlike the somewhat abstract and technical issue of relative mobility, it is these shifts in the *absolute* rate of mobility between the current and the parental generation that are more visible to people. This is because they provide a more immediate and understandable reference point for people in the context of their everyday lives and relationships. In the decades following the Second World War, when there was both more upward social mobility and rising incomes for all, including the immobile, the significance of absolute mobility for issues of social identity and stability was, as Goldthorpe noted at the time, much reduced. However, in the more recent context of sharply rising economic and social inequalities, exacerbated by the financial crisis of 2008, underpinned by a policy regime of austerity, and now, in the wake of Brexit, followed by the uncertain prospects associated with effects of the COVID-19 pandemic, the visibility of mobility and immobility has been significantly enhanced.

Debates and Interpretations: the return to elites

The post-war boom in upward mobility proceeded alongside a series of challenges to established social and cultural interests, which gave an impression that Britain was becoming a more open and meritocratic society. On this basis, a succession of political leaders, from Margaret Thatcher to Tony Blair, claimed that social class no longer mattered, a conclusion that was shared by many academics. However, with the return to levels of wealth inequality not witnessed since the end of the nineteenth century (Piketty 2014), a hasty reappraisal has ensued.

In these circumstances both political and academic attention has been drawn back to an issue that was a founding concern of social mobility research before the Second World War: the problem of elites. The colossal disparities in income that have emerged since the 1980s have stretched the credulity of the meritocratic rhetoric used to justify inequality in the name of social mobility, bringing the issue of social closure at the top back into focus.

Image 15.1 Wealthy friends enjoy bubbly and fizz during the annual Henley Regatta

Source: © Richard Baker/Alamy Stock Photo.

However, one of the limitations of the mainstream approach to social mobility is that national sample surveys have not contained large enough numbers to be able to capture smaller, geographically concentrated elite groups at the very top of the social structure. Here it has been argued that the focus on 'big class' mobility between composite occupational groups collapses important distinctions between smaller 'micro classes' and that occupation itself is a less adequate proxy for social class than it used to be. This was illustrated by research from the *Great British Class Survey*, which drew on the French sociologist Pierre Bourdieu's understanding of social classes as groups distinguished by the differing amounts of economic, social and cultural 'capital' they possess to show the emergence of a distinct elite group concentrated in London and the South-East and the mechanisms they employ to effect social closure (Savage *et al.* 2015).

The latest large-scale study of social mobility in Britain combines a similar 'capitals' approach with a focus on occupational micro-classes to examine social mobility into top jobs (Friedman and Laurison 2019). Using new data from the Labour Force Survey, it reveals the operation of a 'class ceiling' regulating access to elite positions. Not only are the most prestigious professions – like medicine and law – the least accessible to those originating from working-class backgrounds, but also when class outsiders do gain access, they face significant disadvantages in their careers. This is the case even where they have attended elite universities and are better qualified in terms of degree classification than incumbents and is indicated by the large class-pay gap that exists between the upwardly mobile and people in the same jobs who are from professional and managerial backgrounds. This gap then increases when intersections between class, gender and ethnicity are brought into the mix.

Using evidence from interviews with people in a range of elite London-based firms, this study goes on to show how those from privileged class backgrounds start out with a big advantage in terms of the key resources available to them, which accumulate and are passed on within families, facilitating the process of elite reproduction. These include parental economic support ('the Bank of Mum and Dad'), which allows them to take up unpaid internships, and socialisation into cultural understandings, attitudes and behaviours that puts them at ease in elite settings, facilitates their integration into important social networks and marks them out as a good 'match' for top employers. Conversely, those who are upwardly mobile into elite jobs, and who usually cannot access the same type and level of resources, often feel 'out of place' by comparison and lack the confidence to promote themselves.

Conclusion

The study of social mobility in the twentieth century seems to have come full circle. In particular, the problem of social closure at the top is once again an issue of concern. This is because the broader issues of social identity, division and inequality that the process and outcomes of mobility both speak to and shape remain as salient today as they did 120 years ago. Social mobility is a complex, multidimensional phenomenon. How much of it there is, and can be, depends on the way in which social space is conceptualised and calibrated. Social scientists in the UK have mainly focused on individual male intergenerational mobility between social classes, defined by membership of broad occupational groups. In these terms, the overall rate of mobility in Britain has remained high since the First World War, with prospects for social ascent rising on either side of the Great Depression and especially in the 'golden age of mobility' after the Second World War. It is the particular effect of this long boom in upward mobility on Britain's social structure and the circumstances in which it has recently ended that accounts for the contemporary 'crisis' of social mobility.

Further reading

An overview of sociological work on social mobility in twentieth-century Britain and its conceptual foundations is provided by Heath (1981). Miles (2003) gives an historical account of the relationship between social class and mobility in the first half of the century. Bukodi and Goldthorpe (2018) summarise the findings of social scientists on social mobility since the Second World War, while Mandler (2020) brings an historian's perspective to the same period. Elliot Major and Machin (2018) survey changes in mobility from the perspective of economists. Savage (1997 and 2000) and Payne (2017) develop critiques of the mainstream sociological approach to social mobility research. New and revived perspectives on the subject are presented in the collections edited by Miles (2018), de Bellaigue *et al.* (2019) and Lawler and Payne (2018) and by Friedman and Laurison's (2019) study of elites and mobility.

Notes

1 Social mobility is closely related to the topic of inequality, which is one of the themes of Chapter 4 in this volume.
2 For further discussion of inequality in the UK, see Chapter 4.

References

Blanden, J., Goodman, A., Gregg, P., and Machin, S., 2004. Changes in intergenerational mobility in Britain. *In*: M. Corak, ed. *Generational income mobility in North America and Europe.* Cambridge: Cambridge University Press, 122–146.
Bukodi, E., and Goldthorpe, J.H., 2018. *Social mobility and education in Britain: Research, politics and policy.* Cambridge: Cambridge University Press.
Buscha, F., and Sturgis, P., 2017. Declining social mobility? Evidence from five linked censuses in England and Wales 1971–2011. *British Journal of Sociology*, 69 (1), 154–182.
de Bellaigue, C., Mills, H., and Worth, E., 2019. "Rags to Riches?" New histories of social mobility in modern Britain – Introduction. *Cultural and Social History*, 16 (1), 1–11.
Elliot Major, L., and Machin, S., 2018., *Social mobility and its enemies.* London: Pelican.
Erikson, R., and Goldthorpe, J.H., 1992. *The constant flux: A study of class mobility in industrial societies.* Oxford: Clarendon Press.
Floud, J., 1954. The educational experience of the adult population of England and Wales as at July 1949. *In*: D.V. Glass, ed. *Social mobility in Britain.* London: Routledge.
Friedman, S., and Laurison, D., 2019. *The class ceiling: Why it pays to be privileged.* Bristol: Polity Press.
Glass, D.V., ed., 1954. *Social mobility in Britain.* London: Routledge.
Goldthorpe, J.H., Llewellyn, C., and Payne, C., 1987. *Social mobility and class structure in modern Britain.* 2nd ed. Oxford: Clarendon Press.
Halsey, A.H., Heath, A.F., and Ridge, J.M., 1980. *Origins and destinations: Family, class, and education in modern Britain.* Oxford: Oxford University Press.
Heath, A., 1981. *Social mobility.* London: Fontana.
Lambert, P., Prandy, K., and Bottero, W., 2007. By slow degrees: Two centuries of social reproduction and mobility in Britain. *Sociological Research Online*, 12 (1).

Lawler, S., and Payne, G., 2018. *Social mobility for the 21st century. Everyone a winner?.* London: Routledge.

Maas, I., and van Leeuwen, M.H.D., 2016. Toward open societies? Trends in male intergenerational class mobility in European countries during industrialization. *American Journal of Sociology*, 122 (3), 838–885.

Mandler, P., 2020. *The crisis of the meritocracy: Britain's transition to mass education since the Second World War.* Oxford: Oxford University Press.

Miles, A., 1999. *Social mobility in nineteenth and early twentieth century England.* Basingstoke: Macmillan.

Miles, A., 2003. The changing social structure, 1900–1939. *In*: C.J. Wrigley, ed. *The Blackwell companion to early twentieth century Britain.* Oxford: Blackwell, 337–352.

Miles, A., 2018. Introduction to BJS special section: New approaches to social mobility. *British Journal of Sociology*, 69 (4), 1056–1061.

Miles, A., and Savage, M., 2004. Constructing the modern career, 1840–1940. *In*: J. Brown, M.H.D. van Leeuwen and D. Mitch, eds. *The origins of the modern career.* Aldershot: Ashgate, 79–100.

Payne, G., 2017. *The new social mobility. How the politicians got it wrong.* Bristol: Polity Press.

Piketty, T., 2014. *Capital in the twenty-first century.* Cambridge: Harvard University Press.

Renwick, C., 2018. Movement, space and social mobility in early and mid-twentieth-century Britain. *Cultural and Social History*, 16 (1), 1–11.

Roberts, R., 1973. *The classic slum: Salford life in the first quarter of the century.* London: Pelican.

Routh, G., 1987. *Occupations of the people of Great Britain, 1901–1981.* Basingstoke: Macmillan.

Savage, M., 1997. Social mobility and the survey method. *In*: D. Bertaux and P. Thompson, eds. *Pathways to social class: A qualitative approach to social mobility.* Oxford: Clarendon Press, 299–326.

Savage, M., 2000. *Class analysis and social transformation.* Buckingham: Open University Press.

Savage, M., 2010. *Identities and social change in Britain since 1940: The politics of method.* Oxford and New York: Oxford University Press.

Savage, M., Cunningham, N., Devine, F., Friedman, S., Laurison, D., McKenzie, L., Miles, A., Snee, H., Taylor, M., and Wakeling, P., 2015. *Social class in the 21st century.* London: Pelican.

Shahrokni, S., 2018. The collective roots and rewards of upward educational mobility. *British Journal of Sociology*, 69 (4), 1175–1193.

Sorokin, P.A., 1927. *Social and cultural mobility.* New York: Free Press.

16 Gender and sexuality

Stephen Brooke

Introduction

The history of gender and sexuality in Britain from the turn of the twentieth century to the present day brings together the history of the public and private sphere and the history of the social and of the intimate. It is a history that reaches from the home to the street, from bedroom to the workplace to the ballot box, from our bodies to the world.

But first of all, what do we mean by 'sex', 'gender' and 'sexuality'? It is impossible to capture the complex meanings of those words in a few sentences, but we might think about their relationship in the following way: we are born with sexed bodies; 'gender' is the cultural and social meaning that we give to those bodies; 'sexuality' is the desire we feel towards other sexed and gendered bodies.

The meanings of 'sex', 'gender' and 'sexuality' of course have profound implications for individuals' private and public lives. In the most basic fashion, gender and sexuality have been deeply interwoven with the changing sense twentieth century and twenty-first century Britons have had of their own identity, belonging and freedom, whether this is within the family, in the community or as individuals. Gender and sexuality, so central to private life, are also critical to the way twentieth- and twenty-first century Britons have lived in the public sphere in a variety of ways, but particularly as workers and citizens.

A single chapter cannot hope to do justice to such sweeping and important subjects such as gender and sexuality. But it can trace some outlines in the history of gender and sexuality in twentieth-century Britain and raise some questions about their relationship to other historical developments.

What this chapter suggests is that the story of gender and sexuality since 1900 has been about the displacement or deconstruction of dominant ideas about gender and sexuality. In 1900, heterosexuality within traditional marriage was the only licit form of sexuality. Homosexuality was illegal, lesbianism was unrecognized and sexuality outside marriage a point of shame for individuals. In 1900, masculinity was largely defined by work and citizenship, while femininity was defined by motherhood and the home. By the early twenty-first century, such pillars of certainty lay in ruins, even if they had not entirely disappeared from the social landscape. Whether within the family or at the workplace, the meaning of masculinity and femininity has become less clear and more ambiguous. Femininity is, for example, no longer exclusively defined by motherhood, nor is masculinity defined largely by work. The home is no longer only the province of femininity but, theoretically at least, the province of both masculinity and femininity.

DOI: 10.4324/9781003037118-17

Who actually does the dishes, changes the nappies or brings home the larger pay packet remain important questions, but these tasks or goals are no longer as clearly inscribed as masculine or feminine. Similarly, the family and sexuality have been detached from a certain connection to heterosexual marriage or, indeed, to heterosexuality. In the late twentieth and early twenty-first century, reforms involving civil partnerships, marriage, adoption and childrearing and attitudes towards LGBT+ people have meant that ideas about the links among masculinity, femininity and sexuality have changed. In 2004, the Gender Recognition Act was passed. This was a profound change to our understanding of gender itself. An act that enables individuals to change the gender that was registered at their birth; at present, that act is being reviewed and discussed for further amendment. The act and the discussions that have followed this mean that the relationship between gender and the sexed body has itself become more ambiguous.

Thus, a dominant theme in the history of gender and sexuality in twentieth-century Britain is that the very meanings of gender and sexuality are more ambiguous. This is not to say they are less important. Of course, our understanding of our own gender and sexual identity is of fundamental importance to us as individuals. But what kinds of families we grow up in, what we do for work and whom we love and have sex with are now much less rigidly defined and constrained than they were in 1900. In this chapter, I want to think about that change in three specific spheres: the family, work and the economy and sexuality.

The family

Looking back from the twenty-first century is a useful vantage point to reflect upon the changes in gender and family life. A year into the new century, a historian remarked: '[t]he traditional family form has changed in two key respects: the pattern of women's and, to a lesser extent, men's contribution to the family in regard to both financial support and care, and the structure of the family itself' (Lewis 2001, p. 17). This comment came in an era when there were concerns, particularly on the political right, about the survival of the traditional family. Attempts to restore the family and marriage included a recent controversial proposal for a marriage tax incentive (see Guardian 2013; Smith 1994; Durham 1991).

What has changed? If we think about the traditional building blocks of family life, such as heterosexual marriage and childbirth, then we can see that the landscape of the early twentieth century has been transformed. Over the twentieth century, the institution of marriage changed (see chapter by Thane and chapter by Fisher and Charnock in this volume).

Particularly since the Second World War, there have been changing ideas of the home and family and men and women's relationship to it (see Langhamer 2005). Perhaps the greatest visible change is the decline of the breadwinner male as the economic pivot of the home, as is discussed in the following. Changes in the economy, not least the growth of white-collar work and the service sector, have undermined men's position as the sole provider for the home or, perhaps more accurately, revealed the illusion of the breadwinner model. The roles performed by men and women within the family have also changed, at least in our understanding of those roles. At the beginning of the twentieth century, mothers and fathers seemed to occupy strictly defined roles, with women taking on the burden of childcare and domestic work (Davidoff 1990; Ross 1993). Recent work has shown that some roles within the family, such as parenting, were more inclusive of men than we have assumed. There has been an attempt to restore the importance of working-class fathers in everyday domestic life and in the imagination, while other scholarship has illuminated men's roles in the private sphere (see Strange 2015; King 2015; Szreter and Fisher 2010). This work has done much to complicate the boundaries we often place between masculinity and femininity, motherhood and fatherhood and public and private in our understanding of the family and family life.

This does not displace, however, the persistence of inequalities on gender lines. In 2016, for example, the Office of National Statistics reported that women still did a majority of the unpaid labour at home (Office for National Statistics 2016). Working through things like domestic labour and the responsibility for childcare was a key focus of feminism in the 1960s and 1970s, opening up a discussion of the relationship between men, masculinity and the home (Stoller 2018). We might also consider the growing involvement of the state, through healthcare and welfare agencies, in children's lives and upbringing (Thomson 2013).

Another key indication of the changing nature of the family in twentieth-century Britain touches upon what was actually considered a family. The history of lone parenthood over the century is a fascinating example of this. Until the 1980s, single parents and children were regarded as outside the acknowledged and legitimate definition of family. Rather, families of single parents and children were often the objects of either reform, discipline or criticism. But advocacy by groups such as the Child Poverty Action Group and the National Council for One Parent Families and changing demographic patterns, notably a significant rise from the mid-1960s to the present day, forced a recognition of the 'normalcy' of this family structure (Thane and Evans 2012). In 2018, nearly 50 per cent of all births were outside of marriage (Office for National Statistics 2019). Marriage itself fell in popularity as a building block of the family: by 2017, opposite-sex marriage rates were the lowest on record (Office for National Statistics 2020). Divorce has become all the more popular, particularly with parliamentary acts in 1969 and 1973, also complicating the shape of the family in Britain.

As the opening to this chapter suggested, by the end of the period under review, the twenty-first century, family structure and the experience of family life were no longer underpinned by certain or accepted understandings of masculinity or femininity or men and women's roles. Those understandings and roles have changed over the century, making the family a more fluid structure or experience.

Economy

This can also be seen in the relationship between gender and work. In the nineteenth century, the decline of the family economy, the rise of industrial capitalism and a separate-spheres gender ideology meant not that women were excluded from work but that their productive role was perceived as problematic and unequal. Protective legislation excluded women from particular kinds of industrial work or limited their hours. The ideal of the skilled male breadwinner with a dependent wife and family dominated the politics of the labour movement. Many of the professions also excluded women. Women were clustered in industries like textiles and domestic labour.

This gendered economy began to change in the late nineteenth century, with the expansion of retail and innovations such as the typewriter opening up new opportunities for women entering the workforce. In the first half of the twentieth century, total war and changes in industrial production both enhanced the participation of women at the workplace. The two world wars necessitated the entry of women into sectors such as engineering to replace male labour. In 1941, women were mobilized for war work, further undermining any ideological objection to women working. Such wartime changes were coded as temporary, but in the 1920s and the 1930s, the growth of light industries manufacturing consumer goods brought in more women workers, as did labour shortages after 1945 (Todd 2005; Glucksmann 1990; see Chapter 13 in this collection). We might also look to the expansion of the service sector, teaching and local government as sites for increased employment for women.

In Focus: the office

In 1987, the photographer Anna Fox made a series of photographs published the following year by *Camerawork* under the title *Work Stations* (Fox 1988). The photographs were an examination of working life in the Thatcher years, situated principally in the office, with its particular architecture of desks, shelves, files and, notably for the period, the trappings of new technology – desktop computers, hard drives on the floor, printers and screens. What was also notable in Fox's *Work Stations* was the presence of women as workers. Women manned the keyboards and answered phones. In some of the photographs, there was an indication of a long-standing subordination at work – a woman taking dictation from a man, for example, – but in others, there is a new equality and power – a photograph of a man and woman side by side at similar desks, a woman using a brick-like mobile phone on a market floor, men and women celebrating at an office party and a woman striding through the office of an events management company. Fox's photographs cast a critical eye upon the new world of Thatcherite neoliberalism, in which the office was the main sphere of struggle and competition, but they were also a document of the increasing importance of the office as a space of gender change, in particular the presence of women.

This change was in the context of a larger transformation of the labour market in Britain, a shift from manual work to non-manual work. In 1911, for example, 18.7 per cent of the working population could be classified as 'white-collar workers'; by 1961, this had risen to 35.9 per cent (Cook and Stevenson 1988, p. 155). This was matched in the mid-twentieth century by the increase in white-collar unions, often based in the burgeoning public sector. In the early twentieth century, a particular aspect of the shift to white-collar work was the presence of women in clerical positions, dubbed the 'white blouse revolution' (see Anderson 1988). By the late twentieth century, women dominated particular sectors of the service sector; 89 per cent of nurses and midwives and 75 per cent of clerical and secretarial staff were women (Walsh and Wrigley 2001, p. 3, Table 3b). Technology played a central role in both the shift to white-collar work and the feminisation of that work, whether we think of the role of the typewriter, the dictaphone or, more recently, the computer.

One of the points about the expansion of office work is not only about the increased presence of women in that work space; it is also about the way it affects understandings of gender. We should not, of course, forget that the increase in office work and the decrease in manual work also affected understandings of masculinity, which had to be reworked, not least to assert superiority over women in a new space of labour (see Roper 1994). As well, other work has suggested that we need to be attentive to the way women and men not only occupy different positions within the office – as managers or secretaries, for example – but also do different emotional labour, with women often being relied upon to provide care and support (see Hochschild 2004; Langhamer 2017). It is also important to think about the effect of the increase in white-collar work upon questions of equality between male and female workers. A study written in 1988 about clerical feminisation since the Second World War noted the persistence of both occupational segregation between male and female white-collar workers in the office (that is, men and women occupying different jobs) and vertical segregation, in that men enjoyed greater mobility through promotion in the office (see Crompton 1988).

In these ways, that now-familiar work environment – the office – has, through the twentieth century and up to today, mirrored the tension between the progress towards gender equality and the persistence of gender inequality. Indeed, the office has become a crucial forum for that struggle.

Image 16.1 Typing pool typists using old-fashioned typewriters. City of London. *Starsky and Hutch* pin-up posters on the wall (1978)

Source: © Homer Sykes/Alamy Stock Photo.

Changes in the workplace have profoundly changed or complicated understandings of gender. If we look at the increase in married women working, for example, this has altered our understanding of the link between femininity and motherhood. The 'working mother' gained considerable visibility in the post-1945 period as a new social actor (see Brooke 2001; Smith Wilson 2006; McCarthy 2016, 2020). By 2017, 78 per cent of women between 25 and 54 were in employment. This is also related to changes in childbearing (having children later in life) and in the meaning of motherhood (returning to work after childbirth). In 1975, half of mothers were in work; by 2015, the number was 72 per cent (Roantree and Kartik 2018, p. 2).

Men's gender identity was also related to changes in economy. Mass unemployment between the wars tended to affect male workers, particularly skilled male workers, disproportionately, thereby corroding the ideal of the male breadwinner that had long underpinned working-class identity (see Alexander 2000). The period of reconstruction and affluence following the Second World War, with its growth in full-time and part-time work for women, similarly had a destabilizing effect, as did the dramatic loss of manufacturing jobs in the 1980s. The working-class, masculine identity once rooted in the workplace became more and more difficult to sustain as the century went on (see Thompson 1998; Brooke 2001). A bittersweet popular testament to this change in masculinity is the film *The Full Monty* (1997), a chronicle of the impact upon masculinity of a fall from skilled male jobs to either unemployment or service employment. At the beginning of the twentieth century, the road to masculinity led through work, and the road to femininity led largely through motherhood; this is no longer so clear at the beginning of the twenty-first century.

Sexuality

Gender and sexuality are different but intrinsically related spheres. If we talk about changes in women's lives and the meaning of femininity, for example, birth control must be discussed because the growing control over reproduction over the century undoubtedly detached femininity from motherhood, or at least offered women the chance to time motherhood. And, of course, class and gender also shape sexuality, whether heterosexuality or same-sex sexuality. The meaning and practice of same-sex sexuality was different in a working-class context than in a middle-class or upper-middle class context; the meaning of masculinity in a working-class context similarly shaped the understanding of same-sex sexuality (see Houlbrook 2005; Cook 2008; Cocks 2009; Smith 2015). Similarly, heterosexuality was also affected by class position and understandings of, for example, femininity and respectability (see Fisher 2003).

The major trends in birth control ranged over the century, beginning, for example, with a generally declining birth rate; the publication of Marie Stopes' *Married Love* in 1918; the opening of birth control clinics in the 1920s; and the growing acceptance of the use of birth control within marriage by, for example, the Anglican Church, but the critical changes came in the 1960s with increasing use of the oral contraceptive, the Pill; the decriminalization of therapeutic abortion in 1967; and the distribution of birth control to women without reference to their married status that same year with the National Health Service (Family Planning) Act (see Cook 2004). By the late twentieth century, women's sexuality revolved around both sexual pleasure and reproduction. Not least, this meant that femininity was conceptualized less dominantly in terms of motherhood and more in terms of individual rights and selfhood (see Brooke 2011).

The movement towards the recognition of the rights of gay and lesbian people over the twentieth century could also be seen as a way in which masculinity and femininity could be detached from heterosexuality. Before the 1960s, homosexuality was illegal, an offence often rigorously prosecuted by the police (see Houlbrook 2005; Weeks 1981). Lesbian life was not as clearly bounded by legal persecution, but it was, of course, similarly conditioned by social opprobrium (See Jennings 2007a). A major turning point in the discussion and treatment of homosexuality came in 1957 with the Wolfenden Report on homosexuality and prostitution, which advocated tolerance of, though not rights for, homosexuals. Homosexual rights organizations such as the Homosexual Law Reform Society worked hard to change the law, and in 1967, homosexuality was partially decriminalized in England and Wales (the reform extended to Scotland in 1980).

In the wake of the 1967 partial decriminalization of homosexuality, gay and lesbian rights organizations in the 1970s and 1980s such as the Campaign for Homosexual Equality and the Gay Liberation Front helped claim a public space and acceptability for same sex people. In 1970, gay activists marched across Highbury Fields in London in the first major public demonstration for gay rights. This was followed in July 1972 with the first Pride parade in London, an event which eventually became the largest LGBT+ (lesbian, gay, bisexual and transgender – the 'plus' representing other sexual orientations and gender identities) celebration in Europe.

The law may have decriminalized homosexuality, but there remained considerable legal impediments to gay and lesbian life. This was particularly pronounced during the Thatcher years. The 1984 Police and Criminal Evidence Act afforded police greater powers over what could be defined as acts of public indecency. The Chief Constable of Manchester, James Anderton, inveighed against what he called the 'degenerate behaviour' of gay people (Brooke 2011, p. 227). In 1988, the notorious Section 28 of the Local Government Act, aimed at suppressing the discussion of same-sex sexuality, was a clear backlash from a Conservative government determined to police 'normalcy' and uphold the traditional family (see Smith 1994). The mainstream Labour party was hardly more sympathetic. In 1977, the Labour MP Maureen Colquhoun was deselected from her seat after being publicly identified as lesbian. The 1983 Bermondsey by-election witnessed a savagely homophobic campaign against Peter Tachell from within and without the Labour party (Robinson 2007). It was an act of extraordinary political courage, therefore, when Chris Smith, then Labour MP for Islington South and Finsbury became, in 1984, the first MP to come out publicly as gay. The tragic emergence of AIDS after 1981, which in 1987 alone claimed the lives of over 600 people in the UK, on the one hand illustrated the boundaries of the 'permissive' society, provoking some homophobic public and political responses. On the other hand, there was a consensual and relatively humane approach by government to dealing with the disease, at least in the late 1980s. Eventually, the AIDS crisis and the fight against Section 28 lent considerable weight to the campaigning efforts or organizations such as Stonewall after 1989 (see Cook 2017a, 2017b; Berridge 1996).

The increased presence of LGBT+ people and themes in popular culture is also an important factor in the changing meaning of same-sex sexuality in British society. In the 1980s, the success of unapologetically out groups such as Bronski Beat and Frankie Goes to Hollywood and the visibility and importance of LGBT+ dance culture were an important reshaping of popular culture. Television's representation of queer life moved from the clichéd camp figure of Wilberforce Humphries (John Inman) in

Are You Being Served? (1972–85) to the more nuanced character of Colin Russell (Michael Cashman) in *East Enders* in the 1980s and the portrait of Canal Street, Manchester, in *Queer as Folk* in the 1990s.

Since the 1980s, through a combination of factors, including advocacy, campaigning and the need to abide by European human rights legislation, there has been continued progress towards LBGT+ rights (see Brooke 2014). In 1981, for example, the European Court found that Britain was in violation of the European Convention because homosexuality remained illegal in Northern Ireland. Among other things, this has transformed ideas of family, marriage and identity. If we think of 'family' and 'marriage', for example, the exclusive link between these and heterosexuality has been broken. In 2002, same-sex couples were permitted to adopt children on the same basis as heterosexual couples. Two years later, civil partnerships between same-sex people were legalized, paving the way, in 2013, for same-sex marriage. In terms of sexuality and the law, the same age of consent law governs all forms of sexual activity. Under the 2010 Equality Act, sexual orientation is a protected characteristic. Hate crime laws also cover acts committed against people on the basis of sexual orientation. In these ways, heterosexuality no longer shapes the experience of being a man or a woman or the understanding of masculinity or femininity as much as it had in the first six decades of the twentieth century.

The most profound challenge to longstanding conceptions of sex and gender came early in the twenty-first century with the 2004 Gender Recognition Act (GRA). This permitted people to obtain the legal recognition of an 'acquired gender', different than the one registered at their at birth, under particular circumstances, such as gender dysphoria (Gender Recognition Act 2004, c. 7). These criteria are, at time of writing, the subject of a government review (Government Equalities Office 2018). The GRA has been controversial, not least because it highlights the nature of different kinds of discrimination based upon biological sex and acquired gender.

Debates and Interpretations: in what ways has gender influenced the writing of twentieth-century British history?

In 1986, Joan Scott argued for gender to be considered a 'useful category of historical analysis', one that would not simply give depth to writing the history of women but transform the writing of history more widely. Scott argued that building gender into historical analysis would 'yield a history that will provide new perspectives on old questions . . . redefine the old questions in new terms' (1986, p. 1075).

In what ways has gender influenced the writing of twentieth-century British history? This is, of course, a huge question and one that is impossible to answer in a comprehensive way on a small canvas. But looking at the historical understanding of particular questions – the impact of the First and Second World Wars, the perception of a particular era such the interwar period, the development of the welfare state, sexuality, Black British history and political change in the 1970s and 1980s – will show how gender has been 'a useful category of analysis' in shaping a broad understanding of the twentieth-century. Using gender – the discussion of masculinity and femininity – as an analytical prism, historians have deepened our understanding of particular aspects of the war experience, showing, for example, how the war affected discussions of femininity and masculinity in relation to war service and the vote (see Gullace 2002), the relationship between masculinity, combat and the development of psychology (see Roper 2009) and how a 'people's war' was experienced within the framework of new and old ideas of masculinity and femininity (see Gledhill and Swanson 1996; Rose 2003; Francis 2008). In all of these cases, gender becomes a way of understanding broad historical developments related to the experience of war, whether as a causative factor in political change or a framework for understanding new ideas of citizenship or as an influence upon understandings of the self. Similarly, if we look at a particular period – the interwar years – our understanding of that era has been made much richer and been transformed by work that has brought changes in masculinity and femininity to bear on the understanding of a variety of issues, such as politics, the media, leisure, law and culture (see Jarvis 1994; Graves 1994; Bingham 2004; Langhamer 2000; Todd 2005; Bland 2013; Grandy 2014; Light 1991). Another of the most important changes in twentieth-century British history was the development of the welfare state as a central institution of British life. Tracing the history of gender has helped us understand the particular shape of that welfare state, based upon a particular understanding of masculinity and femininity, notably the breadwinner male and the non-working mother (See Pedersen 1993). Gender has also been influential in some work in the history of sexuality. Attention has been given, for example, to the ways in which understandings of masculinity and femininity shaped same-sex sexuality (see Houlbrook 2005; Jennings 2007a). The practice of sex within heterosexuality has also been influenced by gender history, through, for example, the way ideas of masculinity and femininity affected sexual knowledge and practice within marriage or the ways in which understandings of femininity such as the link between motherhood and sexuality influenced the political treatment of questions such as abortion (Fisher 2003; Brooke 2011). Recent histories of Black Britain or the post-colonial state have also woven in the analysis of gender in a narrative about migration, belonging and politics (Matera 2015; Hammond Perry 2015; Connell 2019; Bailkin 2012; Waters 2019; Thomlinson 2015). Finally, gender has been an important theme in recent considerations of shifts in political outlook in the 1970s and 1980s (Robinson *et al.* 2017; Sutcliffe-Braithwaite 2018; Lawrence 2019).

In all of these works, the history of gender has not only been given special attention; it has also been seen as a causative force in important historical developments, a factor central to politics and society and a way in which people structured their identity over the course of the century.

But this should not be seen as a triumphalist narrative, that the narrative of twentieth-century Britain has been entirely imbued with a gender perspective. It has become one way of thinking about that history and one way in which particular experiences, periods and developments have been enriched. But whether we think of the progress of gender equality in politics or the economy, changes in family structure and our understanding of family or identity itself, these remain among other narrative or analytical streams. The question of how or when gender can be incorporated constructively into the broad narrative of Britain in the twentieth century remains an active one.

Conclusion

As suggested in the opening to this chapter, perhaps what the GRA underlines is a theme in the history of gender and sexuality since 1900: we have moved from a period in which meanings of masculinity and femininity and sexuality were more certain to one in which those meanings are fluid and sometimes ambiguous. The meanings we give sexed bodies through the concept of gender have, therefore, become far more complicated and, if not less important, perhaps less binding and more open to change. The same is true of desire. The story of sexuality across the twentieth century should not be told as a story of inevitable, unfolding liberalization and tolerance. Rather, what liberalization and tolerance there has been has had to be fought for and defended and is only relatively recent. But from the beginning of the twentieth century, when only heterosexuality within marriage was a licit expression of desire and all else was either underground or repressed and often beyond the law, Britain has moved to a point where equality between those of different sexual orientations and expressions is guaranteed in law and largely tolerated in society and culture. Whatever our gender or sexuality, we can now live more complex and open lives.

Further reading

Good general studies of sex and gender include Hall (2000), Weeks (1981), Mort (2000) and Weeks (2007). Important studies of birth control include Cook (2004) and Szreter and Fisher (2010). Houlbrook (2005), Jennings (2007b) and Robinson (2007) offer excellent focused studies of same-sex and queer sexuality. The link between politics and sexuality can be explored in Durham (1991), Smith (1994) and Brooke (2011). Fascinating studies of working-class motherhood and working-class father-hood at different points in history over the last century and a half can be found in Ross (1993), Strange (2015) and King (2015). The world of childhood in this chang-ing landscape is beautifully explored in Thomson (2013). How film, gender and class relate in the interwar period is the fascinating subject of Grandy (2014), while the intersection of emotions and feeling with the worlds of work, family, gender and war lie at the heart of Langhamer (2005, 2017) and Francis (2008).

References

Alexander, S., 2000. Men's fears and women's work: Responses to unemployment in London between the wars. *Gender and History*, 12 (3), 401–425.

Anderson, G., ed., 1988. *The white blouse revolution*. Manchester: Manchester University Press.

Bailkin, J., 2012. *The afterlife of empire*. Berkeley: University of California Press.

Berridge, V., 1996. *AIDS in the UK: The making of a policy 1981–94*. Oxford: Oxford University Press.

Bingham, A., 2004. *Gender, modernity and the popular press in inter-war Britain*. Oxford: Oxford University Press.

Bland, L., 2013. *Modern women on trial*. Manchester: Manchester University Press.

Brooke, S., 2001. Gender and working-class identity in Britain in the 1950s. *Journal of Social History*, 34 (1), 773–796.

Brooke, S., 2011. *Sexual politics*. Oxford: Oxford University Press.

Brooke, S., 2014. Sexual rights, human rights, the material and the post-material in Britain, 1970–2010. *Revue Française de Civilisation Britannique*, 19 (1), 114–129.

Cocks, H.G., 2009. *Nameless offences*. London: I.B. Tauris.

Connell, K., 2019. *Black Handsworth: Race in 1980s Britain*. Berkeley: University of California Press.

Cook, C., and Stevenson, J., 1988. *British historical facts 1688–1760*. New York: St Martins.

Cook, H., 2004. *The long sexual revolution: English women, sex and contraception*. Oxford: Oxford University Press.

Cook, M., 2008. *London and the culture of homosexuality, 1885–1914*. Cambridge: Cambridge University Press.

Cook, M., 2017a. AIDS, mass observation and the fate of the permissive turn. *Journal of the History of Sexuality*, 26 (2), 239–272.

Cook, M., 2017b. Archives of feeling: AIDS in Britain, c. 1987. *History Workshop Journal*, 83, 51–78.

Crompton, R., 1988. The feminisation of the clerical labour force since the Second World War. *In*: G. Anderson, ed. *The white blouse revolution*. Manchester: Manchester University Press, 121–143.

Davidoff, L., 1990. The family in Britain. *In*: F.M.L. Thompson, ed. *The Cambridge social history of Britain 1750–1950*. Cambridge: Cambridge University Press, 71–130.

Durham, M., 1991. *Sex and politics: The family and morality in the Thatcher years*. Houndmills: Macmillan.

Fisher, K., 2003. *Birth control, sex and marriage*. Oxford: Oxford University Press.

Fox, A., 1988. *Work stations*. London: Camera Work/Museum of London. Available from: www.annafox.co.uk/work/workstations/

Francis, M., 2008. *The flyer*. Oxford: Oxford University Press.

Gledhill, C., and Swanson, G., eds., 1996. *Nationalizing femininity*. Manchester: Manchester University Press.

Glucksmann, M., 1990. *Women assemble*. London: Routledge.

Government Equalities Office, 2018. *Reform of the Gender Recognition Act 2004, Consultation*. Available from: www.gov.uk/government/consultations/reform-of-the-gender-recognition-act-2004 [Accessed 17 October 2019].

Grandy, C., 2014. *Heroes and happy endings: Class, gender and nation in popular film and fiction in Interwar Britain*. Manchester: Manchester University Press.

Graves, P., 1994. *Labour women: Women in British working-class politics 1918–39*. Cambridge: Cambridge University Press.

Guardian, 2013. Tory Tax Break Marriage Glue. *The Guardian*, 27 September. Available from: www.theguardian.co.uk [Accessed 21 October 2019].

Gullace, N., 2002. *The blood of our sons*. New York: Macmillan.

Hall, L., 2000. *Sex, gender and change in Britain since 1880*. London: Macmillan.

Hammond Perry, K., 2015. *London is the place for me: Black Britons, citizenship and the politics of race*. Oxford: Oxford University Press.

Hochschild, A., 2004. *The managed heart*. Berkeley: University of California Press.

Houlbrook, M., 2005. *Queer London*. Chicago: University of Chicago Press.

Jarvis, D., 1994. Mrs Maggs and Betty: The conservative appeal to women voters in the 1920s. *Twentieth-Century British History*, 5 (2), 129–152.

Jennings, R., 2007a. *A lesbian history of Britain*. Oxford: Greenwood.

Jennings, R., 2007b. *Tom boys and bachelor girls*. Manchester: Manchester University Press.

King, L., 2015. *Family men: Fatherhood and masculinity in Britain, 1914–60*. Oxford: Oxford University Press.

Langhamer, C., 2000. *Women's leisure in England, 1920–60*. Manchester: Manchester University Press.

Langhamer, C., 2005. The meanings of home in postwar Britain. *Journal of Contemporary History*, 40 (2), 341–362.

Langhamer, C., 2017. Feelings, women and work in the long 1950s. *Women's History Review*, 26 (1), 77–92.

Lawrence, J., 2019. *Me, me, me?* Oxford: Oxford University Press.

Lewis, J., 2001. *Should we worry about family change?* Toronto: University of Toronto Press.

Light, A., 1991. *Forever England: Femininity, literature and conservatism between the wars*. London: Routledge.

Matera, M., 2015. *Black London: The imperial metropolis and decolonization in the twentieth century*. Berkeley: University of California Press.

McCarthy, H., 2016. Social science and married women's employment in postwar Britain. *Past and Present*, 233 (1), 269–305.

McCarthy, H., 2020. *Double lives: A history of working motherhood*. London: Bloomsbury.

Mort, F., 2000. *Dangerous sexualities*. London: Routledge.

Office for National Statistics, 2016. Women shoulder the responsibility of unpaid work. Available from: www.ons.gov.uk/employmentandlabourmarket/peopleinwork/earningsandwork-inghours/articles/womenshouldertheresponsibilityofunpaidwork/2016-11-10 [Accessed 11 October 2019].

Office for National Statistics, 2019. *Births in England and Wales: 2018*. Available from: www.ons.gov.uk/peoplepopulationandcommunity/birthsdeathsandmarriages/livebirths/bulletins/birthsummarytablesenglandandwales/2018#biggest-decrease-in-the-rate-of-live-births-within-marriage-since-1973 [Accessed 21 December 2020].

Office for National Statistics, 2020. *Marriages in England and Wales: 2017*. Available from: www.ons.gov.uk/peoplepopulationandcommunity/birthsdeathsandmarriages/marriageco-habitationandcivilpartnerships/bulletins/marriagesinenglandandwalesprovisional/2017 [Accessed 21 December 2020].

Pedersen, S., 1993. *Family, dependence and the origins of the welfare state: Britain and France, 1914–45*. Cambridge: Cambridge University Press.

Roantree, B., and Kartik, V., 2018. *The rise and rise of women's employment in the UK*. London: Institute for Fiscal Studies.

Robinson, E., Schofield, C., Sutcliffe-Braithwaite, F., Thomlinson, N., 2017. Telling stories about post-war Britain: Popular individualism and the 'Crisis' of the 1970s. *Twentieth Century British History*, 28 (2), 268–304.

Robinson, L., 2007. *Gay men and the left in post-war Britain*. Manchester: Manchester University Press.

Roper, M., 1994. *Masculinity and the British organization man since 1945*. Oxford: Oxford University Press.

Roper, M., 2009. *The secret battle*. Manchester: Manchester University Press.

Rose, S., 2003. *Which people's war*. Oxford: Oxford University Press.

Ross, E., 1993. *Love and toil*. New York: Oxford University Press.

Scott, J., 1986. Gender: A useful category of historical analysis. *American Historical Review*, 91 (5), 1053–1076.

Smith, A.M., 1994. *New right discourse on race and sexuality*. Cambridge: Cambridge University Press.

Smith, H., 2015. *Masculinity, class and same-sex desire in industrial England, 1895–1957*. London: Palgrave.

Smith Wilson, D., 2006. A new look at the affluent worker: The good working mother in post-war Britain. *Twentieth-Century British History*, 17 (2), 206–229.

Stoller, S., 2018. Forging a politics of care: Theorizing household work in the British women's liberation movement. *History Workshop Journal*, 85 (1), 95–119.

Strange, J.-M., 2015. *Fatherhood and the British working class 1865–1914*. Cambridge: Cambridge University Press.

Sutcliffe-Braithwaite, F., 2018. *Class, politics and the decline of deference in England, 1968–2000*. Oxford: Oxford University Press.

Szreter, S., and Fisher, K., 2010. *Sex before the sexual revolution*. Cambridge: Cambridge University Press.

Thane, P., and Evans, T., 2012. *Sinners? Scroungers? Saints? Unmarried motherhood in twentieth-century England*. Oxford: Oxford University Press.

Thomlinson, N., 2015. *Race, ethnicity and the women's movement in Britain, 1968–93*. Basingstoke: Palgrave Macmillan.

Thompson, P., 1998. Playing at being skilled men: Factory culture and pride in work skill among Coventry car workers. *Social History*, 13 (1), 45–69.

Thomson, M., 2013. *Lost freedom*. Oxford: Oxford University Press.

Todd, S., 2005. *Young women, work and family in England, 1918–60*. Oxford: Oxford University Press.

UK Public General Acts, Gender Recognition Act 2004 (c. 7).

Walsh, M., and Wrigley, C., 2001. Womanpower: The transformation of the labour force in the UK and USA since 1945. *Recent Findings of Research in Economic and Social History*, 30 (1), 1–4.

Waters, R., 2019. *Thinking Black: Britain 1964–85*. Berkeley: University of California Press.

Weeks, J., 1981. *Sex, politics and society: The regulation of sexuality since 1800*. London: Longman.

Weeks, J., 2007. *The world we have won*. London: Routledge.

17 Healthcare, health and wellbeing

Victoria Bates

Introduction

The twentieth century was a period of remarkable change in relation to medicine and health in Britain. In many ways, too, it was a century of significant progress. There were notable advances in quantifiable measurements of health, such as morbidity or mortality rates and life expectancy. There was an unprecedented rate of discoveries and developments, including new technologies and treatments. The period was marked by the rise of specialisms and transformative new public healthcare systems.

Social historians of medicine have, though, long highlighted the problems of progress narratives. No change was revolutionary; new ways of understanding or treating illness did not replace old ones overnight, and not all members of society benefitted equally from advances in science, health and healthcare. Modern Britain also posed new challenges. Wars brought with them high rates of injury, mortality and psychological trauma. In everyday life, lifestyle changes and higher life expectancy contributed to a rise in chronic illness. New medical technologies improved the accuracy of medical diagnosis, but sometimes at the expense of the patient's voice in clinical encounters. The history of health, healthcare and wellbeing in the twentieth century is not a simple march of 'progress' but rather a number of overlapping stories about culture, society, economics and politics.

Health and wellbeing

Illness

Morbidity and mortality statistics can provide a useful starting point for understanding changes in illness experience, although with a necessary caveat about their notorious unreliability. Morbidity (illness), in particular, often remains invisible. It is highly likely that many non–life-threatening illnesses went unreported or unrecorded over the course of the century, particularly before the National Health Service (NHS) brought free healthcare and more systematic record-keeping in 1948.

Mortality records can provide more reliable evidence. In the nineteenth century, the symptoms of different conditions – such as those affecting the lungs – had often been confused or conflated. However, by the twentieth century, medics and coroners could more accurately pinpoint specific causes of death using new diagnostic tools and technologies. Records of births and deaths kept since the early nineteenth century

DOI: 10.4324/9781003037118-18

can also provide a useful long view of life expectancy and its changes over time, even though the causes of death were not always reliably recorded. Though death rates were already declining in the nineteenth century, particularly infant mortality and deaths from infectious disease, the twentieth century is noteworthy for the increased rate of these improvements.

Figure 17.1 indicates a gradually rising life expectancy at birth over the course of the century. This upward trend can be attributed to a range of factors, including improved sanitation, medical treatments and nutrition. There were some fluctuations associated with exceptional events, for example, a dip in 1918 at the end of the First World War and the start of a Spanish influenza epidemic (1918–19) that killed an estimated 228,000 people in Britain (Honigsbaum 2009). These statistics also of course mask significant geographical and demographic disparities. Inequalities in health and access to healthcare have been grounded in factors such as race, class, gender and socio-economic status. These disparities have remained significant across the century and were not eliminated by the welfare state. That said, the overall picture in broad terms is that of a population with much better health prospects in 2000 than in 1900.

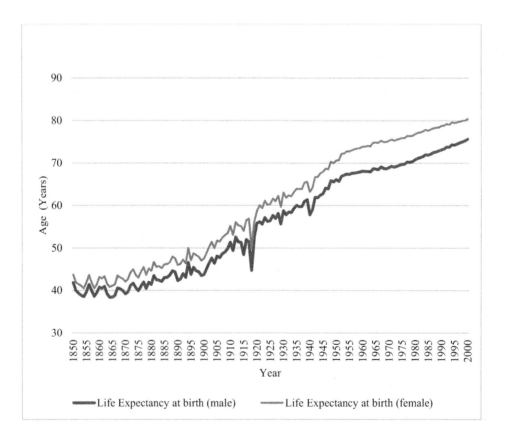

Figure 17.1 Life expectancy at birth in England and Wales, 1850–2000

Source: Office for National Statistics (2012).

There were significant qualitative, as well as quantitative, changes to illness patterns in this period. Chronic illness came to fill a gap left by the earlier decline of infectious disease, although this is not a neat narrative of transformation. Many of the oft-cited Victorian infectious diseases were also chronic, with people living with them and their effects for many years. One such, tuberculosis, continued to pose problems after the Second World War, despite the existence of a vaccination, and is still not eliminated. The development of penicillin and new classes of antibiotics, especially between the Second World War and the 1990s, reduced bacterial infections and facilitated the expansion of surgery, yet antimicrobial resistance was on the rise in the same period (Bud 2007). The idea of a post-infection era in Britain was also shaken by the emergence of HIV/AIDS in the 1980s and most recently by COVID-19.

The reasons for the rise of chronic illnesses are multi-faceted. As the demography of the British population changed, the pattern and nature of its health conditions also shifted. Some existing health conditions became much more significant over the course of the century in connection with migration, such as sickle cell disease, and an aging population, such as Alzheimer's disease. New medical interventions changed the nature of other illnesses from fatal to long-term manageable conditions, such as diabetes and HIV. Some chronic conditions, including cancer, heart disease and diabetes, were not necessarily new but were newly understood in the twentieth century. For example, historians have mapped the long trajectories and reconceptualisation of conditions such as myalgic encephalomyelitis (ME) and post traumatic stress disorder (PTSD), despite apparently being new diagnostic categories in the twentieth century (Gijswijt-Hofstra and Porter 2001). Advances in medical science brought into view some previously invisible chronic diseases associated with genetic conditions. Lifestyle factors – combined with longevity – increased the risk of some chronic conditions, such as those caused by obesity, alcohol consumption, smoking, pollution, and stress.

Cancer provides a case study of the rise of chronic illness in the twentieth century while also complicating this picture. Cancer was already a significant contributor to mortality at the start of the twentieth century. Death rates from many cancers actually dropped over the first half of the century, while others rose. The mortality rates for some cancers fluctuated or affected specific demographics; deaths from lung cancer primarily affected older men and rose over the first half of the twentieth century but then declined for men and increased for women, partly in line with trends in smoking habits (Horn 1962; ONS/PHE 2016). Figures for morbidity do not exist until the late twentieth century, but they do support – in general terms – the claim that there has been an overall increase in cancer rates between 1971 and 2000. The overall picture is one in which the total incidence of common cancers increased over the last twenty years, while the number of cancer-related deaths decreased (see Figure 17.2).

The rise of some cancer rates in the twentieth century can be specifically linked to lifestyle issues, such as the clear relationship between lung cancer and smoking. Others can be attributed to new carcinogens, such as mesothelioma caused by exposure to asbestos. Some forms of terminal cancer would be considered acute rather than chronic – especially those of internal organs. However, others were made 'chronic' with better screening methods and new treatments in surgery, radiation and chemotherapy. The history of cancer shows the difficulty of identifying any single cause of the rise of chronic illness.

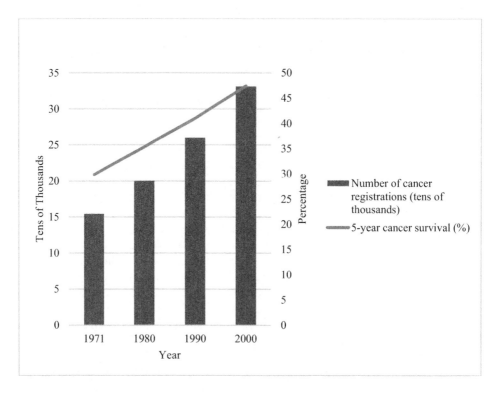

Figure 17.2 Cancer registrations and survival rates in England (1971–2000) based on ONS data[1]

Wellness

Over the course of the twentieth century there was a subtle shift in the tone of discussions around health and illness. With the decline of infectious disease, illness patterns were less likely to adhere to neat binary models of health/illness. The official definition of 'health' expanded to include more holistic models of 'wellness', rather than just the avoidance of sickness. The World Health Organisation declared in its 1948 Constitution that health was 'not merely the absence of disease or infirmity' but rather a 'state of complete physical, mental and social well-being' (Larson 1999).

In the post-war period the growing interest in 'living well' began to connect with emerging counter-cultural movements. In the 1960s, for example, there was a revival of so-called 'alternative' holistic practices such as yoga and 'natural' remedies such as homeopathy. The concept of 'wellbeing' came to transcend health promotion and the avoidance of ill health, including goals such as 'flourishing' in which a healthy life was marked by *positive* embodied, mental and social experiences rather than just the absence of negative ones. Film, photography, literature, advertising, magazines and other cultural forms propagated models for 'living well' that fed the establishment of a so-called 'wellbeing industry' – selling a healthy body and mind – by the end of the century.

In this period the pursuit of health and 'wellness' also became part of a social contract under the welfare state. The NHS provided citizens with free healthcare and placed upon them a growing responsibility for staying as healthy as possible in order to ensure the survival of the system. There was some implicit judgment of people who failed to follow health guidance, sometimes made explicit in scathing tabloid reports on strained NHS resources. Although new in many ways, these ideas about personal responsibility built on a much longer history of public health measures that used education as a tool. Such rhetoric also connected to longer social histories of stigma and the perceived links between illness, gender, class and race.

In line with these trends, public health messages shifted their focus from the prevention of communicable disease to the promotion of 'wellness'. The spatial focus of 'wellness' was no longer the communal street but the individual body. At first the British government engaged in health promotion mainly through advertising, such as the famous 'Go to Work on an Egg' campaign by the Egg Marketing Board in the 1950s and 1960s. The state also began to include messages about health-promotion and risk factors in its public health campaigns, most recently – in 2003, encouraging British citizens to eat 'five [portions] a day' of fruit and vegetables to cut the risk of heart disease and cancer (2003). New technologies, from domestic weighing scales to portable pedometers, supported this trend by allowing citizens to take responsibility for monitoring their own bodies (Sysling 2020).

In Focus: health, self-monitoring and technology

Modern technology made new forms of self-observation and risk management possible in two main ways. First, a number of existing forms of measurement and monitoring moved from the medical sphere into commercial, domestic and personal spaces in the twentieth century. Second, new technologies allowed people to promote their own health and monitor chronic health conditions. This inset looks at some examples of such devices from across the period.

Weighing scales

The history of weighing scales reaches back thousands of years. The *domestic* weighing scale, however, was only developed in the early twentieth century and sold widely in the late twentieth century (Bivins and Marland 2016). This technology moved the self-monitoring of body weight from public spaces into the home, making it increasingly a private process and private responsibility. Advertising that represented or sold weighing scales emphasised their value for enhancing the physical appearance and physical health of the buyer – typically gendered in marketing as a woman (see Image 17.1).

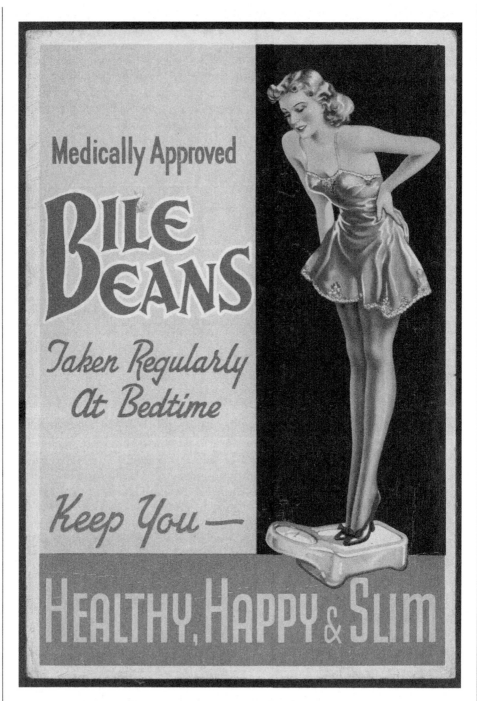

Image 17.1 Bile Beans showcard. Exact date unknown: c. 1940s

Source: © Chronicle/Alamy Stock Photo.

Health had long been connected to diet and nutrition, but it is a relatively recent phenomenon to think about bodily health in numerical terms. In the nineteenth century, a range of international scientists and medical research- ers identified new ways of quantifying the ideal, healthy and 'normal' body. In twentieth-century Britain, many of these methods were popularised for the first time. It became part of mainstream culture to quantify ideal bodies, using tools such as the 'body mass index' and the nutritional calorie (Bivins 2020; Zweiniger-Bargielowska 2005). These ways of thinking about the body began to shape the way that people thought about their own physical appearance and health, supported by the home weighing scale.

Pedometers

Like the weighing scale, the pedometer had a long history but moved into the private realm in the twentieth century. Its development was inextricably woven with the growing interest in walking as recreation and as a healthy pursuit, encouraged in the countryside by new walking groups such as the Ramblers and in urban environments by the legacy of Victorian efforts to clean cities and build public parks. The link between walking and health is most famously demon- strated in the perceived value of 10,000 steps a day, an idea which is commonly linked specifically to the development of a Japanese pedometer named '10,000 steps meter' (*manpo-kei*) in the 1960s (Carter *et al.* 2018).

The pedometer echoes the story of the weighing scale in many ways. It was an old technology that was developed to be smaller, more accurate and more discreet in the late twentieth century. Pedometers improved in accuracy over time as electronics replaced spring-suspended mechanisms (Bassett *et al.* 2017). In spatial terms, they became more subtle devices that could be hidden or invis- ible, changing the nature of health monitoring to an increasingly private activity. Increased accuracy removed the need to position pedometers in specific places on the body. These changes to the pedometer meant that walking no longer needed to be visible or publicly signified as a form of exercise; they provided new opportunities for people who wanted to pursue 'wellness' in private, which might have been particularly important for groups – such as women – for whom public exercise had historically been a less commonplace practice.

Blood glucose monitors

Not all technologies for self-monitoring and quantifying health were in the service of avoiding disease. Over the course of the twentieth century, other new methods were developed to aid the self-management of existing, chronic health conditions. Glucose monitors for the management of diabetes provides one such example.

Medical and technological developments fundamentally transformed the experiences of diabetes patients in the twentieth century. Of particular note are the discovery of insulin (discovered and commercially mass-produced in the early 1920s) and subsequently the development of new technologies for self-monitoring blood glucose levels. Together, these changed diabetes from being almost universally fatal to being a potentially manageable chronic condition. Improved life expectancy and the challenges of long-term management, however, also increased the risk of patients experiencing previously rare long-term complications, from blindness to renal failure.

Home testing kits followed soon after the commercialisation of insulin, first taking the form of a test tube urine test and later using paper reagent strips. Through various iterations, from the 1950s onwards, these self-monitoring systems became smaller and more portable, with the new potential for integration with other technologies such as the personal computer by the end of the century (Clarke and Foster 2012). Such monitoring devices developed alongside new medications, such as oral drugs to lower glucose levels. The first insulin pumps were developed from the 1960s onwards, again becoming more wearable and affordable over time. Such tools for the self-monitoring of blood glucose levels gave people living with diabetes much more control over their own health. It also gave them more responsibility for managing their own chronic health condition and its associated risk factors.

Healthcare

Medicine, science and technology

There were significant developments in diagnostic and curative medicine over the course of the twentieth century. New ways of understanding and diagnosing disease ranged from the rise of bacteriology (the study of bacteria) and virology (the study of viruses) at the start of the century to DNA and genetics at the end.

It is impossible to separate the development of medical treatment in the twentieth century from its two World Wars. These both had a devastating impact on the health of the British population. They caused high death rates and both physical and mental harm, particularly among the young men who served in armed forces and civilian populations subject to aerial bombing. Wartime food shortages had implications for civilian health, although rationing after the Second World War did also ensure some access to food staples, including the expansion of a policy to provide free school milk (a policy famously later ended by Margaret Thatcher). Diverse threats to civilian and army health led to extensive new wartime research into treatments for illness and injury. Commonly cited examples include the development of pioneering blood transfusion apparatus; greater levels of state investment into medical and scientific research; and the stimulation of specialisms including psychiatry, reconstructive therapy and orthopaedics.

Many of these developments had important implications for civilian healthcare. However, they were often limited to soldiers or veterans at first, and there was no straightforward 'revolution' in healthcare resulting from war. The rise of psychiatry and related fields, for example, appears at first glance to be a dramatic story of change. Fuelled in part by research into wartime trauma, these medical specialisms grew rapidly over the course of the century. New developments in psychopharmacology allowed for care outside of institutional settings, with the first anti-psychotic drug Chlorpromazine released onto the market in the 1950s. In 1971 the *Royal College of*

Psychiatrists replaced the *Royal Medico-Psychological Association*, bringing a new professional identity and more formal training structures for the field. However, these advances in psychiatric research, treatment and professional structures took place alongside growing social critiques of these structures in the 1960s and 1970s. Most famously, R.D. Laing, Thomas Szasz and Erving Goffman wrote critiques of psychiatric theory and institutional treatment in what has been loosely termed the 'anti-psychiatry' movement.

The story of medical diagnosis, treatment and cure for physical health is equally complex in relation to the question of 'progress'. Hindsight can be very misleading, and very few medical discoveries were revolutionary at the time, with many taking years to become accepted and established practice within medical practice. That said, they did have an impact over the course of the century. Taking the post-war welfare state as an example, developments in medical science and technology had a tangible effect on people's lives, even if they took some time to do so. In the 1950s the state expanded British school vaccinations to include tuberculosis, polio and diphtheria, some of which had been developed much earlier in the twentieth century. New surgical techniques – some of which were a legacy of wartime research – began to be used more widely, with the United Kingdom's first kidney transplant in Edinburgh in 1960 and first heart transplant in London in 1968.

The post-war period brought a number of developments in women's healthcare that also had life-changing implications. Again, though, these transformations rarely occurred overnight. From 1961 the contraceptive pill was available on the NHS for the first time, albeit at the discretion of general practitioners, who commonly limited prescriptions to married women with children. It was only in 1974 that the pill was made free and freely available, via family planning clinics, to all women irrespective of social, medical and economic factors (Marks 2010). Similarly, research and publications on the benefits of screening mammography emerged during the 1950s and 1960s, but mammograms were not widely used immediately. It was not until the 1980s that the NHS introduced a national breast cancer screening programme that made mammograms available to women in their 50s and early 60s. This hesitancy was in line with some general reluctance to use mass screening and lingering tensions between those who thought the NHS should promote and prevent ill health versus those who thought it should just treat illness.

Welfare

The growth of the welfare state was part of a wider trend to expand state healthcare across Europe and Australasia, particularly in the post-war period (Berridge 1999). There is also a specific national history to its development in Britain, tied closely to twentieth-century politics. After 1906 the Liberal government expanded the role of the state in supporting people through ill health, including through the provision of pensions and healthcare insurance. Without much appetite to raise taxes to pay for this healthcare insurance, under the 1911 National Health Insurance Act the government paid two-ninths of the fixed fees for doctors and worker and employer insurance covered the rest.

These were tentative first steps. The 1911 legislation only covered people in work, while their families could not access benefits such as GP treatment. Changes to the income limit meant that just over half the working population was covered by the late 1930s, but this still left much of the adult population outside the remit of this system (Fraser 1992). There was an important growth in hospital provision during the inter-war years, though with only limited centralisation of healthcare services and certainly no 'welfare state' in the form we would understand it today. Provision was split between a voluntary acute sector funded by philanthropy, worker insurance and direct payment, and local authority institutions for chronic, infectious and elderly patients paid for by local taxes.

The variable nature of local healthcare provision was widely acknowledged, but potential for any large-scale change was disrupted by the Second World War. The idea of a National Health Service was also still a highly controversial one in the mid-twentieth century. Outside of the political sphere, the British Medical Association (BMA) was at first extremely opposed to the system, not wanting to hand professional control over to the state, but a number of compromises to the policy eventually appeased many doctors. The NHS was launched officially on 5 July 1948, based on separate acts for England/Wales, Scotland and Northern Ireland. It was one of the most significant developments in twentieth-century British political and medical history.

The NHS provided – for the first time – primary and hospital care that was free at the point of delivery and centrally funded. That said, the system was not revolutionary. It did not displace private healthcare entirely, and some of its initial principles were compromised in 1951 with the introduction of fees for spectacles and prescriptions. Local authorities continued to keep responsibility for a number of services, including some relating to maternity and child welfare. The system was also not equally transformative for everybody. The democratic aims of the NHS appeared to be met when there was a surge of demand from those who previously had limited access to healthcare, such as working-class women. However, the Department of Health and Social Services' *Black Report* of 1980 showed that overall health inequalities persisted and even grew under the system. Healthcare provision and infrastructure was also geographically uneven.

The new system brought new challenges for the state, particularly in terms of the quality and quantity of healthcare facilities. The early NHS worked with an inherited range of primary care providers and old hospitals, including previous voluntary hospitals and Poor Law infirmaries. It was not until the 1960s that GPs were encouraged to innovate in relation to the provision of primary care, and although there was some building work in the 1950s, the 1962 Hospital Plan accelerated the large-scale building of new NHS hospital facilities. The Hospital Plan scheme was the basis for a number of large, new general hospitals – including teaching hospitals and District General Hospitals. Many were not open until the following decade (see Image 17.2), when they were increasingly criticised as 'white elephants' because expenditure in many building projects had spiralled. The middle of the 1970s brought financial concerns that limited hospital building and scaled down ambitions to smaller, more standardised hospitals.

The NHS not only required buildings to serve the British population's healthcare needs but also a sufficient number of staff members. It would soon become the biggest employer in Britain, and low unemployment levels posed a challenge to recruitment. It was highly beneficial to the new NHS that its launch broadly aligned with the 1948 British Nationality Act, which gave citizenship to Commonwealth citizens. When rules around immigration were tightened in the 1960s,

Image 17.2 Charing Cross Hospital (general teaching hospital), which had 15 floors and cost
£15 million to build. Hammersmith, London, England: under construction

Source: Photograph by H. Windsley, 1972. Credit: Wellcome Collection. Public Domain Mark.

qualified nurses and doctors were excluded from the restrictions; by 1971, almost
a third of English NHS doctors were born and qualified overseas (Snow and Jones
2011).

The NHS faced ongoing challenges over the course of the late twentieth century.
The 1960s were marked by rising expenditure and the 1970s by a disruptive reorganisation. Under a Conservative government (1979–97), expenditure was restricted
again and market forces – including a consumerist model of the patient – came to be
increasingly important. In the very last few years of the century, under New Labour
(1997–2010), these forces remained important in an adapted form. Perhaps the most
famous example is the Private Financing Initiative, which sought to increase capital
expenditure while preserving funding to operational budgets. Each of these decades

brought its own difficulties but continuing public support (Crane 2019). The system survived many decades in which newspapers repeatedly declared it to be in 'crisis', largely due to the extent of this public support, which helped to make the NHS a bedrock of British society, economy and politics. Although changes did not happen overnight, the new system had a transformative effect on British health, healthcare and society.

Debates and Interpretations: the NHS, conflict and consensus

Historians of medicine and health have long used their work to explore 'big' questions, and scholars of the NHS are no exception. There is a tradition of studying the NHS in relation to politics, economics and the state and more recently in relation to society and culture. Taking political histories as a case study here, one of the most significant and enduring debates in NHS historiography is whether the system emerged from a post-war political 'consensus' or from 'conflict' (Gorsky 2008).

The strongest voice on the side of 'conflict' is Charles Webster, who argues that the Labour and Conservative party were in disagreement about launching the NHS. He claims that this tension, and the public opinion that gathered behind the Labour Party, fuelled the founding of the NHS. Within the Labour government there was also conflict between advocates of administration of the NHS through the existing local government structures, and those, victorious in the end, who urged the creation of a new separate, national and regional structure for the NHS (for example, Webster 1990). On the other side of this debate, Rudolf Klein argues that during the interwar years a consensus about the need for reform gradually developed – particularly among civil servants – and that the NHS built on this existing trend (Klein 1983). A number of other scholars broadly align with Klein's view, although they see the 'consensus' as operating in different ways. Daniel M. Fox also presents a picture of broad agreement about the benefits of 'hierarchical regionalism' that aligns with Klein's arguments about the NHS emerging from consensus among technocrats (1986). Differing from the others, however, Fox does not see this as a uniquely British phenomenon and draws comparisons with the United States.

This debate endures in part because it is so difficult to resolve. It is not only a single dispute about 'conflict' and 'consensus' within a given context but also a debate about who was driving change in the late 1940s. While Webster focuses on politics, Klein places the emphasis on civil servants, and Fox on technocrats. Perhaps, then, we should not even be asking the question: 'was the NHS born out of conflict or consensus?' Instead, we should accept that 'conflict' and 'consensus' always existed in relation to the NHS. Taking the existence of both forces as a starting point, the question becomes: how did conflict and consensus shape the new NHS? This reframing of the question also allows us to move the debate forward from its focus on the run up to 1948, as forces of conflict and consensus continued to shape the NHS long after its launch (Seaton 2015).

Care

The welfare state quickly expanded its remit beyond a focus on curative and hospital-based medicine. In particular, there was increased support from the state for a range of forms of community care over the course of the late twentieth century. These shifted spaces of care away from the institution, a move driven in part by financial concerns and by the development of new treatments that allowed for outpatient care. Collectives such as patient groups, service users and disability rights activists also brought into view their criticisms of the conditions of many institutions.

Community care in a range of forms pre-dated the NHS and should not be viewed only as phenomena of the late twentieth century. In the early twentieth century – and before – there were many structures in place to care for people outside of institutional settings; examples include outdoor relief, almshouses, district nurses and hospital outpatient work (Doyle 2014; Doyle and Wall 2018). At this time legislation was brought in to provide state support for after-care, but most support remained informal and relied on existing charitable support networks (Westwood 2007). Social workers also played an increasingly important role in healthcare and support outside of hospitals, for example with the first 'psychiatric social workers' trained in 1929 and 331 working in Britain by 1951 (Long 2011).

In the 1960s and 1970s state intervention escalated following the demands of campaigners and the report of the Seebohm Committee of 1969 that revealed the weaknesses in social care. Legislation was brought in to reform the 'community care' of a wide range of groups, including older people, disabled people, people with learning difficulties and people with mental illness. Each group had distinct needs with specific reforms to address them, but the broad policy goals were the same: where possible, to treat individuals in community settings rather than as in-patients and through local authorities rather than NHS services. Where NHS care was required, it was reformed. Many large hospitals built under the 1962 plan had specialist facilities for short-term in-patient care for older patients and people with mental illness. Longer-term residential facilities were increasingly discouraged, with greater investment instead in supporting independent living and providing outpatient care.

In the 1980s and 1990s these trends accelerated further. The 1990 National Health Service and Community Care Act, for example, made it a requirement for local authorities to undertake assessments of – and arrange appropriate support for – people who might be in need of community care. On paper the policy achieved its aims of decreasing the number of people in long-term, institutional care. For example, systematic and large-scale asylum closures began in the 1980s, but implementation was uneven and resources for 'community care' alternatives were often stretched. The same story was seen with elderly care; the number of older patients in private facilities increased as the state put tighter restrictions on access to local authority financial support and residential care.

The story of care in the NHS is not only one of de-institutionalisation but also of how care – as opposed to acute treatment – was conceptualised and delivered within hospitals. In the late twentieth century there was an increasingly critical examination of what it meant for a patient to be 'cared for'. Such questions were raised particularly in contexts of high-technology medicine and increasing specialisation that it was feared posed challenges to holistic or 'whole person' care. The NHS had always put the patient at its centre, but so-called 'patient-centred care' became increasingly important to its value system over the course of the late twentieth century. Such trends were hand in hand with patient activism in the 1960s and 1970s, which demanded a voice for these groups in clinical encounters. This patient voice articulated itself in a wide range of new forms of political advocacy from patients' groups, which helped to pass the 1991 Patient's Charter (Mold 2015), to new cultural forms ranging from informal patients' newsletters to the new genre of published 'pathographies' (illness memoirs). By the end of the century, patients had an increasing level of influence over their own care, and the so-called 'patient-consumer' was a powerful force in the healthcare system.

Conclusion

It is impossible to do full justice to the changes in healthcare, health and wellbeing that took place over the course of the twentieth century. There were many significant changes to British healthcare and the health of people living in Britain, many of which were positive developments. However, we must also avoid simple stories of 'revolutionary' change or straightforward 'progress'. It is more important to understand what such changes meant to people and how they shaped experiences of healthcare, health and illness. Twentieth-century healthcare, health and wellbeing must not be reduced to a description of scientific discoveries and medical advances, nor to a counter-narrative of the new dangers posed by the modern world. The history of medicine and health in twentieth-century Britain is a more complex, and fundamentally social, story of change.

Further reading

A number of excellent books introduce the social history of medicine, going into more detail about the issues and debates outlined in this chapter. In alphabetical order, some good examples of introductory texts in the field that relate to twentieth-century Britain include R. Cooter and J. V. Pickstone (eds), *Medicine in the Twentieth Century* (Amsterdam, 2000); A. Hardy, *Health and Medicine in Britain since 1860* (Basingstoke, 2001); M. Jackson (ed.), *The Oxford Handbook of the History of Medicine* (Oxford, 2011) and *The Routledge History of Disease* (London; New York, 2016); H. Jones, *Health and Society in Twentieth-Century Britain* (London, 1994); and K. Waddington, *An Introduction to the Social History of Medicine* (Basingstoke, 2011).

Many of the topics discussed here also have their own extensive historiographies. As a starting point for looking up specific research interests, there is an excellent range of history of medicine journals, including: *Bulletin of the History of Medicine, Canadian Bulletin of Medical History, Health and History, History of Psychiatry, Isis, Journal of the History of Medicine and Allied Sciences, Osiris, Medical History, Medicine and the Life Sciences in History* and *Social History of Medicine*.

There are also a number of excellent publications on the history of specific illnesses and conditions, often taking the form of physical and mental 'illness biographies', for example: F. Bound Alberti, *A Biography of Loneliness* (Oxford, 2020); M.D. Moore, *Managing Diabetes, Managing Medicine* (Manchester, 2019), M. Jackson, *Age of Stress: Science and the Search for Stability* (Oxford, 2013); M. Smith, *Another Person's Poison: A History of Food Allergy* (New York, 2015); C. Timmermann, *A History of Lung Cancer: The Recalcitrant Disease* (Basingstoke, 2013) and C. Timmermann and E. Toon (eds.), *Cancer Patients, Cancer Pathways: Historical and Sociological Perspectives* (Basingstoke, 2012).

Note

1 This graph simplifies and combines ONS data on survival rates from the blog 'survival from cancer improving and more people being diagnosed' (https://wordpress.onsdigital.co.uk/40-years-of-cancer/) with published ONS statistics based on frozen/updated data on 1971–2013 cancer registration trends published in 2016 (www.ons.gov.uk/peoplepopulationandcommunity/healthandsocialcare/conditionsanddiseases/bulletins/cancerregistrationstatisticsengland/2014). The websites give further details of what cancers are included and provide the full data sets.

References

Bassett, D.R., Toth, L.P., LaMunion, S.R., and Crouter, S.E., 2017. Step counting: A review of measurement considerations and health-related applications. *Sports Medicine*, 47 (7), 1303–1315.

Berridge, V., 1999. *Health and society in Britain since 1939*, vol. 38. Cambridge: Cambridge University Press.

Bivins, R., 2020. Weighing on us all? Quantification and cultural responses to obesity in NHS Britain. *History of Science*, 58 (2), 216–242.

Bivins, R., and Marland, H., 2016. Weighting for health: Management, measurement and self-surveillance in the modern household. *Social History of Medicine*, 29 (4), 757–780.

Bud, R., 2007. *Penicillin: Triumph and tragedy*. Oxford: Oxford University Press.

Carter, S., Green, J., and Speed, E., 2018. Digital technologies and the biomedicalisation of everyday activities: The case of walking and cycling. *Sociology Compass*, 12 (4), e12572.

Clarke, S.F., and Foster, J.R., 2012. A history of blood glucose meters and their role in self-monitoring of diabetes mellitus. *British Journal of Biomedical Science*, 69 (2), 83–93.

Crane, J., 2019. 'Save our NHS': Activism, information-based expertise and the 'new times' of the 1980s. *Contemporary British History*, 33 (1), 52–74.

Doyle, B., 2014. *The politics of hospital provision in early twentieth century Britain*. London: Routledge.

Doyle, B., and Wall, R. [now Cresswell], 2018. What was healthcare like before the NHS?, *The Conversation* [online]. Available from: https://theconversation.com/what-was-healthcare-like-before-the-nhs-99055 [Accessed 18 August 2020].

Eckstein, H., 1960. *Pressure group politics: The case of the British Medical Association*. Stanford: Stanford University Press.

Fox, D.M., 1986. The consequences of consensus: American health policy in the twentieth century. *The Milbank Quarterly*, 64 (1), 76–99.

Fraser, D., 1992. *The evolution of the British welfare state: A history of social policy since the Industrial Revolution*. London: Macmillan International Higher Education.

Gijswijt-Hofstra, M., and Porter, R., eds., 2001. *Cultures of neurasthenia from Beard to the First World War*, No. 63. Amsterdam and New York: Rodopi.

Gorsky, M., 2008., The British National Health Service 1948–2008: A review of the historiography, *Social History of Medicine*, 21 (3), 437–460.

Honigsbaum, M., 2009. *Living with Enza: The forgotten story of Britain and the great flu pandemic of 1918*. Basingstoke: Macmillan.

Horn, D., 1962. Smoking and health: A report of the royal college of physicians on smoking in relation to cancer of the lung and other diseases. *A Cancer Journal for Clinicians*, 12 (3), 111–112.

Klein, R., 1983. *The politics of the National Health Service*. London: Longman.

Larson, J.S., 1999. The conceptualization of health. *Medical Care Research and Review*, 56 (2), 123–136.

Long, V., 2011. 'Often there is a good deal to be done, but socially rather than medically': The psychiatric social worker as social therapist, 1945–70. *Medical History*, 55 (2), 223–239.

Marks, L., 2010. *Sexual chemistry: A history of the contraceptive pill*. New Haven: Yale University Press.

Mold, A., 2015. The art of medicine: Making British patients into consumers. *The Lancet*, 385 (9975), 1286–1287.

Office for National Statistics/Public Health England (ONS/PHE), 2016. *Cancer registration statistics*. Available from: www.ons.gov.uk/peoplepopulationandcommunity/healthandsocialcare/conditionsanddiseases/bulletins/cancerregistrationstatisticsengland/2014   [Accessed 18 August 2020].

ONS, 2012. *Mortality in England and Wales*. Available from: www.ons.gov.uk/peoplepopulationandcommunity/birthsdeathsandmarriages/deaths/articles/mortalityinenglandandwales/2012-12-17 [Accessed 18 August 2020].

Seaton, A., 2015. Against the 'sacred cow': NHS opposition and the fellowship for freedom in medicine, 1948–72. *Twentieth Century British History*, 26 (3), 424–449.

Snow, S., and Jones, E., 2011. Immigration and the National Health Service: Putting history to the forefront. *History and Policy*. Available from: www. historyandpolicy.org/policy-papers/papers/immigration-and-the-national-health-service-putting-history-to-the-forefront [Accessed 18 August 2020].

Sysling, F., 2020, Measurement, self-tracking and the history of science: An introduction. *History of Science*, 58 (2), 103–116.

Webster, C., 1990. Conflict and consensus: Explaining the British health service. *Twentieth Century British History*, 1 (2), 115–151.

Westwood, L., 2007. Care in the community of the mentally disordered: The case of the guardianship society, 1900–1939. *Social History of Medicine*, 20 (1), 57–72.

Zweiniger-Bargielowska, I., 2005. The culture of the abdomen: Obesity and reducing in Britain, circa 1900–1939. *Journal of British Studies*, 44 (2), 239–273.

Part B
Britain in focus

18 Britain at war 1914–1918 and 1939–45

Linsey Robb

Introduction

The World Wars occupy a huge space in the British collective memory. The 'memories' of these wars have crystallised very specifically into a uniform set of 'truths'. It is believed, for example, that the First World War only happened on the Western Front and men spent the majority of their time fighting in trenches. These 'lions led by donkeys' were innocents sent to a brutal death by uncaring and unprepared politicians. Such images are repeated ad nauseum from the 'war poets' such as Siegfried Sassoon, Wilfred Owen and Robert Graves. If it is thought the British First World War was fought on the battlegrounds, then its Second World War was fought almost entirely on the Home Front (with the notable exceptions of Dunkirk and D-Day). Again, it is 'known' that the British populace pulled together, showing their 'Dunkirk spirit' and 'blitz spirit' at the historically apposite moments and worked tirelessly without complaint to knock out Hitler's Nazis almost single-handedly. Or so it goes. Of course, these narratives have their roots in actual war experiences, and it would be foolish to decry them all as mere myths. Yet they are partial, reflecting fragments of the true breadth of the impacts which these two unprecedented huge wars had on British society. One of the most difficult tasks facing historians is disentangling myths from lived experiences. Therefore, this chapter will introduce the effects of warfare and encourage you to engage critically with received notions about the impacts of the two world wars on British society.

Attitudes to war

Britain entered the First World War on 4 August 1914. Folk memory asserts that the declaration was greeted with glee from the British populace. However, as Adrian Gregory (2008) notes, there is little evidence to support this idea. There was little way of measuring public opinion in 1914, and what evidence there is comes from newspapers and politicians' memoirs, perhaps writing to support the decisions they made retrospectively. Although initial recruitment to the military appeared to reflect enthusiasm, in reality, the response to the reaction to the outbreak of war was mixed. Class, religion, nation and region all impacted war enthusiasm. As Catriona Pennell notes, a nation of 40 million people could never be described with a singular label like 'war enthusiasm' (2012, p. 1).

Of course, war required men to enlist in the military. In both wars millions of men were needed not just to bear arms but to enter the clerical, engineering and logistical roles required to keep the army, navy and, once formally established in 1918, air force

DOI: 10.4324/9781003037118-20

operational. Initially in the First World War, the British state relied on voluntary enlistment to meet the requirements of the armed forces. At the outset this proved successful. In the first two months of the war, 478,893 men enlisted for service. Reasons for doing so were diffuse. Propaganda played a part but so too did peer pressure, financial incentives and the opportunities for 'adventure'. By December 1915 nearly 2.5 million men had joined the armed forces. Yet this was insufficient to sustain the military at the level required. In January 1916 the Military Service Act introduced conscription for single men between 18 and 40. This proved controversial, facing not only opposition from the socialists and pacifists who would become conscientious objectors but also broader opposition for practical and moral reasons. In April 1916, 200,000 protested conscription in London's Trafalgar Square. However, conscription went ahead as planned and was extended to married men in June 1916 and the age limit eventually raised to 51. In total 2.5 million men were conscripted (UK Parliament 2020a).

Conscription in the Second World War was met with little opposition. In January 1939 each British household received a pamphlet, the contents of which were repeated in the press, detailing the roles each member of British society would be expected to play in the event of war, including which professions would be exempt from service, for example, engineering and agricultural trades, as well as details of a measured military call-up. The British government did not repeat the rapid voluntary enlistment (or its subsequent collapse) of the First World War and instead sought to move men into the military in a calculated fashion (Calder 1969). The British reaction to the Second World War's beginning was muted, with little open enthusiasm for war. Both the recent memories of trench warfare and the fear of aerial bombardment weighed heavy on the minds of politicians and the populace. When British Prime Minister Neville Chamberlain declared war on 3 September 1939, many expected immediate aerial bombardment. Instead Britain entered a period known as the 'phoney war' in which little military activity took place until Germany invaded France and the low countries in spring 1940.

Pressure on men to fight was huge in both wars. In the First World War pressure to enlist came from the government with propaganda which insinuated that to avoid service was to be unmanly. Slogans such as 'What did you do in the Great War daddy?' and 'Your country needs you' were common and implied the only correct way to be a man in wartime was to be in uniform. Societal pressure was also prominent, with the famous campaign of white feathers, a traditional symbol of cowardice, handed to men out of uniform just one of the ways men were shamed into enlistment. This level of public pressure was not repeated in the Second World War. While there were intermittent flurries of white feathers, for example, this was not officially condoned (Pattinson *et al.* 2018). Similarly, the state's policy of measured call-up did not lend itself to the didactic haranguing propaganda of the First World War. Despite this, many men of fighting age during the Second World War felt an internalised pressure to 'do their bit' in uniform regardless of their civilian occupation or physical capabilities, with many men in vital reserved occupations, for example, industrial workers, attempting to evade their reserved status and enlist in the military (Pattinson *et al.* 2018).

Working for the war effort

These huge wars needed more than soldiers. They also required industrial production on a vast scale. In the First World War 16.4 million shells were produced in 1915 alone. Similarly, in 1944, 896,636 aircraft bombs were produced in Britain's factories (Howlett 1995). During both wars across the nation, and across the Empire, factories churned out the vast array of goods required for industrialised warfare. The most obvious change to industry in both the First and Second World Wars was the influx of women to new industries. These women dominate both scholarly and popular discussions of the period. With a newly expanded industrial sector and the need to draw men into the forces, women, especially young unmarried women, became the obvious source of labour. During the First World War this had been entirely voluntary. However, in December 1941, the government passed the National Service Act (No 2), which made provision for the conscription of women to industrial and military roles for the first time. Initially only childless widows and single women, 20 to 30 years old, were called up, but this later expanded to include married women and those up to 43. However, neither work itself nor industrial work were necessarily new to the women involved in either war. Before the war began in 1914 roughly 1/3 of all women worked outside the home. 400,000 women did join the labour force in the first year of the First World War, but not all were driven by a patriotic fervour to 'do their bit'. A large proportion were working class, and the higher wages and relative freedoms promised by industrial work (as compared to traditional paid domestic work) were certainly enticing (Grayzel 2002). Similarly, between June 1938 and June 1943 the number of women employed in engineering trades expanded by nearly 4 times (from 488,000 to 1,855,600) (Howlett 1995). However, in both wars women, despite their necessity, were often confined to the 'lighter' end of industrial work, with very few women participating in shipbuilding or other heavy industries. The work women were assigned was often monotonous, and women were paid far less than their male equivalents as well as having to endure sexism and not infrequently sexual harassment alongside high praise from the media and the state.

Factories and workshops in the periods both before and during the First and Second World Wars had often been avowedly 'manly' spaces. Working-class male pride was often built on being able to endure physically demanding work and gruelling hours, not to mention the threat and lived reality of injury. Yet both wars pushed these situations to their limit. In the first months of the First World War production increased dramatically. Many workers were working 70–85 hours a week, leading within a year to decreasing production as workers began to suffer from chronic fatigue (McIvor 2001). While increased state intervention did bring some respite to workers (including the introduction of canteens, rest breaks and the abolition of Sunday working), this was not uniformly applied, and it was the heaviest and most dangerous industries (coal-mining, railway work and construction, for example) which were left largely unaltered, meaning that accident and death rates remained high throughout the First World War (McIvor 2001).

During the interwar period many traditional heavy industrial communities were decimated by the depression of the 1930s. In many ways these communities were revitalised by the Second World War, as once-dead industries were resurrected to produce vital war goods. Yet this did not come without cost. Working hours increased dramatically, especially with spurts around Dunkirk and D-Day. In the immediate aftermath of the evacuation at Dunkirk (with the need to replace equipment lost and a threat of imminent invasion), the average work week was 10–12-hour days and a total of 60–70 hours per week at work (Inman 1957). This often led to an increase in pay, with many men far outstripping their pre-war earnings. However, the stress and exhaustion of these exacting work schedules led to cumulative exhaustion and, like in the First World War, high rates of absenteeism (Mass Observation 1942). Unsurprisingly, given the increased hours worked and the use of newly trained labour, non-fatal accidents increased by 50% between 1938 and 1942 (Waldron 1997). For morale and propaganda reasons these were rarely mentioned. Moreover, during both wars labour tensions continued. Strikes were by no means uncommon, sparked by tensions over pay and conditions as well as specific war grievances, such as, in the First World War, war profiteering (McIvor 2001). In addition, trade unions were in a strong bargaining position due to a shortage of men and a necessity of production (Wrigley 1987, and see also Wrigley's chapter in this volume).

War also necessitated greater regulation of the labour market. Unchecked recruitment early in the First World War left some industries short of manpower and necessitated regulations to 'reserve' vital men for industry rather than military service. From October 1915 essential men, generally in industrial occupations, were placed in reserved occupations (Beckett 2006). This system of reservation was both immensely complex and not infrequently controversial. It was often accused of being a way to 'hide' men in 'cushy' jobs. Similarly, the War Office believed it should have its pick of young healthy men for military service (Grieves 1985). As such, the process of controlling civilian labour changed frequently throughout the war to accommodate changing needs and beliefs. However, one thing was clear: war needed industry, and industry needed skilled workers. By the time of the Second World War this policy was less controversial and more organised. In 1938, as tensions in Europe grew, the Schedule of Reserved Occupations, initially drawn up during the 1920s, was revised, eventually being released to the public in January 1939 alongside the regulations for military conscription. There were echoes of the tensions seen in the First World War, although these were less frequent and more muted. Similarly, the schedule was under constant revision to add and remove jobs, the 'balance of manpower' being a key juggling act the British government had to undertake to ensure the military was both armed *and* staffed (Pattinson *et al.* 2018). At the peak of armed forces employment in 1944 there were as many men in vital reserved occupations as there were in the military, a necessary balance to keep the war machine moving (Howlett 1995).

Civilians at war

The impacts on civilian populations stretched far beyond the factory gates and even into the home. The impact of domestic food shortages should not be underestimated. Severe food shortages played an integral role in Germany's defeat in the First World War. In Britain, the food situation was never as severe, but Britain had been a net importer of food before both the First and Second World Wars. During the First World War the state was reluctant to control food. In the early years of the war food prices rose out of pace with increasing wartime wages, creating a fall in real wages. As 1917 ended, the problems of acute shortages, especially of meats and fat, caused widespread public consternation (Gregory 2008). Rationing was introduced late in the war, with ration books only issued in July 1918. Only sugar and meat were rationed. During the Second World War food was much more tightly controlled. Rationing began in January 1940 and did not end completely until 1954. Rationing was extensive and covered most major foods as well as clothing and furniture. The government heavily promoted the idea that the rationing system ensured a fair share for all. Yet not all adults required the same diet to remain healthy. For example, the flat rate access to food meant many men working in heavy industry felt their rations were too meagre (Zweinger-Bargielowska 2011). Moreover, class, wealth and gender all impacted experiences of rationing. Not all goods were rationed, but off-ration goods were often more expensive due to shortages, meaning they were more accessible to those with higher incomes. In addition, the wealthy generally had better quality and quantity of pre-war clothes and furniture with which it was possible to 'make do and mend' more straightforwardly (King and Andrews 2014). The burden of shopping and preparing nutritious and filling meals with limited resources also fell disproportionately on women, while it was also women who often did without to ensure their husbands and children had full stomachs (Zweinger-Bargielowska 2011).

Overall, the impacts of warfare were much more acutely felt on the home front in the Second World War than in the First. There were very few areas of daily life which were not impacted. Over the course of the war 3.75 million people were evacuated from urban to rural areas to protect them from enemy attack. This figure included not only school children but also children under five with their mothers, pregnant women, disabled people and over 100,000 teachers and 'helpers' (Todman 2016a). Fundamentally, however, the scheme removed huge numbers of children from parental supervision for extended periods, an act simply unthinkable outside of wartime. The war had an impact in ways, big and small, which acted as persistent reminders of the conflict. Street and town signs were removed to confuse the enemy in the event of invasion. From September 1939 until April 1945, with a switch to a 'dim-out' in September 1944, all Britons were subject to night-time blackout regulations to attempt to frustrate enemy bombers. As well as being an ever-present reminder of war, the blackout also brought with it new danger. For example, both breaking and entering and sexual assaults, crimes both made easier by blackout regulations, increased significantly during the war (Howlett 1995). In many ways the changes to daily life in both the First and Second World Wars are too numerous to detail. Nevertheless, even from these few examples, it is clear that war made the familiar unfamiliar and was felt in insidious and ever-present ways.

However, the most significant impact of war, at least psychologically if not numerically, was the attack on British civilians at home. The German Navy attacked the North-East ports of Scarborough, Hartlepool and Whitby on 16 December 1914, resulting in 592 casualties, many of them civilians, of whom 137 died. The attack became a rallying cry, with huge amounts of propaganda centred on the death of women and children. From January 1915 the German forces began using airships, upgrading to aeroplanes in 1917, to attack England's coastal regions. Seventy-eight bombing raids took place over the course of the war. Two thousand UK civilians lost their lives during the First World War (UK Parliament 2020b). Although these numbers are not insignificant, they were not only dwarfed by the civilian casualties in other belligerent nations but also by Britain's losses in the Second World War.

Between 1918 and 1939 aeronautical engineering advanced dramatically. In the 1930s it was assumed that any aerial warfare would be catastrophic, causing widespread destruction and death. Such fears were seemingly confirmed by the hugely destructive bombing of Guernica in 1936 during the Spanish Civil War. State preparations reflect this fear. Civil defence organisations were in place long before the war began. Public air-raid shelters were prepared during the Munich crisis in 1938, when war came perilously close, and home shelters were distributed, free to low-income families, around the country. The reality, for Britain at least, was less dramatic. No bombs fell on Britain until November 1939, when a bomb was dropped on Shetland. It was not until September 1940 that bombing began in earnest. Every night for eight months and five days, 'the Blitz', the German Luftwaffe dropped bombs on the United Kingdom. Although parts of all four nations were at some point targeted, it was London which bore the brunt. From 7 September 1940, London was bombed every night for 57 nights. Bombing after this period was more sporadic, ending completely in March 1945 when German forces were cut off from the UK due to the successful reinvasion of Europe. 70,000 British civilians lost their lives during the Second World War. 40,000 of these deaths took place during 'the Blitz', with almost half of those who died in this period dying in London (UK Parliament 2020b).

Image 18.1 British fire fighters damping down smouldering roof timbers of a church hit by German bombs: June 1940

Source: World War II © World History Archive/Alamy Stock Photo.

Debates and Interpretations: 'Blitz spirit'

In 1940 the British Ministry of Information produced the short propaganda film *Britain Can Take It*. The film focused on the impacts of the Blitz on London, emphasising that rather than being cowed by the nightly onslaught of bombs, the people of London were resilient, continuing their day jobs after gruelling nights of civilian defence work protecting London. This image, of a stoic nation which stood up to danger without complaint and pulled together seamlessly in the nation's hour of need, is now cemented in the British collective memory as a foundational idea of what it means to British. At any nationally difficult moment almost since the end of the war (recessions, housing shortages and global pandemics), politicians and public commentators have asked the British to dig deep and find our own 'Blitz spirit'

Such ideas, however, raise challenges for the historian. Second World War historians have to not only interpret the past but also interpret the past's uses in the present. Historians have long discussed and analysed Britain's particular attachment to the Second World War. Most notably, in 1991, Angus Calder published the seminal book, *The Myth of the Blitz*, which examined the mytholigised events of 1940 and 1941 to provide a more rounded and nuanced view of Britain's war. Mark Connelly (2004) and Malcom Smith (2000) have both examined in depth the ways these stories and ideas grew during the war itself and the various ways they have been deployed since. Yet it is imperative that we do not become 'mythbusters', constantly seeking to constantly undermine collective memory. Not least because, while undoubtedly partial, many of the core components of the 'Blitz myth' have their roots in reality. As Lucy Noakes notes 'it is not enough to dismiss this memory as a creation of the ruling class. . . . The reason for the continued dominance of a memory of unity during the Second World War must lie, in part, in the war itself' (1997, p. 25). Moreover, the production of academic historical knowledge does not take place in an ivory tower but is profoundly shaped by the society in which it is created. As such, many historians of the Second World War, especially cultural, social and oral historians, seek to actively interrogate both their own and society's preset notions about their historical subjects as part of their work (for example, Summerfield 1998; Summerfield and Peniston-Bird 2007; Pattinson *et al.* 2018).

Limits to support

Throughout both world wars support for the war was never universal nor guaranteed. Fundamental to this discord was the United Kingdom's internal composition of four distinct nations. In the period leading up the First World War one of the key domestic issues was Home Rule for Ireland. After decades of debate, two previous bills, and a temporary veto by the Lords, parliament passed the Home Rule Act in 1914 (Jackson 2010). Its implementation was formally suspended, because of the war, for 12 months but never passed into reality. Despite this, many unionists and nationalists volunteered for service in the war. However, Irish separatists never ceased their campaign. Most notably, at about 11.00 am on Easter Monday 1916, insurgents assembled at various prearranged meeting points in Dublin and before noon set out to occupy a number of imposing buildings, most famously the General Post Office (GPO), in the inner city area. Over 1000 people took part in what would become known as the Easter Rising. The insurgents were defeated by the British military after 6 days, including some heavy fighting. Fifteen men were executed for their role in leading the Rising, an act which boosted their popularity within Ireland (McGarry 2010). Irish politics changed dramatically. An attempt to introduce conscription in Ireland in 1918 was extremely controversial, led to outrage in Ireland and further increased support for separatism, as seen in Sinn Féin's victory in the 1918 election and the subsequent Anglo-Irish War of 1919 to 1921. The Government of Ireland Act of 1920 legislated for partition and home rule for both states but was never enacted in the south. In 1921, the Anglo-Irish Treaty ended hostilities, leaving the Irish Free State (now the Republic) independent following a civil war ending in 1922 over accepting the Treaty and Northern Ireland within the United Kingdom. Ireland remained neutral in the Second World War but even Northern Ireland remained slightly different from the rest of the United Kingdom. While subject to wartime rationing and the threats of warfare, conscription was never introduced (Jackson 2010).

While tensions between Britain and Ireland are the least surprising, they were not the only tensions felt between the constituent nations of the United Kingdom. British Second World War films (for example, *In Which We Serve* [1942] and *Millions Like Us* [1943]) often included characters from all the countries of Britain (any Northern Irish representation was very rare) to emphasise the essential unity of British society. However, in reality, relationships between the nations could be strained. One notable controversy came after the introduction of female conscription in 1941. Many young women were sent to jobs in England; this proved especially contentious in Scotland, leading to debates about the underfunding of Scottish industry and the removal of Scotland's women (for fear they would never return) (Rose 2004).

The United Kingdom was also an imperial power. During both wars men from the empire, both colonies and dominions, fought under the British flag. In the First World War alone nearly 9 million men were raised for military and naval service from the empire (Keitch 2017). Their incursion on to the British home front was minimal, although some non-white colonial battalions were stationed in Britain. By contrast, far more war workers and foreign soldiers were present in Britain during the Second World War (Webster 2018). Men came from across the Empire to work in Britain. For example, 1000 skilled technicians and trainees came from the West Indies to work in ordnance factories, with similar numbers coming from British Honduras to work in Scottish forestry (Rose 2004). With the entry of the United States into the war in 1941, a significant number of Black American soldiers were also stationed in Britain during the war. Race became an issue in Britain in a new way. (See Chapter 12 for a discussion of immigrants and minorities.) The British state wished to promote a vision of a tolerant nation and a benevolent paternalistic relationship with its colonies and their inhabitants (Rose 2004). However, in reality, race relations in Britain were mixed. Relationships with white British women were extremely controversial, not infrequently leading to violence against the men involved. While those who worked with and knew Britain's newest arrivals often formed bonds and friendships, the nation as a whole had long been taught that those from the colonies were in some way 'lesser', whether that be intellectually or a lack of 'civility', beliefs which could only lead to tensions (Webster 2018).

Yet while British experience was shaped by national and international events, reactions to war were also localised. For example, due to an influx of industrial workers to the city during the First World War, rents began to rise in Glasgow. This coupled with the rising price of food meant many families were struggling financially.

In February 1915 the Glasgow Women's Housing Association was formed. In May of that year they began a rent strike, with eventually 25,000 people taking part in Glasgow alone as the strikes began to spread across Britain. In response the state passed the Rent Restriction Act, which froze rents at 1914 levels. Region continued to shape experience throughout the Second World War. In addition to the obvious and expected disparities between urban and rural (manifested predominantly in different diets and levels of danger faced), even different urban centres could have incredibly different experiences of war. One reason for this was the varied experiences of the 1930s depression. Those who resided in areas which relied heavily on heavy industry (for example, North-East England, Central and North-Eastern Scotland and parts of Wales) were hit hard by the vast reduction in those crucial industries. Those in lighter industries were, conversely, less affected by economic downturn. War reversed the fortunes of many heavy industries and, in turn, the communities which relied on them. As such many in these areas were happier to remain at home in their now financially lucrative reserved occupations than risk their lives for a state which, as they saw it, had done little to protect them or their families during the economically turbulent 1930s (Pattinson *et al.* 2018).

In addition, many objected to both wars on pacifist or socialist grounds. The conscription legislation of both wars allowed for conscientious objections to service, subject to a tribunal. However, the experience of COs was markedly different during the two wars. During the First World War COs were treated harshly and always viewed with suspicion, often portrayed as cowardly and effeminate. One-third of the 16,000 men who objected to military service between 1916 and 1918 were imprisoned (Ellsworth-Jones 2008). Such actions were not repeated in the Second World War. Only 300 men of the 60,000 who claimed an objection were imprisoned during the Second World War. Instead, the state took a much more pragmatic view of COs, generally choosing to use them to work in mutually agreeable industries. Of those who professed a conscientious objection, 12,204 were turned down completely. Only 3,577 men were granted complete exemption. In total, 45,000 men, the overwhelming majority, were directed to take up work which was deemed of 'national importance', which encompassed both military and civilian roles (Calder 1969). Attitudes to these men had shifted too. While they were rarely openly celebrated, they were largely tolerated, and the ire and hatred of the First World War largely gone.

In Focus: First World War centenary, 2014–2018

2014–2018 saw four years of intense commemorative activity for the centenary of the First World War. Academics, museums, the government, local councils and the public ran events and workshops to commemorate and further understand the war. In many ways, not least scale and variety, it is difficult to summarise the activities which took place. At a local level the events often, but not always, commemorated specific local events or people. Academic historians were also deeply involved in commemorative activities which generally tried to broaden the scope of discussion of the First World War, which is often mired in the mud of the Somme, singularly focused on Britain to the exclusion of even its allies or

Empire, and overly focused on what has been termed a 'pity of war' narrative which emphasises the abject horror and painful deaths of the Western Front over all other aspects of the war (Roper and Duffett 2018).

The stories emphasised tell us a lot about those telling them. As Jay Winter argues: 'Memory is always about the future. When political conditions change, so do narratives about the past' (2017, p. 239). The British Conservative Party came to power in 2010 and was central to state centenary commemorations. Famously, in 2014, during an overhaul of GCSE content, Michael Gove, then secretary of state for education, argued that the history of the First World War was mistaught by left-wing academics and sitcoms as a 'misbegotten shambles' when in fact it was a 'just war' to combat aggressively expansionist German elites (Perry 2014). Such statements risk replacing one partial view of the war with another. Much of the government centenary programme was imbued with this celebration of militarism. For example, the state-organised First World War Centenary Battlefield Tours Programme was offered to every school in England, with each school sending several pupils and an accompanying teacher to key battlefields and cemeteries of the First World War. They were accompanied by serving soldiers and followed a tightly plotted tour which focused predominantly on the Western Front, at the expense of the wider experiences of war. As Pennell notes, 'The risk, therefore, is that rather than encouraging young people to think critically about the past, the tours are emphasizing a particular narrative of remembrance shaped around sacrifice, duty, and loyalty' (2018, pp. 14–15).

Remembrance activities even had an impact at home as TV schedules were packed with centenary content. The BBC especially created a huge amount of commemorative content. Between 2014 and 2018, 2,500 hours of centenary programming was broadcast via TV, radio and online. By their own estimates by November 2014, 75% of the British populace had engaged with some form of centenary content on the BBC (Todman 2016b). There was a cultural onslaught of information, imagery and discussion. However, while the war was incredibly visible, it is not necessarily true that this led to greater understanding amongst the British populace. As Dan Todman notes of this 'cultural blizzard': '[it] allows the already fascinated to confirm their existing beliefs, engages others for a superficial moment, and passes many completely by' (2016b, p. 523).

Conclusion

War is a complex phenomenon. Therefore, wars, especially on the scale of the First and Second World Wars, have multi-faceted and far-reaching consequences which are difficult to capture succinctly. But this chapter has introduced some key ideas with which to approach this topic. Primarily, we must be careful of how we approach the myths which surround each war. To dismiss them entirely as falsehoods would be as problematic as uncritically accepting them. The patriotic pull to defend one's country *was* passionately felt by many. For many the Second World War *was* a period of previously unseen unity and common purpose. Yet, during both the First and Second World Wars, the United Kingdom was a state made up of four distinct nations, not to mention a vast empire, which in turn had divisions, differences and tensions along regional, class, gender and race lines. Moreover, pre-existing tensions could impact British lives as much as the war itself. We must, therefore, begin to understand the multiplicity of experiences and opinions which fall under the broader umbrella of 'British experience' of warfare. It is only by nuancing and complicating our perceptions of these mammoth wars that we have any hope of ever truly understanding them.

Further reading

There are seemingly endless works published on both the First and Second World Wars, and, as such, what follows can only ever be a small section of the wonderful work which exists. This list is far from exhaustive and, by necessity, excludes many fantastic illuminating books. Adrian Gregory (2008) and Dan Todman (2016a and 2020) both provide excellent overviews of the First and Second World Wars, respectively. For research on women's roles, the work of Grayzel (2002), Gullace (2004), Watson (2004), Summerfield (1998), Noakes (1997, 2006) and Pattinson (2020) provides excellent broad-focused research into the female experience in a variety of roles and contexts. There is also a rich literature on the impact of war on labour during both wars; for example, Hinton (1992), Wrigley (1987), Field (2011), Robb (2015) and Pattinson *et al.* (2018). The issue of race remains understudied with regard to both world wars, but Das (2011), Olusoga (2014), Webster (2018) and Rose (2004) provide good starting points. Conscientious objectors remain vastly more studied for the First World War than the Second; see Ceadel (1980) and Bibbings (2011) for the First World War and Barker (1982) for the Second World War. Ireland's and Northern Ireland's relationship to Britain was, and is, complex and contentious, and there is a huge historiography for early twentieth-century Ireland in its own right. However, by way of introduction, for Ireland during the First World War, see Jeffrey (2000), Gregory and Pašeta (2002) and Gallagher (2019), and for Northern Ireland during the Second World War, see Ollerenshaw (2013) and Woodward (2015).

References

Barker, R., 1982. *Conscience, government, and war: Conscientious objection in Great Britain, 1939–45*. London: Routledge.

Beckett, I., 2006. *The Great War 1914–1918*. London: Longman.

Bibbings, L., 2011. *Telling tales about men: Conceptions of conscientious objectors to military service during the First World War*. Manchester: Manchester University Press.

Calder, A., 1969. *The people's war: Britain 1939–45*. London: Jonathan Cape.

Calder, A., 1991. *The myth of the Blitz*. London: Jonathan Cape.

Ceadel, M., 1980. *Pacifism in Britain, 1914–1945: The defining of a faith*. Oxford: Oxford University Press.

Connelly, M., 2004. *We can take it! Britain and the memory of the Second World War*. London: Pearson Longman.

Das, S., 2011. *Race, empire and First World War writing*. Cambridge: Cambridge University Press.

Ellsworth-Jones, W., 2008. *We will not fight . . .: The untold story of World War One conscientious objectors*. London: Aurum Press.

Field, G.G., 2011. *Blood, sweat and toil: Remaking the British working class, 1939–1945*. Oxford: Oxford University Press.

Gallagher, N., 2019. *Ireland and the Great War: A social and political history*. London: Bloomsbury.

Grayzel, S., 2002. *Women and the First World War*. London: Longman.

Gregory, A., 2008. *The last great war: British society and the First World War*. Oxford: Oxford University Press.

Gregory, A., and Pašeta, S., eds., 2002. *Ireland and the great war: 'A war to unite us all'?*. Manchester: Manchester University Press.

Grieves, K., 1985. *The politics of manpower, 1914–1918*. Manchester: Manchester University Press.

Gullace, N., 2004. *"The blood of our sons": Men, women, and the renegotiation of British citizenship during the Great War*. Basingstoke: Palgrave Macmillan.

Hinton, J., 1992. *Labour and socialism: A history of the British labour movement, 1867–1974*. London: Longman.

Howlett, P., 1995. *Fighting with figures: A statistical digest of the Second World War*. London: HMSO.

Inman, P., 1957. *Labour in the munitions industries*. London: HMSO.

Jackson, A., 2010. *Ireland, 1798–1998: War, peace and beyond*. 2nd ed. Chichester: Wiley-Blackwell.

Jeffrey, K., 2000. *Ireland and the Great War*. Cambridge: Cambridge University Press.

Keitch, C., 2017. The empire called to arms [online]. *Imperial War Museum*. Available from: www.iwm.org.uk/learning/resources/the-empire-called-to-arms [Accessed 19 August 2020].

King, E., and Andrews, M., 2014. Second world war rationing: Creativity and buying to last. *In*: M. Andrews and J. Lomas, eds. *The home front in Britain: Images, myth and forgotten experiences since 1914*. Basingstoke: Palgrave Macmillan, 185–200.

Mass Observation, 1942. *People in production: An enquiry into British War Production: Part 1 – A report prepared by Mass-Observation for the advertising service guild*. London: Advertising Service Guild.

McGarry, F, 2010. *The rising*. Oxford: Oxford University Press.

McIvor, A., 2001. *A history of work in Britain, 1880–1950*. Basingstoke: Palgrave Macmillan.

Noakes, L., 1997. *War and the British: Gender and national identity, 1939–1991*. London: I.B. Tauris.

Noakes, L., 2006. *Women in the British Army: War and the gentle sex, 1907–1948*. London: Routledge.

Ollerenshaw, P., 2013. *Northern Ireland in the Second World War: Politics, economic mobilisation and society, 1939–45*. Manchester: Manchester University Press.

Olusoga, D., 2014. *The world's war*. London: Head of Zeus.

Pattinson, J., 2020. *Women of war: Gender, modernity and the first aid nursing yeomanry*. Manchester: Manchester University Press.

Pattinson, J., McIvor, A., and Robb, L., 2018. *Men in reserve: British civilian masculinities in the Second World War*. Manchester: Manchester University Press.

Pennell, C., 2012. *A kingdom united: Popular responses to the outbreak of the First World War in Britain and Ireland*. Oxford: Oxford University Press.

Pennell, C., 2018. Taught to remember? British youth and First World War centenary battlefield tours. *Cultural Trends*, 27 (2), 83–98.

Perry, K., (2014). Michael Gove criticises 'Blackadder myths' about First World War [online]. *The Telegraph*. Available from: www.telegraph.co.uk/news/10548303/Michael-Gove-criticises-Blackadder-myths-about-First-World-War.html [Accessed 19 August 2020].

Robb, L., 2015. *Men at work: The working man in British culture, 1939–1945*. Basingstoke: Palgrave Macmillan.

Roper, M., and Duffett, R., 2018. Family legacies in the centenary. Motives for First World War commemoration among British and German descendants. *History and Memory*, 30 (1), 76–115.

Rose, S., 2004. *Which people's war?: National identity and citizenship in Britain 1939–1945*. Oxford: Oxford University Press.

Smith, M., 2000. *Britain and 1940: History, myth and popular memory*. Abingdon: Routledge.

Summerfield, P., 1998. *Reconstructing women's wartime lives: Discourse and subjectivity in oral histories of the Second World War*. Manchester: Manchester University Press.

Summerfield, P., and Peniston-Bird, C., 2007. *Contesting home defence: Men, women and the home guard in the Second World War*. Manchester: Manchester University Press.

Todman, D., 2016a. *Britain's war into battle, 1937–1941*. London: Allen Lane.

Todman, D., 2016b. 'Something about who we are as a people': Government, media, heritage and the construction of the centenary. *Twentieth Century British History*, 27 (4), 518–523.

Todman, D., 2020. *Britain's war II, a new world, 1942–1947*. London: Allen Lane.

UK Parliament, 2020a. *Conscription: The First World War* [online]. Available from: www.parliament.uk/about/living-heritage/transformingsociety/private-lives/yourcountry/overview/conscription/ [Accessed 8 September 2020].

UK Parliament, 2020b. *The Fallen* [online]. Available from: www.parliament.uk/business/publications/research/olympic-britain/crime-and-defence/the-fallen/ [Accessed 8 September 2020].

Waldron, H.A., 1997. Occupational health during the Second World War: Hope deferred or hope abandoned. *Medical History*, 41, 197–212.

Watson, J.S.K., 2004. *Fighting different wars: Experience, memory, and the First World War in Britain*. Cambridge: Cambridge University Press.

Webster, W., 2018. *Mixing it: Diversity in World War Two Britain*. Oxford: Oxford University Press.

Winter, J., 2017. Commemorating catastrophe: 100 years on. *War & Society*, 36 (4), 239–255.

Woodward, G., 2015. *Culture, Northern Ireland, and the Second World War*. Oxford: Oxford University Press.

Wrigley, C., 1987. The First World War and state intervention in industrial relations, 1914–18. *In*: C. Wrigley, ed., *A history of British industrial relations volume II: 1914–1939*. Brighton: Harvest Press. 23–70.

Zweinger-Bargielowska, I., 2011. *Austerity in Britain: Rationing, controls, and consumption, 1939–1955*. Oxford: Oxford University Press.

19 The impact of the interwar depression on the working class

Stephanie Ward

Introduction

The interwar depression in Britain was part of a wider global phenomenon. From the great dustbowls in the farmlands of the United States to the long snaking queues for bread in Weimar Germany, financial collapse was experienced across industrialised nations. The most devastating consequence of the depression was unemployment on an unprecedented level. In 1932, one of the worst years of the economic crisis, the unemployment rate stood at over 20% in Australia (28.1), Canada (26), Denmark (31.7), Germany (43.8), the Netherlands (25.3), Norway (30.8), Sweden (22.4), the United Kingdom (22.1), and the United States (36.3) (Eichengreen and Hatton 1988, p. 6).[1] While Britain did not experience the depth and extent of economic downfall reached in other states, neither did the population escape mass unemployment. In the United Kingdom, the recorded number out of work (i.e. only those registered at Employment Exchanges) never fell beneath 2 million between 1931 and 1935. It was only in 1941, two years into the Second World War, that the numbers fell beneath 1 million for the first time since the 1920s (Beveridge 1944, p. 111). The former powerhouses of the industrial revolution fared worst as the demand for coal, cotton, and shipbuilding declined. In northern England, industrialised Northern Ireland, urban Scotland, and South Wales, unemployment was stubbornly high for much of the period. It was only the rearmament preparations after 1936 that improved the fortunes of these staple industries.

Yet, while unemployment was one of the key features of interwar British society, outside of the older industrial regions, the picture was one of growth. In the Midlands and South-East of England, car plants and the new 'light' industries of manufacturing brought notable improvements in wages and living conditions. Here, consumerism increased with working-class households buying newly mass-produced goods and moving to modern suburban housing estates. Place was, therefore, crucial to understanding the nature of the impact of the depression. In 1934 in the counties of Glamorgan and Lanark, where the staple industry of coalmining predominated, the rate of unemployment was 36.9% and 29.4%, respectively. In comparison, in Oxfordshire, where car manufacturing had developed, the unemployment rate in the same year was 8.2% (Beveridge 1944, pp. 326–327). It is the stark divide in the living standards between different regions of Britain that begins to explain the often polarised debates within the historiography. The earliest histories of the interwar period focused upon the experience of the unemployed and the levels of poverty and ill health which came in its wake (Mowat 1955). It was from the 1970s that revisionist historians

DOI: 10.4324/9781003037118-21

began to question the traditional approach to the period, and they emphasised relative improvements in living standards, real wages, and consumerism. The most influential of these works was John Stevenson and Chris Cook's *The Slump* (1977). Their call to question the 'myth' of memories of the predominance of hardship and poverty during the depression has since been challenged by historians (for example, Laybourn 1990) who continue to stress the hard reality of life in the depressed regions.

To acknowledge improvements in some areas is not, of course, to deny the real experience of poverty in others. Similarly, there is a risk that in attempting to challenge popular memories of this period, the diversity in the experience of unemployment is lost. The 'unemployed' – usually prefaced by 'mass', 'army', or 'millions' in the contemporary press – was a characterless representation. It hid how experiences of the depression were shaped by factors such as class, age, gender, (dis)ability, race, and place. Moreover, the response to being out of work was formed by the myriad features of previous occupational identity, local political culture, and prevailing governmental attitude. Unemployment was experienced very personally, but this did not mitigate against communal protests as men and women attempted to fight back against their situation. We might also consider the impact of the depression beyond the depressed regions: few working-class men and women would have escaped the fear of losing employment or falling into the clutches of poverty in the midst of economic gloom. Such fear stymied life choices in working-class homes, even in relatively prosperous areas. For William Beveridge, the architect of the welfare state, 'the greatest evil of unemployment is not physical but moral, not the want which it may bring but the hatred and fear which it breeds' (1944, p. 15).

The purpose of this chapter is to explore the impact of the depression upon the lives and lifestyles of the working-class men and women it principally affected. It surveys the diversity in experience of long-term unemployment and privileges the voices of those who were often marginalised in their own period. Beginning with the race rioting in the early years after the First World War, the chapter charts the course of economic slump and recovery, the regional nature of the depression, experiences of unemployment within working-class families, and the response from within and outside working-class communities. Finally, the chapter considers social movements amongst the unemployed, not least because the scale of protest reminds us why popular memories of hardship and want had such lingering political consequences.

Post-war slump

While the depression is synonymous with the 1930s, the 1929 Wall Street crash only exacerbated an existing downturn in many regions. The end of the temporary boom after the Great War saw unemployment in shipbuilding, coal mines, cotton, and building trades steadily increase. As the availability of jobs decreased in some areas, not everyone was perceived to have an equal right to work. Women could be viewed as taking men's jobs and veterans to have a greater claim than non-combatants. Such attitudes shaped how people collectively and individually responded to worlds without work. At their worst, such tensions spilled over into racist attacks upon immigrant minorities, as witnessed in 1919 in port towns and cities across Britain. Race rioting erupted first in Glasgow in February, and in subsequent months similar patterns of violence occurred in North Shields, Hull, Liverpool, London, and Cardiff (Jenkinson 2009).

For immigrants, especially people of colour, the end of the post-war boom signalled a particularly uncertain period in finding and securing work. John James Ernest, who was born in St Lucia and arrived in Cardiff in 1915 to work at the docks, recalled how he was unemployed for five years during the depression and did not receive any form of benefit (British Library Sound Archive 1973). Black seamen faced the dual injustice of employers' preference for white workers and the decision by local authorities to openly discriminate in the granting of payments. Such instances were ever more present as unemployment steadily increased and remind us that amongst the unemployed, all were not affected equally (see Chapter 12).

Regional nature of the depression

In the early 1920s, the number of strikes within the staple industries is indicative of the deep-seated structural problems principally facing coal mining, cotton, and shipbuilding. The loss of overseas markets, the return to the Gold Standard in 1925, and decreasing domestic demands saw thousands of workers laid off. While the fortunes of mining and shipbuilding might have dominated the headlines, the downturn here had a rippling effect on subsidiary trades such as transport and building. The nine days of nationwide stoppage of industry in the General Strike of 1926 and subsequent seven-month lockout in the coalfields was something of a turning point in the fortunes of the older industrial regions. Short-term work was replaced by longer periods of unemployment. Following the 1929 Wall Street crash and the onset of a global economic depression, unemployment steadily increased across the UK. It rose from 1.5 million in January 1931 to 2.7 million by the end of the year. The financial crisis precipitated the downfall of the second Labour government and the formation of a coalition National government which remained in power for the duration of the decade.

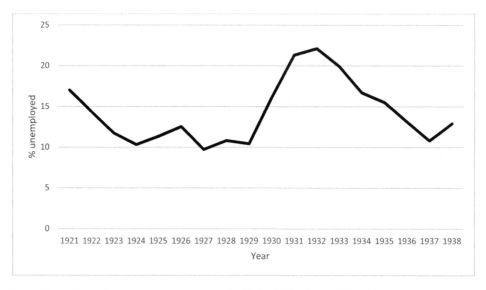

Figure 19.1 General unemployment rate in the United Kingdom, 1921–38

Source: Beveridge (1944, p. 47).

Table 19.1 Average number of unemployed persons on the registers of employment exchanges in the United Kingdom, 1928–1941

Year	Number of unemployed
1928	1,254,904
1929	1,248,588
1930	1,974,501
1931	2,697,868
1932	2,813,042
1933	2,588,358
1934	2,221,063
1935	2,106,121
1936	1,821,700
1937	1,557,001
1938	1,881,357
1939	1,589,801
1940	1,034,672
1941	391,521

Source: Beveridge (1944, p. 111).

The figures recorded by labour exchanges, although a useful guide to historians, were not actually a true reflection of the number unemployed. Farm workers, casual labourers, domestic servants, nurses, and teachers were not covered by the government's National Insurance scheme, nor the estimated millions who had exhausted their right to benefits. The national figures also hide stark variations between different trades. Between 1927 and 1936 the average rate of unemployment in tramway and omnibus services was 4.4%. In the same period in shipbuilding, it was 40.8% (Beveridge 1944, pp. 49, 83). The statistics for different towns are similarly revealing.

The assault on the powerhouses of Victorian industry was assisted by the continued process of mechanisation. Just as craftsmen and cottage industries fell to the forces of modernity with the stirrings of industrialisation a century earlier, so too did swathes of the British workforce in the face of the technological advancement of the post-war era. Skilled coal cutters, coachmen, and farm labourers found their trades rendered obsolete in the face of electric drills, motorcars, and combine harvesters. This process within the wider uncertain economic climate meant that even

Table 19.2 Employment exchange areas with the highest and lowest average rates of unemployment in 1934[2]

Place	Average unemployment rate (%), 1934
Great Britain and Northern Ireland	16.7
Cottenham (Cambridgeshire)	2.3
Hemel Hempstead (Hertfordshire)	2.5
Pontlottyn (Glamorganshire)	64.9
Blaina (Monmouthshire)	75.5

Source: Beveridge (1944, pp. 324–327).

in more prosperous regions unemployment still lingered. The Pilgrim Trust's 1937 social investigation, *Men Without Work*, reported that, contrary to popular belief, there were high numbers of residual long-term unemployed in relatively prosperous places like Leicester and Deptford; there were opportunities to work, but either low wages, lower-status work, or different skill levels prevented men and women taking up such opportunities (1938, pp. 47–100). In counties like Glamorgan and Durham, it was, however, chronic unemployment which plagued the population, with large numbers experiencing unemployment for months and years rather than days or weeks. The Victorian staple industries increasingly appeared obsolete against the prosperous modernity of car plants, tinned food factories, and newly established trading estates.

Social policy

The governmental response to unemployment was central to how people experienced the depression. Conservative (1922–24, 1924–29), Labour (1924, 1929–31), and National (1931–35, 1935–37, 1937–39) governments all followed three basic principles in the official response to mass unemployment: maintain individuals and their dependants at a basic level of subsistence through unemployment insurance; eradicate abuse from the system; and encourage migration from the depressed regions through the 1927 Transference Scheme, which offered financial assistance to help unemployed men and women to relocate to more prosperous areas (Garside 1990). The 1934 Special Areas Act, which legislated for dedicated investment in the most economically challenged areas, was the only attempt by a government to move beyond these three principles. There were some work programmes, but these were limited in their impact and the subject of vociferous condemnation from many of the unemployed.

The unemployed had three possible avenues for claiming financial assistance. The first was unemployment benefit from the National Insurance Scheme established in 1911 and extended to cover 20 million workers in 1920 as part of the transition to peacetime conditions (Levine-Clark 2010). Second, rather than disallow hundreds of thousands of workers following the exhaustion to the right to benefits after 26 weeks, 'transitional payments' were introduced. Payments were generally lower, subjected to intense scrutiny through a household means test, and administered through Public Assistance Committees (PACs), leaving Labour councillors in particular susceptible to local pressure. Last, if disallowed from other schemes, the unemployed had to prove destitution and apply for relief from the Board of Guardians or, from 1929, its successor, the PACs. This was very much a last resort, as it carried with it the taint of the Poor Law.

As the Unemployment Fund grew to become one of the largest areas of domestic spending, successive governments focused on removing abuse from the system. The Genuinely Seeking Work Test (1921) and the Anomalies Act (1931) removed millions from claiming benefits, mainly married women and single men, but the 1931 household Means Test was the most-hated feature of the system. The Means Test saw inspectors cross the threshold of respectability into working-class homes to calculate any income, or even items of value, within a household. Hard-earned savings and the wages of all family members were weighed up, and transitional payments were lowered or stopped accordingly. There was also controversy over benefit levels nationally, as governments tried to calculate a basic level of subsistence; advancements in the field of nutritional science allowed the British Medical Association to make recommendations on calorific minimums for adults and children. Differences in rents, costs of living, unexpected costs for illnesses, extra fuel in winter, and clothing led to many reports which highlighted how benefits did little more than prevent outright starvation (Boyd Orr 1937). In the end, after two decades of heated public debate, the National government introduced the autonomous Unemployment Assistance Boards (UABs) in 1934 to remove the issue of unemployment benefits from politics nationally and locally. Although highly controversial in its initial year, the UABs paved the way for the centralised administration of the welfare state.

Experiences of unemployment

Black-and-white photographs of crowded pavements outside of Labour Exchanges have become synonymous with the depression. The long queues of men patiently waiting to 'sign on' are stark evidence of the extent of unemployment. But along with images of men standing idle on street corners, such visual representations hide the personal experience of unemployment and its impact upon the rest of the household as well as the wider community. There was no universal experience of being out of work for long periods; whether it was met with bitterness or acceptance, emasculation, or rebellion depended upon the individual and their immediate social situation (McKibbin 1998, p. 161). Caradog Jones's findings for Liverpool were applicable across the country: 'The truth of the matter is that the unemployed differ among themselves as much as do the employed' (1934, p. 365). Yet, while this holds true, we are able to discern some broader trends in the experiences of unemployment based upon factors such as place, age, class, and gender. You were more likely to be out of work if you worked in particular trades, if you were a young adult or over 45 years old, and if you lived in the older industrial regions (Ward 2013, p. 51).

Image 19.1 London, England: c. 1923, unemployed men in London standing in line at the Employment (dole line) Exchange

Source: © Underwood Archives/UIG/Bridgeman Images.

Through social surveys, documentary films, newspaper articles, collections of oral testimonies, and, later, oral histories, the voices of those marginalised within their own period can be heard. They provided a counterpoint to the impression of those like Lily Coleman, the chair of the Belfast Board of Guardians, who commented that if the poor worked as hard at looking for a job as they did under the blankets, unemployment would be less of a problem (Munck and Rolston 1987, p. 25). As valuable as these sources are for historians, it is important to recognise that not all voices are heard equally, and the experiences of women and ethnic minorities are less well documented. I draw here, therefore, upon a range of sources to provide a snapshot of the experiences of long-term unemployment for the unemployed and their families.

The collected reflections of men and women in *Memoirs of the Unemployed* show the horror of long periods of unemployment for men and women used to regular employment (Lambert and Beales 1934a). They speak of the futility of attempting to find work in alternative trades or other areas. The loss of friendships; families separating; above all, they reveal the mental exhaustion, tested nerves, and anxiety caused by the constant worry over money and the acute inferiority complex that long-term unemployment brought. Whether a former colliery banksman, skilled engineer, rulleyman, or casual labourer, long-term unemployment disrupted all aspects of life. From the decision over whether to buy new school shoes or pay off a debt to the grocer to larger decisions of moving from the family home to rent a few rooms, unemployment imposed a constant worry over working-class families. Working lives were regulated by hooters and bells, clocking in and out of a factory, with clearly defined leisure time. Regular pay meant the comforting routine of a Sunday roast dinner; savings to meet the unexpected demand of medical bills; coal in the grate in winter; and rare, but planned, excursions to the seaside. Without work, there were long, long hours to fill, and routines and plans dissipated.

For the older unemployed worker, filling time was a particular issue, especially with little prospect of returning to work. A 44-year-old former labourer in an artificial silk factory felt after two years of unemployment that 'time hangs heavily on my hands' (Lambert and Beales 1934e, p. 127). In the depressed regions, the futile tramp for work provided only a temporary reprieve during the initial months of unemployment. Thereafter, the desire to escape the domestic space of the home saw men going to libraries, working on allotments, or standing on street corners. As breadwinners found themselves reliant upon their wives and children, their presence at home was a reminder of the emasculating loss of status in the rigid gendered hierarchy of working-class families (Penlington 2010; Ward 2013). A skilled wire drawer, financially reliant on his wife, questioned whether his was 'a man's life' (Lambert and Beales 1934d, p. 180). Even in severely depressed areas, unemployed older men still suffered from the psychological impact of idleness. John Evans, an unemployed miner from South Wales, offered a heartfelt and honest summary of his position in the comment that 'one moment I feel I could almost lick a man's boots for a favour: another time I feel I could bash him in the face' (1935, p. 95). Working women felt the sense of loss and isolation of unemployment just as acutely as their male counterparts (Alexander 2000). A 43-year-old woman unemployed for over a year explained that, 'I don't welcome the change after nearly nine years of work that I liked and did well. I hate this nothing-to-do' (Lambert and Beales 1934b, p. 87). The situation for women was worse, as their status as worker could never trump their position as wife or their perceived inferiority to their male counterparts: if they stayed in work, they were wrongly taking a man's job, and, out of work, they struggled to receive their rightful benefits if married.

For young men and women coming of age, the reality of attempting to find work in urban Scotland, South Wales, the North-East of England, and industrialised Northern Ireland was all too real. After leaving school at 14, many found low-paid casual work until turning 18, when higher wages were demanded. Young men could find themselves in a perpetual state of youth, as without regular work, they did not progress through the expected stages in the lifecycle. A 28-year-old engineer from the Midlands felt like a 'hunted animal whose holes have been stopped up' (Lambert and Beales 1934c, p. 154). Like other young men, he expressed little hope of marriage until he was back in work. Young women found opportunities for work seriously limited by the depression. Shop work and, above all else, domestic service were often the only outlets for many girls upon leaving school. Both demanded long hours for little pay. It was for these reasons that young single men and women were most likely to migrate to other parts of the country in search of work.

The dynamics of home and family life were seriously disrupted by long-term unemployment and short-term working. Adult sons and daughters left at an earlier age to attempt to ease financial strains, while husbands were thrust into a world of domesticity. But it was upon housewives that the burden fell for stretching meagre budgets and maintaining standards and morale within homes. Mothers, and not fathers, were overwhelmingly blamed in the popular press if the children of the unemployed were underfed or poorly clothed. Many women would go without proper meals to see their families fed. These sacrifices did help, alongside school feeding programmes, to protect the health of children (Thompson 2006). But such actions were not without personal cost. The Pilgrim Trust reported how 'undernourishment, combined with the strain of "managing" on very limited resources and dealing with domestic crises . . . make heavy demands on the physical and psychic resources of mothers of families' (1938, p. 139).

It was the plight of working-class mothers and children that generated the most heated criticism of the National government's response to long-term unemployment. The Communist Party of Great Britain even went so far as to accuse the government of starving mothers and children (Brown 1935). But public outcry came not just from the expected quarters of the Left. *The Times* in 1928, for example, ran a series of special investigations into the position in coalfields.[3] Academics used unemployed villages as almost scientific experiments to uncover the psychological benefits of regular labour (Bakke 1935; Cameron *et al.* 1943). Even royalty took an interest, with King Edward VIII visiting South Wales in 1936. Standing on top of the ruins of the Dowlais Steel Works, he boldly declared that 'These works brought all these people here. Something should be done to get them at work again' (*Western Mail*, 19 November 1936). For its part, the Left produced a steady stream of literature to urge the government to take action and refute claims about ignorant mothers and workshy youths (Orwell 1937; Hannington 1937; Wilkinson 1939). The attention afforded to the depressed regions encouraged voluntary movements to provide practical support. Settlement movements, charities, university students, and political parties organised everything from jumble sales, clothes drives, and soup kitchens to farmsteads, adopting depressed towns, and providing holidays. Such efforts certainly helped to relieve some of the impact of long-term unemployment, although not universally so. Charitable relief could be an affront to pride and an unwelcome panacea to government inaction. Moreover, without regular employment, the psychological and physical cost of unemployment was inescapable for not only individuals but all family members. Recognising this aspect helps explain why a particular legacy of the period was etched in popular memories of the 1930s.

In Focus: social movements and unemployment

Historians have long called into question the influential findings of the Austrian study *Marienthal* that the long-term unemployed tended to pass through a series of psychological stages ending in apathy (British Library Sound Archive 1973; Jahoda *et al.* 1972; McKibbin 1991, p. 253). From the first signs of economic downturn in the immediate aftermath of the First World War, groups of unemployed men and women took to the streets to protest against the lack of work. There were marches of occupational groups; miners marched from South Wales to London (1927) and across Scotland (1928), and, most infamous of all, Jarrow shipbuilders marched to London in 1936. Over time, the demands of protestors shifted to lobbying for better levels of relief, and more concerted movements of the unemployed began to emerge as men and women who were out of work organised around the identity of 'the unemployed'. The introduction of a household means test as a requirement for benefit for the long-term unemployed in 1931 became a major focus of campaigns, given that scales of relief could be influenced by local pressure. Few trade unions provided an active role or leadership for unemployed members, and the Labour Party's more patient approach for change through parliamentary channels could prove frustrating. It was the Communist Party–affiliated National Unemployed Workers' Movement (NUWM) which bridged the gap for those who wanted to see more direct action.[4]

The NUWM operated like a trade union for its members, providing guides to unemployment benefit schemes; representation to Labour Exchange appeal meetings; advice on all aspects of unemployment; and, from the pen of its leader Wal Hannington, countless tracts on the social impact of unemployment. The NUWM also organised some of the most high-profile protests of the period in the national hunger marches of 1922, 1929, 1930, 1932, 1934, and 1936, where marchers set off from across Britain to converge in London at the same time. Home Office files reveal how closely the hunger marchers were monitored and the unease in Westminster. While not all of those who marched were Communist Party members, its association was enough to encourage police enforcement and the dismissal of protests as propaganda for the Left in the conservative press.

Outside of the national marches, the NUWM played an important role in organising local demonstrations. Indeed, it is at a local level that the scale of the social movement against unemployment can be best appreciated, including the role that women played often marching with young children in arms. There are notable regional patterns. In urban Scotland, the unemployed in Dundee and Glasgow marched on the streets in their tens of thousands on numerous occasions in the 1920s and 1930s. But the unemployed in the South Wales coalfield were undoubtedly amongst the best organised and most persistent, producing the largest protests of the interwar period. On 5 February 1935 alone, an estimated 300,000 people took to the streets of South Wales in a remarkable, albeit temporary, demonstration of unity between the NUWM, Labour Party, Communist Party, religious leaders, trade unions, teachers, and shopkeepers. While the majority of marches were peaceful affairs, there were dramatic outbursts of action. In 1932 there were reports of riots in Birkenhead, Bristol, Durham City, and London. In Belfast, in a rare example of non-sectarian violence, Protestants and Catholics united in the Outdoor Relief Strike, which ended in the armed forces firing upon demonstrating crowds.

Organising under the identity of 'the unemployed' could only ever provide a temporary focus for a social movement and a transitory membership. This helps to explain the pattern of more concerted bursts of action and the otherwise sporadic nature of protest movements. So, what were, if any, the achievements of the protest movements? There were little material or practical gains in the raising of levels of benefits (aside from a temporary repeal of the new means test regulations in 1935) or introduction of genuine work programmes, and the abolition of the means test did not come until 1941. The importance of the social movements of the unemployed might, however, be measured in a less tangible way. Street protests kept the plight of the out of work in headlines throughout the period, even if many only made it into the local press. They helped ensure that unemployment was one of the chief causes of the labour movement. Crucially, they also provided an avenue for men and women to make their voices heard. When a public discourse of dole cheats and fecklessness dominated, protest was a means of challenging this narrative. Marching through towns and villages in a Sunday best suit was a public display of respectability. On a more personal level, it gave men and women something to do.

For men emasculated by unemployment, attending meetings and organising and joining in demonstrations was a performance of masculinity. The military overtones of the marches, with the strict line formation, the tramping to the beat of a drum, and the undoubted intimidation it provided, was a macho display. But the material culture of the marches is also suggestive of the importance of the pomp and ceremony of participating in the larger marches for men and women. Bright banners were carried; jazz bands, or fife bands in Scotland, headed the marches; and crowds lined the streets to watch marchers process. It all gave a certain theatrical air and contributed to the drama of the occasion. The marches of the unemployed were an important platform to vocalise opposition, but they also gave meaning and purpose to directionless days without regular employment. Such popular action was not to resurface in later periods, and the scale and nature of such action against unemployment was confined to the interwar period.

Debates and Interpretations: mass unemployment and the legacy of the 1930s

The post-1945 settlement undoubtedly influenced interpretations of the depression. Martin Pugh argued that the British Left 'scored a belated victory in writing the history of the interwar period as one of poverty, failure and reaction' (2009, p. vii).

Following the revisionist literature of the 1970s, the rise in unemployment in the 1980s encouraged other historians to look again at the impact of mass unemployment (Nicholas 1986; Glynn and Booth 1987). There were also more detailed studies into health and welfare which, while revealing a mixed picture of improvements depending upon age and sex, also stressed the undoubted impact of long-term unemployment (Webster 1985; Thompson 2006). The protest movements against unemployment have also received much attention along with explorations of social policy (for example, the special issue of *Labour History Review*, 73:1 2008 and Ward 2013). Beyond these more focused studies, historians have continued to question the legacy of the depression within the wider context of the twentieth century.

John Stevenson and Chris Cook were quite right to emphasise the importance of consumerism and improvements in living standards. They drew upon A.J.P. Taylor's question of 'which was more significant for the future – over a million unemployed or over a million private cars?' to frame their challenge to the myths of the so-called 'Devil's decade' (Stevenson and Cook 1977, pp. 3–5). Martin Pugh's *We Danced All Night* proceeds in a similar vein (2009, pp. vii–xii). In setting out to challenge myths, there is, of course, a danger in overlooking the importance of popular memory. *Why* the imagery of hardship, dole queues, and a hatred for the means test lingered in public debates and oral histories is as important as determining *whether* such views were exaggerated (Perry 2000, p. 201). Richard Overy's *The Morbid Age* (2009) and Juliet Gardiner's *The Thirties* (2010) are important in showing the wider cultural context that helped to inform and shape memories of the depression.

There are also areas which historians have yet to fully tackle. The experiences of women, disabled and immigrant workers, and people of colour are the most notable. How these groups were affected by unemployment and participated in the political arena awaits further attention. For example, Black seamen in Cardiff successfully lobbied the National government with the help of the League of Coloured Peoples to secure the right to claim relief in the 1930s. Further regional studies which address the importance of place and how the experiences of unemployment were shaped by gender and age will continue to complicate the image of mass unemployment and enrich our understanding of the cultural legacy of the 1930s.

Conclusion

In assessing the significance of the interwar depression, it is difficult to escape the stark contrast between the modernity of new housing estates, mass car ownership, and shiny Art Deco factories on the one hand and the deteriorating older industrial regions on the other (Priestley 1934). But we must also consider how, even within the depressed regions, the relentlessly grim picture given by some social surveys must be punctuated by the reality of how children and young adults still found pleasure and release. Dance halls, cinemas, and adult education movements thrived in working-class communities across Britain. This does not diminish the experience of hardship; rather, it is to appreciate the rich cultural life of working-class villages and towns. While the depression certainly overshadowed the depressed regions, it did not block out the light entirely.

The post-war welfare state was one of the most significant legacies of the depression years in its ambitions of full employment, social security, and free access to healthcare. The Labour Party's 1945 election victory must be seen in light of the lingering consequences of the depression as well as the social upheaval of the Second World War. When arguing for the importance of the welfare state, Minister of Social Insurance Jim Griffiths declared in parliament in 1946, 'It is insecurity that destroys. It is fear of tomorrow that paralyses the will' (1969, p. 89). And, for those living and who went on to live in the depressed regions, the welfare state proved vital as the entrenched regional inequalities stubbornly persisted and grew in the face of deindustrialisation. For some, memories of protest from the 1930s became a rallying cry in the face of the challenges of the future.

Further reading

John Stevenson and Chris Cook's classic revisionist account of the depression (which has been reissued a number of times) remains a very good starting point for understanding the historiography of the interwar period (1977). Likewise, Martin Pugh's *We Danced All Night* is a very readable social history which attempts to offer a more rounded picture of life in the more prosperous regions in the twenties and thirties (2009). As a counter-view, Ross McKibbin's *Classes and Cultures* is unchallenged in its coverage of working-class culture and politics (1998). Richard Overy's impressive *The Morbid Age* (2009) and Juliet Gardiner's *The Thirties* (2010) offer an excellent balance between social and intellectual responses to mass unemployment. Gardiner also provides a lucid account of the reasons for polarised debates of the period in a later article (2011).

For more detailed studies of particular issues: Craft and Fearon's edited collection on the economy is highly recommended (Crafts 2013); for a longer perspective on social policy and poverty, see Gazeley (2003) and Boyer (2019); on women's unemployment, Sally Alexander (2000) and Keith Laybourn (2003) highlight the nature of an often-overlooked issue; and for studies of health, Charles Webster's classic 'healthy or hungry thirties' debate is an invaluable starting point (1985). Regional perspectives on the depression, political culture, and protest movements are provided on South Wales and the North-East of England by Ward (2013), Thompson (2006), and Nicholas (1986) and for urban Scotland by Petrie (2018).

Notes

1 The figures given are the unemployment rates in industries as calculated from the records of trade unions, private companies, insurance societies, and governments. They do not reflect the true level of unemployment, as not all occupations or individuals of working age were included in the figures.
2 Beveridge, *Full Employment in a Free Society*, pp. 324–27.
3 *The Times*, 28 March–2 April, 10–13 September 1928.
4 Originally named the National Unemployment Workers' Committee Movement, it was formed in 1921.

References

Alexander, S., 2000. Men's fears and women's work: Responses to unemployment in London between the wars. *Gender & History*, 12 (2), 401–425.
Anon, 1938. *Men without work: A report made to the Pilgrim Trust*. Cambridge: Cambridge University Press.

Bakke, E.W., 1935. *The unemployed man: A social study*. London: Nisbet and Co. Ltd.

Beveridge, W., 1944. *Full employment in a free society*. London: Allen & Unwin.

Boyd Orr, J., 1937. *Food, health and income*. London: Macmillan.

Boyer, G.R., 2019. *The winding road to the welfare state: Economic insecurity and social welfare policy in Britain*. Princeton: Princeton University Press.

British Library Sound Archive, 1973. *Family life and work expereince before 1918, John James Ernest interviewed by Win Preece*.

Brown, M., 1935. *Stop this starvation of mother and child*. London: CPGB.

Cameron, C., Lush, A., and Meara, G., 1943. *Disinherited youth: A report on the 18+ age group enquiry. Prepared for the trustees of the Carnegie United Kingdom Trust*. Edinburgh: Constable.

Caradog Jones, D., 1934. *The social survey of Merseyside: Vol. 2*. London: Hodder & Stoughton, Ltd.

Crafts, N., and Fearon, P., ed., 2013. *The great depression of the 1930s: Lessons for today*. Oxford: Oxford University Press.

Eichengreen, B., and Hatton, T., 1988. Interwar unemployment in international perspective. *Institute for Research on Labor and Employment, Working Paper Series*.

Evans, J., 1935. Time to spare. *In*: F. Greene, ed. *Time to spare: What unemployment means by eleven unemployed*. London: Allen & Unwin.

Gardiner, J., 2010. *The thirties: An intimate history*. London: Harper Press.

Gardiner, J., 2011. "Searching for the gleam": Finding solutions to the political and social problems of 1930s Britain. *History Workshop Journal*, 72, 103–117.

Garside, W.R., 1990. *British unemployment 1919–1939: A study in public policy*. Cambridge: Cambridge University Press.

Gazeley, I., 2003. *Poverty in Britain, 1900–65*. London: Palgrave Macmillan.

Glynn, S., and Booth, A., eds., 1987. *The road to full employment*. London: Allen & Unwin.

Griffiths, J., 1969. *Pages from memory*. London: J. M. Dent & Sons Ltd.

Hannington, W., 1937. *The problem of the distressed areas*. London: Victor Gollancz Ltd.

Jahoda, M., Lazarfeld, P., & Zeisel, H., 1972. *Marienthal: The sociography of an unemployed community*. English ed. London: Tavistock.

Jenkinson, J., 2009. *Black 1919: Riots, racism and resistance in imperial Britain*. Liverpool: Liverpool University Press.

Lambert, R., and Beales, H., eds., 1934a. *Memoirs of the unemployed*. London: Victor Gollancz Ltd.

Lambert, R., and Beales, H., eds., 1934b. "I hate this nothing-to-do" – A married woman factory worker. *In: Memoirs of the unemployed*. London: Victor Gollancz Ltd.

Lambert, R., and Beales, H., eds., 1934c. My fatal "inferiority complex" – An unmarried engineer. *In: Memoirs of the unemployed*. London: Victor Gollancz Ltd., 149–155.

Lambert, R., and Beales, H., eds., 1934d. "The wife works while I look after the home": A skilled wire drawer. *In: Memoirs of the unemployed*. London: Victor Gollancz Ltd.

Lambert, R., and Beales, H., eds., 1934e. Keeping eleven on 68s. 6d. a week – An unskilled labourer. *In: Memoirs of the unemployed*. London: Victor Gollancz Ltd.

Laybourn, K., 1990. *Britain on the breadline: A social and political history of Britain between the wars*. Gloucester: Alan Sutton.

Laybourn, K., 2003. "Waking up to the fact that there are any unemployed": Women, unemployment and the domestic solution in Britain, 1918–1939. *History*, 292 (88), 606–623.

Levine-Clark, M., 2010. The politics of preference: Masculinity, marital status and unemployment relief in post-First World War Britain. *Cultural and Social History*, 7 (2), 233–252.

McKibbin, R., 1991. *The ideologies of class: Social relations in Britain, 1880–1950*. Oxford: Oxford University Press.

McKibbin, R., 1998. *Classes and culture: England 1918–1951*. Oxford: Oxford University Press.

Mowat, C.L., 1955. *Britain between the wars, 1918–1940*. Chicago: Chicago University Press.

Munck, R., and Rolston, B., 1987. *Belfast in the thirties: An oral history*. Belfast: Blackstaff Press.

Nicholas, K., 1986. *The social effects of unemployment on Teesside, 1919–39*. Manchester: Manchester University Press.

Orwell, G., 1937. *The road to Wigan Pier*. London: Victor Gollancz Ltd.

Overy, R.J., 2009. *The morbid age: Britain between the wars*. London: Allen Lane.

Penlington, N., 2010. Masculinity and domesticity in 1930s south Wales: Did unemployment change the domestic division of labour? *Twentieth Century British History*, 21 (3), 281–299.

Perry, M., 2000. *Bread and work: The experience of unemployment, 1918–1939*. London: Pluto Press.

Petrie, M., 2018. *Popular politics and political culture: Urban Scotland, 1918–1939*. Edinburgh: Edinburgh University Press.

Priestley, J., 1934. *English journey*. London: Harper & Brothers.

Pugh, M., 2009. *We danced all night: A social history of Britain between the wars*. London: Vintage.

Special Correspondent, 1936. The King's Concern for South Wales Unemployed. *Western Mail*, 19 November, 11.

Stevenson, J., and Cook, C., 1977. *The Slump: Society and politics during the depression*. London: Jonathan Cape.

Thompson, S., 2006. *Unemployment, poverty and health in interwar south Wales*. Cardiff: University of Wales Press.

Ward, S., 2013. *Unemployment and the state in Britain: The means test and protest in 1930s south Wales and north-east England*. Manchester: Manchester University Press.

Webster, C., 1985. Health, welfare and unemployment during the Depression. *Past and Present*, (109), 204–230.

Wilkinson, E., 1939. *The town that was murdered: The life story of Jarrow*. London: Victor Gollancz Ltd.

20 Civil society, voluntary action and citizenship, c. 1918–1960s

Helen McCarthy

Introduction

Across the twentieth century, most British people spent some of their spare time occupied in a variety of voluntary associational pursuits, from joining sewing circles and working men's clubs to attending political meetings and demonstrations. These activities formed part of the backdrop of collective life in cities, towns and villages up and down the land, as well as involving Britons in networks of friendship, activism and aid across borders, including in Britain's extensive overseas empire. These forms of organized sociability and voluntary action played a key role in the development of British society and democracy and were integral to shifting understandings and practices of citizenship. They also became ever more closely wrapped up in questions about the responsibilities and reach of the state, both central and local, in people's everyday lives.

This chapter explores how the associational realm of civil society was made and remade in Britain, focusing particularly on the period between the introduction of universal suffrage and the rise of radical social movements from the later 1960s. It traces change and continuity in patterns of voluntary action, explores the role of civil society organizations within debates about citizenship and democracy and considers how relations between the state and voluntary sector have evolved, particularly regarding the provision of social services to the public. The chapter defines civil society broadly, exploring the activities of British people overseas as well as in the metropole, and considers how the dynamics of class, gender and race shaped the participation of different groups. As will become clear, associational life in Britain was varied and diverse, and its relationship with the state fluctuated over time, but not all citizens had an equal stake in it. Whilst civil society provided a space for identifying social needs, asserting rights and fostering solidarities, it also reflected and sometimes magnified wider social inequalities and relations of power.

Mapping civil society

'Civil society' is a complex category open to multiple definitions. This chapter conceptualizes it loosely as the space existing between state, market and family where collective forms of social action and sociability can flourish. There has been a long tradition of theorizing the relationship between state and society within European political thought, but from the eighteenth century a vision of civil society took hold which, in Jose Harris's (2008, p. 131) words, was 'quintessentially composed of voluntaristic, non-profit-making, civic and mutual-help movements, coexisting with but nevertheless quite distinct in ethos and function from the spheres of both states and markets.'

DOI: 10.4324/9781003037118-22

The philosopher Jurgen Habermas (1989) linked this vision to the emergence of the 'bourgeois public sphere,' which he described as a realm of sociability where private individuals could engage in conversation and rational debate beyond the control of established church or state. This 'public' was the product of modernizing forces at work in European societies, from the rise of print culture and the spread of literacy to urbanization and industrialization, and found its primary expression in the growth of coffee houses, philosophical and literary societies, charities and clubs. These mostly middle-class associations were soon joined by what other scholars (Eley 1992) have termed the 'plebeian public sphere,' encompassing trade unions, friendly societies and radical political movements like Chartism. From the later nineteenth century, the outlines of what might be viewed as a 'global' civil society took shape, driven by accelerated international trade, communications and migration. These helped to connect individuals and groups across national borders, forming networks and associations to agitate for peace, evangelize for religious causes, campaign for workers' rights or facilitate intellectual collaboration (Arsan *et al.* 2012).

In short, 'civil society' has been closely identified with the associational life of communities and with diverse modes of voluntary action of different scales. In more recent times, politicians and voluntary sector leaders have adopted this language of 'civil society' imprecisely, often conflating it with 'community', 'voluntarism', 'localism' and 'citizenship'. In 2010, the UK government established an Office for Civil Society, which had multiple functions, from supporting social enterprise and encouraging volunteering to launching Prime Minister David Cameron's 'Big Society' agenda (Hilton *et al.* 2010). The very capaciousness of civil society as a concept poses problems for historians hoping to map the landscape of voluntary action and to evaluate its character over time. One possible approach is to use available data to produce statistical snapshots of civil society participation for particular periods. Between the wars, for instance, the total individual membership of the three main political parties in Britain approached 4 million, whilst some of the major pressure groups of the era generated huge followings: the League of Nations Union (LNU), an advocate of international cooperation, had over 400,000 subscribers in the early 1930s, whilst the National Council of Women (NCW), an umbrella body for women's organizations, consisted of 17,000 individual members and 1,268 affiliates representing about 2.5 million women in total. In the sphere of organized leisure, the Club and Institute Union had 918,000 working-class men registered as members in 1929, whilst across Britain in 1937, there were 657 Masonic Lodges covering 102,000 men. The British Legion was another notable presence, with over 400,000 members around this time, and the Scout and Guide Associations had enrolled a million or more of the nation's children. Finally, organized religion remained a major hub of associational activity. In the late 1920s there were around 2.7 million Anglican communicants, 3.3 million members of the various Nonconformist denominations and about 2.6 million members of the Roman Catholic Church (McCarthy 2011a).

Other scholars have pieced together data for voluntary organizations over longer periods of time. This approach has provided a crucial corrective to popular narratives of civic decline in the later twentieth century, often imagined to be a product of the expanding welfare state, mass consumerism or growing individualism. Examining membership figures for a range of organizations between 1951 and 1991, the political scientist Peter Hall found no evidence of a steady downward curve. Participation in youth and outdoor recreational bodies continued to expand into the early 1980s, from which point membership of environmentalist groups climbed dramatically. Survey data suggest that the average number of associational memberships amongst adults grew by 44% over this period, with one study finding that two-thirds of the population belonged to at least one formal association and 36% belonged to two or more in the mid-1980s (Hall 1999). Historians have confirmed and developed this picture, pointing to the growing supporter base of new high-profile non-governmental organizations (NGOs) founded since the Second World War, including Oxfam, Amnesty International (AI) and Friends of the Earth (FOE) (Hilton *et al.* 2013), as well as the continuing popularity of older charities, such as the Save the Children Fund (SCF) and St John's Ambulance Brigade (SJA) (Ramsden and Cresswell 2019). These NGOs sustained mass memberships: at its peak in the mid-1980s, the Campaign for Nuclear Disarmament (CND) had 100,000 members, whilst the Royal Society for the Protection of Birds (RSPB) had half a million and the National Trust over twice that figure (Hilton *et al.* 2012). The evidence suggests that volunteering has remained similarly buoyant. The proportion of the population volunteering at least once a month hovered around 25–30% between 1980 and 2010, whilst figures for those doing voluntary work at least once a year were even higher, ranging from 54% to 76% over the same period (Ibid., p. 293). The swelling size of the retired population might have played a role in sustaining these trends, with older people providing a range of voluntary services to family members and the wider community in the later twentieth century (Thane 2000).

If levels of civil society engagement thus remained reasonably strong, the types of voluntary associations which British people have joined or supported experienced

Image 20.1 Julie Fox, American folk singer, at CND Rally, 1960

Source: © Keystone Pictures USA/ZUMAPRESS/Alamy Stock Photo.

greater change over the century. The work of campaigning pressure groups became increasingly professionalized and policy focused, whilst many charities became significant providers of public services, delivered in partnership with the central or local state. The largest NGOs developed elaborate management and financial accountability structures and became expert publicists and media communicators. Over time, the language of 'voluntary action' was gradually replaced by the concept of a 'voluntary sector' with shared interests and defined career paths for those employed within it. Long-established causes, such as alleviating poverty or campaigning for women's rights, were pursued within these shifting structures and in some cases acquired a radical political edge, influenced by the new social movements which prioritized new issues, such as human rights and gay rights, from the late 1960s. Change was also evident in the international arena: the United Nations played a similar role to its inter-war predecessor – the League of Nations – as a focus for non-governmental action, but NGOs broadened their horizons to include a wider range of targets from the 1970s, including global financial institutions and multinational companies (McCarthy 2011b; Sasson 2016; Iriye 2002). Finally, developments in technology shaped civil society participation, whether through televised charity appeals, 'telethons', charity music singles or, more recently, the growth of online activist communities and petitions (Jones 2015; Robinson 2012). It is striking that the increasing presence of new information and communication technologies in the home, such as television, video gaming and the internet, appears to have done little to undermine civic engagement of this kind.

Debates and Interpretations: change and continuity in patterns of voluntary action over time

These questions of change and continuity in patterns of voluntary action over time have formed a focus for scholarly debate. As noted, narratives of civic decline were prominent in public discourse around the start of the millennium, prompted in part by falling voter turn-out at elections, and were reinforced by the accounts of some scholars, including political scientist Robert Putnam (discussed below) and historian Frank Prochaska. In a pamphlet published in 2002, Prochaska argued that the decades following the Second World War 'saw the triumph of planning, as people looked to the state to provide them with everything from health care and education to transport and telecommunications,' whilst the 1980s, by contrast, 'saw the triumph of the market', leaving little space for a vibrant civil society. Prochaska subsequently developed this interpretation in his 2006 book, *Christianity and Social Service in Modern Britain*. This declinist narrative was convincingly challenged by a body of research produced by historians at the University of Birmingham and published in *The Politics of Expertise: How NGOs Shaped Modern Britain* (2013) by Matthew Hilton, James McKay, Nicholas Crowson and Jean-Francois Mouhot. The authors argue that the history of non-governmental action is better captured through narratives of change rather than a simplistic story of decline from some mythical 'golden age' of voluntarism. They show that civil society became increasingly dominated after 1945 by large, professionalized NGOs which provided opportunities for citizens to engage with a wide range of social and political causes. This type of engagement was more individualized than in earlier times, but it was no less vibrant or significant for facilitating political participation and shaping political agendas.

Civil society, democracy and citizenship

The previous survey suggests that Britain has sustained a vibrant civil society across the twentieth century, even if the exact character of popular involvement has changed over time. This section moves on to consider how these changes both shaped and were shaped by shifting understandings of democracy and practices of citizenship. Many modern political theorists have drawn a close link between civil society and the functioning of democratic politics. In his classic 1830s work, *Democracy in America*, Alexis de Tocqueville observed how strong networks of voluntary self-help enabled Americans to organize within their communities and hold formal power to account: 'I have frequently admired,' he wrote, 'the endless skill with which the inhabitants of the United States manage to set a common aim to the efforts of a great number of men and to persuade them to pursue it voluntarily' (Tocqueville 2003, p. 596). Over a century and a half later, the political scientist Robert Putnam reworked this idea as 'social capital', which he defined in terms of 'social networks and norms of reciprocity' and the 'trustworthiness that arise from them' (2000, p. 19). Societies rich in social capital, Putnam argued, were more likely to have stable democratic governments because citizens could use their associational ties to solve problems collectively, as well as to bring issues to the attention of elected officials.

Many commentators have followed this line of thought in suggesting that the embeddedness of Britain's associational traditions has contributed to its pluralistic democratic culture. The social policy expert William Beveridge argued in 1948 that

> vigour and abundance of Voluntary Action outside one's home, individually and in association with other citizens, for bettering one's own life and that of one's fellows, are the distinguishing marks of a free society. They have been outstanding features of British life.
>
> (1948, p. 10)

Studying Britain in the early 1960s, the political scientists Gabriel Almond and Sidney Verba observed a healthy mix of citizen engagement, public trust and strong representative institutions (1963). Britain, they concluded, possessed an exemplary 'civic culture', founded on its peaceful transition from absolutism to democracy in the nineteenth century. A few years later, sociologist Ralf Dahrendorf (1968) offered a similar explanation for why democracy had flourished in Britain but foundered in countries with histories of totalitarianism, such as Germany. In Dahrendorf's view, the development of civil society institutions over the previous two centuries had played a key role in entrenching democratic values in Britain, in contrast to their weak and shallow hold in Germany.

Historians have partially endorsed these narratives. In his 2001 book, *Democratisation in Britain*, John Garrard argues that civic participation prepared the ground for the formal enfranchisement of new groups of voters by demonstrating their political fitness. From the late eighteenth century, the expanding urban sphere of assembly rooms, charities and voluntary societies helped to establish the social virtue and social power of the rising middle classes. In the mid-nineteenth century, friendly societies, mechanics institutes and working men's clubs demonstrated the democratic capacities of working-class men. Suffrage societies, charity work and municipal activism achieved the same for women a few decades later. Once universal suffrage was achieved, civil society organizations appeared to play an even stronger role in mobilizing voters around cherished causes and hence stabilizing democracy. Writing of the interwar period, AJP Taylor noted the existence of innumerable voluntary societies which 'protected animals and children; defended ancient monuments and rural amenities; gave advice on birth control; asserted the rights of Englishmen, or encroached upon them.' This 'great army of busybodies,' Taylor concluded, 'were the active people of England and provided the groundswell of her history' (1965, p. 175).

More recent scholarship on the women's movement between the wars reveals how voluntary organizations such as the National Federation of Women's Institutes, the Townswomen's Guilds and the Mothers Union helped newly enfranchised women to exercise collective power on issues ranging from child and maternal welfare to the improvement of transport and utilities for rural housewives (Beaumont 2013; Thane 2001). As totalitarian ideologies pervaded civil society in other European countries in the 1930s, associational life in Britain seemed able to preserve its pluralist traditions. Many interwar associations were explicitly non-partisan in orientation, seeking to carve out a space for activism and sociability which could bridge political and sectarian lines. Bodies as diverse as Rotary, the Women's Institutes, the British Legion and the LNU maintained their 'no party' rules as a means of building broad-based memberships, a goal in which they achieved considerable success (McCarthy 2007).

Yet historians have also looked critically upon idealized visions of civil society as the incubator of democratic values. Voluntary organizations could be inclusive, but they were frequently hierarchical and exclusionary, a striking feature of associational life both before and after the establishment of universal suffrage. The preservationist and town planning movements which flourished from the end of the nineteenth century were primarily vehicles through which landed and urban elites were able to claim a role as guardians of the natural and urban environment. Amongst the founding members of the Glasgow Civic Society in 1896 were lord provosts, city councillors, prominent businessmen, medical officers and university professors. The Birmingham Civic Society, founded just over two decades later, was led by George Cadbury Jnr of the confectionary dynasty, and its membership included Neville Chamberlain, soon to be MP for the city; the architects William Haywood, Herbert Buckland and Charles E Bateman; and the artists Arthur Gaskin and Joseph Southall. As Lucy Hewitt and John Pendlebury have shown, these bodies purported to speak for local residents and the public at large whilst remaining dominated by 'professionally qualified, politically literate and networked individuals with high levels of social capital and strong commitment to their sphere of interests' well into the later twentieth century. (Pendlebury and Hewitt 2018; Hewitt 2012, p. 29).

The voluntary aid societies, including St John's Ambulance Brigade and the British Red Cross Society, offer a different example of how civil society could shore up existing social relations of power. Both were founded in the nineteenth century and remained wedded to the welfare paternalism of that era and to values of duty and patriotism, reflected in their uniformed rituals and the patronage they enjoyed from the Royal Family. Personal testimonies collected by Stefan Ramsden and Rosemary Cresswell suggest a strong 'sense of respect for social hierarchy' amongst the ordinary membership. One publication compiling the memories of elderly members of SJA was heavy on encounters with royalty. Chapter headings included: 'To Tea with the Queen', 'The Day I Met the Queen', 'The Queen Mother's Birthday', 'Trooping the Colour' and 'Our Trip to Buckingham Palace'. One woman who had belonged to the

Image 20.2 Sir R. Birchall inspecting P.O. units of St. John's Ambulance Brigade, 1939

Source: © British Postal Museum & Archive/© Royal Mail Group Ltd 2021 courtesy of The Postal Museum/ Bridgeman Images.

Brigade in the 1960s recalled with pleasure her participation in rigidly choreographed remembrance day parades: 'they were part of showing the public what we were and what we stood for. . . . [I felt] very much a sense of pride' (Ramsden and Cresswell 2019, p. 526).

Notions of duty and service could acquire different meanings when embraced by voluntary organizations linking Britons to the wider world. Before the 1970s, most NGOs saw their overseas work through the lens of empire. The belief that the British had a special responsibility towards less 'civilized' peoples and possessed great stores of governing expertise was widely held during the interwar decades. The LNU encouraged its members to embrace an ideology of 'enlightened patriotism' through which they could seamlessly combine their loyalty to king, country and empire with an equally strong commitment to fostering international understanding (McCarthy 2011c). This formula for legitimizing Britain's imperial status was reconfigured in the era of decolonization by bodies such as Rotary, the Women's Institutes and Christian Aid, who were all active in overseas aid projects, pen-pal schemes and exchange programmes in the 1960s. As Anna Bocking-Welch has shown, these organizations made sense of their nation's declining international power 'through a pre-existing narrative of global benevolence in which they, as British citizens and participants in associational life, could play an active part' (2019, p. 4). Recent research on Save the Children (SCF) reveals further continuities in how Britons clung on to notions of superiority over 'lesser' nations and to global racial hierarchies. SCF activists typically conceptualized the beneficiaries of overseas aid as ignorant and helpless, a tendency established in their humanitarian work with African children in the 1930s. This attitude persisted amongst SCF fieldworkers recruited in the 1950s from military backgrounds, men who had little interest in the structural causes of global poverty or in thinking through the damaging legacies of colonialism for the developing world (Baughan 2013; Hilton 2015).

In short, civil society did not always function in inclusive ways or present a model of engaged citizens practicing deliberative democracy. Nor was voluntary action always wedded to 'progressive' causes, even in the era of the new social movements. As well as giving rise to student protest and the radical counterculture, the 1960s saw the establishment of the anti-permissive National Viewers and Listeners Association, which campaigned against sex, violence, blasphemy and swearing in the media; the Society for the Protection of the Unborn Child, which lobbied for the reversal of the 1967 Abortion Act; and numerous anti-immigrationist lobbies formed in areas home to large populations born outside Britain. One can argue that these non-governmental organizations contributed to the pluralism of Britain's political culture, providing spaces for communities of interest to find a collective voice. Yet they remind us that civil society could be a battleground for conflicting ideas and causes as well as an arena of cooperation and exchange.

Civil society, social welfare and the state

As well as mapping voluntary action and evaluating its democratizing effects, historians have sought to understand the relationship between civil society and the state, particularly in the arena of social welfare (Harris 2010). In broadest terms, the direction of travel since the early nineteenth century has been towards greater state provision, although this expansion occurred in an uneven and non-linear fashion. Government issued grants to voluntary schools to educate working-class children from the 1830s, whilst mid-Victorian municipal authorities funded workhouses, asylums and hospitals and invested in urban infrastructure and civic amenities. By the late nineteenth century, a mixed economy of statutory and voluntary services shaped the landscape of welfare in most towns and cities, with charities and volunteers working alongside an army of publicly employed medical officers, health visitors, district nurses, sanitary inspectors and school attendance officers, sometimes harmoniously and sometimes less so. From the 1870s, efforts were made to coordinate this provision through a more efficient division of labour between the rate-payer-funded Poor Law, which formed the last resort of the destitute, and the vibrant world of Victorian philanthropy and mutual aid. Charitable institutions targeted a huge variety of needy groups in these decades: the elderly, the disabled, the temporarily or long-term unemployed, widows, unmarried mothers, orphans, prisoners and members of particular faith or occupational groups fallen on hard times (Prochaska 1990; Finlayson 1994).

The drive for greater efficiency continued after the First World War. In 1919, the National Council of Social Service (NCSS) was founded as a coordinating body which built on collaborative models pioneered locally through the Guilds of Help movement and by the Councils of Social Welfare operating in many towns. Partnership with the state lay at the heart of the Council's vision, which aimed

> to promote the systematic organisation of voluntary social work, both nationally and locally, with a view to securing (i) the co-ordination of the voluntary agencies, and (ii) their co-operation with the official agencies engaged in the same sphere of work.
>
> (Brasnett 1969, pp. 22–23)

In 1934, the social worker Elizabeth MacAdam named this spirit of cooperation 'the new philanthropy', noting the evolution of 'a new technique of organization, a close interrelation between private philanthropic effort and State control' (1934, p. 17). Yet she also observed how the Liberal welfare reforms of 1906–14, which included old-age pensions, free school meals and unemployment and sickness benefit, had shifted the weight of provision decisively towards the state. Reliance on charity to maintain basic subsistence – food, shelter, clothing – was increasingly rare by the 1930s, a trend much welcomed by socialists and progressive liberals. One such Liberal, William Beveridge, was a vocal advocate of state action to pool the risks of unemployment, sickness and old age. In his famous report of 1942, *Social Insurance and Allied Services*, he argued for wide-ranging reforms to extend the state safety net further and ensure material security for all citizens from 'cradle to grave' (Harris 1977).

For the Labour politicians who delivered these reforms after 1945, the establishment of a generous and comprehensive welfare state meant finally consigning the paternalistic regime of Victorian philanthropy to the past. Speaking in 1973, the former Cabinet minister Richard Crossman recalled the hostility which he and his party colleagues had felt towards 'the do-good volunteer,' whom they had wanted to see replaced

> by professional and trained administrators in the socialist welfare state of which we all dreamed. Philanthropy to us was an odious expression of social oligarchy and churchy bourgeois attitudes. We detested voluntary hospitals maintained by flag days. We despised Boy Scouts and Girl Guides.
>
> (Crossman 1973, p. 9)

For the sociologist TH Marshall, the universalist principles of the post-war welfare state represented a milestone on the road towards 'social citizenship', whereby individuals would enjoy

> the whole range [of rights] from the right to a modicum of economic welfare and security to the right to share to the full in the social heritage and to live the life of a civilised being according to the standards prevailing in society.

British society had moved on from its nineteenth-century inheritance, in which 'the common purpose of statutory and voluntary effort was to abate the nuisance of poverty without disturbing the pattern of inequality of which poverty was the most obviously unpleasant consequence' (Marshall 1950).

Yet even the strongest advocates of an expanded welfare state accepted that voluntary action still had a legitimate role to play in a modern, progressive society. Beveridge wrote a long report in 1948 entitled *Voluntary Action*, which described how charity and self-help could identify and meet complex welfare needs more effectively than the state (see inset box). Many post-war socialists remained supportive of voluntary action as an arena for mutuality and active citizenship, conscious of how their own Labour movement had been shaped by progressive traditions of social work and workers' education. Prime Minister Clement Attlee, for example, had as a young man joined Toynbee Hall, a philanthropic settlement in east London which gave university graduates an opportunity to live alongside, aid and educate the urban poor. This experience established Attlee's dislike of charity administered by 'smug and self-satisfied' middle-class volunteers, but he admired the 'associative instinct' evident amongst the working classes of east London and exemplified on a national scale in the friendly societies and cooperative movement (Deakin and Davis Smith 2011, p. 73). This sentiment was rearticulated in the late 1940s by Michael Young, who urged Labour to embrace new models of neighbourhood democracy as a counterweight to the top-down planning of the socialist state. Through his later work at the Institute of Community Studies and the part he played in founding dozens of innovative voluntary initiatives, Young helped to sustain and extend Labour's commitment to a vibrant civil society into the later twentieth century (Beach 1998). Tony Blair would take up this mantle in the late 1990s through New Labour's 'Compact' (Compact on relations between Government and the Voluntary and Community Sector in England 1998) with the voluntary and community sectors, which declared voluntary action 'fundamental to the development of a democratic, socially inclusive society.'

This did not mean that the role of voluntary sector involvement in welfare provision or its relationship with the state was uncontested. As already noted, some charities became major players in the delivery of public services, receiving significant grants-in-aid from the state or, later in the century, bidding for contracts alongside for-profit competitors. The Women's Royal Voluntary Service (WRVS), for example, was founded in 1938 by the National Government as a vehicle for mobilizing volunteers for the home front in the event of war. After 1945 it adapted to a peacetime role supplementing local welfare and emergency services and received a regular grant from the Home Office to support its central staff, who managed the unpaid labour of thousands of volunteers. As competitive tendering became the norm under Margaret Thatcher's Conservative governments, WRVS found itself obliged to bid for local authority contracts to deliver its flagship Meals-on-Wheels service to the elderly and housebound, promising value for money and high levels of accountability. Many other charities underwent a similar transformation in the 1980s and 1990s, adapting to the new 'contract culture' whilst seeking ways to avoid over-reliance on state funding and to preserve their voluntarist ethos.

Against this shifting social policy landscape, tensions could arise between welfare professionals and volunteers. As Georgina Brewis has shown, volunteer labour played a significant part in the extension of state welfare after 1945: volunteers provided trolley, canteen and home visiting services for hospitals; ran youth clubs; assisted at maternal and child welfare clinics and school medical inspections; and sat on numerous committees, boards and advisory groups across local and central government. A report published by the NCSS in 1952 paid tribute to this wealth of voluntary service but noted that public authorities often viewed volunteers as unreliable workers. As more services moved within the remit of the trained professional employed by the state, volunteers were left with lower-skilled, less interesting tasks to do and found their work more closely supervised and monitored. An influential report authored by the retired social worker Geraldine Aves in 1969 called for better training and management of volunteers, but efforts at capacity-building within this unpaid workforce could also backfire. Those who struggled to acquire the required skills felt discouraged, whilst too great a degree of competence exhibited by volunteers threatened the professional status of paid workers (Brewis 2013). Most controversial of all was the use of volunteer labour to maintain public services during periods of industrial action. Memories of middle-class strike-breaking during the General Strike of 1926 informed trade unionist attitudes as late as the 1970s, when the Confederation of Health Service Employees passed a motion to bar all volunteers from hospitals, fearful of how this pool of labour might be used by employers. Tensions ran especially high in 1978 during the Winter of Discontent when volunteer groups became involved in government emergency planning (Davis Smith and Oppenheimer 2005).

In Focus: William Beveridge and *Voluntary Action* (1948)

William Beveridge (1879–1963) turned to the study of social problems following a privileged upper middle-class upbringing and education. Like the Labour politician Clement Attlee, Beveridge spent formative years as a young Oxford graduate at Toynbee Hall, working with the urban poor of east London. Beveridge admired the spirit of selfless service which he found in the settlement movement but considered its philanthropic ethos an inadequate response to the structural causes of unemployment and poverty. These experiences shaped Beveridge's thinking as a civil servant and prominent policy expert over the following decades, which culminated in the publication of his influential blueprint for a comprehensive welfare state in 1942.

Less well-known is the substantial tome which Beveridge published six years later on the subject of voluntary action. As a lifelong Liberal, Beveridge believed that insuring citizens against unemployment, poor health and old age should not remove all incentives for self-help or encroach upon the rich associational traditions of British society. He was dismayed by the post-war Labour government's decision to centralize the administration of the reformed benefits system, having argued for the role of the friendly societies to be preserved, as it had in the earlier National Insurance legislation of 1911. It was, in fact, the national leadership of the friendly societies which commissioned Beveridge's 1948 report, which outlined in detail the crucial role which volunteers and voluntary organizations should continue to play in a modern, advanced society like Britain. Beveridge identified a range of needs which, he believed, would never be fully met by national welfare systems. The elderly, for instance, often suffered from isolation and loneliness which could be best tackled by informal befriending services and community-based clubs. Some of the most effective institutions for children in care, Beveridge argued, were run by charities like Barnardo's and the Church of England Children's Society, whilst the National Society for the Prevention of Cruelty Against Children served a vital function in identifying and prosecuting cases of abuse and pushing lawmakers to tighten protections. Beveridge extended his analysis to groups with complex needs, such as those with physical disabilities, unmarried mothers and recently discharged prisoners. Some of his more imaginative proposals included homes for 'tired housewives' who needed a break from housework and childcare and night nurseries which might allow married couples to enjoy an evening out.

Voluntary Action reiterated the values of partnership embraced by the NCSS in the early twentieth century, articulating a strong case for ongoing cooperation between voluntary and statutory services in the era of a universalist welfare state. Beveridge was in no doubt that 'the State must in future do more things than it has attempted in the past,' but he was equally sure that 'room, opportunity, and encouragement must be kept for Voluntary Action in seeking new ways of social advance.' These principles were reiterated by the influential report of the Wolfenden Committee, *The Future of Voluntary Organisations* (1974), which described the sector 'in terms of the ways in which it complements, supplements, extends and influences the informal and statutory systems' in a 'pluralistic system of government and social structure.' Political efforts to roll back the state recalibrated this relationship again in the 1980s, as did New Labour's enthusiasm for 'civic renewal' in the late 1990s and David Cameron's hopes for a 'Big Society' after 2010. Nonetheless, the model of partnership described by Beveridge and evident throughout the history of British state welfare seems likely to shape the character of British civil society for some time yet.

Conclusion

As the analysis in this chapter has demonstrated, the history of civil society in Britain points in many directions, connecting with debates about democratization, associational life, empire and the evolution of the welfare state. As such, the topic does not fit neatly into a single area of historiography but features in a wide range of scholarly literatures produced by political scientists, sociologists and social policy experts as well as by historians. Part of the challenge of historicizing civil society is this difficulty of delimiting it as an area of study.

Further reading

General studies mapping non-governmental activism include Hilton *et al.* (2012, 2013) and Hall (1999). For conceptual histories of 'civil society,' see Harris (2008) and Eley (1992); for political science perspectives, see Almond and Verba (1963) and Putnam (2000). On voluntarism after the welfare state, see Brewis (2013) and Deakin and Davis Smith (2011); for gender and voluntarism, see Thane (2001) and Beaumont (2013); and for global and imperial contexts, see Baughan (2013), McCarthy (2011b) and Hilton (2015).

References

Almond, G., and Verba, S., 1963. *The civic culture: Political attitudes and democracy in five nations*. Princeton: Princeton University Press.

Arsan, A., Lewis, S.L., and Richard, A., 2012. Editorial – The roots of global civil society and the interwar moment. *Journal of Global History*, 7, 157–165.

Baughan, E., 2013. 'Every citizen of empire implored to save the children!' Empire, internationalism and the save the children fund in inter-war Britain. *Historical Research* 86, 116–137.

Beach, B., 1998. Forging a nation of participants: Political and economic planning in labour's Britain. *In:* A. Beach and R. Weight, eds. *The right to belong*. London: I.B. Tauris, 89–115.

Beaumont, C., 2013. *Housewives and citizens: Domesticity and the women's movement in England, 1928–1964*. Manchester: Manchester University Press.

Beveridge, W., 1948. *Voluntary action: A report on the methods of social advance*. London: George Allen & Unwin.

Bocking-Welch, A., 2019. *British civic society at the end of empire: Decolonisation, globalisation and international responsibility*. Manchester: Manchester University Press.

Brasnett, M., 1969. *Voluntary social action: A history of the national council of social service, 1919–1969*. London: National Council of Social Service.

Brewis, G., 2013. *Towards a new understanding of volunteering in England before 1960?* London: Institute of Volunteering Research.

Compact on relations between Government and the Voluntary and Community Sector in England, 1998. Available from: www.compactvoice.org.uk/sites/default/files/compact_1998.pdf.

Crossman, R.H.S., 1973. *The role of the volunteer in the modern social service*. Oxford: Oxford University Press.

Dahrendorf, R., 1968, *Society and democracy in Germany* (English translation). London: Weidenfeld & Nicolson.

Davis Smith, J., and Oppenheimer, M., 2005. The labour movement and voluntary action in the UK and Australia: A comparative perspective. *Labour History*, 88, 105–120.

Deakin, N., and Davis Smith, J., 2011. Labour, charity and voluntary action: The myth of hostility. *In:* M. Hilton and J. McKay, eds. *The ages of voluntarism: How we got to the big society*. Oxford: Oxford University Press, 69–93.

Eley, G., 1992. Nations, publics, and political cultures: Placing Habermas in the nineteenth century. *In:* C. Calhoun, ed. *Habermas and the public sphere*. London: MIT Press, 289–339.

Finlayson, G., 1994. *Citizen, state and social welfare in Britain 1830–1990*. Oxford: Clarendon Press.

Garrard, J., 2001. *Democratisation in Britain: Elites, civil society, and reform since 1800*, Basingstoke: Palgrave Macmillan.

Habermas, J., 1989. *The structural transformation of the public sphere: An inquiry into a category of bourgeois society*. Cambridge: MIT Press.

Hall, P., 1999. Social capital in Britain. *British Journal of Political Science*, 29, 417–461.

Harris, B., 2010. Voluntary action and the state in historical perspective. *Voluntary Sector Review*, 1, 25–40.

Harris, J., 1977. *William Beveridge: A biography*. Oxford: Oxford University Press.

Harris, J., 2008. Development of civil society. *In:* S.A. Binder, R.A.W. Rhodes and B.A. Rockman, eds. *The Oxford handbook of political institutions*. Oxford: Oxford University Press, 131–143.

Hewitt, L.E., 2012. Associational culture and the shaping of urban space: Civic societies in Britain before 1960. *Urban History*, 39, 590–606.

Hilton, M., 2015. Ken Loach and the save the children film: Humanitarianism, imperialism, and the changing role of charity in postwar Britain. *Journal of Modern History*, 87, 357–394.

Hilton, M., *et al.*, 2010. *The big society: Civic participation and the state in modern Britain*. London: History and Policy.

Hilton, M., *et al.*, 2012. *A historical guide to NGOs in Britain: Charities, civil society and the voluntary sector since* 1945. Basingstoke: Palgrave Macmillan.

Hilton, M., *et al.*, 2013. *The politics of expertise: How NGOs shaped modern Britain.* Oxford: Oxford University Press.

Iriye, A., 2002. *Global community: The role of international organisations in the making of the contemporary world.* London: University of California Press.

Jones, A., 2015. The disasters emergency committee (DEC) and the humanitarian industry in Britain, 1963–85. *Twentieth Century British History*, 26, 573–601.

MacAdam, E., 1934. *The new philanthropy: A study of the relations between the statutory and voluntary social services.* London: George Allen & Unwin.

Marshall, T.H., 1950. *Citizenship and social class and other essays.* Cambridge: Cambridge University Press.

McCarthy, H., 2007. Parties, voluntary associations, and democratic politics in interwar Britain. *Historical Journal*, 50, 891–912.

McCarthy, H., 2011a, Associational voluntarism in interwar Britain. *In:* M. Hilton and J. MacKay, eds. *The ages of voluntarism: How we got to the big society.* Oxford: Oxford University Press, 47–68.

McCarthy, H., 2011b. The lifeblood of the league? Voluntary associations and league of nations activism in Britain. *In:* D. Laqua, ed. *Internationalism reconfigured: Transnational ideas and movements between the wars.* London: I.B. Tauris, 187–208.

McCarthy, H., 2011c. *The British people and the League of Nations: Democracy, citizenship and internationalism, c. 1918–1945.* Manchester: Manchester University Press.

Pendlebury, J., and Hewitt, L.E., 2018. Place and voluntary activity in inter-war England: Topophilia and professionalization. *Urban History*, 45, 453–70.

Prochaska, F., 1990. Philanthropy. *In:* F.M.L. Thompson, ed. *The Cambridge social history of Britain 1750–1950, volume III: Social agencies and institutions.* Cambridge: Cambridge University Press, 357–394.

Prochaska, F., 2002. *Schools of citizenship: Charity and civic virtue.* London: Civitas.

Prochaska, F., 2006. *Christianity and social service in modern Britain: The disinherited spirit.* Oxford: Oxford University Press.

Putnam, R., 2000. *Bowling alone: The collapse and revival of American community.* London: Simon & Schuster.

Ramsden, S., and Cresswell, R., 2019. First aid and voluntarism in England, 1945–1985. *Twentieth Century British History*, 30, 504–530.

Robinson, L., 2012. Putting the charity back into charity singles: Charity singles in Britain 1984–1995. *Contemporary British History*, 3, 405–425.

Sasson, T., 2016. Milking the third world? Humanitarianism, capitalism, and the moral economy of the Nestlé Boycott. *American Historical Review*, 121, 1196–1224.

Taylor, A.J.P., 1965. *English history, 1914–1945.* Oxford: Oxford University Press.

Thane, P., 2000. *Old age in English history: Past experiences, present issues.* Oxford: Oxford University Press.

Thane, P., 2001. What difference did the vote make? *In:* A. Vickery, ed. *Women, privilege and power: British politics, 1750 to the present.* Stanford: Stanford University Press, 253–288.

Tocqueville, A., 2003. *Democracy in America, and two essays on America.* London: Penguin.

21 Heterosexual sexuality in Britain, 1918–1972

Hannah Charnock and Kate Fisher

Introduction

Historians of sexuality have produced a vibrant seam of work on cultures of homosexuality and queer sexual practices. Much of this work has sought to historicise homosexuality and interrogate how 'deviant' sexualities were labelled and experienced in the past. Being attentive to the ways in which power operated through and around human relationships, much of this scholarship has been concerned with how normativity was mobilised against non-conformers. However, the normal sexual behaviours upon which constructions of the transgressive depend have not themselves been subject to the same critical, historical dissection. Indeed, the antinormative stance of many 'queer' approaches to the history of sexuality projects an unexamined stability onto the lives of people deemed 'ordinary'. Antinormativity relies on the assumption that normative sexualities were unambiguous and rigidly policed. As such, historical scholarship on sexual attitudes and behaviours outside of the transgressive are not approached with the same critical eye that has so enriched our understandings of homosexualities. Yet, as this chapter explores, we can adopt a 'queer' approach to understanding the practice and experience of heterosexuality that views heterosexual identities and practices as historically specific and inherently unstable and which acknowledges the multiple ways in which relations between men and women might not conform to dominant norms or expectations.

Indeed, the period between the end of World War One and the mid-1970s is sometimes characterised as a 'golden age' of heterosexual normativity, and Gert Hekma has argued that Western sexual practices and ideologies in the twentieth century promoted 'a heterosexualisation of society' (2011). The rise in the rate of marriage during this period, alongside recognitions of marriage's cultural purchase, inform this view. However, this chapter argues that an assumption of powerful heteronormativity is to miss the turbulent upheavals and wide-ranging variations in lived experiences and the anxieties that underpinned the cultural championing of marriage, respectability and nuclear family-building. Drawing upon interventions by Laura Doan and Matt Houlbrook, who have called for scholars to 'queer' heterosexuality, we explore the kaleidoscopic nature of heterosexual sexuality (defined as the ways in which different-sex relations were performed) (Doan 2013; Houlbrook 2013). Rather than treating differences in heterosexual experiences according to gender, class, age, race, location and so on as simply variations on a theme, we draw attention to the need for an intersectional analysis that explores how individuals' material conditions shaped how and why they engaged with and formed relationships with the opposite sex.

DOI: 10.4324/9781003037118-23

Historical accounts of heterosexual experiences in the first two-thirds of the twentieth century are often centred on marriage and the reproductively active years. This chapter takes a broader view of the heterosexual lifecycle. It acknowledges the importance of marriage in structuring the lives of many Britons in the mid-twentieth century but draws attention to the limitations of this narrow focus. This chapter has three parts: the first considers pre-marital heterosexuality, and the second part examines marriage, while the final part explores non-marital 'adult' heterosexuality. While accepting that identity categories and distinctions between the normal and the deviant were part and parcel of individuals' own conceptual frameworks, we nonetheless show the inherent tensions that clouded distinctions between normal and deviant and how these evolved over time. As such, the chapter explodes notions that heterosexuality in this period was static and uncomplicated, revealing instead the messiness of different-sex relationship formations and individuals' navigation through the life-course.

Pre-marital heterosexuality

Scholarship on early twentieth-century femininity has suggested that expectations of marriage structured the lives of young women. What they learned at school, what jobs they were encouraged to undertake, the management of their social lives and their engagements with popular culture all gravitated towards their imagined destinies as wives and mothers. While the cultural scripts available to boys and young men were somewhat more varied (emphasising work and military service as sources of masculine identity), they too were raised to expect futures as married heads of households. In these ways, marriage was seen as the defining milestone in the transition from child to adult.

Histories of youthful heterosexuality have therefore framed adolescent social and leisure activities in terms of spousal searches, and adolescent experience is primarily viewed through the prism of courtship. Viewed in this way, one of the most striking shifts in heterosexuality between 1918 and the early 1970s was the changing nature of this journey to marriage. In the early decades of the century, courtship rituals were often formal and ritualised. Public (chaperoned) courtship was common across class divides, although the working-class 'monkey walk' (a weekly parade of young people) looked and sounded very different to the church fetes, bazaars, tennis clubs, chaperoned walks and society events attended by the well-to-do. By the 1940s, some of these had fallen out of favour, giving way to more informal types of romantic introductions such as those made at dance halls, cinemas and coffee bars. However, across the period, much of young people's lives continued to involve the active pursuit of marriage partners; direct matchmaking persisted in the form of marriage bureaux and computer dating from the 1960s. As gender-mixed forms of education, work and leisure practice became more common, new rhythms and rituals of relationships emerged, but for most individuals the goal of finding a marriage partner remained. In the years after the Second World War the average age at first marriage fell continuously until 1971, suggesting an increasing immediacy in young people's pursuit of this life transition, facilitated by full employment and the attendant ability of couples to establish an independent household at an earlier age.

That young people's leisure revolved around courtship for much of the twentieth century, should not, however, be used to suggest that marriage was at the forefront of all people's minds. What marriage signified and what young people looked for in a partner transformed over this period. Changing views of the nature of marriage, especially the emerging emphasis on marriage as a locus for long-term fulfilment and happiness, made courtship emotionally charged, requiring the testing of social, cultural and personal compatibility. Individuals might 'court' numerous partners in the process of settling for one.

While 'flirting' remains an unexplored area of heterosexual culture, with almost ten years between the onset of heterosexual relationships and the average age of marriage, experimenting and sexual exploration were additional goals of heterosexual relationships. Of course, these cultures were highly gendered and offered more opportunities for sexual experience to young men. Nevertheless, teenagers, students and the career-driven in particular enjoyed romantic and/or sexual relationships without anticipating marriage. War disrupted social scenes, bringing visitors from across the empire and the world (Rose 1998). The tensions, uncertainty and life-threatening jeopardy associated with military postings, war work and bombing raids could be marshalled to justify otherwise daring or unlikely relationships, as revealed by Lucy Bland's research into the 'Brown Babies' fathered by American GIs during World War Two (2019). Beyond wartime, public anxieties about good-time girls masked a preparedness among many young people in the 1930s to engage in petting in casual relationships. By the 1960s and 1970s, non-condemnatory discussions of summer romances and 'flings' were a staple of young women's magazines. Indeed, by the 1960s and 1970s, young people were commonly advised to use their early adult years to exhaust potentially destructive sexual impulses and to play the field as part of determining their ideal match. Readers were encouraged to test the long-term viability of attractions to the sexy rocker with the motorbike or the intellectually challenging girl. In short, the vast majority of young people expected to get married, and much emphasis was placed on the processes of finding a suitable spouse, but this was never the intended outcome of all heterosexual relationships or interactions.

Looking at youthful sexual behaviour, historians often stress the 'chastity' of early twentieth-century heterosexuality. Historians have emphasised the absence or limitations of formal education about puberty, menstruation, reproduction and sex in the early decades of the century. Citing low levels of pre-marital pregnancy and the stigma of illegitimacy, historians have implicitly suggested that sexual activity was not a core aspect of pre-marital heterosexuality; young people's sexuality is seen to have comprised what they knew (or did not know) and what they felt rather than what they did (Cook 2005; Davis 2012). As such, a major turning point in British sexual culture is perceived to have occurred during the Second World War, accelerating in the 1960s and 1970s as premarital sex became more common and a greater openness in sexual matters emerged. The provision of school-based sex education from the 1940s is deemed to reflect a progressive change over time from sexual ignorance to the expectation of some (limited) sexual knowledge; while this transformation was not complete (at no point in the twentieth century was sex education compulsory in British schools), it is seen to indicate a growing acceptance that young people were both sexually curious and active (Pilcher 2005).

The notion of a mid-century watershed looks somewhat different, however, if we incorporate non-penetrative sex into our definitions of sex. Undoubtedly, many young people in the early twentieth century avoided penetrative intercourse until marriage, but, as oral history studies suggest, kissing, cuddling, fondling, (heavy) petting or coming close to sex all formed a central aspect of youthful sexuality either side of the 'sexual revolution' (Szreter and Fisher 2010, Charnock 2020). These acts were central to the construction of intimacy and compatibility testing. There was some change in the nature of this activity over the course of the period. While many of these activities were frequently adopted by couples in anticipation of marriage, by the 1970s expectations of pre-existing intimacy and emotional commitment had, for many, diminished, meaning that kissing, cuddling and even having sex with relative strangers were no longer unusual or necessarily 'deviant'. By the end of our period, it was more common for individuals to engage in intimate sexual activity with a member of the opposite sex outside the context of a long-term relationship, but this represented an evolution in sexual practices rather than a dramatic break from the past.

Marital heterosexuality

In twentieth-century Britain, heterosexual marriage was perceived to be ubiquitous and was understood as taking a very particular form. Ideal marriages, depicted in the popular culture of this period and which have preoccupied historical narratives, were composed of two *young* people who had a *monogamous* relationship, founded upon *romantic love*. Heterosexuality was indistinguishable from the nuclear family and was assumed to be both *domestic* and *reproductive*. As Pat Thane has suggested, however, 'happy families' as imagined here were far from universal; heterosexuality transcended marriage, sexual and emotional happiness took many forms and marital experiences mapped very poorly onto this ideal (Thane 2011).

Image 21.1 'Teenage' bride in her wedding dress with bridal veil and groom in a three-button suit of the era, standing together outside the entrance to a modern church building, England, UK, 1960s

Source: © Allan Cash Picture Library/Alamy Stock Photo.

Monogamous

Religious and legal definitions of marriage saw marriage as the exclusive union of one man and one woman. While the wording of wedding vows shifted, commitments of fidelity remained core. In England and Wales, adultery was the only grounds under which a marriage could be legally terminated through divorce until 1937, and prior to 1938 adultery was one of only two grounds for divorce under Scots law. Wifely adultery was more severely sanctioned than that of husbands; prior to the 1923 Matrimonial Causes Act, a woman's ability to secure a divorce in England and Wales required evidence not only of the husband's infidelity but also guilt of an additional offence (usually cruelty) (Cretney 2005). Even after the legal discrepancy was eradicated, grounds for divorce were highly gendered. In 1979, adultery was cited as the cause of divorce in around 25 per cent of cases brought forward by women, but this figure rose to almost 40 per cent among men filing for divorce (ONS 2020).

Ever-increasing divorce rates (rising from 2.8 per 1,000 married population in 1950 to 9.6 in 1975) suggest that unfaithfulness and other transgressions threatened many marriages across the twentieth century (Zweiniger-Bargielowska 2014). Although the law defined 'adultery' in narrow terms (consensual sexual intercourse between two adults where at least one party was married to someone else), individuals' definitions of betrayal might include non-sexual indiscretions such as flirting or intense friendships.

Alternatively, some married couples did not require monogamy. In the early twentieth century, several high-profile commentators (such as socialist feminist writer and campaigner Dora Russell) articulated the potential benefits of 'free love', and by the 1970s wife-swapping was a much-discussed cultural sensation. It was also possible for marriages to incorporate or move beyond adultery. Context was central to understandings of fidelity: notions of mid-life crisis informed accommodations of some middle-aged men's indiscretions, and wartime infidelity might be accepted as another 'cost' of war. Helen Smith's work on male same-sex desire in the north of England has demonstrated how some working-class men saw sexual activities and/or relationships with other men as compatible with continued satisfaction in marital and domestic heterosexuality (2015). In these ways, then, some marriages survived (and indeed thrived) despite 'affairs' or breaches of monogamy.

Domestic

Twentieth-century welfare reforms were premised on the belief that 'the home [was] the very essence of family life' and that families should have a home of their own. These values informed post-war reconstruction efforts such as the Homes for Heroes initiative of the 1910s and 1920s, the 1946 New Towns Act and the 1947 Town and Country Planning Act. Not all heterosexuality was 'domestic', however, and housing policies reflected the politics of a messier reality, in which many working-class families lived in shared overcrowded housing stock, even in the age of mass affluence. While slum clearance, suburbanisation and the increased availability of council housing transformed the living conditions of many married couples and aided nuclear domesticity, for many others, a private family home remained elusive – housing shortages and moving in with the in-laws upon marriage remained common.

We should be wary of assuming, however, that a shared home was the goal of all heterosexual formations. In addition to non-marital forms of heterosexuality that were conducted in non-domestic spaces (i.e. courtship and adulterous relationships), many married couples also had living arrangements that precluded shared domesticity. Physical separation was an important aspect of many couples' experiences. Military service, slow demobilisation and overseas deployments kept spouses apart beyond the years of total war in 1914–18 and 1939–45. Separation could be romantic and prompt new forms of intimacy, but it could also have the effect of dulling emotional bonds and isolating couples from one another (Twells 2016; Abrams 2017). Long-term marital separation was also a fact of life for many migrant workers who had travelled to Britain alone to find work. Elsewhere, the travel associated with colonial administration, sales work and maritime industries meant that significant numbers of men spent much of their time outside the home and away from their wives. Across this period, the nature of shift work often meant that spouses sharing the same home experienced domesticity very differently to middle-class ideals of shared evenings of slippers and supper.

Romantic

The history of heterosexuality in the early to mid-twentieth century has traditionally focused on the 'rise of companionate marriage'. This model suggests that marriage moved away from representing a duty and form of social security to an emotional commitment between individuals based on friendship, sexual compatibility and romantic love. Most influentially, Claire Langhamer has argued that the period from the 1940s to the 1970s witnessed an 'emotional revolution' in which romantic love became the foundation of marriage, with sex increasingly understood as an expression of that emotional bond (2013). Marriage was the central emotional space in which individuals sought, and frequently found, fulfilment and satisfaction.

Yet the centrality of emotional meaning to a successful marriage was not entirely new in the mid-twentieth century, and, conversely, pragmatic understandings of marriage also endured. Even in the 1970s romantic love competed with other motivations for 'tying the knot' and provided alternative routes to loving or contented partnerships. As post-war migration saw the expansion of Muslim, Hindu and Sikh communities, arranged marriages became an increasingly common element of British heterosexuality. Paradoxically, as Langhamer has noted, the growing emphasis on marriage as a form of self-fulfilment fuelled the understanding of marriage as an expectation, which underpinned choices across the class spectrum, including queer individuals, who saw marriage (or long-term monogamy) as the desirable progression of the life-course. Moreover, older notions of duty did not necessarily disappear. Joanna Bourke's research on the League for the Marrying of Broken Heroes (an organisation that garnered considerable press support for its attempt to find 'noble' and 'plucky girls' prepared to marry disable or disfigured servicemen) demonstrates how in the years after World War One women were praised for seeing marriage as a national duty that involved self-sacrifice and selflessness (2016). Notions of duty also underpinned the hastily arranged marriages brought forward (or, in many cases, initiated) by extra-marital pregnancy, a fate faced by many in the mid-century as sex before marriage became more common while the stigma associated with illegitimacy and lone parenthood persisted (Thane and Evans 2012).

Furthermore, the rhetoric of marriage as a mutually-fulfilling emotional bond could enable forms of domestic violence and emotional coercion that exploited notions of devotion and commitment. On top of the financial and logistical difficulties that prevented individuals from leaving abusive relationships, ideas of love often made it difficult for individuals to acknowledge dysfunction, a situation compounded by the fact that marital rape was legal until 1991. Abuse might be conflated with ideas of uncontrollable passion, and abusers' articulations of remorse also drew on the romantic gestures and demonstrations of love. Far from being universally life-enhancing, then, romantic love was potentially toxic and deeply damaging.

Reproductive

Marriage in this period was inextricably linked with having children, which was seen by many throughout the twentieth century as women's natural destiny, assumed to be fundamental to their health and happiness. As with all these idealised visions, however, the reality was less straightforward; not all marriages were reproductive, and not all families were genetically linked. Some marriages were characterised by difficulties in conceiving children, others by repeated miscarriages. Although some couples were aware of their infertility upon marriage (as in the case of the League for the Marrying of Broken Heroes), for many this was unplanned and unexplained, leading to much unhappiness. Adoption provided an alternative, and the mid-century saw legislation designed to formalise adoption processes and bestow legal rights to children and their adopters. Moving into the late twentieth century, so-called 'blended families' would become more common as marital breakdown, divorce and remarriage led to new family formations.

At the same time, the twentieth century witnessed sustained and determined efforts to limit conception. In the early decades this was primarily achieved by withdrawal and abortion and aided by low rates of penetrative coitus, with contraceptive technologies such as condoms, caps, the pill and the coil becoming increasingly used. Of course, unplanned pregnancies (both within marriages and outside them) continued, but faith in contraceptives and the value placed on planning a family as of modern, harmonious and companionate partnership meant that couples marrying from the 1960s confidently adopted non-reproductive forms of intercourse (Cook 2005).

Young

Given the emphasis on marriage as a reproductive union, it is perhaps unsurprising that the dominant imagery of twentieth-century marriage depicted newlyweds or the young families of twenty- to thirty-somethings. Yet many marriages across this period spanned decades and shifted significantly over the life-course. While this remains one of the most under-researched aspects of heterosexuality in the twentieth century, we should be attentive to how aging informed the identities of married couples.

Any assumption that marriages shift from passionate, sexual relationships to companionate (semi-)celibacy over time needs reassessing. In the first instance, many married couples continued to engage in sexual activity after the birth of their children, into middle-age and beyond. Moreover, we should be wary of falling into the trap of assuming that a decrease in (hetero-)sexual activity necessarily reflects the diminution of a relationship; the very idea that sexual intercourse forms an integral component of healthy and satisfying marriages is a cultural construct and by no means universal. The dominance of reproductive years in historical accounts of marital sexuality has limited our understanding of sexuality during mid- and later-life transitions such as having adult children, menopause, widowhood, divorce, retirement and old age.

In Focus: 'Little Kinsey' (1949)

In 1949, the social research organisation Mass Observation undertook the first major survey of sexual attitudes in Britain. With the financial backing of the *Sunday Pictorial* newspaper, which would go on to publish the study's findings, the 'Little Kinsey' survey recorded the attitudes of Britons from a wide range of social backgrounds and was presented as 'the most important human document' of its time.

The Mass Observation survey's title referenced the research of sexologist Alfred Kinsey, who had interviewed over 10,000 men and women to study the sexual practices of the American population in the 1940s. The British survey did not aim to replicate Kinsey's American reports: the Mass Observation study was much smaller in scale and was designed to focus on attitudes to sex rather than sexual behaviour. The reference to Kinsey can instead be understood as an attempt to claim legitimacy for the survey by likening it to Kinsey's 'scientific' study and capitalise on its notoriety. The most substantial aspect of the research consisted of a street survey in which trained interviewers questioned a sample of 2052 individuals about their opinions on various aspects of sexual culture, including marriage, birth control, prostitution and extra-marital sex. Three thousand clergymen, doctors and teachers were also invited to complete this attitude-based survey so that the views of the 'man on the street' could be compared to those held by these 'leaders of opinion'. A smaller survey completed by 450 members of Mass Observation's National Panel of Observers recorded details of individuals' sexual activities and behaviours, and two small ethnographic studies were carried out in a small cathedral city and an industrial seaport. In bringing together these qualitative methodologies, Tom Harrison (the director of Mass Observation), hoped that their survey would highlight 'more of the actuality, the real life' of sexual culture than Kinsey's quantitative study.

The findings of 'Little Kinsey' were published in the *Sunday Pictorial* in June and July 1949 as a series entitled 'The Private Life of John Bull'. Across five instalments, the paper addressed different themes of the report: the opening feature offered a broad overview of Britons' understandings of the role and function of sex and sex education; part two centred on the matter of heterosexual relationships and attitudes towards marriage, divorce and 'free love'; the third part focused on the smaller survey of sexual behaviour answered by Mass Observation panellists; part four investigated family planning; and the final instalment brought these individual themes together under the headline: 'Are Our Morals in Decline?' Initially, there had been concerns that British reserve would prevent individuals from participating in the survey, but Mass Observation was

convinced that they had obtained meaningful findings. While they acknowledged that many interviews were characterised by 'a faint suggestion of uneasi-
ness', only 1 per cent of people approached refused to answer the survey (a
figure in line with market research questionnaires), and interviewers detected no
obvious traces of lying.

On the whole, the survey concluded that views on sex were varied and in
flux. The topic which elicited the most positive agreement was sex education.
The survey indicated that, viewed simply as a way of imparting the 'facts of
life' to young people, sex education was approved of widely: 76 per cent of the
street sample and over 90 per cent of the 'opinion leaders' were in favour of formal sex instruction. These findings were echoed in the report's findings that sex
education was becoming more common: almost a third of under-25s surveyed
had received some formal sex education compared to only 1 in 12 over-45s.
This development was clearly welcomed by the authors of the reports who were
relieved that 'the battle had been won' and who hoped that formal sex instruction delivered by teachers and parents would replace traditions of informal 'education' offered through peer learning, reading and observation.

On other topics, opinion was less clearly defined. The report uncovered a
messy mixture of views, with individuals' attitudes sometimes in conflict with
their own behaviours. On topics such as divorce and birth control, responses to
the street survey tended to fall between the disapproval of church leaders and
the more pragmatic opinions of doctors and teachers, with many (non-religious)
individuals reluctantly accepting both as necessary evils that needed to be care-
fully controlled. Similarly, public opinion on marriage appeared to sit between
the spiritual institution of the church, the romantic model of the movies and the
antagonistic relationship of music hall comedy. The report noted that much of
this ambiguity stemmed from the complicated relationship between what people
thought and what individuals actually did. Extra-marital sex was the survey topic
on which the most people most strongly disapproved: 63 per cent of the street
sample disapproved of extra-marital sex, and the qualitative responses suggested
that there was no widespread acceptance of sex relations outside of marriage. Yet
at least 31 per cent of those who completed the sexual habits questionnaire indicated that they had engaged in intercourse prior to marriage with someone other
than their spouse, and responses to the street survey also indicated that people
who had themselves engaged in intercourse prior to marriage nonetheless rejected
the principle of pre-marital sex. Although they did not explicitly comment on the
validity of particular sexual attitudes, on the whole, the report's authors found
these apparent contradictions reassuring and celebrated the nation's seemingly
'healthy' approach to sex in which individuals formed attitudes from personal
experience rather than relying on the opinions of others.

Little Kinsey concluded that Britain was in the late 1940s 'a world of rapidly
changing moral values', in which there was little correlation between what so-
called 'opinion leaders' thought and the views and expectations of the lay population. Ultimately, the survey's major conclusion was there were no core British
sexual values but instead a conflicted and confused nation struggling to make
sense of their thoughts, feelings and experiences of sex.

Non-marital adult heterosexuality

While marriage was the quintessential heterosexual relationship in the mid-twentieth century, a variety of 'alternative' heterosexual forms also flourished. These experiences may not have been perceived as 'the norm', but they were far from unusual. Some of these relationship forms sit in parallel to narratives of the rise of 'companionate marriage' and 'emotional revolution' insofar as they appeared to embody the prioritisation of individual emotion and happiness over official recognition. For example, Tanya Evans (2011) and Joanne Klein (2005) have shed light on the experiences of women in long-term relationships with married men. Similarly, fugitives of the state such as criminals and 'illegal' migrants had permanent relationships outside marriage. On the surface, at least, many of these relationships were marriages in all but name – couples might have a home and children together and be sexually and emotionally monogamous – but the lack of official recognition could create problems for the legal recognition of parenthood, financial responsibility and inheritance.

Other forms of heterosexuality had a long history prior to the twentieth century but took on new forms or were considered differently in this period. One-off sexual encounters (later termed 'one-night stands') became more common. People had engaged in casual sexual interactions before the 1960s, but from this point the act of engaging in sexual activity with little-known partners or people with whom a longer-term relationship was not sought became a form of normal sexuality. As feminist campaigners later noted, the boundaries of acceptability were elastic and gender specific; while women's promiscuity might be condemned, men's might be excused on the assumption that their sex drive was greater and less controllable.

Important too was the changing nature of the sexual economy and sex work (broadly defined). The first half of our period saw significant institutional attempts to regulate and control the buying and selling of sexual activity (Laite 2012). Ongoing concern about the issue informed the Report of the Departmental Committee on Homosexual Offences and Prostitution 1957 (known as the Wolfenden Report after the chair of the Committee Sir John Wolfenden) and led to further legislation. The 1956 Sexual Offences Act and the 1959 Street Offences Act increased police powers to arrest and prosecute brothel owners and women suspected of soliciting. This legislation did not eradicate street-walking or brothel-keeping, but these laws led to an intensive police crackdown which, along with the expansion of the phone network, contributed to the emergence of 'call girls' and appointment-based sex work in the later part of the period.

Moreover, the lines between 'sex work' and 'recreational' sex were never clear cut. Fears articulated by social hygiene reformers of the 1920s regarding so-called 'amateurs', young women who were engaged in relationships with men seemingly for financial advantage, would be echoed 40 years later during the Profumo affair, when Christine Keeler and Mandy Rice-Davies's relationships with elite men became the subject of intense social and legal scrutiny, eventually leading to Stephen Ward's prosecution for profiting from immoral earnings. Erotic entertainment pre-dated the twentieth century, but Soho's burlesque revues became synonymous with 1960s 'Swinging London', and the rise of striptease in the mid-century tapped into a growing monetisation of heterosexual desire. The Lady Chatterley Trial in 1961 and the end of theatre censorship are often viewed as watersheds in the increasing sexualisation of British popular culture in the latter decades of the century; topless models were a daily feature in tabloid papers by the mid-1970s (most notoriously in *The Sun*'s 'Page 3'), while the sex comedy *Confessions of a Windowcleaner* became the top-grossing British film of 1974 (Leach 2004). The critiques of 'sexploitation' and 'sleaze' culture launched by second-wave feminism and conservative lobbyist groups indicate that these changes were not universally welcomed, and we should resist simplistic notions that these changes were inherently liberating. Nevertheless, the movement of the sexual economy into the 'mainstream' in this way only further muddied the distinctions between normal and deviant heterosexual identity, desire and practice.

Debates and Interpretations: measuring and classifying sexual activity

While sexual activity has long been implicitly quantified in birth and baptism statistics, a new preoccupation with measuring and classifying sexual activity emerged in the mid-twentieth century. American-based studies conducted by Kinsey and Masters and Johnson remain the most well-known of these interrogations of sexual interactions, but British researchers conducted similar (though generally smaller-scale) surveys of their own in the second half of the century. As mentioned previously, a small subsample of volunteers in the 'Little Kinsey' survey completed an additional questionnaire on aspects of their sexual practice in 1949. In the following decades Eliot Slater and Moya Woodside interrogated the sexuality of a large sample of married couples (1951), Eustace Chesser quantified the sexual histories and conduct of English women (1956), Michael Schofield explored the sexual behaviour of teenagers (1965) and Geoffrey Gorer used surveys to examine sex and marriage and the workings of the 'sexual double standard' (1971).

Against the backdrop of the AIDS epidemic in the late 1980s, a large-scale survey of sexual practices was designed on the grounds that more effective health education strategies required a better mapping of the transmission of sexually-transmitted diseases. The first National Survey of Sexual Attitudes and Lifestyles (Natsal) was conducted between May 1990 and November 1991; it interviewed a random sample of 18,876 individuals and attempted to quantify sexual histories (e.g. numbers of partners, age at first intercourse) to measure patterns in sexual orientation, the extent of risk-bearing sexual practices and generational changes in sexual lifestyles. While the immediate crisis of AIDS abated in the 1990s, ongoing concerns regarding teenage pregnancy and sexual health ensured a persistent demand for up-to-date information on sexual behaviour from public health bodies. As such, Natsal-2 was undertaken in 1999–2001 and Natsal-3 conducted in 2010–12; Natsal-4 is underway at the time of writing. While the scope and coverage of the survey changed between iterations, central to the mission of Natsal has been determination to maintain a consistent methodology and a sustained belief in the survey's importance for providing evidence to inform sexual health interventions (www.natsal.ac.uk/home.aspx).

Reflecting broader epistemological shifts from the mid-twentieth century, the statistical 'data' offered by these surveys have often been celebrated as offering unique scientific insights into British sexual practices. The data generated are often deployed by historians (ourselves included) as evidence of sexual cultures in the past; figures generated by Chesser and Gorer on rates of premarital intercourse underpin arguments about cultures of chastity or promiscuity, while Natsal data on non-vaginal sex are used to make claims about queer sexuality. As Liz Stanley (1995) has suggested, however, there are critical questions to be asked about the how and why we value quantifiable measures of sexuality. Part of a distinctive post-war approach to knowledge, the sex survey is a product of its time that shapes and is shaped by assumptions about what is normal and what is transgressive. The commitment to quantifiable data means that surveys often measure what can be measured rather than what we want to know. Subsequently what can be measured is elevated to occupy a privileged place as telling and crucial evidence. Evidence that the age of first intercourse fell during the course of the twentieth century has become highly significant in exploring the period of 'sexual revolution' in the 1960s. Yet we do not know the meaning of a falling age at first intercourse simply through documenting its occurrence; we need instead information about the circumstances, choices, beliefs and relationships that underpinned this change in behaviour.

In these ways, despite the growth and sophistication of sex surveys, the meaning and significance of sexual behaviours and choices remains elusive. The challenge remains making sense of the material surveys produce. There is therefore a fundamental relationship between sexual knowing and sexual feeling which is central to understanding changing sexual cultures, and more and more detailed sex surveys are only part of the process of this investigation.

Conclusion

This chapter began by calling for the queering of heterosexuality as part of the historical approach to understanding individuals' lives and experiences. We suggested that normativity should no longer be simply the foil to a critically queer lens but should itself be subjected to that lens and deconstructed as having its own particular historical trajectory, internal contradictions and social power. The chapter has sought to show the value of embracing the complexities of heterosexuality (as a form of physical sexual practice, a sexual preference, a relationship form or lifestyle) in understanding the shifting nature of different-sex relationships during the course of the twentieth century.

When the Kinsey Report was published in the 1940s, reviewers and commentators were quick to conclude that it destabilised the idea of normal sexuality. The *American Journal of Public Health* responded: 'our conception of what is normal sexual behaviour must be radically revised', while Albert Deutsch concluded that 'terms such as abnormal, unnatural, oversexed and undersexed . . . have little validity. . . . There is tremendous variety in the frequency and type of sexual behaviour in normal Americans' (Winslow 1948, p. 573; Deutsch 1947, p. 495). This variety was equally true of Britain. Even in the so-called 'golden age of marriage', heterosexuality manifested in a variety of forms. This variation reflected the personalities and sexual preferences of individuals but was also a product of the material conditions within which they lived. Expectations and the lived reality of relationships and sexuality were shaped by class, gender, race and age, and the heterosexuality of even the most orthodox of individuals was likely to change in meaning and expression over the course of their lives. While being 'normal' or living an acceptable heterosexual life has lost none of its cultural power or appeal during the twentieth century, historians need now to fully embrace the capacious power of normal sexuality in shaping individual lives that were far from straightforwardly conventional or stuck rigidly to heteronormativity. Normal heterosexual lives were profoundly varied, interesting and dynamic.

Further reading

A rich literature exists on the changing nature on heterosexuality, for example, Harris and Jones (2015), Hall (2013) and Weeks (2007). Brooke (2011) explores how legislation shaped and reflected heterosexuality. Bingham (2009) examines shifts in the public representation of sexuality. The history of emotions has done much to interrogate shifting notions of romantic love; see Cohen (2013) and Langhamer (2013). King (2015) considers married heterosexuality from the perspective of husbands and fathers. Brown (2019) explores the relationship between sexuality and religion.

Historians have begun to interrogate the intersections of sex, race, nationality and (post-)colonialism. See Ghosh (2006) for a colonial perspective. Frost (2019) and Jenkins (2014) examine mixed-race relationships and the politics of miscegenation. The (hetero)sexual cultures of migrant and BAME communities are an area calling out for future study.

References

Abrams, L., 2017. A wartime family romance: Narratives of masculinity and intimacy during world war two. *In:* L. Abrams and E.L. Ewan, eds. *Nine centuries of man: Manhood and masculinity in Scottish history*. Cambridge: Cambridge University Press.

Bingham, A., 2009. *Family newspapers? Sex, private life, and the British popular press 1918–1978*. Oxford: Oxford University Press.

Bland, L., 2019. *Britain's 'brown babies': The stories of children born to black GIs and white women in the Second World War*. Manchester: Manchester University Press.

Bourke, J., 2016. Love and limblessness: Male heterosexuality, disability, and the Great War. *Journal of War & Culture Studies*, 9 (1), 3–19.

Brooke, S., 2011. *Sexual politics: Sexuality, family planning, and the British left from the 1880s to the present day*. Oxford: Oxford University Press.

Brown, C.G., 2019. *The battle for Christian Britain: Sex, humanists and secularisation, 1945–1980*. Cambridge: Cambridge University Press.

Charnock, H., 2020. Teenage girls, female friendship and the making of the sexual revolution in England, 1950–1980. *The Historical Journal*, 63 (4), 1032–1053.

Chesser, E., 1956. *The sexual, marital and family relationships of the English woman*. London: Hutchinson's Medical Publications.

Cohen, D., 2013. *Family secrets: Shame and privacy in modern Britain*. London: Viking.

Cook, H., 2005. *The long sexual revolution: English women, sex, and contraception 1800–1975*. Oxford and New York: Oxford University Press.

Cretney, S., 2005. *Family law in the twentieth century: A history*. Oxford: Oxford University Press.

Davis, A., 2012. *Modern motherhood: Women and family in England, 1945–2000*. Manchester: Manchester University Press.

Deutsch, A., 1947. The sex habits of American men: Some of the findings of the Kinsey report. *Harper's Magazine*, December, 490–497.

Doan, L., 2013. *Disturbing practices: History, sexuality and women's experience of modern war, 1914–1918*. Chicago: Chicago University Press.

Evans, T., 2011. The other woman and her child: Extra-marital affairs and illegitimacy in twentieth-century Britain. *Women's History Review*, 20 (1), 47–65.

Frost, G., 2019. "Not always logical": Biracial and binational unions in Britain, 1880–1940. *History of the Family*, 24, 585–607.

Ghosh, D., 2006. *Sex and the family in colonial India: The making of empire*. Cambridge: Cambridge University Press.

Gorer, G., 1971. *Sex and marriage in England today.* London: Thomas Nelson & Sons.

Hall, L., 2013. *Sex, gender and social change in Britain since 1880.* 2nd ed. Basingstoke: Palgrave Macmillan.

Harris, A., and Jones, T.W., eds., 2015. *Love and romance in Britain, 1918–1970.* Basingstoke: Palgrave Macmillan.

Hekma, G., ed., 2011. *A cultural history of sexuality in the modern age.* Oxford: Berg.

Houlbrook, M., 2013. Thinking queer: The social and the sexual in interwar Britain. *In:* B. Lewis, ed. *British queer history: New approaches and perspectives.* Manchester: Manchester University Press.

Jenkins, S., 2014. Aliens and predators: Miscegenation, prostitution, and racial identities in Cardiff, 1927–1947. *Cultural and Social History,* 11, 575–596.

King, L., 2015. *Family men: Fatherhood and masculinity in Britain, 1914–1960.* Oxford: Oxford University Press.

Klein, J., 2005. Irregular marriages: Unorthodox working-class domestic life in Liverpool, Birmingham, and Manchester, 1900–1939. *Journal of Family History,* 30 (2), 210–229.

Laite, J., 2012. *Common prostitutes and ordinary citizens: Commercial sex in London, 1885–1960.* Basingstoke: Palgrave Macmillan.

Langhamer, C., 2013. *The English in love: The intimate story of an emotional revolution.* Oxford: Oxford University Press.

Leach, J., 2004. *British film.* Cambridge: Cambridge University Press.

Office of National Statistics (ONS), 2020. *Divorces in England and Wales: 2020 data tables* [online dataset]. Available from: https://www.ons.gov.uk/peoplepopulationandcommunity/birthsdeathsandmarriages/divorce/datalist?filter=datasets.

Pilcher, J., 2005. School sex education: Policy and practice in England 1870 to 2000. *Sex Education,* 5 (2), 153–170.

Rose, S.O., 1998. Sex, citizenship, and the Nation in World War II Britain. *American Historical Review,* 103 (4), 1147–1176.

Schofield, M., 1965. *The sexual behaviour of young people.* London: Longmans.

Slater, E., and Woodside, M., 1951. *Patterns of marriage: A study of marriage relationships in the urban working classes.* London: Cassell.

Smith, H., 2015. *Masculinity, class and same-sex desire in industrial England, 1895–1957.* Basingstoke: Palgrave Macmillan.

Stanley, L., 1995. *Sex surveyed 1949–1994: From mass observation's 'Little Kinsey' to the national survey and the Hite reports.* London: Taylor and Francis.

Szreter, S., and Fisher, K., 2010. *Sex before the sexual revolution: Intimate life in England, 1918–1963.* Cambridge: Cambridge University Press.

Thane, P., 2011. *Happy families? History and family policy.* London: British Academy.

Thane, P., and Evans, T., 2012. *Sinners? Scroungers? Saints? Unmarried motherhood in twentieth-century England.* Oxford: Oxford University Press.

Twells, A., 2016. "Went into raptures": Reading emotion in the ordinary wartime diary, 1941–1946. *Journal of Women's History,* 25 (1), 143–160.

Weeks, J., 2007. *The world we have won: The remaking of erotic and intimate life.* London: Routledge.

Winslow, C.-E.A., 1948. Sexual behavior in the human male. *American Journal of Public Health,* 38.

Zweiniger-Bargielowska, I., 2014. *Women in twentieth-century Britain: Social, cultural and political change.* London: Routledge.

22 Britain and Europe since 1945

Neil Rollings

Introduction

Britain formally joined the European Economic Community (EEC) (the forerunner of today's European Union) on 1 January 1973, as part of the EEC's first enlargement.[1] Nearly fifty years later, on 31 January 2020, it became the first country ever to leave. A belated entry, then 'an awkward partner' before stepping away from membership typify the often fraught and reluctant attitude of the UK to European integration. Yet that relationship has often been more complex than commonly perceived, raising a host of diverse questions about Britain's past and its future. With whom would it be best to form trading links? How could Britain best maintain its status in the world? With whom did it feel most comfortable associating? Who should decide government policy? Britain's relationship with European integration provides an excellent lens, therefore, through which to gain a richer understanding of Britain's economic and social, as well as political, history. Moreover, just as that relationship has a history that goes back well before 1973, so it will continue to develop into the future.

From the end of the Second World War to British membership of the European Community 1945–73

The Schuman Plan

The official historian of Britain and the European Community suggests that in order to understand Britain's relationship with European integration, one has to go back to the Reformation (Wall 2020, p. 2). However, with limited space we begin with the aftermath of the Second World War. At that time, Britain saw itself as lying at the centre of three separate spheres of influence: the United States, the Commonwealth and Europe. In British eyes at least, the Second World War had strengthened both the first of these – in the form of 'the special relationship' between Britain and the United States – and the second – with Commonwealth soldiers standing side by side with their British counterparts. Given this, Britain's relationship with the rest of Europe was seen as important but very much the third ranked of these relationships: there was a commitment to building relations with the rest of Europe but not to the extent that it harmed the other two spheres of influence. Also, Britain deserved a special status in Europe. As Ernest Bevin, the foreign secretary in the Labour government after the war, put it: Britain 'was not simply a Luxembourg' (Plowden 1989, p. 94).

DOI: 10.4324/9781003037118-24

It was in this context that Jean Monnet and other French officials drafted proposals which set out the idea of creating a new Europe. The starting point, announced by Robert Schuman, the French foreign minister, on 9 May 1950, which became known as the Schuman Plan, was the proposal to pool coal and steel resources equally between the two countries plus any others who wished to participate. This would prevent any single member state using its steel and coal industries for war purposes; that is, national governments would hand over control, or sovereignty, of policy in these two industries to a supranational body operating above national governments. To a significant extent, this reflected the underlying goal of European integration – the creation and maintenance of peace – and the recognition that this could only be achieved through co-operation.

For a variety of reasons, some short term – lack of notice, the relative size of the British coal and steel industries and their recent nationalisation – some more long term – concerns about the loss of sovereignty and that Britain had not experienced invasion like the other founding member states – the British government felt unable to participate at that time. Accordingly, Britain played no role in the talks which led to the signing of the Treaty of Paris in April 1951 and the resulting creation of the European Coal and Steel Community (ECSC) (Lord 1996). Those who did become members of the ECSC were France, West Germany, Italy, Luxembourg, the Netherlands and Belgium, otherwise known as 'the Six'. Setting the tone for Britain's sustained ambivalence towards European integration, the government was not willing to sign up to full membership but was afraid of the consequences of being completely excluded. Instead, Britain sought a half-way house and in 1955 became 'associated' with the ECSC.

The creation of the European Economic Community

After the success of establishing the ECSC, European integration then faltered with two initiatives in the fields of political and defence co-operation failing to come to fruition. In response the Six returned to the field of economic integration in the mid-1950s to try to move European integration forward. A conference was held in June 1955 at Messina in Sicily. Following the conference the Six began negotiations which were to lead to the signing of the Treaty of Rome in March 1957 and the creation of the EEC in January 1958. Britain sent a representative to these negotiations, but he withdrew in November 1955. However, again Britain was afraid of exclusion: if West Germany, Britain's main economic rival at the time, was a member and Britain was not, there was a potential threat to Britain's economic competitiveness. Britain responded with its own 'alternative' proposal, a free trade area consisting of most of Western Europe (Ellison 2000).

Ultimately, the British proposal failed, and with the EEC in operation the British government had to adopt the fall-back position of helping to create the European Free Trade Association (EFTA), consisting of Britain, Ireland, Portugal, Denmark, Sweden, Norway and Austria. EFTA came into operation in 1960 but was always regarded as a second-best means to an end – Britain still hoped for a wider and looser form of integration covering both the Six and the EFTA countries. EFTA was a way for the non-EEC member states to keep together to strengthen their bargaining position with the EEC.

It soon became clear that a bridge was not going to be built between EFTA and the EEC in the near future: the Six seemed more intent on deepening integration amongst themselves. In addition, elements in British industry were becoming convinced of Britain's need to join the EEC. Large firms, responsible for a significant proportion of Britain's exports and seeing opportunities to exploit economies of scale, were an important voice pushing for British entry into the EEC in the early 1960s. From a sectoral perspective, the chemical industry and the car industry were in favour of British entry, while opposition came from those industries fearing that they could not compete against their continental counterparts.

More generally, informed opinion was moving in favour of British membership of the EEC: trade with Western Europe was growing, while that with the Commonwealth was stagnating, even if it was still larger than trade with western Europe. With growing concerns over Britain's economic performance there was a strengthening belief that joining the EEC would not only offer 'a cold shower of competition' but would impose the same institutions on Britain and that this might be economically beneficial. Politically, as well, there was a feeling that swapping the Commonwealth and EFTA for the EEC would enhance Britain's influence in the world. Accordingly, in July 1961, less than two years after Britain had signed the convention which created EFTA, Harold Macmillan, the prime minister, announced the government's intention to open negotiations with the Six about the possibility of applying to join the EEC (Milward 2002). Negotiations lasted until January 1963 at which point President de Gaulle, the French president, famously vetoed Britain's application, in part because France wanted to ensure it was the leading country in the EEC but also because he remained unconvinced of Britain's commitment to European integration.

Britain was left treading water: it was still a member of EFTA and the Commonwealth but had shown that it did not value either body highly while trying to ensure that the EEC reduced its barriers to trade with the rest of the world so that British exporters could gain access to the markets of EEC member states. A second application was launched in 1967 by the Labour government but it was again vetoed by de Gaulle. It was only after de Gaulle had lost power in 1969, dying soon after, that a new application from Britain stood any chance of success. Formal negotiations opened in the autumn of 1970, which, after some hiccups, finally led to Britain joining the EEC in January 1973, eleven and a half years after the first application (Wall 2013).

Britain as a member of the European Community (EC) and the creation of the European Union (EU)

Denmark and Ireland became members of the EC at the same time as Britain, transforming the Six into 'the Nine'. Membership for Britain did not, however, end the issue of Britain's relationship to the EC. A significant body of opposition to membership had developed. More generally, the early 1970s were not a propitious time to join the EC for a number of reasons. First, the general economic environment was becoming less favourable as economic growth rates began to diminish, the Bretton Woods international monetary system was beginning to fall apart and the oil crisis was about to break. Second, the EEC itself did not look so enticing. Its policies had developed over the 1960s, and it was feared that the Common Agricultural Policy in particular would impose a considerable burden on Britain, both financially in terms of Britain's contribution to the Community's budget and on the cost of living because of higher food prices.

It was in this context that the Labour government held a referendum on British membership in 1975 with the outcome being confirmation of British membership (see 'In Focus' box). This endorsement of British membership of the EEC did little, however, to resolve Britain's position, and it was no more supportive of initiatives to further European integration after the referendum. There was no rise in public engagement with the EEC: in the first direct elections to the European Parliament held in June 1979 Britain had the lowest percentage turnout of voters of all the member states. Most famously, the new Conservative prime minister, Margaret Thatcher, was determined to renegotiate Britain's financial contribution to the Community. It took four years to resolve the issue of a British rebate, during which time further integration stalled (Wall 2019).

With the financial issue finally resolved in 1984, progress was once more possible. Most crucial in this respect was the emergence of the Single Market Programme. The idea of creating a Single Market had widespread political and business support. It was seen as a way of relaunching European integration, it offered a potential solution to Europe's declining competitiveness and it chimed with liberal notions of removing barriers to trade and increasing competition by freeing market forces (Warlouzet 2018). In many ways there was nothing new with the notion of a Single Market – the idea underpinned the removal of tariffs which lay at the heart of the Treaty of Rome – but many other barriers, relating, for example, to differences in taxation and in technical standards remained and had even increased during the 1970s. There was a broad consensus within Europe, including Margaret Thatcher and the British government, that such barriers needed to be removed, and this was the aim of the programme. As a result, the 1986 Single European Act (SEA) was drafted. This set out a programme of measures to create a Single Market by the end of 1992 but also revised the Treaty of Rome with the aim of speeding up decision-making within the European Community and should, therefore, be also seen as part of the broader development of European integration in the 1980s (Ludlow 2017).

What was still unclear, however, and remained a source of contention was the extent to which the creation of a Single Market required the adoption of common practices and policies. To some member states it seemed logical that a Single Market required considerable tax harmonisation and a single currency, others, such as the British, saw no need for deeper integration of this sort. Consensus, therefore, was short lived, with divisions emerging once more over proposals for economic and monetary union (EMU). These proposals were published in 1989 in what has become known as the Delors Report, after Jacques Delors, the president of the European Commission and chairman of the committee that drafted the report. Not long after this the EC Commission also published a 'social charter' to protect worker rights. Like EMU this was again at odds with Thatcher's view of European integration – in general she favoured the removal of barriers to trade and some degree of foreign policy co-operation but opposed increased spending and increased powers being given to EC institutions (and hence was also against the extension of EC-level interventionist policies). A further challenge to Thatcher's line on Europe came from her own ministers, who were pushing for Britain to join the Exchange Rate Mechanism, which it finally did in 1990. This was symptomatic of the prime minister's increasingly weak position in the Conservative Party, and later that year she was replaced by John Major.

Major was now faced with the situation of maintaining unity in his party between the Eurosceptics, those opposed to further integration, and the Euroenthusiasts, while also negotiating with his counterparts from other member states about how best to take European integration forward. At the Maastricht summit in December 1991 talks on the future of Europe came to a head. Out of the summit came the Treaty of European Union, signed on 7 February 1992. This turned the European Community into the European Union by taking further steps to political integration and also agreed a programme to bring about EMU.

In Focus: business and the 1975 and 2016 referendum campaigns: a comparison

As a parliamentary democracy Britain does not have a history of holding public referenda on policies. The issue of Europe is an exception, as there have been two during the near fifty years of British membership. The first was in 1975. The Labour Party's February 1974 election manifesto promised a referendum on Britain's EEC membership. Labour having been elected, the referendum duly occurred the following June with a straightforward remain/leave choice. Although the Labour Party was split on the issue, the government campaigned to stay in. On a relatively high turnout of nearly 65 per cent of the electorate, over two-thirds voted in favour of continued membership. Support was strongest in the South-East of England and weakest in Scotland, but only in the Shetlands and Western Isles were there majorities against. The background in 1975, therefore, was very similar to that which led to the 2016 referendum, apart from it being a Labour government in the 1970s rather than a Conservative one.

The outcome, however, was markedly different. Many accounts have tried to explain the result of the 2016 referendum, and Saunders (2018) has provided a detailed history of the 1975 campaign. Some point to long-term factors; others emphasise chance and accident. One difference was the role of the economy and economic actors in the two campaigns. In 1975 economic arguments were dominant and appear to have swung an initially sceptical population in favour of staying in. In contrast, in 2016 the same economic arguments held less sway and were often neutered by the 'Leave' campaign. Instead, issues like immigration, (English) identity and 'taking back control' were more influential. Indeed, perhaps the main impact of economic considerations was that sustained austerity had meant that arguments about the detrimental economic impact of leaving the EU had less resonance.

Yet the share of British trade with the EU was significantly larger in 2016 than in 1974, foreign direct investment flows were also larger and, perhaps most significant of all, the Single Market had resulted in the reduction of non-tariff barriers and standardised regulations. In all these ways, therefore, the UK was far more embedded in the EU in 2016 than was the case in 1975, and, hence, depending in part on the form of departure from the EU, there was far more to lose. One might expect, therefore, that economic arguments about the losses from leaving the EU would have been even more influential. Certainly, all the main estimates of the economic impact of Brexit forecast losses to the

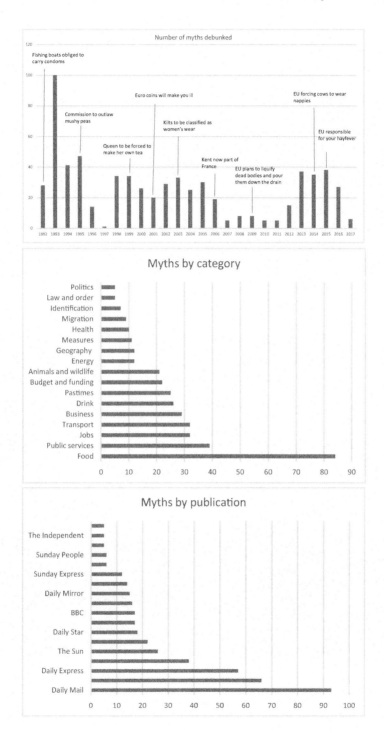

Figure 22.1 EU debunking of British media myths

Source: European Commission (European Commission in the UK – European Commission (archive-it.org).

economy even on the softest of Brexits, with the losses growing the harder the Brexit.

Similarly, the arguments of economic actors, notably business, appear to have been far less influential in 2016 than in 1975. In part this reflected greater distrust of business, especially big business, in 2016, but the position of business is also important. In both referenda the Confederation of British Industry (CBI) strongly endorsed continued membership. In other respects, however, there were important differences. In 1975, although the CBI liked to depict itself as 'the voice of industry', it remained behind the scenes but maintained a network of contacts with many companies to which it supplied various pro-Europe materials. The main voice of industry came from individual companies, which were almost universally in favour of continued membership. These companies not only contributed financially to the campaign to stay in but also took explicit campaign positions which they spread through a variety of methods. There were adverts, organised talks and letters to employees threatening that if there was a vote to leave then the company would have to move its production to Europe with job losses in the UK, while Tesco bags carried the slogan 'Yes to Europe'.

Image 22.1 Demonstrators display banners that read 'CBI = Voice of Brussels' during a speech by Britain's Prime Minister David Cameron at the Confederation of British Industry (CBI) annual conference in London, Britain, 9 November 2015

Source: © Reuters/Toby Melville/Alamy Stock Photo.

Much of this contrasts with the 2016 referendum campaign. The CBI's voice was neutered by claims that it was the 'voice of Brussels' (Figure 22.1). This mattered because companies in 2016 were much more reluctant to declare overtly for the campaign to remain. Significant financial support was forthcoming for the 'Remain' campaign, but companies were often reluctant to go further. There was concern that company brands might be damaged, and PR consultants advised companies to remain publicly neutral unless there was a very clear and significant gain from continued EU membership. Since there was an expectation of a Remain victory, companies appear to have adopted this safety-first approach. Some companies and sectors went further, seeing an opportunity to put pressure on the EU to reduce regulation without wanting to leave the EU. This was even though the British economy was already one of the most lightly regulated ones in the developed world, according to the Organisation for Economic Cooperation and Development, partly because British governments had been so successful in gaining various opt-outs from EU agreements (*The Economist* 2015). Similarly, small business had more of a political voice in 2016 compared to 1975, and they also complained about EU regulation because for many only selling in the UK, it was seen as an unnecessary burden. Finally, whereas in 1975 there were literally virtually no business supporters supporting leave, this was not the case in 2016, where a number of very wealthy individuals were able to bank roll the Leave campaign.

All of this highlights one final aspect relevant here. Even in 1975 British business was aware that European integration was about more than the removal of trade barriers: European integration was a multi-faceted and complex phenomenon. By 2016 that complexity had multiplied, which meant that a simple remain/leave choice did not reflect the different dimensions of business opinion, which were often of the form of Remain but reform.

Britain and the European Union

John Major believed that he had achieved the near impossible in these negotiations as Britain obtained two key opt-outs from the treaty – to the final stage of economic and monetary union and to the Social Chapter (Wall 2020, pp. 208–220). However, within the Conservative Party this outcome only papered over the cracks between the Eurosceptic and Euroenthusiast factions. These divisions became steadily more obvious, particularly after 'Black Wednesday', 16 September 1992, when Britain was forced out of the ERM. Thereafter British policy consisted of pushing for enlargement and emphasising that there was no single model of European integration which fitted all member countries. It was, in Major's own words, 'multi-track, multi-speed, multi-layered', a concept which resonated with Britain's position in the 1950s when proposing the free trade area and which not only allowed flexibility but could also mean almost anything one liked (Young 1998, p. 165).

With the election of Tony Blair's Labour government in May 1997 rhetoric and policy became more positive towards European integration. One of the first tasks of the new government was to sign the Social Chapter, and there was much talk about Britain wanting to be a leading country at the heart of Europe. In practice, the shift was more of tone than substance. Britain only began to participate in very specific aspects of the Schengen Agreement, continuing to refuse to agree to the abolition of border checks between signatories. Similarly, on the central issue of economic and monetary union, Britain continued to opt out and so did not join the Eurozone, the group of EU countries covering most of western Europe which introduced economic and monetary union in 1999 (James 2012).

In many respects this latter decision seemed prescient in light of the Eurozone debt crisis which developed from 2009 following the Global Financial Crisis. Tensions between creditor and debtor Eurozone members (notably Germany and Greece) threatened not only the Eurozone but European integration more broadly. Yet the crisis coincided with the introduction of the Lisbon Treaty, signed in 2007. The treaty introduced significant reforms to the way the EU operated. Ironically, given the popular British critique that the EU is dominated by the unelected Commission, the treaty extended the powers of the European Parliament and (to a lesser extent) the European Council, which is made up of the heads of states of the member countries.

By this stage Euroscepticism was growing in popularity. During the 2000s UKIP became increasingly successful in European elections and in 2014 achieved the extraordinary result of winning that European election in the UK. Given this, and with rising Euroscepticism within the Conservative Party, David Cameron, leader of the Conservatives since 2005 and prime minster after the 2010 election, responded with policies likely to appeal to such sentiments, despite being the head of a coalition government with the strongly pro-EU Liberal Democrats. In 2011 he vetoed an EU draft treaty aimed at tackling the Eurozone debt crisis, and in 2013 he promised an in-out referendum if the Conservative government formed the next government. In many respects this seemed a hollow promise, as the expectation was that the Conservatives would require the continuing support of the Liberal Democrats if they were to form the next government – the Liberal Democrats would veto any such referendum. One consequence, therefore, of the Conservatives' surprise election victory in 2015 was that this promise now had to be fulfilled, and so on 23 June 2016 Britain held its second referendum on its continued participation in European integration, this time voting to leave by 52% to 48% (O'Rourke 2018, and Evans and Menon 2017). Thereafter, Britain not only had to negotiate the terms of its departure from the EU but also to determine the nature of its future relationship not just with the EU but with the rest of the world. This has been fraught and meant that British business has had to operate in conditions of enormous uncertainty about its future environment. Expectations were initially for a 'soft Brexit' where access to the Single Market would be maintained, but as time passed, the outcome became increasingly a harder Brexit, with the possibility of a 'no deal' scenario becoming increasingly likely. Under such a scenario British companies would be forced to trade with the UK's largest trading partner as if it were just another member of the World Trade Organisation. While this has been avoided, British business will still face tariff walls, the requirement for significant amounts of documentation and delays at cross-border checkpoints – trade will no longer be frictionless. In addition, labour from the EU, important for some sectors of the economy, will no longer have free access. For the City of London, the ability to operate freely within the EU will also be curtailed.

To sum up, the story of Britain's relationship with the European Union and its predecessors is now one characterised by change in the light of Brexit. But much of the recent change has been the outcome of long-term continuities. Surveys of public opinion consistently put the UK at the bottom or near the bottom when asking about support for the EEC or EU. It has been consistently easy to depict the UK as an awkward partner or a reluctant European. Yet, in other respects, this interpretation hides the extent to which the UK has influenced and engaged with European integration. It has had a lasting impact on the course of European integration – on the creation of the Single Market and on the emergence of a multi-tier form of integration where member states are able to opt out of aspects of deeper integration, for example.

Debates and Interpretations: Britain's relationship to European integration

The ever-expanding literature on Britain's relationship to European integration has been dominated by two interpretations. First, there is a school of thought which emphasises how Britain's late entry into the EEC was a missed opportunity which had long-term detrimental political and economic impacts on the UK. The second, more popular accounts emphasise the costs of EEC/EU membership, a position which has been at odds with key academic studies of the history of European integration. Let's look at these in turn.

A missed opportunity?

Euroenthusiasts point to Britain's postwar history as one of missed opportunities, particularly in rejecting the initial steps towards European integration in the 1950s. As Tony Blair put it in 2001:

> The tragedy for British politics – for Britain – has been that politicians of both parties have consistently failed, not just in the 1950s but on up to the present day, to appreciate the emerging reality of European integration. And in doing so, they have failed Britain's interests.

From a Conservative perspective, Geoffrey Howe voiced exactly the same sentiments a decade earlier when resigning from the Thatcher government. Thus Roy Denman, a civil servant who was involved in the negotiations for British entry, entitled his book on the subject *Missed Chances* (1996), and more recently Stephen Wall has again adopted this perspective (2008 and 2020). Nor is this simply related to politics: it is also common to argue, as Geoffrey Owen (1999) does, that earlier membership of the EC would have improved Britain's economic performance just at the time when Britain's relative economic decline was at its most problematic. Entering the EEC in the 1950s, it is argued, would not only have given British manufacturers open access to the large markets of the Six but would also have removed protection at home, and this increased competition would have improved economic performance by breaking down 'the cosy relationship' between business and labour. Underpinning all of this 'if only' school of thinking is criticism of past policy.

However, the historiography has gradually moved away from this position with the emergence of a more sympathetic picture. A better understanding of British policy has emerged; in particular there has been a recognition that the 'missed opportunities' argument is too simplistic: the argument ignored the realities of the postwar world, underestimated the constraints that these imposed on British policy and downplayed the complexity of the situation (Rollings 2007). It has also become accepted that Britain did not turn its back on Europe after the war but that British policy was based on co-operation between governments rather than via supranational bodies.

This view has developed as records have become available to historians, beginning with Britain's decision not to join the ECSC. Academic debate on this, the free trade area proposals and the failure to gain entry in the 1961–63 negotiations have emerged, though critics of each of these still remain. De Gaulle's vetoes, therefore, had a major effect.

One other key feature of the developing historiography on the period before UK entry into the EEC has been its broadening away from diplomatic history to consider other forces behind European integration and other actors. Alan Milward, who wrote one of the most influential books on European integration as well as the first volume of the official history of Britain and the European Communities, was highly critical of the narrowness of these diplomatic accounts, himself stressing the economic forces that underpinned the early years of European integration (Milward 2000 and 2002). Partly in response to his work, more recent historical research has moved towards considering the views and records of the economic departments of British government, notably the Treasury and the Board of Trade. However, Milward himself has been criticised for overemphasising the role of national governments. Several authors maintain that other non-state actors need to be incorporated into the picture (Kaiser 2005 and Rollings 2007), and slowly attention is moving in this direction.

However, perhaps the most significant recent trend has been the lack of detailed historical research on Britain and European integration. Historical studies of aspects of European integration remain an active field, but, apart from the continuation of the official history series after Milward's untimely death, and even then by a retired diplomat rather than an academic historian, there have been no major research-based monographs developing our understanding of the historical development of this relationship. Whether Brexit will stimulate a resurgence of research in this field or push it further from the field of study remains to be seen.

Costs of EC membership

While the popular debate on the period before Britain became a member of the EC has been dominated by Euroenthusiasts, the same cannot be said of the period since 1973. Contemporary popular debate is generally critical of the EU, fed by media attacks on the institutions of the EU. *The Sun*'s famous reaction to the Delors Report on EMU was the front page headline 'Up Yours Delors'. Yet it is important to note that at the time of the 1975 referendum, the paper was staunchly in favour of staying in and that its reporting reflects the tastes of its readership. For example, its coverage of the launch of the Euro into public circulation was completely different in the Republic of Ireland compared to that in the UK edition of the paper – the former full of praise, the latter simply condemning. Over the years it has been easy journalism to create false scare stories about the EU, be it about bent cucumbers, sausages or even condoms, all stressing 'Brussels bureaucracy' and the loss of British sovereignty to it. Whilst a *Daily Telegraph* journalist, Boris Johnson was one of those who contributed to this.

Britain's unique history is often a key element of this Eurosceptic discourse which emphasises the burden and costs of EC/EU membership and which fed into the tide of popular attitudes towards the EU (Forster 2002 and Booker and North 2016). Eurosceptics point to Britain's global history, it being an island nation and its ties to the Commonwealth. Historians have responded to this in two ways. First, there have been critiques of this Eurosceptic portrayal of European integration. In part this has been a consequence of the position that most historians working on European integration being interested in the topic because they are sympathetic to the cause of European integration and of Britain's involvement in that process. This factor alone does not explain one significant difference between the historiography and popular debates. A key theoretical debate amongst historians and political scientists has been over the driving force behind European integration and, therefore, what European integration may look like in the future. One group emphasises the growing powers of the supra-national institutions of the EU and its predecessors. Apart from seeing this generally in a positive light there is little difference between this body of research and popular debate. However, the argument of the second group is at odds with popular percep-tions. This group, often called inter-governmentalists, believe that European integra-tion has been, and remains, controlled by national governments, who only hand over sovereignty to supranational bodies on their terms and in their own interests: Euro-pean integration has been an inter-governmental process. Alan Milward has played a crucial role in the development of these ideas, building up his argument from research on the start of European integration and entitling his key work *The European Rescue of the Nation-State* (1992 and 2000). He argued that postwar European integration was just one part of the postwar reconstruction of the state in western Europe. This reconstruction centred upon the notion of a strong national government which man-aged the economy and provided a welfare state, amongst other things. However, it was not possible for national governments on the Continent to achieve this solely by their own actions because of their interdependence with other nations – by the 1950s, for example, 40 per cent of the national income of the Netherlands was earned outside of its national frontiers. European integration provided a solution, Milward suggests, to this problem of interdependence by helping to provide increased security and greater prosperity. In other words, national governments in the Six were willing to hand over a small amount of sovereignty to supranational institutions in return for this extra security and prosperity which followed from European integration and which, in turn, then buttressed the popular allegiance and legitimacy of these national governments.

Milward's conclusions, along with those of other inter-governmentalists, are dis-puted but they remain as a corrective to the view that European integration inevitably meant the emergence of a supranational European state. Rather, the institutions of the EU are seen to have created a new level of decision-making *in addition* to local, regional and national governments, what is called multi-level governance. If nothing else this debate has shown that it cannot be taken for granted that 'Brussels bureau-cracy' has simply taken over a wide range of powers away from Westminster and other national governments across Europe and will inevitably continue to do so until a European state has been created, as is commonly presented in popular discussion of Britain and European integration.

The second strand of the historiography is a more recent development and looks to explain the popularity of Euroscepticism in Britain and the result of the 2016 ref-erendum. Much has already been written by social scientists and commentators on the latter with regard to the factors influencing the way people voted, the way the campaigns were run and the potential consequences. The historical dimension has also been explored in terms of culture and identity. In particular, the historical legacies of empire have been a focus of attention (for example, Dorling and Tomlinson 2019 and Gildea 2019). Such accounts question the popular imagery of Britain as an heroic island nation with a past of which to be proud. Such narratives, it is argued, are based on historical myths and misconceptions of Britain's past and its imperial legacies and, as such, are part of the wider movement towards restitution for imperial exploitation.

Conclusion

In many respects UK policy can be described as 'cakeism', as Kevin O'Rourke calls it (2018, p. 213), that is, wanting to have its cake and eat it. In the 1950s this meant wider and weaker European integration in the form of the free trade area so that Britain had access to the EEC markets but also maintained its preferential trading relationship with the Commonwealth. As part of the renegotiation which preceded the 2016 referendum, David Cameron managed to get his counterparts to agree that the founding principle in the Treaty of Rome of 'ever closer union' would no longer apply to the UK. And by the time of the Brexit negotiations this was evident in a desire for frictionless access to the Single Market but where the European Court of Justice had no say over UK policy. This might be regarded as a lack of realism on Britain's part but can also be seen as evidence of the difficulty the country has had in negotiating multiple and complex demands and expectations in a changing world.

Further reading

The most informative popular account of the earlier period remains Young (1998). The most authoritative works are the three volumes of the official history of Britain and the European Communities up to 1985: Milward (2002) and Wall (2013 and 2019). Wall has also contributed two broader histories (2008 and 2020). All of these, however, tend to focus on various negotiations and political actors. Broader economic and social accounts remain thinner on the ground. The best recent one is O'Rourke (2018), while the most influential account of the process of European integration from an economic history perspective remains Milward (1992 and 2000). Saunders (2018) provides the first historical account of the 1975 referendum. A number of analyses of the impact of historical legacies on English identity have appeared recently (for example, Dorling and Tomlinson 2019; Gildea 2019).

Note

1   At the same time as the EEC was created, Euratom was also created. With the ECSC this made three communities, and so it was common to refer to the EEC or the European Communities. In 1967 the three communities were merged, and so there was then just one European Community (EC). This then became the European Union (EU) in 1992.

References

Blair, T., 2001. Available from: http://news.bbc.co.uk/1/hi/uk_politics/1671114.stm [Accessed 15 October 2018].

Booker, C., and North, R., 2016. *The great deception: Can the European Union survive?* London: Bloomsbury Continuum.

Denman, R., 1996. *Missed chances: Britain and Europe in the twentieth century.* London: Indigo.

Dorling, D., and Tomlinson, S., 2019. *Rule Britannia: Brexit and the end of empire.* London: Biteback.

Ellison, J., 2000. *Threatening Europe: Britain and the creation of the European Community, 1955–58.* London: Palgrave Macmillan.

Evans, G., and Menon, A., 2017. *Brexit and British politics.* Cambridge: Polity.

Forster, A., 2002. *Euroscepticism in contemporary British politics: Opposition to Europe in the Conservative and Labour parties since 1945.* London: Routledge.

Gildea, R., 2019. *Empires of the mind: The colonial past and the politics of the present.* Cambridge: Cambridge University Press.

James, H., 2012. *Making the European Monetary Union.* Cambridge: Harvard University Press.

Kaiser, W., 2005. From state to society? The historiography of European integration. *In:* M. Cini and A.K. Bourne, eds. *Palgrave advances in European Union Studies.* London: Palgrave Macmillan, 190–208.

Lord, C., 1996. *Absent at the creation: Britain and the formation of the European Community, 1950–1952.* London: Dartmouth Publishing.

Ludlow, N.P., 2017. More than just a Single Market: European integration, peace and security in the 1980s, *British Journal of Politics and International Relations*, 19 (1), 48–62.

Milward, A., 1992. *The European rescue of the nation-state.* London: Routledge.

Milward, A., 2000. *The European rescue of the nation-state.* 2nd ed. London: Routledge.

Milward, A., 2002. *The rise and fall of a national strategy, 1945–1963: The United Kingdom and the European Community, volume I.* London: Frank Cass.

O'Rourke, K., 2018. *A short history of Brexit: From Brentry to Backstop.* London: Pelican.

Owen, G., 1999. *From empire to Europe: The decline and revival of British industry since the Second World War.* London: HarperCollins.

Plowden, E., 1989. *An industrialist in the Treasury: The post-war years.* London: Andre Deutsch.

Rollings, N., 2007. *British business in the formative years of European integration, 1945–1973.* Cambridge: Cambridge University Press.

Saunders, R., 2018. *Yes to Europe: The 1976 referendum and seventies Britain.* Cambridge: Cambridge University Press.

The Economist, 2015. The reluctant European, 17 October. Available from: www.economist.com/leaders/2015/10/17/the-reluctant-european [Accessed 20 October 2018].

Wall, S., 2008. *A stranger in Europe: Britain and the EU from Thatcher to Blair.* Oxford: Oxford University Press.

Wall, S., 2013. *The official history of Britain and the European Community volume II: From rejection to referendum, 1963–1975.* London: Routledge.

Wall, S., 2019. *The official history of Britain and the European Community volume III: The tiger unleashed, 1975–1985.* London: Routledge.

Wall, S., 2020. *Reluctant European: Britain and the European Union from 1945 to Brexit.* Oxford: Oxford University Press.

Warlouzet, L., 2018. Britain at the centre of European Co-operation (1948–2016). *Journal of Common Market Studies*, 56 (4), 955–970.

Young, H., 1998. *This blessed plot.* London: Macmillan.

23 The 1960s and the cultural revolution

Marcus Collins

Introduction

What immediately comes to mind when you think of Britain in the 1960s? Chances are that it will be the Beatles and the Stones, miniskirts and Minis, Mods and Rockers, the World Cup and the Pill. Put all these images together and you have a vision of the 'swinging sixties', when a buttoned-up nation transformed into a permissive society.

This image of Britain as a modernising, liberalising nation was much publicised during the 1960s and continues to beguile down to the present. YouGov (2016) asked respondents to name the decade in which 'Britain was at its greatest'. While half of them had no preference, the 1960s was over twice as popular a choice as its nearest rival, the 1980s, and as popular as the 1940s, 1950s and 1970s combined. Only 1 per cent of people thought Britain to be in its prime in 2016 itself: the year of the Brexit referendum.

The 'swinging sixties'

Despite – or perhaps because – of its popular appeal, the 'swinging sixties' has attracted surprisingly little serious historical research. The first major historical study of the period was Arthur Marwick's *The Sixties: Cultural Revolution in Britain, France, Italy, and the United States c.1958–c.1974* (1998). Marwick advanced three arguments that did much to define the parameters of debate. The first was to propose a 'long sixties' that extended backwards to 1958 and forwards to 1974 (Marwick 1998, p. 7). He chose 1958 as his starting point because of the emergence in the late 1950s of a number of phenomena emblematic of the 1960s, including new kinds of youth culture and sexual liberalisation. The oil crisis of 1973–1974 marked the end of the postwar economic boom and with it, he argued, the era of affluence which served as a precondition for rapid social and economic change.

Marwick's second argument was that this 'long sixties' had experienced a 'cultural revolution' or 'mini-Renaissance' (1998, p. 6). To him, 'the vast number of innovative activities taking place simultaneously, by unprecedented interaction and acceleration' (Marwick 1998, p. 7) in virtually all artistic fields did not simply make the 1960s an exciting and enriching time to be alive. Like the Renaissance itself, the sixties in his view were a turning point after which people could not create or appreciate culture in quite the same way again. And, much as Italy was the fulcrum of the Renaissance, 'Britain assumed a surprising primacy' (Marwick 1998, p. 36) in Marwick's account of the 'cultural revolution'.

DOI: 10.4324/9781003037118-25

Marwick's third argument went still further by claiming that the sixties reshaped society every bit as much as it transformed culture. While accepting that Western nations experienced 'no fundamental redistribution of political and economic power', he maintained that there was nonetheless 'a "revolution", or "transformation" in material conditions, lifestyles, family relationships, and personal freedoms for the vast majority of ordinary people' (Marwick 1998, p. 15). The sixteen outstanding 'Characteristics of a Unique Era' (Marwick 1998, pp. 16–20) which he identified made the case for the sixties' transformative power:

1. The formation of new subcultures and movements, generally critical of, or in opposition to, one or more aspects of established society.
2. [A]n outburst of entrepreneurialism, individualism, doing your own thing.
3. The rise to positions of unprecedented influence of young people . . .
4. Important advances in technology . . .
5. The advent . . . of 'spectacle' as an integral part of the interface between life and leisure.
6. Unprecedented international cultural exchange . . .
7. Massive improvements in material life, so that large sections of society joined the consumer society and acquired 'mod cons' . . .
8. Upheavals in race, class, and family relationships . . .
9. 'Permissiveness' – that is to say, a general sexual liberation, entailing striking changes in public and private morals and . . . a new frankness, openness, and indeed honesty in personal relations and modes of expression.
10. New modes of self-presentation . . .
11. A participatory and uninhibited popular culture, whose central component was rock music . . .
12. Original and striking (and sometimes absurd) developments in elite thought . . .
13. The continued existence, and indeed expansion, of a liberal, progressive presence within the institutions of authority . . .
14. [T]he continued existence of elements of extreme reaction . . .
15. New concerns for civil and personal rights . . .
16. The first intimations of the electrifying challenges implicit in the concept of the entire West as a collection of multicultural societies.

Was there a 'cultural revolution' in 1960s Britain?

So was there a 'cultural revolution' in 1960s Britain? And if so, when did it start and end; where did it take place; whom did it involve; how did it relate to the political, social and economic developments of the period; and what were its long-term effects? The breadth of the topic and the patchiness of research mean that there is little agreement among historians about the answers to these questions or even how to answer them. Inasmuch as there is a consensus, it is that Marwick's model is flawed. Let's begin with Marwick's claim (1998, p. 5) that the 1960s were 'a self-contained period . . . of outstanding historical significance'. Even when the decade is elongated into Marwick's 'long 1960s', many of the phenomena he describes are part of much longer-term trends stretching back into the earlier twentieth century and forward towards the present. There was self-evidently sex before the 'sexual revolution', youth cultures before rock'n'roll, mass media before television, consumerism before Carnaby Street, civil liberties before permissive reforms and bohemianism before hippies. Marwick readily accepted these precedents but argued that their manifestations in the sixties were different in scale and effect. Such was their impact, he argued, that the 1960s set 'the cultural and social agenda for the rest of the century, whatever the subsequent political vicissitudes' (Marwick 1993, p. 565). Here he was thinking of the ascendancy of Margaret Thatcher, who as early as 1970 was blaming the 'permissive society' for the decline of self-discipline, moral standards, 'family' values and the rise of drug abuse, pornography and sexual licence. Yet she and her successor John Major, who moralised about the need to get 'back to basics', did little to reverse permissive legislation and much to accelerate the individualistic ethos at its core (Collins 2007, p. 27).

The extent of a 'cultural revolution' and Britain's pre-eminence in it are both open to challenge. The few writers who share Marwick's view that the sixties ushered in a wholesale change in mentality are conservative moralists diametrically opposed to his liberal politics. Marwick broadly celebrated the liberating effects of the 1960s. In contrast, the right-wing journalist Peter Hitchens (2008, p. 343) identifies the same 'Cultural Revolution' as destroying the 'customs, manners, methods, standards and laws which have for centuries restrained us [the British] from the sort of barbaric behaviour that less happy lands suffer'. Hitchens indicts the sixties for having created the drug-addled, crime-ridden, secular and sexually deviant Britain of today. In his view (p. 272), 'the laws have grown more permissive and society more violent, selfish and chaotic'.

Whereas conservative moralists present a catastrophist account of the same narrative outlined by Marwick, most historians take issue instead with his notion of a 'cultural revolution' in the 1960s accompanied by wholesale social transformation. The word 'revolution' connotes a sudden and decisive overthrow of an existing order, which Marwick's critics simply do not see as happening in the 1960s. The influential revisionist writer Dominic Sandbrook (2005, 2006) contrasts the eye-catching attitudes and behaviours of a small elite with the more unadventurous attitudes, tastes and behaviours of the majority. Sandbrook's conservative politics lead him to celebrate the unrevolutionary climate of sixties Britain which was so frustrating to the left at the time. Radicals were chagrined that Britain staged no mass student uprising in 1968 and viewed women's liberation, gay liberation and Black Power as battles to be fought, not as victories already won.

Marwick's claim that Britain spearheaded a cultural revolution can be challenged from two angles. The first is that he conflated Britain with the 'swinging London' mythologised in Piri Halasz's famous *Time* magazine article of April 1966. Halasz took a small collection of boutiques and clubs in Chelsea, Soho and Mayfair to be emblematic of a 'bloodless revolution' (1966, p. 30) which had liberated Britain from a stifling Victorianism. Many accounts have contrasted the London scene to the decidedly less permissive and fashionable way of life elsewhere. Outside of London, they claim, 'the sixties' appeared to happen to other people in other places. Marwick addressed this issue by portraying Britain as being unusually open to provincial culture during the 'long sixties'. These included the novels and plays of Angry Young Men; the films of 'British New Wave' directors; and the music of beat groups from the Midlands, North and West. Although on-trend boutiques and clubs popped up in dozens of British towns and cities like Newcastle and Edinburgh sustained thriving artistic scenes, Halasz (1966, p. 30) observed that creative types gravitated towards the metropolis. The Beatles were famously sons of Liverpool but decamped to London and the Home Counties as soon as they secured a record contract.

Second, even if we accept that Britain underwent some sort of 'cultural revolution' in the 1960s, it is debatable whether Britain 'led the way' in the manner proposed by Halasz and later echoed by Marwick. The global reach of the Beatles was truly remarkable, and any account of Western culture in the 1960s could not afford to omit Mary Quant's miniskirt, the Rolling Stones and groundbreaking BBC programmes such as *Monty Python's Flying Circus*. Yet – and at the risk of playing a kind of cultural Top Trumps – Britain did not seriously challenge American cultural dominance in most other fields during the 1960s. There were no British figures of the same stature and influence as the actor Marilyn Monroe, the artist Andy Warhol, the critic Susan Sontag, the journalist Tom Wolfe, the composer John Cage, the trumpeter Miles Davis, the boxer Muhammad Ali, the photographer Diane Arbus, the feminist Betty Friedan, the environmentalist Rachel Carson, the counterculturalist Timothy Leary, the documentary filmmakers Albert and Davis Maysles and the choreographers Martha Graham and Alvin Ailey. Many of the most quintessentially sixties cultural and intellectual currents were American imports modified for British use. Black Power, gay pride, the counterculture, second-wave feminism and the early civil rights campaign in Northern Ireland bore a strong American imprint. Of these, only activists in Northern Ireland achieved politically what the Beatles and Stones did culturally by transmuting American influences into something quite distinct.

Living conditions during the 'long 1960s'

In social terms, it is hard to dispute Marwick's argument that affluence and technology transformed living conditions for most British people during the 'long 1960s'. Table 23.1 shows how luxury goods at the beginning of the period became staples by its end. Using electricity to wash clothes, clean floors, heat rooms, preserve food, deliver entertainment and communicate with others changed lives immeasurably. Much less clear is how these changing material conditions affected social attitudes. Marwick's claim (1998, p. 18) that the 1960s simultaneously witnessed upheavals 'subverting the authority of the white, the upper and middle class, the husband, the father, and the male generally' is highly controversial. Revisionists have argued that changes that attracted publicity during the decade proved to be more rhetorical than actual. Affluent manual workers did not undergo 'embourgeoisement' but maintained a working-class outlook and lifestyle that set them apart from their white-collared counterparts. (See Chapter 8 for a discussion of the movement to the suburbs in this period.)

Talk of a newly 'companionate marriage' was as ideal as reality. The 'generation gap' was bridged by a generation of baby boomers who followed in their parents' footsteps upon leaving school by finding employment, getting married, leaving home, having children and starting the life cycle all over again. The minority of adolescents who appeared to threaten this norm were subjected to 'moral panics' that reinforced the social order. When Mods fought Rockers on the beaches in 1964, both of these subcultures lost by being labelled as 'folk devils' ostracised by the respectable majority (Cohen 1972). The much-vaunted 'emancipation' of women was rudely contradicted by the ongoing sexual division of labour within the household and at the workplace, where men performed largely separate jobs for higher pay. Some feminists saw the

Table 23.1 Availability of consumer goods in households (percentages)

	1955	1975
Vacuum cleaner	51	90
Washing machine	18	70
Refrigerator	8	85
Freezer	–	15
Television	35	96
Telephone	19	52
Central heating	5	47

Source: Adapted from Obelkevich, 2002. Consumption. *In*: Catterall and Obelkevich, eds. p. 145.

women's liberation movement as a reaction against the sexual exploitation and objectification of women on show in the fashionable sixties scene. The most pronounced reaction to non-white immigration was not integration or multiculturalism but racism. Five years after Martin Luther King's 'I have a dream' speech, Enoch Powell's nightmare vision of race war producing 'rivers of blood' was endorsed by two-thirds or more of the native British population (NOP 1968, p. 9; Gallup 1968, p. 65).

Such stolid conservatism made a mockery of contemporary speculation about the emergence of a 'permissive society'. Most of the permissive legislation lacked strong public backing. What's more, the laws were arguably not permissive in intent. Legislators had no more intention of encouraging abortion, divorce, pornography and sex between men through legal reform than they had had of encouraging suicides by the 1961 Act or murders by the suspension and subsequent abolition of capital punishment. Abortion and male homosexuality were accordingly decriminalised, not legalised. Paternalism was enshrined in the requirement for a woman to obtain permission for an abortion from two doctors, while the age of consent for male homosexuality was set five years higher than that for heterosexuality. Betting shops were screened off from public view, and hard-core pornography was sold illicitly under the counter. Pirate radio was banned, the Wootton report which advocated the decriminalisation of marijuana possession was shelved and many forms of discrimination against women and ethnic minorities would only be outlawed in the second half of the 1970s.

Debates and Interpretations: what do opinion polls tell us about the nature, degree and scope of permissiveness before, during and after the 1960s?

It has proven simpler to punch holes in Marwick's model of sixties Britain than to develop a fully fledged alternative. Historians studying subordinate social groups simultaneously expose the elitism, sexism, xenophobia and homophobia rampant in the sixties and identify the decade as a hothouse of identity politics. Sandbrook tries to have it both ways by writing about much the same people and events familiar to any account of the 'swinging sixties', only to disclaim their wider significance (see the 'In Focus' section on the Redlands Affair). His attempt to replace Marwick's model of change in the sixties with one of cultural continuity is overstated. It is premised on claims that the great British public preferred Cliff Richard to the Beatles and *The Sound of Music* to *Sgt. Pepper* (Sandbrook 2005, p. 446, 2006, pp. 389–390), which do not withstand sustained scrutiny. According to official sales data, the Beatles released 17 of the 60 top-selling singles of the 1960s compared to just three by Cliff Richard and seven of the ten top-selling albums of the decade, with *Sgt. Pepper* outselling *The Sound of Music* and every other LP (Collins 2014, pp. 90–91).

One way out of this impasse is to engage more methodically with the abundant evidence surviving from the period. The political scientist Ivor Crewe (cited in Johnes 2011, p. 22) once wryly observed that

> Airy generalizations about cultural change are the most superficial form of social comment. Take a few casual impressions, add some personal hunches, sprinkle with some statistics, and a plausible case can be made for almost any thesis about how the values of the British have changed.

Though Marwick was an indefatigable researcher, his attempt to demonstrate cultural change through focusing of groundbreaking artistic works was something of a self-fulfilling methodology. Sandbrook legitimately questions whether everyday life in sixties Britain is captured in arthouse films or countercultural magazines. Yet, for all his assiduity in detecting the sensationalist aspects of media coverage, his footnotes demonstrate an inordinate dependence on Fleet Street clippings for his portrait of an age. Equally limiting is his lack of engagement with academic social histories of the period, which are proliferating rapidly from an admittedly small base.

Both Marwick and Sandbrook, in common with historians of the period more generally, make sparing and unsystematic use of the least worst sources to gauge attitudes in sixties Britain. These sources are opinion polls. Like any historical source, opinion polls needs to be treated with care and judgement. The data are fragmentary, polling questions can be loaded or ambiguous and the answers given by respondents may not adequately convey their opinions, still less their motivations. That said, unlike other historical sources save for surveys and elections, polls explicitly aimed to collect a diversity of opinions fully representative of the population of mainland Britain (excluding Northern Ireland). Polls therefore provide better measurements of public opinion in the sixties than do Sandbrook's journalists or Marwick's artists and memoirists.

A signal virtue of Marwick's work was that he presented a series of testable hypotheses which are not so much disproved as for the most part unproven. The remainder of this chapter investigates what opinion polls tell us about the nature, degree and scope of permissiveness before, during and after the 1960s. Permissiveness, which can be defined as a libertarian attitude towards personal behaviour and group differences, is central to any claims for a 'cultural revolution'. During the sixties, the term was used to refer to an sequence of liberalising legislation from the Obscene Publications Act of 1959 to the Divorce Reform Act ten years later. In each case, permissive legislation expanded the civil rights of individuals by relaxing prohibitions or controls exercised by the state. The concept of a 'permissive society' envisioned legislative reforms to be part of a wider cultural shift towards heterodoxy and self-expression.

If a 'cultural revolution' did indeed happen in sixties Britain, we should be able to spot three things in polling data. The first would be that there is an increase in permissive attitudes during the 'long sixties'. This shift would have to be dramatic, even unprecedented, to qualify as being truly revolutionary. Second, we should expect to see permissiveness form an identifiable cluster of issues, with clear divisions between those holding permissive opinions on one side and those holding anti-permissive opinions on the other. The third sign that a 'cultural revolution' has occurred would be for such permissive attitudes to become prevalent within the British public as a whole.

Time-series data enable us to test whether permissive attitudes increased during the 'long sixties'. These data consist of answers to identical or near-identical questions asked two or more times. They are commonplace for political issues such as voting intentions, for which the same question has been asked every month since 1948, but much rarer for matters concerning permissiveness. Though time-series data are available for fewer than thirty such questions polled by Gallup and NOP from 1945 to 1980, the results are nonetheless informative. Figures 23.1 to 23.5 display the answers to questions on five themes: crime, ethnicity and immigration, religion, sex and marriage and women and the young. The net score provided for each answer is calculated by subtracting the percentage of anti-permissive responses from the percentage of permissive responses. For example, the net scores for 'Capital punishment A' in Figure 23.1 show that 58 per cent more respondents in 1952 opposed abolishing the death penalty than supported it, resulting in a net score of –58 per cent. When the same question was posed to respondents in 1954, the net score was –36 per cent. This striking diminution of the gap between those for and against capital punishment in just two years was probably due to the controversial murder trials of Derek Bentley in December 1952 and John Christie in June 1953. Answers to all but one of the other questions displayed in Figure 23.1 show the same softening in attitudes to criminal justice during the 1950s, 1960s and 1970s, although there remained anti-permissive majorities in almost every case. In contrast, Figure 23.5 shows that those in favour of providing contraceptive advice to single young people grew from a small majority in 1966 (a net score of +16 per cent) into a large majority in 1975 (a net score of

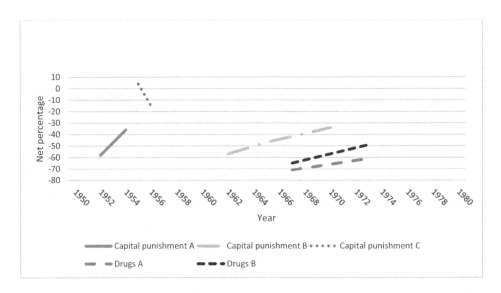

Figure 23.1 Attitudes to crime (Gallup and NOP polls, 1950–80)

Questions

> *Capital punishment A:* In this country most people convicted of murder are sentenced to death. Do you agree with this or do you think that the death penalty should be abolished? (net abolish minus keep, 1952–54)
>
> *Capital punishment B:* Should the death penalty be abolished altogether, or not? (net abolish completely minus keep, 1962–70)
>
> *Capital punishment C:* If Parliament were to remove the death penalty for an experimental period of, say five years, would you approve or disapprove? (net approve minus disapprove, 1955–56)
>
> *Drugs A:* What do you think should be the legal position on 'hard' drugs such as heroin and cocaine other than on medical prescription? Should it be a criminal offence to take them? (net should minus should not be criminal offence, 1967–73)
>
> *Drugs B:* What do you think should be the legal position on 'soft' drugs such as cannabis and marijuana other than on medical prescription? Should it be a criminal offence to take them? (net should minus should not be criminal offence, 1967–73)

+57 per cent). The same upward trajectory appears in most answers about sex and is evident well before the 'long sixties' in questions concerning divorce (Figure 23.4). The 'death of Christian Britain' thesis proposed by historian Callum Brown (2013) in sixties Britain receives some corroboration in polls which show the growth of secular sentiments over mixed marriages, Sabbatarianism and core tenets of Christianity (Figure 23.3). The civil rights of women, the young and ethnic minorities present a more mixed picture. Support for equal pay for women rose markedly from the 1940s until its enactment in 1970, but support for voting rights at 18 fell shortly after they became law (Figure 23.5), and there was no clear liberalisation in attitudes towards non-white immigrants from the late fifties to the late seventies (Figure 23.2).

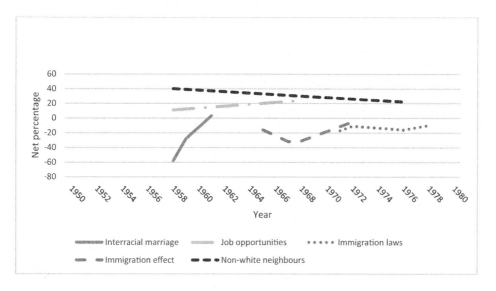

Figure 23.2 Attitudes to ethnicity and immigration (Gallup and NOP polls, 1950–80)

Questions

Interracial marriage: Do you approve or disapprove of marriage between white and coloured people? (net approve minus disapprove, 1958–61)

Job opportunities: Do you think that coloured people from the Commonwealth should be allowed to compete for jobs in Great Britain on equal terms with people born here? (net agree minus disagree, 1958–68)

Immigration laws: Do you think that coloured people from the Commonwealth should have the right of completely free entry into Britain, should there be restrictions on entry, or should they be kept out completely? (net free entry minus no entry, 1971–78)

Immigration effect: Do you think that on the whole this country has benefitted or been harmed through immigrants coming to settle here from the Commonwealth? (net benefitted/no difference minus harmed, 1965–72)

Non-white neighbours: If coloured people came to live next door, would you move your home? (net wouldn't move minus would/might move if next door, 1958–76)

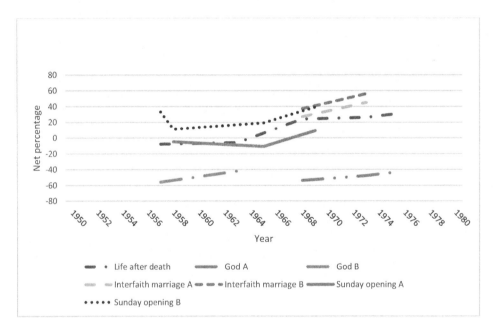

Figure 23.3 Attitudes to religion (Gallup and NOP polls, 1950–80)

Questions

Life after death: Do you believe in any form of life after death? (net no/don't know minus yes, 1957–75)

God A: Do you believe in God? (net no/don't know minus yes, 1968–75)

God B: There is a personal God/There is some sort of spirit or vital force which controls life. (net no/don't know minus yes, 1957–63)

Interfaith marriage A: Do you agree or disagree with marriage between Jews and non-Jews? (net agree minus disagree, 1968–73)

Interfaith marriage B: Do you agree or disagree with marriages between Catholics and Protestants? (net agree minus disagree, 1968–73)

Sunday opening A: Would you approve or disapprove if the present laws were changed to allow public houses to open same hours Sunday as weekdays? (net approve minus disapprove, 1958–69)

Sunday opening B: Would you approve or disapprove of theatres being allowed to open on Sundays, just as they do on other days? (net approve minus disapprove, 1957–69)

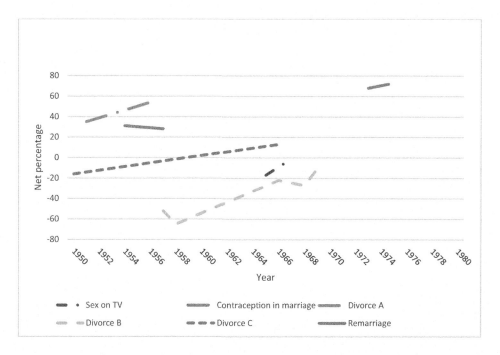

Figure 23.4 Attitudes to sex and marriage (Gallup and NOP polls, 1950–80)

Questions

Sex on TV: Do you agree or disagree with people who say that there is too much sex on TV? (net disagree minus agree, 1965–67)

Contraception in marriage: Do you approve or disapprove of the use of contraceptives (birth control) in marriage? (net approve minus disapprove, 1973–75)

Divorce A: It has been proposed that after 7 years separation a married couple should be able to get a divorce. Do you agree or disagree? (net agree minus disagree, 1951–56)

Divorce B: What's your attitude towards divorce: it should not be allowed at all; it should be easier than at the present time; it should be more difficult than at present? (net easier minus harder/same/impossible, 1957–69)

Divorce C: Would you approve or disapprove if it were made possible to get a divorce simply by agreement between the two parties? (net approve minus disapprove, 1950–66)

Remarriage: The Archbishop of Canterbury says that the Church of England should not remarry a divorced person, so long as the other party is still alive. Do you agree with this ruling or not? (net disagree/less strict minus agree, 1954–57)

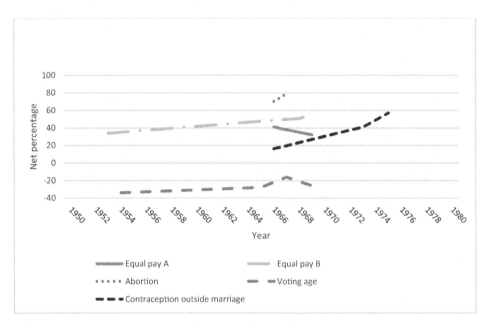

Figure 23.5 Attitudes to women and the young (Gallup and NOP polls, 1950–80)

Questions

Equal pay A: Adopting the principle of 'equal pay for equal work' between men and women? (net good thing minus bad thing, 1966–69)

Equal pay B: Do you approve or disapprove of paying women the same wages as men if they are doing the same work? (net approve minus disapprove, 1953–69)

Abortion: Do you think abortion operations should or should not be legal in cases where the health of the mother is in danger? (net should minus should not, 1966–67)

Voting age: Do you agree or disagree that the voting age should be reduced to eighteen? (net agree minus disagree, 1954–69)

Contraception outside marriage: Do you think contraceptive advice should or should not be available in public clinics to young people who are not married? (net approve minus disapprove, 1966–75)

For evidence of the cohesion and prevalence of permissive attitudes, it is necessary to examine polls in greater detail. In a different study (Collins 2020, pp. 36–43), I survey over 200 answers concerning permissiveness given in forty polls. Here, I will trade breadth for depth by analysing just four answers polled by a single polling company, NOP, in a single year, 1968. The full datasets for these four polls have survived, meaning that we can break down the results along lines of party preference, gender, socioeconomic class, age, region, marital status and whether respondents had children still living with them at home. British polling organisations did not sample for ethnicity until the early 1980s, when the UK census recorded 3.5 per cent of the population as being non-white (Ballard 1999, p. 5).

The results shown in Table 23.2 require careful interpretation. The first thing to note is that the degree of permissiveness varied widely from issue to issue. Eight times as many respondents disapproved as approved of Pope Paul VI's prohibition on artificial birth control. Conversely, most people had little tolerance of student radicalism, which is often portrayed as being as quintessentially a sixties phenomenon as the Pill. Respondents divided fairly equally over the other two issues. Two-fifths of them espoused anti-permissive sentiments saying that they would dislike living near ethnic minorities and favoured the reintroduction of hanging as a matter of priority.

The large majority opposed to student demonstrations and large minorities in favour of capital punishment and racial discrimination suggest that Britain was far from being a 'permissive society' in 1968. Permissiveness does not appear to be prevalent on the basis of these numbers; nor does it appear to be cohesive given the great disparity in the popularity of various permissive causes. However, permissiveness can be considered cohesive inasmuch as some population groups were consistently more permissive in their answers than were others. On each of the four questions, relatively more permissive responses were given by Liberals, men, the highest classes, the youngest age group and those with dependent children. London and the South was the most permissive region in its answers to three of the questions, and married respondents tended to be more permissive than unmarried ones. These crosstabulations cannot tell us the reason why permissiveness was relatively stronger in some sections of the British population. For example, the greater religiosity and political conservatism of women in sixties Britain may account for their relatively unpermissive attitudes, but that would need further investigation. The results nevertheless correspond to Marwick's identification of the young, the affluent and the metropolitan as forming a permissive vanguard. As he would have expected, Conservatives were more socially conservative, and Liberals were more socially liberal. However much he exaggerated the pace and scale of the 'cultural revolution', he pinpointed the most dynamic groups within society.

Table 23.2 Public attitudes to permissive issues in 1968

		Would you please tell me whether you agree or disagree with these statements? I would not want an ethnic minority family as neighbours. (March 1968; net disagree minus agree)	Do you think students are or are not justified in holding demonstrations on political subjects like the war in Vietnam? (May 1968; net justified minus not justified)	Here is a list of things which some people would like the government to do. Would you please tell me which three of them you think are the most important? (July 1968; percentage *not* selecting 'Bring back capital punishment' from nine options)	Do you approve or disapprove of the Pope's decision to ban artificial methods of birth control for Roman Catholics? (August 1968; net disapprove minus approve)
Voting intention	Conservative	+5.5%	−49.5%	55.1%	+74.8%
	Labour	+17.7%	−48.8%	64.3%	+63.9%
	Liberal	+19.5%	−37.3%	64.8%	+82.6%
Gender	Men	+15.4%	−42.4%	60.4%	+77.4%
	Women	+10.7%	−49.9%	57.9%	+66.5%
Class	AB	+15.7%	−34.9%	60.9%	+80.1%
	C1	+4.2%	−41.5%	59.4%	+72.8%
	C2	+14.4%	−47.3%	60.6%	+75.6%
	DE	+15.1%	−54.4%	56.3%	+64.1%
Age	16–24	+33.3%	−19.0%	74.5%	+78.1%
	25–34	+28.2%	−29.7%	67.3%	+70.3%
	35–44	+20.6%	−40.7%	63.8%	+77.5%
	45–54	+10.9%	−43.9%	57.7%	+70.4%
	55–64	+12.3%	−65.5%	51.7%	+72.9%
	65+	−13.4%	−63.9%	50.8%	+64.8%
Region	Scotland	+32.6%	−50.0%	45.8%	+48.4%
	North	+22.1%	−51.3%	58.6%	+66.0%
	Wales and West	+14.0%	−56.4%	60.7%	+72.1%
	Midlands/East Anglia	0.0%	−38.9%	60.5%	+76.7%
	London and South	+7.3%	−38.0%	60.8%	+81.7%

		Would you please tell me whether you agree or disagree with these statements? I would not want an ethnic minority family as neighbours. (March 1968; net disagree minus agree)	Do you think students are or are not justified in holding demonstrations on political subjects like the war in Vietnam? (May 1968; net justified minus not justified)	Here is a list of things which some people would like the government to do. Would you please tell me which three of them you think are the most important? (July 1968; percentage *not* selecting 'Bring back capital punishment' from nine options)	Do you approve or disapprove of the Pope's decision to ban artificial methods of birth control for Roman Catholics? (August 1968; net disapprove minus approve)
Marital status	*Married*	+14.1%	−44.8%	58.5%	+74.5%
	Unmarried	+8.8%	−52.0%	60.9%	+62.2%
Children	*Dependent children*	+22.8%	−36.0%	64.5%	+75.0%
	No dependent children	+5.6%	−54.0%	55.5%	+69.6%
	Net total/total	+12.8%	−46.4%	59.1%	+71.8%
		(51.8% disagree; 40.0% agree; 9.2% don't know)	(24.5% justified; 70.9% not justified; 4.6% don't know)	*not selecting* 'Bring back capital punishment' from nine options	(81.5% disapprove; 9.7% approve; 8.8% don't know)
	Sample number	1753	1935	1898	1213

Source: NOP National Political Surveys, 1968; datasets available at UK Data Archive, https://beta.ukdataservice.ac.uk/datacatalogue/studies/study?id=68020#!/resources.

In Focus: The Redlands Affair

Image 23.1 The Rolling Stones pictured in Green Park, London, for a press conference prior to their departure for America, where they are due to appear on the Ed Sullivan coast-to-coast show. Right to left: Brian Jones, Keith Richards, Bill Wyman, Mick Jagger and Charlie Watts. 11 January 1967

Source: © Trinity Mirror/Mirrorpix/Alamy Stock Photo.

The Redlands Affair of 1967 provides an insight into why sex and drugs and rock'n'roll provoked scandal in the 1960s and why their significance remains a matter of historical controversy. The Affair concerned the arrest, conviction and brief imprisonment for drugs offences of two members of the Rolling Stones, Mick Jagger and Keith Richards, after a raid on Richards' country residence of Redlands. Their trial, which took place during the Summer of Love, became a test case for competing models of permissiveness. To their accusers, the Stones represented how easily liberty degenerated into licence. They tied drug abuse to the Stones' long record of incivility and to the immodest behaviour of Jagger's girlfriend, Marianne Faithfull, when the raid occurred. An opposite case was made by the countercultural magazine *Oz* (1967, n.p.), which applauded the Stones for 'symbolis[ing] the new permissiveness' in the face of draconian punishments. A more qualified defence of permissiveness was espoused by *Times* editor William Rees-Mogg (1967, p. 11), who argued that the incarceration of Jagger for possession of a small quantity of amphetamines was a disproportionate response liable to alienate the younger generation. The writer, musician and anarchist George Melly considered the Affair something of a sideshow. The eventual quashing of Richards' conviction and the suspension of Jagger's sentence displayed the 'comparatively permissive attitude of the authorities', but the consequences were limited by the fact that 'the right to smoke pot or strip naked in public are not going to affect the structure of society' (Melly 1970, pp. 119–120).

These contemporary interpretations of the Redlands Affair broadly correspond to subsequent historical interpretations of permissiveness in the 1960s. These might be termed the 'hell in a handbasket' model of conservative moralists, the 'paradise lost' model of disillusioned radicals, the 'onwards and upwards' model of liberal progressives and the 'storm in a teacup' model of sceptical mythbusters. The 'hell in a handbasket' model is forcefully stated by Peter Hitchens (2012, p. 3), who portrays sex, drugs and rock'n'roll as an unholy trinity of 'self-indulgences . . . on which modern morality rests'. The Redlands Affair, in his view, witnessed the defeat of Britain's traditional 'religious and conscience-based moral system' (Hitchens 2012, p. 111) by this new hedonistic ethic of 'Jaggerism', aided and abetted by a liberal elite. The 'paradise lost' model appears in the autobiographies of Keith Richards and Marianne Faithfull. Faithfull claims (Faithfull and Dalton 1994, p. 97) that 'the cantankerous, ancient custodians of a crumbling empire' sought to teach a lesson to dissolute youth by 'plotting the downfall of the Rolling Stones'. A more sophisticated version of the same idea is advanced by the distinguished academic Martin Cloonan (1996, p. 6), who interprets the Redlands Affair as part of 'a backlash against the permissiveness which appeared to have pop at its core'. The 'onwards and upwards' model was exemplified by Arthur Marwick. In his view, '[m]easured judgement prevailed' (Marwick 1998, p. 562) once the terms of imprisonment passed on Jagger and Richards were overturned on appeal. The 'storm in a teacup' model favoured by Melly in the immediate aftermath of the Affair has been revived by Dominic Sandbrook. He questions whether the Affair represented a showdown between authority and rebellion by characterising the Stones (Sandbrook 2006, pp. 518, 524) as having 'often led much more conservative lives than people imagined' and dismissing as 'ridiculous' their belief that they were 'scapegoats for the permissive society'.

I would argue that none of these approach fully captures the significance of the Redlands Affair or, by extension, the nature of permissiveness in sixties Britain. Conservative moralists cannot account for the fact that the Wilson government sought to crack down on drugtaking at the very time when they were enacting permissive legislation in other fields. These same reforms undermine the idea that the Affair formed part of a concerted backlash against permissiveness. This mixture of liberal and illiberal measures and the unintended consequences that ensued cast doubt on Marwick's concept of 'measured judgement'. Drugs laws – like those concerning obscenity, betting, immigration, abortion, male homosexuality and divorce – were confounded in their intentions by poor drafting and the refusal of large sections of society to behave as politicians envisaged or desired. The Rolling Stones were an extreme example of such intractability, contrary to Sandbrook's claims of their covertly 'conservative' inclinations.

To me (Collins 2019), the Redlands Affair can be understood within the context of what I term an 'anti-permissive permissive society'. Most people in sixties Britain were opposed to most aspects of permissiveness. Recreational drugs, whether 'soft' or 'hard', were among the most reviled manifestations of sixties culture. Only 3 per cent of respondents in a 1967 opinion poll said that they or others in their household know someone who had taken illegal drugs. Other polls showed that drugtaking was considered one of the most serious problems faced by society. This intense concern illustrates both the 'anti-permissiveness' of opposing drug use and the consciousness of a 'permissive society' in which drug use appeared to be increasing, irrespective of respondents' personal experience of the problem. Much the same process can be seen in the Redlands Affair. Again, opinion polls registered widespread disapproval of drugtaking, with the majority of adults wishing that Jagger received more the three months' imprisonment to which he was originally sentenced. But their wishes were not heeded, and the release of Jagger and Richards – when paired with the publicity accorded by the trial to countercultural rebellion – reinforced the idea that sixties Britain was becoming ever more permissive in the face of public opposition.

Conclusion

If we revisit the sixteen 'unique characteristics' identified by Marwick, we see that they would make for a poor characterisation of the half century before the 'long sixties' but a compelling one of the half-century to come. The impact of globalisation, mass communications, consumerism and individualism has accelerated and intensified since the sixties, ushering in what social theorists have termed postmodernity. Anglophone youth culture is more dominant than ever, and the civil rights of subordinate social groups continue to be matters of urgent public concern. The sixties therefore was a turning point, establishing much of the political, social and cultural framework right up to the present day. Any triumphalism would be misplaced. Women and ethnic and sexual minorities continue to press for equality and recognition. The unresolved nature of their struggles suggests that Marwick underestimated the complexity of their claims and overestimated the strength of 'liberal, progressive' forces. By the same token, however, the legacy of the sixties is far from spent.

Further reading

Overviews of the sixties Britain include Marwick (1998), Donnelly (2005), Sandbrook (2005, 2006), Collins (2007) and Harris and O'Brien Castro (2014). The politics of permissiveness are surveyed in Holden (2004), Jarvis (2005) and Davidson and Davis (2012). Other histories of the 'cultural revolution' can be divided between those focusing on genres and social groups. Genre studies examine newspapers (Bingham 2009), the alternative press (Nelson 1989), drama and film (Aldgate 1995), visual art (Hewison 1986), arts festivals (Bartie 2013), television (Schaffer 2014) and popular music (Randall 2008; Collins 2020). Notable works on social groups include those on Londoners (Mort 2010), Christians (Brown 2013; Brewitt-Taylor 2018), immigrants

(Wills 2017), second-wave feminists (Browne 2014; Jolly 2019), heterosexuals (Szreter and Fisher 2010), homosexuals (Robinson 2007), students (Hoefferle 2012) and youth subcultures (Weight 2013; Gildart 2013).

References

Aldgate, A., 1995. *Censorship and the permissive society: British cinema and theatre, 1955–1965*. Oxford: Oxford University Press.

Ballard, R., 1999. Britain's visible minorities: A demographic overview. *Cross Asia-Repository* [online], 5. Available from: http://crossasia-repository.ub.uni-heidelberg.de/286/1/demography.pdf.

Bartie, A., 2013. *The Edinburgh festivals: Culture and society in postwar Britain*. Edinburgh: Edinburgh University Press.

Bingham, A., 2009. *Family newspapers? Sex, private life, and the British popular press 1918–1978*. Oxford: Oxford University Press.

Brewitt-Taylor, S., 2018. *Christian radicalism in the Church of England and the invention of the British sixties, 1957–1970: The hope of a world transformed*. Oxford: Oxford University Press.

Brown, C.G., 2013. *The death of Christian Britain*, rev ed. London: Routledge.

Browne, S.F., 2014. *The women's liberation movement in Scotland*. Manchester: Manchester University Press.

Cloonan, M., 1996. *Banned! Censorship of popular music in Britain, 1967–92*. Aldershot: Arena.

Cohen, S., 1972. *Folk Devils and Moral Panics: The creation of the mods and rockers*. London: MacGibbon and Kee.

Collins, M., 2007. Introduction: The permissive society and its enemies. *In*: M. Collins, ed. *The permissive society and its enemies: Sixties British culture*. London: Rivers Oram, 1–40.

Collins, M., 2014. We can work it out: Popular and academic writing on the Beatles. *Popular Music History*, 9 (1), 79–101.

Collins, M., 2019. Permissiveness on trial: Sex, drugs, rock, the Rolling Stones and the sixties counterculture. *Popular Music and Society*, 42 (2), 188–209.

Collins, M., 2020. *The Beatles and sixties Britain*. Cambridge: Cambridge University Press.

Davidson, R., and Davis, G., 2012. *The sexual state: Sexuality and Scottish Governance, 1950–80*. Edinburgh: Edinburgh University Press.

Donnelly, M., 2005. *Sixties Britain: Culture, society, and politics*. Harlow: Longman.

Faithfull, M., and Dalton, D., 1994. *Faithfull*. London: Little, Brown.

Gallup, 1968. *Gallup political index*, May, 65.

Gildart, K., 2013. *Images of England through popular music: Class, youth and rock'n' roll, 1955–1976*. Basingstoke: Palgrave Macmillan.

Halasz, P., 1966. London: The Swinging City – You can walk across it on the grass. *Time*, 15 April, 30–34.

Harris, T., and O'Brien Castro, M., eds., 2014. *Preserving the sixties: Britain and the 'Decade of Protest'*. Basingstoke: Palgrave Macmillan.

Hewison, R., 1986. *Too much: Art and society in the sixties 1960–75*. London: Methuen.

Hitchens, P., 2008. *The abolition of Britain: From Winston Churchill to Princess Diana*. London: Continuum.

Hitchens, P., 2012. *The war we never fought: The British establishment's surrender to drugs*. London: Bloomsbury.

Hoefferle, C., 2012. *British student activism in the long sixties*. London: Routledge.

Holden, A., 2004. *Makers and manners: Politics and morality in postwar Britain*. London: Politico's.

Jarvis, M., 2005. *Conservative governments, morality and social change in affluent Britain, 1957–64.* Manchester: Manchester University Press.

Johnes, M., 2011. On writing contemporary history. *North American Journal of Welsh Studies,* 6 (1), 20–31.

Jolly, M., 2019. *Sisterhood and after: An oral history of the UK women's liberation movement, 1968 – present.* Oxford: Oxford University Press.

Marwick, A., 1993. Six novels of the sixties – Three French, three Italian. *Journal of Contemporary History,* 28 (4), 563–591.

Marwick, A., 1998. *The sixties: Cultural revolution in Britain, France, Italy, and the United States, c.1958 – c.1974.* Oxford: Oxford University Press.

Melly, G., 1970. *Revolt into style: The pop arts in Britain.* London: Allen Lane.

Mort, F., 2010. *Capital affairs: London and the making of the permissive society.* New Haven: Yale University Press.

Nelson, E., 1989. *British counter-culture 1966–73: A study of the underground press.* Basingstoke: Macmillan.

National Opinion Polls (NOP), 1968. NOP bulletin, May, 9.

Oz, 1967. How I jailed Jagger, *Oz Sheet,* 1 May.

Randall, A.J., 2008. *Dusty! Queen of the postmods.* New York: Oxford University Press.

Rees-Mogg, W., 1967. Who breaks a butterfly on a wheel? *The Times,* 1 July, 11.

Robinson, L., 2007. *Gay men and the left in post-war Britain: How the personal got political.* Manchester: Manchester University Press.

Sandbrook, D., 2005. *Never had it so good: A history of Britain from Suez to the Beatles.* London: Little, Brown.

Sandbrook, D., 2006. *White heat: A history of Britain in the swinging sixties.* London: Little, Brown.

Schaffer, G., 2014. *The vision of a nation: Making multiculturalism on British television, 1960–80.* Basingstoke: Palgrave Macmillan.

Szreter, S., and Fisher, K., 2010. *Sex before the sexual revolution: Intimate life in England 1918–1963.* Cambridge: Cambridge University Press.

Weight, R., 2013. *Mod: A very British style.* London: Bodley Head.

Wills, C., 2017. *Lovers and strangers: An immigrant history of post-war Britain.* Harmondsworth: Penguin.

YouGov., 2016. *Survey results 9–10 May 2016* [online]. Available from: https://d25d2506s-fb94s.cloudfront.net/cumulus_uploads/document/7r92ujavz0/InternalResults_160510_Best-Year.pdf.

24 Resisting racism in 1970s and 1980s Britain

The experience of young South Asians

Anandi Ramamurthy

Introduction

The need for Black[1] people to defend their own communities was a key motivating factor for the establishment of the Asian Youth Movements (AYMs) across Britain in the late 1970s and early 80s. This chapter will explore the experiences of racism and deprivation which led to the formation of independent grassroots organisations amongst Asian youth during this period. It will offer an understanding of how this generation of migrants saw both the UK and the wider world and outline the actions that they took to try to make the world a better place. It will consider the ways in which their political identity intersected with those of others, nationally and internationally. It will reflect on how they contributed to the contestation of British identity, which continues to impact how Britain sees itself today (Gilroy 1987, 2019).

Context

Although South Asian workers had been welcomed to Britain in the immediate post–Second World War period when Britain, like all European powers, was 'desperate for labour' (Sivanandan 1982, p. 3), as the supply and demand for labour changed, South Asians and other migrants from the former colonies were increasingly framed as 'a problem'. Rather than recognising migrants' contribution to economic growth, as well as the savings that the state made through employing 'ready-made workers' (Sivanandan 1982, p. 103), Black people were blamed for economic problems such as housing shortages and presented as a drain on the state purse. In education, migrant children were viewed as responsible for lowering educational standards and were often siphoned through state sanction into remedial classes or 'bussed' out of their areas. Trade unions, too, failed to defend the rights of Black workers, leading to strikes such as those at Red Scar Mill in Preston in 1965 and at Imperial Typewriters in 1971 in which South Asian communities without the full backing of trade unions were forced to organise themselves to challenge racist discrimination in working practices and in defence of equal pay and conditions for South Asian workers (Ramdin 1999, pp. 217–220).

While the trigger to the rise of racist violence and 'paki bashing' in the 1970s is often attributed to the inflammatory ideas espoused in Enoch Powell's 1968 'rivers of blood' speech, by 1962 the state itself had created structures to 'nationalise' racism (Sivanandan 1982, p. 12) through the Commonwealth Immigration Act of

DOI: 10.4324/9781003037118-26

1962 and subsequent immigration acts that were constructed to prevent African, Asian and other non-white Commonwealth citizens from entering the UK. The 1962 Act introduced a permit scheme to limit migration from the commonwealth. The 1968 Commonwealth Immigration Act was railroaded through parliament in three days by the Labour Party to prevent entry from Kenyan Asians, with British passports, forced to leave Kenya after changes in Kenyan labour laws. The new law required British passport holders to prove that they had a parent or grandparent born in the UK in order to be granted the right of abode, inevitably discriminating against Kenyan Asians. The 1971 Immigration Act brought in by the Conservative Party consolidated the 1968 Act and removed the right of Commonwealth citizens to remain in the UK unless they had 'ancestral' connections, creating a two-tiered system of citizenship: patrials and non-patrials. Such political actions and the media stoking of racism with inflammatory headlines about immigration numbers inevitably created tensions. In 1972 when Ugandan Asian refugees with UK passports were forced to flee Uganda, the National Front mobilised racist sentiment for what they described as 'the biggest ever anti-immigration demonstration in Leicester' (Marett 1989, p. 56; Eames 2009).

By the mid-1970s the children of the first generation of South Asian migrants were growing up. While the 'myth of return' (Anwar 1979) continued to predominate amongst first-generation migrants, for their children who had very few memories of their parent's homeland, their vision and aspirations for the future lay in Britain. Experiencing racism in housing, in school and on the street, young South Asians felt they had no choice but to challenge their dehumanisation and assert their self-worth. As Anwar Qadir, an AYM (Bradford) member, reflected: 'We were a generation that was saying . . . life has a lot more to offer to us than working in the foundries and the mills, and driving the buses and cleaning hospitals, so we were a generation that was saying "no"' (2005).

Schooling

It was not just through immigration laws that the state framed Black people as problems. The policy of bussing, for example, which at least a dozen local authorities implemented in the 1970s, forced South Asian children as young as five to travel up to an hour to school. The authorities argued that migrant children were lowering school standards and therefore sought to prevent more than 30% of migrant children being in one school. There was a disregard for pupil welfare, not simply through travel, but also through the unfamiliar environments in which children were placed, often exacerbating racist bullying and violence.

Many of the young people who joined the AYMs in the 1970s and 1980s have an overriding memory of racist violence in school from both pupils and staff. One member from Bradford remembers being forced to eat a sausage by a teacher although he was a Muslim. Others refer to racist bullying from white pupils. The extent of violence was well known by the school authorities, who sometimes organised for Asian pupils to leave school early in order to separate them from white pupils. Fridays in some parts of Bradford were known as 'paki-bashing', days and many Asians therefore did not attend, impacting their education.

Apart from racist violence, the undermining of self-worth also took place through the curriculum. For those siphoned into English as a Second Language classes, there was only one subject: English. Some pupils placed in these classes spoke fluent English anyway; others were left there despite having learned English and had to negotiate with the school authorities to be able to move, indicating such practices were a form of racial segregation rather than instituted for educational purpose (Ramamurthy 2013, pp. 17–22). The curriculum, too, framed entirely through a colonial lens, narrated Britain's contribution to the subcontinent as a narrative of paternal development with no mention of the exploitation or destitution caused by the extraction of wealth. From holding a 23% share of the global economy at the beginning of the 18th century, India's share dropped to less than 4% by the time Britain left India in 1947 (Tharoor 2017). According to Patnaik, between 1765 to 1938, Britain extracted $45 trillion from India (2017, p. 311).

While the dominant memories of school by AYM members are of racism and violence, a number of former members have powerful recollections of teachers who stood up against racist bullies and racist ideas and encouraged young Asians to do the same (Ramamurthy 2013, pp. 20–22). School in this sense was a microcosm of the various forms of racism and resistances in society.

Racist violence and the formation of the youth movements

By the mid-1960s the Secretary of East Pakistan House claimed 'a growing mass hysteria against Pakistanis' (Kabir 1965), and youth workers in the Spitalfields (East London) area noted the growing violence against Pakistanis (Leech 1980). Racist attacks against Yemini and Pakistani workers took place in Sheffield in 1968, and the police did nothing to investigate these. In 1968 and again in 1971 Pakistanis were robbed and murdered in the East End of London. The United Coloured People's Association and the Pakistani Progressive Party demonstrated outside the Houses of Parliament in 1971 to raise awareness of the issue, but nothing was done.

While the establishment of the youth movements was an expression of second-generation migrants' determination to carve out their place in Britain, the young people involved in the AYMs were also influenced by the organisational experiences and politics of the previous generation. In the 1960s Indian Workers Associations (IWAs) and other groups had already begun to show 'vigour and initiative in combating racial discrimination and opposing racist immigration policies'(Hiro 1991, pp. 139–140). In 1961 the Coordinating Committee Against Racial Discrimination was formed by Jagmohan Joshi of the IWA and the anti-fascist campaigner Maurice Ludmer. Links between South Asians and the US Black Panthers were also forged by the IWA (GB) when the leader Jagmohan Joshi hosted a joint meeting in 1971 in Wolverhampton.

The climate of racism was exacerbated by the press. When 20,000 South Asians were expelled from Malawi in 1976, headlines such as 'Scandal of £600 a Week Immigrant' and 'New Flood of Asians to Britain' fuelled racial tension. Clergy on Brick Lane raised concern (Leech 1980, p. 7). Organisations such as the National Front capitalised on these wider racist articulations to foster fear and mobilise support. In 1976 two students from the Middle East were murdered in the East End of London, and growing racist attacks were catalogued by the Spitalfields

Bengali Action Group. It was in this climate that 18-year-old Gurdip Singh Chaggar was murdered in Southall in June 1976 (Ramamurthy 2019). When the youth marched to the police station to demand justice, two of them were arrested. Youth held a sit-in outside the police station to demand their release. The following day the Southall Youth Movement was formed. The image of Asian youth demanding their rights on the television news inspired young Asians in other towns and cities to organise.

In April 1976, South Asians in Bradford had already mobilised, with the Trades Council, against the National Front who had decided to hold a meeting in Manningham, an area in which the South Asian community lived.

'We'd picked up on the activity of the National Front and how they were mobilising and wanting to essentially repatriate the Asian community – all this talk about, the Asian community stealing our jobs, stealing our homes, stealing our women' (J. Rashid 2005).

But the Trades Council marched to the city centre, leaving Manningham unprotected. Many young Asians left the main march 'because Manningham was ours and we had to protect it. It was there that we really started thinking that we've got to get our own house in order' (Tariq Mehmood 2005).

In 1977, with the support of the IWA, young people established the Indian Progressive Youth Association. A year later, recognising that it was essential to fully represent all parts of the subcontinent, they went on to establish the Asian Youth Movement (Bradford). The formation of a youth movement in Bradford was followed by the establishment of youth movements in Brick Lane, Manchester, Leicester and Nottingham. In Bolton and Blackburn Asian Youth Organisations were also formed by anti-fascists. Later Sheffield, Birmingham and Luton established youth movements. While each movement was impacted by the structure of feeling in the city in which they formed, the individual movements shared broad political perspectives and networked between each other to build support for their local campaigns.

Black consciousness matters

Embracing a Black political identity, the youth were inspired by and offered solidarity to the struggle against apartheid in South Africa, the Black Power movement in the United States, and the Palestinian national struggle. This political Blackness was symbolised through their adoption of the Black Power fist on their badges and publications and the titles of their magazines: *Kala Tara* (Black Star) and *Kala Mazdoor* (Black Worker).

As one former member from Bradford recalled, 'South Africa made our blood boil'. In the East End, the affinity felt towards the children of Soweto gunned down by government forces when they protested the introduction of Afrikaans as the medium of instruction can be seen by the adoption of the slogan used by the children of Soweto: 'Don't mourn, organise' by the fledgling Newham Youth Movement. The majority of youth movements not only challenged street racism but also sought to challenge the racism of the state through campaigning against the immigration laws as well as the racism of the police (Ramamurthy 2006).

AYMs in Bradford, Manchester and later Sheffield and Birmingham all produced magazines to articulate their 'views and feelings' and develop their own political

KALA TARA

PAPER OF ASIAN YOUTH MOVEMENT BRADFORD.   No. 1.   20p.

Image 24.1 Cover of *Kala Tara: Magazine of the Asian Youth Movement* (Bradford) 1979
Source: Courtesy: tandana.org.

analysis. *Kala Tara*, published in 1979 by the Asian Youth Movement (Bradford), was the first such magazine. It centred the struggle on their right to be in Britain through the slogan 'Here to Stay, Here to Fight'. Emblazoned with the Black Power fist, they established the AYM as part of a broader international movement for racial justice. Apart from discussing the struggle against racist violence and the right to self defence, the magazine discussed a range of issues such as the struggle against racism in the workplace and the racism of the immigration laws. The AYMs were keen to point out Labour's complicity and consolidation of discriminatory immigration legislation (Solomos 2019). They often chanted 'Labour, Tory both the same, both play the racist game' (AYM Bradford 1979). The magazine also featured AYM solidarity with anti-imperialist struggles in Ireland through support for the North of England Irish Prisoners Committee. Education was an important part of political activism for AYM members. As Gurnam from Bradford recalls:

> We used to go in the library cafe . . . we used to share what we were reading and then it would get into disputes about certain politics, . . . And so the library was like our kind of reference. . . . I can remember reading Marx's *Capital*, . . . discussing Gramsci and all these other people and becoming politicised.
>
> (G. Singh 2006)

The question of women's liberation, however, was not effectively addressed in *Kala Tara* or in the working practices of the majority of AYMs, reflecting the primarily male membership of the youth movements. In many cities machoism and organisational practices (such as meeting in pubs) as well as a lack of priority regarding sexual and domestic violence led most women to organise independently. In London, women established Awaz (Voice) and exposed the racist and abusive practice of 'virginity tests' in 1979, after a 35-year-old woman spoke of her ordeal at Heathrow when entering the country as a fiancé (Wilson 2006, p. 162). In Southall and Birmingham, Southall Black Sisters and Birmingham Black Sisters campaigned against domestic violence and the state's racism (Southall Black Sisters 1989). These women's organisations however, worked on joint campaigns with the AYMs. Birmingham Black Sisters (BBS) mobilised in support of the Kewal Brothers strikers (women who were struggling against low pay and the right to join a union), with the AYM and IWA. BBS challenged the decision making processes that undermined women. AYM Manchester was an exception. They set up a women's section and argued that 'Asian women are the most oppressed section of our community, . . . the emancipation of women is a pre-requisite for the liberation of society at large' (AYM Manchester 1981, p. 6). They also invited women such as Amrit Wilson to speak about the work of Awaz, the London-based Asian women's action group, but the women's wing of the movement was small and spent a lot of time supporting women who were at the centre of deportation campaigns rather than steering the movement as a whole (Ramamurthy 2013, pp. 86–96).

The AYMs also recognised culture as a tool for resistance, creating poetry, banners and magazines. They gained strength from anti-imperialist poetry by Amilcar Cabral, Pablo Neruda and Faiz Ahmed Faiz, for example (Ramamurthy 2013, pp. 80–86), but they argued, 'you can't dance racism away'. On 1 May 1978, when fascists marched to the East End of London, a coalition of antiracist organisations, including the AYMs and the Hackney Committee Against Racism (HCAR), mobilised to defend the community. But when HCAR called for support from the organisers of a Rock Against Racism Carnival on that day, they 'were met with virtually a blank wall'. Carnival organisers refused to make an announcement from the platform (HCAR 1978). While Rock Against Racism acted as a space to symbolically oppose racism, opposition to fascist meetings declined in 1978 according to HCAR. 'At Ilford by-election the picket was about 2,500, at Bristol the opposition was less than 1000, on May Day the opposition was nil' (HCAR 1978).

In Focus: bring my children home – the case of Anwar Ditta

Anwar's story highlights the social impact of immigration policy. While a large number of campaigns were conducted to stop people being deported from Britain, Anwar's story highlighted how families with social ties in two continents were divided by a system that appeared set up to disbelieve rather than believe them. For the AYMs, by highlighting an individual case, it was possible to humanise the debate surrounding the immigration laws. It was a case of turning numbers into names so as to narrate people's stories. For the AYMs, Anwar's case exposed the depths of inhumanity and racism in a system that attempted to divide a mother from her children.

Anwar Ditta was born in Birmingham in 1953. In 1962 her parents separated when she was nine years old. Her father was given custody of the children, and she and her sister were sent to Pakistan. She was married in 1967, although below the age of consent, and had three children. In 1975 she decided to return to England with her family. She and her husband left the children in Pakistan while they found work and a place to live. On returning Anwar and her husband remarried, believing that their Islamic marriage would not be recognised under English law. Because of this belief, they gave their status as bachelor and spinster. This was to prove a costly mistake. After two and a half years of waiting, in May 1979, the Home Office declared that they were 'not satisfied that the children Kamran, Imran and Saima were related to Anwar Sultana Ditta and Shuja ud Din'. The Entry Clearance officer even came up with the absurd idea that 'no clear evidence of Anwar Sultana Ditta ever having been in Pakistan had been produced. . . . It appeared that there might be two Anwar Ditta's'. Anwar had photographs of herself in Pakistan with her husband, her family and her children. She had birth certificates for all her children and despite having asthma in England as a child and needing frequent medical attention, there were no medical records for her in Britain for 13 years until she re-registered in 1975. When Anwar's fourth child was born in Rochdale, the hospital also confirmed that this was her fourth child. None of this evidence was adequate to accept the children were hers.

The Anwar Ditta Defence Campaign organised pickets and demonstrations in Rochdale and Manchester, with 'energetic petitioning' (Campaign Against the Immigration Laws [CAIL] 1980).

Image 24.2 Anwar Ditta Defence Campaign demonstration, Manchester
Source: Courtesy: tandana.org and Anwar Ditta.

But despite the provision of more evidence, Anwar lost her appeal. The Home Office upheld the adjudicator's decision on the basis that they believed Anwar and Shuja were deceptive. The Home Office argued that Anwar lied by applying for her passport on return to the UK under her maiden name (a result of believing her marriage was not recognised). Anwar's age had also been registered on her marriage certificate as 20 when she was 14. Yet as a minor this had clearly not been in her control. Losing the appeal left no legal avenue open to Anwar. Although there was no legal avenue left, the youth movements stuck by her to demand justice, supporting Anwar to become a powerful speaker:

> People think why did I leave my children? This is not a crime. I didn't know English Law. I didn't know I could bring my children straight away and that the home office would have provided them with accommodation, money. . . . I didn't want my children to suffer. . . . Do you think it's easy to campaign? . . . It's really ridiculous making black people suffer and destroying their families. What kind of a law is this?

The strength of the campaign, along with the determination of Anwar Ditta herself, led to interest from Granada TV. World in Action sent a camera crew to Pakistan with Ruth Bundey, Anwar's new solicitor. She collected evidence from teachers, religious figures and the local community that Anwar and her children were who they said they were. Blood tests were analysed in London to prove that the children were undoubtedly hers. The day after the documentary was screened, in March 1981, the Home Office refusal was overturned. Anwar went on to support others struggling for justice in the years to follow. Having been disbelieved and asked to provide evidence of her past that she did not have, Anwar kept all the records of her campaign in case she would ever need evidence again. These documents are now in the Ahmed Iqbal Ullah Race Relations Archive, Manchester.

Police violence, racism and the Bradford 12

Police inertia in investigating racist incidents and often arresting the victims rather than the perpetrators was well established by 1978. In 1977, for example, the Virk brothers were attacked by five fascists when fixing their car. The brothers called the police and tried to defend themselves, but on arriving the police arrested them rather than the perpetrators of the attack. The brothers were charged with grievous bodily harm and eventually convicted by a white jury after a judge refused to permit the defence lawyer to raise the issue of racism and the police failed to interview any Asian witnesses to the attack (Singhji 2010).

In Southall, the police's inaction in protecting the community came to a head in 1979, when the National Front (NF) decided to hold a meeting in Southall. The tactic of holding election meetings in communities where migrants lived was one adopted by the NF during the 1979 election in which they fielded 300 candidates[2] as a strategy to gain media attention. Black people and anti-fascist activists marched to protest in their thousands and were confronted with police violence that led to a thousand people being injured and the death of the school teacher Blair Peach:

> It was their day, the police abused us, called us black bastards, black whores, wogs and n*****s. . . . One man had his kidney damaged by the kick of a horse, one youth was so badly kicked that his testicles had to be removed. Another person woke up in an intensive care unit with a blood clot on his brain. And Blair Peach was killed.
>
> (Parita in AYM Bradford 1979, p. 4)

The police's criminalisation of the community was exposed by witnesses at the time who noted: 'on the evening of the arrests, defendants found that upon arrival at the police station type written charge sheets were ready, waiting for any random name to be put on them' (Suresh in AYM Bradford 1979, p. 4). Such aggression led the youth to believe that they had no choice but to organise to defend themselves: 'We must organise ourselves so that any racist attack can be dealt with effectively. We cannot rely on the police. We must defend ourselves. Black self-defence is no offence' (Singh in AYM Bradford 1979, p. 3).

In January 1981, 13 young Black children were burned to death when a 16-year-old's birthday party was firebombed. On 1 July 1981 Mrs Khan and her children were burned to death in Walthamstow, London, after a petrol bomb was thrown into their home. Just two days after the Khan family lost their lives, fascists attempted to stage a skinhead concert at the Hambrough Tavern in Southall (Page 1981). The police response was ineffective. With the events of 1979 still resonating, the pub was burned down in a night of civil unrest. The rolling out the government's Swamp 81 police operation, which licenced the increased use of stop and search powers, was also a signal to Black communities that they were perceived as the problem, leading to unrest in Bristol, Brixton and Liverpool in 1980 and early 1981. On 11 July 1981 unrest exploded across the country. Areas with Asian communities such as Handsworth, Luton, Woolwich, Camden, Kilburn, Hounslow and Southall all mobilised against fascists. The same weekend also saw the 'dispossessed working class youth' erupt in anger with incidences of violence and looting in over 30 cities (Harman 1981).

In Bradford, on 11 July when rumours of fascists coming to the city were heard, members of the United Black Youth League (a recently formed group after a split in the Asian Youth Movement Bradford over the issue of accepting state funds) took the information seriously. They made petrol bombs that were never used in order 'to be prepared should the need arise, to protect themselves and their community against fascists'. Three weeks later on 28 July over a dozen members were arrested, and 12 young men were charged with 'conspiracy to make explosives' and 'endanger life'. The Bradford 12 case and campaign acted as a national focal point against repressive policing policies and practices towards Black people (Ramamurthy 2013, pp. 120–147).

The leading defendants in the Bradford 12 case had been key campaigners in the AYM during the previous six years, defending the rights of others. They had campaigned for Anwar Ditta to be reunited with her children and had defended communities against racists and fascists both in Bradford and nationally. When the case came to trial it was clear that Special Branch had been involved in the arrests and the investigation. Campaigners nationally mobilised support under the slogan 'the only conspiracy is police conspiracy'. They felt that the arrests were an attack on themselves. The Bradford 12 included young Asians from a variety of backgrounds struggling against racism. The 12 included Muslims, Sikhs, Hindus and Christians.

When the case came to trial the defendants argued that they had made petrol bombs to defend their community in the wake of police failure to do so. When fascists had not visited they had not used the petrol bombs, proving that their intent was self-defence. The trial exposed the depths of police racism, with Detective Inspector Holland, Deputy Head of CID in Bradford, revealed to have publicly declared:

> Police officers must be prejudiced and discriminatory to do their job. Prejudice is a state of mind drawn from experience. Searching long haired youths in bedraggled clothing produces drug seizures, and searching West Indian youth wearing tea cosy hats and loitering in city centres could detect mugging offences. . . . Subordinate officers are expected to act in a discriminatory way; that is against those

Image 24.3 Free the Bradford 12 poster
Source: Courtesy: tandana.org.

people who by their conduct, mode of life, dress, associates, transport, are most likely to be criminals.

(Telegraph and Argus 13/9/81)

But the core issue was not the racism of individual police officers but the force as a whole. Dave Stark, a prominent anti-fascist campaigner in Bradford, researched information on racist attacks in West Yorkshire, information that was presented alongside the Home Office's own reports on the national picture (Stark 1982). With a supportive defence team and a powerful national campaign, the 12 were eventually acquitted, making legal history in the right of a community to self-defence.

The Bradford 12 Campaign gives evidence of the connections and solidarity that existed across communities struggling for social, economic and human rights at the time. The Bradford 12 Campaign legacy booklet listed hundreds of local, national and international organisations that included workers organisations, Black organisations, welfare organisations, trade unions, socialist organisations, communist parties, anti-deportation campaigns, temples, mosques, gurdwaras, national liberation organisations, women's groups, law centres, film cooperatives, feminist and socialist publishers, disabled groups and students organisations who in turn raised the case of the 12 in their constituencies (Bradford 12 Campaign 1982, p. 23). The campaign encouraged communities in other towns and cities to organise. The Sheffield Asian Youth Movement was formed in 1982 after a restaurant worker was attacked by racists and yet was arrested as the perpetrator of violence when he defended himself.

While the need to challenge street racism, police racism and the racism of the immigration laws continued, the state recognised the need to offer concessions to communities suffering systemic racism in housing, the job market, wider opportunities and policing. In 1982 the Scarman Report on the Brixton riots recognised the importance of increased provision for job opportunities and housing for inner-city communities. The report did not recognise the racism of the police, and throughout the 1980s campaigns against police racism and criminalisation of Black communities continued, with cases such as the Newham 8 and Newham 7. Frequently building solidarity links, Asian and African-Caribbean communities marched together as in the case of the Newham 8 (who were arrested after defending themselves from attacks by white plainclothes police officers in 1984) and Colin Roach Family Support committee (a man who was killed by the police for whom the family was seeking justice).

It took until 1999 for the state to acknowledge institutional racism in the police after the death of Stephen Lawrence (Macpherson 1999).

Debates and Interpretation: challenging racism inside or outside the state

As the youth articulated in their literature, the primary struggle against racism was not to challenge personal acts of discrimination but to challenge the state's racist policies and practices. Racism in this sense was not an issue of ignorance that could simply be challenged through education but was an exercise of power.

BENEFIT

VENUE: Sheffield University Students
Union Building.

DATE: Friday,16 Sept.

TIME: 8p.m.-late   PRICE:£1.oo.

Image 24.4 Black Community on Trial benefit

Source: Artist: Mukhtar Dar. Courtesy: tandana.org.

This understanding of the role of the state in practising racism led to debates between the youth about the best way to challenge it. Was it better to advocate outside of state structures, as grassroots organisations, or would it be more effective to work within state structures, which would permit access to state resources and could enable work that could not be afforded without financial backing? The youth were divided on this issue. In the 1980s the number of ethnic minority organisations that began to emerge across county councils in the UK mushroomed. There were ethnic minority units in the Greater London Council and other metropolitan councils, Section 11 youth projects, education projects and a vast array of cultural organisations. The shift in direction of some Asian Youth Movements from campaigning to service-oriented organisations was part of a wider social and political process. In 1980 Michael Heseltine's (Conservative Cabinet member) report *It Took a Riot* already emphasised the government's belief in the need to act to prevent 'infiltration . . . which burnt the Liberal's fingers' and to control community organisations (1981, p. 8).

As one AYM member from Bradford recalled:

> They wanted to talk to us, incorporate us, . . . and I applied for this job – unqualified social worker, Section 11. . . . They had 300 applications . . . and I got the job! 'Cos in my interview I said that I was active in the Asian Youth Movement. . . . And he said, 'You're the person we want' . . . for me it was a clear illustration of the incorporation of Black politics into the state. . . . We were all now being picked off the streets as it were and given jobs.
>
> (G. Singh 2006)

Some of the work that the AYM did during this period continued to be transformative. With AYM support, Drummond school parents in Bradford resisted the racism of their headmaster, Ray Honeyford, who criticised multicultural policies of cultural enrichment as 'the approved term for the West Indian's right to create an ear splitting cacophony' and condemned bilingual education by suggesting it prevented South Asian children from learning English (Singh 1984). While challenging Honeyford, the AYM also challenged developing multicultural education policies as failing to address the core issue of racism. They asserted that rather than developing a multicultural education policy, schools should focus on an anti-racist policy: 'Multi-cultural education is not necessarily anti-racist', they argued, but 'anti-racist education must be multicultural'. Today the failure of the education system to address Britain's history of racism continues, with campaigners arguing for the importance of including the history of both the British Empire and the history of the Black experience in Britain in the curriculum (Goodfellow 2019).

The shift in direction of the AYMs, however, was to have a profound effect on the sustainability of the organisations. As a former chair of Bradford AYM acknowledged,

> you have to decide what kind of an organisation you want to be. If you want to be an advocacy organisation it's less appropriate to look at funding. If you want to be a delivery organisation, then you apply for funding because that's what it's all about.

By 1984,

> quite frankly [AYM (Bradford)] just became a community project . . . and that's why it actually collapsed, because it was no longer an advocacy organisation on quite challenging issues around . . . prejudice and discrimination etc. for the community.
>
> (N. Rashid 2006)

However, for Jasbir from Newham Monitoring Project:

> if the question is, would it have been a better world or would things have been significantly different and progressive if the funding was not there, I probably would have to disagree. The two organisations that come to mind are Newham and Southall and despite all the stories that have gone with regards to funding I think it did help . . . because people who were involved in some of these organisations were really solid people, they gave their hearts and minds to that work.
>
> (J. Singh 2006)

To members of the monitoring projects, it was organisations such as the Commission for Racial Equality (CRE) that had the most detrimental effect on anti-racist organisation. As Jasbir recalls,

> they were mostly white individuals who staffed the CREs . . . and they would always come down when there were racist attacks or any incidents and discuss things with the police. . . . We took a very hard line, we would talk to the police but we would not sit on any police liaison groups or police consultative committees, . . . because how can you sit with your enemy and discuss your own issues?
>
> (J. Singh 2006)

It is clear that within the state, different bodies represented conflicting positions. Some have argued that all of these organisations formed part of an 'apparatus created by the state, to house a class of political middle-men' that would eventually 'sabotage the aspirations of the youth by activating the policy of "divide and rule"' by buying activists off the street (Mukherjee 1988, p. 221).

Conclusion

The Asian Youth Movements were powerful grassroots organisations that sprang up to defend communities from state and street racism. They gave voice to their communities and highlighted gross injustices. The political Blackness to which they adhered enabled the building of progressive political alliances across the different ethnic and religious communities of South Asia and communities of colour. These were political movements that wished to create a more just society to which they would be proud to belong. As Tariq Mehmood from Asian Youth Movement Bradford reflected, 'The British culture that we loved and adored was the culture of those who were fighting against British capitalism, British colonialism and there were many of those, it's not like today where we seem atomised into many different groups' (Mehmood 2005). As Amrit Wilson, the founder of Awaz, reflected,

> the 1970s and 80s was a period of intense struggle . . . there was a lot of repression but people did actually fight back. . . . The campaigns were ours, they were not run by professionals, we owned them and were propelled by a sense of justice which gave rise to a very powerful solidarity.
>
> (Ramamurthy 2013, p. 207)

Further reading

Ramdin (1999) provides a longer historical overview of Black working-class history and resistance to racism. Also see Ramdin (1987 republished 2017). Sivanandan and Prescod (2008) and Field (2019) both provide essays written contemporaneously that reflect on the struggle against racism in the 1960s, 70s and 80s. Wilson (1978, republished with new essays in 2018) and Wilson (2006) focus on South Asian women's struggles and resistances both in the 1970s and more recently. Shukra (1998) explores Black political consciousness since the 1950s, narrating the experience of anti-racist organisation in the GLC and the Labour party in particular. Narayan (2019) offers new reflections on the British Black Power movement, its anti-colonial legacies and its foregrounding of the relationship between race and class. For a fictional account of the experience of the Asian Youth movements, Tariq Mehmood's novel *Hand on the Sun* (1983), written partly while he was on remand as a member of the Bradford 12, offers a raw and sensitive account (to be republished 2021).

Notes

1 I am using the term 'Black' since it was employed by activists at the time to mean people of colour whose families had experienced exploitation as a result of colonialism or the transatlantic slave trade.
2 The NF only polled 200,000 votes in total in the 1979 elections, an average of just 66 votes per seat.

References

Anwar, M., 1979. *The myth of return: Pakistanis in Britain*. London: Heinemann.

AYM Bradford, 1979. *Kala Tara: Paper of the Asian youth movement (Bradford)*. London: Bradford.

AYM Manchester, 1981. *Liberation: Organ of the Asian youth movement*. Manchester.

Bradford 12 Campaign, 1982. *Self defence is no offence! How the Bradford 12 won their freedom'*. Leeds: Leeds Other Paper.

CAIL, 1980, *CAIL news: Newsletter of the campaign against the immigration laws*. New York: Spring.

Eames, F., 2009. ITV and the Ugandan migration. *Media History*, 15 (4), 453–469.

Field, P., 2019. *Here to stay, here to fight : A race today anthology*. London: Pluto Press.

Gilroy, P., 1987. *There ain't no black in the union Jack*. London: Routledge.

Gilroy, P., 2019. 'Still ain't no black in the union Jack'. *Tribune Magazine*. Available from: https://tribunemag.co.u k/2019/01/still-no-black-in-the-union-jack.

Goodfellow, M., 2019. Put our colonial history on the curriculum – then we'll understand who we really are. *The Guardian,* 5 December. Available from: www.theguardian.com/commentisfree/2019/dec/05/britain-colonial-history-curriculum-racism-migration.

Harman, C., 1981. The summer of 1981: A post-riot analysis. *International Socialism,* 2 (14), 1–43. Available from: www.marxists.org/archive/harman/1981/xx/riots.html#n5.

HCAR (Haringey Campaign Against Racism), 1978. 'ANL Carnival, they did pass', *Campaign Against Racism and Fascism (CARF) Magazine.*

Heseltine, M., 1981. *It took a riot.* Available from: www.estatesgazette.com/pdf/It-Took-A-Riot.pdf.

Hiro, D., 1991. *Black British, white British: A history of race relations in Britain.* London: Grafton.

Kabir, A., 1965. The growing campaign against Pakistanis in Britain. *Peace News,* 19 March.

Leech, K., 1980. *Brick Lane 1978: The events and their significance.* London: Stepney Books Publications.

Macpherson, W., 1999. *The Stephen Lawrence inquiry.* London: Home Office.

Marett, V., 1989. *Immigrants settling in the city.* Leicester: Leicester University Press.

Mehmood, T., 1983. *Hand on the Sun.* Hamondsworth: Penguin.

Mehmood, T., 2005. Interview with the author, Manchester.

Mukherjee, T., 1988. The journey back. *In:* P. Cohen and H.S. Bains, eds. *Multi-Racist Britain.* Basingstoke: Macmillan Education, 211–225.

Narayan, J., 2019. British black power: The anti-imperialism of political blackness and the problem of nativist socialism. *The Sociological Review,* 67 (5), 945–967.

Page, M.F., 1981. Relf launches race onslaught. *New Statesman,* 10 July.

Patnaik, U., 2017. Revisiting the "Drain", or Transfer from India to Britain in the Context of Global Diffusion of Capitalism. *In:* Shubhra Chakrabarti and Utsa Patnaik, eds. *Agrarian and other histories: Essays for Binay Bhushan Chaudhuri.* Tulika Books: New Delhi, 277–318.

Qadir, A., 2005. Interview with the author, Bradford.

Ramamurthy, A., 2006. The politics of Britain's Asian youth movements. *Race & Class,* 48 (2), 38–60. Available from: https://doi.org/10.1177/0306396806069522.

Ramamurthy, A., 2013. *Black star: Britain's Asian youth movements.* London: Pluto Press.

Ramamurthy, A., 2019. Racism, self defence and the Asian youth movements. *Discover Society.* Available from: https://discoversociety.org/2019/04/03/racism-self-defence-and-the-asian-youth-movements/.

Ramdin, R., 1987. *The making of the black working class in Britain.* Aldershot: Wildwood.

Ramdin, R., 1999. *Reimagining Britain: 500 years of Black and Asian history.* London: Pluto Press.

Rashid, J., 2005. Interview with the author, Bradford.

Rashid, N., 2006. Interview with the author, London.

Shukra, K., 1998. *The changing pattern of black politics in Britain.* London: Pluto.

Singh, G., 2006. Interview with the author, Coventry.

Singh, J., 2006. Interview with the author, London.

Singh, M., 1984. *Education and race: A reply by Marsha Singh.* Available from: www.tandana.org SC105.

Singhji, M., 2010. Who made black history. Available from: www.irr.org.uk/news/who-made-black-history/.

Sivanandan, A., 1982. *A different hunger: Writings on black resistance.* London: Pluto Press.

Sivanandan, A., and Prescod, C., 2008. *Catching history on the wing: Race, culture and globalisation.* London: Pluto Press.

Solomos, J., 2019. "Strangers in their own land": Powellism's policy impact. *Patterns of Prejudice,* 53 (2), 200–209.

Southall Black Sisters, 1989. *Against the Grain: Southall black sisters 1979–1989.* London: Southall Black Sisters.

Stark, D., 1982. *A report on racist violence in Bradford – 1981.* unpublished document written for the legal defence team of the Bradford 12.

Tharoor, S., 2017. *Inglorious empire.* London: Penguin.

Wilson, A., 1978. *Finding a voice: Asian women in Britain.* London: Virago.

Wilson, A., 2006. *Dreams, questions, struggles: South Asian women in Britain.* London: Pluto.

Glossary

1958 Birth Cohort Study – Also know as the National Child Development Study (NCDS). This collects a wide range of data on the lives of 17,415 people in England, Scotland and Wales born in a single week in 1958, who have been followed up 11 times since the study began.

1970 Birth Cohort Study – Also known as BCS70. Like the NCDS, this longitudinal study follows the lives of 17,000 people in England, Scotland and Wales born in one week in 1970. The tenth follow-up wave of the study (2021) is currently under way.

Alternative vote – A voting system in which the voter chooses candidates in rank order. If no candidate secures more than 50% of first preferences, the bottom candidate is eliminated and the second preferences are redistributed. The process is repeated until one candidate has 50%. It is not guaranteed to provide a proportional result.

Blue-collar worker – A skilled or unskilled worker who performs manual work. The term covers a broad range of work, and examples may include mining, manufacturing and construction. Blue-collar workers are usually contrasted with white-collar workers and are seen as being of lower social status than those who work in offices (see: entry for 'White-collar worker'.)

British Household Panel Survey – This survey began in 1991, interviewing a representative sample of 10,300 members of 5,500 household units across Britain about a range of social and economic factors. The panel was subsequently extended and ran until 2009, when it was partly merged with the then new, more wide-ranging, UK Longitudinal Household Study, also known as *Understanding Society*.

Cartel – A collection of firms operating in the same industry that collaborate on fixing minimum prices and allocating market share. Some cartels also shared technical information.

Chain migration – This type of migration occurs when migrants from one location follow others to the same destination. Those who migrate first often subsequently encourage, help and support the migration of family members, friends and social acquaintances. One common consequence of chain migration is that migrants form new communities that share similarities with those they left behind.

Cohabitation – Cohabitation refers to the living arrangements of individuals who share a household with a partner/partners to whom they are not married or do not have a civil partnership. For much of the twentieth century, cohabitation was understood as a form of unorthodox heterosexuality and was associated with adultery and other forms of 'illicit' unions that would or could not be sanctioned by marriage. However, challenges in obtaining a divorce meant following marital breakdown, new relationships might gain informal legitimacy through cohabitation. While cohabitation existed across the century, it became a more common and accepted living arrangement, particularly from the 1970s. In the last quarter of the century, cohabitation was increasingly normalised both as a precursor to marriage (i.e. couples living together prior to getting married) and as the basis of a family unit for those who could or did not wish to have their relationships legally registered through marriage or civil partnership.

Comprehensivisation in secondary education – Comprehensive schools are mixed-ability schools that do not select students on the basis of academic achievement or parental wealth. The comprehensive sector expanded after 1965 as a result of the Labour government's instruction to local authorities to convert from the selective, tripartite system of education implemented in 1944.

Conscientious objector – A person who refuses on moral or religious grounds to serve in the armed forces or to bear arms in a military conflict.

Corporate governance – The system of rules, practices and processes by which a company is directed and controlled, including the allocation of power and accountability and who makes decisions.

Educational Maintenance Allowance – First introduced in 1999, this is a means-tested scheme that provides financial support paid directly to 16–19-year-olds in the UK who want to undertake post-compulsory education or unpaid training. It was scrapped in England in 2010, where it was replaced by a bursary scheme administered by educational institutions.

Eurozone – The Eurozone is the group of countries who have joined European economic and monetary union and, as a result, use the Euro as their currency and have their monetary policy set by the European Central Bank.

Exchange Rate Mechanism (ERM) – The ERM was part of the European Monetary System established in 1979 to encourage monetary coordination. The ERM set fixed margins within which the currencies of member states could fluctuate against each other.

Externality – An externality is a cost or a benefit which lacks a price, usually because of an absence of property rights. Examples of negative externalities commonly include pollution, while a positive externality might be my being inoculated or having a fine garden which gives you pleasure as you pass.

FDI (foreign direct investment) – The amount of money spent by firms on overseas assets.

First Past the Post – The system used for elections to the House of Commons. The winning candidate in any constituency needs only to secure a simple majority – that is to say the candidate who gets the most votes wins; he or she does not need to secure more than 50% of all votes. The system makes it possible for a party to win a majority of seats in the Commons even if the other parties between them secured more than 50% of the national vote.

Free-riding – Free-riding behaviour occurs when someone seeks to benefit from expenditure or actions by others without contributing themselves.

Gender – Gender is a construct. It can mean how we are characterised as male or female and how other psychological, social, cultural and ideological meanings and structures can flow from that characterisation. 'Masculinity' and 'femininity' are gender constructs, denoting aspects of male or female identity.

Gold Standard – A regime in which each national currency could be exchanged for a constant weight of gold. Consequently, exchange rates between currencies were fixed firmly. The Gold Standard came to an end in the 1930s.

Industrial districts – A distinct geographical region which is dominated by either a single or series of closely related industries (e.g. Lancashire cotton).

Labour Force Survey – This collects data on the employment circumstances of people in the UK. Administered by the Office for National Statistics, it is carried out quarterly and involves 44,000 households.

M-form – The multidivisional form characterised by a high level of delegation to departments or divisions of a firm, with strong central co-ordination through the board of directors and supporting staff.

Macroeconomics – The study of the behaviour of the economy as a whole. (By contrast microeconomics is the study of components of the economy such as the household, the firm, or the industry.) Modern macroeconomics originated in the work of the Cambridge economist John Maynard Keynes (1883–1946). Other schools of macroeconomics emerged after the Second World War to challenge Keynesian dominance.

Malthusian – These approaches posit that while population size can potentially increase at an exponential rate (2, 4, 8, 16 . . .), output from restricted resources is only likely to grow at an arithmetic rate (2, 3, 4 . . .) resulting in a falling level of output per capita.

Oligopolistic – A market dominated by a small number of firms.

Pacifist – Someone who opposes warfare and violence as a means of settling disputes.

Parliamentary Commission on Social Mobility – The Social Mobility Commission – formerly known as the Social Mobility and Child Poverty Commission – is an advisory public body attached to the Department for Education. Originally set up in 2010, its remit is to monitor and improve social mobility chances in the UK.

Plutocratic elite – This is an elite whose membership is based on wealth, rather than, for example, heredity or status.

Proportional voting system – (or proportional representation) – Any voting system which, unlike First Past the Post (see previously), delivers seats in the legislature in rough proportion to the votes cast for the parties standing for election. The Single Transferable Vote system is a widely used example.

Protectionism – A system by which governments impose import tariffs on selected products, normally employed as a means of protecting indigenous industries.

Sex – Sex is a way of identifying the biological or physiological characteristics of a person's body, sometimes with reference to reproductive function. Sex indicates characteristics that have been or can be understood as male or female or characterised as neither male nor female. Sex can also mean a sexual act.

Sexuality – Sexuality can mean one's sexual identity or orientation, the sexual preference or desire one has for another gender or sex, or the same gender and sex as oneself.

Short-term capital flows – Movements of funds between countries with a view to obtaining a short-term advantage, for example, to enjoy a higher interest rate or in anticipation of a change in exchange rates. These flows were regarded as speculative and potentially destabilising.

Social Chapter – The Social Chapter was a draft chapter of the Treaty of European Union which set out proposed worker rights. It was removed on UK insistence and was turned into a separate Social Policy Agreement signed by the then-11 other member states.

Social marginal cost and benefit – The use of the adjective 'social' reflects those costs and benefits to others which exceed my private costs. The adjective 'marginal' reflects the change in total costs resulting from an increase in a unit of output.

Stock-flow approaches – Stock-flow approaches to pollution often cite the plug-less bath tub. Water (current emissions) enters the bath (stock of pollution), while water exits through the plughole. If the emissions (tap water) rise faster than the stock breaks down (exiting plughole), then the stock of water rises in the bath. Stock-flow approaches to fisheries are more complex, since for a period the flow (catch) of fish can leave more for other fish to eat. However, in both cases the stock can reach a level at which the effects of future flows (catches, emissions) cause increasing damage.

Sure Start – This is a programme introduced by the New Labour government in 1998, which was designed to improve the life chances of economically and social disadvantaged children. It provides support to children under four years of age, including through Sure Start Centres, to help families access childcare and early years education. The programme has been severely cut back since 2010.

Tragedy of the Commons – Refers to the overuse or overconsumption of a resource because of an absence of property rights.

Transactions costs – The costs of doing business through the market. With respect to foreign exchange markets, transactions costs are higher when currencies are floating because this creates uncertainty about the value of payments and receipts in the future.

Tripartite education system – The 1944 Education Act created a system of free secondary education defined by three types of school, with the distinctions between them drawing on the prevailing notion that there were 'three types of mind'. Thus, grammar schools were for the supposedly more academically able, and technical schools were for those with an aptitude for more applied, commercial and vocational subjects, while secondary moderns taught more elementary and practical skills. Pupils were selected for, or allocated to, different schools on the basis of their performance in an intelligence test known the 11+ exam, taken at the end of their primary schooling.

White-collar worker – A worker who works in an office and whose job does not usually involve manual labour. Although white-collar workers are usually seen as being of higher social status than blue-collar workers, this category covers a wide range of jobs, ranging from managerial roles with considerable power and authority to data entry clerks who are often considered to be at the bottom of the organisational hierarchy (see: entry for 'Blue-collar worker'.)

Index

Printed in Great Britain
by Amazon

42826169R00223